THE OLD NORTHWEST

IN THE

AMERICAN REVOLUTION

An Anthology

★ ★

Edited with Introductions by

David Curtis Skaggs

The State Historical Society of Wisconsin
Madison   1977

Library of Congress Cataloging in Publication Data

Main entry under title:
The Old Northwest in the American Revolution.

Bibliography: p. 467.
CONTENTS: The West on the eve of independence: Sosin, J. M. The French settlements in British policy for the North American interior, 1760–1774. Van Every, D. The great crossing. Alvord, C. W. Virginia and the West. Curry, R. O. Lord Dunmore and the West. Marshall, P. Imperial policy and the government of Detroit. [etc.]

1. Northwest, Old—History—Revolution, 1775–1783—Addresses, essays, lectures. 2. Northwest, Old—History—To 1775—Addresses, essays, lectures. 3. Northwest, Old—History—1775–1865—Addresses, essays, lectures. I. Skaggs, David Curtis.
E263.N84043   973.3'0977   77–1757
ISBN 0–87020–164–6

To the memory of my grandparents

CHARLES JOHN BAER
1888–1972
and
ARLINE NEFF BAER
1891–1975
of
Topeka, Kansas

PREFACE

The inception of this volume undoubtedly came when a native of the Great Plains found himself employed in Ohio. The historian's natural curiosity about the region in which he lives caused a limited inquiry about the area. This curiosity expanded when in January, 1971, Governor James A. Rhodes named me one of his lame-duck appointments to the Ohio American Revolution Bicentennial Advisory Commission. Because I was the only academic appointed, the other commissioners and many acquaintances in the general public expected me to know everything about the American Revolution in Ohio. Rather than display my ignorance, I began to study the history of the Ohio valley-Great Lakes region in the revolutionary era, a period I usually expanded to include the years 1763–1787. Two things became apparent. First, few people really comprehended the role of the West in the period; either they thought nothing worthwhile happened at all or they assumed George Rogers Clark was embodiment of all that was worth knowing. Second, there was little secondary literature that would provide the interested citizen the essence of what he or she should know of the age. From these beginnings there appeared a need to provide such information to residents of the Old Northwest. Similarly, I found most bibliographies slighted the amount of scholarly study about the region. It seemed the bicentennial provided an opportunity to compile such a list in the hope it might provoke an understanding of the depth of academic interest in the region that has existed and does exist now, as well as possibly prod interested scholars to fill in the gaps of research that appear.

To this editor, three basic areas of inquiry seemed apparent: the West as a contributing cause to the Revolution; warfare in the western theater (a region which had to be extended to include bordering states and provinces) with the diplomacy that resulted in the region's incorporation into the United States; and the solutions of the immediate western problems facing the young republic before the adoption of the Constitution. Keeping these themes in mind, efforts were made to find concise, readable, and accurate descriptions and analyses of various related problems. Not only were leading scholarly journals and books investigated, but also so-called popular histories whose scholarship was of high quality. The result is a gathering of articles and book excerpts from a variety of sources reflecting the views of both academics and popular writers.

This anthology is the product of efforts of many persons and institutions from the region with which it is concerned. Their collective work is combined to provide a better understanding of the vast woodlands between the Great Lakes and the Ohio River.

Several of the authors reside in the Old Northwest today. In Illinois are William Pattison, Staughton Lynd, and Jack Eblen. Merrill Jensen is in Wisconsin, Robert Berkhofer in Michigan, and James O'Donnell in Ohio. Most of the others lived, studied, and/or taught in the Old Northwest at one time or another. Moreover, this endeavor involved an editor from Ohio and a publisher from Wisconsin.

As in any work of this type, a number of people significantly assisted in its development. Drs. Thomas H. Smith of the Ohio Historical Society, Michael Devine of the Ohio American Revolution Bicentennial Commission staff, and James Morton Smith of the State Historical Society of Wisconsin have been particularly helpful. Besides allowing their essays to be printed, Otis Rice, James O'Donnell, and Robert Berkhofer have offered suggestions that contributed to the introductions and the bibliography.

Paul H. Hass of the Society Press of the State Historical Society of Wisconsin has made important suggestions. Other assistance came from Dr. Lester J. Cappon of the Atlas of Early American History being developed at the Newberry Library in Chicago. The maps themselves have been produced through the excellent work of the University of Wisconsin Cartographic Laboratory. The inter-library loan office at the Bowling Green State University library has been of considerable assistance in securing copies of journal articles not available in the library itself. My undergraduate assistant, Kevin Diels, diligently put most of the bibliography into the LAPLUME program at the Bowling Green Computer Center, a task which allowed for an expansible bibliography with a minimum of retypings. The co-operation of the computer center staff has also been of great assistance to a novice. As usual, the history department's secretarial staff has made my load lighter and my work neater. Financial assistance for this volume was received from the Bicentennial Council of the Old Northwest through the participation of the bicentennial commissions of the states of Illinois, Indiana, Ohio, and Wisconsin. Additional financial support came through gifts from Fred W. Uhlman and Company of Bowling Green, Ohio, and Ms. Jeanne Feightner of Chicago. This aid is most gratefully appreciated.

An unrepayable debt is owed each of the contributors whose love of learning made each of these essays worthy of an additional audience. In particular, I am grateful to them for allowing me to reprint or publish these essays without the usual scholarly annotation. It is hoped the interested reader will want to learn more by going to the original essay.

Finally, my wife and sons have contributed importantly to this project not only with their interest, but also with their patience and understanding during these bicentennial years.

DAVID CURTIS SKAGGS

Bowling Green, Ohio
November, 1976

CONTENTS

Eight maps pertaining to the sites
mentioned in the essays follow
page 150.

PART I

THE WEST ON THE EVE OF INDEPENDENCE

THE BRITISH DECISION to receive Canada rather than the West Indian sugar island of Guadaloupe as part of the Peace of Paris of 1763 opened new responsibilities, possibilities, and problems in imperial governance. There were a variety of interest groups contending for preferential treatment from the government—American Indians, fur traders, land speculators, and settlers.

Of these, the fur traders had powerful allies in Montreal, Philadelphia, Albany, and London. They saw the West as a haven for Native Americans and a source of pelts which decorated and warmed the fashionable of Europe. This group received at least short-term satisfaction from the Proclamation of 1763 which confined settlement east of the mountains except for the St. Lawrence valley area. But trade with the Native Americans by local firms received a setback in 1764 when the Board of Trade adopted a regulation depriving the colonies of control over Indian diplomacy and trade by placing all such activities in the hands of two superintendents of Indian affairs—Sir William Johnson for the area north of the Ohio and Colonel John Stuart for the district south of it. While this system never operated effectively, its potential disturbed many colonists interested in open commerce and diplomacy with the tribes. Moreover, it represented an imperial intrusion upon interests traditionally handled by colonists.

More influential were the speculators, both British and American, who gathered like vultures ready to pick off any piece of property left on the bones of Indian treaties. As early as

1748 trans-Appalachian communities began on the upper reaches of the Tennessee valley and in 1754 another grant began a settlement along the Greenbrier branch of the Kanawha. Speculative fever swept across the colonies when the 1763 treaty eliminated the French menace to such areas. George Washington and fellow holders of military land bounties sought to buy a common holding near the mouth of the Ohio River which they called the Mississippi Company. The largest of all was the Grand Ohio Company which sought to create a proprietary colony of Vandalia stretching from Pittsburgh westward and encompassing most of modern West Virginia and eastern Kentucky.

All this happened because the cabinet allowed Stuart and Johnson to move the Proclamation Line westward, which they did under the treaties of Fort Stanwix, Hard Labor, and Lochaber. Both the Iroquois and Cherokee made concessions to channel settlement into Kentucky and West Virginia thereby avoiding their villages and hunting grounds.

The various land schemes had reasonable chances of success until 1772 when Lord Hillsborough secured cancellation of them. From that time the pressure was to incorporate the Northwest into Quebec while Virginia worked independently to settle the Monongehela, Kanawha, and Kentucky river valleys under its charter provisions.

As if speculation problems were not enough, the English had to control and govern the region. As originally planned the army would exercise nominal governance of whites in the region through outposts on the frontier. To carry out the massive military committment required funds, and these were to come from the stamp tax. When colonial and commercial protests forced abandonment of this scheme, the natural consequence was retrenchment and withdrawal of armed forces from the West. This left a compelling need for civil government in the region, a need fulfilled by the Quebec Act of 1774 which brought the French *habitants* at Detroit, Kaskaskia, Vincennes, and elsewhere under provincial government.

The Quebec Act was a marvel of statesmanship. Its provisions included a liberal treatment of Roman Catholics, utilized the best access route into the region—the Great Lakes-St. Lawrence basin—and provided a measure of territorial security for the

Indians which they had heretofore never enjoyed. But it outraged many colonists. Toleration of "popery" warmed few hearts in areas recently menaced by Indians attacking in the name of a Roman Catholic monarch. New England clergy were particularly offended by this policy and raged against it from their pulpits, calling the act intolerable and linking it to the same Parliamentary conspiracy that recently enacted the coercive acts. Virginia's claims to the Northwest were particularly jeopardized by this law. Coupled with a policy designed to raise the costs of newly patented lands five times their current low price and to place perpetual Crown quitrents on such properties, the expansion-minded colonists found much to take offense at. Requirements that all of the enlarged Quebec fur trade be channeled through Montreal offended fur traders in Albany and Philadelphia.

In the midst of this colonists began to stream into the trans-Appalachian west. By 1776 three significant areas were being settled—the upper Ohio valley between Pittsburgh and Wheeling, the Kanawha valley, and the Kentucky bluegrass region. In 1774 the Moravians established a mission among the Delawares in the Muskingum valley of Ohio. To the west there remained the settlements and fortifications of the former New France at Detroit, Mackinac, Prairie du Chien, Kaskaskia, Cahokia, and Vincennes. All across the region the Native American awaited the expected onslaught with foreboding. The redcoats brought them little protection, the Americans promised even less.

There can be no doubt that British imperial policy constituted a contributing cause to the American Revolution. By 1774 it offended a variety of diverse interests—fur traders, land speculators, anti-Catholics, frontiersmen, and anti-Parliamentarians objecting to that legislature's intrusion into colonial policy embodied in the Quebec Act. While the totality of actions relative to the West did not constitute sufficient cause for armed rebellion, they did solidify animosity towards British rule.

The French Settlements in British Policy for the North American Interior, 1760–1774

Jack M. Sosin

Traditionally most Americans have seen the Quebec Act of 1774 as just one more example of the British trampling on American liberties during the imperial crisis following the Boston Tea Party. Since the act came at the same time as the "coercive acts" against Massachusetts, since it apparently deprived the seaboard colonies of their land claims to the region northwest of the Ohio, and because it instituted governmental procedures inimical to many colonists of English extraction, American polemicists lumped it with the Massachusetts bills into a category called the "intolerable acts."

Professor Jack M. Sosin (1928——) has taught at the University of Nebraska at Lincoln since 1958. A distinguished student of eighteenth-century British imperial history, Sosin is best known as the author of Whitehall in the Wilderness: The Middle West in British Colonial Policy, 1760–1775 *(1961),* Agents and Merchants: British Colonial Policy and the Origins of the American Revolution, 1763–1775 *(1965), and* The Revolutionary Frontier, 1763–1783 *(1967). In this article he describes how the evolution of British policy toward the former French colony of New France and its inhabitants came as the result of administrative problems having little to do with the seaboard colonies. He argues that the Quebec Act "did not stem from the colonial crisis of 1774" but rather it "represented the final solution of the Ministry for administering the northern district of the interior." The coincidence of its passage at the time of the Coercive Acts does not mean it was a retaliatory measure against colonial unrest. It was "an honest attempt to insure the stability and security of the interior by granting to the inhabitants a form of government following the traditions and circumstances of the French inhabitants."*

From Jack M. Sosin, "The French Settlements in British Policy for the North American Interior, 1760–1774," in the *Canadian Historical Review*, 39: 85–208 (September, 1958); reprinted without footnotes with permission of the author and the University of Toronto Press.

AMBIGUOUSLY SITUATED in Canada or Louisiana at various times during the French régime, the settlements at Vincennes and in the Illinois country later presented a thorny problem for British administration of the North American interior. Formulated in part as a consequence of the negotiations of the Treaty of Paris by which the interior was annexed to the British Crown, the original British policy was to a larger extent a result of the conduct of the Seven Years' War in America. The final disposition of these settlements followed a decade of experimentation. During this time several considerations impinged on the decision of the British ministers.

British control over much of the northern district of the interior had come with the fall of Canada at the capitulation of Montreal to General Jeffery Amherst in September, 1760. At that time an important concession—one destined to influence policy in the future—was made, for under Articles 37 and 38 of the Capitulation, the French inhabitants were guaranteed their possessions and property. A more immediate question arose, however, as to the area which had been surrendered. Shortly after the Capitulation, Colonel Frederick Haldimand, acting on behalf of the British Commander-in-Chief, asked the French Governor for a definitive map of Canada. On the pretence that he had no charts, the marquis de Vaudreuil refused the request, but dictated orally a line to Haldimand while the British officer traced the boundary of the province on a map of North America. Thus drawn, the line went up the Ohio and Wabash rivers to the Wabash-Maumee portage, and then extended along the watershed to Red Lake near the headwaters of the Mississippi. Vaudreuil later claimed to the French minister, the duc de Choiseul, that he had rejected the boundary indicated on a map presented by Haldimand, and had verbally substituted another, adding roughly a hundred leagues to Louisiana at the expense of Canada by extending the former colony as far as the Maumee portage.

Whatever the case, the boundaries of the two provinces were not clear when, five days after the surrender at Montreal, Amherst dispatched Major Robert Rogers with two hundred rangers to Detroit, Michilimackinac, and Ouiatanon to accept the surrender of the garrisons at these posts. Reinforced by regulars from Niagara and Fort Pitt, the detachment arrived at Detroit on November 29 when the post was turned over and the inhabitants took the oath of allegiance. Prevented by inclement weather and the advanced state of the season from fully executing his orders, Rogers returned to army headquarters in New York after leaving instructions for the occupation of the lesser posts. By the spring of 1761, British military units had a tenuous hold on most of the French posts in the northern district, although they had not as yet taken possession of the Illinois settlements or Vincennes. These districts were to be contested that spring when formal peace negotiations between France and Great Britain were initiated.

Compelled by overwhelming British victories to cede Canada, the French throughout the negotiations sought to restrict the cession as much as possible. The duc de Choiseul proposed to the British envoy in Paris, Hans Stanley, "une fixation des limites du Canada dans la partie de l'Ohio determinées par les eaux pendantes" so as to avoid further territorial or boundary disputes. The proposal to set the boundary at the watershed of the Ohio was rejected by the British ministers, however, when they voted unanimously on June 24 to demand Canada in its entirety. William Pitt, the Secretary of State for the southern department, instructed the British envoy in Paris to demand the cession of the province "total and entire, not mutilated or dismembered. . . ." After conferring with Pitt, the French envoy in London, François Bussy, pointed out to Choiseul that since the boundary between Louisiana and Canada had never been clearly distinguished, the Ohio and Wabash rivers should be designated as appertaining to Louisiana. Since various French publications had listed the Ohio as part of the northern province, however, it would now be necessary to procure a statement from the Ministry of Marine establishing the best possible boundaries for Louisiana.

While Pitt demanded Canada as delineated by the line drawn on the Vaudreuil map, Bussy held out for a boundary which would have assigned much of the area east of the Mississippi to Louisiana. To the British ministers this indicated that the French were endeavouring "to chicane about the limits of Canada on the side of the Ohio." With the British maintaining an inflexible attitude, by the end of August, 1761, the French apparently gave in to the British claims and agreed that Canada as delineated on the Vaudreuil map would remain with Great Britain.

At this point, however, the Franco-British negotiations were disrupted by France's interjection of the claims of her ally, Spain. Favouring a strong line against Spain, Pitt found himself almost isolated in the cabinet and resigned early in October, 1761. Although they were forced to declare war against Spain the following January, the British ministers again resumed diplomatic negotiations with the court of Versailles that spring.

In the meantime, Pitt's successor as Secretary of State for the southern department had begun an inquiry in order to institute a definitive policy for the North American interior. In December, 1761, the Earl of Egremont requested from the Commander-in-Chief in America a full account of the territories recently taken from France, instructing Amherst to transmit orders to the commanders of the conquered French area to dispatch with all convenient speed an exact report of the country. In particular Egremont asked for information as to the extent of Canada under the French régime so that the boundaries of the province could be ascertained. In compliance, Amherst referred the request to the commanders at Montreal, Quebec, and Three Rivers. The report of Colonel Thomas Gage, commanding at Montreal, was particularly important in that his seat of government controlled the route to the interior by way of the St. Lawrence and Ottawa rivers. Dated March 20, 1762, Gage's report was transmitted by Amherst on May 12, 1762.

With regard to the limits of Canada vis à vis Louisiana, Gage was unable to find that they were "distinctly described," so as to be known specifically under the French régime. Consequently he transmitted what were generally believed to have been the boundaries of Canada, and his own conclusions based on the fur trade as it had been conducted by the Canadians under the authority of the northern governors. Using this standard he concluded that not only the Lakes but also the course of the Mississippi from its source to the mouth of the Illinois River fell within Canada. The Illinois district, thought formerly within Canada, had been annexed to Louisiana after some dispute between the Governors of the two provinces. Gage pointed out that a line drawn southeast from the portage of the Illinois with the headwaters of Lake Michigan would lead to the post of Ouiatanon, eighty leagues down the Wabash from the portage with the Maumee. This post was the last trading fort in Canada and "was certainly the Boundary of Canada. . . ." About sixty leagues below Ouiatanon on the Wabash was the post of Vincennes, served by traders from Louisiana, and marking the limits of the southern colony. Based on the best information he could obtain, Gage believed these constituted "the real Boundaries betwixt the two Provinces."

Although this report on the interior was to play an important part in helping to formulate Egremont's future programme it arrived too late in England to have any bearing on the issue of the Canadian-Louisiana boundary dispute. Indeed, as far as the peace negotiations were concerned, the issue had become academic. Because of further British military victories in the war, the cabinet, on the resumption of negotiations in the spring of 1762, had been able to increase their demands, especially with regard to the North American interior.

The issue was taken up by the ministers at the first of two meetings on April 30 when it was decided that France should cede Louisiana for the restitution of Martinique, recently captured by British forces. At a second meeting called that day, the Earl of Bute, favouring an early peace, persuaded the cabinet that since France would be expected to reject such harsh terms and the war would thereby be prolonged, England should limit its demand to the area east of the Mississippi River. During the summer of 1762, after heated arguments in the cabinet, the Mississippi River, with the exception of the "island" on which New Orleans was situated, became the accepted boundary between the two powers in North America. The line was incorporated in the preliminary peace treaty signed in Paris on November 3. Since Havana had been captured in the meantime, the cabinet had instructed the British plenipotentiary, the Duke of Bedford, to insist on the cession of either Florida or Puerto Rico as compensation for the restitution of Havana. Spain chose to relinquish Florida, and the day after the preliminary treaty was signed, Louis XV ceded Louisiana west of the Mississippi and New Orleans to Charles III as compensation.

The definitive treaty was signed in Paris on February 10, 1763. Two months later final orders were given for the evacuation of the French West Indian islands and for the military occupation of Florida and Louisiana east of the Mississippi.

Garrisoning the new acquisitions was to be a key consideration in future British policy for the interior. By the end of 1762, independent of the final settlement of the peace negotiations, Amherst had almost nine thousand troops in America, dispersed in a line from Nova Scotia to Quebec and Montreal, along the New York and Pennsylvania frontiers to the Great Lakes, and Detroit and its dependent posts. No garrisons, as yet, had been sent to the Illinois country or the lower Wabash. After the preliminary peace treaty had been signed, however, the Commander-in-Chief in America had been instructed by the Secretary of State to consider a permanent arrangement for the forces on the continent, and early in February, 1763, the Secretary at War had notified Amherst that the Ministry had decided to assign twenty battalions for the North American service. The Commander-in-Chief was instructed to consider the fortifications and the disposition of the troops necessary to maintain the newly acquired territories and the defence of the continent. In order to support the garrisons, the Ministry had also been considering an American revenue measure. It had been postponed that parliamentary session until more information could be obtained, but it was clear that an over-all programme was projected, for in March, 1763, Egremont informed Amherst that "a General Plan" for the future regulation of North America was "now actually under consideration. . . ."

At this time both Secretaries of State, Egremont and the Earl of Halifax, were conferring on a programme for the newly acquired territories, but it was not until the formation of the Grenville Ministry in the spring that Egremont referred a policy directive to the Board of Trade on May 5 stipulating the outlines of a programme for the new territories. At most the Board could be expected to fill in the details of a comprehensive policy within the general framework set down by the Secretary of State. With regard to the interior, Egremont's programme was based on precedents evolved by the military commanders in North America and the Indian superintendents during the war to guarantee the tribes against encroachments on their lands and to give them a uniform trade under imperial regulation. Unauthorized settlements and the chaotic state of the trade as conducted by the individual colonies—the source of repeated Indian complaints during the war—had led to the tribes' supporting the French during the conflict. After the fall of Canada, Sir William Johnson, with the support of Amherst, had established imperial regulation of the trade to be conducted at the posts under the supervision of the commandants. The policy of restricting settlements to prevent encroachment on lands claimed by the Indians had originally been instituted by the military in America. It had been in operation for some time, having been approved by the Board of Trade under the Earl of Halifax in 1760 and the Privy Council in 1761.

Egremont's policy directive of May 5, 1763, also proposed limiting the area of Canada, reserving the interior for the use of the Indians for the present, and erecting two governments for Florida as well as an establishment for the smaller West Indian islands acquired by the recent treaty. Some aspects of the policy raised by the Secretary of State's directive were actually being implemented by other departments. Revenue for the new establishment was to be undertaken by Grenville at the Treasury, and, as the Secretary at War informed the president of the Board of Trade, the Earl of Shelburne, the disposition of the troops and the interior forts was left to the judgment of the Commander-in-Chief in America.

There was then very little for the Board of Trade to decide for every point raised in Egremont's directive was either in actual operation, or left to the purvey of some other executive department. With regard to the North American interior, the Board of Trade was able to obtain only one minor alteration from the policy presented by Egremont. In the correspondence exchanged between the Board and the Secretary of State that summer, Egremont objected to leaving the interior outside the jurisdiction of some civil government. He proposed that the Indian country, although reserved for the use of the natives, be assigned to the government of Quebec. Disagreeing with this procedure in their report of August 5, the Board of Trade suggested an alternative arrangement by which a commission would be issued to the Commander-in-Chief to exercise jurisdiction over the interior so as to enable him to send criminals and fugitives to their respective colonies for adjudication.

When Egremont died suddenly that month, a political crisis ensued. It finally led to the resignation of the Earl of Shelburne as First Lord of Trade after he had unsuccessfully attempted to overthrow his colleagues. The programme for the new acquisitions was again taken up in September by the Earl of Halifax when, on assuming the seals for the southern department, he accepted the arguments of the Board of Trade against extending the jurisdiction of the government of Canada over the Indian reservation. No decision was to be made at present for granting a commission to the Commander-in-Chief for the government of the interior, however. If this step should be found necessary in the future, Halifax felt that such action could then be taken. The Board was instructed to complete a proclamation respecting the new acquisitions and to begin formulating specific regulations for the Indian trade. Under the presidency of the Earl of Hillsborough, the Board completed the proclamation, issued on October 7, 1763.

As the Secretary of State pointed out to Amherst in transmitting the document, it was to be hoped that the new directive, in addition to the plan regulating the Indian trade and the ten thousand troops in America, would insure stability and security for the continent. It was not until July of the following year, however, that the Board of Trade completed the detailed plan for the management of Indian trade, a project entailing the regulation of Indian affairs, both commercial and political, by imperial officers under one uniform system. Based largely on the recommendations of the Indian superintendents, the plan of 1764 was not brought into Parliament at this time in the absence of an imperial fund to defray the expense of the programme. The issue of an American revenue for the Indian department as well as the royal garrisons in the new acquisitions was to prove an explosive issue. The measure designed for this purpose was George Grenville's Stamp Act.

While a revenue measure for the maintenance of the forces was being implemented, the garrisons in the interior presented a pressing problem. Shortly after the Proclamation of 1763 was issued, it became evident that the Commander-in-Chief, assigned the decision for the distribution of the interior garrisons and fortifications, had been unable to make a general disposition because of the Indian uprising of that year. During Pontiac's Rebellion, the tribes had made devastating inroads on British military strength in the interior. Of all the posts, only Fort Pitt, Niagara, and Detroit had been able to withstand the onslaught. Whatever the cause of the revolt, many military officials in America believed that the French inhabitants were responsible, in part, for the uprising. Major Henry Gladwin, commandant at Detroit, felt that the uprising was caused by disaffected French traders who circulated the rumour that the cessation of hostilities was a British fiction, and that French forces were coming to eject the British from the interior. Amherst himself thought it not impossible that the French traders may have gone to great lengths in attempting to engross the fur trade and to exclude British rivals. In Montreal Gage, convinced of collusion between the Canadians and the Indians, held that the savages had been stirred up by rumours circulated by the French that the British planned to deprive the Indians of their lands. So great was the reaction of some British officials to the supposed perfidy of the French inhabitants that Colonel William Eyre, chief military engineer in America, advised removing "every Canadian from all our Posts to the inhabited Parts of Canada . . . to prevent their doing Mischief. . . ." Governor James Murray of Quebec, sharing this view, recommended to Halifax that all the French inhabitants in the interior be evacuated to the settled area of the northern province.

While nothing was done to implement this drastic proposal the Indian uprising did have a marked reaction on the officers in America. Gage, having replaced Amherst as Commander-in-Chief, was now convinced of the vulnerability of isolated garrisons in the interior, and welcomed the establishment of a series of military colonies on the frontier, at Niagara and Fort Pitt, in order to check Indian incursions. "We may by such means," he advised Halifax, "become formidable on the Ohio. . . ." No action was taken on this suggestion, however; on the contrary, Amherst before departing America in November, 1763, had ordered the reoccupation of all the interior forts.

A complicated and difficult task confronted the new Commander-in-Chief in these circumstances as Gage pointed out to the Treasury officials. The army had to administer an extensive territory ranging from the St. Lawrence to the Mississippi; it was involved in an Indian war; it supported the infant colonies; and it bore the expenses of the Indian department. Gage's position was made more difficult by the decision of the Treasury Board in London to impose strict controls over military expenditures. So constrained was the Commander-in-Chief by the new arrangement that he confessed to Sir William Johnson that he was thrown into difficulties in executing the services of the military and Indian departments whose operations were so vital for the administration of the interior. The posts served several rôles in addition to being the only authorized locations for the conduct of the Indian trade. Not the least of their functions was to maintain the legal authority of government in the interior. The provisions of the Proclamation of 1763 had not provided for the satisfactory exercise of legal jurisdiction by the commanding officers, and although the Proclamation called for the apprehension and extradition of criminals from the colonies taking refuge in the Indian reservation, there was no method to punish crimes committed by civilians in the interior. To meet this situation Gage recommended that a clause be added to the Mutiny Act providing that accused persons might be tried by court martial for crimes committed in areas where the civil judicature had not been established. The Mutiny Act of 1765 (5 Geo. III, c. 13) merely allowed the officers at the posts to arrest and confine accused persons. They were to be sent to the colonies for trial in civil courts.

By this procedure legal jurisdiction was extended over the French inhabitants in the interior, especially in the Illinois country when British army units finally occupied that area in 1765. Earlier attempts via the Ohio and Mississippi rivers had been frustrated by opposition from the tribes, but the situation was made especially acute in the spring of 1765 when Gage learned that the French, in the Illinois country and west of the Mississippi, were supplying the tribes with goods. Unless the British could provide the natives with supplies, they might be driven into an alliance with the French, and the security of the interior once more endangered. With this in mind, Sir William Johnson warned the Board of Trade of the influence of the French inhabitants in the Maumee and Wabash valleys. Occupation by the British of the Illinois country, he felt, would in some measure check their activities. Following a hazardous but successful journey by Johnson's deputy, George Croghan, to negotiate with the western tribes, British army units occupied the Illinois country late in 1765. Although Croghan in his journal had recorded stopping at Vincennes, a village he described as containing eighty or ninety families, no attempt was made to occupy the Wabash Valley due to the hostility of the Indians.

With the responsibilities of the army thus further extended, the reaction to the revenue measures passed by Parliament to support the American garrisons complicated Gage's task. The passage of the Stamp Act initiated widespread riots in the urban centres on the seaboard, marking the first step in the process leading to the outbreak of the Revolution a decade later. In the summer of 1765, many of the colonial governors, fearing that they would not be able to maintain order with the resources at their disposal, requested the aid of military detachments. As Gage pointed out, however, it would be difficult to comply with their request in view of the scattered and distant disposition of the troops in the interior and without stripping the forts in the Indian country of their garrisons. Nevertheless, Gage did offer to make some detachments available; the army already over-extended was thus further depleted. The process was attenuated as revolutionary tension increased in the East. In time, the need for troops on the revolutionary seaboard loomed larger than the requirements for the western garrisons in the eyes of the British ministers. At that point, a basic decision had to be made with regard to the West.

One of the first to recognize the issue was Viscount Barrington, Secretary at War, who instituted a private correspondence with Gage on the question of interior fortifications shortly after the Stamp Act riots. Aware of the inadequacy of troop arrangements in the face of any sudden emergency on the coast, and conscious of the cost to Great Britain involved in maintaining interior garrisons, Barrington sought the opinion of the Commander-in-Chief on the problem. On the basis of information supplied by Gage as to the situation of the interior forts and the alternatives open for western policy, Barrington, by the spring of 1766, had drawn up a plan calling for a drastic reduction of the garrisons in the interior and returning the control of Indian affairs and trade to the colonies in order to reduce the expense falling on Great Britain. The Secretary at War would retain only Niagara, Detroit, Michilimackinac, and Fort Chartres in the Illinois country, concentrating the bulk of the troops on the coast where they would be readily available for any emergency. Completed by early May, 1766, the Barrington plan was referred to Gage for emendation and correction by the Secretary at War, and then circulated among the ministers.

By the spring of 1766, in order to concentrate the forces and reduce expenses, Gage, with the approval of the Whig Ministry, had already begun to reduce the garrisons, ordering a retrenchment on the lower Mississippi and the evacuation of some of the lesser posts in the northern district. Aware of the unique value of the Illinois country as a counterbalance to the French west of the Mississippi, however, he urged an arrangement similar to the one he had proposed for Niagara and Fort Pitt, suggesting to the ministry that semi-military colonies be established in the Illinois country in order to relieve the problem of provisioning the troops stationed in such a remote district.

No decision was possible at this time owing to the instability of the ministry in London, but the issue of the expenses of the American forces and, by implication, British policy for the interior became involved in the political struggle marking the parliamentary session in January, 1767, during the early months of the succeeding Chatham Administration. The question of revenue for the American forces was especially urgent in view of the repeal of the Stamp Act the previous year. The matter came up again in January, 1767, when Barrington as Secretary at War brought into the House of Commons the estimate for the American army. £400,000 would be required for the coming year. The Opposition attacked so great an expense; George Grenville objected particularly to Britain's paying the cost of protecting colonists who refused to recognize the right of the mother country to tax them. The following month Barrington brought in the extraordinary expenses of the American army, an outlay not previously provided for by Parliament. The sum came to £300,000 over what had been appropriated. The particular disposition of the troops at a great distance from the settled areas of the colonies, the difficulty in transporting supplies and provisions, and the expenses of the

Indian department were the reasons given to the House of Commons for so great an expense. This caused Grenville to move that the troops be withdrawn from the interior or that the colonists be made to bear some portion of the cost. Although Grenville lost the vote on his motion, he won the substance of the debate when Charles Townsend, the Chancellor of the Exchequer, demanded in the cabinet the following month that an American tax be introduced, that the American expenses be reduced by withdrawing the forces from the interior, and that the conduct of the Indian department be returned to the colonies, in order to relieve the burden on Great Britain.

Because of the instability of the Chatham Ministry, the question was not resolved that year, but following a reorganization of the cabinet at the end of 1767, and the admission of the Earl of Hillsborough as the newly created Secretary of State for the colonies, a decision was finally reached which contained the substance of the proposals favoured by Barrington, Grenville, and the now deceased Charles Townsend.

By January, 1768, Barrington was able to assure the Commander-in-Chief in America that a decision on the disposition of the troops—a decision he had "long wish'd, & begun to despair of"—would soon be forthcoming. The next month he noted that the new Colonial Secretary would soon bring the matter before the cabinet. "He knows my Ideas & seems not to disapprove them," he confided. A decision was finally reached by the cabinet after two meetings on March 11 and March 18 when it was agreed to transfer control of commercial relations with the tribes to the colonies and to abandon all of the interior posts with the exception of Detroit, Niagara, and Michilimackinac. In addition, either Fort Chartres or some other post in the Illinois country was to be retained, along with Fort Pitt, pending a report by the Commander-in-Chief in America on these fortifications. By this new programme, the Ministry hoped to lessen the present heavy expense and to preserve the unity and discipline of the army so that it could operate effectively in an emergency. Welcoming the decision, Gage immediately ordered the posts on the lower Mississippi evacuated. He was especially concerned with Fort Chartres where the cost of the Indian department was particularly high. With Fort Pitt, it accounted for half the outlay of the Indian department in the northern district. In addition, almost all of the posts in the interior—constructed of perishable materials—were in a ruinous state.

The Illinois country presented a unique problem because of the influence of the French and their drain on the fur trade. To counter their activities, and at the same time to maintain British authority, Gage proposed that the inhabitants be collected at one point and formed into a military colony, headed by a governor and appointed council with priests to be named by the Bishop of Quebec. Three years were to pass, however, before the Ministry came to any decision. In the interval, the Commander-in-Chief was plagued with problems stemming from the administration of the interior.

In addition to preventing violations of the Indian boundary line and encroachments on lands reserved for the tribes—even after the line had been extended by the treaties of Hard Labour and Fort Stanwix in 1768—there was also the continuous problem of controlling the traders who refused to be restricted to the posts, where they would be under the surveillance of the officers and could be prevented from defrauding the natives. The burden of the Indian trade still fell on the imperial government, for the colonies failed to evolve a uniform system of regulation.

Another problem was presented by the French inhabitants in the interior—"Those cursed French Settlements," Gage complained, "with the Strolling French and Canadians"—who inhabited every Indian village and constantly aroused the animosity of the tribes against the British. So perplexed was he with the situation in the interior that he confided to Barrington that he wished "most sincerely that there was neither Settler nor Soldier in any part of the Indian Country" and that Great Britain was free of both the trouble and expense of Indian affairs.

A decision by the Ministry was precipitated, however, when it became necessary to abandon Fort Chartres, then in an advanced state of decay. An added inducement to a settlement was the continuing high cost of supplying the interior posts. Meeting on December 1, 1771, the cabinet agreed that Gage, at his discretion, be allowed to abandon Chartres and its supply post, Fort Pitt, and to submit to the cabinet the plan he had previously outlined for an establishment in the Illinois country "on the lowest plan of Expence." He was empowered to retain a temporary garrison at Kaskaskia in the Illinois country. With regard to the other forts in the interior, however, it was "agreed on all hands" in the cabinet that they be retained for the present. By the following September, Fort Chartres had been razed, a detachment of only fifty men left at Kaskaskia, and Fort Pitt evacuated.

The reduction of military strength in the Illinois country intensified the problem of the inhabitants in that district. Hillsborough, not too sanguine over any immediate solution by a mixed civil and military government as suggested by Gage, had considered the matter too complex for any decision in the near future. The matter was further complicated by the objections that the inhabitants raised to military rule. A British trader in the Illinois country, George Morgan, of the Philadelphia firm of Wharton, Baynton, and Morgan, had written his partners that, because of the "Tyranny & Oppresion" experienced by the inhabitants under the British commanding officer, he had proposed a petition to the Board of Trade requesting a civil government. The inhabitants also offered resistance to the attempt to form them into regular companies of militia in order to relieve the burden on the army. They declared that they were not obliged by their oath of allegiance to bear arms, and that their doing so would antagonize the Indians. Stating their intention of remaining neutral in case of an Indian war, they threatened to leave their settlements and cross the Mississippi should the British government press the issue.

The French at Detroit had no aversion for militia duty, however, hence it was proposed to use them to remove "vagabond" French settlers from the Indian villages. The itinerant French presented a particularly acute problem at Vincennes where there was no British military establishment, and consequently no legal authority. A count taken in 1767 and transmitted to the Colonial Secretary in January, 1769, listed a total population of 429 and 168 persons being classified as "Strangers." The settlement had increased within a short time, Gage informed Hillsborough. He found that "Strollers and Vagabonds" from Canada, Detroit, and the Illinois country had assembled there either to "live a lazy kind of Indian life," or to take refuge there from justice. So disturbed was the Commander-in-Chief over the situation on the Wabash that he considered a detachment of troops necessary for the Vincennes settlement. He wrote to the commandant at Fort Chartres: "I wish you was near enough to send down all vagabonds and Strollers" for the interior settlements must not be allowed to increase with the "fugitive French and Canadians" who went there to escape the law. They would become too formidable within a short time, he predicted, if allowed to increase.

Although Gage wished that there were no settlements at all in the Indian country, he realized that since the French were already established, the government was obliged to allow them to continue. The situation was disturbing, however, with the commandant at Fort Chartres and the Indian superintendent charging that the French at Vincennes were inciting the Wabash tribes against the British. The migratory tendencies of the inhabitants presented an additional problem. In December, 1770, it was reported that several families at Detroit had "slip'd away" to the Maumee River "under a pretense to Trade," but it was feared that they had prevailed on the Indians to grant them lands for a proposed settlement. The following year Gage confided to Sir William Johnson that the settlement at Vincennes was increasing to such an extent that some form of government was required or else the "vagabond French" should be removed. The Indian superintendent agreed, but pointed out that while it would be difficult to evacuate them, it would also be difficult to keep them under proper control.

By the end of 1771, however, with the decision to reduce the establishment in the Illinois country, Hillsborough was able to give Gage definite instructions concerning the French in the interior. Although he felt that the inhabitants in the Illinois country should be removed to Quebec or some other colony, he feared that there were too many obstacles to such a project. Since a final disposition for that district would depend on the "inclinations of the Inhabitants," the ministers would delay reaching any decision. On the other hand, he noted, it was evident that the "Settlement forming at the Post of St. Vincent" was in every respect "of the most dangerous Tendency" and would keep the British perpetually at odds with the Indians. He ordered that the inhabitants be required to evacuate.

Concurring that it would be futile to attempt to remove the

French from the Illinois country—they would merely move to the west bank of the Mississippi—Gage recognized at the same time the need for some government to insure their allegiance to Great Britain. A regular government would not be appropriate, however, in view of the scattered location of the settlements. He urged instead that a governor and judge be appointed with the approval of the inhabitants. With respect to the French at Vincennes Gage concurred with Hillsborough, informing the Colonial Secretary that they would be ordered to retire from their settlement as directed from England. On April 8, 1772, the Commander-in-Chief issued a proclamation to this effect; it was then transmitted to the inhabitants by courier via the commandant at Kaskaskia.

In view of the difficulty in communication with the remote Wabash village, it was not until December that Gage received a letter from the inhabitants addressed to Captain Hugh Lord at Kaskaskia, claiming that they held their lands by title and offering to send two delegates to prove their contention. The nature of the French claim caused some speculation between Sir William Johnson and the Commander-in-Chief. The Indian superintendent felt that an Indian title would not be admitted without setting a dangerous precedent. Although the former French régime had been liberal in its grants, Johnson had never heard that any were made on the Wabash.

In his report to the newly appointed Colonial Secretary—the Earl of Dartmouth—Gage on January 6, 1773, transmitted the letter from the inhabitants, but informed the minister that the delegates promised by the settlers to inform him of the nature of their titles had not as yet appeared. It was necessary, however, to deal with the Vincennes population in the larger context of policy for the inhabitants of the interior as a whole, and owing to pressure from the settlers of the Illinois country for some form of civil government, Dartmouth informed Gage in March that he considered some type of establishment to be necessary. Although the proposals made by the Illinois inhabitants were "too absurd and extravagent to afford the least ground for consideration," yet it did seem to him that they had a right, under the Treaty of Paris, to continue in their possessions. It would be both "dangerous and disgraceful," Dartmouth felt, to leave the Illinois country without regulations so as to insure the inhabitants the rights they were entitled to expect, and to secure their allegiance. It was to be hoped that Gage, who was shortly to return to England for consultation, would be able to supply the information necessary for a new policy. The status of the Wabash settlement would also be considered, since, by Gage's last dispatch, the inhabitants there no longer appeared "a lawless Banditti" as had been represented, but rather subjects claiming possession of their lands by right of title.

Before receiving this dispatch, however, Gage in April transmitted a memorial to the Colonial Secretary from the Vincennes settlers who declared that they were not affected by Gage's proclamation since it dealt with vagabonds and not peaceful settlers cultivating lands granted by the French King. Since their grants had been made to them as French subjects prior to the Treaty of Paris and before the agreements by the British with the tribes restricting settlements, they were not affected by Gage's proclamation. In transmitting their statement to Dartmouth, Gage pointed out that it had been customary under the French régime to empower the commandants in the Indian country to grant lands contiguous to some posts. When approved and confirmed by the governor of the province on which the fort depended, the grants were then deemed valid and entered on the registers. Some commandants had exceeded their authority, however, and their grants had not been confirmed. Since recourse had been made to the registers at Quebec, the British had been able to validate the claims of the inhabitants at Detroit. Gage had been informed that the same procedure had been used by the French in the Illinois country, but he had never heard that any grants had been made on the Wabash. It would be difficult to confirm any made by the officers at Vincennes, as well as in the Illinois country, for the registers were in New Orleans, the capital of Louisiana, now in Spanish hands. The inhabitants, he speculated, must claim under titles from the commandants or by Indian grants. The latter, as far as Gage could ascertain, had never been admitted by the French, and could not now be allowed by the British without setting a dangerous precedent. If any credit was to be given to reports concerning the inhabitants on the Wabash, many had "strolled" there from Detroit, and from settlements on both sides of the Mississippi, settling without any permission, or any title. In order to ascertain the validity of their claims, Gage had instructed the inhabitants to transmit a list of all the settlers, as well as the date of each grant, by whom confirmed and granted, and the location of the register. If the settlers were to comply with this demand, some light might be thrown on the nature of their claims. If necessary, permission might be obtained to search the archives at New Orleans.

On receipt of Gage's remarks, Dartmouth, acting on the assumption that the Commander-in-Chief was then *en route* to England for consultation, directed his further instructions to the temporary commander in America, General Frederick Haldimand. The inhabitants at Vincennes were to be informed that the royal government would consider their claims with the most favourable indulgence. Until the situation was clarified, however, the inhabitants would not be molested as long as they behaved as faithful subjects obeying the instructions of the Commander-in-Chief.

By the time these orders had arrived Gage had left for England, but the two delegates promised to present the claims of the Vincennes inhabitants had not as yet appeared. In fact, it was not until September of that year that Captain Hugh Lord, commanding at Kaskaskia, was able to transmit to Haldimand some documentary evidence to support the inhabitants in their contention. In addition to the list requested by Gage earlier that year, Lord had obtained a certificate from Louis St. Ange, former commandant at Post St. Vincent and Fort Chartres, and a deposition from Etienne Phillibert, currently acting as notary at the settlement, stating that his predecessor, one Clouvier, before fleeing the country, had lost many of the contracts for land concessions. Further, the transfer of the record office to the Illinois country in 1761 had resulted in the loss of additional documents. A further explanation was given by another former commandant at Vincennes, one St. Marie, who charged that the fugitive, Clouvier, had carried away some records while others were "eaten by rats etc."

Whatever the case, Captain Lord reported to Haldimand that it was Phillibert's contention that his predecessor had "destroyed more than half the Papers entrusted to his care," and that by this "unfortunate accident" the inhabitants were prevented from sending copies of their grants. Lord had conducted a full inquiry but could not obtain any authenticated information as to the first establishment of the post. Should the certificate by St. Ange be deemed insufficient, he for one believed that the inhabitants could not produce any better proof.

By January, 1774, having received the certificates by St. Ange and Phillibert, as well as the "Verifications of Title" requested by Gage, Haldimand transmitted the documents to Dartmouth, at the same time observing to Gage that it would be best not to molest the inhabitants any further, but to give them some sort of government. Even before receipt of the depositions in England, it was apparent that the Ministry would follow this procedure. As early as September, 1773, Gage, after conferring with Dartmouth and Lord North, was able to report that they seemed willing to oblige the French in the Illinois country and at Vincennes "whether they hold their Possessions by good or bad Title." Gage himself could think of no other solution but that he had proposed for some time—"to give them some sort of government adapted to their Situation. Within three months it was apparent that the ministers had come to a comparable decision. Dartmouth on December 1 revealed the outlines of a new policy for the French inhabitants in the interior, a policy to be adopted shortly in the Quebec Act of 1774. By the end of the year 1773, the British Ministry came to a decision; to grant civil government to the French inhabitants of the whole interior, north and west of the Ohio River. Strong pressure for this had come from the French in the Illinois country as well as from the British merchants at Detroit. Before his departure for England, Gage had received two delegates from the French in the Illinois country, Daniel Blouin and William Clajon. The Commander-in-Chief had refused to entertain their suggestions for a civil government, however, unless the proposals were made through the commanding officer in the Illinois district.

Dartmouth had expressed some interest in the views of the two Frenchmen, however, indicating that they probably would not be considered as inadmissible by the ministers. Gage had replied that Blouin and Clajon had merely presented a sketch of a form of government by which the populace would choose its own governor and magistrates, a system, Gage described, as patterned after "some Republican Model, a good deal similar to that of the Colony of Connecticut." He expressed his apprehensions to Lord at Kaskaskia, however, that Blouin and Clajon had deceived the inhabitans by instilling in them "Ideas of an English Government quite incompatible with our Constitution. . . ." Bloudin pressed the issue of a civil government nevertheless, and, after the Commander-in-Chief departed for England in June, 1773, the Frenchman wrote to Dartmouth emploring the intercession of the Colonial Secretary for the "Establishment of a Civil Government . . . on British Principles. . . ."

In response, the Colonial Secretary on December 1, 1773, informed Daniel Blouin that some form of government was necessary in the Illinois district. Although he did not think that a civil government independent of any other royal colony could be adopted, yet he could assure Blouin that the interests of the inhabitants would not be neglected. They might rest assured of enjoying "every Privelege that their Situation can with propriety admit of." At the same time, Dartmouth informed Hector Cramahé, Lieutenant-Governor of Quebec, that the affairs of the province, then actually under consideration, would be settled shortly. The limits of the colony, reduced by the Proclamation of 1763, would in Dartmouth's opinion constitute "a necessary part of this very extensive Consideration." There was no longer any hope, he continued, of perfecting the policy contemplated at the time the Proclamation of 1763 was issued. Several considerations now induced him to doubt the propriety of restricting the colony to the narrow limits prescribed by the Proclamation.

Several factors did influence the ministers in the decision to extend civil jurisdiction to the inhabitants in the interior by enlarging the boundaries of the colony of Quebec. The measures designed to raise revenue for the support of the troops garrisoning the interior country had failed, and the turbulence on the seaboard colonies had necessitated the withdrawal of the garrisons from the Indian country. Further, the entire programme of 1763 and the modification instituted in 1768 proved unsuccessful. The frontiersmen and land speculators had repeatedly violated the boundary line set by the Proclamation of

1763 and the treaties of Fort Stanwix in 1768 and Lochaber in 1770. Flagrant encroachments on Indian lands went far to antagonize the tribes already dissatisfied over the chaotic state of the Indian trade. Given the opportunity as early as 1768, the colonial assemblies had failed to regulate the traffic in a uniform system. Thoroughly aroused by 1773, the tribes were believed to have formed a confederacy and a general Indian war seemed likely. A revision in policy was necessary, and it paralleled the demands of the French inhabitants in the interior for a civil government.

It is clear from the evidence of Dartmouth's letters of December 1, 1773, that the programme for the interior as incorporated in the Quebec Act passed in the spring of 1774 did not stem from the colonial crisis of 1774. This measure cannot be considered as one of the bills directed against Massachusetts in retaliation for the Boston Tea Party, and termed by the American colonists as "Coersive Acts." Rather it was the only effective alternative left to the ministers after more than a decade of experimentation. Providing a governmental and religious settlement suited to the situation of the French Canadians, the Quebec Act extended the boundaries of the colony to include the area north and west of the Ohio River. Coupled with the additional instructions issued to Governor Guy Carleton early the next year, the Act represented the final solution of the Ministry for administering the northern district of the interior. Promulgated after other measures had proved unsuccessful, it represented an honest attempt to insure the stability and security of the interior by granting to the inhabitants a form of government following the traditions and circumstances of the French inhabitants.

The Great Crossing

Dale Van Every

The end of Pontiac's war in 1765 allowed the colonists from Pennsylvania southward to cross the Appalachian divide and enter into the fertile grounds between the bluegrass region of Kentucky and Pittsburgh. Despite quarrels over the Virginia-Pennsylvania border and vague titles to land consequential to the Proclamation of 1763 and various Indian treaties, movement into the region continued at an increasing pace before 1775. Begun by the famous long hunters who moved through the Cumberland Gap before the last Anglo-French war for empire, they were followed by surveyors, and eventually by an army of Virginians commanded by Lord Dunmore who established the Old Dominion's claim to the region.

The occupation of Kentucky, begun at Harrodsburg in 1774, constituted only part of the total transmontane migration. Pittsburgh, Wheeling, and the Kanawha valley also found new white settlements developing. In mobilizing the southwest Virginia settlements for Dunmore's campaign and in his successful defense at Point Pleasant at the mouth of the Kanawha on October 10, 1774, Colonel Anthony Lewis demonstrated frontier leadership potential of the highest order. That defeat of Chief Cornstalk and the subsequent treaty of Camp Charlotte, Ohio, constitute an important chapter in the clearing of the region south of the Ohio for settlement. Moreover, Dunmore's war brought a galaxy of frontiersmen together, men who would in the subsequent decade dominate western campaigns and politics.

Dale Van Every (1896—) was born in Michigan, but he has spent most of his life in California, where between 1928 and 1942 he produced films and wrote screenplays. The author of several books dealing with the West, he is most famous for his trilogy on the "American Frontier" which contained volumes entitled Forth to the Wilderness *(1961),* A Company of Heroes *(1962), and* Ark of Empire *(1963). Collectively they constitute the most readable account of the American West between the French and Indian War and the purchase of Louisiana.*

From Dale Van Every, *Forth to the Wilderness: The First American Frontier, 1754–1774* (New York, 1961), 313–345; used with permission of William Morrow and Company.

THE FIRST AMERICANS to look beyond the mountains for the fulfillment of their expectations called themselves Men of the Western Waters. No allusion could more clearly emphasize how complete had been the readjustment of their every major interest. By western waters they meant streams which flowed westward toward the Mississippi instead of eastward into the Atlantic. There were not yet wagon roads, canals, or river steamboats and they were committing themselves to a separation from old associations as radical as had they or their fathers in making their original move across the Atlantic. Travel from the new homes they were seeking back to the cities of the seaboard would become a longer and more arduous journey than from those cities back across the Atlantic to Europe.

The western waters nearest to the very early frontier were in a unique area. On account of comparative ease of access it amounted to a southern extension of the Valley of Virginia and was to be reached not by travel west but by travel south. Yet its streams flowed westward. The crestline of the Alleghenies, elsewhere so unmistakable, took here a jog to the east while at the same time losing much of its prominence. By a kind of geographical accident, here the real mountain barrier lay far to the west of the actual divide, for two of the greatest rivers of the west, the Tennessee and the Kanawha, rose inside this angle side by side. Each had eroded the head of its watershed until its upper tributaries had penetrated into a region well to the east of the main bulk of the Appalachian range. Divided only by steep but narrow and easily surmountable ridges, their headwaters were interlaced with each other's and with those of the eastward flowing Roanoke and James. A man on foot or horseback found awaiting him a rough but readily passable route when seeking to reach the upper Roanoke, whether he came southward down the Valley or westward from tidewater, and from the Roanoke on he was separated only by local watersheds, each to be crossed in a short day's journey, from New River, flowing north-north-west into the great Kanawha, and, successively, beyond, the Holston, Clinch, and Powell, flowing south-southwest into the Tennessee. This singular region with its paradoxical centrifuge of rivers and its even more paradoxical distortion of the mountain barrier was to assume a strategic importance in the western movement second only to the Forks of the Ohio. But this importance was late in becoming apparent.

The first Englishmen of certain record to enter it and thus to be first to stand on western waters were Thomas Batts and Robert Fallam in 1671. They crossed the piedmont, scaled Blue Ridge, turned down the Valley, and just beyond the next ridge came to their astonishment upon a westward flowing river. They called it the Great River. Later Virginians called it New River. So long had seemed its discoverers' journey from the then westernmost Virginia settlements that they imagined that they might have approached the Western Ocean. They measured the river for tidal rise and fall and brought back the story that they were certain that they had caught a distant glimpse far down its valley of waves and sails.

It was another three quarters of a century before the first settlers appeared on New River. They were introduced under the sponsorship of James Patton, the great forerunner of Virginia's first generation of great expansionists. He was an English sea captain who had made more than a score of Atlantic crossings with shiploads of immigrants and redemptioners. Becoming at last fired with a desire himself to become a part of this beckoning new world to which he had brought so many others, he persuaded the same Governor Gooch of Virginia who made the first Ohio Company grant to assign him 120,000 acres of land in the wilderness to the southwest of Virginia's then frontier. His venture was more than a land speculation for he proposed to take personal charge of the grant's development and himself to introduce actual settlers. In 1748, continuing to extend his colonizing, he established two seventeen-year-old Irish youths, William Ingles and John Draper, on New River. Their station became the first English settlement on the western slope of the Allegheny divide.

Patton's initiative and success led to a sudden increase in Virginia's interest in western lands. The Ohio Company was formed by northern Virginians whose attention was fixed on the northwest and the Forks of the Ohio. Central and southern Virginians formed the Loyal Company to investigate the possibilities to the more remote southwest. Dr. Thomas Walker, whose intellectual and scientific attainments commanded the widest respect and who was later to become the guardian of the

young Thomas Jefferson, took active lead of this new enterprise. Instead of confining his promotional efforts to political
and financial activities in Williamsburg and London he went
into the wilderness to see for himself what kind of land and how
much land might be available. The Company had been granted
800,000 acres but to find anything like that amount of accessible
land beyond the already settled or pre-empted portion of
Virginia was far more of a problem than to coax the grant from
Virginia's complacent government. To look for it up the Kanawha to the northwest was useless. The river wound for
hundreds of miles through deep gorges in rugged mountains
and finally joined the Ohio too close to the towns of Indians
under French influence to suggest this as an appropriate site for
a settlement. To look southwestward down the Tennessee was
equally inadvisable since any move in that direction must at
once offend England's uncertain friends, the Cherokee, and
soon thereafter get into country to which North Carolina had a
stronger claim. There was therefore nowhere to look but west
and this Walker did. In 1750 he set out with five companions on
his famous exploring journey, crossing the Holston, Clinch,
and Powell rivers, picking up the Great War Path used by
Cherokee and Shawnee warriors in their attacks on each other,
and keeping on to the discovery of Cumberland Gap. By now he
had put what he had hoped was the principal part of the
mountain barrier behind him yet there seemed nothing but
more mountains and even wilder wilderness beyond. In April
he erected the first log cabin to be built by white men in
Kentucky as a token that he had come not merely to look but to
possess. Continued circling to the north and northeast disclosed, however, only more of these densely thicketed and
nearly impassable mountains. In July he struggled back to
Staunton, having found no land beyond the Gap worth his
company's attention. One item in his report, however, stirred
many pulses. He wrote: "We killed 13 Buffaloes, 8 Elks, 20
Deer, 4 Wild Geese, about 150 Turkeys, besides small game. We
might have killed three times as much meat, if we had wanted
it."

Meanwhile the little settlement on New River, named
Draper's Meadows for John Draper's father, George, who had
failed to return from a hunting trip, continued modestly to

flourish. William Ingles married John's sister, Mary, and founded a family whose absorbing adventures dramatically illustrate, because they chanced to be recorded in some detail, the kind of stresses to which every frontier family of the time was subjected. Draper's Meadows was overwhelmed by the first Indian attack of the French War to strike the Virginia frontier. On July 8, 1755, the day before Braddock's disaster on the far off Monongahela, a Shawnee war party swept in upon the little settlement. James Patton himself was present, being engaged, with the aid of young William Preston, in distributing a fresh supply of ammunition to the more outlying stations. He was then 63 but the old sea captain was as fiercely vigorous as ever. He cut down two Indians with his broadsword before being borne down by numbers. In the sudden desperate confusion of the attack Ingles and Preston both escaped death, each fortunately spared for an ensuing lifetime of service to the frontier.

Mary Ingles and her two children, four-year-old Thomas and two-year-old George, were among those carried off by the Indians. The third day after her capture she gave birth to a baby girl but managed nevertheless to keep up with the war party during its three-hundred-mile return over the mountains to the Scioto. Three months later she came to grips with her fearfully difficult decision. Determined to return to her husband, she realized any attempt to escape was hopeless with an infant in arms. She therefore left the baby behind in a Shawnee salt-making camp at Big Bone Lick and after weeks of starving and freezing made her way through the winter wilderness back to Virginia.

Though Mary bore her husband four more children and Ingles' station became one of the most substantial on the Wilderness Road she never ceased to brood over the baby girl she had abandoned. During the next ten war years both parents were continually absorbed in the duties and demands of frontier defense but both likewise were continually oppressed by the thought of their captive children. Nothing was ever heard of the fate of the little girl but eventually they learned that George had failed to survive the first year of his captivity. Ingles never relaxed his efforts and the year of the Fort Stanwix Treaty he finally succeeded in locating and ransoming Thomas. Seventeen by now, Thomas had forgotten every word of English and had become a complete Indian. For a time after his return to his parents only constant watchfulness restrained him from escaping back to the Shawnee. Educated by a no less distinguished tutor than Dr. Thomas Walker, he eventually became reconciled to life among the whites, set up a place for himself, and married. After another fourteen years he suffered exactly as had his father. His home was burned in a 1782 Indian attack in which his wife in her turn was carried off.

Such afflictions as these suffered by the Ingles family were common on the southern Virginia frontier during the repeated attacks and perpetual threat of attack of the French War, the Cherokee War, and Pontiac's War. During this ten-year-long strain the frontier did not advance. It did well to hold its own, which it did on the whole, aside from withdrawal from some of the outlying and more exposed stations. The demands of continued conflict provided, meanwhile, a training school for woodsmen, for local militia, and, above all, for citizen commanders destined to meet the greater demands to come. It was a hard school. Men who were not quick to learn were no longer quick.

With the restoration of a troubled peace in 1765, the southwest Virginia frontier first rebuilt and then began to contemplate the new land beyond New River. The first to venture westward were the long hunters. Most were but dimly aware of the immense service they were about to perform. They were chiefly impelled to see country they had never seen before. At first they hunted across the Holston, the Clinch, and the Powell. But Cumberland Gap, discovered by Walker 15 years earlier, drew them like a magnet. They passed through it and roamed on westward, hunting, trapping, marveling at the height of the cane and the number of buffalo, until the more venturesome had emerged from the last mountains into the beautiful lowland valleys of central Kentucky. Most of those restless wanderers have remained nameless. But one of them has given his name to an era. Though Daniel Boone had been preceded by many others, his own first excursion into Kentucky in 1767 was noteworthy as a preparation for later achievements. Accompanied by Samuel Harrod and Michael Stoner, he passed through the Gap and wintered in the same thicketed maze of eastern Kentucky mountains which had so disillusioned Walker. But so far Boone was looking for room to hunt not to plant and he was more attracted than dismayed. In 1769 he went back, this time accompanied by John Finley, an old ex-trader whose stories of the Kentucky country had excited Boone when the two had served together with Braddock. Finley had not seen Kentucky since in 1752 he had for a few weeks had a trading post there but he still remembered vividly what he had seen there. Boone and his companions, who included his brother, Squire, roved for almost two years across Kentucky, exploring, hunting, trapping, becoming in the course of their wanderings as familiar with the enchanting Bluegrass as with the Barrens or the Wilderness. For years the Shawnee had been increasingly disturbed by these insolent invasions of their favorite hunting grounds by white hunters. As yet unwilling themselves to accept sole responsibility for breaking the peace they contented themselves for a while with catching as many of the interlopers as they could, confiscating their arms, horses, traps, and furs, scolding them, threatening them, and turning them loose. Boone and members of his party were twice captured and plundered. The Shawnee chief's grimly succinct advice to them is recorded as: "Now, brothers, go home and stay there."

Tales of the wild paradise in Kentucky brought back by long hunters stirred the imagination of their stay-at-home neighbors. On the southwestern Virginia frontier practical attention was so far, however, too intent on the immediately adjacent valleys of the Holston, the Clinch, and the Powell to be as yet seriously distracted by a prospect so far, however fair, as Kentucky. But any advance across even this nearest threshold was ostensibly denied them. By the terms of the Proclamation, which defined the western limit of legal settlement as the line of the watershed dividing eastward and westward flowing rivers, even the twenty-year-old settlements on New River were illegal. Virginia was appealing to the cabinet for some adjustment of this manifest injustice. The cabinet declined to budge, ruling that there could be no exceptions and that the New River settlers must withdraw. But the King's ministers were far off and concerned with many other problems. The settlers were right there on the ground and concerned with but this one. They sat tight. Those who had been tenants merely ceased paying their quitrents. The cabinet relented enough to consent to the New River settlers remaining, providing the consent of the Cherokee could likewise be obtained.

Stuart undertook to negotiate this question with the Cherokee and they readily agreed in 1768 to the Hard Labor line which left the New River settlements on the Virginia side. The cabinet accepted this solution but decreed that under no circumstances were there to be further grants west of the Proclamation Line. This disapproval was never relaxed and the governors of Virginia were repeatedly and sternly instructed to conform to the injunction. But the wave of frontier excitement produced by 1768's promise of at least temporary Indian peace, which had led to the rush of settlers to the upper Ohio, stirred a similar reaction in southern Virginia and western North Carolina. There was an immediate pressing by bolder borderers into the inviting valleys of the Holston and the Clinch even though this was regarded at the time as all but certain to draw Cherokee attack. That they were violating English law concerned them least of all.

Stuart was fully prepared to hold the Line and to protect Cherokee interests but his intentions were frustrated by the Cherokee themselves. Their older and more influential chiefs, including particularly Attakullaculla and Oconostota, had on their visit to the Iroquois in 1768 been deeply impressed by the dexterities of Iroquois statecraft. The Iroquois had contrived to guard their own borders by turning the time of white advance off to the west. The Cherokee proposed now to do the same in their sphere. Without regard for Stuart's advice they began offering the Virginians even more than the Virginians were asking. The successive Lochaber and Donelson lines, revising the boundaries between Virginians and Cherokee, each readily if not eagerly approved by the Cherokee, were like gates swinging open, inviting white settlers to push westward toward Kentucky rather than southward toward the Cherokee homeland. As a result, settlers were able to occupy, unresisted, the upper valleys of the Holston and Clinch and to begin to trickle into the Powell. Their number swelled so rapidly that in 1772 the new county of Fincastle was formed to conduct the affairs of Virginians living west of New River. This advance and the coincidental advance of settlers into western Pennsylvania at the other end of the active frontier were like the two horns of a crescent, each aimed at Kentucky. Cherokee policy had combined with Iroquois policy to dump the entire burden of Indian resistance to white encroachment upon the shoulders of the forsaken Shawnee. It was the ensuing lodgment of American frontiersmen in the middle of the Mississippi Valley, however limited and precarious a lodgment at first, that was to sever the main Indian defense line, frustrate every imperial purpose of England and Spain, and make the new United States a continental power almost from the date of birth.

But these were distant prospects to those frontier leaders, farsighted as they were, who in 1773 made the actual decision to undertake at once the occupation of Kentucky. The stupendous difficulties lying in wait were far more visible. Kentucky was very far away indeed and to be reached from the existing frontier only by a passage of hundreds of miles through an unbroken wilderness inviting Indian attack at any mile or any hour. It had been but eight years since Gage and Bouquet had concluded that such a passage was a task too difficult for a fully organized professional army. The westernmost settlements from which the long leap must be launched, on the Monongahela and the Holston, had been themselves so recently occupied that people had as yet scarcely begun clearing their land and were in many cases still uncertain whether they were in Pennsylvania, Virginia, or North Carolina. They already had problems too many and too pressing to have attention to spare for an entire new set of problems. Their greatest need was a pause to consolidate gains that had already been made too fast. But with that willful self-assurance that was a frontier characteristic so new nobody yet recognized it, it was nevertheless determined to reach straight away for Kentucky.

Ironically enough, the groundwork for the move was laid by Lord Dunmore, the new Governor of Virginia, whose official duty it was to prevent it. In this new frontier crisis, exactly as had his predecessor, Dinwiddie, in the frontier crisis of 1753, he ignored his government's instructions and confounded his government's policy. Most royal governors had accepted their posts in the hope of improving their private fortunes. Most had instead become involved in tedious and protracted disputes with provincial assemblies who objected to every exercise of executive authority. Dunmore was no exception in this respect, for in 1773 Virginia was seething with rebelliousness. But he was at the same time able to please at least those relatively few Virginians who were directly interested in western lands. His support of their designs, which we may infer may have included some of his own, violated cabinet directives to an extent made possible only by the length of time required for the transmission of official dispatches to and fro across the Atlantic. His arbitrary pronouncements had effect during the many weeks before a cabinet veto could arrive and meanwhile his acts were beyond recall. He was also shrewd enough at the outset to foresee that it would be safe to oppose the Vandalia project, which offended eastern as well as western Virginians since if it became a reality it must constitute a barrier cutting Virginia permanently down to the size of other provinces. His political perspicacity on this score was demonstrated by the cabinet's ultimate rejection of the project.

Dunmore's chief western interest was concentrated on the anarchic situation occasioned by the Pennsylvania-Virginia dispute over the upper Ohio. The flood of settlers pouring into the area was daily adding to the confusion and continually inviting intervention. Gage was still issuing proclamations calling upon illegal settlers wherever located to "quit these countries instantly and without delay" but words alone, however official, carried now even less weight than they ever had before. Fort Pitt had been abandoned and dismantled in 1772 and with it the last physical vestige of imperial authority west of the mountains had vanished. Dunmore went himself to Pittsburgh, proclaimed the area a part of Virginia to be designated the District of West Augusta, appointed Virginia justices, and privately encouraged his principal supporter, Dr. John Connolly, Croghan's nephew, to raise the standard of civil war, if necessary, to maintain Virginia's claim. Further to encourage his supporters he offered to grant them land anywhere, including Kentucky. The cloud on his authority to do this, cast by the fact that the cabinet had repeatedly and specifically forbidden it, did not trouble the men who rushed to accept. They were not men who held authority in high regard.

Dunmore's arbitrary display of energy at Pittsburgh was to have but passing effect. It was not Virginia but Pennsylvania which was presently to establish claim to the region. But in the

Holston and Clinch settlements of Fincastle County, three hundred miles away, there were effects which were never to pass. William Preston had been born on the frontier, had grown up with the frontier, and had fought in all the wars of the frontier. He was now county lieutenant and county surveyor. The latter office was if anything the more important. Nothing except survival was more important on an advancing frontier than acceptable surveys of new land being claimed. They were not important as efforts to establish title under the laws of Virginia or of England, since so far all titles west of the Proclamation Line remained invalid. They were important in that they were required to provide a clear designation of each man's claim in order to mitigate boundary disputes with adjoining claimants. Preston seized with instant vigor the opportunity opened by Dunmore's extravagant offer of grants. The western boundary of Fincastle, Virginia's newest county, was presumed to extend indefinitely westward. Preston claimed the authority, as Fincastle's surveyor, to order and to supervise surveys in Kentucky while at the same time denying the legitimacy of surveys made there by any other authority than his. The little group of extraordinarily vital and vigorous local leaders of Virginia's southwestern frontier had suddenly determined not only that Kentucky must be forthwith preempted but that they themselves must take command of the process. Control of events was not to be left to land companies, or royal governors, or infinitely distant cabinet ministers, but was to be taken by the frontier and exercised in the frontier's own interests. This was a position they were about to prove themselves abundantly able to maintain.

They realized, moreover, that whatever was to be done had to be done immediately. The excuse provided by Dunmore's grants might soon pass. He was certain soon to be suppressed or recalled by his indignant superiors in London. There was still every prospect that even sooner the projected province of Vandalia would be set up, thus erecting a permanent barrier of prior claims, unsympathetic officials, and politically powerful influences to every aspiration of the Virginia frontier. Under less pressing circumstances a much more cautious program would have been indicated. So precipitate a thrust as deep into the Indian country as Kentucky would without the slightest

doubt bring on an Indian war. But the other threats left no time
for discretion. There was literally no time to lose. None was.

In 1773 the previous invasion of Kentucky by long hunters
was succeeded by a new invasion by surveyors. Guided and
guarded by long hunters with previous experience with the
country, they ranged across Kentucky with their chains, com-
passes, and little red flags, selecting and marking the more
attractive tracts. The outraged Shawnee sought to discourage
them as they had formerly the hunters. Many were despoiled
and later in the year a number of the more persistent were
killed. But like the long hunters they were not to be discouraged.

Not all of these 1773 surveyors were subject to Preston's
supervision. Thomas Bullitt, for one, had advertised in newspapers of Pennsylvania as well as Virginia for volunteers to
accompany him. To Preston's even greater dissatisfaction Bullitt paused on his way down the Ohio to treat with the Shawnee
for permission to conduct his surveys. Other parties were led by
William Thompson, James Finley, James Harrod, James Smith,
and James McAfee. But Preston began soon to gather the reins
more firmly into his own hands. Later in the year he organized a
larger and more formal surveying party under John Floyd
which was to make a more complete and authoritative survey
superseding the earlier piecemeal ventures.

None of these surveys was clothed with any authority more
substantial than Preston's assertion that as surveyor of Fincastle
County his jurisdiction extended indefinitely westward. No one
making them imagined the surveys were establishing titles of
any legal validity. But the frontier had by now well learned that
actual occupation could be depended upon to lead to practical
possession. What the surveyors were achieving was to select and
designate prior claims to land for the benefit of themselves, of
their frontier friends, relatives, neighbors, and associates still
east of the mountains, and of a select few figures of political and
economic influence whose support and sympathy were worth
enlisting. Among this latter group were Washington, Patrick
Henry, Colonel Richard Byrd III, and John Connolly.

Daniel Boone, for his part, saw no compelling virtue in
fooling with or waiting for surveys. On the road to possession
occupation in person was in his view a longer step than pre-

emption on a map. In late September he started for Kentucky with forty-odd actual settlers, some of them his former neighbors from the Yadkin and others his more recent neighbors from the Clinch. The risks confronting and the hopes animating the little expedition were precariously balanced but fully understood. So far the Shawnee had been kept isolated by the diplomatic maneuvers of Johnson and Stuart and the self-serving intertribal machinations of the Iroquois and the Cherokee. Boone's risk was that the Shawnee had by now been made so desperate that they might feel compelled to go to war even though they must fight alone. His hope was that they might continue to hesitate until he had had time to build a stockade in Kentucky. If they gave him that much time he counted on being able thereafter to hold it. The Shawnee were not long in dispelling every doubt. They attacked him before he had reached Cumberland G ap. Among the five whites killed were Boone's son, James, and Henry, son of William Russell, a Fincastle justice and an outstanding leader of Clinch River settlers. The Shawnee had served grim and unmistakable warning. Were the Virginians to keep on coming at Kentucky then they must expect war.

Boone, somewhat reluctantly, turned back. He was not so much perturbed by Shawnee hostility, which he had more than half expected, as he was by his uncertainty about the Cherokee attitude. The Shawnee attack on the Cherokee side of the mountains suggested progress toward an understanding between these traditional enemies. The more than two-hundred-mile-long trail over the mountains to Kentucky was an incredibly perilous line of communications at best. Were the Cherokee to support Shawnee resistance by attacking its Virginia end it must become an impossible one. There had been recent indications that such a development was far from impossible. For the last three years persistent Shawnee delegations had been seeking better relations with the Cherokee and beseeching them to realize that the Shawnee cause against the whites was a common Indian cause. A lively faction among the Cherokee, particularly among the younger warriors, had begun to agree with this point of view.

After the Cumberland Gap attack on Boone, frontier leaders made urgent representations to the Cherokee, demanding to know their intentions. It presently became evident that the peace faction, headed by Attakullaculla, was still in control of their councils. With Cherokee neutrality assured, at least for the moment, Preston ordered Floyd to proceed. As soon as spring made wilderness travel feasible the advance into Kentucky was to be resumed and the Shawnee challenge to be accepted. The frontier began to prepare for the coming war. The Frontier People had come a long way since the days they had cowered in despair awaiting the succor of an English regular army. They were now boldly seeking a war and proposing when it came to wage it unassisted.

The winter was filled with alarms which each week became more strident. The fierce animosity between the races led people almost to welcome every rumor of trouble. The long frontier with its isolated farms and stations offered innumerable opportunities for local provocations, altercations, and incidents. The nearer Cherokee and Mingo who had promised neutrality were more often involved than the more distant Shawnee. By 1774 the frontier was more than ever disposed to feel that any and every Indian was after all just another Indian. Reports of instances of whites killing Indians and Indians killing whites flared like heat lightning along the border.

The Shawnee dispatched delegations to other nations in one last frantic effort to rally support. But in the north the Iroquois more sternly than ever admonished the Mingo and Delaware to stand aside, in the south the opinion of the peace faction among the Cherokee that Cherokee interests were not involved continued to prevail, and in the west the Miami and Wyandot offered the Shawnee no support more tangible than their profound sympathy. A Shawnee delegation came also to Pittsburgh to remind Alexander McKee, Croghan's successor as Deputy Superintendent, that this white encroachment below the Kanawha was a flagrant violation of solemn treaties and a repudiation of every assurance offered them under the Proclamation. It was McKee's official duty to listen. But he had been stripped of the power to offer redress. He could only agree with the justice of their protests, condole with them, and counsel them to remain patient.

The Pennsylvania-Virginia territorial dispute was serving all that late winter and early spring to heighten every other border

tension. Connolly announced that he had been commissioned
Virginia's commander on the Ohio by Dunmore, called up the
Virginia settlers of the area for militia service, and erected a
stockage on the ruins of Fort Pitt which he called Fort Dunmore. Rival Pennsylvania officials placed Connolly under arrest
but his Virginia militia forced his release. Since the Virginia
militia constituted the only even partially organized military
force in the region, Virginia partisans were able to establish
Connolly's temporary supremacy and to harass, imprison, mal-
treat, and expel Pennsylvania sheriffs and justices. The
Shawnee had been sufficiently observant to be by now making a
distinction between the settlers from the two provinces and to
be asserting that only the Virginians were their enemies. Connolly, for his part, was equally aware that an Indian war would
improve Virginia's position in the boundary dispute with Pennsylvania. He circulated reports along the Ohio frontier advising
all settlers to prepare at once to defend themselves and declaring that the long-threatened war with the Shawnee had to all
intents and purposes already begun. Anxious to assure the
safety of the sympathetic Pennsylvania traders residing in their
towns, the Shawnee conducted them to Pittsburgh with a
Shawnee escort commanded by Cornstalk's brother. In spite of
its having been engaged in a mission committed to saving white
lives, Connolly attempted to seize and then to assault the escort.
The Shawnee were only saved from this turbulent militia by the
sagacity of Croghan and McKee in contriving to smuggle them
out of Pittsburgh and back to their country.

Cornstalk still hoped to keep his nation out of a war which he
well realized must surely be lost if fought without allies. But he
was also being forced to realize that the one alternative was
abject surrender. For that portentous spring of 1774 the ever
more imminent threat of war produced no slackening in the
compulsive surge of the white frontier toward Kentucky.
Floyd's expedition made its way down the Ohio and resumed
the provocative surveys. James Harrod conducted a party of
actual settlers to Kentucky where they began the erection of the
houses of Harrodsburg, destined soon to be the capital of
Kentucky. George Rogers Clark, then only twenty-two but
within three more years to become the greatest of all frontier
leaders, was camped near Zane's Station with another party of

90 settlers on their way to Kentucky who were lingering there only while they decided whether to go on or first to strike a warning blow at the nearest Shawnee. War had by now become without doubt inevitable before the summer was over but it was precipitated immediately by an instance of white brutality even more shocking than had been the Stump murders.

On the west bank of the Ohio River, near the present Steubenville, Ohio, there was a small Mingo village presided over by a jovial, middle-aged subchief whose Indian name was Tachnechdorus. He was better known to his many white friends as Logan. Most other Indians of the region had long since withdrawn into the interior of Ohio but this handful of Mingo were not alarmed by their proximity to the white frontier since they were a colony of the Iroquois who were as clearly recognized as allies by Virginia and Pennsylvania as by England and their chief, Logan, had for long been as clearly recognized as a staunch friend of the whites with whom all of his life he had lived in close and amiable contact. Logan's mother was a Cayuga and his father had been a Frenchman who after having been captured as a child by Oneida had grown up to become an important Iroquois chief. Logan had formerly lived on the Susquehanna and had taken his white name as a mark of his attachment to James Logan, the Quaker Indian agent and later governor who for half a century had been much respected by all Pennsylvania Indians. During the French War and Pontiac's War Logan had clung to his white loyalties at so great a risk to his life that he had finally been forced to flee to Philadelphia for refuge.

Just across the river from the Mingo village was a white settlement usually known as Baker's Bottom inasmuch as its principal edifice was a bar kept by Joshua Baker. Its inhabitants were grimly aware of their exposed location at the very edge of the Indian country but their relations had been amicable with their immediate Mingo neighbors who had been accustomed often to paddle across the river to trade, visit, or drink. Baker's wife had a cow and frequently gave Mingo women milk for their children. Connolly's warning that the frontier must prepare at once to defend itself roused among the settlers that ferocious antipathy to all Indians with which from childhood all border people had been imbued. As was the case with the Paxton Boys and the Conestoga their implacable attention became fixed on the nearest Indians. When four of the Mingo, two unarmed men and two women, came unsuspectingly across the river they were made drunk and butchered. Five more Mingo who came at intervals to inquire what had happened to the others were shot down before they could get out of their canoes. Among the nine dead were Logan's mother, brother, sister, and several cousins. Strapped to his sister's back, and surviving, was the infant son of John Gibson, then a trader and later a Revolutionary colonel, a judge, and secretary of Indiana territory.

The bereaved Logan fiercely renounced his lifelong partiality for whites. His vengeance was terrible. Gathering about him a band of his previously neutral Mingo which was soon joined by numbers of ardent young Shawnee who had become impatient with Cornstalk's inaction, he began his extraction of an eye for an eye. He did not attempt a single invasion. Instead, he divided his followers into small packs which were directed to lurk in the wilderness until they could descend by surprise upon isolated farms and outlying settlements. No tactic could have been more cruel or more effective or more nearly impossible to counter. His stabbing attacks were scattered from the Allegheny to Cumberland Gap so that the frontier was terrified from end to end and at no point could the inhabitants feel that they might not be the next to suffer. Logan later said that he himself halted his depredations after he had personally killed 13, which according to his count was the number of his relatives, friends, and acquaintances the whites had killed that spring, but his followers pretended to no such restraint. The frontier's recent advance across wide expanses of new country had left it sprawled, disorganized, and most difficult to defend. Soon thousands of these new settlers were in flight. Most sought refuge in the nearest larger settlement but many of the fainter-hearted kept on eastward across the Monongahela and even across the mountains. The frontier now had the war that it had so deliberately sought.

The government in London was perhaps not too disturbed that the Americans should have a border war which it could be hoped might distract them from their seditious concern with petitions, protests, and riots but was nevertheless incensed by Dunmore's many irresponsibilities. In the colonies, however, there was little disposition to regard it as an American war and less intention of becoming involved in it. Everybody who did not live on the frontier, which included nineteen out of every twenty Americans, charged those who did live there with having forced the war on the inoffensive Indians. American abhorrence of the Logan murders was universal but the bitterest public denunciations were directed at Dunmore and the principal frontier leaders, in that order. Pennsylvanians asserted that he with the connivance of such fellow conspirators as Connolly and Preston had fomented Indian trouble to aid Virginia in tearing away the western portion of their province. Tidewater Virginians were no better pleased. They charged that the same combination had embarked upon an indefensible land-grabbing program for their personal profit which could prove of no conceivable benefit to the province as a whole. Most patriot leaders from Charleston to Boston accused Dunmore of engaging in a Royalist plot to embroil the colonies in an Indian war in order to draw American attention away from their just quarrel with George III and his ministers. All in all the conviction of seaboard people was all but unanimous that the frontier should be left to stew in its own juice. Pennsylvania's assembly declined to call up a single company of militia, though a grudging allowance was made for the hiring of a hundred rangers to assist in the defense of some of Pennsylvania's more exposed settlements. At Williamsburg the House of Burgesses was nearly as much opposed to the appropriation of defense funds. Dunmore's sole recourse in the emergency which he had done so much to bring on was to call up the militia of the frontier counties which amounted to notifying them that they could expect no help.

All along the more exposed edges of the frontier people were either fleeing or "forting," as they termed the hasty resort of the inhabitants of each neighborhood to the nearest community stockade for refuge and mutual defense. Fincastle County was beset in addition to its general defense problem by two other concerns. The first was that the increasingly restless Cherokee might enter the war, an apprehension that had been deepened by the recent peculiarly gratuitous murder by one Isaac Crabtree of an inoffensive Cherokee visitor, commonly known to the whites as Cherokee Billy, while the victim was innocently observing an afternoon of horse racing at a Watauga settlement. The second was fear for the fate of their surveyors scattered through Kentucky who might not yet have realized how much more dangerous their situation had suddenly become.

With regard to the Cherokee threat it could only be trusted that they would swallow this last provocation, as they had so many others, since there was no possibility of appeasing their wrath by penalizing Crabtree. On any frontier it was regarded as utterly irrational to consider punishing a white man for any injury, including murder, done an Indian. But something could be done about the surveyors. Daniel Boone and Michael Stoner were dispatched to search Kentucky for them. The two combed the Kentucky wilderness as far as the Falls of the Ohio and in two months returned safely after dodging Indians during the most of an 800-mile journey. They had been in time to warn many of the surveyors. A few had already been killed, but some escaped by canoe down the Mississippi, and most of the others were able to get back over the mountains. Harrod's party broke off their construction of Harrodsburg and marched to the Holston where they enlisted in a body in the frontier army then being organized. By midsummer there was not a white man left in Kentucky.

For Dunmore, with a war on his hands for which his government, his province, and public opinion everywhere held him chiefly responsible, there was no alternative to getting on with it as best he could. This turned out most unexpectedly to be very well indeed as a consequence of a development nobody then was prepared to believe possible. First reports of fleeing settlers had indicated another sad repetition of the helpless frontier panic that had followed the outbreaks of the French War and Pontiac's War. But there was something different about this 1774 frontier and how great was that difference was about to be demonstrated. It presently became apparent that many more people were forting than fleeing and that instead of waiting for help they were themselves already preparing to strike back.

Having no semblance of a regular army at his command and having been refused by his assembly the appropriation that would have permitted him to mobilize the militia of eastern Virginia, Dunmore's campaign plans were necessarily limited to whatever use could be made of the totally untried and most sketchily organized frontier militia. His only thought at first was of defense. He directed the militia of the northern Virginia frontier to construct a fort on the Ohio at Zane's Station and the militia of the southern frontier to march up the Kanawha to construct another fort on the Ohio at the mouth of that river.

In the north the task was simplified by the existence of wagon roads, nearby settlements, and an available food supply. The northern commander, Major Angus McDonald, whose previous military experience as a sergeant under Bouquet had included an attempt to expel the trespassing "vagabonds" of 1762 in this same region, was able promptly to obey his instructions. The new fort was called Fort Fincastle since it was just far enough west to be within the far-flung boundaries of Preston's Fincastle County. But more was to come of the maneuver. Contingents of frontier militia were seldom so much commanded by their officers as were their officers by the opinions of their men. Infuriated by the continued depredations of Logan's raiders, the 400 militiamen of McDonald's command held angry meetings and voted to move from defense to offense. Dropping down-river in bateaux and canoes, McDonald marched ninety miles into the wilderness and burned several of the nearer Shawnee towns after encountering no resistance beyond some scattered sniping and skirmishing. The Shawnee were fully able to have overwhelmed so small a force as McDonald's, as they were soon to prove, but they declined to give battle. Cornstalk was well aware that a rout of McDonald could not become a victory that could win a war. He was still casting about desperately but unsuccessfully for the support of allies to enable him either to strike back hard enough to deter white aggression or at least to negotiate from a position of strength. McDonald's frontier militia withdrew to the Virginia side of the Ohio, delighted with their success and animated by a new confidence in their prowess. They had some reason to feel pleased with their temerity. Theirs had been the first offensive engagement undertaken by an independent frontier force since Armstrong's Kittanning raid eighteen years before in 1756. Aside from having demonstrated the new frontier resolution, the campaign was perhaps chiefly significant for having provided George Rogers Clark with the first military experience of his memorable career.

The southern commander, Colonel Andrew Lewis, was confronted by an infinitely more formidable task. Among his problems was almost every classic difficulty known to military science. He was undertaking to march his army 200 miles through forested mountains and keep it fed and supplied over a lengthening line of communications made by the nature of the terrain peculiarly susceptible to disruption in order to seek battle with an enemy in the heart of that enemy's country. Meanwhile his main base, together with the homes and families of his men, was exposed to an ever more serious threat of Cherokee assault which must be made even more likely by the departure of the majority of its defenders. Possibly not least among his burdens was the oppressive memory that in every former campaign in which he had commanded he had encountered disaster. If so he did not permit this thought to swerve him a hairsbreadth from his purpose.

Almost his only element of strength, aside from his own indomitable spirit, was the stature of the men who rallied to his standard. Not until the days of a Scott, a Grant, or a Lee, was an American commander to be blessed with such an array of supremely qualified lieutenants. His colonels, William Preston, Charles Lewis, William Christian, and William Fleming, were men whose outstanding capacities were rivaled only by those of his junior officers, among whom were James Robertson, Evan Shelby, Arthur Campbell, William Ingles, Benjamin Logan, Daniel Boone, William Russell, John Field, James Harrod, William Cocke, John Floyd, Matthew Arbuckle, Valentine Sevier, and James Ward. Upon his muster rolls were most of the greatest names in frontier annals.

Dunmore's astonishing proposal that quotas of the militia of Augusta, Botetourt, and Fincastle counties, representing respectively the middle Valley, the southern Valley, and the new southwestern frontier, be organized into an expedition to make the infinitely difficult Kanawha advance to the Ohio was taken under consideration by the frontier's local leaders. At first glance it seemed to border on the fantastic to expect a crowd of untrained and unequipped settlers, not all of whom had guns and no one of whom had more than enough powder to do a little hunting, to make such a march into the Indian country as had only been made before by a Braddock, a Forbes, or a Bouquet with a regular army supported by artillery, wagon trains, and ammunition by the ton. Everybody, moreover, was aware that nobody could command the services of a single militiaman. All that was possible was the suggestion that a man might feel like volunteering, after he had been able to persuade himself that this was at least a halfway rational project. There was as little respect for another man's opinion on this side of the frontier as on the Indian side. But the more people thought about it and talked about it the more most warmed to the idea. In the course of attempting to arrive at a decision the military commanders of each community undertook an exchange of letters with their fellow commanders which resembled on a smaller but equally vital scale the exchange of views and news undertaken by the contemporary committees of correspondence in the course of attempting to hit upon the most effective means by which patriots might resist the impositions of the King's ministers. It presently became apparent that the frontier consensus favored any move to hit back at their Indian tormentors. But in one respect they differed with the governor. No one could see the use in making so great an effort just to build a fort. What was much preferred was to keep on across the Ohio until the Shawnee, together with any other Indians who might side with them, could be met and fought on their own ground. Augusta and Botetourt began at once to muster their regiments and to wrestle with the so much greater task of arranging for their supply while in the field.

Upon Fincastle's county lieutenant, Preston, fell the heaviest burden of all, for his southwestern border was more exposed to Indian raids and was increasingly threatened by the possibility of a general Cherokee attack. It was for Preston to attempt to decide how many men must be retained for home defense before allotting men to the expeditionary force and for each man who volunteered for distant service to decide if it was really his duty to leave his family for his neighbors to guard. Uppermost that summer in every responsible settler's mind was the dread that meanwhile, in some sudden gust of panic, the whole frontier might be abandoned, as had so often happened in former wars. Some inkling of the resolution with which people were facing up to this danger may be gained from extracts from messages being exchanged by Preston and his local commanders:

The frenzied labors of emergency stockade building were touched upon in a July 13th note from William Russell on the Clinch which closed with, "Pray excuse haste, my Hands are so sore at work about the Fort, I can scarcely write." James Robertson was writing from Watauga on July 26th, "Onless you send Some men down the Case will be Bad So that I must stay with (no) more than Six men unless I kill part and tye the Other. I Expect we will have a war amongst our Selves without that of the Indians." The tension continued and on September 25th, when the expeditionary army was already hundreds of miles away, William Cocke was getting off a circular letter to Holston inhabitants, saying, "I would therefore advise and Request you not to Give the Indians one foot of Ground for by Flying we not only make them Sensable of Our incapasity to Receave them but give up our property for their surport." On September 29th Arthur Campbell was more confidently reporting to Preston from the Holston, "I have had the good fortune notwithstanding the late alarms occasioned to keep the people from flying the country." That there was still anxiety on the Holston was indicated, however, by George Adams' message of October 4th, "Amunition is very scarce With us Which is ye ocasion of abundanc of Feare." On October 6th Campbell was remarking dryly on his defense supervisory difficulties, "The most of the people in this Country seem to have a private plan of their own for their own particular defense" and was adding a grim footnote, "The Boy that was scalped is dead, he was an extraordinary example of patience and resolution to his last, frequently lamenting 'he was not able to fight enough to save his mammy.' "

In spite of these preoccupations with immediate border defense Fincastle had furnished nearly three hundred men for the Kanawha expedition in response to Preston's July 20th call for volunteers: "Our Cause is good; & therefore we have the greatest Reason to hope & expect that Heaven will bless us with Success in the Defense of ourselves & families against a parcel of murdering Savages. Interest, Duty, Honor, self preservation and everything which a man ought to hold Dear or Valuable in Life ought to Rouze us up."

Light is thrown on the realities involved in raising a contingent of volunteers on this already beleaguered border by the experiences of James Robertson, the future founder of Tennessee but now concerned with the defense of Watauga of which he had been one of the earliest settlers. Robertson had been taught to read and write by his wife but his having come so late to learning had not inhibited the vigor of his expression. In responding to Preston's call to arms he wrote, "Since rec'd your letter I have been continually on Horse Back amongst the People. I will get 18 or 20 men Ready to start Thursday Evening or Friday morning." The next day he was writing a shade less confidently, "I thought to get them march'd today but it was not in my power. Some had grain to put up . . . Pray sir if Possible Procure me a Quire of Paper as I cannot get one Sheet." By August 11th his troubles were multiplying: "I have had a Severe Spell of a Great Cold and the worst tooth Ache that ever was." The next day he reported: "This morning Our Scouts met with a Couple of Poor Little Boys between this and Bluestone that made their Escapes from the Indians Last Tuesday night about midnight . . . I had A thought of Seting home next Monday but I wont Atempt it untill I See if we Can Rub up these Yalow Dogs A Little. I supose my helpless famyly is in Great fear and Indeed not without Reason . . . N.B. Sir I have been in the greatest misery Ever any felow was in. Since last Monday with A pain in my Jaw one of my Eyes Has been Shut Up Ever Since and has hardly Either Eat or Slept I Declare." By September 1st he was already late for the army rendezvous and his aggravation was again centered on his difficulties with his detachment of volunteers: "I gather them all Together Saturday and Pretends to make A Draft by your Orders I tell them, and dont want to Concern with any that has famylys, but Only these Hulking younge Dogs that Can be well Spar'd." Still, by September 12th he was well enough satisfied and even a little proud: "I thought it was meerely Impossible to do it in the time and I am sure there is not Such an Other Company for the Quaintyty of men." He and his little band of neighbors had arrived and were now a part of the army.

The commander of that army, Andrew Lewis, was tough, cold, stern, and with a look about him to shake even the most truculent frontier volunteer. His driving insistence on conformance and performance had given the bold outlines of reality to a project which had in the beginning seemed as unlikely a military enterprise as could well have been imagined. By September 1st his shuffling, elbowing, brawling rabble of volunteers had begun to behave enough like an army to be achieving an orderly rendezvous at Camp Union on the Greenbrier and on the 7th he was able to begin his northward march over the mountains. [*See* Map 2.]

Two days before the First Continental Congress had assembled. The last glimmer of imperial influence was fading from the frontier scene. Johnson, Pontiac, and Bouquet were dead. Croghan, his last bright dream of fortune ended, was beginning to drift into a penniless and invalid obscurity. By the next spring patriots would have exiled Stuart. The frontier arena had been cleared of every figure who formerly had dominated it. To take the place of its one-time masters the frontier had bred sons of its own to take command. Their readiness for this sudden presumption to self-sufficiency was now to be tested by the conduct of this homespun and buckskin army, the first of all frontier armies, which with every step of its northward march was setting precedents and establishing traditions.

Christian with the larger portion of the Fincastle regiment had been enough delayed by the greater distance to be covered and by his border's special difficulties to be the last to arrive at the rendezvous. As a result, much to his men's disgust, he was given the duty of guarding the convoy. Lewis partly reassured them with the promise that he would give them time to catch up with the main army before he crossed the Ohio into the Shawnee country. No regular officer but must have fallen in a faint if confronted by the demand that he prepare plans for the supply and security of such an army on such a march through such a country. Former armies marching into the wilderness had paused to build roads over which wagon trains could be dragged and had still found the supply problems all but insoluble. But the problem of supplying this army was solved almost in passing by men who by long frontier experience had learned to adapt and to make do. Beef was driven on the hoof over the steep mountain trails and flour was transported by an ingeniously alternating use of pack horses and of canoes which were constructed as needed. The army's security en route was as imperturbably maintained. Cornstalk's reconnoitering parties shadowed the march, kept constant track of its progress, sniped at stragglers, and watched for chances to stampede the horses. But this was not an army with masses of slow-moving regulars to offer fat targets. It was rather an army so lean, active, and alert that it was never safe to stray within a long gunshot of it.

Lewis kept on north through the Kanawha gorges and over the wooded ridges and on October 8th camped on the Ohio to await the arrival of Christian and his convoy guard. Here in a hollow tree was found a letter left there by scouts from Dunmore's army and soon Lewis was able to exchange repeated messages with the governor. For Dunmore had before the end of August been so impressed by the vigorous response of the frontier to his originally forlorn call to arms that he had decided himself to take the field. Marshaling the militia of the northern Virginia frontier, he had started down the Ohio in boats and canoes with 700 men while another body of 500 under Major William Crawford, Washington's land agent, marching overland, crossed the Ohio at the mouth of the Hockhocking. Reassembling his army, Dunmore dispatched orders to Lewis to make haste to join him and began slowly to advance into the wilderness toward the main Shawnee towns on the Scioto.

Cornstalk had closely observed this formidable convergence of white armies advancing upon his country. The last faintest hope of support from other Indian nations had faded. His nearest and friendliest neighbors had remained as unmoved by the Logan murders and now by these white invasions as had the self-centered Iroquois or the self-hypnotized Cherokee. He was left with no alternative to war but submission. Yielding at last to the importunities of his warriors he chose war as the lesser evil. Having finally decided to fight he struck shrewdly, swiftly, and with terrible force. Concluding the more sensible way to deal with an enemy so superior in total numbers was to assail it in detail, he determined to destroy Lewis before he could join Dunmore or had himself been joined by Christian. Crossing the Ohio in canoes and rafts with 800 warriors the evening of

October 9th, he planned to storm Lewis' camp the morning of the 10th.

The attacking Shawnee were as confident as they were enraged and determined. The force that they were stalking was in their estimation not a real army but a mere aggregation of settlers and they had learned by long experience that settlers were more often quailing victims than serious antagonists. So certain were they of an easy victory that in their battle plan they had posted warriors along the banks of both rivers to dispatch white fugitives who might try to escape by swimming.

Two hunters out at dawn to shoot turkeys detected the presence of the advancing Shawnee while they were still a mile from camp. One was shot but the other got back with the alarm. Most of the men being awakened by the sudden shrilling of fifes and rattle of drums had never before been on a battlefield. For weeks they had been talking of the day they might at last come to grips with the Indians. Now they were realizing with a stabbing intensity of comprehension which they could not possibly have foreseen that not only the day but the very hour was upon them. The veteran Lewis well understood how critical was that moment. He had all too often before seen untried men break, men who had seemed in all outward aspects as bold as these. He knew that the issue of the battle, the fate of his army, and, perhaps, the outcome of the war could be decided in the next few minutes. Inexperienced soldiers were never prepared for the shocking violence of the first blast of enemy gunfire.

He ordered his two colonels, William Fleming and Charles Lewis, to lead detachments of 150 men each out to meet the Indian advance with a view to determining its strength. It proved strong enough to throw back and for a time to threaten to destroy the reconnaissance force. The initial collision with the Indian onrush was made the more dismaying by the almost immediate fall of both colonels. Charles Lewis was killed and Fleming suffered wounds observers considered mortal.

The howling Shawnee rushed forward, certain that the recoil must become a rout and then the familiar panic. But the frontier militia did not break. Their retreat was slow, they fought stubbornly for each foot of ground that they were forced to give up, and they kept their line intact. To the astounded Indians these no longer seemed settlers. They seemed rather to be white warriors as resolute in battle as the most dedicated red warrior.

Lewis ordered out fresh companies to thicken and lengthen his battle line. Finally the Shawnee advance was stemmed. For hours the struggle continued with unabated ferocity while the issue appeared to tremble in the balance. These were adversaries who for generations had visited nightmarish miseries upon the other and on this field they were giving vent to animosities bred in them from the cradle. On the thicketed slopes and in the swampy bottoms the battle lines were interlocked, often at hand to hand, and the fighting was at all times so close up that each side was continually yelling taunts, threats, and imprecations. In later accounts of the battle both belligerents paid the highest tribute to the other's extreme aggressiveness. The Indian warrior caste was committed to courage in combat by training, experience, and immemorial tradition. The frontiersmen had had no such tradition. They were founding one that day.

By noon it was the Indians who were beginning, almost imperceptibly at first, to give way. Painfully, foot by foot, the whites recovered the ground that they had lost. But only darkness put an end to the battle. From dawn to dusk the brutal testing of one another's will to fight had continued without quarter offered or sought. It had been a conflict as desperately sustained as at Bushy Run but there had here been one great difference in that this new kind of borderer had proved himself as adept at woods fighting as his Indian antagonist. Again, as at Bushy Run, the two forces were about equal in number, roughly 900 whites to 800 Indians. White casualties ran to a quarter of the number engaged and the Indian losses were probably as many.

That night Cornstalk withdrew across the Ohio while Lewis built breastworks to shelter his wounded. Tactically the battle had been a draw but strategically it was an overwhelming Indian defeat. Cornstalk's only hope had been to crush Lewis as Braddock had been crushed, with the chance that panic might seize the frontier, Dunmore feel compelled to withdraw, and other Indian nations be so impressed that they must rush to join the victors. Instead, he could now only look forward to the junction of Christian, Lewis, and Dunmore and his own hopeless inferiority from then on. The war was already over. He presented himself to Dunmore with an unqualified appeal for peace.

In the resulting Treaty of Camp Charlotte the significant clause was a Shawnee acknowledgment of the white man's right to Kentucky. In its first war the frontier had failed to punish the Indians as it had been hoped they might be punished but it had won the new land it had sought to win. This opening of its own way west had come at the last possible moment for with the outbreak of the Revolution the next year that opportunity must otherwise have been lost, perhaps forever.

Historians have fixed the name Dunmore upon this war between the Shawnee and the Virginia frontiersmen. It would be difficult to find one more inapt than that of an English governor for a conflict which was so intrinsically and essentially American and which produced results so detrimental to every English interest. It was a war provoked by frontiersmen, waged by frontiersmen, and won by frontiersmen for the sole benefit of frontiersmen. In striving for what they alone wanted they won much more than they then realized. Far broader vista were opened by their victory than the way to Kentucky. It provided an example suggesting to all Americans the possibility of a self-sufficiency such as the frontier had discovered, a reminder that patriots everywhere could without professional aid plan and organize means of defense and, if need be, raise an army, feed an army, lead an army. The lessons learned at Point Pleasant were instructive on wider fields than the coming series of desperate frontier wars. There were not only veterans of Point Pleasant at Vincennes, Piqua, and King's Mountain. There were also men who had learned on that field and on their way to it at Saratoga, Brandywine, Cowpens, and Yorktown. Washington, who had known Lewis since Lewis had served with him at Fort Necessity, was so impressed with his conduct of the Point Pleasant campaign that in 1775 he proposed Lewis be made commander-in-chief of the Continental Army.

The war with the Shawnee had scarcely been won before the men who had been harried from Kentucky were back there again. Clark, rushing down the Ohio to Kentucky in the earliest spring of 1775, found them everywhere. That impetuous young man was fired with an enthusiasm for the new country that was presently to make him the frontier's greatest champion, to save Kentucky for Virginia, and to win the entire northwest for the United States. The Harrod brothers and their hardy companions had already returned to reoccupy Harrodsburg on March 15th and to make it the first permanent settlement in Kentucky. By mid-April Benjamin Logan was building his station near the present Stanford and Isaac Ruddle his on the South Fork of the Licking.

So far the frontier's advance over the mountains into Kentucky had proceeded under the umbrella of a pretended regard for at least a shadow of legality. The initial occupation of Kentucky had been a flouting of the laws of England but had paid lip service to the laws of Virginia. The first settlers in Kentucky were able to consider themselves outlying communities of Virginia's Fincastle County. The presumption of Virginia's jurisdiction had rested originally on the terms of Virginia's charter, had been denied by the Proclamation, and had then in practical effect been reasserted by the military success of Virginia's frontier militia under the nominal command of Virginia's royal governor.

Virginia and the West

Clarence W. Alvord

Few colonies were more interested in transmontane developments than Virginia. The massive territorial claims of its charter and the land speculation fever of its gentry combined to provide an exceptional interest in western America. To the Virginians, several ministerial policies impeded their movement across the Appalachian chain—the Indian boundary, the proposed colony of Vandalia, and the incorporation of the Northwest into Quebec.

Professor Clarence W. Alvord (1868–1928) taught at the University of Illinois, Urbana, from 1901 to 1920, and at the University of Minnesota from 1920 to 1923. He was one of the foremost scholars of the region, writing and editing numerous books and articles on its history. The most famous of these, The Mississippi Valley in British Politics *(2 vols., 1917), is still the standard study for imperial policy relative to the Old Northwest. All subsequent works are mere expansions upon or modifications of Alvord's work. His most enduring monument was the* Mississippi Valley Historical Review *(now the* Journal of American History*) of which he was the first editor, from 1914 to 1923. This article places particular emphasis upon Virginia's role in the coming of the Revolution and its continuing interest in westward expansion that resulted in the George Rogers Clark expedition of 1778 and subsequent efforts to lay claim to the region north of the Ohio.*

After noting the colony's long-term interest in the West, Alvord turns to Clark's efforts, and he plays down the importance of surprise in the Virginian's conquest of the Illinois settlements. Instead, he argues that the support of the Spanish in New Orleans and of American fur traders in the area prepared the way for Clark's achievement. Moreover, he concludes that the "summer of 1779 marked the zenith of Virginia's power north of the Ohio; from that date there was a steady decline." He concludes in words that will be echoed in subsequent readings, that the cession of the Old Northwest to the Americans came not as the result of American arms, but rather because of "the liberal principles held by a British statesman"—the earl of Shelburne.

From Clarence W. Alvord, "Virginia and the West: An Interpretation," in the *Mississippi Valley Historical Review*, 3:19–38 (June, 1916); reprinted without footnotes by permission of the *Journal of American History*.

T HE SCIENTIFIC STUDY of western American history is a child of yesterday, so recently born that when writers make the attempt to give the correct perspective to western happenings they find their effort thwarted by the inadequacy of their knowledge. Exactly what did occur west of the mountains has been so infrequently made the subject of that careful and painstaking investigation which must precede any right interpretation, that the meanings of most occurrences in regions remote from the eastern settlements are still subjects of speculation. An excellent example of this ignorance is found in the most dramatic western event of the eighteenth century: the occupation of the Illinois country by the Virginia troops under George Rogers Clark during the revolutionary war. The story of that enterprise is more or less familiar because it is the central event in a well known historical novel. It is the dramatic character of a Clark's expedition that has attracted the attention of historians so that what may be called the annals of the western hero's anabasis may be found in most of the histories of this country; but there have been few attempts to place the event in its proper setting and to interpret its significance in the history of the revolution as a whole. Even today historians do little more than guess at the influence which the occupation of the Illinois villages exerted upon the negotiations of the final treaty of peace in 1783.

The account of this episode as usually narrated is based very closely upon Clark's own reports and may be epitomized as follows: the British at Detroit were sending Indian war bands against the frontiers of Pennsylvania and Virginia; and the most remote posts of the latter state, situated in modern Kentucky, were especially subject to the ravages of these relentless savages. A young frontiersman, George Rogers Clark, formed a plan for striking a blow at the British in the north and proposed it to Patrick Henry, governor of Virginia, who in the most secret way provided money from the state funds for the enterprise. Keeping his purposes to himself, the young commander collected troops to the number of about two hundred and with these landed near Fort Massac, situated in the southern part of modern Illinois, and marched across the prairies to Kaskaskia, which, taken completely by surprise, surrendered without a blow. Clark was able to hold the whole Illinois country throughout the war; and without doubt, say most historians, the success of this event was the cause of the cession of the west as far as to the Mississippi river in the final treaty of peace.

This whole narrative is, as a rule, dragged into the general history of the United States as if it were a startling episode unconnected with preceding events and as if it had little relation to the men and measures of the time, its chief importance depending on the later development of the region. Thus, lacking perspective, the composition of the picture as a whole is untrue, in spite of the accuracy of its details.

The occupation of the Illinois country by Virginia has a long history preceding it, but in this time and place it will be possible only to hint at the most important steps in the development which led up to the sending of the frontiersman to the remote regions on the Mississippi. The fact that the charter claims of Virginia stretched northwestward so as to include most of what is the old northwest is too well known to delay us; but this very fact is fundamental in the interpretation of the revolutionary episode; and it must, therefore, be constantly borne in mind, for the whole history of the revolutionary war in the west is a mystery which can be solved only by an understanding of Virginia's persistent attempt to make good her claims to this vast territory.

It was not until the middle of the eighteenth century that the colonists began to realize that great wealth was to be obtained by exploiting the western domain; but from that time onward one scheme of colonization after another was started in the hope of making fortunes for the promoters. It was a company of Virginia gentlemen backed by London capital that made the first definite trial at settlement. The attempt of the Ohio company to establish colonists on the upper waters of the Ohio river was the immediate occasion of the French and Indian war, which ended in the cession to Great Britain of the west as far as the Mississippi. After this event the activities among the colonists, particularly in Virginia and Pennsylvania, in pushing settlements westward became more and more important in the history of the country, and the land fever spread rapidly among the speculators of both the new and the old world. In a letter dated 1768, which discusses the possibilities of investments in

America, particularly in western lands, there occurs the statement: "It is almost a proverb in this neighborhood (Philadelphia) that 'Every great fortune made here within these fifty
years has been by land.' " When the famous western pioneer,
George Croghan, was in England, he found his associates "land
crazy." Most of the public men of the eastern colonies, such as
Washington, Henry, and Franklin, at one time or another
entered into some "get-rich-quick" scheme for exploiting and
colonizing the west; and the shares of every company for
promoting settlement west of the mountains found a ready
market.

This speculative interest in western lands was associated with
the advance of the fur traders into the wilderness. Previous to
the French and Indian war, many British traders were engaged
in the fur trade; but after the close of that war there was a wild
rush across the mountains, and traders in unprecedented
numbers were to be found from Mackinac to the gulf of Mexico.
In 1767, the Philadelphia firm of Baynton, Wharton, and
Morgan employed about three hundred and fifty boatmen on
the Ohio river for the transportation of their merchandise to
the Illinois country. These advance agents of the British westward movement added fuel to the fire of speculation by their
glowing descriptions of the new land.

The vacillating attitude of the successive British ministries
tended still more to excite the desires and imagination of the
promoters. It was well known both in America and Great
Britain that the most influential politicians of the various factions which made contemporary British politics chaotic were in
favor of some method of developing the west. Even the king
himself could be counted among the expansionists. It was,
therefore, expected that there would soon be removed the
temporary prohibition of settlement west of the mountains,
published in the famous proclamation of 1763 for the purpose
of quieting the fears of the Indians. In order to be prepared for
the mad westward rush that was sure to come as soon as this
should be done, the various companies which had been formed
for the exploitation of the territory maintained agents in the
British capital to win the favor of the ministers. There were at
one time in London agents representing the old Ohio company,
formed by Virginians in 1747; a group of merchants claiming

an indemnity in land for losses suffered at the outbreak of Pontiac's conspiracy; Virginia soldiers claiming payment in western lands for their services in war; officers and soldiers of Connecticut petitioning for land in a colony to be situated on the Mississippi; a company of officers who served in Pontiac's war who wished to found a colony at Detroit; a company of Philadelphia merchants and others, petitioning for the establishment of a colony in the Illinois country; and the great Mississippi company, composed of the most prominent Virginians, asking for an extensive grant on the Mississippi. In addition there are evidences of other schemes which have not left such clear traces of their purposes. [*See* Map 1.]

It is very probable that the multiplicity of plans with their conflicting claims made it difficult for the ministers, open to varying influences, to reach a decision in regard to the best method of opening the west; but in the spring of 1768, a plan for imperial expansion was accepted by the Grafton ministry, and the imperial agents, particularly General Gage and the two superintendents of Indian affairs, were instructed to put it into execution. The underlying principle on which the instructions were based was that expansion westward was to be gradual and under the control of the imperial agents, who were to purchase the Indians' hunting grounds for settlement as rapidly as the growth of population in the colonies demanded. In order to carry this policy out, the ministers ordered that a boundary line between the settlements and the Indian territory should be agreed upon by treaty with the Indian tribes. Across the boundary thus run no white settler was to be allowed to pass until by treaty the line was pushed farther westward. In this way western expansion could be controlled and the rights of the Indians protected. Such a boundary line was completed within two years after the orders were sent out from London. Beginning at Lake Ontario, it bent westward so that it opened up for settlement the upper waters of the Ohio river as far west as the mouth of the Great Kanawha; thence it turned south and east, closing for settlement the back country of the southern colonies; then turning around the Florida peninsula it bent again westward till it reached the Mississippi.

This boundary made available for settlement new territory within the colonies of New York, Pennsylvania, and Virginia.

The land opened in the royal colony of Virginia was regarded as imperial domain by the majority of British ministers since it had been purchased by imperial money; consequently its disposition was under the control of the home government. An opportunity to form a new colony west of the mountains was therefore offered. There were capitalists ready to relieve the treasury of all the expense involved in such an enterprise. Under the careful management of a Philadelphian, Samuel Wharton, there was formed a company composed of some of the most prominent public men both in America and Great Britain, such as Benjamin and Sir William Franklin, Thomas Walpole, Thomas Pownall, Lord Hertford, George Grenville, and many others, among whom were the most influential under-secretaries of state and of the treasury. The political connection was strengthened by taking into the company two members of the ministry, the Earl of Rochford and Lord Gower, who were able to win the support of the king himself. In this way the project of the new colony of Vandalia was forwarded, and all the preliminary steps had already been taken to launch the project when the revolutionary war broke out. One fact is of great significance: the new colony would have shut off Virginia completely from the west, for its boundaries as finally agreed upon stretched from North Carolina to Pennsylvania.

While the ministers had the subject of this newly purchased land under consideration, they came to a momentous conclusion concerning another part of the western territory, namely the old northwest. This was the most productive fur region contiguous to the settled parts of the country; and from the first the influence of the fur traders had been thrown against every project to form new settlements within its boundaries. The fur industry of Canada had passed rapidly into the hands of the Scotch, who exercised a very strong influence in favor of maintaining the great lakes region in its primitive condition. They were able to advance many strong arguments in support of their own interests, the most convincing being based on the necessity of protecting the hunting grounds of the Indians from the cupidity of speculators and frontiersmen. In 1774 the ministry determined to take action; and by the Quebec act parliament added all the territory between the lakes and the Ohio and Mississippi to the province of Quebec, thus removing the possibility of its exploitation by Virginia and other colonies. By this action the ministry closed for immediate settlement the land to the north of the Ohio and left for possible colonization only the southwest.

By these three decisions of the ministry, the running of the Indian boundary, the plan to establish the colony of Vandalia, and the union of the old northwest to the province of Quebec, the interests of Virginia were directly injured. Land speculation in the west had been for years the most important interest of Virginia's public men and it is not strange, therefore, that this imperial encroachment upon Virginia's charter rights, this curtailment of the ambition of her citizens, drove the latter almost unanimously into the party of the American revolutionists. To them the very existence of their colony seemed to be at stake. The conditions existing in the year 1774 predestined the course of the future war in the west.

Before the appeal to arms came, Virginia tried to defeat the ministerial plans by indirect methods. When John Stuart, southern superintendent of Indian affairs, first mentioned his intended purpose of running the Indian boundary line the colony of Virginia refused to listen to the proposal; and it was only when blunt directions from the ministry were received that the colony yielded; and even then means were found to thwart, in part, the ministerial intentions. It was Virginia's influence that caused Sir William Johnson, northern superintendent of Indian affairs, to permit the Iroquois to cede all their claims to lands south of the Ohio as far west as the Tennessee river. This extinguished the most important Indian claim to Kentucky and partially opened for settlement lands west of the Virginia Indian boundary which began at the Great Kanahwa. But the Virginians had other successes. In running the Indian boundary line back of their colony from North Carolina to the Ohio, they managed to persuade the Cherokee Indians to grant them a larger extent of territory on their western frontier. By this change lands belonging to such men as George Washington, Patrick Henry, Colonel Lewis, and Thomas Walker were opened to immediate settlement.

The plan to found the colony of Vandalia was decidedly a more serious danger to Virginia's interests than the temporary expedient of the boundary line, and naturally aroused the greatest fear in the hearts of the colonists. It is possible that the open opposition to the new colony shown by Lord Hillsborough, the British colonial secretary at the time,—an opposition which cost him his office,—may have been due to his advocacy of the cause of the Virginians; at any rate his appointee to the governorship, Lord Dunmore, became the strongest champion of Virginia's claims to the west. Immediately on his arrival, in 1771, Dunmore allied himself with the western speculators and gave little heed to the instructions of a new colonial secretary, Lord Dartmouth. The policy of Lord Dunmore was dictated by his own financial interest, for he wished to become a great landholder, possibly a proprietor of a western colony. He immediately began making grants of land not only within the limits of the proposed new colony of Vandalia but even on the other side of the Indian boundary line as far west as the site of modern Louisville. He joined a company of Virginians which purchased from the Indians two large tracts of land in the Illinois country and had the audacity to recommend the company's enterprise to his superiors in England, being careful, however, not to disclose his own connection with it.

This particular scheme seems to have been only a first step in the larger plans of the governor. He realized that Virginia's right to the old northwest would be made stronger if a colonial army were to march into that territory and subdue the Indian tribes. While the ministry in England, by means of the Quebec act, were closing the land north of the Ohio to possible settlement, Lord Dunmore, through his agents, stirred up an Indian war in that region; and, after parliament had extended the province of Quebec to the Ohio, Lord Dunmore led his colonial militia into the region and administered a severe chastisement to the Indians. Exactly what the governor planned may never be known, for, on his return from the war, the series of events which ultimately led to the revolutionary war was well under way and Dunmore was obliged to give his attention to matters nearer home.

In spite of the acts of Virginia's governor and prominent citizens, the British government would undoubtedly have been able to carry out its plans and to have shut off Virginia completely from the territory west of the mountains, had not the revolutionary war broken out at the critical time and thus given

Virginia the opportunity to strengthen her claims to the west by actual occupation.

The success of Dunmore's war in 1774 had for the time intimidated the Indians on the frontier, and there was a rush of settlers into the Ohio valley in spite of the fact that the prohibition of settlement by the British government was still in force, for, as has been seen, the colony of Vandalia was not yet established. During 1775 and the years following, this illegal settlement was pushed well down the Ohio and into the heart of Kentucky. The majority of these settlers, who came into the new country after the Indian war, were Virginia citizens and preferred, for the present at least, to retain their connection with the mother colony. Such settlements as Harrodsburg, Boiling Spring, and St. Asaph were formed and the new inhabitants voluntarily looked to Virginia for the protection of their rights. Virginia's sovereignty was thus stretched over the west by the initiative of her own citizens.

Just at the moment when Virginia through her frontiersmen seemed to be getting the better of the mother country in the dispute over the possession of the west, her sovereignty was threatened by another claimant. In the years just before the outbreak of the revolutionary war, there was handed around among the land speculators an opinion of two famous British jurists, Lord Camden and Lord Chancellor Yorke, to the effect that the Indian nations were sovereign powers and could, therefore, grant titles to lands which the British courts would be obliged to sustain. This opinion gave rise to great activity among the westerners and on the strength of it land purchases were made in the Illinois country, on the Wabash river, and elsewhere. Acting on this opinion a company of North Carolinians, with Colonel Richard Henderson at their head, purchased of the Cherokee the land south of the Ohio and west of the Indian boundary, which had been ceded to Great Britain by the Six Nations at the treaty of Fort Stanwix in 1768. Within these boundaries, which included most of Kentucky and some of Tennessee, the proprietors proposed to establish the colony of Transylvania, and settlers were immediately sent into the region. In order to assure their purchase the proprietors sent a representative to the continental congress, where they were certain of finding sympathizers among the delegates of those colonies whose western boundaries were definitely fixed by their charters.

The Virginian authorities naturally took action to thwart the purposes of the North Carolinian proprietors. Lord Dunmore, although in the midst of the revolutionary struggle and deserted by many who had shared his western interests, issued a proclamation directed against this usurpation of the rights of the Virginia colony. The Virginia delegates to the continental congress were able to prevent that body at the critical moment from taking action against their interests. Still more important, however, was the action of the adherents of Virginia in Kentucky. The settlers in that region were incensed at the assertion by the North Carolina proprietors of claims over lands which they had taken up in accordance with Virginia law; and they found in a young frontiersman, George Rogers Clark, a leader who was to win fame for himself as the most effective promoter of the claims of his mother state.

Clark was at this time a young man in his early twenties, but he possessed those qualities of courage and determination that fitted him preëminently for the leadership of a rough pioneer community. He had already identified himself with Virginia's interests in Dunmore's war, in which he had fought under General Lewis. He had gone to Kentucky to advance himself by land speculation and was naturally enough opposed to the North Carolinian usurpers; it was the decisive action of this young Virginian that ultimately thwarted the plans of the latter. The smouldering discontent against Henderson was blown to a flame, and an assembly of Virginians chose Clark as one of the two representatives commissioned to go to the mother province to lay their complaints before the assembly. Clark met with ready sympathy for his plans from Patrick Henry, who had been one of the close advisers of Lord Dunmore in his opposition to the British ministerial plans. It was not difficult, therefore, to arouse him to the necessity of taking such action as would secure the claims of Virginia against usurpation. The county of Kentucky was formed, and the mantle of Virginia sovereignty was thus thrown over the land south of the Ohio extending to the Mississippi. It was, therefore, the action of the pioneers acting under their rights of popular sovereignty that saved Virginia's claims.

In the old northwest, however, the British power seemed firmly established. In accordance with the purpose of the Quebec act, the administration of Canada was extended into this region, lieutenant-governors being appointed for Detroit, Mackinac, Vincennes, and Illinois, although on account of the course of events no permanent government was established at the two last named places. After the appointment of these British officers, the border warfare was better organized and Indian parties were sent in every direction to distress the American pioneer settlements. In spite of the efforts by the Americans to retain the Indians in their service, the aborigines naturally enough preferred to wield the tomahawk against those who were actually invading their hunting grounds. Their fight had always been against the pioneer settler, and in the contest between the mother country and the colonies, the Indians saw their opportunity to stay the westward advance of the white man.

The united colonists realized keenly the importance of conciliating the Indians and of driving the British from their stronghold on the lakes; and accordingly congress appointed commissioners and agents for the Indians. The officials who had charge of the old northwest were stationed at Pittsburg; and their executive agent was Colonel George Morgan, who as representative of the Philadelphia trading firm of Baynton, Wharton, and Morgan had had ample opportunity to familiarize himself with the western territory and to make connections with the Indians. He was particularly well acquainted with the conditions in the Illinois country, where during his sojourn of many years he had made many warm friends. During the years 1776 to 1778 Morgan was constantly planning the conquest of the territory under his charge. His correspondents at Detroit and Kaskaskia informed him that the Americans would find no difficulty in winning the French inhabitants to throw in their lot with the American colonies. He, in turn, encouraged them to hope that an American army would soon occupy all the great lakes and Mississippi region. As a matter of fact the continental congress was willing to send out an expedition, but the necessary funds for such a far reaching undertaking were not to be found.

Virginia's opportunity, therefore, came to her through the

financial embarrassment of the confederacy. Her interests on account of her charter claims were much more definite than those of the united colonies; her citizens had for years been reaching out into the west in the hope of making fortunes both through the fur trade and by land speculation. Many Virginians were looking to the region across the Ohio river as to a land of promise for their future enterprises, and some even had a direct stake in the territory through their association with the Wabash land company. Furthermore, the Virginia settlements in Kentucky were directly threatened by the British troops and the Indians. On the other hand, they occupied an extremely good strategic position from which to make an offensive movement against the poorly defended British posts north of the Ohio; and the continuous attack of the Indians on their homes in the blue grass region furnished these settlers with an incentive to decisive action.

Were the region of Illinois as unknown and seemingly remote as it has been frequently pictured by historians, the suggestion of an invasion of the country would probably not have been favorably received by even the boldest of the men of the Virginia frontier. But the truth is that the Illinois country had become a fairly well known region since 1765. Hundreds of traders from Pennsylvania and Virginia had visited the quaint villages of Kaskaskia and Cahokia to traffic with the French inhabitants, and this intercourse was continued up to the time of the famous expedition of George Rogers Clark. Not only did the English colonists visit the Illinois villages, the Frenchmen in turn were frequent visitors to the Ohio river and some of them were seen within the new settlements of Kentucky and even as far east as Philadelphia. By this commercial intercourse attachments had been formed in the French villages of the Mississippi which generated sufficient magnetic force to attract across the Ohio representatives of the revolutionary party in the colonies. In the year 1777 there were in Kaskaskia and Cahokia several members of the American trading class who had retained their commercial connections with the east and were even closely affiliated with men who had cast their lot with the revolting colonies. These distant representatives of Americanism took every occasion to discuss with their French neighbors the struggle for liberty and were so successful as evangelists of the novel ideas that a large party of American sympathizers was developed among the French population; among its members were to be found most of the officers of the militia, who were destined to exercise a potent influence when the crisis arose.

There are, however, indications of a much closer relation between the Virginia expedition and the Illinois inhabitants than the growth of an American party in the Illinois country. For many years there had lived at Kaskaskia as trader and land speculator William Murray of Philadelphia. He was the moving spirit in the formation of both the Illinois and the Wabash land companies, and his future was bound up in the development of the purchases of these companies. It was William Murray who had persuaded Lord Dunmore of Virginia and some of the latter's associates to make investments in this region. With the outbreak of the revolution Murray seems to have felt a still greater dependence upon Virginia where he had many supporters. In 1776 he was in New Orleans when Captain George Gibson and William Linn came thither to purchase munitions from the Spaniards for the colonies. It is not evident how far Murray entered into relations with Gibson, but it seems most probable that a letter to his brother advising him to assist an American military expedition on its arrival in Kaskaskia was carried by Gibson's boats on their return voyage in 1777. Certainly Murray was well informed of Virginia's activities in the west, for he appeared at Williamsburg to urge the claims of his land companies as soon as the news reached that city of George Rogers Clark's success.

Another Kaskaskian who had commercial interests in the success or failure of Virginia's enterprise was Thomas Bentley. He had been in the Illinois country only a few years but had cemented his relations with the French population of Kaskaskia by marrying a daughter of one of the most prominent families of that village. His trading enterprises carried his boats up and down the Mississippi and on the Ohio. There is indubitable evidence that one of his boats met Gibson's expedition at the mouth of the Ohio in March, 1777, when Bentley received certain information of events that were still in the future. He must have been informed at this time that spies were to be sent from Kentucky to investigate conditions at Kaskaskia. From the interest George Rogers Clark showed in Bentley in later years it must be that at this time some communication passed between the two men. The British commander of the Illinois country, Philippe de Rocheblave, declared later that Bentley was chiefly responsible for the coming of the Americans to the Mississippi.

One other factor in the western situation needs to be noted. In spite of the reluctance of the Spanish government to enter into a treaty of alliance with the Americans, the representatives of that monarchy in America were distinctly friendly to the cause of the revolting colonies. It has already been seen that Americans were permitted to purchase munitions of war in North America; but it is not so well known that the agent of the Spanish government in America, Don Juan de Miralles, was confidentially informed of the campaign planned by George Rogers Clark and regarded himself and Patrick Henry as co-partners in sending the expedition against Kaskaskia. This prior understanding between the Virginia government and the Spanish explains the friendly reception of the colony's military leader at St. Louis.

The main events of Clark's expedition: how he sent spies to Kaskaskia, and induced Patrick Henry to furnish supplies; how he collected a company of about two hundred pioneers with whom he descended the Ohio, marched across the prairies of Illinois and on the night of July 4–5, 1778, took Kaskaskia, have already been sketched. Clark's own narrative needs correction in one important detail. It pictures the occupation of Kaskaskia as a complete surprise and as causing a fear among the inhabitants, scarcely to be understood in view of the fact that the latter had been bred among the dangers of the frontier and that there had been frequent intercourse between the French and Americans for many years. When it is further known that the French had been warned of the approach of the Virginians several days before their arrival and had refused to prepare for the defense in spite of the urgent entreaties of their acting commandant, Clark's classic description of the poltroonery of the French must be very much discounted indeed. The American sympathizers in the Illinois villages had done their work so well that almost all the French officers of militia had been won over, and their commandant was left helpless to defend the territory entrusted to his care. After the refusal of his own soldiers to serve him, the latter sent post haste to Vincennes for support; forty men were sent out from there but they arrived too late to prevent the Virginians' success. The countrymen of Kaskaskia and Cahokia were already throwing up their hats in joy at the sound of the words of independence and the French alliance. There had been no need of a conquest by arms; there had only been an occupation by friends. Clark's task had, indeed, proved an easy one. [*See* Map 3.]

The maintenance of the possession of this territory by the Virginians was a much more difficult and dangerous problem. The people of Vincennes, on the Wabash river, were persuaded by Dr. Jean Baptiste Laffont and Father Gibault to throw in their lot with their relatives and friends and change their allegiance; they were allowed to be American citizens only for a short time, however, for in the fall British forces under Lieutenant-Governor Hamilton of Detroit occupied the village.

With a formidable force of the enemy within striking distance, the position of the Virginians in Illinois was now seen to be untenable unless some desperate measures should be taken. Half of Clark's troops had already returned to Kentucky, leaving him with less than a hundred American followers. To increase his embarrassments, he was without resources. The French people of the Illinois villages saved him from danger; two companies of militia were raised among them, and the necessary money and supplies were willingly furnished in return for drafts on Virginia. With this support Clark was able to make one of the most dramatic military campaigns of the war. Fighting his way through the frozen marshes of the prairies, he led his men to Vincennes and captured the place easily, since Major Hamilton, regarding an attack by Clark as impossible, had diminished the garrison. Thus with Vincennes in his control, Clark's position at Kaskaskia and Cahokia was rendered fairly secure.

The summer of 1779 marked the zenith of Virginia's power north of the Ohio; from that date there was a steady decline. In 1780, the British made an attack on St. Louis and the Illinois villages; although it was repulsed by the combined efforts of the Spaniards and Clark, the affair demonstrated so significantly the returning energy of the British that Clark felt it dangerous to maintain the posts north of the Ohio any longer. Accordingly the garrisons at Vincennes and Kaskaskia were withdrawn. For a year more there were a score of soldiers in those posts, acting as scouts; but even these were recalled in the following winter, and the villages were left to shift for themselves. In spite of this withdrawal, it was acknowledged by the Spanish governor of St. Louis that the region which had been actually occupied by the Virginians in 1778 belonged to the revolted colonies. In extent this territory was, however, only a small part of the old northwest, for it comprised merely the region bounded by the Illinois river as far as Peoria, by a line from that village to Vincennes, and thence by the Wabash river to the Ohio, in other words, approximately the southern half of what is now the state of Illinois. Outside of these boundaries lay the British territory governed by officers with headquarters at Mackinac, Detroit, and Niagara; and over the whole extent of this region, almost within sight of the American troops at Pittsburgh, roamed the Indian allies of Great Britain. Virginia had really only weakened the hold of the mother country on a small corner of the disputed territory; and neither the establishment of a few scouts at Peoria by the Spaniards nor their seizure of St. Joseph,—now in lower Michigan,—in January, 1781, brought the question of dominion into dispute in any way. [*See* Maps 4 and 5.]

There exists some doubt as to whether or not this very slight occupation of the old northwest by the Virginians influenced the final disposition of territory in the treaty which closed the war. Most western writers, anxious to magnify the importance of their own region, have been inclined to give Clark the credit of securing for the United States this important acquisition; the easterners have had too little information on the subject to express an authoritative opinion, but many have allowed their skepticism to become evident. The following statement is a typical expression of the western view: "Few events have had a vaster influence upon the future of the nation than this expedition of Clark's. Not only did he secure the western gate of the republic, but he gained these western lands the ownership of which greatly advanced the idea of union." If such a view is correct, Clark's expedition must be looked upon as one of the most important episodes of the revolutionary war and should be classed with the campaigns that ended in the surrender of Burgoyne and of Cornwallis; in such a case, Virginia's service to the United States, when she sent forth her men to protect her frontiers and to make effective her western claims, can scarcely be measured. The question, then, of the influence of the occupation of the Illinois villages upon the negotiations of the peace is of real importance in any attempt to interpret the final treaty.

It is possible that the American commissioners may have felt that their position in claiming the west for the new republic was somewhat strengthened by the knowledge of the success of Clark, but it is unbelievable that they would have demanded less, even had he failed, since the first boundaries proposed by Benjamin Franklin included all Canada as well as the west; and his argument in support of his proposal was that such generosity would win the affection of the Americans and separate them from France. Furthermore, he pointed out that the long extended frontiers between Canada and the United States were occupied by "the most disorderly of the people, who being far removed from the eye and control of their respective governments, are the most bold in committing offences against neighbors, and are forever occasioning complaints, and furnishing matter for fresh differences between their states." Although the demand for the cession of Canada was not persisted in, still the demand of the American commissioners was for the cession of a large extent of western territory, most of which was occupied by British troops, and which could not be claimed from the fact that in one corner of the region there were a few French villages, who, though without American garrisons, acknowledged the sovereignty of the thirteen colonies.

The interest of France and Spain were not in accord with this extensive demand of the United States; in fact the interests of Spain were directly opposed to any extension of the United States's boundaries in the west, since her possessions on the right bank of the Mississippi river in such an event would always be endangered by the restless and lawless frontier population. Spain's principal interest, however, was to preserve the navigation of the Mississippi for herself; and her statesmen thought the best means to accomplish this end was to secure for her a narrow strip of territory along the eastern bank, extending from the gulf to the Ohio river. Beyond this, her ambition did not extend; but in order to limit still further the expansion of the Americans, Spain proposed that England should retain at the treaty of peace all territory lying between the Ohio and the Mississippi rivers which had been united to Canada by the Quebec act of 1774.

French diplomacy during the American revolution has been a subject of dispute among historians. One school of interpreters, following the unreasoning suspicions of Jay and Adams, has insisted that the French minister Vergennes was guilty of playing a double game and used his influence to restrict the new nation on its western boundaries. The interpretation of the opponents of this school, who have listened to the more temperate language of Benjamin Franklin, is now known to be better established, for a careful examination of the most secret dispatches of Vergennes proves that he was most friendly to the revolting colonies and promoted their interests as far as it was in his power. Naturally enough, however, his attitude toward the extension of the boundaries of the United States to the west was limited by his many obligations to Spain, which country had been induced to enter the war only after a definite promise from the French minister of an addition to her territories. From the first, Spain had insisted on the sole right of navigation of the Mississippi river, and Vergennes' tentative consideration of Spain's plan for the peace, outlined above, can only be explained by his desire to secure peace, a desire which might be thwarted by the conflicting interests in the west of the allies of France.

The machinations of Spain were of little moment in the final treaty, for Great Britain had determined, in spite of the ease with which she might have secured more favorable boundaries in the west, to yield to the demands of her revolted colonies in this particular. This compliance is the adequate explanation of the treaty; and the reason for it is to be found in the attitude of Lord Shelburne, who was prime minister at the time of the final settlement. Twice before, Lord Shelburne had been intimately associated with the affairs of western America. When he was president of the board of trade in 1763, he had drafted the proclamation of 1763, which was the fundamental law of the west in the years preceding the revolutionary war; and from 1766 to January, 1768, he was the secretary of state in whose department the care of colonial affairs fell. During this period the chief American interest in his eyes had been the rapid settlement of the west. In September, 1767, he laid before the ministry a comprehensive plan for the development of the region, in which he set forth the desirability of establishing colonies along the Mississippi river, wherein the following argument is of significance: "It is impracticable to prevent along such a Frontier, the taking Possession of unoccupied Land and resisting a general Inclination of Settlement." The whole paper revealed Shelburne's belief in the inevitable movement of the Americans westward until the whole territory should be occupied. During the negotiations of 1782 he gave expression to the same thought in a letter to his agent in Paris in the following words: "For the good of America, whatever the Government may be, new provinces must be erected on those back lands and down the Mississippi."

To a man holding such a view of the future of the west, whose principles had been completely liberalized by the free trade teachings of Adam Smith, Franklin's argument that a stable peace could only be made by ceding sufficient territory in the west for the expansion of the restless frontier population was convincing; and there seems never to have entered Lord Shelburne's mind a doubt as to the expediency of granting such extensive boundaries, even though the territory was garrisoned by British troops. He granted what seemed to him necessary for the completion of a permanent peace. The basis then for the success of American diplomacy had been laid not by the victory of the arms of Virginia, not through the boldness of George Rogers Clark in winning the old northwest for the United States, but in the liberal principles held by a British statesman. There is certainly a note of justifiable pride for his act, the noblest of his life, in the following words penned by Lord Shelburne to an American friend in 1797: "I cannot express to you the satisfaction I have felt in seeing the forts (of the northwest) given up, I may tell you in confidence what may astonish you, as it did me, that up to the very last debate in the House of Lords, the Ministry did not appear to comprehend the policy upon which the boundary line was drawn, and persist in still considering it as a measure of necessity not of choice. However it is indifferent who understands it. The deed is done: and a strong foundation laid for eternal amity between England and America."

Lord Dunmore and the West

Richard O. Curry

As ministers and speculators sought to influence decisions in Whitehall relative to the disposition of the Ohio valley lands, the frontiersmen of Virginia and Pennsylvania also sought to determine the settlement of the Northwest. Most vigorous in pressing Virginia's claims for at least the lands south of the Ohio was John Murray, earl of Dunmore, Royal Governor of Virginia. Dunmore's motives in the 1774 punitive expedition against the Shawnee, usually known as Dunmore's War, have long been suspect. Dunmore maintained that he was punishing Indians who had violated the treaty of Fort Stanwix and had attacked white settlements south of the Ohio. But close examination shows that Dunmore had personal economic interests at stake in the settlement of the region, that he violated various imperial orders that he not allow more settlement in the area, and that he allowed others with similar vested land claims to advise and assist him in the effort. Moreover, the war was part of a Virginia versus Pennsylvania feud over which colony had title to the forks of the Ohio River at modern Pittsburgh. The war may also be seen as part of a failure of British policy to control colonial expansion. The British evacuation of Fort Pitt in 1772 paved the way for Dunmore and the Virginians to seize the initiative and move into the power vacuum left by the departing redcoats, before either the Indians or the Pennsylvanians did so.

In this article, written while he was a graduate student at the University of Pennsylvania, Richard O. Curry tries to rehabilitate Dunmore's reputation. Dunmore is seen as one protecting the "rights" of Virginians against the claims of Pennsylvania and court sycophants trying to erect the colony of Vandalia. His audacity in moving down the Monongahela, in establishing a Virginia garrison at the forks in old Fort Pitt, and in instituting a Virginia county government for the area constituted a bold step by a partisan of the interests of the Old Dominion. Curry, now a professor at the University of Connecticut who has devoted most of his recent scholarship to the Civil War era, argues that Dunmore's treatment of the Shawnee was more humane than that of the frontiersmen he commanded. Rather than exterminate the Indians, Dunmore merely chastized them and kept them north of the Ohio.

75

Certainly what happened at Gnaddenhutten, Ohio, eight years latter might bear Curry out on this point. Curry also exonerates Dunmore of any treachery toward Colonel Andrew Lewis, whose wing of the Virginia army received the full brunt of Chief Cornstalk's attack.

Whatever Dunmore's motives, the Ohio expedition of 1774 helped keep three years of relative peace on the frontier. During that brief span of time, settlers spilled over into the Monongahela, Kanawha, and Kentucky river valleys in enough numbers to hold the region for the Americans in the ensuing War for Independence.

★★★★★★★★★★★★★★★★★★★★★★★★★★★★★

Great Dunmore our General valiant & Bold
Excels the Great Heroes–the Heroes of Old;
When he doth command we will always obey,
When he bids us fight we will not run away.

Theodore Roosevelt, in his history, *The Winning of the West*, was the first historian to call attention to the importance of Dunmore's War in the history of westward expansion. Not only did the battle of Point Pleasant break the power of the Shawnee Indians in the Ohio Valley, but opened up Kentucky, the "dark and bloody ground," to settlement. Even more significant, this expedition commanded by John Murray, the last Royal Governor of Virginia, was to have an indirect bearing on the terms of the Peace of Paris, 1783. Without Kentucky as a base of operations, it is doubtful that George Rogers Clark could have led his band of "western" Virginians against Kaskaskia and Vincennes in the Illinois country. Had this daring mission failed, the western border of the United States well could have been established at the crest of the Alleghanies rather than at the banks of the Mississippi. Furthermore, this campaign—conceived, planned and executed under the direction of Lord Dunmore—broke the savages' power so completely that the frontier was quiet for nearly two years after the American

---

From Richard O. Curry, "Lord Dunmore and the West: A Re-evaluation," in *West Virginia History*, 19:231–243 (July, 1958); reprinted without footnotes with permission of *West Virginia History*.

Revolution broke out at Lexington and Concord in the spring of 1775.

Lyman Copeland Draper characterized the war against Shawnee as the most popular event in Dunmore's whole administration. And indeed, Virginians did have ample reason for rejoicing. In retrospect, some historians tend to emphasize the significance of Dunmore's War solely in the broad framework of national development. Yet a large number of Virginians had more immediate, more personal reasons for celebrating Lewis' victory over Cornstalk. Now that the Indian menace was removed, it was possible for settlers to violate the Proclamation of 1763 in relative safety, and for speculators to have existing claims surveyed. "Land hunger" can scarcely be overemphasized when explaining the grievances of Virginians against George III. As the cultivation of tobacco was the mainstay in the economic life of the colony, the planter aristocracy turned to land speculation as a means of extricating themselves from an overwhelming burden of indebtedness to British merchants. The tobacco trade in the 1760's was at best a precarious occupation. If speculation in western lands was to be denied by royal fiat, how then was the landed gentry to continue to support itself in the manner to which it had become accustomed?

Even though the Royal Proclamation of 1763 originally had been intended as a temporary measure until a more comprehensive western land policy could be worked out, Virginians were none too happy to await the king's pleasure before securing new grants or having existing claims opened to settlement. A temporary proclamation line beyond which no settlement was allowed was distasteful enough; but when it became apparent that no satisfactory, long range policy was forthcoming, it is a massive understatement merely to say that Virginians were restless and dissatisfied.

Even more ominous from the Virginians' point of view was the possibility that when the West was opened for development, exploitation would be undertaken by English land companies rather than by Virginia interests. Such an eventuality conflicted with James Mason's visions of a Virginia empire in the West. Then too, for example, the Lees of Virginia had organized the Mississippi Land Company. Dr. Arthur Lee was sent to London as its principal agent. And eventually, Thomas Jefferson went so far as to deny the right of any control whatsoever over western lands to the imperial authorities.

In 1769 a petition was made to the British Crown by an English company, headed by Thomas Walpole, requesting the right to purchase and colonize a large tract of land which had been ceded by the Iroquois at Fort Stanwix. The Privy Council actually authorized the grant in 1773. Only because of the growing unrest in the American colonies did the project fail to meet final approval. The proposed new colony was to be known as Vandalia, and its seat of government was to be located at the mouth of the Great Kanawha. From a Virginian's viewpoint, Great Britain, in considering the transmontane region as imperial domain, had ignored the charter rights of his colony with impunity. Though Virginia never officially contradicted the imperial assumption of sovereignty, she was determined not to abandon her claims to western lands without a struggle.

In Lord Dunmore, Virginia land speculators found a willing ally. Dunmore, who had come to the American colonies to increase his own personal fortune, had no serious objections to the occupation of the transmontane region, despite the policy of the imperial government. Dunmore had visions of acquiring western estates of his own and found many congenial associates and advisors among the land speculators of Virginia— including George Washington and Andrew Lewis. He became Governor of Virginia in 1771 and as early as April, 1772, the earl expressed his interest in acquiring a tract of land which had been secured at the Treaty of Lochaber in 1770. "Lord Dunmore," wrote a contemporary, "and several gentlemen of that country determined upon petitioning the king for some part of it." In November of the following year Dunmore petitioned the Board of Trade for a personal grant of 100,000 acres. Unfortunately for the earl, his request was rejected.

The last Royal Governor of Virginia not only pushed his own interests vigorously but upheld the "rights" of the colony which he administered. In the controversy with Pennsylvania over the location of its western boundary, Dunmore aggressively supported Virginia's claim to the region around Fort Pitt. When Governor Penn sent a committee to Williamsburg to seek a compromise solution, Dunmore refused to make even the slightest concession. The dispute was not finally settled until after the Revolution, but Dunmore had been so outspoken in promoting the claims of his colony that when he ordered the expedition against the Shawnee, it was rumored in Virginia that Dunmore was going to fight the Pennsylvanians.

John Murray was sympathetic to the aspirations of Virginians in other ways. For example, the Proclamation of 1763 had made provision for granting tracts of land to British officers and soldiers which could be located west of the proclamation line. There was considerable doubt as to whether Virginians (colonials) were included under the terms of this act. Yet, on December 15, 1773, Dunmore announced that colonials "should be at liberty to locate the lands, they claimed under the Royal Proclamation of . . . 1763, WHEREVER they should desire; and that every officer should be allowed a distinct survey, for every thousand acres." For this decision, Dunmore was severely reprimanded by Lord Dartmouth, the British Colonial Secretary, who wrote that:

> independent of the general impropriety of laying out lands within that tract until His Majesty's pleasure be finally known, it seems to me very doubtful whether provincial officers and soldiers are included in that proclamation, and therefore I trust that you will grant no patents for such locations or allow further locations to be made upon such claims until you have received further Orders from the King.

On his return from the western campaign, Dunmore found another letter from Dartmouth awaiting him. This communication was even more emphatic and instructed Dunmore to make no grants "beyond the Limits of the Royal Proclamation of 1763" under any conditions whatsoever. Then when the Colonial Office learned of Dunmore's expedition against the Indians, he was threatened with dire consequences for his action. Not only had Dunmore acted without consulting Sir William Johnson, the Superintendent of Indian Affairs in the Northern District, but was accused by Dartmouth of being personally interested in land speculation. Dunmore denied the accusation. Rather than violating British policy, the earl maintained that the Shawnee could have been pacified only by resorting to force; and "I think there is a greater probability that these scenes will never be renewed, than ever was before. Furthermore," said the Governor, "no power on earth could restrain the Americans who do not conceive that Government has any right to forbid the settlement of unoccupied lands or to prevent the killing of Indians—their inveterate enemies whose stage of development was little removed from Brute Creation." As no frame of government had been established for the western region which Virginians were settling despite the proclamation line, the Earl of Dunmore observed that the only alternative to a "Set of Democratic Governments of their own" was to extend the boundaries of Virginia so that the pioneers could be kept under the governmental authority of England. Undoubtedly there was more than measure of truth in such a viewpoint. Seemingly, it was more realistic and more practical than the policies, or lack of them, which were pursued by the British government. But Dunmore, in view of his own personal application for a tract of 100,000 acres, hardly could have expected the Colonial Office to believe that he had no interest in land speculation. Nevertheless, he further defended his honor by stating that the "Philadelphia Papers, and I dare say other means, have been used to make it believed, that I acted only in conjunction with a parcel of Land Jobbers. . . . The Indian disturbances have . . . been wonderfully aiding to Mr. Penn's purpose, and he has not neglected them." Without doubt, Dunmore's Pennsylvania adversaries represented his activities to the Colonial Office in the most odious light; yet the earl's self-characterization as a misunderstood patriot can hardly be accepted at face value.

Regardless of his motivations, Dunmore's direction of the campaign against the Shawnee was one of enlightened action. He was not interested in a war of extermination; and before resorting to final measures, he did attempt to negotiate a peaceful settlement. Furthermore, after the battle of Point Pleasant, the Royal Governor offered liberal peace terms. His prevention of a war of annihilation which Lewis' branch of the army wanted to pursue in Ohio visibly angered the Virginians. Evidently this factor contributed to the accusation in later years that Dunmore had been guilty of treacherous conduct. But undoubtedly, his decision was wise. His object was to secure a lasting peace. What useful purpose would have been served in wreaking unnecessary vengence? After the Revolution began, Virginia agents, attended by representatives of the Continental

Congress, pursued the governor's policy to its logical conclusion. A peace treaty was signed the following year at Fort Pitt.
Nevertheless, Dunmore's reputation has suffered at the hands
of historians.

Thomas Perkins Abernethy pointed out that the last Royal
Governor of Virginia could well afford to offer generous terms
to the Shawnee. Abernethy reasoned that Dunmore had speculative interests in Kentucky, not in Ohio. Other historians have
also concluded that his actions were largely if not entirely
determined by the desire for personal gain and/or that he was
the tool of "land jobbers." For example, Isaac Harrell stated that
Dunmore's War was fought to gratify the western aspirations of
"would be landholders" who held unsurveyed claims. Clarence
W. Alvord states that there is no absolute proof for such a view
but he strongly suspects a close connection between speculative
aspirations and the campaign against the Shawnee. In a similar
vein, Randolph C. Downes interpreted the earl's conduct as a
"complete surrender to land-hungry frontiersmen and speculators." Of course, Theodore Roosevelt had no words of
condemnation for Dunmore. Ardent nationalist that he was,
questions concerning the motives of Dunmore or the activities
of land speculators were of minor significance in comparison to
the tremendous surge it gave to western expansion. One can
nearly picture an image in Roosevelt's mind of the last far
western pioneer standing on a California shore looking sadly at
the Pacific Ocean.

It appears, however, that historians have been too severe in
their negative appraisal of Dunmore's career. It can hardly be
denied that John Murray had economic interests in the West or
that "land hunger" was the most significant factor which motivated speculators and frontiersmen. But to picture the Earl of
Dunmore as a greedy, grasping speculator who probably welcomed war for selfish economic reasons is by no means a
complete picture of motivation. Documentary evidence suggests that Dunmore acted for a variety of reasons. Interest in
land speculation was only one important factor.

Efforts to find a solution to western land and government
problems virtually defied solution for blundering, inept or
ill-informed British politicians. In opposing a short-sighted
British policy, there was merit in Lord Dunmore's contention

that westward expansion could not be prevented and that the extension of Virginia's authority was the only alternative to a "Set of Democratic Governments of their own." Dartmouth, who wrote to Sir William Johnson that "I am at a loss to guess at the motives which led to the hostilities against the Shawnee," apparently could not appreciate the governor's position that his campaign against the Indians was designed to avert a more serious uprising against the advancing frontiersmen—a frontier advance which neither Dunmore, the British Government, nor the Indians could turn aside. Indeed, his conduct of negotiations at Camp Charlotte, and his prevention of unnecessary bloodshed was well-considered statesmanship. Dunmore certainly was not guilty of perpetrating a needless war. Lyman Draper estimated that as many lives were lost on the frontier in the decade preceding Dunmore's campaign as were forfeited as a result of the war itself.

In addition, Lord Dunmore was not unconscious of humanitarian considerations in hoping for an early pacification of the Shawnee. He was well aware that "Longknives" were guilty of committing atrocities as were the Indians. In a letter to Dartmouth, Dunmore stated his intention of trying to discover and prosecute renegade whites who shared a large portion of blame for the seemingly unending process of attack and retaliation. Only the unreserved skeptic can accuse Dunmore of complete hypocrisy when on the eve of his departure for the West he wrote to Dartmouth that:

> ... I expected a War with the Indians, since the Shawnees, Mingoes, and some of the Delawares, have fallen on our frontiers, killed, scalped and most cruelly murdered a great many, women and children . . . , but I hope in eight or ten days to march . . . over the Alleghany Mountains, and then . . . to the mouth of the Scioto, and if I can possibly fall upon these lower towns undiscovered I think I shall be able to put an end to this cruel war in which there is neither honor, pleasure, nor profit.

Dunmore's campaign against the Shawnee was swift and decisive. For a short time, his popularity in Virginia reached unparalleled heights. On the return march from the West, the officers of his army passed a resolution praising their commander, "who, we are confident, underwent the great fatigue of this singular campaign from no other motive than the true interest of this country." When he arrived in Williamsburg, Dunmore was presented with congratulatory addresses from the city, the College of William and Mary and from the governor's council. Then in March, 1775, even the Virginia Convention, assembled in opposition to imperial authority, resolved that:

> the most cordial thanks of the people of this colony are a tribute justly due our worthy Governour [sic], Lord Dunmore, for his truly noble, wise, and spirited conduct, on the late expedition against our Indian enemy; a conduct which at once evinces his Excellency's attention to the true interests of this colony, and a zeal in the executive department which no dangers can divert, or difficulties hinder, from achieving the most important services to the people who have the happiness to live under his administration.

The last Royal Governor of Virginia "who during the campaign of 1774 shared its hardships with the privates, marching on foot and carrying his own knapsack" richly deserved this acclaim. He had served Virginians well. Surely Dunmore deserves a far more favorable evaluation from historians than it has been his fortune to receive. Up to this point in his career as Governor of Virginia, the earl displayed a remarkable talent for statesmanship and foresight. Despite the fact that he disagreed with established imperial concerning western lands, his activities would suggest that he combined self-interest and colonial "rights" with a genuine desire to maintain the authority of George III. In urging the extension of Virginia's boundaries westward, Dunmore obviously recognized the inadvisability of the proposed Vandalia enterprise, and other attempts to resolve the western problem which conflicted with Virginia's charter rights. The Quebec Act may have been a piece of enlightened legislation in-so-far as the French Canadians were concerned. Yet the fact that Americans considered this piece of legislation as one of the Coercive Acts suggests that British statesmen would have done well had they embraced Dunmore's program—a program which would not have clashed so violently and inevitably with the hopes and aspirations of colonials. By no means does such a conclusion signify that Dunmore was a reformer with a theoretical program who strived to show the British government the error of its ways. Nevertheless, it is clear that from a variety of motivations, the policies which John

Murray actively put into operation demonstrated his recognition of fundamental issues which the authorities in London failed completely to grasp.

Fate, however, was not kind to the last Royal Governor of Virginia. Dunmore, the champion of colonial "rights" in pre-Revolutionary Virginia, was none the less a loyal subject of George III. When war came in 1775, his zeal in opposing revolutionary forces earned for him the burning hatred of his former supporters. On one occasion Dunmore exploded "that he had once fought for Virginians, and that by God he would let them see he could fight against them." Never to be successful, the royalist forces under Dunmore were defeated by none other than General Andrew Lewis, the hero of Point Pleasant. Defeated, humiliated and without hope for victory, the earl left Virginia in July, 1776.

Now that Dunmore had earned the hatred of Virginians, all former acts and activities were viewed with suspicion. No longer was he to be hailed as the grand and glorious conqueror of the Shawnee. In the minds of many Virginians, Dunmore's War was now considered as a plot against the frontier militia—a conspiracy planned with diabolical cleverness. The earl's intentions had not been to pacify the Shawnee or pave the way for future settlement. Rather, the frontiersmen concluded that the Earl of Dunmore must have been secretly in collusion with the Shawnee. By isolating Andrew Lewis at Point Pleasant, Dunmore hoped for his destruction at the hands of Cornstalk. Even Lewis made a statement to this effect before he died in 1781. These charges, however, were not confined to contemporaries. They were repeated with variations by a whole generation of "border" historians. Indeed, this viewpoint has been carried over into the twentieth century by "local" historians who have erroneously repeated the rationalization that the battle of Point Pleasant was the first battle of the American Revolution.

Even if Lord Dunmore had been guilty of treachery, the conclusion that the encounter at Point Pleasant was the first battle of the American Revolution is illogical enough—not to say absurd. Rarely, if ever, can the "devil" theory of historical causation be substantiated. Aside from the evidence which depicts Dunmore as a far-sighted champion of colonial "rights," an accurate account of the expedition itself exonerates the earl from these wild accusations which were distorted in the heat and passion of war.

In essence the charge of treachery stems from the fact that Dunmore and Lewis did not rendezvous at the Ohio River. The governor's first instructions directed Lewis to proceed to Point Pleasant where the two branches of the army would converge. A later communication, however, instructed Lewis to proceed to the mouth of the Little Kanawha instead of Point Pleasant. Lewis refused to comply and sent word to the earl that he could not alter his route. Evidently this information did not reach Dunmore. When the Governor did not find Lewis at the Little Kanawha, he sent messengers south to locate Lewis with instructions for him to proceed to the mouth of the Big Hockhocking, about sixty miles north of Point Pleasant. When Lewis arrived at Point Pleasant, he found Dunmore's message in a hollow tree and sent word to the earl that he could make no further advance until his rear guard arrived with supplies. Then on October 8, 1774, two days before the battle, Lewis received more dispatches from Dunmore and replied that he would march northward to join his commander-in-chief as soon as possible. Then Dunmore changed his plans. Rather than delay the progress of the expedition by awaiting the arrival of Lewis, the governor sent a dispatch instructing Lewis to cross the Ohio at Point Pleasant and march toward the Indian towns. The two wings of the army, converging at an angle, would rendezvous and proceed to attack the Shawnee villages. Before this new plan of action could be put into operation, Cornstalk with a force of 800 to 1000 Indians attacked Lewis' army of 1100 frontiersmen. Dunmore's treachery then, consisted of failing to rendezvous with a subordinate who did not comply with the instructions of his commander-in-chief. Had Lewis fulfilled the instructions of Dunmore, there would have been no battle at the confluence of the Great Kanawha and Ohio Rivers between a group of colonial frontiersmen and a band of Shawnee Indians. [*See* Map 2.]

Nevertheless, as has been mentioned before, Dunmore's reputation has suffered at the hands of historians. Alexander Scott Withers, in his famous volume, *Chronicles of Border Warfare,* reasoned that in 1774 Dunmore knew that revolution in the colonies was inevitable. Therefore he tried to seek the aid of the Indians in reducing Virginians to subjection. Thus he concluded that:

> the battle of Point Pleasant, virtually the first in the series of those brilliant achievements which burst the bonds of British tyranny; and the blood of Virginia, there nobly shed, was the first blood spilled in the sacred cause of American liberty.

Writing in the *Virginia Magazine of History and Biography* in 1902, a "local" historian, J. T. McAllister, was even more explicit. The encounter at Point Pleasant was the "first battle of the Revolution." McAllister concluded that everyone in Virginia was aware as early as June, 1774 that the American Revolution was inevitable. By "aiding Lewis to overcome these foes" Dunmore would have performed an invaluable service to the cause of independence. But to "cripple him or have him exterminated" would have assured the suppression of the revolutionary movement in Virginia. Yet, in the final analysis, McAllister conceded that "the evidence sustaining absolutely a charge of this kind is hard to produce." Since such evidence is non-existent, McAllister had to resort to the process of fallacious reasoning and perversion of facts.

Historical myths, however, die a slow death. On December 4, 1907 Senator Nathan Bay Scott of West Virginia introduced the following bill in the Senate of the United States:

> A bill to aid in the erection of a monument or memorial at Point Pleasant, W. Va., to commemorate the battle of the Revolution fought at that point between the colonial troops and Indians October 10, 1774.

The bill was approved by the Senate on February 21, 1908. Thus was official sanction given, "but only obliquely" as historian Elizabeth Cometti phrased it, to the rationalization that the battle of Point Pleasant was the first encounter in the War for Independence—a myth which persists among the people of the Trans-Alleghany region down to the present day.

Imperial Policy and the Government of Detroit

Peter Marshall

In our history books, access to the West is generally viewed from an Anglo-American bias. We usually associate it with routes through Pittsburgh and the Cumberland Gap and fail to recognize the significance of the St. Lawrence and the Mohawk valleys. While much attention has been focused on the expansive interests of Virginians and Pennsylvanians in such enterprises as the Grand Ohio and Illinois companies, little emphasis has been placed on the efforts of those connected with interests in Quebec and New York upon colonization attempts. Moreover, we tend to place more importance on communities like Boonesborough and Harrodsburg than upon Detroit and Kaskaskia.

Peter Marshall (1926———), professor of American history and institutions at the University of Manchester and formerly on the faculty of the University of Bristol and of McGill University, the latter in Montreal, is one of the foremost authorities on the imperial connections between London and the Middle West. In numerous articles in scholarly journals he has examined the interaction of colonial and imperial interests in the period between the Great War for the Empire, 1754–1763 (the French and Indian War) and the American War for Independence.

This article examines Colonel John Bradstreet's attempts to interest New-York-based associates in the development of a colony centered on Detroit. Like most colonial servants of the crown, Bradstreet's fortunes rose and fell with those of his friends in the English court. Thus one sees how the changing of ministerial positions contributed to the failure of a colony using the Great Lakes as its principal avenue of transportation. In particular, the fall of George Grenville and the earl of Shelburne were significant misfortunes for Bradstreet. (Lord Shelburne, in 1782, was to contribute significantly to the awarding of the Northwest to the United States by the treaty of peace.) The emergence of such officials as the viscount of Hillsborough and the earl of Dartmouth reoriented British policy away from the type of colony envisioned by Bradstreet. It was Dartmouth's decision to place the whole of the region lying between

87

Hudson's Bay and the Ohio River under the domain of Quebec that finally doomed Bradstreet's design.

Also of interest in this article is the emergence of local government in Detroit itself. To keep civil authority from remaining "suspended" throughout the twelve-year period after Detroit's occupation, the military officers of the western posts devised "their own means of resolving local civil disputes." Under a grant of authority from the local commander, Philip Dejean served as civil majestrate for the Detroit region from 1767 until 1774. But the temporary nature of this system and the failure to condemn or deny these proceedings left civil government in the region in limbo. It was this situation that Dartmouth sought to remedy when he annexed the region to Quebec, even though he knew he offended interests in Virginia, Pennsylvania, New York, and London. By the time all this was done, Marshall notes, "imperial policy was entering, rather than escaping, its years of larger crisis."

* *

ON 29 November 1760, eighty-two days after the capitulation of New France, a force commanded by Major Robert Rogers received the surrender of the garrison at Detroit. When, at the end of January, news of the successful carrying out of his orders reached General Amherst, the commander-in-chief did not conceal his delight. Leaving Montreal only five days after Vaudreuil's submission, Rogers had won the race to reach his principal destination before winter closed the Lakes to navigation. Amherst now hastened to inform the Indian superintendent, Sir William Johnson, that there were 'incredible quantities' of furs amassed at Detroit. He therefore proposed, once the weather improved, to garrison the Great Lakes posts properly, and 'to appoint a Person of knowledge & probity to be Governor at the Detroit', with orders to open a free and fair trade with the Indians. He invited advice from Johnson concerning 'the Government of the Indians, and the maintenance

From Peter Marshall, "Imperial Policy and the Government of Detroit: Projects and Problems, 1760–1774," in the *Journal of Imperial and Commonwealth History*, 2:153–189 (January, 1974); reprinted without footnotes with permission of the author and Frank Cass & Co., Ltd.

of this great & important post of the Detroit and its Natural Commerce with the Subject . . .'. Amherst was never to waver from this initial expression of belief in the value of the new acquisition.

Fifty years after its establishment, Detroit remained best appreciated from afar. Its value as a centre for trade with the Indians, the terminus of a line of commercial communication that passed through Niagara and Montreal or New York to the markets of Europe, caught the imagination as its physical appearance would not. The fort, protected by a wooden stockage about twenty-five feet high and 1,200 yards in circumference, contained, even when enlarged by the British, only a hundred houses, crowded together on unpaved streets. In 1763 some forty merchants and their *engagées* were resident there. Settlement had taken place on both banks of the river which linked Lakes Erie and St. Clair, adding considerably to the total population and providing supplies for the garrison. Early population estimates did not allow for the considerable seasonal fluctuation in numbers due to the presence or absence of traders nor distinguish between the inhabitants of the fort and of its environs. Excluding the garrison, which in the first decade of British rule contained about 200 men, the region may have contained some 600 settlers. Rogers reported to Amherst that 500 French had taken the oath of allegiance, most of whom exercised their right to remain under the terms of the peace. By the outbreak of the revolution the population had probably increased to over 1,000 but French still outnumbered English inhabitants.

During 1761 and 1762 Amherst completed the occupation of the West—with the important exception of the French forts on the Mississippi—so that Detroit became the most substantial of a number of posts stretching from Michilimackinac in the north to Ouiatenon in the south. Although this may have appeared an impressive achievement in terms of an extension of territorial influence, the military and administrative problems thus created were, or should have appeared to be, daunting. The West lacked civil administration: it was excluded from the limits of the older colonies and even if recognised as a part of Quebec would be attached to a region under military rule. Following the murder, in the summer of 1762, of a Detroit trader by his two Indian slaves, Amherst authorised a local military tribunal to pass sentence of execution upon the offenders. Other breaches of the peace were bound to occur, for the maintenance of order in the West was continually endangered by the conflicts arising from the irreconcilable interests of the four principal elements of society: the military, the Indian officials, the traders, and the Indians. Differences appeared on a number of fundamental points of policy. Amherst was prepared to allow Johnson to regulate prices for goods traded at the posts, but refused the superintendent's request to restrict the number of passes issued to traders. Although Johnson secured control over permits for New York traders making for Niagara and Detroit, his deputy at Montreal, Daniel Claus, was denied similar powers by Gage, the military governor. Johnson's traders were refused permission to carry rum; Gage enforced no such prohibition. The resumption of the old rivalry between New York and Canadian interests was accordingly marked by the bestowal of an unassailable superiority on those able to offer spirits to the Indians. The traders resented both the restriction of their activities and the regulation of their profits: no gratitude was displayed by the Canadians for their relatively free circumstances.

Amherst's establishment of military control in the West was accompanied by an attitude of contempt towards commercial interests: in his view the traders considered nothing but their profits, even if these were secured at the cost of inciting an Indian war. Gage, Amherst's successor as commander-in-chief, reflected military opinion when he asserted that 'the Canada traders are a terrible set of people; and stick at nothing true or false'. This was not simple national prejudice, for he subsequently admitted that the French traders

> were in general of a better stamp than . . . ours . . . The people sent with our trade, if not confined to the Forts ramble every where, they are generally of no Character, and of desperate fortunes, and for the consideration of a present profit have never thought of consequences, or of what Mischief they entailed upon their Country.

Protecting the traders was a thankless task while the Indians, the objects of their greed, were no more worthy of respect. Amherst saw no need to conciliate or supply the tribes: 'when men of what race soever behave ill, they must be punished but not bribed . . .' he informed Johnson, affirming a few months later that 'it is not my intention ever to attempt to gain the friendship of Indians by presents'. Johnson, who had held an Indian conference at Detroit in the summer of 1761, was of a very different opinion, but the commander-in-chief, who had never seen the West, held inflexibly to the view that no Indian menace existed. From this it followed that the value of the Indian officials and the cost of their services were to be questioned. Johnson and his deputy George Croghan spent lavishly on Indian conferences: Amherst saw no justification for such prodigality. Expenditures were to be entrusted to commanding officers in preference to Indian officials.

The problem posed by Western conditions, arbitrarily disposed of through Amherst's initial moves but demanding more substantial political decisions which could only be reached by the ministry if a lasting solution was to be found, was of a complex nature. Conflicting interests needed to be reconciled to permit the conduct of trade, the management of the Indians, the regulation of settlement, and the most efficient disposition of a military force which, for the first time, would be maintained in a North America at peace. Amherst's attitudes compounded the difficulties which any endeavours to achieve a satisfactory situation would encounter.

Amherst, Johnson, and Gage agreed that the Indian trade required the presence of garrisons but differed as to the provision and extent of the financial costs involved. Amherst demanded a reduction of Indian expenses, while Gage displayed continual alarm at the size of the bills submitted for payment. Two possibilities of economy were suggested: gifts of goods, arms and ammunition to the Indians should be drastically reduced; the forts might be manned by settlers who would be granted lands in the vicinity on military tenures, thereby removing both the need of regular detachments and the high cost of transporting supplies and provisions from the East. Amherst had approved a project of this kind at Niagara in 1762; Gage would offer this remedy for the difficulties raised at Fort Pitt in 1764 and at Natchez in 1767. It was a device now advocated by Colonel John Bradstreet as the means by which a new colony might be established at Detroit.

By the end of the war Bradstreet had completed a quarter of a century's military service in North America. Rising to prominence as the 'first projector' of the expedition of 1745 against Louisbourg, he had thereafter pursued connections, promotion, and appointments with unremitting zeal and a constant sense of overlooked merit. He had first attached himself to Governor William Shirley of Massachusetts; as Lieutenant-Governor of St. John's, Newfoundland, he had inspired an attempt by Lord Baltimore to revive the family's proprietary claim to the island; during the French and Indian war he had become aide-de-camp to Loudoun, had been assigned to quartermaster duties, and in 1758 had led a provincial force to reoccupy Oswego and cross Lake Ontario to capture Fort Frontenac and destroy supplies intended to maintain the French posts in the West. This success won him a military reputation which would seem otherwise undeserved if his correspondence, when dwelt on hopes of advancement rather than on the glories of battle, is to be taken as a guide. Success at Oswego greatly strengthened his belief in a right to be rewarded for his 'great work': at the least, his military appointment, which enabled him to combine his duties as deputy quartermaster general at Albany with an avid interest in acquiring New York lands, should not be terminated. In subsequent appeals his hopes soared much higher. Might he become Governor of New York? Lieutenant-Governor of Montreal or Trois Rivières? Colonel Commandant of the four New York Independent Companies? He was prepared to accept any governorship in Northern America, but refused to consider an appointment in the southern colonies or the West Indies: even Bradstreet's ambitions knew climatic limits.

Throughout this search for place Bradstreet depended heavily upon the friendship of Charles Gould, deputy judge advocate general, who for twenty years prior to becoming judge advocate general in 1769 had fulfilled the duties of that office. How he had formed this connection is not clear though prior to his death in 1756 King Gould, Charles's father, had been agent for Nova Scotia, where Bradstreet had spent his early years. The first letter from Bradstreet preserved by Gould is of April 1754, and records the securing of votes in the interests of Sir Richard Lyttelton during the parliamentary election at Poole.

After the war, Bradstreet's hopes of advancement rested largely on the support of Gould and Lyttelton. When Bradstreet despatched his assistant, Philip Schuyler, to England in March 1761 in order to expedite the clearing of his financial accounts, he provided a letter of introduction to Gould.

Schuyler had been associated with Bradstreet in military affairs since the winter of 1755–56; although he had resigned in disgust at the outcome of the campaign of 1756 he had rejoined Bradstreet in 1758, and on Bradstreet's promotion to deputy quartermaster general had continued to serve under him. From this wartime connection a joint interest developed in the acquisition of New York lands which would continue until Bradstreet's death. The laborious task of clearing his superior's accounts kept Schuyler in England until October 1762. During his stay he was able to add some potentially useful acquaintances to those already possessed by Bradstreet.

The proposal to establish a colony at Detroit was put forward well before Schuyler's return to North America. Writing to Sir William Baker in February 1762, Bradstreet referred to current reports of difficulties in settling the limits of Canada and of the desire of the French to maintain their interests among the Great Lakes Indians. The establishment of a government in that area would overcome the problem:

> This will secure the Frontier of our colonies, give us the whole of the Indian Trade in safety, effectually put a stop to the great and dangerous French Plan of surrounding us with Inland Colonies and enable us to execute that Plan ourselves in its full extent when it may be thought necessary.

Detroit was well suited to become the principal seat of government. It had good lands, was well placed for the Indian trade, possessed between two and three hundred French families to which Bradstreet, if he was put on the British establishment, would add a further thousand men from the colonies. These men would raise sufficient provisions within a few years to support both themselves and the garrison. The best of the provincial field officers had offered to raise the men at their own expense if placed in command and commissioned as captains on the regular establishment.

By the autumn of 1762 the plan to establish a colony at

Detroit had been fully conceived and appeared likely to succeed. It would implement the views of the highest authority in
North America, Sir Jeffery Amherst, who had recommended to
Lord Egremont, the secretary of state, the making of 'a seat of
government and a separate Government of the Detroit'. Although he also favoured further governments at Crown Point
and Niagara he did not consider these 'so essentially necessary'.
Bradstreet had already despatched a copy of his project to
Gould for submission to Egremont, but he entrusted another
copy to Captain Mungo Campbell of the 55th Regiment. It was
hoped that Campbell, who had been serving in New York, could
use an influential family connection, the Earl of Breadalbane, to
present the plan to Lord Bute. Bradstreet had prepared a
further memorial for Lord Halifax, the secretary of state for the
northern department; Schuyler, recently returned, had written
to Thomas Brand whom Bradstreet considered, for no good
reason, 'a man of weight'. The economic purpose of the colony
was now declared to be the growing of hemp. This justification
may well have been devised by Schuyler, who had noted the
offering of premiums to encourage its production by the Royal
Society of Arts, and had made the acquaintance of Brand
through that institution.

Campbell, at first denied leave by Amherst, was allowed to sail
for England early in December 1762. Gould had promised to
discuss the Detroit project with Halifax and Charles Townshend, then president of the Board of Trade, but Campbell cast
doubt on Bradstreet's willingness to settle in so distant a post as
Detroit and offered to take his place. Halifax and Townshend
professed friendship for Bradstreet, but any favourable developments were put out of the question by the rapid succession of
changes which occurred in the ministers responsible for American affairs, the outbreak in July 1763 of the Indian attacks on
the frontier posts, and the delay in reaching major decisions
which preceded the issuing of the proclamation of 7 October
1763.

A period of less than nine months saw the presence in office
of four presidents of the Board of Trade, the most spectacular,
if not necessarily the most important, indication of the phase of
ministerial instability which marked the resignation of Bute and

the promotion of Grenville. The preparation of a system of government for the new acquisitions was not assisted by the death of Egremont while the details and implications of the measure were in course of debate. Between May and October 1763 the process of organisation was perhaps inevitably protracted but dangerously disconnected, with consequences in failing to define the status of Detroit that were of the first importance.

The Board of Trade was requested on 5 May by Egremont to prepare a report on the administration of the new possessions. The documents forwarded for information and guidance drew attention to a basic problem: the need to distinguish between a frontier of settlement and a limit of government, a contrast rendered unavoidable by the necessity of permitting trade with the Indians. To resolve this difficulty it was suggested that officers commanding military posts in unsettled territory should be empowered to return offenders to be dealt with by the civil power in the seaboard colonies. Subsequently, John Pownall, secretary to the Board of Trade, submitted more specific proposals for the restriction of settlement. This should be generally prohibited beyond the Alleghanies and in the Great Lakes region, which would be reserved for a regulated trade conducted among Indians protected by military detachments.

When the Board submitted its report on 8 June its recommendations sustained these objections to the westward spread of settlement. The new acquisitions were considered in the light of their value as measured in mercantilist terms: by this yardstick, priority of importance was accorded to ensuring the exclusive fishery of the Gulf of the St. Lawrence, followed by the Indian fur and skin trade and the market for commodities offered in return by British traders; settlement in the coastal colonies, whether to the north or to the south, was considered certain to provide valuable primary products, and in such cases the immediate establishment of regular governments was indispensable. In other instances,

> as no such regular civil Government is either necessary or indeed can be established, where no perpetual Residence or planting is intended; It will there be sufficient to provide for the Free Trade of all Your Majesty's Subjects under such Regulations, and such Administration of Justice as is best suited to that End.

This denied the claims of Newfoundland, Senegal, and, at least for the moment, the Indian territory of North America, where a regulated free trade should be established under military supervision.

The number of troops and their stations would require a further report. For the moment, the boundaries of the Indian territory would be defined by those established for Canada and Florida in the north and south, and by the Mississippi in the west. Canada was adjudged suitable for settlement, and would therefore immediately receive a regular government, but its interior limits would be restricted by a line extending from Lakes Champlain to Nipissing, in effect making the Ottawa river the furthest discernible extent of the province.

The principles which underlay the report were clearly those of ensuring the permanent supremacy of British interests, at last freed from French competition, in North America, and of facilitating their expansion for the economic benefit of the mother country. Their application would threaten the established economy of the St. Lawrence: if D. G. Creighton's assertion that in consequence 'A great inland commercial empire . . . was to become a normal colony . . . The stunted little colony which the British named Quebec was but a contemptible fragment of what they had conquered as New France . . .' seems to import more to the proposals of the Board than is justified—the Board had clearly distinguished between areas of trade and of settlement—it remains clear that this attempt to restrict British interests in North America could not hope for success. In particular, the French settlements at Detroit and in the Illinois country, which the Board seemed content to ignore, could not be disposed of by simple omission.

The Western problem might have emerged if an objection to the Board's report had been sustained. One of Egremont's advisors—possibly Henry Ellis—objected to the definition of colonial limits. He took it for granted that the new boundaries would refer only to settlements and that the governors' commissions would include all territory as far as the lands of the Hudson's Bay Company. This was essential, 'that the French may never claim a right to come upon the back of our settlements, upon the pretence of its being derelict land, & not included in the Commission of His Majesty's Governor, nor the

Jurisdiction of His Crown . . .' Egremont accepted the criticism and informed the Board that, while agreeing that land grants and settlements should not be permitted, it was necessary that the commission of the Governor of Canada should extend over all the Great Lakes as far as the limits of the Hudson's Bay Company and the Mississippi. From this amendment the Board vigorously dissented.

The presence of Shelburne as president of the Board may have stimulated this somewhat uncharacteristic resistance. In its reply of 5 August the Board objected on three grounds to the annexing of the Indian country to Canada: first, that the acceptance of limits formerly claimed by the French would appear to admit the substance of a title which had never been acknowledged by Britain; secondly, that since the territory would become subject to the laws of Canada, the province would secure great advantages in respect to the whole of the Indian trade; thirdly, that the area would contain the greatest part of the military force retained in North America and depend upon the garrisons to control the Indians and traders. The governor would either virtually become commander-in-chief or fall into constant conflict with the military. The argument was pursued literally to the death, for on 21 August Egremont expired of an apoplectic fit. His successor, Halifax, was not disposed to insist upon the point. On 16 September a cabinet found only Grenville concerned over the assertion of sovereignty; on 19 September the Board was instructed to prepare a proclamation excluding Indian lands from the boundaries of the established colonies. Its provisions would be restricted to a prohibition of settlement and private land purchases among the Indians, and empowering

> all Military Officers and Agents for Indian Affairs, within the reserved Lands, to seize such Criminals and Fugitives, as may take Refuge in that Country, and to send them to be tried in any of the Old Colonies (if That can legally be done) or else to that Government, from which They respectively fled.

The proclamation issued on 7 October 1763 therefore merely asserted the crown's 'Sovereignty, Protection, and Dominion' over Indian territories which were excluded from governors' commissions and in which no practical or theoretical provision was made for civil administration. No mention was made of means by which criminal or civil cases arising in the West would be adjudicated: presumably these were thought to fall within the powers of military and Indian officers, but the legal basis for any action on their part was not discussed or defined.

Events in the West during the summer of 1763 rendered, at least for the moment, the omission of arrangements for its administration a matter of unimportance. The Indian rising, contemptuously dismissed as a serious threat by Amherst, had broken out on a scale which even Johnson, its predictor, had not foreseen. Of the western posts only Detroit and Fort Pitt resisted the initial onslaught: from Michilimackinac to Venango isolated detachments were overwhelmed, betrayed, or surrendered on treacherously broken terms. The need of Detroit was not a government but a relief column. Although the tribes were unable to capitalise on their initial successes and abandoned the siege of Detroit despite the loss on the Lakes of reinforcements, British prestige demanded the despatch of punitive expeditions. This task fell to Gage, who had been left in command by Amherst when he returned to England on leave in November. His instructions required the assembling of two contingents, formed from regular and colonial troops, which would in the spring take the offensive against the Indians. One force of 1,500 provincials and some regular companies was to set out from Fort Pitt to punish the Delawares and Shawnees held responsible for the depredations on the Pennsylvanian frontier; another 2,000 men were to be raised in New York and New Jersey, and would proceed from Niagara to chastise the tribes which had led the attacks on Detroit and the neighbouring posts. Bradstreet had solicited and been given that command before Amherst left for England.

By obtaining this appointment, which could be justified on the grounds that it involved an amphibious operation comparable to that conducted against Fort Frontenac, Bradstreet had succeeded, almost certainly with Amherst's approval, in combining prospects of military advancement and of land speculation. He had already used the news of the Indian attacks as proof of the need to execute his plan for settling 3,000 men at Detroit to raise hemp. Gould had been pressing Bradstreet's case with the ministry, though progress had been hampered by the continual changes of office: in January 1763 he had approached Robert Wood, under-secretary in the Southern department, who had considered neither command of the independent companies nor a peacetime post of quartermaster general to be practicable, but had hoped that some good government might be obtained on the settling of North American affairs. In March Gould was encouraged by the appointment of his friend, Charles Townshend, to the presidency of the Board of Trade. By May ministerial changes required the exertion of new pressures: Townshend and Bute, both of whom had been approached by Campbell, had resigned, but Gould, through the friendship of Charles Jenkinson, had contrived to reach George Grenville. Although general promises of rewards for Bradstreet were forthcoming neither Grenville nor Egremont, who had been reminded of the case by Wood, made any particular offer. During the summer of 1763 Gould's letters could only counsel patience. The death of Egremont and the retirement of Wood seem to have improved Bradstreet's prospects: Halifax, transferred from the Northern to the Southern secretaryship of state was prepared to appoint him lieutenant-governor of either Montreal or Trois Rivières, allowing Colonel Burton the first choice of posts. The new secretary had also been reminded of the Detroit scheme, which Campbell had meanwhile submitted to Bute's brother, James Stuart Mackenzie.

Before Halifax's offer could reach him, Bradstreet had accepted command of the expedition against the Indians. Feeling that the burdens of command justified his promotion to brigadier general, and that advancement in rank would be preferable to appointment in an office which he had held, at St. John's, since 1746, he declined to move to Canada. He did not embark on his military task, however, in the spirit which distinguished his services during the French and Indian war. Bradstreet's letters indicate that he had, from the outset, persuaded himself that his force would be insufficiently large or well trained to overcome tribes supported by the French still active on the Mississippi. Asserting the superiority of his own scheme of a military settlement, Bradstreet had clearly, by January 1764, determined his policy for the coming summer, since he then informed Gould of his hopes to receive orders to make strong alliances with the Indians of the Mississippi-Great Lakes region. The slowness to assemble of the provincial levies, the lack of regular troops, the inexperience of the men who did arrive in Albany, all contrived to provide Bradstreet, before he had even set out, with excuses for inactivity. Rather than reducing the savages to dependence, he predicted, he might well have to act on the defensive.

During the winter of 1763–4 Gage attempted, without much success, to obtain precise commitments from the colonies concerning the troops they would provide Bradstreet and Bouquet, the commander of the southern expedition. Their assemblies proved generally reluctant to raise and pay contingents, seeking refuge in an habitual unwillingness to take the first step—Governor Bernard reported that the New England colonies would not act before New York and New Jersey, nearer the danger, announced their contribution, while those colonies had refused to raise men until New England made its intentions known. The widely circulated report that the Indians around Detroit had proposed surrender and were suing for peace presented a further obstacle. As Gage admitted to Bradstreet, 'Those cursed overtures at Detroit, which I could not conceal, for I saw what hurt they would do us, has given all the Provinces a handle to make excuses.'

At the beginning of April Bradstreet received his campaign instructions from Gage; he was to assure possession of Niagara, where deputies from the Detroit Indians would be received to discuss peace; he was then to attack the Wyandottes of Sandusky and subsequently the Delawares and Shawnees installed on the Muskingum river; on arriving at Detroit, any French found to have acted traitorously were to be made examples of, and he would then proceed to Michilimackinac. The 17th regiment, with a detachment of one hundred despatched to the northern fur post, would form the Detroit garrison.

A month later, Bradstreet was still awaiting the arrival of the provincial contingents at Albany and predicting that he would receive only half the necessary number of troops. By early June, two months after he had proposed to set out, the last of his force was arriving, and large numbers were deserting daily as they discovered the nature of their service. Instead of the 3,600 good men which Bradstreet considered to be the least he required, he commanded 700 regulars, 300 men from Canada entitled the *Volontiers Canadiens* but composed of all nationalities, and about 800 provincials. Although great numbers of the Six Nations were to join him as Oswego and Niagara, Bradstreet believed them to be of uncertain loyalty and intent only on securing immense presents. The news that Major Loftus had failed to ascend the Mississippi and take over the French forts in the Illinois country had greatly raised the Indians' spirits, and the Detroit Indians would most likely attack his force if they considered themselves strong enough to prevail.

The correspondence between Gage and Bradstreet during May and June attested to their impatience and exasperation: the New York and New Jersey contingents were being reduced by desertion while the Connecticut troops seemed indefinitely delayed. Gage, who had concluded, from the hostile reception given news of Grenville's reform of the laws of trade, that no assembly would vote funds for moves against the Indians in another year, declared of current colonial behaviour that 'I am out of all patience with these cursed people'. Bradstreet did not leave Oswego until 3 July for Niagara, where he had intended to remain three days but was detained a month while Johnson held an Indian conference. He defended the delay by arguing that, had he not halted, the Six Nations might well have resumed hostilities and given the signal for the Western Indians to renew their attacks. He left Niagara on 7 August with a force of about 1,500 men and 500 Indians.

Bradstreet had already concluded that he would not have time to reach the Scioto, and that information about the closeness to Sandusky of the Shawnees and Delawares was incorrect. Nine days later he informed Gage from Presq'Isle, where he had been forced to land by a storm on Lake Erie and had encountered a small group of Shawnees and Delawares, that he had agreed to a mutual halt to hostilities, pending a formal conference to conclude peace which would be held at Sandusky at the end of the month. The Indians were to surrender their prisoners and grant the British liberty to build forts and send traders throughout their country; Indians who broke the treaty were to be delivered up at Fort Pitt and there tried by a court of six Englishmen and six Indians. Six hostages were to be provided by the Indians as a guarantee of their observance of the terms of the treaty; henceforth they would take up arms against the enemies of the British.

Gage, six weeks distant in New York, had, before receiving news of this agreement, been ordering Bradstreet either to make a 'formal and regular peace' with the Great Lakes Indians or attack them; he must ensure that he attacked the Delawares and Shawnees on the Scioto at the time Bouquet reached there from Fort Pitt; only if the tribes surrendered for execution ten of the chief promoters of the war and agreed to sue for peace before Johnson should the fighting cease. Bradstreet's announcement of peace reached Gage on the same day as a letter from Bouquet, written immediately on receiving the news. It had filled him with astonishment since the Delawares and Shawnees had only five days previously committed further crimes on the Pennsylvania frontier. Had Bradstreet known this 'he never could have compromised the honour of the nation by such disgraceful conditions: and that at a time when two armies, after long struggles, are in full motion to penetrate in to the heart of the enemy's country'. Bouquet was outraged that a younger officer should make peace, not only without consultation but while assuring the Indians that he would halt his superior's operations. He proposed to take no notice of the peace.

On the day he received these two letters Gage returned a blistering letter of rebuke to Bradstreet. The articles of peace were totally unacceptable; he had completely disregarded his instructions; power to offer peace was quite distinct from that to conclude and dictate its terms, an authority possessed only by Johnson; he had not consulted his superior officer, who was totally correct in his refusal to abandon the campaign. Bradstreet was sent a further copy of Gage's letter of 16 August. Seemingly unaware of the fury that his decisions were arousing, Bradstreet continued his way to Detroit, where he arrived on 27 August. From there he despatched details of a general peace which he concluded on 7 September with all the tribes of the region; trade with the Indians was declared reopened on the following day. Immediately after announcing this success, Bradstreet received Gage's letter of 16 August: he replied that the peace he had made at Sandusky was in fulfilment of his instructions and that he assumed Bouquet's troops had been halted. He was about to return to Sandusky and would receive the Indians' prisoners. If they did not deliver them up, severe punishment would be inflicted.

Bradstreet withdrew from Detroit, ignoring his instructions to proceed to Michilimackinac, highly satisfied with his achievements: before leaving he found time to send Gould copies of his Indian transactions, requesting that they be passed to Amherst and Lyttelton. The main force had remained less than three weeks at Detroit but its stay was long enough for speculative assessments of the region to be made. On 4 September Montresor handed Bradstreet proposals for securing a land grant and settling families which would provide the garrison and the outlying forts with forage and provisions. Three days later, immediately after the treaty of peace had been confirmed, Bradstreet proposed that his officers should apply for land grants. His argument was that

> either the Government must dispossess the present Inhabitants of their lands and entirely remove them from hence or support this feeble colony [Montresor asserted that it contained only 280 men capable of bearing arms] with a numerous body of English sufficient to cultivate the vacant lands in this streight and subordinate the savages who are powerful in this neighbourhood . . .

The alternatives were logically defensible, but the circumstances of their assertion offered little prospect of a respectful hearing.

The return to Niagara proved protracted and something less than triumphant. The Indians did not assemble at Sandusky to make peace, and Gage's renewed instructions to move south to join Bouquet, who was now ready to advance from Fort Pitt, in occupying the Delaware and Shawnee country, had to be acknowledged. Bradstreet called a meeting of his officers to consider the orders. Two officers of the *Volontiers Canadiens,* another French Canadian, and a French-speaking Huron all testified to the distance and difficulty of the route: since no evidence to the contrary was offered it was not surprising that the commanding officers of the units concluded that 'Genl Gage's orders to Colonel Bradstreet are not practicable, nor the troops in a condition to attempt so long a march'. Although news of Bouquet's progress led the Six Nations Indians with the

force to agree, after an initial refusal, to attack the Delawares
and Shawnees, third thoughts led them to reject the proposal.
Hampered by deteriorating weather and storms on Lake Erie,
Bradstreet's troops did not reach Little Niagara until 4 November.

To the commander-in-chief Bradstreet's failure was accen-
tuated by the complete success of Bouquet, who had obeyed
orders, occupied the Indian country, recovered the prisoners,
and made no peace treaty. Bradstreet wholly rejected this
assessment of his conduct and refused to admit that he had
disregarded Gage's instructions or bungled his task. A further
scathing denunciation of his entire proceedings in making
peace, usurping Bouquet's authority and trusting tribes who
were still sending out war parties against the Pennsylvania and
Virginia frontiers, was returned the answer that 'it gives me
some satisfaction to find you approve of all my conduct except
my mistaking your intentions in making a formal peace'. Even
this represented a withdrawal from an initial position of arguing in outraged fury, with copious quotations from his instructions, that he had been empowered to make peace.

Bradstreet's willingness to admit error did not grow as he
approached Albany. Visiting Sir William Johnson, he showed
him many papers relative to his conduct in the campaign and
declared 'that he is determined to do what I think, and what I
told him, he had better let alone, but had declared he would
vindicate his conduct to the utmost, and show the world he
acted up to his instructions'. Johnson, when asked his opinion,
replied that he thought things were often made worse by
publication. Bradstreet retorted that he would defend himself
and supposed that Gage had written a great deal home to his
disadvantage. 'I told him that in such delicate points, a man
should not act upon supposition. His answer was much the same
with the former, and in a very high strain.' Despite returning
with an army which, in Johnson's view, could easily have been
destroyed by an Indian attack, and which resembled a routed
rabble rather than a victorious force, Bradstreet assumed the
air of a conqueror.

Bradstreet's conduct during and after the campaign was
barely defensible and personally foolish. His behaviour was

dictated by the ambition which constantly stimulated his correspondence. He had procured the command primarily to advance his military career and overcome the difficult obstacles to peace-time promotion; secondly to strengthen his claims to a governorship; thirdly to establish his interest in Detroit lands. The tone of his letters from early summer onward suggests that he had no intention of engaging in Indian warfare: he preferred the triumphs of peacemaking to the hazards of battle. If he believed that this would win him greater recognition he was dangerously mistaken: by flouting his instructions and usurping the functions of the Indian superintendent, Bradstreet lost all chance of support from either Gage or Johnson for his schemes. His controversy with the commander-in-chief over his authority to make peace with the Indians saw him argue as a lawyer, not as an officer. Although he retained the friendship of Amherst it was certain that in future Bradstreet's project for Detroit would not receive the aid of the two imperial representatives in North America most able to assist it.

Gage's opposition soon became apparent. He had already denied any power to effect land grants when replying to an application from Lieutenant Edward Abbott, a petitioner whose promptness was matched by his pertinacity in maintaining hopes of securing benefits from his stay at Detroit. 'The Detroit', Gage explained, 'will probably be assigned to some one of the Governments, and most likely that of Canada. And it will be in the Governor's power only to make grants within his jurisdiction.' When, in the aftermath of his bitter dispute, the commander-in-chief received the request of the Detroit expedition's officers for land, his refusal to sponsor the application was curt: he did not, he wrote Bradstreet, care to forward the request home 'for many reasons'. He was no doubt influenced by the contents of a letter which he had received on the day of his reply. Johnson had written at length to catalogue the misdeeds and failures of Bradstreet, among them 'the handing away lands to several officers, and even to some French inhabitants at and about Detroit and the mouth of the river, expressly contrary to His Majesty's proclamation'. Bradstreet would not be afforded aid either on grounds of policy or of friendship.

Gage impeded but was unable to crush a proposal which Bradstreet was aware would be unlikely to gain his support.

Before receiving the General's refusal he had forwarded a copy of the officers' memorial to Gould, explaining that he wished him to present it to the ministry if Gage 'should forget, as he is very apt to do'. The bearer of the memorial was Lieutenant Thomas Mante of the 77th Regiment, who had served as Major of Brigade on the expedition. Mante was described by Bradstreet as 'a very deserving man', a judgment hardly confirmed by the details of his career. His abilities were, at best, facile; his integrity was negligible; his eagerness to succeed was accompanied by chronic impecuniosity; in later years he was to serve, with disinterested incompetence, both Britain and France as a double agent; his identification as Junius vastly exaggerated his talents. Bradstreet's memorial reached Gould through Mante in the early months of 1765.

The proposal was considered by the Privy Council on 8 May 1765 as a consequence, according to Mante, of George Grenville's regard for Bradstreet. It was presented on behalf of sixty petitioners who were prepared to transport 624 families to Detroit. There they would flourish in a good climate and on rich soil; hemp and flax could be raised, and wild grapes gathered for their juice. The region contained at present few English but about 600 French inhabitants, who were content under British rule. The Indians in the vicinity required careful handling, and the sale of arms and ammunition to them should be kept out of private hands; other Indian trade should be regulated by a superintendent. Honest dealing would be insufficient to retain Indian friendship: a respectable force must exist to overawe them, and this would be supplied by the families to be settled at Detroit. Its distance from the established colonies and enlarged size would require a civil government and regulations for military discipline, since the garrison could not undertake the defence without additional aid. The erection of Detroit 'into a species of distinct government' was therefore requested.

The petition was referred a week later to the Board of Trade, where it remained unexamined during the long summer recess. Mante failed to write to Bradstreet, but drew on him for £50, over and above the £100 he had secured on his arrival from Gould; Bradstreet protested the second bill. Although Gould wrote optimistically in June that the Detroit scheme was receiving attention, Bradstreet concluded that the Stamp Act disorders would compel the ministry to devote attention to existing rather than future colonies. He himself seemed, having heard of Bouquet's death, to be resuming hopes of military promotion.

On 8 November the Board of Trade noted Mante's petition and ordered him to attend for a hearing in six days' time. Mante then requested a further delay until the nineteenth, so that Amherst could attend and testify to the condition of Detroit. This duly took place with, according to Mante but without mention made in the Journal of the Board, evidence also being given by Monckton. The Board then decided on 2 November in favour of delay: it would be premature to reach a decision until the larger and outstanding question of establishing a general system for the regulation of Indian affairs had been settled.

A plan for the conduct of Indian relations had been drawn up by the Board of Trade and circulated on 10 July 1764 to governors and superintendents for their comments and criticisms. Replies began to be received at the beginning of 1765, and the Board considered the question on three occasions in the first quarter of the year. The last of these discussions was held on 26 March and it was agreed that the subject would be raised again on the following Tuesday; the minutes of that meeting do not mention Indian affairs. The passing on 22 March of the Stamp Act offers a sufficient explanation of delay. The fall of Grenville and his replacement by Rockingham signalled a period of political instability during which disorder in the older colonies dominated American policy. Western problems remained, both in distance and priority, more remote, but the Detroit interests persisted in pursuing their case.

During the winter of 1765–6 prospects of securing approval for the colony had not entirely disappeared. Gould, while admitting that the formation of the Rockingham ministry had deprived him of his influence with Halifax, saw hope in the improved position of Amherst, who not only thought the settlement of Detroit desirable but was also Bradstreet's friend. Mante, though still financially distressed, had announced that he would become lieutenant-governor. Bradstreet, while willing to become governor, preferred to press the need for additional troops to restore order in the wake of the Stamp Act riots—a step which would also improve his chances of promotion. In any event, he asserted that the safety of the new colony could only be ensured by combining the governorship with command of an enlarged garrison. Meanwhile he maintained touch, through Gould and Mante, with Charles Townshend.

It was Townshend who, during 1766, became increasingly the main hope of exerting influence upon the ministry; as paymaster-general he was accessible to Gould, through whom Bradstreet extolled the great benefits to be gained from the establishment of hemp manufacture at Detroit. Mante wrote in the spring that 'he is well with Mr. Townshend; it appears to me the latter does or may know the intention of administration on the affair of Detroit & would say as much as would put it out of doubt'. The change of ministry in July seemed to improve the outlook, since in becoming chancellor of the exchequer Townshend had apparently gained advancement. Gould urged Bradstreet to write a congratulatory letter, which he promised to deliver personally. Bradstreet had heard of the changes before receiving this advice: he was delighted at the news that Pitt, who had supported him in the past, had accepted office, and particularly by the accompanying rumour that Grenville, who had favoured the Detroit settlement, had also returned to power. A source in the War Office had assured him that Detroit would be made a government, with lieutenant-governors residing at Niagara and Oswego. The letter for Townshend was composed on the day Gould's advice was received, Bradstreet commenting that 'perhaps, after the Ministry is settled they may think of Detroit and Mr Townshend remember his promise . . .'. He had hopes of double benefits, for 'Mr Townshend directed Mr Mant to write me that I might be assur'd of the appointment of Brigr in America'.

Promises from Townshend were of no more value than notes of hand from Mante, of whom Bradstreet remarked in November: 'As I never write to Mr. Mant I know nothing about him but by report—the last account of him was that he was gone to France and talk'd much of the affair of Detroit.' The new administration was preoccupied with East Indian affairs, beginning to suffer from the idiosyncratic behaviour of its leader, and possessed, in Shelburne, a secretary of state who refused to disclose his plans for America before he had undertaken a thorough review of the situation. But if this forced the future of Detroit to remain unresolved, Bradstreet's military prospects appeared to brighten. In December he visited New York and was reconciled with Gage, being received 'in so obliging a manner as puts an end to all resentment upon the old affair'. The general's fury had been slow to subside, since his anger at the management of the expedition had been maintained by a prolonged wrangle over the financial accounts which he had found unacceptable. Gage now promised to support Bradstreet's proposals to raise a regiment in America—the names of His Majesty's or the Queen's Loyal Americans were suggested—and to provide recruits for the force stationed in the southern colonies. Gage was said to be writing to Amherst on Bradstreet's behalf to push the matter of the regiment.

This change of attitude may have owed more to political considerations than to a belated recognition of Bradstreet's merits. The commander-in-chief's correspondence home contains no indication of any subsequent endorsement of Bradstreet's schemes, but Gage's military problems in America and political developments in Britain combined to indicate the advisability of adopting a flexible attitude towards Western policy. The likelihood of a confirmation of the plan of July 1764 for the imperial regulation of Indian affairs had dwindled steadily; Barrington's counter-proposal to return control of Indian relations to the colonies and effect as complete a military withdrawal as possible from the West had been presented to the ministry of May 1766 after its author had obtained Gage's private opinions at some length: the recruitment of men for the force in North America was proving chronically difficult; Shelburne's entry into office could be construed by Gage as a sign of a revival of Amherst's influence, since his predecessor was known to be consulted by the new secretary of state; Bradstreet's long-established connection with Amherst was a matter of public knowledge. By November Gage was aware that Barrington's plan had been placed before the ministry and that Shelburne, confronted with the problems of Indian trade and Western settlement, had declared that any policy must be 'well digested' before being put into effect. Major decisions of this kind would inevitably involve an assessment of the future rôles of both Bradstreet and Detroit.

Under British occupation the problems of Detroit had persisted and grown: the government of a settlement excluded
from the bounds of the colonies but lacking alternative administration presented many practical difficulties. Military justice
could be dispensed while Detroit was under direct threat of
Indian attack. Gage informed Major Henry Gladwin that he
was free to court-martial two French inhabitants accused of
spying for the Indians and, if found guilty, to execute them.
This he regarded as a point not only of law but also of policy.
'When ever you can, you must carry it with a very high hand
with the French, or you will lose all authority over them; it is
absolutely necessary in your present circumstances'. In less
dangerous times more persuasive methods became necessary:
in September 1765 the commanding officer explained the
arrangements he had inherited.

> We have got a judge (one Mr legrand) appointed by Col Bradstreet
> who by his commission is empowered to decide all controversial
> causes or disputes in this settlement, and likewise Vendue Master. I
> find he is very ill qualified for such an office and hitherto unable to
> decide any cause that came before him with any kind of justice,
> therefore I have found it necessary, to have any controversies that
> happens here amongst the traders or inhabitants, examined into
> and decided by arbitrators mutually chosen by the parties con-
> cerned. A proper person to officiate here as judge in civil causes is
> very much wanted, as our present judge is of no manner of use,
> rather a disservice, nor do I know any frenchman here that I could
> recommend for such an office. . . .

The problems posed by the inhabitants were surpassed by
those introduced by the traders. Commanding officers were
supposed to restrict their activities to the posts, but the only
means of enforcing the rule was by reporting an offender to the
colony with whom he had posted a bond for good behaviour
and securing its confiscation. In many cases traders had evaded
this requirement and were prepared to challenge the legality of
military control. In January 1767 the commanding officer at
Detroit reported that

> There are Liberty Boys at Detroit as well as elsewhere, who if they
> are talked to about the King's Proclamation for trade will readily
> answer that it is not an Act of Parliament, and what is most unlucky
> there is only two English merchants in the whole Place that are
> provided with Governor's passes, and when People are on such a
> footing without any bond or security for their good behaviour it is

impossible for any commissary or Commanding Officer to manage them.

Gage could only reply that entry into 'the uninhabited country'—an obvious contradiction of fact—was restricted by royal authority; that the Governor of New York had issued a proclamation forbidding traders to leave without proper passes, and that Turnbull should assist the commissary to put his instructions into effect, and leave him the management of Indian affairs.

The commander-in-chief was only too well aware of the impotence of government in the absence of imperial regulations and authority for their enforcement. Canadians threatened the peace of the West more substantially than did the New Yorkers. The Indians of the Great Lakes' region were thought, in 1767, so hostile to the traders as to be preparing an outbreak comparable to that led by Pontiac. Gage expressed at some length his alarm and frustration at the situation to Lieutenant-Governor Carleton:

> They [the Indians] complain at all the posts, as well the commanders as the Indian commissaries, of the French settled amongst the Indians, spiriting them up to mischief, aided and abetted by the inhabitants of the Detroit, the traders from Canada and those at the Illinois, who all ramble over the country without restraint, holding conferences with each other, planning mischief by exciting the savages against us, and carrying on illicit trade. That the traders from Canada pay no regard to the King's regulations about the trade, and neither the commanders of the posts or the Indian officers can obey the orders they have received, whilst those people pass their posts with impunity, which they can do at all times, if they choose it, unknown to the garrisons. And if there is no way to punish them but to prosecute them upon their bonds, without which neither the regulations which the King had made or any other which he shall hereafter judge proper to make will be of any signification. . . .

Continual dealings with Western problems rendered Gage sympathetic to suggestions that military commitments should be reduced or eliminated where practicable. Yet no proposal, including the most sweeping put forward, Barrington's plan, involved the abandoning of Detroit. If this represented a general acknowledgement of the importance of the settlement as a centre of the fur trade, retention also displayed recognition of an inability to ignore the continuation of European rivalries in the Mississippi valley.

The military conflict between Britain and France for supremacy in North America was resolved in 1760 but in other terms the outcome of their rivalry was less decisive. Although Article VII of the Treaty of Paris ceded to Britain all lands other than New Orleans on the east bank of the Mississippi, occupying the new acquisitions proved a lengthy and frustrating task. The problem centred on the transfer of the scattered settlements on the Illinois country and the replacement of the French by a British garrison. Although Amherst had given orders in August 1763 for this to be done, Major Arthur Loftus did not set out with the 22nd Regiment from New Orleans until the end of February 1764, and proceeded no more than two hundred miles up river before an encounter with hostile Indians determined him to abandon the attempt. It was well over a year before a further effort was made: the 24th Regiment under Major Farmar left New Orleans at the end of June 1765 while Gage, determined to avert a repetition of the previous year's fiasco, dispatched a detachment of one hundred men from the 42nd Regiment stationed at Fort Pitt, which proceeded down the Ohio at the end of August. This force reached Fort Chartres on 9 October, where it was joined on 2 December by Farmar's regiment. The French garrison then withdrew. It had taken almost three years to arrange this event.

The Illinois settlements were neither individually nor collectively impressive in size: five villages, of which the largest was Kaskaskia, contained some 500 French inhabitants, about half of those who lived in the region, together with a roughly equal number of blacks. Many traders had simply crossed the river into Spanish territory, securing a safe base from which they would continue to dominate the Indian trade. The situation gave rise to two major fears: first, that the remaining French inhabitants of the Illinois and Detroit would connive with these traders and Indian tribes against British interests; secondly, that a free trade would confirm the superiority of the Mississippi over the Ohio and the Great Lakes as an outlet for peltry. To avert these consequences drastic steps would have to be taken: either the French inhabitants would be forced to quit the region or a military presence would have to be maintained sufficient to control the West. Failure to act would merely renew, in a more distant and disadvantageous setting, the struggle against old enemies which had so recently seemed to have been brought to an outright conclusion. With these considerations in mind ministers in London and the commander-in-chief in America were forced to ponder the consequences of adopting policies which would meet the pressing need to husband and concentrate military resources. It was to an examination of this dilemma that Shelburne, with characteristic thoroughness, now addressed himself.

Shelburne's progress towards defining the problem and proposing a solution was fatally impaired by his membership of a leaderless administration and a consequent growth, from the beginning of 1767, of his differences with Townshend. Gould blamed the delay in reaching a decision about Detroit on these circumstances; by March 1767 he had jettisoned the plan for raising a regiment but saw some reasons for hope that the colony would be approved. Amherst remained its supporter and Mante had made large promises in Townshend's name which Gould wished he would make good.

On 12 March, under guise of the approaching budget, Townshend offered an open challenge to Shelburne by delivering an ultimatum

> that if the reduction of them [the American extraordinaries] was not determined before the closing of the committee of supply, by drawing the troops nearer the great towns, laying the Indian charges upon the provinces and by laying a tax on the American ports, he would not remain chancellor of the exchequer . . .

Shelburne's response was to prepare a paper explaining why costs could not be cut that year in America. Such a step would involve the reduction of expenditure upon the military and Indian departments. This would require the withdrawal of troops from the outposts. Amherst, Monckton, and Gage were of opinion that this could not be done. Although Barrington was urging that most of the posts be abandoned and trade with the Indians via the Mississippi be completely discarded, Shelburne felt that a choice between these recommendations could not be made without a thorough examination of their respective merits. Views on the management of Indian affairs were even more numerous and confusing. If Shelburne felt able to reject a plan 'founded upon a Basis which can have neither weight nor duration, to wit, the will of the Superintendents almost uncontrolled by either the civil or military Power', he felt that the whole question of the Mississippi trade which, 'if not diverted into other Channels, might be estimated at one half of all the Indian Trade of North America' had to be carefully considered. 'If', he concluded, with cutting reference to Townshend, 'no person has such a plan yet in readiness, a reasonable time must be granted to those who are willing to produce it.'

Chatham's continual absence from business benefited neither side. Barrington was plunged into despair of ever obtaining a decision. Early in May the cabinet considered the disposition of troops: Barrington gave his opinion and Amherst one that 'differed from it in every respect'. Nothing was resolved, and in July Barrington was reporting that 'I impatiently wait for the *resurrection* of Lord Chatham'. Shelburne was meanwhile proceeding to evolve a policy. By early summer he had determined to restore control of Indian affairs to the colonies, decided that the advantages of establishing new colonies in the interior outweighed the drawbacks, and concluded that he therefore supported the establishment of governments at the Illinois and at Detroit. This would enable most troops to be withdrawn and allow foodstuffs to be raised locally for the needs of the remaining garrisons. At Detroit the crown could collect the revenues already established by the French. Economy therefore favoured colonisation. Indian resentments could be assuaged by formal land purchases, and the problem, inherited with the peace, resolved as to the future of the 'many hundred Families . . . who must either receive some Form of Government from hence or remain altogether without any preserving their old Attachments dangerous to us and what we cannot be too careful to guard against'. Acceptance of this solution could not be rapidly secured: it was 11 September before the cabinet moved to refer the three central questions—the management of the Indian trade, the maintenance of the posts, and 'the Several applications made for New Governments or Settlements at the Detroit and the Illinois'—for the consideration of the Board of Trade. A further month passed before Shelburne requested the Board to frame its recommendations: on the question of the new governments extracts of letters from Amherst and Gage, as well as private proposals, were forwarded.

Throughout this waiting period Bradstreet received sufficient encouragement from his correspondents to sustain, and possibly strengthen, his hopes. By the spring of 1767 he had learned that three governments were proposed at Detroit, Fort Chartres, and further south on the Mississippi. In June Amherst's continued support had been assured, together with his view that the Detroit affair was not over. By the autumn letters expressed optimism and reported the exertion of influence. Mante, after a period of absence, had resumed his activities and was maintaining connections between Amherst and Gould. Amherst had been alerted to the rumour that Bradstreet possessed a rival for the governorship and was inquiring into the matter. On learning of this, Gould wrote directly to Shelburne, pressing Bradstreet's claims for appointment as Governor of Detroit. By November, with the question referred to the Board, no certain news could be forwarded to Bradstreet, but Gould wrote optimistically that 'it seems now on the point of being determined, and I think in your favour. Sir Jeffery Amherst, who is truly your friend, is entirely of that opinion . . .'. Even Mante, who was frequently with Amherst, had contrived to be consulted, and would not endanger Bradstreet's chances. Bolstered by this news, Bradstreet, while still refusing to accept the certainty of his appointment and alarmed lest the death of Townshend should suppress the economic arguments in support of the new colony, could allow himself to discuss details of its civil and military establishment, express the hope that Gould would become agent, and elaborate his proposals for the cultivation of hemp and the manufacture of rope as the principal activities of the settlers.

If the death of Townshend in September 1767 gave rise to concern, the political conflicts and reconstruction of the ministry which concluded the year represented a far more dangerous change of circumstances. Shelburne, reaping the rewards of personal and political unpopularity, was driven by Grafton towards resignation: his secretaryship was to be divided between ministers responsible for European and American affairs. Declining an offer of the new American post, Shelburne clung to the Southern department for a further nine months, isolated, without influence, and replaced in the conduct of American policy by Hillsborough. The Board of Trade thus delivered its report on Western affairs to a politician whose views differed greatly from those of the initiator of the inquiry.

The reference had been taken seriously. The Board engaged in a diligent examination of all the relevant evidence before its recommendations were signed on 7 March 1768. Answers were provided to Shelburne's three questions. Management of the Indian trade should be returned to colonial control, with the Indian superintendents being retained as diplomats and negotiators rather than as wielders of authority. This would permit the abandonment of many posts: garrisons would be required only at Detroit, Michilimackinac, and Niagara, supported by two, or at most three, armed vessels on the Lakes for the maintenance of communication. The question of new colonies was considered as a major point of principle, since the projects reviewed by the Board had 'nothing less in view, than the entire possession and peopling of all that country, which has communication with the rivers Mississippi and St. Lawrence. . . .' A decision on this point involved not merely the particular merits of the proposals but a statement of the general aims of imperial policy.

It is evident from the report that the question of establishing a colony at Detroit was treated more seriously than the two other requests to approve governments at the mouth of the Ohio and in the Illinois country. The Board acknowledged Detroit as 'the great Center of Indian Commerce'. It was situated among many Indian tribes and possessed a considerable French population which had remained there under the terms of the peace. Of the three posts to be kept its maintenance 'does appear to us to be by far the most important Object, not being confined merely to the Convenience of any particular Colony, but embracing every Advantage, upon which the Safety and Extension of our Indian Commerce do depend'. This importance led the board to reject any suggestion of a compromise which would maintain an imperial presence at no financial cost:

all such Forts ought to be garrisoned by Troops in Your Majesty's pay commanded by Officers appointed by Your Majesty, as it would, in our humble Opinion, be dangerous to publick Safety, and inconsistent with the true Principles of this Government, that Forts and military Establishments, intended to answer such important Objects, should be entrusted to any other Hands. . . .

Bradstreet's offer to raise a regiment of military settlers was therefore unacceptable.

The purpose of colonial development was defined in strictly mercantilist terms—'to improve and extend the commerce, navigation and manufactures of this kingdom'. This justified the acquisition and settlement of Nova Scotia, Georgia, and the Floridas. Additional inland colonies had been advocated on five grounds. First, that an increase of population would stimulate the demand for British manufactures. The Board considered that it was more likely to encourage industrial activity in the colonies. Secondly, that the fur trade would be secured and the Indians protected from French and Spanish influence. This argument was rejected since settlement would reduce, rather than enlarge, a trade which in any event could never be excluded from competition as long as New Orleans remained the best market. A third assertion that new colonies would protect the old was flatly denied: in fact, precisely the opposite would occur. The fourth point, that a reduction in the cost of supplying the Western posts would be achieved, was admitted, but its importance would depend upon a determination of the garrisons' future strength. The Board believed that the present French population was sufficient to furnish the posts with necessary provisions. The final claim, that these settlements required a form of civil government, was not accepted. There was no precedent for instituting a government in order to supply troops, and no need to create one in respect of the French settlements 'which, being formed under Military Establishments; and ever subjected to Military Authority, do not . . . require any other Superintendance than that of the Military Officers commanding at these Posts'.

The cabinet considered this report on 18 March, basing its discussion on a minute prepared by Hillsborough, Barrington, and Major-General Harvey. Acceptance of the proposals for the abandonment of all the Western posts proved too sweeping for the ministers, two refusing their approval. It was therefore decided to retain the Illinois and Fort Pitt for the time being and to allow Gage to judge which other posts should be maintained or abandoned.

Unwillingness to apply radical measures did not, however,

serve the cause of the Detroit colony: Gould wrote in July to report that progress was at a standstill and to regret his lack of close acquaintance with Hillsborough. Bradstreet was not totally downcast by the news since, as always, the governorship was but one of many ways of advancement, and not necessarily the most attractive. He had heard that the salary would be no more than five or six hundred pounds. If this was so, he would be better provided for as deputy quartermaster general. Contemplating life in a settlement lacking fortifications, public buildings, or any house suitable for the residence of a governor, Bradstreet preferred to pursue the possibilities opened by the death of Sir John St. Clair, the senior deputy quartermaster general, and by the promotion of Carleton to the governorship of Quebec. Detroit never became the isolated summit of his ambitions.

During the next four years neither policies nor ministerial connections favoured any revival of hopes that a colony might be established. Pressure for Western expansion was dominated by the activities of the Grand Ohio Company, a much more formidable force than that constituted by Bradstreet, Gould and Amherst, and one able to acquire much more political support in Britain. Bradstreet limited his ambitions to pressures for preferment, as a successor to Sir Henry Moore, the late Governor of New York, or as a replacement for Carleton, whom he understood had left Quebec permanently, provided that he might be appointed as both governor and brigadier—a double reward was needed to compensate for such an expensive and disagreeable location. Mante disappeared for long stretches of time and had failed to repay his debts to Bradstreet and Gould. This did not put an end to begging letters: in August 1771 he requested Gould to loan him a further ten guineas so that he might appear properly dressed before Lord Albemarle. He explained that he had prepared a pamphlet highly critical of Albemarle's conduct at the taking of Havana and was now being persuaded to suppress it. This may have represented a blackmailing off-shoot of the full-scale history of the war in America on which Mante had been engaged for some time before the spring of 1772 and of which he had promised to send Gould those parts relating to Bradstreet's activities before its publication. Gould commented that he seldom saw Mante and believed 'he is in some sort under the protection of the Minister'. Mante's career as a double agent for Britain and France was under way.

Gould professed himself unable to aid Bradstreet. All business was at a stand, he wrote in September 1771, and since he hardly knew Hillsborough, Bradstreet should visit London to make a personal application to the secretary. Amherst held to his belief that withdrawal of the Western garrisons would strengthen Indian capacity to lay waste the frontier, a view which Bradstreet's letters encouraged him to maintain. He continued to advocate the establishment of inland colonies:

> The neglect of not taking hold of the Utmost Bounds of our Conquest by forming Seats of Government on the Mississippi and the Detroit, and the suffering the Posts of Communication to go to ruin, would give an Enemy such advantage as I should be very sorry to see them commence hostilities with. . . .

With the departure of Shelburne, however, Amherst's views no longer received a respectful hearing.

The appointment of Hillsborough as American secretary had substituted a hostile for a sympathetic minister. Sir Jeffrey's brother, General William Amherst, asserted that Hillsborough had 'adopted a plan which he found ready cut & dry, in the hands of his Friend & associate of the War Office'. This was a reference to Barrington and his proposals for abandoning the West, declared by William Amherst to be 'the most incongruous & monstrous heap of absurdities, that perhaps ever were before produced', yet now only awaiting Sir Jeffery's approval before their adoption. This, despite repeated urging, Amherst refused to give, since he considered that this step must lead to a final undermining of British strength in America. By William Amherst's account when 'the little junto' found its efforts insufficient to destroy his brother's influence over the other ministers, Hillsborough in July 1768 conspired to destroy his reputation. Amherst was titular Governor of Virginia and, like his predecessors, non-resident. The needs of the colony and of the impoverished Lord Botetourt combined to justify a change. Amherst could not assume his duties, since this would require him to serve under Gage, his junior as an officer. Hillsborough knew this, and proposed that he should surrender his office with suitable compensation, in the belief that Amherst's acceptance of 'so dirty a proposal, would effectually ruin him in the eyes of the Publick'. Detecting the trick, Amherst spurned the exchange and an enraged minister 'snatched what he could not gain by Artifice'. Amherst may have preserved his honour but the Detroit lobby had lost its principal support.

The ministry could depreciate but not eliminate Western problems. If Hillsborough's main concern was to resist the efforts of the Grand Ohio Company to establish the colony of Vandalia on lands ceded by the Indians at the Treaty of Fort Stanwix, the maintenance of British authority in the larger region bounded by the St. Lawrence and the Mississippi formed a commitment which, however burdensome, could not be discarded. Hillsborough was only too willing to receive any scheme which would enable imperial responsibilities to be reduced. Gage was urged to provide a solution to difficulties which Hillsborough, despite 'a mature consideration', found insoluble. The commander-in-chief's reply was both lengthy and guarded. He doubted the value of forts as effective controls of the fur trade or as frontier defences against Indian attack. He agreed that the economic argument for expansion was unacceptable: trade with the interior could be maintained 'by proper management, without either Forts or Settlements'. It could be said that forts 'have kept the French Settlers in Subjection, and if the Settlers can't be removed, or such a Government established over them as to render Troops unnecessary, that Forts may be said to be of use to ensure their Obedience'. The case for interior settlements seemed justified neither by need for additional land nor by the products likely to be forthcoming. They might supply cheaper provisions for the troops, but the forts themselves had no other function 'than to protect the Settlements and keep the Settlers in subjection to Government'. Gage had provided ample support for the adoption of a policy of withdrawal but had declined to propose its outright implementation.

This cautious approach was rapidly vindicated by the onset of the Falkland Islands crisis. By the beginning of 1771 Hillsborough considered an Anglo-Spanish war to be imminent: hopes of withdrawal from the Mississippi gave way to orders for Gage to plan and personally command an attack on New

Orleans; no further abandonments of forts were to be undertaken. Although Gage's assessment of the value of the Western posts was accepted, Hillsborough's views had been transformed by the new situation. Those Lake posts were not to be left in an insecure state 'as by their situation on the Passes between the great Waters of Communication give Security to the Dominion of the Country . . . in the present Conjecture'. The most fervent and constant ministerial opponent of Western expansion had been forced to yield his position. By the end of the year he instructed Gage to keep the Lake Posts in a state of repair, since 'it is agreed on all hands that they ought to be kept up and supported, at least for the present'. The Illinois might require a permanent establishment, though the secretary still clung to the belief that the best answer would be 'the Removal of the Inhabitants to situations within the Limits of Quebec or of some other established Colony'. On the eve of his resignation in the summer of 1772 Hillsborough was still promising to consider the question of a civil establishment in the Illinois, once he had received the views of the inhabitants. He continued to agree with Gage, however, that the introduction of a 'regular Government' would be 'highly improper'. Whatever their differences in outlook, both Shelburne and Hillsborough had equally failed in their efforts to resolve imperial problems in the West.

Twelve years after its occupation, Detroit continued to lack an acknowledged form of government. Civil authority could not remain suspended throughout this period but such provisions as were made to meet the needs of the Illinois and Detroit rested on a highly uncertain basis. In Quebec, the years of the *règne militaire* had seen jurisdiction exercised over a wide range of criminal and civil matters by general courtsmartial. This situation was not, however, comparable with that which persisted in the West: the period of military rule had been ended by the proclamation of October 1763. The establishment of courts in the new province was accompanied by the amputation of its westernmost extent: Detroit, the furthest inland point to which the legal system of New France had reached, was now severed from the successor régime. The settlement was consigned by the proclamation to Indian territories where the need for order, but not law, was recognised.

Officers commanding the Western posts were therefore

forced to devise their own means of resolving local civil disputes. Court records for Detroit in this period have not survived, but Pierre St. Cosmé and Gabriel Le Grand acted in judicial matters before the outbreak of Pontiac's conspiracy. In September 1764 Bradstreet, before withdrawing his force, instructed John Campbell, the officer commanding the post, to model his method of government after that of Montreal. If obeyed, this would have required all criminal cases to be tried by courts-martial, leaving civil cases to be heard by the captains of militia, with a right of appeal to Campbell. Since a regular militia was not established, the duties of the inhabitants being limited to assisting the garrison in times of need or danger, this method could not be followed. Local appointments of an informal nature were made, which approximated to those of justices of the peace, involving arbitral rather than judicial powers. Public as well as private concerns were regulated in this manner: St. Cosmé and Le Grand acted as spokesmen for the inhabitants in resisting the demands of commanding officers for financial contributions towards the maintenance of the fort and garrison, and arranged a compromise solution. In the wake of the Stamp Act disorders Gage, while insistent that revenues dating from the French period be collected, ordered 'that no kind of Tax is to be levied upon any account whatsoever'.

Commanding officers gave increasing emphasis and imparted added formality to these local procedures. In April 1767 Captain Turnbull commissioned Philip Dejean as justice of the peace, permitting him to act as notary for wills and deeds and, where both parties requested it, to arbitrate between disputants. Judgments were to be recorded in English. Three months later a new commanding officer, Major Bayard, appointed Dejean as 'Second Judge'—reserving for himself the right of judicial primacy—with power to hold court twice a month and there decide on all actions of debt, bond, bills, contracts and trespasses above the value of £5 NY. In May 1768 a court of inquiry, appointed by Captain Turnbull at the request of Dejean, confirmed that the fees established by the committee appointed to organise the court of justice were 'just and reasonable and ought not to be less'. Fees, payable by prisoners released after confinement for debt or misdemeanour and on canoes arriving with merchandise belonging to traders not owning property in Detroit, would be applied to maintaining the fortifications, as had been the case during the French régime. No complaints against Dejean were received by the court of inquiry.

Dejean's functions went unchallenged and grew in extent during the next six years: he adjusted practically all civil matters, probated wills, collected debts, certified property transfers, arranged bonds of indenture between master and servant, and began to assume powers in criminal matters. The provision that all proceedings be recorded in English was ignored. Gage was content, failing instructions on the conduct of judicial affairs, to confirm the propriety of referring all disputes to arbitration. He did not 'know any other manner to decide them, unless they go to the King in Council; and that you will say is an expence and delay too great for people to think of'. Any attempt to extend the limits of the existing settlement was, however, to be absolutely resisted. Only grants registered and approved during the French régime could be maintained. All claims dating from 1760 were to be publicly annulled and those made by British commanders cancelled. Buildings on such lands must be demolished.

A situation was thus knowingly created of local judicial procedures, meeting immediate needs but lacking formal authority and restricted to matters arising out of rights established prior to the arrival of British authority. A court for the settlement of all civil disputes had been established at the Illinois by Colonel Wilkins in November 1768. The confirmation or denial of these arrangements hung upon constantly deferred ministerial decisions. Inevitably, not all were satisfied by these temporary provisions. Major Henry Bassett raged at his inability to prevent an unregulated trade, largely in rum, taking place in the woods outside Detroit, which had resulted in drunkenness and murder. 'The traders in general that are on these Posts' he informed the commander-in-chief,

> are the outcasts of all Nations, and the refuse of Mankind. I sincerely wish there was a Police form'd for these upper Country's, to make these Vagabonds tremble, a commanding officer here has not authority to punish these Villains & if he takes any steps to recover debts, or any other civil affair, they think together & raise a power to torment him, when he goes down there, these fellows call English Liberty . . . it is impossible [to regulate trade] without a

commanding officer risking a persecution at Law, until its fully in his power to put these fellows in the guard house, and send them by the first opportunity down to New York, or Canada . . .

In dealing with the problems brought before him, Bassett was discomforted by his inability to speak or understand French. James Sterling, an English merchant but 'by marriage connected with the best part of this settlement', had acted as his interpreter and correspondent: Bassett urged that these services should be officially rewarded. Pressure for patchwork improvisation to be supplanted by defined authority could not be indefinitely resisted.

The replacement in August 1772 of Hillsborough by Dartmouth as American secretary coincided with the need to act in mitigation of the failure of administrations to implement the provisions of the proclamation of October 1763 relating to Quebec and the West. Dartmouth was not uninformed of these questions: as president of the Board of Trade in the Rockingham ministry he had grown acquainted with their complexities. His predecessor's policies had been inflexible though not totally ignorant; they had failed to settle the crucial issues of establishing an assembly in Quebec and preserving a distinction between Indian and settled territory. Dartmouth thus inherited problems of government over a region extending from the Gulf of the St. Lawrence to the Mississippi valley.

The new secretary appeared more sympathetic to Western settlement and proved receptive to the pressures applied by the promoters of Vandalia. He also showed an interest in the problems of civil government in the French settlements, requesting further information from Gage about the state of the Illinois and what arrangements 'may be further necessary, considering it in the light of a Colony of the King's Subjects'; a report from Cramahé, conducting the administration of Quebec during Carleton's absence in England, praising Dejean for charging with murder and despatching a suspect from Detroit to Montreal for trial, led him to question the basis of Cramahé's jurisdiction and 'by whom the magistrates there are appointed'. As, during the winter of 1772–3, the remorseless proliferation of reports began grudgingly to give way to recognition that the process must terminate in legislation on the future government of Quebec, it became clear that the extent as well as the constitution of the province was under review. When Gage, on leave in England, met Dartmouth, he was questioned by John Pownall about the number of inhabitants at Detroit. Edward Abbott was invited to furnish details of the settlement and assured Dartmouth of the inhabitants' wish for civil government. By the end of 1773 the secretary had concluded that the provision of separate arrangements for the Indian territory was impracticable and that in consequence he doubted 'both of the justice and propriety of restraining the colony to the narrow limits prescribed in that Proclamation'. Imperial decisions were at length to determine the future of Detroit.

Four courses of action could be proposed as answers to the problem of the West. First, its complete abandonment: this, however tempting, was put out of the question by the Spanish and French presence in the Mississippi valley. Secondly, the West could be placed under a uniform system of imperial regulation: the financial cost and the diversion of British military strength to the region invoked problems of taxation and of excessive demands upon a limited body of troops sufficient to render the plan unacceptable. Thirdly, new colonies could be established. Dartmouth was willing to approve the creation of Vandalia, but this limited concession met with sustained opposition, both within the ministry and from imperial officials in America. Gage had refused to support inland colonies since 'The Pretence of forming Barriers will have no End, wherever we settle, however remote, there must be a Frontier . . .'. Dartmouth acknowledged this point in resisting a general expansion of settlement: when, in December 1772, Gould heard that something was intended at Detroit, and proposed to approach the American secretary on Bradstreet's behalf, further inquiries damped his hopes and indicated that interest was centred elsewhere. The Detroit venturers were now of slight significance: Gould had little access to the ministry; Amherst had lost political influence: Lyttelton was dead; Mante found it financially prudent to reside at Dieppe. Their decline favoured the adoption of the fourth possibility, that of placing the West under the jurisdiction of existing colonies. Quebec seemed the obvious choice once it proved possible to discard the argument that an enlargement would acknowledge past French claims and prejudice the British position in any future negotiations.

The ministry's conclusion did not meet with universal acceptance. During the debates on the Quebec bill, opponents laid much stress on the undesirability of extending the limits of the province and forced its proponents on to the defensive. North argued that territorial expansion provided the only solution to the problems of providing civil government and discouraging settlement. Since the present inhabitants were all former French subjects and all Roman Catholics, a return to government from Quebec was entirely justifiable. The ministry's case was not strengthened by Carleton's behaviour when he appeared before the committee upon the bill: his evidence was offered in tones of indifference, ignorance, and insolence. This may have reflected an accurate assessment of the strength of the opposition, but it rendered the validity of the ministry's stand less evident.

Much of the debate concerned the disposition of an extent of territory of which almost all the participants revealed themselves to be ignorant, whether arguing for the opposition, as did Thomas Townshend, that 'Near the Illinois and Fort du Cane, I am informed there are at this time upwards of five-and-twenty thousand British settlers', or whether retorting, in the Solicitor-General's justification of the enlargement of Quebec, that 'as to British subjects within the limits, I believe there are not five in the whole country'. Sufficient was known, however, of the importance of Detroit in the operation of the Quebec and New York fur trades for a measure of attention to be given to its fate.

The entry of British interests into the St. Lawrence fur trade after the conquest of New France had confirmed rather than reduced the old rivalry between Montreal and Albany. Carleton had energetically espoused the cause of the Canadian traders, particularly in opposing Johnson's aim of restricting dealings with the Indians to a limited number of specified posts. From 1767 widespread protests, in which both English and French traders at Detroit joined, led Shelburne to recommend that traders be allowed to travel freely north of the Ottawa river and of Lakes Superior, Huron and Michigan. This concession, which fanned the discontent of traders at posts such as Detroit where liberty of movement was still denied, indicated the imminent discarding of the plan of regulation. That decision served to heighten the ambitions of Quebec, particularly as it became apparent that an alternative system of control would not be achieved by agreement between the colonies involved in the Indian trade. In April 1769 a committee, appointed to consider memorials from the English and Canadian merchants and traders of Montreal urging the issue of new regulations, reported to the Quebec council. Dismissing the possibility that the colonies could create their own system and stressing the futility, except through military administration, of controlling posts which were neither annexed to colonies nor subject to civil administration, the committee staked a claim to management by Quebec. This provided the best solution if it could be agreed that the regulation of the Indian trade and the hearing of civil cases should be referred, as the Mutiny bill had already provided in criminal matters, to existing colonies.

By 1774 the case of Quebec for the inclusion of Detroit within its sphere of interest and, by the provisions of the Quebec bill, within its territory, appeared more substantial than the rival ambitions of New York. Although Maseres, in his evidence before the House, considered it preferable to extend the limits of New York, while Carleton's indifference to detail extracted the statement that 'I do not know the settlement of Detroit very accurately' as he did not consider the post as his current responsibility, parliamentary proposals of specific alternatives were totally lacking. Even Edmund Burke, whose concern for colonial boundaries was directly linked with his duties as agent for New York, did not attempt to secure Detroit for his principals.

The absence of public controversy reflected with reasonable accuracy the relative strengths of the Montreal and Albany trading interests. Although each was periodically alarmed at the activities of the other, the superiority of Quebec over New York in the trade was apparent at many posts, including Detroit. John Lees, a merchant who visited the settlement in 1768, considered the Canadians to possess two major advantages:

These [Schenectady] Batteau's Carry usually 25 or 26 [fur] packs, a french Canoe holding very nigh Double what they will—on which Account, and from the Cheapness of Labour in Canada, it is

reckoned the Indian Trade is carried on, on cheaper Terms in
Canada, than from Albany or Schenectady. . . .

Commercial rivalry in Detroit did not embitter personal relations between the two communities. Correspondents of William
Edgar harked back nostalgically to the 'happy place', declared
from New York that they 'would rather live at Detroit upon
three hundred a year than at this place upon five, provided it
was in a Civil Government', and demanded news of marriages,
scandals, and squabbles over precedence at assemblies. In 1770
a Canadian trader from Montreal, landing at Grosse Isle, was
stabbed by an Indian:

> On the news reaching here both French and English Canadian
> traders, about 40, went over, surrounded the cabins, got the Indian,
> who struggled about coming. He was immediately put from ever
> hurting another, by getting a Passport to the other World. This is
> Better and less Expence to the Government than Sending Down the
> Country.

Such frontier justice was now to give way to civil administration.

As the implications of the changes initiated by the Quebec Act
became appreciated in North America, hopes vied with fears
among those concerned with the future condition of Detroit.
Major Henry Bassett, the commanding officer at Detroit in the
period prior to 1774, had ambitions to become its first governor, an aim now extinguished. Gould, who could not have
paid much attention to detail, understood that the extension of
Quebec had revived the prospect of establishing a new colony
and once more proposed Bradstreet for office. Those nearer at
hand understood more accurately the import of the decision.
Isaac Todd, receiving the news in Montreal, wrote Edgar that
'you see this Will intirely frustrate Maj. Bassett and Mr. Sterling's Scheme, and you at Detroit . . . will be Canadians,
perhaps Mr. Sterling may be appointed Judge for Detroit . . .' Alarm grew among English traders at the prospect of
the imposition of Canadian laws, Roman Catholicism, and
parliamentary duties on imports. A new form of trade restriction was threatened. If the duty stood, how would the Detroit
traders secure rum? It could no longer be brought up from
Schenectady and all supplies would have to be obtained from

Quebec. Although the majority might benefit from the return of Detroit to its former connections, the traders, true to their outlook, would continue to resist rules and regulations of any kind.

Bradstreet's desire for preferment survived the collapse of his plans for Detroit. The news of the passing of the Quebec Act was of less interest to him than the possibilities opened by the death in July 1774 of Sir William Johnson. He urged Gould to secure his appointment as Indian superintendent. Gould dutifully raised the question with Amherst, who promised to take it up with Dartmouth, though of the opinion that 'it will be much for his advantage and more consistently with his Rank, that he get into the line of Governments'. On 25 September Bradstreet's ambitions were stilled by death: nothing less would have silenced his claims.

The problems posed between 1760 and 1774 by the existence of Detroit incorporated a modest degree of significance in their own right and possessed considerably more importance when examined in the context of imperial policy towards Western expansion. Throughout these years ministerial views remained obstinately indecisive when confronted with the needs to maintain a British presence at Detroit and to place that presence on a formal footing. In the absence of instructions Gage, saddled with 'these cursed French Settlements, with the Strolling French and Canadians, who Seat themselves in almost every Indian Village', found himself responsible for large areas with small detachments and even smaller powers. The refusal of successive ministries to extend, even in some modified form, colonial government, while unwilling or unable to abandon territory, found specific illustration in the condition of Detroit during its first years of British rule. If circumstances did not become as disorderly as theory might have ordained, practical difficulties became steadily more apparent and were not resolved until the passing of the Quebec Act. The degree to which its provisions would have ameliorated western problems is impossible to assess: imperial policy was entering, rather than escaping, its years of larger crisis.

PART II

THE REVOLUTIONARY
WAR
IN THE NORTHWEST

ONCE the War for Independence began, the conflict in the trans-Appalachian west constituted a sideshow from the main theater on the Atlantic Coast. American independence could neither be won nor lost in the West, but the future of the United States might be determined there in a more indirect manner. If the West had remained in the hands of some other power—Britain or Spain—then the American states might have become more oriented toward the Atlantic than towards the continental interior, as became the case. How much the loss of the West might have determined our manifest destiny, is, of course, a matter out of the province of historians.

The conflict in the Northwest was dominated by three major geographic features—the Appalachian Mountains, the Mississippi River Valley, and the Great Lakes basin. The British controlled the lakes and they provided the best route for transportation and logistical support into the North American interior. There were several vulnerable points along this route which, if occupied by an opponent, could deprive the British of this critical lifeline—Montreal, Niagara, and Detroit. The British lost Montreal for a brief period in 1775–1776 and during that time the redcoats' role in the Northwest virtually ceased. After Governor Sir Guy Carleton retook Montreal in the summer of 1776, control of the lakes became the major focus of the royal effort to retain the Middle West. Only once was a serious threat launched against any of the other vulnerable locations. General John Sullivan's punitive expedition of

1779 against the Iroquois threatened Niagara but never went beyond the Finger Lakes region of New York. Despite hopes in Kentucky and Pittsburgh and fears in Detroit, the Americans never launched a concerted attack on the critical garrison at the juncture of Lakes Erie and St. Clair.

The Appalachian chain severely limited the American effort in the Northwest. With the principal east-west route into the region controlled by the British and with the Mohawk River route similarly blocked, the rebels had to use two less desirable avenues of approach. The Cumberland Gap in modern Southwestern Virginia provided secure access into Kentucky, but one that was slow and expensive. Crossing the mountains over either Braddock's or Forbes' road into the upper Ohio valley, another way west, was less expensive but highly vulnerable to interdiction by Indian raiding parties at almost every bend in the river west of Pittsburgh.

The Spanish dominated the other route west, up the Mississippi and its major tributaries. The Spanish government cooperated with James Willing, who took a small expedition down the Mississippi in 1778, but his initial opening of that river was negated by a British counterattack at Natchez. Other Spanish efforts moderately assisted George Rogers Clark. When Spain entered the war in 1779, her officials conducted their own operations with no intention of aiding American expansion into the lands east of the Mississippi. In fact, all Spanish efforts on the east bank reinforced His Catholic Majesty's claim to trans-Appalachia.

If the British lacked anything in their western war effort it was manpower. Only 500 regular redcoats were west of Montreal, a thin red line that could stop very little. The French *habitants* provided additional manpower, but their loyalty was questionable, as events in Illinois proved. The British effort depended mostly upon the Indians, and a few loyalists. While the Indians constituted the balance of power in the region, the tribes were divided in their loyalties or were located too far from the scene of action to have decisive affect on the results. The military effort affected primarily the tribes of modern Ohio— the Delaware, Mingo, Wyandot, Shawnee, Potawatomie, and Miami. While British defeat portended unmitigated disaster for all tribes in the region, one could hardly expect the Sauk, Fox,

Iowa, Ottawa, Chippewa, Winnebago, and Menominee to perceive their danger.

The Americans found their manpower pool small, but larger than the British without the Indians. Their objective was to eliminate, if possible, British garrisons which threatened to supply the Indians with the firearms and firewater that set the frontier aflame. Clark's drive into the Illinois country accomplished this objective and, combined with the subsequent activities of the *habitants* and the Spanish, effectively neutralized any threat from that region against the vulnerable settlements in Kentucky. This caused the battleground to be located between the Wabash and Wheeling, between Detroit and the bluegrass region, with the bloodiest fighting occurring in 1780–1782.

Neither side mounted the sustained offensive necessary to inflict fatal damage on the other. The garrison and militia at Pittsburgh and the few regulars and militia in Kentucky never co-operated with one another nor did they ever have supplies sufficient to achieve victory. The victory of Clark at Piqua in 1780 and his destruction of the Shawnee villages on the Miami in 1782 and the triumphs of British Captain Henry Bird at Ruddle's Station and Martin's Station in 1780 and of loyalist Alexander McKee at Blue Licks in 1782 indicate they might take ground, but they could not hold it. By the end of the war the Indians were mostly out of the upper Ohio Valley and settled in the Lake Erie basin. But no Americans could settle in the vacant lands for fear of destruction by a raiding party. Thus the war ended in a stalemate. The British nominally dominated everything east of Lake Michigan, the Indians conceded nothing north of the Ohio, the Spanish influenced the vast area drained by the Illinois, Rock, and Wisconsin rivers, and the Americans controlled Pittsburgh and central Kentucky and had vague claims, based upon colonial charters, extending northwestward to the territory of the Hudson Bay Company.

Despite the mythology of Clark's conquests, not a single American soldier was north of the Ohio when the treaty was signed in early 1783. The question puzzling all who observe this fact, is, why did the British concede the Old Northwest to the Americans? In part, they did not realize what they were giving away. The ministers in Whitehall really never held great visions of agricultural, commercial, mineral, and industrial wealth which could be developed in this vast wilderness. Moreover, the British prime minister, Lord Shelburne, made concessions to the Americans to wean them from the French alliance. If the Americans were out of the war, the British could shift military and naval resources against the French and Spanish. Thus a quick peace with the Americans might insure success in the West Indies and India where the British navy was sorely pressed. Finally, Shelburne wanted to heal the wounds of the Revolution with a generous peace, one which might bring the new nation and the mother country into close co-operation in the future. For the United States the consequences of these predispositions were most favorable.

Three other interests had to be contended with in Paris— those of the Spanish, French, and Indians. The Spanish tried desperately to keep the Americans out of the Mississippi basin. When this seemed impossible, their negotiator, the Conde de Aranda, sought to limit the extent of the American advance to roughly the modern state of Kentucky east of the Cumberland River and to the upper Tennessee River Valley. Led by the Comte de Vergennes, the foreign minister, and Joseph Mathias Gerard de Rayneval, his secretary, the French sought to reinforce the Spanish in private negotiations with Shelburne. Because the Spanish held out too long for Gibraltar, they lost the cis-Mississippi west to the Americans, who came to terms first.

The one party not privy to these councils, the Native Americans, received short shrift. In the end, only those Indians living in modern Ontario were spared from the less-than-tender mercies of the Americans. Whatever the American Revolution represents to the former colonists, to these aboriginal inhabitants it was an unmitigated disaster, one whose proportions were only too soon to become obvious.

The Peace of Paris terminated the military aspects of the war in the West, but by that time new problems emerged on how this vast region should be settled and governed. The end of the War for Independence meant the beginning of the American Revolution in the Old Northwest.

The Ohio Valley in the American Revolution

Otis K. Rice

Brief overviews of the war in the Northwest are difficult to find. Even more difficult are those which perceive, as this one does, that the war in the West and the revolution in the West did not necessarily occur concurrently. The author weaves the history of the several transmontane settlements—around Pittsburgh, Wheeling, and Point Pleasant—and the bluegrass region into a cohesive whole. Professor Otis K. Rice (1919———) is a former high school teacher who is now at West Virginia Institute of Technology where he combines administrative duties with scholarly inquiry and teaching. His The Allegheny Frontier: West Virginia Beginnings, 1730–1830 *(1970) is a widely acclaimed account of Virginia's western district. This paper was originally delivered before a symposium, held at Ohio University in November, 1974, commemorating the bicentennial of Lord Dunmore's War.*

* *

HISTORIANS probing the causes of the American Revolution have usually emphasized events and attitudes in the seaboard sections of the colonies. They have drawn attention to the political, constitutional, and economic clashes stemming from British efforts to tighten control over the colonies and have examined in infinite detail a series of provocative incidents which heightened tension and made any settlement of differences increasingly difficult.

Where the West has been concerned, most writers have concentrated upon the effects of the Proclamation of 1763, which, among other provisions, forbade settlement west of the

From Thomas H. Smith, ed., *Ohio in the American Revolution: A Conference to Commemorate the 200th Anniversary of the Ft. Gower Resolves (The Ohio American Revolution Bicentennial Conference Series,* Number 1, Columbus, 1976), 5–13; reprinted without footnotes with permission of the author and the Ohio Historical Society.

Allegheny Mountains. That essential feature of the proclamation was first set forth in the Treaty of Easton of 1758, concluded between Sir William Johnson, acting for the proprietors of Pennsylvania, and the Six Nations. In 1761 Colonel Henry Bouquet extended the ban on settlement west of the mountains to transmontane Maryland and Virginia. These attempts to restrict settlement were highly unpopular, but the outcry against them was mild compared with that raised against the Proclamation of 1763. The bitter remark of David Robinson, a resident of Augusta County, Virginia, who held military warrants for western lands, that recently won territory was now to be given "as a Compliment to our good Friends and faithfull Allies, the Shawnee Indians" accurately reflected the anger of speculators and settlers, who were to rankle under the restriction for no less than five years.

Yet, too much can be made of proscriptions upon settlement in the Ohio Valley during the time when the British Government was groping for some means of reconciling the interests of the fur trader with those of the speculator and the settler and of averting a costly and bloody Indian war. Indeed, just as some of the British regulatory and fiscal policies most offensive to the New England merchants had been removed by 1770, so had tensions over restrictions upon western lands also eased somewhat after 1768. By the treaties of Hard Labor and Fort Stanwix with the Cherokees and the Six Nations, respectively, and by subsequent agreements with the former, lands south of the Ohio River had been opened to settlement as far west as the Kentucky. The treaties represented a substantial victory for speculators and settlers and quieted much of the dissatisfaction with British western policy.

Perhaps equally as serious but also to some extent defused was the proposal to establish the colony of Vandalia. Embracing most of the territory between the Allegheny Mountains and the Ohio River and extending from the Monongahela River to the Kentucky, Vandalia would have included territory claimed by both Virginia and Pennsylvania. The scheme had its origins in a compensatory grant made by the Six Nations in the Treaty of Fort Stanwix to Philadelphia merchants who had allegedly lost trading goods valued at more than £85,000 during Pontiac's uprising. Under the successive corporate titles of the Indiana

Company and the Grand Ohio Company, the merchants and their associates undertood one of the most ambitious speculative ventures in the history of the American colonies. [*See* Map 1.]

Neither the infringements of the Vandalia project upon the charter rights of Virginia and Pennsylvania nor the possibility of the establishment of a large proprietary colony at a time when such aristocratic regimes were becoming anachronistic excited any violent reaction in the colonies. Older Virginia combines such as the Loyal and Ohio companies and other organized groups such as the Military Associates had serious reservations about the proposed colony but were lulled into acceptance by promises of recognition of their prior rights. Even George Washington, who in 1774 and 1775 sought to attract settlers to his lands on the Kanawha, pointed to the proximity of his holdings to Point Pleasant, likely to be the capital of Vandalia.

By the end of 1772 prospects for Vandalia were declining, and the time had come for a vigorous reassertion of colonial rights to territory west of the Alleghenies. At this propitious moment John Murray, the Earl of Dunmore, was at the helm of the Virginia Government. Like his fellow Scotsman, Robert Dinwiddie, Dunmore proved a strong protagonist in pressing the rights of Virginia. He himself succumbed to the allurements of land speculation and followed policies with respect to the West that could hardly have failed to endear him to the most ardent expansionists. In 1773 he visited the Forks of the Ohio, asserted Virginia authority over the region, then in dispute with Pennsylvania, and named the aggressive but imprudent John Connolly his agent at Fort Dunmore, as the post at the Forks of the Ohio was renamed.

In 1773 Dunmore also authorized a large party of surveyors, under Colonel Thomas Bullitt, to lay out lands in Kentucky. Although the territory south of the Ohio had been cleared of claims of the Cherokees and the Six Nations, the rights of the Shawnees to the land had been pointedly ignored. Continuing to disregard the claims of the Shawnees, other surveying companies left for Kentucky in the spring of 1774, and James Harrod founded the first settlement in the Bluegrass region. By then immigrants were pouring into the upper Ohio Valley.

Shawnee hostility to the intruders mounted steadily. An increasingly fragile peace in the Ohio Valley was punctuated by cruel Indian forays against isolated settlements and by bloody retaliation by those determined to have the Indian lands. During the spring and summer of 1774 Dunmore collaborated with George Croghan, the deputy Indian superintendent under Sir William Johnson, to isolate the Shawnees and prevent their forming a strong confederacy of disaffected northern Indian tribes. He further earned the plaudits of speculators and settlers by organizing a large expedition for the purpose of crushing Shawnee resistance. He himself led a northern wing of his army by way of Fort Dunmore. The other, under Andrew Lewis, marched down the Kanawha with the expectation of joining the governor on the Ohio. Nearly every important land speculator in territory then claimed by Virginia participated in Dunmore's War, and many were present at the battle of Point Pleasant. [*See* Map 2.]

In the action against the Shawnees at Point Pleasant, the only battle of Dunmore's War, and by the terms of the Treaty of Camp Charlotte, Dunmore accomplished his limited objective of making the region south of the Ohio River safe for settlement. His willingness to treat with the Indians, however, aroused deep dissatisfaction among the militia, who desired to crush the Shawnees. Recollections in later years of deep distrust of Dunmore at the time of the agreement, nevertheless, were generally those of ultra-patriotic veterans or of historians and antiquarians who read their history of the Revolution backwards. Even the Fort Gower resolves were coupled with professions of appreciation to the governor, who continued to receive similar pledges of friendship and support from the western country.

On the other hand, within six months after the Treaty of Camp Charlotte Dunmore had become a detested figure in the Ohio Valley. Once the Revolution had broken out, he cast aside plans made at Camp Charlotte for a great council of western tribal leaders for the purpose of working out a definitive solution to the Indian claims to land south of the Ohio. Instead, he began to seek pledges of Indian support for the British in the war with the American colonies. In addition, he ordered the disbanding of the garrisons at Fort Dunmore, Fort Henry at

Wheeling, and Fort Blair at Point Pleasant, the posts which constituted the outer ring of protection for upper Ohio Valley pioneers.

Effective countermoves by the Virginia Convention largely nullified Dunmore's actions. On August 7, 1775, the Convention ordered Captain John Neville with about a hundred men from Winchester to Fort Pitt, the name restored to the post at the Forks of the Ohio. More important, it named a commission, which in October, 1775, concluded the Treaty of Pittsburgh whereby the Shawnees, Delawares, Mingoes, Senecas, Wyandots, Pottawattomies, and Ottawas agreed to remain neutral in the conflict between England and the colonies. For more than a year the tribes kept their promise, making possible an uninterrupted advance of settlement into western Pennsylvania, transmontane West Virginia, and eastern Kentucky. By the time that most of them deserted their neutrality in 1777, most sections of the Ohio Valley were in a better defensive position then they had been at the beginning of the Revolutionary War.

Although Ohio Valley residents were overwhelmingly devoted to the American cause, a source of considerable concern at the outset of the war lay in Loyalist proclivities, especially conspicuous on the upper Ohio. John Connolly convinced both Dunmore and Thomas Gage, who was in charge of British forces in America, that the reduction of Fort Pitt, with troops from Detroit, would seriously undermine American defenses in the Ohio Valley and encourage the Loyalists to openly espouse the British side. To gather such a force, he and two companions set out by way of Maryland and Virginia for Detroit. John Gibson, a Pittsburgh trader with whom Connolly had earlier corresponded, alerted the West Augusta Committee of Safety to the threat, with the result that Connolly and his associates were arrested and their plans thwarted.

With the Connolly plot nipped in the bud and Indian affairs generally quiescent, land speculation and settlement in the Ohio Valley proceeded with little interruption. Taking advantage of the situation, Judge Richard Henderson, a North Carolina speculator, and several others organized the Transylvania Company in January, 1775. Shortly afterward Henderson arranged a council with the Cherokee chiefs at Sycamore Shoals on the Watauga, where, in spite of imperial regulations prohibiting private purchases of land from the Indians, he bought from them all the land between the Kentucky River and the highlands south of the Cumberland and a strip between the Holston River and the Cumberland Mountains. Older chiefs, including Attakullakulla, Oconostota, and The Raven, knowing that Cherokee claims to the region were somewhat nebulous, approved the transaction, but young chiefs opposed it, and Dragging Canoe, their spokesman, warned Henderson that Kentucky would become "a dark and bloody ground."

Acting on the assumption that in the event of a war between England and the colonies the actual possession of the territory thus acquired would constitute a decided advantage, Henderson pursued his plans with vigor and dispatch. The very day that his council with the Cherokee chiefs ended he sent Daniel Boone and twenty-eight axmen to blaze a trail, later known as the Wilderness Road, along the south bank of the Kentucky River to the Bluegrass region. Ten days later Henderson himself set out with about thirty riflemen, Negro slaves, and a large packhorse train laden with provisions.

In addition to Boonesborough, which was established under Henderson's auspices, three other Kentucky settlements—Harrodsburg, Boiling Spring, and St. Asaph's—were made in Kentucky in the spring of 1775. Although few of the inhabitants were willing to concede the rights which Henderson claimed, they recognized the need for some kind of common government. Henderson seized the opportunity and invited them to send representatives to Boonesborough on May 23 to enact laws for the colony of Transylvania. In response to his call, eighteen men assembled under a large elm tree. With Henderson endeavoring to play the role of a forest Demosthenes, they set up a court system, established a militia, and provided for the punishment of criminals, the preservation of game, and, interestingly enough, the breeding of horses. Although sheer necessity evoked a measure of temporary cooperation among the Kentucky stations, Henderson's dream of founding a proprietary colony and instituting a feudal land system was anathema to most Kentuckians. Upon the advice of George Rogers Clark, they addressed a memorial to the Virginia General Assembly protesting the pretensions of Henderson.

On June 6 the independent settlers of Harrodsburg, styling themselves "a Respectable Body of Prime Rifle Men," called upon the General Assembly to grant them representation in that body and designated Clark and John Gabriel Jones their delegates. Although they coupled their request with a vigorous assertion of loyalty to the American cause and a profession of hatred of British tyranny, they were motivated primarily by a desire for secure land titles and an adequate defense structure, which Virginia could provide but which Henderson could not. Fortunately for their petition, the General Assembly of Virginia recognized a need to clothe all of the Ohio Valley settlements with a canopy of government. To that end it not only created Kentucky County but also divided the District of West Augusta into Monongalia, Ohio, and Yohogania counties, all before the year was out.

As Henderson's fortunes waned, speculators once more began to lay grandiose plans for the upper Ohio. In the summer of 1776 residents of the area in dispute between Virginia and Pennsylvania petitioned Congress to create a fourteenth state, Westsylvania, the boundaries of which coincided almost precisely with those earlier determined for Vandalia. The petitioners pointed to problems arising from uncertain jurisdictions and geographical conditions, but they also sought to give their memorial a philosophical basis by declaring that they had, as "emigrants from almost every Province of America" generally "imbibed the highest and most extensive Ideas of Liberty." Annexation to either Virginia or Pennsylvania, they argued, would deprive them of the country to which they, as the first occupants, were entitled by the "Laws of Nature and of Nations." Despite their eloquent plea, the Continental Congress, unwilling to antagonize either Virginia or Pennsylvania and rightly suspicious that the Indiana Company was behind the move, turned down the petition.

Political moves were not entirely separated from the defense needs of the frontiers. By the summer of 1776 settlements extended from the Forks of the Ohio to the mouth of the Kanawha, with the density of population generally decreasing toward the south. Nevertheless, an important vanguard of pioneers had reached central Kentucky either by following the Wilderness Road from the Holston Valley or by making the long journey down the Ohio and up the Kentucky. For the protection of her upper Ohio Valley settlements, Virginia established a defense perimeter along the Ohio River, with Forts Pitt, Henry, and Randolph as key points in the shield. Kentucky's security rested upon the inadequate militia stationed at the three posts of Harrodsburg, Boonesborough, and St. Asaph's until the creation of Kentucky County, when a full complement of militia officers was appointed and transfers of ammunition from Fort Pitt were authorized.

British authorities took advantage of the mounting anger of western Indians over the expanding settlements in formulating their military strategy for 1777. Plans called for three separate expeditions, launched from Canada, Fort Oswego, and New York, to converge in the Hudson Valley, with the object of severing New England from the remainder of the states. To enhance the likelihood of success of this three-pronged offensive, Lieutenant Governor Henry Hamilton, the commandant at Detroit, convened a council of Ohio Valley tribes for the purpose of inducing them to join the British. He succeeded in winning over the Ottawa and Chippewa chiefs and some of the Wyandots and Mingoes, but he was unable to secure pledges of support from the Delawares and Shawnees, whose lands were more exposed to the dreaded Virginia "Long Knives." Yet even the latter soon began to falter in their neutrality.

Following the council Hamilton acted quickly. In the summer of 1777 he dispatched fifteen war parties to the Ohio Valley frontiers. British direction gave to the tribal associations a unity of purpose and durability seldom attained when the Indians were acting alone. At the same time that he unleashed his reign of terror, Hamilton held forth offers of food, lodging, and humane treatment to settlers in the backcountry who would desert their American allegiance and present themselves at a British post. To any who would join the British forces and serve until the close of the war he promised pay equal to that which they would receive in American service and two hundred acres of land.

Hamilton's offer, along with fears of a general Indian war and residual attachments to England, was probably at the root of a Loyalist uprising in the Monongahela Valley in the late summer of 1777, which was suppressed only with the timely arrival of Colonel Zackquill Morgan and five hundred militia. Benjamin Logan, at his fort at St. Asaph's in central Kentucky, so feared the appeal of Hamilton's offer that he made every effort to prevent news of it from reaching the men there. By this time a number of well-known frontier figures, among them Simon Girty and his brothers, Matthew Elliott, and Alexander McKee, had deserted the Americans and joined the British.

Although the defeat at Saratoga on October 17 doomed British plans for 1777, they and the Indians achieved greater success in the Ohio Valley. The largest of their attacks was launched against Fort Henry, at Wheeling, on September 1, when about two hundred Wyandots and Mingoes, accompanied by a few Delawares and Shawnees, lured about half the garrison outside the walls of the fort and killed twenty-three of them. Later that month they ambushed Captain William Foreman and a reconnoitering party south of Wheeling, killing Foreman and twenty of his men. Hardly a frontier area escaped some blow. Within six months after Hamilton had sent out his war parties he had received seventy-three prisoners and 129 scalps.

As the situation became more ominous, Brigadier General Edward Hand was ordered by the Continental Congress to coordinate all defenses on the upper Ohio. Hand arrived at Pittsburgh on June 1, 1777, and immediately made preparations for an invasion of the Indian towns, particularly those of the Wyandots and the Pluggy's Town confederacy. The worsening conditions on the frontiers, however, forced him to rely upon such protection as the stationing of 150 militia in each of the frontier counties could provide during the ensuing winter.

Winter, normally a season of restricted military activity, brought no respite to the shaken Ohio Valley. In early November Cornstalk, the Shawnee chief, arrived at Fort Randolph, ostensibly to inform Matthew Arbuckle, who was in charge, that he could no longer prevent his tribe from joining the British. Suspicious of Cornstalk's story, Arbuckle detained him at the fort. Cornstalk's son, Elinipsico, and companions who came in search of the chief were also held. When two hunters from the fort were attacked by Indians a few days later, the angry garrison, now convinced of Indian duplicity, fell upon the Shawnee emissaries and killed them.

Meanwhile, a critical shortage of ammunition had developed on the upper Ohio. To relieve the situation, General Hand, in February, 1778, led five hundred men to the mouth of the Cuyahoga River, where the British had reportedly established a powder magazine. Hand succeeded only in killing three old Indians and capturing two squaws and in earning for his expedition the derisive appellation of the "Squaw Campaign." [*See* Map 3.]

As expected, the tempo of the war picked up in the spring of 1778. On May 16 about three hundred Indians, mostly Wyandots and Mingoes, tried unsuccessfully to reduce Fort Randolph. They then moved up the Kanawha and into the Greenbrier region, where an assault upon Fort Donnally proved equally futile. In June Daniel Boone, who had been captured at Blue Licks while on a saltmaking expedition, learned of an anticipated attack upon Boonesborough. Knowing that the fort could not withstand a surprise invest-ment, Boone contrived to escape and warned the Kentuckians of the impending danger. Delays in the arrival of the Indians, together with criticisms of his role in the capture of the salt-making party at the Blue Licks, raised deep suspicions of Boone's story. At last, on September 7, about four hundred Indians under the Shawnee chief, Blackfish, and the French Canadian, Dagniaux De Quindre, laid siege to Boonesborough. The fort's seventy-five defenders resisted a variety of tactics by the Indians, ranging from offers of a treaty to the use of fireballs and an attempt to dig a tunnel beneath the walls of the structure. After ten days of frustration, the weary attackers withdrew.

The successful defense of Boonesborough not only enabled the insecure Kentucky settlements to survive but it also made possible a shift from a defensive to a partially offensive strategy by the Americans in the Ohio Valley. Already Governor Patrick Henry and the General Assembly of Virginia had given ap-proval to a highly secret plan laid before them by George Rogers Clark. The authorization measure was so ambiguously phrased that only its sponsors were aware of its real purpose. In addition to his public orders to raise eleven companies of militia and proceed to Kentucky, Clark had private instructions to attack the British post at Kaskaskia in the Illinois country. With about 150 men gathered from the upper Ohio Valley, to which were added about twenty-five Kentuckians, among whom was the noted scout and hunter, Simon Kenton, Clark left Fort Massac, about ten miles below the Falls of the Ohio, on June 26. Traveling by land rather than the more frequented river routes, Clark stole upon the post at Kaskaskia on July 4, leaving its surprised garrison no choice but surrender. In quick succession Vincennes and Cahokia also fell. Clark's audacity drew a number of western tribes into more friendly relations with the Americans. It also set the stage for a relatively close association between Clark and Spanish authorities west of the Mississippi River. [*See* Map 3.]

Clark's conquests confronted Hamilton with an intolerable situation. American retention of Kaskaskia and Vincennes threatened the British position in the Ohio Valley. Gathering a force of British, Canadians, and Indians, of whom perhaps no more than thirty-three were regulars, Hamilton set out for the Illinois country by way of the Maumee and Wabash rivers. In late December he made a successful surprise attack upon Vincennes, but as the weather could only be expected to become worse, he then went into winter quarters at nearby Fort Sackville. Relying upon the elements for protection, he permitted the Canadians to return to Detroit and the Indians to their villages. Taking advantage of the same elements, Clark left Kaskaskia for Vincennes in the midst of winter. Hamilton, taken unawares, capitulated on February 25, 1779, and was sent as a prisoner of war to Williamsburg.

Despite his spectacular successes, Clark knew that his victories rested upon audacity and surprise and not upon any genuine military superiority. He also knew that only the capture of Detroit could insure the desired erosion of British power in the West and durable relief from the distresses suffered by Ohio Valley residents. Nevertheless, Governor Henry and the council of Virginia opposed a proposal by the Board of War in June, 1779, for an attack upon Detroit with some 5,500 men under the command of General Lachlan McIntosh, Hand's successor at Fort Pitt. Their opposition sprang from a mistaken belief that Clark might be able to take Detroit and from fears that a successful assault by McIntosh might undermine Virginia's claim to the territory northwest of the Ohio River. Deprived of broad support, McIntosh accomplished little, and

Forts McIntosh and Laurens, which he constructed at the mouth of Beaver Creek and on the Tuscarawas River, respectively, served more as irritants to the Indians than as bastions of strength for the Americans. [*See* Map 3.]

The optimism exuded by Virginia authorities was not without foundation, for the situation in the Ohio Valley in the summer of 1779 appeared brighter than at any time since the Indians had become allies of the British. Settlers continued to move into the region in substantial numbers. Colonel John Bowman was able to gather three hundred Kentuckians for an assault upon the Shawnee village of Chillicothe, and, although the outcome has sometimes been regarded as a defeat for Bowman, the attack demonstrated to the Indians that the Americans could strike with swiftness and effectiveness. Moreover, Bowman's expedition forced the British to give up a plan to lay siege to Fort Laurens by depriving them of at least two hundred needed Indian warriors. Any threat that might have been posed to the Kentucky settlements from the Cherokees was also averted when an expedition led by Evan Shelby laid waste their villages in the Chickamauga country.

As a result of the gains of the Americans, delegations of Wyandots and Shawnees journeyed to Fort Pitt for the purpose of arranging a peace, and Indian attacks on settlements south of the Ohio diminished in both frequency and intensity. At Fort Nelson, the new post erected at the Falls of the Ohio by George Rogers Clark, the mood was one of confidence and was celebrated with a great ball to which settlers from the other stations in Kentucky were invited. The party, which lasted for several days, offered a welcome diversion from the stern demands of wartime living.

Only a thin line, however, separated optimism and gloom. On October 4, 1779, several hundred Indians, accompanied by Matthew Elliott, Simon Girty, and the latter's two brothers, attacked a party under Colonel David Rogers, which was returning from New Orleans with five batteaux loaded with gunpowder, medicines, and other needed supplies. Although Rogers and his men had sighted a large number of Indian rafts emerging from the Little Miami River and had taken refuge on an island, they were too late. The Indians surrounded the island and killed all but ten of Rogers' men. From dispatches which

Rogers was carrying to Clark, they found corroboration of suspected American weakness in the West.

Capitalizing upon the changed situation, the absence of Clark in building Fort Jefferson in the land of the Chickasaws, and a general pessimism then prevailing among Americans in the Ohio Valley, the British mounted two offensives in the spring of 1780. One army, commanded by Emanuel Hesse, was to move south from Mackinac, regain control of the Illinois villages, descend the Mississippi River, and recapture West Florida from its Spanish conquerors. Anticipating Hesse's plan, Clark lay in wait at Cahokia. His presence so overawed Hesse's Indian allies that the British moved on to St. Louis, where they were again expected and met by withering cannon fire. In disgrace, Hesse beat a retreat to Mackinac. [See Map 4.]

The other expedition, under Captain Henry Bird, enjoyed greater success. In April Bird left Detroit with 150 white men, about a thousand Indians, and six pieces of artillery. He descended the Miami with the intention of striking at Fort Nelson. When he reached the Ohio he found that the Licking River was in full flood and that he could ascend it to the central Kentucky settlements. He attacked Ruddle's Station, which became the first Kentucky station to surrender, and then moved on to Martin's Station, which also capitulated. By then the waters of the Licking River were receding, and Bird, with about a hundred prisoners, returned to Detroit.

The threat to the Kentucky settlements and demands for retaliation against the Indians induced Clark to hasten from Cahokia to Louisville. From there he went to Harrodsburg, where he laid plans for an expedition against the Shawnee towns. With nearly a thousand men he left the mouth of the Licking River on August 1. Five days later he reached the Indian villages, which he found deserted but which he laid waste. At Piqua, on the Miami River, the Indians, led by Simon Girty, had prepared to make a stand, but when confronted with the cannon which Clark had brought, they broke and ran. Clark's show of strength, however, had been no more impressive than that of Bird, and the tribes were not yet ready to rally to the American side. [See Map 4.]

Until British power at Detroit was broken the Ohio Valley settlements could expect no lasting peace. Twice in 1780 the

Americans sought to launch expeditions against that bastion of British strength. The first, authorized by the Continental Congress and planned by George Washington, was to be under the command of Colonel Daniel Brodhead of Fort Pitt. Brodhead, however, proved unable to obtain sufficient militia to man the Ohio Valley forts while the regulars were away on a campaign, and Congress failed to provide the necessary supplies. Consequently, Brodhead did little more in the summer of 1780 than beat off attacks by the Shawnees, who ranged as far south as the Monongahela Valley.

The other campaign against Detroit was projected by the government of Virginia. To that end, George Rogers Clark was named a brigadier general of Virginia troops, with headquarters at Louisville, and instructed to raise a force of about two thousand men. Everywhere on the frontiers men continued to exhibit their usual reluctance to leave families behind for the purpose of striking at such a distant objective. When Clark mustered his men at Wheeling, he had only four hundred, not half the number he had expected there. Even then, desertions were so numerous that he set out down the Ohio without waiting for a detachment of Westmoreland County militia under Archibald Lochry. Upon arriving at Wheeling, Lochry, although inadequately supplied, hastened on down the Ohio. About twenty miles below the mouth of the Licking River he was ambushed by a large party of Indians under Alexander McKee and Joseph Brant. Sixty-four of Lochry's men were killed, and the remaining forty-two were captured. Kentuckians, disenchanted with Clark's Illinois venture, his construction of patrol boats for use on the Ohio, and the erection of Fort Jefferson, likewise showed little enthusiasm for an expedition against Detroit. Reluctantly, Clark was obliged to accept the fact that no blow could be mounted against the British stronghold at that time.

News of the British surrender at Yorktown again lit the fires of hope for residents of the Ohio Valley that peace might return to their beleaguered land. But such was the character of the war in the West that the conflict continued for more than a year after the defeat of Lord Cornwallis. In September, 1781, at a time when an expedition under Colonel John Gibson was being readied for a strike against the Wyandots, the Indians themselves took the initiative. A small army, led by the Delaware, Buckongahelas, and the Wyandot, Half-King, set out for Wheeling, but the inhabitants of the upper Ohio were given timely warning by David Zeisberger, a Moravian missionary, and serious consequences for the settlers were averted.

The frontier inhabitants held the Delawares responsible for their woes and increasingly called for vengeance. To that end Colonel David Williamson led an expedition against the Delaware towns in October, 1781, but he found them apparently permanently deserted. By then the Delawares had migrated to the Sandusky and had forced the Moravian Delawares, some four hundred Indians Christianized by Moravian missionaries, to accompany them. During the following winter some of the Moravian Indians, often on the verge of starvation, returned to their homes for provisions which they had left behind. Despite the removal of the Delawares, Indian depredations continued along the frontiers, and in early March, 1782, Williamson once more led his militia into the Indian country.

At the village of Gnaddenhütten, near Coshocton, Williamson came upon ninety Moravian Indians, who had returned to their abandoned town for food and supplies. With them were four hostile Indians. When the militia discovered that some of the Indians who had attacked the frontiers had been at Gnaddenhütten, they gave vent to uncontrolled rage. On the morning of March 8 they fell upon the unsuspecting Moravian Delawares and killed all of them, sparing not even their women and children.

The wanton slaughter of the friendly Delawares enraged tribes north of the Ohio and resulted in new onslaughts upon the trans-Allegheny settlements. To deal with the continued attacks, about four hundred mounted militia from Westmoreland and Washington counties, acting largely on their own initiative, chose Colonel William Crawford as their commanding officer and on May 25 left Mingo Bottom, near present Steubenville, Ohio, for the Indian villages on the Sandusky. On June 4 the Americans were attacked on the upper Sandusky by a large force of Indians, augmented the following day by reinforcements of British and Shawnees. Fifty of Crawford's men were killed, and the others fled in wild disorder. Crawford was among the captives. In an act of supreme contempt, his captors put him to death, but only after inflicting upon him almost every variety of torture in the Indian repertoire. [*See* Map 5.]

With the coming of autumn, Captain William Caldwell and Alexander McKee concluded that their fears of an American attack upon Detroit and an invasion of Canada had been without foundation and that they should launch their own offensive moves against the Ohio Valley settlements. Intending to strike first at Fort Henry, they changed their plans upon receiving a report, later proved false, that Clark was at the mouth of the Licking River with two gunboats. With about three hundred Canadian rangers and Indians, they proceeded to Kentucky, where on August 16 they unsuccessfully stormed Bryan's Station, a few miles from Lexington.

Emboldened by their success in beating off their attackers and by the arrival of an additional 182 mounted men, the Kentuckians, led by Colonel John Todd, set off in pursuit of the enemy. They overtook the Indians and the Canadians at Blue Licks, at a horseshoe bend in the Licking River. There they fell into a cleverly-set trap, and seventy-two of them lost their lives. A relief force of 470 men under Benjamin Logan arrived too late to save them, but it did bury in a common grave forty-three stripped and mutilated bodies, not one of which was identifiable. [*See* Map 5.]

Fort Henry, the post against which the attack had originally been directed, did not escape. In September over two hundred British and Indians, with Joseph Brant as their leader, laid siege to the fort. Their effort, however, proved in vain, foiled, according to one of the most persistent legends of the upper Ohio Valley, by the daring feat of young Betty Zane, who obtained a supply of much-needed gunpowder from the nearby residence of her brother during the heat of the battle.

With the signing of the Treaty of Paris on September 3, 1783, peace officially returned to the Ohio Valley. Prior to the conclusion of the treaty, however, John Jay, Benjamin Franklin, and John Adams, the American negotiators, experienced some anxious weeks. In order to hasten the proceedings and to compensate Spain for her failure to recover Gibraltar, the Comte de Vergennes, the French foreign minister, proposed that the territory north of the Ohio should be retained by

England and that south of the Cumberland should be awarded to Spain, leaving to the United States the region between those two rivers.

Stunned by the suggestion of Vergennes, the American diplomats arranged a separate peace with the British. By the terms of the agreement, the new nation acquired all the trans-Appalachian region north of Florida, but the boundary between the United States and Florida temporarily remained in some doubt. Even in the French proposal, however, there had been recognition of the fact that the American advance into Kentucky and Tennessee constituted a basis for awarding those regions to the United States. On the other hand, a controversial literature has grown up concerning the significance of George Rogers Clark with respect to the decision that the Northwest Territory should be American.

Historians have long since ceased to equate the Revolution with the war. To be fully understood, the Revolution in the Ohio Valley, as distinguished from the Ohio Valley in the Revolutionary War, must also be considered in its political, social, and economic aspects. Large scale land speculation, for example, did not cease with the war but assumed new forms and adapted to new conditions, thus insuring a continuation of certain aristocratic bases for western society. Yet, the Northwest Ordinance, which placed national restrictions upon human slavery, assured new states a republican form of government and equality in the Union with existing states, and encouraged education, enunciated great principles clearly in the Revolutionary tradition. Their impress was indelibly stamped not only upon the Ohio Valley but also upon the entire nation.

Exploration of these and other effects of the Revolution upon the Ohio Valley lies beyond the scope of this brief essay. In some respects the observation of John Adams that the real revolution occurred in the minds of the American people and was ·in essence accomplished before the war began might be reversed as far as the Ohio Valley is concerned. To an extent, the fruits of the Revolution coincided with the occupation of much of the region. It may be said, with some truth, that for the Ohio Valley the Revolution began, rather than ended, in 1783.

Lake
of the Woods

SCALE

0   100   200 Miles

CANADA

LAKE SUPERIOR

NESOTA

Lake
Nipissing

M
I
C
H
I
G
A
N

LAKE HURON

WISCONSIN

R.

Fox R.

LAKE ONTARIO

Wisconsin R.

LAKE MICHIGAN

Lake
St.Clair

IOWA

Mississippi R.

Rock R.

LAKE ERIE

NEW YORK

M
O
U
N
T
A
I
N
S

R.

Maumee R.

Illinois R.

Muskingum R.

OHIO

INDIANA

R.

Scioto R.

PENNSYLVANIA

ILLINOIS

Wabash R.

Miami R.

Gt. Miami R.

MD

WEST
VIRGINIA

A
P
P
A
L
A
C
H
I
A
N

MISSOURI

Kentucky R.

Licking R.

Kanawha R.

VIRGINIA

R.

R.

KENTUCKY

CUMBERLAND
GAP

RKANSAS

Cumberland R.

TENNESSEE

Tennessee R.

NORTH CAROLINA

———— Ohio Land Company, 1748
•••••• Indiana Company, 1765
———— Illinois Company, 1766
———— Military Associates, 1766
———— Vandalia, 1769

Map 1: Land Speculation, 1748-1769

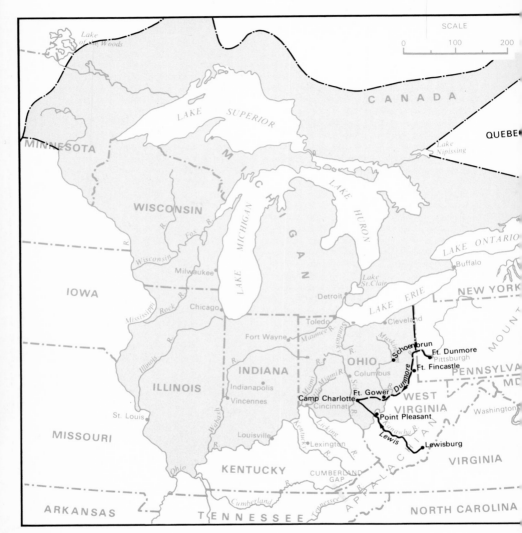

Map 2: Quebec Act and Military Campaigns, 1774

Added to
Quebec, 1774

Map 3: Military Campaigns, 1778-1779

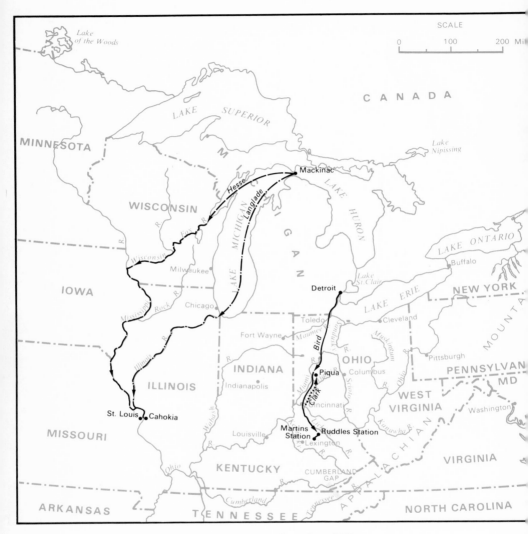

Map 4: Military Campaigns, 1780

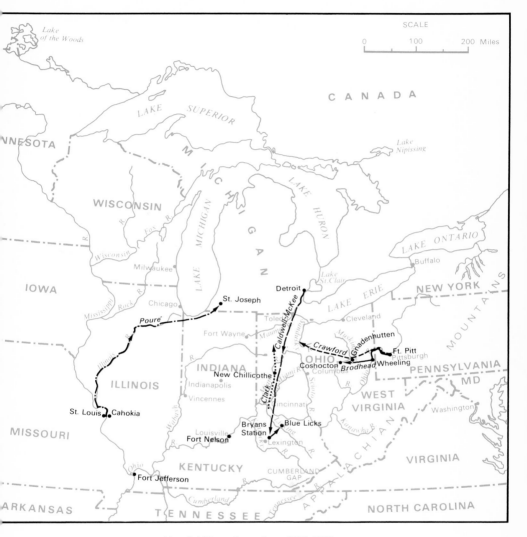

Map 5: Military Campaigns, 1781-1782

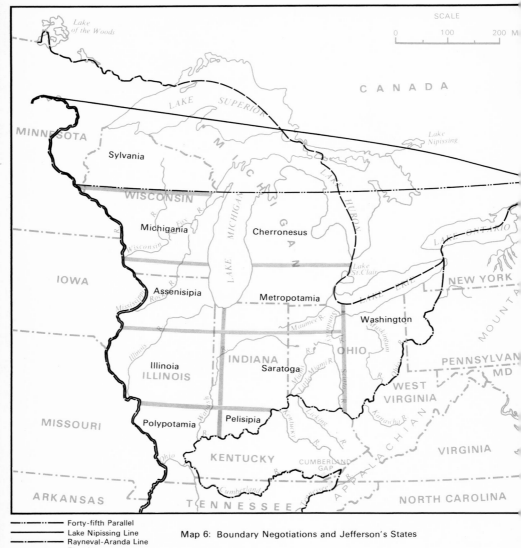

SCALE

0   100   200 Mi

CANADA

Lake of the Woods

Lake Superior

Lake Nipissing

MINNESOTA

Sylvania

WISCONSIN

Michigania

Fox R.

Wisconsin

Cherronesus

Lake Michigan

Lake Huron

Lake St. Clair

Lake Erie

Lake Ontario

NEW YORK

IOWA

Rock R.

Mississippi R.

Assenisipia

Metropotamia

Washington

Maumee R.

Raisin R.

Washington R.

Illinois R.

Illinoia

ILLINOIS

INDIANA

Saratoga

OHIO

Little Miami R.

Big Miami R.

Scioto R.

Muskingum R.

Kanawha R.

PENNSYLVANIA

MD

WEST VIRGINIA

MOUNTAIN

MISSOURI

Polypotamia

Wabash R.

Pelisipia

Kentucky R.

Licking R.

VIRGINIA

KENTUCKY

CUMBERLAND GAP

Ohio R.

APPALACHIAN

ARKANSAS

Cumberland R.

TENNESSEE

Cumberland R.

NORTH CAROLINA

Forty-fifth Parallel
Lake Nipissing Line
Rayneval-Aranda Line
Final Line
Proposed State Boundaries

Map 6: Boundary Negotiations and Jefferson's States

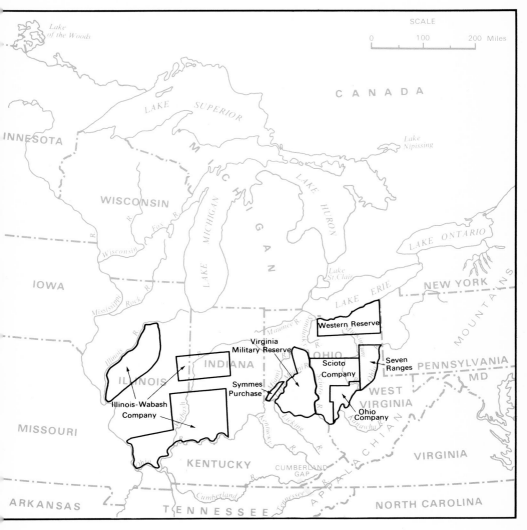

Map 7: Land Speculation, 1783-1790

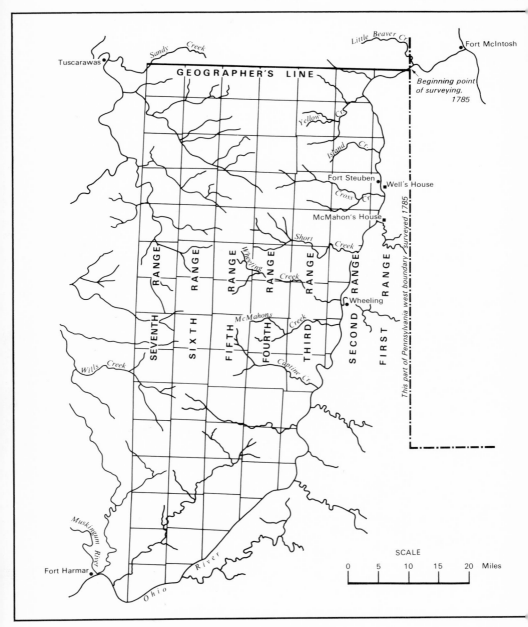

Map 8: The Seven Ranges

The Native American Crisis in the Ohio Country, 1774–1783

James H. O'Donnell III

Normally little attention is given the role of the American Indian in the Revolution and even less to the consequences of that event upon the Native American. Of particular importance in this essay is the account of Anglo-American attitudes toward the aboriginal inhabitants of the Northwest. In using excerpts from the play Ponteach, *Professor James H. O'Donnell III (1937———) of Marietta College graphically illustrates the "condescending and murderous attitudes held by whites" toward the Indians. Moreover, he describes the internal divisions among the Indians, using the Delawares as an example, that contributed to a lack of cohesion among the tribes relative to policy in the Revolutionary era. From the murder of Logan's family in 1774 to the massacre at Gnaddenhütten in 1782 the war in the upper Ohio valley pitted Indian against frontiersman in an unequal struggle that could only result in cultural or actual genocide for the indigenous inhabitants.*

Professor O'Donnell is the author of Southern Indians in the American Revolution *(1973) and numerous scholarly articles. His research has turned to the northern Indians in the same period and this paper, originally presented at an Ohio University symposium on the bicentennial of Lord Dunmore's War, represents an initial contribution to this scholarly redirection.*

* *

W HEN Thomas Jefferson wrote his well known *Notes on Virginia,* he sought to answer a number of questions, including a formal list sent to him by his French correspondent, and a broad

From Thomas H. Smith, ed., *Ohio in the American Revolution: A Conference to Commemorate the 200th Anniversary of the Ft. Gower Resolves (The Ohio American Revolution Bicentennial Conference Series,* Number 1, Columbus, 1976), 17–21; reprinted without footnotes with permission of the author and the Ohio Historical Society.

philosophical one posed by certain European intellectuals as to the nature of American genius. In seeking to establish the validity of the New World experience, Jefferson cited numerous examples of American creativity. In describing indigenous rhetoric, he included a speech attributed to Logan, an Indian chief who was well known on the Pennsylvania-Virginia frontier and in the Ohio country.

Evidently Thomas Jefferson had seen this speech in the *Virginia Gazette* for 4 February 1775 and copied it into his Memorandum Book; later he transferred it to the draft of his *Notes on Virginia*. Whatever Jefferson's motives for using this speech and whatever its true form and sources, we are interested in it for the revealing glimpse it provides of Indian-white relations. As recorded in the *Virginia Gazette* it reads:

> I appeal to any white man to say that he ever entered Logan's cabin but I gave him meat; that he ever came naked but I clothed him. In the course of the last war, Logan remained in his cabin an advocate for peace. I had such an affection for the white people, that I was pointed at by the rest of my nation. I should have lived with them had it not been for Colonel Cresap, who last year cut off, in cold blood, all the relatives of Logan, not sparing women and children: there runs not a drop of my blood in the veins of any human creature. This called upon me for revenge; I have sought it, I have killed many, and fully glutted my revenge. I am glad that there is a prospect of peace, on account of the nation; but I beg you will not entertain a thought that any thing I have said proceeds from fear! Logan disdains the thought! He will not turn on his heel to save his life! Who is there to mourn for Logan? No one!

Here is a core sample drawn from the depths of Indian-white relations on the colonial frontier. Although it is cast in a prose style similar to that of the King James version of the Bible, Logan's description outlines the attempts of the two races to live together, the failures of their efforts, and Logan's realization of his earthly finitude.

One of the fundamental reasons why the two races could not live in harmony is contained in Logan's comment that he "should have lived with them [the whites] had it not been for Colonel Cresap, who last year cut off, in cold blood, all the relations of Logan, not sparing women and children." Indeed, later editions of the *Notes* contained appendices in which Jefferson printed a number of corroborative letters from frontiersmen. Despite slightly different accounts of the individuals involved and the numbers of Indians killed, the witnesses agreed that in April of 1774 a group or groups of whites moved down the Ohio River, killing any and all native Americans whom they found along the way.

In the Logan speech we confront that fundamental assumption of the frontiersman—*that Indian life was of absolutely no value!* Nowhere is this demonstrated by actions better than by these incidents from the Ohio frontier. By why this attitude? To answer the *why* we will have to do more than quantify. Numbers of murders may tell us we *are* becoming more murderous and more violent, but they do not tell us *why* we are more murderous and more violent.

Finding an articulation of such attitudes is not easy. Fortunately for our cause we may find many of the ideas we seek expressed in the dialogue of a play written by an author who was intimately familiar with the eighteenth-century frontier. To us it does not matter that the play was not performed in the eighteenth century, or if it has ever been performed; what matters is that *Ponteach, A Tragedy* is a play which affords us profound insights into the mind of the frontier.

Published in London in 1766, *Ponteach* has been attributed to Robert Rogers, the famous ranger of the French and Indian War. Some doubt his authorship, but at the moment we are interested in the attitude which the play reveals, for whoever wrote the play knew, or had learned, the frontier and its outlook. The author has cast his characters into sets, so that the dialogue may be used to instruct us. From the two hunter-frontiersmen, the two traders, the two British governors, and the three British military officers, we may glean much helpful information.

At the outset of the play, the hunters and the traders reveal their attitudes about the trade with the Indians and the value of Indian life. While alive the native American was only something to be used, a means to an end in the fur trade. By cheating an Indian a man could gain riches, and of course there was no sin in cheating an Indian. For as the character McDole, who is one of the traders, says: "Our fundamental maxim is this, That it's no crime to cheat and gull an Indian." To which his partner Murphey responds: "How! Not a Sin to cheat an Indian say

you? Are they not Men? havn't they a right to Justice as well as
we, though Savage in their Manners?" Then in response we
hear an account of the nature of white guile in the trade.

Ah! If you boggle here, I say no more;
This is the very Quintessence of Trade,
And ev'ry Hope of Gain depends upon it;
None who neglect it ever did grow rich,
Or ever will, or can by Indian Commerce.
By this old Ogden built his stately House,
Purchas'd Estates, and grew a little King.
He, like an honest Man, bought all by Weight,
and made the ign'rant Savages believe
That his Right Foot exactly weigh'd a Pound:
By this for many Years he bought their Furs,
And died in Quiet like an honest Dealer.

When Murphey suggests that by now the Indians should
know of such simple trickery, McDole then reveals the favorite
device of the traders, the use of that demonic spirit, rum, made
even more baneful by drugging it with tincture of laudanum
and tincture of cantharides (known today as opium and Spanish
Fly). Explains McDole:

A thousand Opportunities present
To take Advantage of their Ignorance;
But the great Engine I employ is Rum,
More pow'rful made by certain strength'ning Drugs.
This I distribute with a lib'ral Hand,
Urge them to drink till they grow mad and valiant;
Which makes them think me generous and just,
And gives full Scope to practise all my Art.
I then begin my Trade with watered Rum,
the cooling Draught well suits their scorching Throats.
Their Fur and Peltry come in quick Return:
My Scales are honest, but so well contrived,
That one small Slip will turn three pounds to One.

After the Indians have been cheated roundly on the stage
before us, they and the traders exit, to be succeeded by two
frontiersmen out hunting without luck, a misfortune which
they blame on the Indians, whom they say are taking all the
game. The dialogue between the two characters Honnyman
and Orsbourn is filled with venom toward the natives.

HONNYMAN
These hateful Indians kidnap all the Game.

Curse their black Heads! they fright the Deer and Bear,
And every Animal that haunts the Wood,
Or by their Witchcraft conjure them away.
No Englishman can get a single Shot,
While they go loaded home with Skins and Furs.
"Twere to be wished not one of them survived,
Thus to infest the World, and plague Mankind.
Curs'd Heathern Infidels! Mere savage Beasts!
They don't deserve to breathe in Christian Air,
And should be hunted down like other Brutes.

ORSBOURN

I only wish the Laws permitted us
To hunt the savage Herd where ever they're found;
I'd never leave the Trade of Hunting then,
While one remained to tread and range the Wood.

HONNYMAN

Curse on the Law, I say, that makes it Death
To kill an Indian, more than to kill a Snake.
What if 'tis Peace? these Dogs deserve no Mercy;
Cursed revengeful, cruel, faithless Devils!
They killed my Father and my eldest Brother
Since which I hate their very Looks and Name.

ORSBOURN

And I, since they betrayed and killed my Uncle;
Hell seize their cruel, unrelenting Souls!
Tho these are not the same, 'twould ease my Heart
To cleave their painted Heads, and spill their Blood.
I abhor, detest, and hate them all,
And now could eat an Indian's Heart with Pleasure.

At this point in the play, these two gentle souls spy two
Indians coming toward them, whom they kill, scalp, and rob of
their peltry and weapons. As they complete their cowardly
work, Orsbourn has one fleeting twinge of conscience, but
Honnyman assures him that:

It's no more murder to crack a Louse
That is, if you've the wit to keep it private.
And as to Haunting, Indians have no Ghosts,
But as they live like beasts, like Beasts they die.
I've killed a Dozen in this self-same Way,
And never yet was troubled with their spirits.

These condescending and murderous attitudes held by
whites were painfully well known to all native Americans, but

they were acutely familiar to the tribes of the Ohio country. The two major groups living in the Ohio country at the time of the Revolution, the Delawares and the Shawnees, had been driven across the upper reaches of the Ohio River by the expansion of Europeans westward from the seacoast. In the seventeenth century the Delawares and even some of the Shawnees would have been found living in New Jersey, Delaware, and eastern Pennsylvania.

Then in the course of the decades that followed, the Shawnees and the Delawares had suffered at the hands of the Europeans many times over. That trinity of dispossession composed of land, trade, and rum, repeatedly had exacted heavy sacrifices from these tribes and their brethren. From their pre-contact locations on the east coast, these two groups had been pushed west by successive waves of land hungry whites. Along the way of course, traders like those whom we have met took their measure, exchanging paltry for peltry and cheating the Indians at every turn. Rum was of course a curse which all the native Americans bore by mid-century. The life of the Delaware leader Teedyuscung and his numerous bouts with the bottle is an example too well known to bear repeating.

By the year 1774, the cycle was in process once more. The Delawares, the Shawnees, and their fellows in Ohio had not had even a half-century's respite from pressures. Again their lands were envied by the whites and once more they were drawn into war, this time with the Virginians. Parenthetically, I should explain that to the native Americans of the eighteenth century, "Virginian" was a derogatory term used to mean any of the land greedy whites who peopled the frontier. So strong was the feeling implied by this term, that it was used by the Indians as a color word. Thus when a native American wished to identify the worst sort of prevarication, it was labelled a "Virginia lie!"

But in 1774 it was Virginians specifically, not frontiersmen generally, who troubled the Ohio Indians. Desire for more lands on their western borders had pushed the Virginians westward again as they had gone in the 1750s when they helped start the Great War for Empire. This time they encountered no French resistance, but instead the Shawnees, who had been driven westward by the Europeans at least twice before and now were trying to hold the central Ohio country for their own, with the Bluegrass of Kentucky as a kind of hunting ground and buffer zone. But Lord Dunmore and his troops put an end to that and established by force the colony's intention to settle its great Kentucky country.

As if the total pressures on the Ohio Indians had not reached sufficient levels otherwise, there was yet another force at work, this one also of white origins, but restricted in the main to the Delawares. The force of which I speak here was the efforts of the Christian missionaries. While I am not at this point questioning the good intentions of the members of the United Brethren, I am concerned with the cultural, social and political impact which this was having on the Delawares at the time of the Revolution.

In the first instance, the natives were being asked to commit cultural suicide. Follow Christianity, urged the preacher, which meant putting aside *everything* which was Indian, so that you could worship God (who was of course a Caucasian!) in the proper way by thinking, praying, dressing, eating, living, and working like a white man. Converts were urged to separate themselves into model Christian communities where they could put aside all ways that were Indian in order to take up that which was Christian, i.e., white.

The mission effort then was splintering the tribe from within while the white desire for land and profits from the trade were devastating it from without. As a result of these several forces at work, the Delawares were being divided into factions. For the purposes of identification, the groups may be labelled as follows: (1) those members of the tribe remaining in Pennsylvania and the east which we may call *Delaware Party P;* (2) those who had emigrated westward, were traditionalist in culture, and leaned toward the American cause in the Revolution, whom we shall label *Delaware Party A* (which was led by Captain White Eyes and Killbuck); (3) those who lived in Ohio also and were traditionalist in lifestyle, but who favored the British cause in the Revolution, whom we shall call *Delaware Party B* (which was led by Captain Pipe); and (4) those who had opted for the Christian lifestyle, lived in model Christian villages, and, claimed little or no interest in the American Revolution, which will be our *Delaware Party C* (which was under the leadership of the missionary, David Zeisberger).

As if these factions did not present problems enough, the geographical location of the tribe proved deadly when the war came. The principal trail from Pittsburg to Detroit lay directly through the Delaware country. I need not tell you that native Americans travelled by trail as we would travel by highway, so that a party going from Pittsburg to Detroit would follow the trail along the east bank of the Ohio River, then cross the Big Beaver River and go west to Tuscaroras where the path divided into a southerly branch toward the Shawnees and a northerly one toward Sandusky and Detroit. Consequently the Delawares lay astride any invasion route which the British planned to use against Fort Pitt or which the Americans might follow to Forts Sandusky and Detroit.

Moreover, native American hospitality demanded that a village entertain any delegation of Indians who came along the way, regardless of the intent of the travellers. This way-station position afforded the Delawares much information about activities in the Ohio country. Indeed, Captain White Eyes and David Zeisberger funneled information to the Americans at Fort Pitt (although they would of course deny this), while Captain Pipe and certain pro-British traders passed the news along to Detroit.

At Revolution's eve then, the tribes in the Ohio country well knew the ways of the people without color, feared that the worst might come, and yet never ceased to hope that their lands might be guaranteed them. After all these native Americans of whom we speak were settled agriculturalists, who cultivated extensive fields of corn, beans, squash, potatoes, and pumpkins. Captain White Eyes, the well-known Delaware leader who espoused a policy of friendship with the Americans, had a tract of about thirty thousand acres on the Muskingum where he planted crops, raised cattle, used horses and plows and occasionally "hired white men" to help if he needed extra labor. Loss of land had a real meaning for these tribes, all assertions to the contrary notwithstanding.

On the Ohio frontier intrigue preceded warfare early in the Revolution, as each party sought to know the other's strengths. A Loyalist attempt to gain control of Fort Pitt failed and the pro-British traders and agents were forced to take an oath of neutrality, which they would later denounce when they had reached the safety of Detroit. American success at Fort Pitt, on the other hand, meant that the military commanders there as well as the Indian commissioners appointed by the Continental Congress would seek to gain information from the Indian country.

In the course of the eight years of warfare that followed, the Ohio Indian country was alive with activity. But first, let us not assume that the natives were pawns on a field of peril. They were aware that they must be ever vigilant to protect their lands and lives. Preferably they would have stayed out of the white man's war, but their geographical position made this impossible. Moreover they were encouraged in their resistance to American expansion by the British.

After the loss of Fort Pitt, Detroit fell heir to the supervision of the Indians within the Western division of what was known in British imperial structure as the Northern Indian department. Agents and commissaries who had used Fort Pitt as a headquarters would escape to Detroit and then re-enter the Indian country whenever possible. Thus it was only natural that Detroit would be regarded as an anathema by the Americans while it was a place of refuge to the British and their native supporters. Over the months and years then, numerous parties went out from Detroit to harass the American frontier from Fort Pitt to Kentucky. If you are interested in having this quantified, I can provide you with the information that during the summer of 1777, a total of 32 parties went out, in which there were 386 Indians and 43 non-Indians.

Likewise Fort Pitt became the focus of defense on the northwestern frontier as the Americans sought to protect their borders against British invasion and Indian attacks. As it was the focal point of defense, naturally it drew numbers of hostile parties into its vicinity at certain times and yet at other times it served as a place for conference when the Americans sought to parley with the tribes. Moreover, it would be from Fort Pitt that expeditions into the Indian country would go out and it would be to that post that reports of murder, murder, foul murder would come in from the tribes.

Anti-Indian violence, you see, did not cease when the American Revolution began. You might assume with some degree of reason that once the war began one might no longer need to speak in such terms. Such, alas, was not the case. Not even acts of friendship or flags of truce stopped whites from murdering Indians, as distinguished from casualties in battle. In 1777, the celebrated Cornstalk and several of his followers surrendered themselves as hostages to the Virginians to satisfy demands that without such prisoners no peace and treaty negotiations could begin. While in this state of voluntary confinement, Cornstalk and his companions were assassinated by some Americans. While this seems to have been the act of some outraged militia, rather than an organized death plot against native American leaders, it certainly did not augur well for Indian-white relations.

As if the murders in 1774 and 1777 were not enough, I must relate to you that in 1778 the Delaware chieftain, Captain White Eyes was murdered while in the act of guiding a group of American troops through the wilderness toward some hostile Indian towns. This episode was covered over by a story that he had contracted small pox, the truth being concealed lest it turn the pro-American Delawares away from the Patriot cause. Indeed the act seems all the more pointless in the case of White Eyes since he had been loyal to the Americans, guided whites to safety out of the Indian country, journeyed east for a meeting with the leaders of the Continental Congress, and led his followers in signing what is recognized as the first treaty between the United States and an Indian nation.

Pointless as the killing of White Eyes might seem, since there was no stretch of the imagination which could label him a potential hostile, the most atrocious absurdity occured in 1782 in the My Lai of the American Revolution, when Americans executed almost one hundred of the Christian Delawares. Indeed these cases serve only to confirm the nature of the notions evidently held by the frontiersmen toward the Indians.

Taken in the long view it would appear that the frontier mind had accepted a philosophy of genocide toward the Indians. Eradicate them like so many lice from the universal body of mankind, thought the woodsman, leaving the corpus free of their infestation. For the Indians of the Ohio country, the crisis of the American Revolution brought "all the Noise and Miseries of War, And Blood and Murder [to] stain our Land again."

George Rogers Clark in Kentucky and the Illinois Country, 1772–1778

Dale Van Every

By far the best-known American warrior in the Northwest was George Rogers Clark (1752–1818). Almost the archetype Virginia frontiersman, Clark represents the virtues and liabilities of the advance guard of Americans that crossed the Appalachians. His thirst for land, his disrespect of authority, his impatience, and his audacity, all combined to create one of the most amazing successes of the American war effort—the seizure of the Illinois country and the recapture of Vincennes.

Clark's dominant role in these years is well-illustrated in Dale Van Every's trilogy on the trans-Appalachian frontier from 1753 to 1803. In this extended excerpt from A Company of Heroes, he examines Clark's role in the West in a lucid and compelling manner. He argues that although Clark's conquests were temporary, they did frustrate British attempts to dominate the Northwest. Had Clark not succeeded at Vincennes, writes Van Every, "the massive English-Indian invasion already underway could have been expected to gather a momentum certain to carry every American settlement west of the mountains and to have left to the peace commissioners no basis for discussion of a more favorable western boundary than the original Proclamation Line" of 1763.

Moreover, Van Every contends, Clark's success prompted thousands to stream "westward to lend the support of their numbers to the harassed stations of Kentucky. . . . Soon they were to be subjected to new dangers, even more oppressive than before, but their coming had brought by the narrowest of margins enough added strength to withstand them."

Abridged from Dale Van Every, *A Company of Heroes: The American Frontier, 1775–1783* (New York, 1962), chapters IV, VI, IX, and XII; with permission of William Morrow and Company.

IN THE FAR LONGER and more storied roll of remarkable frontiersmen, there has been not one whose exploits and achievements have ever approached those of George Rogers Clark. For the frontier's ten most dangerous years he was the defender toward whom all turned in every recurrent crisis. It was largely due to his tireless exertions and the extraordinary force of his personality that, during the Revolution, the westernmost frontier was everywhere held in the face of odds which so apparently dictated a retreat.

He came later to the scene than other great leaders of the early frontier. He was born 32 years after Andrew Lewis, 23 years after William Preston and William Fleming, 20 years after Washington, and 10 years after James Robertson and William Christian. But once he had appeared he lost little time making his presence felt. At twenty he was descending the Ohio by canoe, exploring shores notoriously perilous to all white men other than a few Indian-tolerated traders. He was surveying in Kentucky while the stockade poles of Harrodsburg and Boonesborough were just beginning to rise. At the outbreak of the Revolution, leadership was thrust upon him by the handful of Kentucky settlers the defense of whose four weak and scattered stations seemed beyond the range of human capacities. He conducted that defense so aggressively that he was soon embarking upon the only successful invasion of enemy territory achieved by American forces during the Revolution. In six wilderness campaigns—a form of warfare demonstrated during the preceding century and a half of border conflict to be the most difficult and precarious of all military undertakings— he was never surprised, never discomfited. Again and again he snatched victory when by every circumstance defeat appeared foreordained. Lafayette, with ample opportunity to judge, rated him as second only to Washington among American commanders. Certainly no one after Washington served the Revolutionary cause with more enduring effect. His unflagging defense of Kentucky, his inspired trans-Ohio conquests, and his persistent demoralization of the western Indians gave unanticipated substance to American postwar claims to the west. The Mississippi boundary, conceded at the peace table, seems to us now an English surrender somewhat less fantastic than it was then universally considered, because of his efforts. All this he achieved before he was thirty.

In the frontiersman, Clark, there appeared fully developed every quality which most clearly identified him as a completely representative frontiersman. In the depths of the wilderness he was as much in his element as any Indian or long hunter. He was a master of those accomplishments, skills, and crafts most valued on the frontier. In physique, strength, and endurance he had few equals and in the common frontier predisposition to violence, belligerence, and reckless daring he had none. He was able to command the devotion of his normally recalcitrant and insubordinate followers by a continuing demonstration that whether in the woods, on the river, on the march, or in forest battle he was more ready than any other man for every wilderness test. High among the fashions in which he appealed to them was the degree to which he shared their contempt for consequences, moral as well as physical, and their volcanic impatience with every restraint, notably that of governmental authority. Perhaps strongest of all his appeals to them was that he shared the nearly universal frontier inclination, in whatever situation, to look first for personal advantage, an inclination that reached its apogee in an insatiable hunger for land, including land already claimed by another settler, previously granted to a land company, or repeatedly pronounced Indian by treaties.

Yet absolute self-reliance, the key virtue in the frontier character, could reach an extreme from which flowed more weakness than strength. Clark did not escape this extravagance. His impatience of restraint led him during his most brilliant campaigns to keep official accounts so heedlessly that his personal affairs never recovered from the disorder; his scorn of authority, particularly the plodding decisions of the central government, led him to independent enterprises which bordered on treason; and, eventually, frustrations of his freedom of action led him to alcoholic excesses which undermined his health. But these were weaknesses that became manifest later. During the Revolution, when the fate of his country and of his countrymen on the frontier rested so heavily upon him, he rose unfailingly to every demand.

His preparation as a child and boy to meet these demands

upon his young manhood could not have been more effective had it been consciously planned with that end in view. He was born November 19, 1752, in a cabin on the banks of the Rivanna River on what was then tidewater Virginia's western frontier.

He was not, however, destined to grow up among the deprivations and limitations of life in a frontier cabin. When he was five, the family moved east again to a small plantation in Caroline County inherited from an uncle. Here, though he could continue to satisfy a boy's natural appetite for riding, hunting, and fishing, he could also be subjected to a certain amount of schooling. This last was imperative since in the years ahead there would be need to prove himself more than the superlative woodsman. There would be the need also to handle the staff work of distant commands, to address assemblies, to correspond with governors, to draft dispatches announcing the conquest of provinces.

Undoubtedly, however, the greatest influence bearing upon his development was family associations. From the year of his first departure from home, his letters were filled with evidences of his devotion to those with whom he had been in such close communion until then. There is some justice in Clark's conviction that he came of most superior stock. The closely knit Clark-Rogers clan formed a loyal, vigorous, and enterprising unit which admitted dependence only on each other. His parents were individualists who impressed all who knew them by their force and character, and all of his brothers were distinguished by their readiness for public responsibilities. . . .

In common with every Virginian familiar with the frontier all the members of the Clark family were intensely interested in western lands. George Rogers Clark, the second son of John and Ann, was delegated to be the clan's scout and forerunner in the search for the best available. The spring before he was twenty he set out. He was now six feet tall, straight, graceful, handsome, with sinews like whipcord, a thatch of red hair, and sparkling black eyes. No young man about to become a frontier hero could more perfectly have looked the part.

He crossed the mountains by the route made memorable by Nemacolin, Gist, Washington, and Braddock, by the repeated ebb and flow of Indian invasion, and more recently by the astounding post-Stanwix surge of westbound settlers toward the upper Ohio. By that spring of 1772 thousands had swarmed over the mountains, grasping at land to which none could hope to gain legal title. All of it was blanketed by the prior claims of immense land companies which were in the course of being blessed by cabinet sanction. Moreover, with both Pennsylvania and Virginia claiming jurisdiction over the region, Pennsylvania and Virginia land seekers were almost as ready to fight each other as they were the Indians. . . .

The next two years were marked, even for a man of Clark's inexhaustible energy, by an almost incredible activity. He pushed his inspection of the Ohio 300 miles down river. He blazed his claim to land on Fish Creek, built a cabin, and planted a corn crop. He made repeated trips back over the mountains to Virginia to report to the family on the results of his explorations and once brought his father out to see the Fish Creek claim. . . .

The Fish Creek location, 130 miles down river from Pittsburgh, was far beyond the mountain crestline which for so long had seemed a permanent barrier to any possible further advance of the frontier. But already it seemed too near, too accessible, to be highly prized. Kentucky, waiting at a more glamorous distance, offered rich level land not constricted in narrow mountain valleys, land described by the few who had seen it as more beautiful than any other on earth. . . .

In the spring of 1774 Clark was on the Ohio at the mouth of the Little Kanawha as one of the leaders of a group of some 90 land seekers headed for Kentucky. It was a more or less chance assembly of venturers seeking the safety in numbers in event of a Shawnee attack en route. That same spring James Harrod, with a smaller but similar group, had gained an earlier start and was already well down river on his way to the establishment of Harrodsburg. Informed that the Shawnee appeared at last determined to resist the occupation of Kentucky, Clark's party returned to Wheeling to inquire how they might best serve the white cause. It was his firsthand knowledge of events at this juncture that enabled him later to testify that Michael Cresap had had nothing to do with the atrocious murder of the Logan family and had instead counseled against any aggressive move upon Logan's village. The outrage had in any event made certain that the impending war could no longer be postponed.

Clark was commissioned captain of militia and gained his first military experience with the two expeditions into the Indian country, commanded by Angus McDonald and Lord Dunmore. . . . Among his companions were fellow frontiersmen who had already won or were destined to win some of the greatest names in frontier annals: Daniel Morgan, Simon Kenton, John Floyd, James Wood, Michael Cresap, Joseph Bowman, William Harrod, Thomas Nicholson, Jacob Drennon, Peter Parchment. There was one more of that company of heroes who then was among those most trusted and best liked: Simon Girty.

The outbreak of the Shawnee war had forced every white man to flee from Kentucky and the lower Ohio, but the Shawnee surrender after Point Pleasant reopened the way west. In the spring of 1775 all who had withdrawn rushed back, accompanied by a host of new land seekers. Clark had previously explored the river as far as the Falls and he now turned his attention to the interior of Kentucky. He had been engaged as deputy surveyor by the Ohio Company but his primary purpose was to find land for his family and himself. . . .

Clark took time off from his surveying duties to inspect all of central Kentucky and to visit Harrodsburg, Boonesborough, and Logan's Station in the first weeks of their existence. He was enchanted by the region, as was every other early viewer. . . .

This rich and beautiful land was being claimed by men who had every need for their boundless enthusiasm. No single one of them could feel that he had more than the faintest shadow of a legal right to the possession he was asserting. All had ventured so far and risked so much on the mere assumption that one way or another all would somehow work out well in the end. Most were never to succeed in justifying their hopes. Daniel Boone, for one notable example, was never able finally to establish a permanent legal title to a foot of Kentucky soil, and moved eventually to the Spanish side of the Mississippi. Each of these first Kentucky settlements or projected settlements based such claim as it could cite on a different theory of land rights. Each theory conflicted with provincial and English law and of necessity with that advanced by local rivals. The Ohio Company's claim to the tract Clark was surveying near what was later to become Leestown was based on the hope of gaining a royal grant which had already in fact been specifically disapproved.

The Harrodsburg group of independent Pennsylvania settlers argued that all wild land had previously belonged to no company or state or Indian nation and therefore could become the property of the first man to take, use, and develop it. John Floyd and Benjamin Logan were erecting Logan's Station on land Floyd had surveyed by authority of William Preston, surveyor of Virginia's Fincastle County, whose authority to do so was far from clear inasmuch as by the English law on which his commission depended all settlement was forbidden west of the 1768 readjustment of the Proclamation Line. Boonesborough was being established on land purchased from the Cherokee, whose title to it the Cherokee themselves did not seriously assert, by Richard Henderson's Transylvania Land Company.

All settlements were illegal under English law, but Henderson's claim was additionally clouded by the ringing denunciations of the governors of Virginia and North Carolina. As though this superfluity of disapproval were in itself sufficient reason to prefer it, the other settlers decided to pool all their claims under Henderson's dubious sponsorship. Representatives of all four settlements (Harrodsburg had already sprouted a short-lived offshoot at Boiling Spring), meeting in convention at Boonesborough, asserted their right to govern themselves, declared that fidelity to the King, and petitioned the Continental Congress for recognition as a separate province.

Important as was the question of title validity, the problem it presented was for the future. More immediate concerns were more pressing. None of these 350 men who had swarmed to Kentucky in the spring of 1775 was as yet a bona fide settler. Not one had brought his family with him. All so far were adventurers and gamblers, feverishly blazing trees to mark the boundaries of land that they felt there was a chance they might one day own, living in temporary huts, hunting to gain food from day to day. Essentially they were as much land speculators as were the great land companies. It was a speculation in which they had invested themselves, in lieu of money. The price offered was the risk of survival. The news of Concord and Lexington convinced many that the price was too high. The two major factors bearing on their situation combined to demonstrate how desperate were the odds. These were, first, that the two most belligerent of all Indian nations, the Shawnee and the

Cherokee, were crouched on either flank and, second, that the only connection with possible support from the main frontier was the tenuous threat of a 200-mile-long mountain trail. To the majority of the adventurers it had become clear that their position was obviously indefensible. Most of them bolted. By mid-July not more than fifty men had remained in Kentucky. Again, as in 1774, the reach for the new promised land seemed to have been premature.

Then, in the first week of September, came the startling event that changed the whole aspect. Boone returned from a hasty trip back to his former home on the Clinch. With him were his wife and daughters. They were the first white women to stand on the banks of the Kentucky. With their coming what had been before a temporary camp of itinerant land seekers had made the vital transition to a permanent community of homemakers. Of all Boone's services to the foundation of Kentucky this moment, in which his wife, Jemima, shared, represented his greatest. . . .

That summer of 1775 the inhabitants of every one of the thirteen colonies were being required to make difficult decisions. But there could have been no choice inviting so grievous an ordeal as that made by these men and women inhabiting the farthest wilderness. Clark's personal decision was typical of a self-confidence so complete as to suggest a belief in his own destiny. He had been captivated by his first view of Kentucky. He had promptly decided to make it his home. The next conclusion was obvious. A home demanded defending. His was a temperament that welcomed responsibility. He accepted the survival of Kentucky as his. In any military sense the successful defense of a position so remote and feeble was utterly impossible. Forthwith he began to plan to achieve the impossible. . . .

The few young and unattached men left in Kentucky were continuing to leave that late summer of 1775. Apprehension of Indian descents upon the weak and isolated settlements was not alone responsible. Henderson's Transylvania Company, maintaining that the Cherokee purchase gave it claim to the whole region, was raising the price of land. Men who had come so far and risked so much were not content to contemplate the payment here of the same quitrents that might have been expected east of the mountains.

Clark was one of the young men leaving Kentucky that fall, but early the next spring he was back. . . . During the winter in Virginia he had given much sober thought to the Kentucky problem and had been struck by the mixed opinions among influential Virginians with regard to the legitimacy of Henderson's operations. As a result of his thinking he had brought with him to Kentucky a fully considered, clear-cut program. His principal proposal was that conversations be opened with Virginia to explore the possibility of some form of political link between Williamsburg and Harrodsburg. Most of the settlers would have preferred to remain free, not only of the Transylvania Company but of any of the three nearer provinces from which practically all had come. But the circumstances of the growing Indian threat indicated a positive need for some kind of support from east of the mountains. Even that absolute necessity, gunpowder, was already in critical short supply. A population required to live largely by hunting spent powder sparingly even if steadily, but with war the need must increase tremendously. The first Indian attack on a stockade would oblige the defenders to use more in an hour than they might otherwise use in a year. The settlers were prepared, therefore, to give Clark an attentive hearing. In angling for their approval of his plan he could dangle a double bait. In addition to the possibility of some military support there was the possibility of Virginia sympathy with the settlers' resistance to Henderson's land exactions. Most of his fellow Kentuckians began soon to regard this Virginia connection as probably the least of the several evils with which they were confronted.

Meeting in convention at Harrodsburg June 6, 1776, the settlers in their impatience failed to leave the room for negotiation that Clark had advised. Instead, they impetuously elected him and John Gabriel Jones, a newly arrived young attorney, Kentucky's delegates to the Virginia assembly with instructions to proceed to Williamsburg and demand their seats. This application for acceptance as a Virginia county was in conformance with the process by which for generations newly settled counties had progressively been organized along Virginia's western border on the Atlantic side of the mountains. But Kentucky's distance, isolation, and disputed territorial status made the overture a long and important step toward future acceptance on a broader scale of the most consequential of all American governmental principles, the doctrine that new territories in the west were free to seek admission as new and equal members of the existing union of states.

Setting out over the notoriously difficult Wilderness Road, which for the next twenty years was to remain the same narrow pack trail climbing a succession of forested, rockbound ridges beyond each of which it dropped into another cane-choked gorge, the two candidates rode hard in the hope of reaching Williamsburg before the assembly's scheduled summer adjournment. This was Clark's first experience with the land route connecting Virginia and Kentucky and, as with every undertaking of his extravagantly active career, it was an eventful one. . . .

Governor Patrick Henry was ill at his home in Hanover. From his bed he listened to Clark's account of conditions in Kentucky. . . . In 1775, the great issue confronting the American people was whether or not their initial insistence upon comparative freedom of action was to develop into that opportunity freely to express their native genius represented by total independence. Pursuit of this objective raised at once a second issue. Would the new nation prove to have seized in time the opportunity to gain west of the mountains the room for unlimited growth required *fully* to express that same native genius?

Many hundreds of thousands of Americans were deeply and desperately conscious of the first issue; all but a few were ignorant of or indifferent to the second. The inclination of their national leaders became therefore of vital importance. Upon their judgment, whether informed or not, depended to a large degree the new nation's inheriting a chance to grow along with the chance to live. Among these national leaders those who held three posts were in a position during the Revolution to exert the most critical influence: the commander in chief of the continental armies, who must determine the use made of the limited military force available; the ambassador to the court of France, the Revolution's prospective ally; and the governor of Virginia, the province with the longest and most exposed frontier. The first of these required to grapple with the problem was Patrick Henry, Virginia's first Revolutionary governor. Here again, as so often in our country's early history, sheer providence appeared to have taken a hand. He had been prepared to understand the nature of the problem by a phase of his personal experience in no way connected with his rise to political power.

He was a self-educated lawyer who had represented so many humble clients that their votes could become more important to him than their fees. Few of the causes he had represented had enjoyed the favor of Virginia's ruling oligarchy of great land-owners. He had been a spokesman for the landless. He had been a flagrant rebel while most of his fellow Patriots were still fumbling with petitions and remonstrances. The arenas in which he had battled had been provided by the courtroom, the statehouse, and the platforms. Yet this radical eastern lawyer, all of whose foreground activities were connected with popular movements and class struggles in the east, was himself a great proprietor in the west. From the moment he first began to accumulate some capital and more political influence he had invested both in western lands. He had been associated with Dr. Thomas Walker, founder of the Loyal Company and first explorer of Kentucky, in his plans for opening to settlement hundreds of thousands of acres on Virginia's southwest frontier, and with William Fleming, hero of Point Pleasant, in his 1767 proposal to establish a colony at the mouth of the Ohio. His own land agent was Joseph Martin, already notable as the founder of the first station in Powell Valley. Though in 1775 he drove Dunmore, the last royal governor, from Virginia, he had only the year before warmly approved of Dunmore's expansionist activities. The Kentucky surveyors had taken the same care to designate superior tracts for him that they had for Washington. While remaining an easterner, he had identified himself with the westward movement. These western sympathies had been strengthened by family ties. His sister Anne married William Christian, the noted frontier colonel who commanded a regiment in the Point Pleasant campaign, and his sister Elizabeth married William Campbell, commander at King's Mountain, and then William Russell, the Clinch River colonizer. His long, if vicarious, experience with the frontier had therefore well prepared him to listen with sympathy and understanding to Clark's plan to save Kentucky.

He sent Clark on to the council at Williamsburg with his hearty endorsement. The council was less sympathetic. . . . Most Virginians had no western land interests and were inclined to regard the distant Kentucky settlements as a dangerous liability certain to interfere with Virginia's nearer and far more important commitments in the expanding war. But there was some important support for the Kentucky petition. . . . Patrick Henry was led by his general democratic principles plus his belief in the west's future to take a firm stand in favor of Kentucky's admission. The compelling persuasion, however, was Clark's central and unanswerable argument that the maintenance of the Kentucky settlements provided a buffer which, if abandoned, would open the way to more direct Indian assaults on Virginia's present frontiers. On December 7, 1776, the assembly voted to admit Kentucky as a Virginia county.

Hurrying westward, Clark met Jones at Pittsburgh. The powder was still there. Clark's letter having miscarried, the Kentuckians had naturally failed to send for it. He and Jones were therefore faced with the task of delivery. Other frontier news awaited them. The major Ohio Indian nations were still professing their former uneasy neutrality. But there were many portents that the mounting tension was soon to break. The English supply line was again open. Colonel John Butler was at Niagara assembling Tory refugees soon to be organized into a regiment of partisans widely and terribly known as Butler's Rangers. Lieutenant Governor Henry Hamilton, commanding at Detroit, was stocking his magazines with the food and ammunition required if the western Indians were to take an organized part in the general English war effort. Meanwhile, repeated incidents had kept the upper Ohio frontier in a state of concern at times bordering on panic. Occasional stray parties of Indians, too impatiently vindictive to wait for the planned campaigns of the future, were committing minor mischief calculated to provoke both sides to greater excesses. A number of whites had been killed or taken on the Ohio and in Kentucky. . . .

With his amazing talent for attracting volunteers no matter how desperate the venture, Clark found seven men willing to help man the little boat carrying the cargo of powder upon which the fate of Kentucky depended. The existence and importance of the powder supply were no secret on the Indian side of the frontier. Little that happened at Pittsburgh had escaped the attention either of the swarms of resident Tory spies or of the throngs of Indian delegates flocking there for the recurrent peace conferences. . . .

But in his 400-mile dash down the Ohio Clark managed to evade ambush and elude pursuit. At the mouth of Limestone Creek, now Maysville but then uninhabited though already the Ohio River gateway to Kentucky, he buried the powder in five different spots rather than attempt to pack it inland. Its weight was too great and its value too precious to be carried and protected by so few men with the Indians in such close and active pursuit. He went on down river a few miles, set the boat adrift further to mystify the pursuers, and started overland for Harrodsburg to get help.

Near McClelland's Station he left Jones and five of his exhausted men behind and pressed on toward Harrodsburg with the two most able to travel. Returning to McClelland's with James Harrod and a strong party he was met by heartbreaking tidings. After his departure, John Todd, one of the most prominent of Kentucky's first settlers, had appeared with a party of eight surveyors and had persuaded Jones to guide him to the hiding place of the powder instead of waiting for help from Harrodsburg. Proceeding along the great buffalo trace leading to the mouth of the Limestone, they had on Christmas Day encountered and been overwhelmed by . . . Indians. Of the little party of ten Jones and William Graden had been killed and four others taken captive. In Jones' short wilderness career he had experienced enough action and excitement to crowd a long and adventurous lifetime, but the gallant young attorney had so soon come to the end of it.

Harrod, fearing for his station, rushed back to defend it. Clark remained to help hold McClelland's which the Indians promptly and furiously attacked. . . . It was a battle so grueling as to lead both antagonists to recognize defeat. The Indians failed to take the fort and withdrew. The defenders, anticipating stronger attacks to come, decided to abandon the station and add their remaining manpower to the defenses of Harrodsburg.

Harrod had meanwhile been informed by his scouts that Harrodsburg was not in immediate danger. Possession of the gunpowder was of such incomparable importance that in any event to secure it was considered worth any hazard. Leading a party of 30 determined men, Harrod made for the Limestone by a circuitous route, encountered no Indians, found the five caches of gunpowder undisturbed, and successfully returned with the great prize to Harrodsburg on January 2, 1777.

The settlements in Kentucky had by now been reduced to two stations, Harrodsburg and Boonesborough. But few as they were, the defenders of Kentucky could now face the future with new confidence. Thanks to Clark's initiative they had won an enormous advantage which formerly they had lacked. They were armed. . . .

On March 5, 1777, Clark held the first muster of Kentucky militia. The next day the first two settlers were killed in the opening action of the Indian invasion which continued throughout the summer to threaten Kentucky with extinction. Yet, in the midst of all his desperate concern with keeping the three little settlements alive, he was looking forward not so much to making a counterattack as to launching a counterconquest. On April 3rd he made his first considered move toward this objective by dispatching two young hunters, Samuel Moore and Benjamin Linn, as spies instructed to bring him a report on the state of enemy defenses in the Illinois. Already fixed in his mind was the contemplation of a campaign destined to affect the future of his country more decisively than any other of the Revolution excepting only Saratoga and Yorktown. He was then twenty-four.

It was not chance or accident that had drawn his attention to the Illinois. No region in the west has ever or for so long held so glittering a place in frontier imagination. The mystery of distance had gilded its glamour. Illinois had been a familiar word long before the name Kentucky had ever been mentioned. . . . Traders had envisaged immense profits in the Illinois. Land companies had competed for preferment there. George Washington, Benjamin Franklin, and Patrick Henry had been actively interested in schemes for establishing colonies there. George Croghan, the frontier magnate, George Morgan, the present American Indian agent, and William Murray, the last English commandant at Fort Pitt, had devoted years to efforts to gain commercial advantage there. Every individual frontier land seeker had dreamed of the possibility of establishing himself there.

Clark, himself a confirmed land seeker, shared this general interest in Illinois opportunities, but his more immediate concern was with the strategic bearing of the Illinois on the defense of Kentucky. The French towns of Kaskaskia, Cahokia, and Prairie du Rocher were centers of influence over a large Indian population. Were the Illinois Indians to be persuaded by the English to join the Ohio Indians in their attacks on the American frontier, then Kentucky was surely doomed. On the other hand, a counterstroke in time might forestall this development and even turn the tables of military advantage. This was the essence of his plan.

His spies returned on June 22nd, having aroused no suspicion by their visit. Footloose American frontiersmen ranged so widely that they excited little surprise wherever they chanced to appear. Neither Moore nor Linn nor any of Clark's fellow Kentuckians had any idea as yet of what was in his mind. Had they guessed they would have thought him mad. That summer there seemed too few defenders to hold Kentucky. Any thought of invading the faraway Illinois could only have been considered preposterous. The spies' report made continued secrecy the more imperative. The one chance of success for the project lay in no hint of warning being allowed to reach Hamilton in Detroit, for the young hunters had discovered the Illinois to be for the moment undefended by the English. . . . The Illinois now depended for defense upon local French militia under the command of Philippe de Rocheblave, a former French officer now in the English service. With receipt of his spies' report Clark's notion became at once a firm intention. If he moved with sufficient stealth and speed, he foresaw the possibility of seizing the whole territory with an expedition numbering as few as 500 sufficiently resolute men. As was soon to become evident, he was determined to make the attempt with no matter how few.

Clark's responsibility for the defense of Kentucky held him there through the summer and into the fall. Then, as the second necessary step in the advancement of his great design, on October 1st he started for Virginia. . . .

Governor Patrick Henry had been given an outline of Clark's proposal in a preliminary letter. He had been nonplussed by the obvious hazards and difficulties involved. But he was converted by Clark's personal presentation of his plan and soon became as enthusiastic as he had formerly been dubious. Henry was naturally attracted by the prospect of striking so shrewd and unexpected a blow against the enemy, and his lifelong interest in western lands had prepared him to recognize the future value of establishing a solid American claim to the territory. There was still the same need to maintain complete secrecy. Only a very narrow circle of Virginia's most influential leaders, such as Thomas Jefferson and George Mason, were informed of what was afoot. All approved. Clark was commissioned lieutenant colonel, authorized to raise seven 50-man companies of militia by calling for volunteers in any county, and granted £ 1200 to meet the expedition's incidental expenses. His public orders directed him to devote this special force to the defense of Kentucky. His secret orders directed him to proceed with it against Kaskaskia.

Clark now had that freedom of action of which he so often was to prove abundantly able to take advantage. According to his carefully considered plan, he was to raise a portion of his force on the upper Ohio frontier and then, after descending the Ohio, to be joined at the mouth of the Kentucky by other contingents coming overland from the Holston and Kentucky. But when he arrived at Redstone on February 1, 1778, he was at once confronted by unforeseen recruiting difficulties. The depredations of 1777, the violence of the Shawnee hostility aroused by Cornstalk's murder, and the Squaw Campaign fiasco had combined to leave the frontier in no mood for distant ventures. The Pennsylvania-Virginia dispute made Pennsylvanians disinclined to support any Virginia enterprise and Virginians reluctant to offer the advantage of their absence to their Pennsylvania rivals. Widespread apprehension of Tory plots, highlighted in March by the flight of Alexander McKee, Matthew Elliott, and Simon Girty to the Indian country, persuaded many others of the need to stand guard at home. Had Clark been in a position to reveal his real intentions, he might have met with a more ready response. But not many were so eager to share the bleak and unrewarding trials of Kentucky's defense. People on the upper Ohio who had discovered the difficulty of holding a border as populous as their own were inclined to feel settlements as weak, exposed, and isolated as Kentucky's were better abandoned, thus sparing a drain on the resources needed to defend the main frontier.

Nevertheless, by persistent persuasion and unflagging spirit, with valuable recruiting help from William Harrod and boats and supplies furnished by Hand, Clark rounded up 150 volunteers and was able to sail from Redstone on May 12th. With him went 20 families of settlers who may only be regarded as truly indomitable. . . .

At Fort Randolph, Clark's fleet of barges was joined by others commanded by Captain James O'Hara, also on his way down river. For Clark's, though by far the most important, was only one of three American expeditions proceeding westward that year. On January 10th, Captain James Willing, with 27 men in a small armed galley, had left Pittsburgh, dispatched by authority of Congress to raid the English posts and presumably Tory settlements on the lower Mississippi. O'Hara was on his way to support Willing who had meanwhile been enjoying successes in the Natchez area which the English bitterly described as more piratical than military. In June, the third expedition set out under the command of Colonel David Rogers who had been instructed by Virginia to establish commercial and other relations between Virginia and the Spanish authorities in New Orleans and then to return with a shipment of munitions.

Clark changed his rendezvous with the overland forces from the mouth of the Kentucky to the Falls of the Ohio, the latter being on a more natural route between the Kentucky settlements and the Illinois. There he pitched his camp on Corn Island, a seven-acre islet just above the rapids, selecting the midriver site as one from which desertions must prove more difficult as well as one more defensible by the 20 settlers' families who were to be left here. The settlers promptly began to plant their corn and to build a blockhouse. . . .

Clark's situation had become one to dismay any commander. Judged by every military standard he was confronted by a totally unacceptable risk. He had based his original plan on the assumption that a force of 500 men was a minimum necessity. In Virginia the state's limited resources had required a reduction to 350. After recruiting failures and desertions he now had but 178. His so-called army of invasion would be outnumbered 5 to 1 by the resident militia of the region it was presuming to invade, and 25 to 1 by the surrounding Indians it was presumed to impress. Nevertheless, he determined to keep on. . . .

On June 26th Clark embarked upon the last lap of his memorable venture. The final issue of his year-long struggle was now immediately before him. As the boats bounced through the rough water of the rapids, the day was darkened by a total eclipse of the sun. The timing of the phenomenon excited various reactions among men who were accustomed to believe in signs and wonders and, above all, in luck. Some were much disturbed. Clark, always on the alert to take advantage of any opportunity to raise the spirits of all around him, proclaimed it a certain portent of the imminence of great events. His confidence in the omen soon appeared justified. Rowing night and day, the 425 miles to the mouth of the Tennessee were made in four days without mishap.

More luck ensued. A boatload of American buffalo hunters was captured. They were wanderers who had been in Kaskaskia eight days before. Their information was of inestimable value, for Clark had had no word of conditions in the Illinois since the return of his spies twelve months before. They said the region's sole defense still consisted of local French militiamen who remained unaware that an American invasion was in immediate prospect. They also said, however, that there was no chance that they would readily accept or even tolerate an American invasion but that, on the contrary, they were determined to resist with all their strength, inasmuch as they were convinced that all Americans, and particularly the Virginians, were barbarians. With his usual immediate impulse to see in each discovery of new difficulty a revelation of new advantage, Clark decided that "no part of their information pleased me more than that the Inhabitants viewed us as more savage than their Neighbors the Indians." The hunters supported the reliability of their report by readily volunteering to accompany the expedition.

Even better luck immediately followed. The flotilla was overtaken by a lone man in a canoe. He was William Linn who had remained at Corn Island with his family to help his fellow settlers hold the new post there. With him he had a letter for Clark from Colonel John Campbell in Pittsburgh, informing him that France had come to the aid of the American Revolution. The letter had arrived the day after Clark had left the Falls and, realizing its supreme importance, Linn had undertaken the extraordinary risk of coming on with the message. Clark could now hope that, when the Illinois French learned that their mother country had declared war on England, they might the more easily be persuaded to forsake their half-hearted attachment to their present English rulers.

He left his boats near the ruins of Fort Massac, the French post abandoned by them in 1758 and never occupied by the English. He proposed to march the last 125 miles overland through the wilderness. To have continued along the normal water route by way of the Mississippi would have denied him the complete surprise upon which all still depended. . . . They had been unable to bring enough food to last. The final two days they marched hungry. At dusk on July 4th, 1778, the starving and exhausted Americans stood in the edge of the Kaskaskia clearings. [*See* Map 3.]

The surprise was total. After so long and agonizing an effort, the triumph when it came was complete and gained without the firing of a shot. In the night the invaders swooped silently upon the town in two divisions. The sleeping inhabitants were restrained within their houses. The gates of the fort were open and unguarded. The first Rocheblave knew of the attack was upon being awakened in his bed by Simon Kenton tapping him on the shoulder. It took a little time to get the commandant dressed and out on the parade ground to deliver in person his formal surrender for his summoners were routed from the bed chamber by Madame Rocheblave's shrewish cries of outraged modesty.

At daybreak the inhabitants peered fearfully from their doors and windows at the ragged, bearded, uncouth intruders patrolling their streets. Clark had established guard lines around the town to prevent the dispatch of messengers to summon assistance or spread the alarm and had instituted a search for and a confiscation of weapons. The strain and the suspense continued. Finally the priest, Father Pierre Gibault, approached Clark to beg for clemency. Having subjected the townspeople to hours of terror, Clark was suddenly overflowing with friendliness. He was astonished by the good father's alarm. The inhabitants' persons, property, and religion would of course be protected. The Americans had come not as enemies but as friends, saviors, and allies. He broke the sensational news that France had joined the United States in the war with England. The sudden relief from their fears swept the impressionable and volatile population to the other extreme of rejoicing. They rushed to the church to give thanks, danced in the streets, and took the barbarous invaders to their bosoms. Most of them readily subscribed to the oath of allegiance demanded by Clark. Cahokia fell as painlessly. The better part of the Illinois had been delivered into his hands literally for the asking.

So much had been achieved, but if possession were to be held, Vincennes, 180 miles away on the lower Wabash, a principal control post on the great portage route connecting the Mississippi with Detroit, the Lakes, and the St. Lawrence, must be secured. Simon Kenton with two companions was dispatched to spy out the situation there. He sent back word that Vincennes likewise had no English garrison. The English high command had entertained no thought that there could be the faintest possibility that the harassed American frontier could be capable of any sort of a counterstroke. Father Gibault, by now an energetic American partisan, rushed to Vincennes to persuade the French militia and population there also to change sides. With a readiness as cheerful as that shown by Kaskaskia and Cahokia, a celerity which was becoming suspicious, they agreed. Leonard Helm with a single platoon was dispatched to take possession of Vincennes. . . .

Clark's was a meager force indeed with which to hope to maintain control over an area 600 miles from the slight help he could expect from Kentucky, 1000 miles from his nearest significant source of military support in Virginia, and 1300 miles from his only available source of supplies in New Orleans. Yet it was with the backing of only these 100 men scattered among the garrisons of four towns that he was undertaking to influence the inclination toward war or peace of surrounding Indian nations capable of placing 5750 warriors in the field, according to Croghan's authoritative Indian census of 1765.

He put up a bold front. He assured his already uneasy new French friends that they need feel no concern for the apparent weakness of his forces. His major army, he said, was at the Falls of the Ohio where it could be called upon whenever necessary. And he summoned the Indians to a general peace conference with all the insolence of a conqueror absolutely certain of his superiority. . . .

The Indians of the region had been astounded by the sudden appearance of armed Americans in the Illinois. This was country into which the English army at the peak of its power, after having so overwhelmingly manifested its might during the French War, had nevertheless been unable to penetrate during Pontiac's War. Only three years before there had been no Virginians within a thousand miles. Now they were here in the very heart of the Indian country. Indians swarmed to the proposed conference, indignant, suspicious, antagonistic, but burning with curiosity to see for themselves what manner of men these interloping strangers really were.

The Indians of the immediate Illinois area did not represent a serious threat. They had been weakened by the disease, indolence, and dissipation connected with their long association with their French neighbors, their tribal disciplines had been impaired by intermarriage with the French and with the Santo Domingo Negroes introduced in Mississippi Bubble days, and their military power had never recovered from the stresses of the Iroquois invasions of 1680 and 1684. But among the nations occupying the region's perimeter, the Miami, Ottawa, Potawatomi, Chippewa, Ojibwa, Kickapoo, Winnebago, Sauk, Fox, were included some of the most belligerent and dangerous on the continent. The number of their delegates to the conference at Cahokia far exceeded the number of Clark's soldiers. . . .

Themselves traditional virtuosos of eloquence and oratory, Indians were notoriously impressionable in council and not even Johnson or Croghan had been equipped with a presence and personality capable of more forcibly impressing them. The great achievement of Clark's 1778 campaign was not the uncontested occupation of the Illinois, but his success in neutralizing so considerable a segment of the Indian military power upon which English strategy had depended. The whole English program for the full employment of Indians against the American frontier was for months thrown off balance and off schedule.

As winter came on Clark could well feel a surge of satisfaction. He had apparently succeeded in all he had set out to achieve. Through the patriotic co-operation of the American merchant, Oliver Pollock, his New Orleans supply line was functioning. Though he had not yet heard from Virginia, he could be confident his services were appreciated by his own people. He had been informed of the projected advance of

General Lachlan McIntosh from Pittsburgh and, as Christmas approached, he expected to hear any day of the fall of Detroit. . . .

Then the Illinois' midwinter merrymaking was disrupted by a thunderbolt. Instead of word of new American victories there burst upon the celebrants the worst of all possible news. Far from having been contained by McIntosh, Hamilton, breathing wrath and vengeance, was making a sudden advance upon the Illinois with an army of 600 regulars, militia, and Indians. He had already recaptured Vincennes, and advance parties of his counter-invasion force were in the woods within three miles of Kaskaskia.

The real battle for the Illinois was only now beginning. . . .

No commander could have been animated by higher hopes, firmer determination, or more ambitious plans than Hamilton when he set out from Detroit on October 7, 1778. He contemplated no less than the conquest of the third of a continent. His recent concern for the safety of Detroit had been relieved by the construction of a new and stronger fort and the arrival of reinforcements under Captain Henry Bird, a fellow regular officer whose experience with frontier warfare had been broadened at Oriskany. Detailed and accurate intelligence from Hamilton's many agents in the Pittsburgh area had made it clear that there was no longer anything to fear from McIntosh's stumbling advance into the edge of the Indian country. He had long chafed under the conditions of his Detroit command which had condemned him to the irritating supervision of an irresponsible French population and the inglorious organization of Indian raiding parties. Before him now there loomed instead the dramatic opportunity to achieve a personal triumph reminiscent of a Clive's empire-building feats. His immediate objective was the reconquest of the Illinois and the establishment of forts to control the mouths of the Ohio and Missouri, and as a consequence the trade and navigation of the entire Mississippi. But his attention was fixed upon a wider vista. He had sent messages to Stuart urging him to raise the southern Indians to act in conjunction with the thousands of northern Indians already being rallied to follow his own advance across the Ohio. He foresaw as his campaign developed, support from English troops at Pensacola. On his horizon gleamed the prospect of restoring the whole vast region west of the mountains to English dominion.

With him in the boats and canoes in which he embarked at Detroit were 60 English regulars, 115 French militia, and 60 Indians. This was but the advance guard of the army that was soon to be, but he had no occasion to doubt that it was ample for his preliminary purpose, the reconquest of the Illinois. As he progressed from one Indian town to the next along the main water route connecting Lake Erie with the Wabash, he could be sure that he would be joined by hundreds of Indians. When in the spring he resumed his advance from his base in the Illinois, many more wild legions already in the process of enlistment among nations as distant as the fabled Sioux would swarm to augment his invading horde.

At the outset all proceeded as he had foreseen except the weather. Indians, always eager to add strength to strength, joined him at each town until his force exceeded 600. The weather, however, remained unprecedently bad. . . . He had expected to reach Kaskaskia by late November. Instead, his floundering and frost-bitten army was 71 struggling days making the 600 miles between Detroit and Vincennes even though he had kept driving his men on in the face of whatever hardship and difficulty. The magnitude of the design upon which he had embarked had made no effort seem to him too painful.

His final approach to Vincennes was a soldierly masterpiece in which he provided for every contingency which could occur to a commander. He surprised and captured the scout patrols sent out by Captain Leonard Helm, the American commander. He threw out a net of his own patrols to make certain Helm could not get off a warning to Kaskaskia or Kentucky. He dispatched stronger patrols to watch the mouths of the Wabash and the Tennessee. . . .

Hamilton's entrance into Vincennes, December 17, 1778, was unopposed. The French population accepted the return of the English as cheerfully as they had recently accepted the intrusion of the Americans. The French militia as readily turned their coats again. Deserted by his French allies, Helm's garrison had dwindled to one American and he had no alternative to the surrender of the fort on demand. . . .

The continuing heavy rains had flooded the valley of the Wabash for tens of miles around the town. Surveying the preposterous terrain with the judgment of a professional soldier, Hamilton came to what seemed to him the only possible conclusion: To attempt this late in the winter to continue his advance to Kaskaskia was totally inadvisable; no army could conceivably make such a march. Nothing, in any event, was to be lost by a pause at Vincennes until the weather improved. Clark was too remote to receive American reinforcement in the meantime, while the delay synchronized with Hamilton's overall plan. The great rendezvous of his northern Indians with Stuart's southern Indians on the Tennessee was not scheduled until spring. He could easily deal with Clark and Kaskaskia en route to it with the overwhelming northern force he would then have at his disposal.

In Kaskaskia, Clark was estimating the bearing upon his situation of the same conditions. He had heard through his French agents of Hamilton's departure from Detroit, but had at first assumed he must be moving to resist McIntosh. Late in December he learned through the apprehension of an English spy in Cahokia that McIntosh had turned back long before he had posed any slightest threat to Detroit. This unwelcome revelation raised at once the suspicion that Hamilton might instead be advancing upon the Illinois. Clark had had no word from Vincennes for weeks, suggesting the possibility that it could already have fallen. The same practical considerations that had so impressed Hamilton led him, however, to doubt any threat of an immediate attack on Kaskaskia. The excessively inclement weather, the long-recognized difficulty of persuading Indians to campaign in midwinter, the flooding of every stream in the intervening 200 miles of wilderness, all indicated that even were Hamilton at Vincennes he would hold there. Nevertheless, Clark ordered out scouts to watch every trail to the east. . . .

It was now obvious that Hamilton was in possession of Vincennes. But his strength or intentions remained an enigma. Clark dispatched new messengers and spies toward Vincennes.

Not one returned. The suspense continued for weeks. Finally, on January 29th, it was ended by Francis Vigo's appearance at Kaskaskia. Vigo was an Italian trader of St. Louis who had been captured by one of Hamilton's patrols near Vincennes. After an interrogation Hamilton had released him on his undertaking to transmit no information to Kaskaskia. . . . Vigo's information was complete, detailed, and accurate. He said that Hamilton had taken Vincennes with an army of 600 soldiers and Indians, that to conserve his supplies he had returned most of his Detroit militia to winter in Detroit, that most of the Indians who had not been released for their winter hunting had been dispatched on various raids, that he was holding Fort Sackville with a garrison of 80 soldiers supported by artillery, that to his reassembling army in the spring were to be added not only many more hundreds of Indians from the north but 500 from the south, and that he proposed to resume his advance as early in the spring as weather permitted.

The suspense had ended but very much for the worse. To Hamilton's coming invasion from so near a base with so overwhelming a force there could be no adequate resistance. It was already too late to hope for any assistance from faraway Virginia, from which Clark had had no word since he had crossed the mountains more than a year before. More than the Illinois must fall. Kentucky, too, was doomed; possibly even the Pittsburgh area. To Clark the situation was so desperate that all was very simple. Since to wait for Hamilton to reassemble his main army in the spring was to invite certain destruction, the one alternative was to attack him at once. The chance that with his fort surrounded by miles of seemingly impassable flood water Hamilton might be off guard offered a possible opportunity for surprise which provided the project's sole hope of success. As Clark so clearly put it in his letter to George Mason: "I saw the only possibility of our maintaining the Country was to take advantage of his present weakness, perhaps we might be fortunate." He consulted his officers. All stoutly agreed.

His campaign plan contemplated an attack by water as well as by land. He armed a large oared barge with 2 cannon and 4 swivels, manned her with a crew of 40 under the command of his cousin, Lieutenant John Rogers, and named the so hastily commissioned warship *Willing*. The galley was to sail by way of

the Mississippi, the Ohio, and the Wabash and, upon approaching Vincennes, to cooperate with his land force in any
way that then seemed indicated.

After manning the galley, there remained to Clark fewer
than 90 Americans for his overland expedition. There were
manifestly too few for the venture, even for a commander of
Clark's temerity, and he was driven to the expedient of calling
for French volunteers. . . .

Clark had pressed his preparations so vigorously that on the
seventh day after receipt of Vigo's report on Hamilton he had
equipped and dispatched his navy and was marching eastward
from Kaskaskia at the head of his army. Various accounts have
estimated his force at as few as 130, but according to the
testimony of both Clark and his second in command, Joseph
Bowman, it numbered 170. Roughly half were hard-bitten
American frontiersmen most of whom had been with him since
passage of the Ohio rapids, but the other half were so far
untried French volunteers. The moccasined and leather-
shirted column, winding in single file off into the storm-beaten
wilderness, was less an army than a band of adventurers whose
one element of military cohesion was their instinctive reliance
upon a great commander. [See Map 3.]

The icy rains continued. All the lower Illinois was a wind-
whipped morass. They waded in water that was by turns ankle
deep, knee deep, and waist deep. At night they built scaffolds
upon which to place their baggage and especially their scant
reserve store of powder, while they slept on the ground in the
slush and mud. During the first week they passed among herds
of buffalo, providing them with at least the one comfort of all
the meat that they could eat in camp at the end of each
exhausting day. But after that there was only an occasional
raccoon or opossum marooned by the rising flood water. Once
they brought down a fox that had most unnaturally taken
refuge in a tree. It clearly was weather fit for neither man nor
beast. They had been unable to transport enough food and
were presently weakened by hunger. The farther they marched
the deeper became the water. As they approached the Wabash,
the flooded earth had become an inland sea across which they
could barely distinguish the tops of the submerged trees on the
farther side. As Clark well said: "This would have been enough

to have stop'd any set of men that was not in the same temper that we was."

The wilderness Frenchman was a born boatman. Clark set his Frenchmen to contriving makeshift canoes and rafts. The first raft was used to look for land on the eastern shore and the first canoe was sent down river to look for *Willing,* for which they had now such desperate need. But the galley had been delayed by the difficulty of making headway against the sweep of flood waters and, to the vast mortification of the crew, eventually proved unable to reach Vincennes until the second day after Clark arrived. He could not wait. His men were starving and each hour's delay reduced the chance of the surprise upon which the whole enterprise depended. They were already so near Vincennes that they could hear the thud of the morning and evening gun at the English fort. With the completion of a second canoe he began ferrying his army by driblets to the eastern shore. A canoe with five Frenchmen appeared. The astonished hunters were swiftly taken. Their canoe was a god-send and their information even more welcome. They said Vincennes was still unaware of Clark's approach. . . .

They were now within seven miles of Vincennes but what still lay before them was worse than all that had gone before. The eastern shore of the Wabash was more deeply inundated than had been the west. The five captured Frenchmen who knew the country were certain that in the intervening lowlands the water was too deep for men to get to Vincennes on foot. Clark decided, nonetheless, that either resort to continued ferrying in the three canoes or delay while more were constructed was bound to make their approach too slow to preserve the essential element of surprise. As had been his custom throughout the march when the going was exceptionally difficult, he set off at the head of the long column of men plodding on through the water in single file. The most ordinary men, no matter how weary or discouraged, are prone to follow such a leader. But these were not ordinary men. By now their exertions and sufferings had transfixed them with a fanatical resolution to get on to the end of this fearful march.

There was an attendant hazard in following in Clark's foot-steps. He was six feet tall. When he strode on into water until it rose to his chin it was over the head of many of those behind attempting to keep up. The three canoes paddled back and forth, helping shorter men to keep their heads above water and rescuing others who were at the point of collapse. They were all day the 22nd making the next three miles. That night they spent on a half-acre patch of slightly higher ground on a maple knoll where there had been a sugar camp. The weather turned colder, so benumbing many of the more exhausted men that the next morning they were only able to get to their feet when lifted by their companions.

On this last day of the march Clark was obliged continually to break the half-inch crust of ice with a stick as he pushed on through the water. So many men had reached the absolute limit of their endurance that these early hours of the 23rd were the most harrowing of the whole march. . . . Toward noon they came out on a slight rise which Clark termed "a delightfull Dry Spot of ground." The sun had also come out, and he afterwards referred to the 23rd as that "delightful Day." A passing squaw in a canoe was captured. She had with her a half quarter of buffalo. There was enough broth to provide every man a swallow.

The last lap became suddenly the easiest. There was a lake too deep to be waded, but so narrow that all could be ferried across in the three canoes. Early in the afternoon the starving, half-drowned, and utterly exhausted army of conquest staggered and crawled up among the trees of a low eminence known as Warrior's Island. From it they could see, two miles away across a rolling pond-dotted meadow, the town of Vincennes and, just above it, Fort Sackville. . . .

After having struggled so desperately to achieve surprise, Clark determined to relinquish that tactical advantage for the sake of the psychological advantage of advertising his confidence in his own complete superiority. He was not so much concerned with Hamilton's garrison as he was with the nearly 700 French inhabitants and with the hundreds of Indians in nearby Indian towns. A few of the French were pro-American, others had enlisted in the English service, most were resolutely neutral, but all had intimate relations with the Indians. Were his actual weakness suspected, he could be soon overwhelmed by any combination of the two. Taking care that the duck hunter learned nothing of his numbers, though informing him that this was an invading army not from the Illinois but from Kentucky, Clark dispatched by him a written message to the townspeople. In it he advised them that he was attacking at once, that those who favored the English should take refuge in the fort, that all others should remain in their homes, and that all found in the streets would be treated as enemies.

In late evening, a few minutes after the town had been stunned by his sensational message, Clark marched. His company flags and standards were attached to the tops of long poles. While moving obliquely across the rolling prairie, his men were hidden by the intervening low rises and only the raised flags were visible to indicate the size of his force. The French volunteers were partial to flags, each little group had its own, and the two dozen emblems waving in the gathering dusk suggested a very considerable army. The stratagem was a complete success so far as the townspeople were concerned. They were so impressed by the arrogance of his message and the array of banners that there was no thought of resistance or of appealing to Hamilton for advice. For fear of offending Clark no one from the town even informed Hamilton of Clark's message.

Clark's occupation of the town was accomplished without difficulty. The inhabitants were delighted to find so many of their Illinois friends and relatives among the invaders. Many local militiamen joined his ranks, changing sides for the third time in hardly more than as many months. A secret store of gunpowder was disclosed and turned over to him. Food was urged upon his starving men. The investment of the fort was meanwhile completed and every loophole and gun port kept under persistent rifle fire. Hamilton replied with artillery salvos, damaging a number of houses in the town, including the church. In this exchange Hamilton's fire was more thunderous but less effective. No Americans were injured, while so expert was their marksmanship that a number of gunners were hit during the recurring intervals when a port was opened to aim and fire a cannon. . . .

At nine the next morning Clark suspended firing and demanded the fort's surrender, accompanying the summons with the threat invariably made in wilderness warfare that he could not vouch for the conduct of his men were he obliged to take the place by storm. . . .

Clark was well enough aware that his position was not so superior as he was endeavoring to indicate. Until *Willing* arrived with artillery to breach the walls, he had too few men to attempt to storm a fort defended by so strong a garrison. Meanwhile, an English supply party from Detroit was approaching from the north which, if diligently directed, could speedily raise a swarm of Indian allies. Hamilton, for his part, was dwelling morosely only upon his own disadvantages. Though he could rely on his English regulars, the French half of his garrison was becoming increasingly nervous. His principal weakness, however, was the most enervating that can afflict a commander. He had permitted his thinking to be dominated by the bewildering initiative of his bolder and more aggressive opponent.

As the firing continued, several more of the garrison were wounded and one American finally was hit. Hamilton was still unable to adjust to the sudden, monstrous alteration in his situation. Yesterday he had considered himself a commander on the verge of a conquest of limitless extent. Today he was shut up in one little backwoods fort. Unable to endure his own uncertainty, he requested another parley for the sake of inquiring what terms Clark proposed to impose. Clark, as usual pressing every slightest suggestion of an advantage, refused to consider anything but unconditional surrender. Hamilton declined but asked for a three-day truce. Clark refused. The exchanges of views and arguments continued, Helm acting part of the time as go-between. Clark finally and grudgingly agreed to a meeting with Hamilton on the parade ground in front of the gate.

At this juncture there developed a bizarre interruption which for sheer timeliness at a critical moment in a campaign can surely never have been excelled. From the nearby forest burst an Indian war party, just returned from raiding Kentucky, whooping and firing their guns in the air to announce to their patrons in the fort the good news of their success in having taken prisoners and scalps. The Americans could for a moment scarcely credit the full breathtaking extent of their miraculous good fortune. Not in their fondest dreams had any of them ever imagined an opportunity of such consummately rounded perfection as to be in a position to preside over the homecoming festivities of a pack of red-handed Indian raiders. . . . Seven of the Indians were seized, five were shot down, and only one escaped. The two white captives were released and the captured Indians brought into town.

Clark ordered them tomahawked in the street in full view of the garrison. They were forced to sit in a circle with bowed heads while awaiting the death stroke. Some accounts maintain that Clark himself performed the hatcheting, others that an American sergeant, estimated to have lost more relatives to Indians than had any of his companions, was granted the coveted privilege. Several perplexities briefly delayed the executions. Two of the condemned were discovered to be Frenchmen who, while accompanying the raiding party, had been painted and accoutered to give them the appearance of Indians. One of these was suddenly recognized as his son by a French lieutenant in Clark's army and the other turned out to have relatives in Vincennes. Clark reluctantly spared both. Then Captain Richard McCarty of the Cahokia company learned that one of the genuine Indians was the 18-year-old son of Pontiac and interceded for his life on the plea that his own life had once been saved by Pontiac. Clark spared him, too. The other four Indians were axed.

Clark then walked toward the fort to meet Hamilton. If he had not himself wielded the tomahawk, he had stood so near the proceedings that blood had splattered on his face and hands. While Hamilton stared, he paused to wash his face and hands in a pool of rainwater that had accumulated in a beached canoe. He straightened and the two adversaries stood face to face. The English commander made no effort to conceal his disgust with the American's barbarous violence, and yet could not conceal his own secret agitation. His every impression since Clark had so incredibly materialized out of flood and darkness had forced him to realize his opponent's terrifying aggressiveness. The angry debate between the two continued on into the afternoon. Hamilton kept reiterating his determination never to surrender unconditionally, and Clark kept re-emphasizing his preference for a resumption of the assault to provide an opportunity sufficiently to punish white men who lent themselves to the ignominy of setting Indians on fellow white men. Each kept characterizing the other as a "Murderer." Again and again

Hamilton furiously turned away, but each time he turned back. Once he re-entered the fort to consult his officers. This served only to remind him that, while the English portion of his garrison remained steadfast, the demoralization of the French half had been completed by the execution of the Indian raiders. Finally Clark sensed that his prey was ready for the kill. He offered at least the shadow of terms, permitting the defenders to march out before laying down their arms. Hamilton grasped at the straw of this small indulgence and surrendered. On the morning of February 25, 1779, the Americans took formal possession, and the fort became again Fort Patrick Henry. The ceremony of firing a cannon salute to commemorate the victory was marred by the explosion of a powder cask, seriously burning a number of the celebrants and providing the only significant American casualties of the campaign.

The victory had been a frontier triumph achieved by frontiersmen. They had taken more than an English fort, a garrison of English regulars, and an English lieutenant governor. They had had the deeper and even more rewarding satisfaction of inflicting a public, ritualistic punishment upon representative Indian raiders and of inflicting humiliation upon . . . the most noted of all promoters, organizers, and partisan leaders of Indian outrage in the west. . . .

Clark saw the capture of Vincennes as only a prelude to the far more important capture of Detroit. Though without formal military training, his sense of strategic values was nevertheless so well developed that he clearly comprehended that only by reduction of the English base at Detroit could the Indian threat to the frontier be suppressed and the war in the west ever be brought to a successful conclusion. Many ensuing years of disaster were to demonstrate the soundness of this judgment, but never during those years was the capture of Detroit to prove again to be as nearly within reach as on the morrow of the capture of Vincennes. . . .

The temporary nature of Clark's Illinois conquest has led many historians to argue that it could have had little bearing on the eventual cession of the northwest to the United States by England at the peace table. But the significance of a victory may usually be most clearly identified by considering the contrary consequences had it not been won. Had Clark not taken the

English lieutenant governor at Vincennes, the massive English-Indian invasion already under way could have been expected to gather a momentum certain to carry every American settlement west of the mountains and to have left to the peace commissioners no basis for discussion of a more favorable western boundary than the original Proclamation Line.

The English commanders in the west had reacted swiftly and diligently during the winter of 1778–79 to repair the disarray into which their Indian program had been thrown by Clark's insolent conferences at Cahokia after his occupation of Kaskaskia. In re-establishing English prestige they had relied heavily on the support of the wilderness French in the more northern areas as yet unaffected by Clark's advances. Many of these traders, voyageurs and former French officials, whose influence over Indians had been developed during the generations they had lived among them, were willing to employ this in the English interest in return for various forms of privilege and pay. By early spring of 1779, five expeditions in which Indians of more than a dozen nations had been incorporated were en route to the projected rendezvous with Hamilton in the Illinois. Each as it progressed from one Indian center to the next was gathering recruits by the scores and hundreds. Three of them had been organized by Captain Arent de Peyster, commandant at Mackinac, that great junction of wilderness water routes and chief focal point of Indian population and trade. One, under Charles Langlade, a veteran of wilderness warfare the first of whose countless exploits had been the celebrated capture of Pickawillany in 1752, was skirting the western shore of Lake Michigan, gathering in Chippewa, Menominee, and Winnebago recruits. Langlade's nephew, Charles Gautier, was heading southward by way of the Wisconsin and the Mississippi, recruiting Sauk, Outgami, Sioux, and Iowa. Lieutenant Thomas Bennet, his less familiar repute supported by an initial force of 20 soldiers and 60 militiamen, was proceeding down the eastern shore of Lake Michigan, picking up northern Ottawa and Chippewa recruits, with the intention of uniting with Langlade at the foot of the lake. Working out of Detroit, McKee was assembling a rapidly accumulating force of Shawnee, Potawatomi, Kickapoo, and southern Chippewa and Ottawa that had reached a total of 600. At Sandusky, Henry Bird, with assistance from Simon Girty, was rallying Wyandot and Mingo who had already evidenced their readiness to fight by keeping the starving American garrison at Fort Laurens in a state of siege since January.

This whole imposing effort, so instinct with menace to the American frontier, was disrupted by the electrifying news of the capture of its commander in chief. By calculated English policy, Hamilton had been elevated in Indian estimation to a height upon which his person represented English power in the wilderness. His sudden descent from the role of prospective conqueror to that of humiliated captive, therefore, had a corresponding impact. Frenchmen who had lent themselves to the recruiting project were serving with no love for the English, so long their traditional enemies, but only because they had considered it politic to associate themselves with the stronger side. They began at once instead to fear that they might have chosen the weaker. Upon their counsel and example the Indians had always been accustomed to rely. As a consequence of this sudden tidal wave of doubt, all five musters were shattered by wholesale desertions long before they had reached any scene of action. Gautier was forced to turn back at Rock River on the Mississippi, Langlade at Milwaukee River, Bennet at St. Joseph's. Bird's and McKee's assembled levies as suddenly melted away. As evidence of the seriousness of the disaffection, among the Indians as well as the French, Half King, the principal Wyandot chief who had since the war's outset been among the most aggressive leaders of frontier attacks, hastily made a formal offer of peace to the Americans and presently visited Pittsburgh to press his overture in person. Informed of the course of events by his western commanders, Governor Haldimand in September was gloomily reporting to the cabinet, "It is much to be apprehended that our Indian allies have it in contemplation to desert us." Much of the damage was repaired in time to regain Indian support in the following campaign season. But, meanwhile, the loss of Kaskaskia and Vincennes to Clark had set back the timetable of the English war effort in the west by a full year. As ensuing events were to prove, that year of delay was vital.

A second effect of Clark's initiative, even more significant than the confusion spread among French and Indians, was the encouragement given the inhabitants of the frontier. In the midst of all the extremities that they were enduring they remained a people ever eager to detect the first sign that the general danger might be sufficiently abating to countenance a renewed reach for the land in the west they so yearned to possess. News of Vincennes, supported by the spectacle of the captive Hamilton's progress eastward over the mountains, was accepted by many as such a sign. In the late summer of 1779, through the winter and well into the spring of 1780, thousands streamed westward to lend the support of their numbers to the harassed stations of Kentucky and to establish totally new settlements in Tennessee. Soon they were to be subjected to new dangers, even more oppressive than before, but their coming had brought by the narrowest of margins enough added strength to withstand them. Few victories, surely, have had decisive effects more immediate or more enduring than Clark's at Vincennes.

The British-Indian Attack
on St. Louis,
May 26, 1780

Don Rickey, Jr.

In 1780 the British staged a counterattack designed to dislodge both the American and Spanish holds on the Northwest. Emmanuel Hesse, a fur trader based at Prairie du Chien, Wisconsin, recruited a large party of Indians to attack St. Louis, the principal western outpost. The successful defense of that community by Captain Fernando de Leyba constitutes one of the important defeats for British forces in the western campaign. Spanish influence in the Illinois country rose as a consequence and paved the way for two expeditions from the area into modern southwestern Michigan. Never again were the British able to launch an attack west of the Wabash.

Don Rickey, Jr. (1925——) has spent most of his career as a historian for various federal government agencies. Currently he is with the Bureau of Land Management in Denver. He is best-known for his study of the frontier soldier entitled Forty Miles a Day on Beans and Hay *(1963). He wrote this article while working at the National Park Service's Jefferson National Expansion Memorial in St. Louis.*

★ ★

ST. LOUIS, as the Spanish administrative capital of Upper Louisiana, the "Illinois country" of the French and Spanish eras, became a military objective following Spanish entry as an American ally in the Revolutionary War in 1779. The war had spread to the Old Northwest and the Mississippi Valley in the summer of 1778, when George Rogers Clark led his command of Virginia militiamen to attack the British posts of Kaskaskia,

---

From Don Rickey, Jr., "The British-Indian Attack on St. Louis, May 26, 1780," in the *Missouri Historical Review*, 55: 35–45 (October, 1960); reprinted without footnotes with permission of the author and the *Missouri Historical Review*.

Vincennes, and the smaller settlements along the east bank of the Mississippi. Gabriel Cerré, influential trader and merchant of St. Louis and Kaskaskia, threw in with the Americans, providing them with supplies and influence essential to their cause. Other supplies, and especially ammunition, reached the Americans from Spanish New Orleans, via the Mississippi and Ohio Rivers, through the active cooperation of the Spanish governor of Louisiana. Captain Fernando De Leyba, Lieutenant Governor of Louisiana, had already given Spanish diplomatic support to Clark from his headquarters at St. Louis and had offered reinforcements to the Americans if the British should undertake the reconquest of the Old Northwest.

Even before the formal outbreak of war between Spain and England, British plans had envisioned a campaign to seize the entire Mississippi Valley, as Spanish aid to the Americans was common knowledge and a source of irritation to the British. The 1779 British plan of offensive called for two campaigns, one from the north and one from the south, to sweep the Spaniards and Americans from the Mississippi Valley. The southern campaign never got underway, as the energetic Spanish governor at New Orleans, Bernardo de Galvez, stole a march on his foes in the fall of 1779 and captured the British posts on the lower Mississippi and Gulf coasts from which the British had expected to launch their campaign. The northern campaign, originating from Michilimackinac, was aimed at reducing the Spanish-American settlements in the northern Mississippi Valley, with St. Louis as its major objective.

No regular British troops could be spared for the upper Mississippi Valley campaign. Lieutenant Governor Patrick Sinclair was compelled to carry out his instructions by using Indian allies and such white traders as he could persuade to undertake the assignment. Emanuel Hesse, a trader at Prairie du Chien, was given command of the expedition. Hesse, a Pennsylvanian, had held a lieutenant's commission in the King's Royal American Regiment during the French and Indian War. In February, 1780, he was directed to establish a rendezvous for most of the Indian allies at the portage of the Fox and Wisconsin rivers and await further orders from Sinclair at Michilimackinac. Meanwhile, British traders were sent out to enlist Indian war parties for the campaign.

Late in March a Sergeant Phillips of the King's 8th Infantry Regiment and a Highland soldier brought Hesse a set of secret orders, written in Gaelic, to his Fox-Wisconsin portage encampment. The two soldiers had accompanied the Chippewa chief Matchekewis and his war party from a council at Michilimackinac to the rendezvous. Lieutenant Governor Sinclair's message to Hesse directed him to move down the Wisconsin River to its mouth at Prairie du Chien and there establish a base camp for the campaign. From there he was to descend the Mississippi to the mouth of Rock River, near modern Rock Island, Illinois, where he would add a large Sac and Fox war party to his command, and then proceed down river to attack St. Louis, Cahokia, and the other "Illinois" settlements. [*See* Map 4.]

By the first of May, Hesse had assembled a force of about 750 Indians and about two dozen white traders and their *engagees*. The Canadian traders had been offered exclusive trade rights on the Missouri River in return for their aid, and the intense trade rivalry between themselves and the Spanish-French traders out of St. Louis did much to spark their interest in the campaign. Joseph Calvé, a British trader-agent whose relatives lived in St. Louis, and Jean Marie Ducharme, whose trade goods had been seized by Spanish authorities, were to act as leaders of Indian contingents.

Most of Hesse's Indian allies gathered at the Fox-Wisconsin portage were Chippewas, Menominees, Winnebagoes from the Green Bay area, and Santee Sioux. Small parties of Ottawas, Mascoutens, Kickapoos, and Pottawatamies helped swell the command. The 200 Sioux were led by the most influential Santee chief, Wapasha of the Wakpekutes band, whose village occupied the site of modern Winona, Minnesota. Wapasha, or "Red Leaf," was given a British general's commission and a uniform to match, as was the Chippewa Matchekewis. He was violently pro-British and had been "received" by the colonial governor in Quebec. The Sioux, Menominees, and Winnebagoes were the fiercest and most warlike of Britain's Indian allies. Energetic diplomacy, plus gifts of English muskets and ammunition and the promise of abundant loot, had bound them firmly to the King's cause.

The attack force departed downriver from Prairie du Chien on May 2. Sgt. Phillips was left in charge of the base camp. Near the mouth of Rock River, Hesse stopped at the large Sac and Fox village of Saukenuk. The unlooked for arrival of Hesse's force took the vacillating Sac and Fox completely by surprise. Joseph Calvé had been with the Indians for some time, attempting to obtain their commitment to participate in the campaign. A strong pro-American and neutralist element among them had served to balk Calvé's efforts. However, the presence of Hesse's overwhelming force of Indian allies compelled the Sac and Fox to assent to his threats and persuasions and agree to accompany him in the campaign. If a total of somewhere near 1,000 Indians participated in the May 26, 1780, attacks on St. Louis and Cahokia, Hesse must have "recruited" about 250 Sac and Fox warriors. The addition of these reluctant allies may actually have been far more of a hindrance than a help to the British plans. From Saukenuk, Hesse's motley assortment of Indian allies and white traders went down the Mississippi to what they believed would be an easy capture of St. Louis and Cahokia.

News of Spain's declaration of war on England had reached St. Louis on February 20, 1780. Rumors of British plans to attack from the north were soon circulating in and around the town. At the end of March an upriver trader, John Conn, arrived in St. Louis bringing word of the build-up of Hesse's expedition at the Fox-Wisconsin portage. Up to this time there were no defense works in or around the town. Fort Don Carlos, at the mouth of the Missouri River, was a decayed mud and log shambles. Its garrison of a corporal and a few regular soldiers of the Stationary Regiment of Louisiana had moved out of the decrepit fort and were living in a nearby cabin. Captain Fernando De Leyba, Lieutenant Governor of Spanish Upper Louisiana, at once began preparations to fortify the town. Realizing the uselessness of old Fort Don Carlos, De Leyba had its armament of five cannon and the garrison moved into St. Louis. The ramshackle fort was blown up.

Having no public funds to fortify the town, De Leyba exorted its citizens to contribute money by public subscription. He planned to build four stone towers as bastions in a defense line around St. Louis. As the town was most vulnerable to attack on the west and north, the captain ordered that construction begin on the west tower. This tower was located at what is now the intersection of Fourth and Walnut Streets, on the height of land commanding the town from the west. The first stone was laid on April 17, and the tower was almost completed by May 26. It was about 30 feet in diameter and 30 to 40 feet high. Cannon mounted in this tower commanded all parts of the defense lines and could provide a cross fire in the event that enemies came near the lines. A second tower, at the north end of town, was begun while work was in progress on the first. After excavating for this north tower all funds were exhausted, leaving only a circular hole available as a defensive strong point at the northern end of the lines. Neither of the other two towers were begun prior to the attack.

To fortify St. Louis as rapidly as possible, De Leyba had two entrenchments dug surrounding the town. The two entrench-ments ran from the west tower, along the height of land, and thence down to the river bank. The north trench was 2,280 feet long, and the south trench extended for 3,800 feet. Auguste Choteau's "1780" map indicates a sturdy log palisade around St. Louis, *but* this palisade was erected after the May 26 attack.

Earth from the trenches was probably piled up on the outside to form an additional parapet where "the earth was supported by the trunks of small trees to form a sort of wall." Writing in 1823, Elihu H. Shepard said the defense lines consisted of "a trench about the town protected by a stockade and pointed brush [abatis?] with three gates. . . ." From these and other descriptions the small logs seem to have been placed in the mound of earth thrown out in digging the trenches, forming a palisaded wall about five or six feet high in front of the trenches.

Cannon were mounted in the nearly finished but still roofless west tower and at each end of the defense lines near the river bank. James Musick states in his St. Louis As a Fortified Town that "in 1787 the tower still had its original [1780] armament of three four-pounder cannon and two of a calibre of six." The guns at each end of the entrenchments were probably four-pounders, as these were the most common artillery available. Small swivel guns may also have been mounted at various locations along the defense lines.

In addition to fortifying the town, De Leyba had ordered 60 Ste. Genevieve militiamen to come to St. Louis in two swivel armed bateaux. These reinforcements arrived on May 13.

Captain De Leyba further augmented his defense force by calling in all the hunters [chasseurs] within about 20 leagues of St. Louis. This added another 150 men, mainly from along the Copper and Meramec rivers. By May 26 the St. Louis garrison numbered about 350 men: a handful of Spanish regulars, militiamen, hunters, and townsmen.

Reconnaissance parties were sent up the Mississippi to find the enemy and send back intelligence to De Leyba. On May 23 the scouts returned, having sighted the British Indians. From what he had been able to learn, De Leyba expected an attack by a force of about 900 Indians and some British and Canadians. Following the scouts' return, mounted pickets were posted outside the town to warn of an imminent assault, and arrangements were made for the firing of a signal gun at first sight of the enemy.

Hesse's expedition probably cached most of its boats and canoes on May 24 on the east bank of the Mississippi several miles north of St. Louis and Cahokia. The next day several Indian scouting parties were sent across the river to reconnoitre for the projected attack. May 25 was the feast of Corpus Christi, and many St. Louisians were out in the fields and pastures picking flowers and wild strawberries as part of their holiday celebration. Considering that Captain De Leyba had received information that the attackers were only a short distance up river on May 23, it is somewhat puzzling that he apparently allowed the town's defensive posture to slouch considerably in permitting the scattering of his people into the fields on the fete day of Corpus Christi. However the presence of so many people in the country surrounding the town kept the Indian scouts from approaching as closely as they would have liked, so that they were not able to relay detailed information on the settlement's defenses to their commander. As far as Hesse knew, the place had no fortifications, and he and his Indians expected to easily capture the town by surprise.

The morning of May 26, Jean Marie Ducharme split off from the main command with a contingent of Indians to attack Cahokia on the east bank of the river. Hesse and the remaining force of about 650, including perhaps two dozen British and Canadian traders, crossed the river several miles north of St. Louis and began his advance on the long awaited objective.

Bearing down on St. Louis from the north, the attackers

surprised and killed a few citizens and slaves working in the fields. If De Leyba's mounted pickets carried in any warning of the Indians' approach, it was apparently not in time to allow everyone to get safely inside the defense lines. However several people did manage to reach the lines, and one party, including some women, dashed through the Indians to the north gate in a horse drawn cart. Some of those in the cart were wounded by bullets and arrows. A citizen running for the lines was killed just north of the town, about half way between the breastworks and the big mound. A slave had better luck in his race for life. Sprinting toward safety, he suddenly whirled about and grappled with a pursuing warrior. Wrenching the Indian's musket from his grasp, the slave shot him with his own gun and brought the weapon into the town as a trophy. One man was captured "by the Winnebagoes, within 300 yards of the lines. . . ."

The first shock of the attack on the town itself fell about 1:00 p.m. at the north end of the entrenchments when the British Indians, reported Captain De Leyba, began to advance like madmen, with an unbelievable boldness and fury, making terrible cries and . . . firing." About the same time, said P. L. Cerré, what later proved to have been Ducharme's Indians en route to attack Cahokia were opposite St. Louis, on the east bank of the river, and "with some of their long and large bored [army] muskets, fired across the river and actually made some of their balls rattle on the roofs of the houses of St. Louis." The tower signal gun was fired as soon as the Indians began to break from cover.

At the opening of the attack, De Leyba ordered all the women and children into the commandant's large stone house [Laclede-Choteau house] with a guard of 20 militiamen under Lieutenant Cartabona. The captain personally directed the firing of the cannon in the stone tower, where he had posted six hunters and a few soldiers. All of the remaining 300 men: soldiers, militiamen, hunters, and townsmen, occupied the trenches and breastworks and began firing on the attackers. Cannon fire greatly dismayed the Indians, as they had an awesome fear of artillery. Most of the warriors were very careful not to expose themselves to the defenders' musketry and guns, contenting themselves with firing from a safe distance and concealed by such cover as they could find.

The Winnebagoes and Sioux pressed closest to the defense lines on the north and west, where the action was fiercest. The Sioux chief, Wapasha, was especially active and was later highly praised in British reports of the campaign. He was no doubt a striking figure, dressed in his general's bullion trimmed, scarlet coat and laced cocked hat. A Winnebago chieftain and three warriors were killed, while four other Winnebago were badly wounded. The Canadians and white traders hung back, keeping up only a desultory and ineffective long range fire. Calvé's hesitant Sac and Fox contingent withdrew at the beginning of the attack, to the consternation of the Sioux and Winnebagoes who feared treachery on the part of the Sac and Fox warriors. Wapasha's Sioux and the Winnebagoes made several feints to enter the entrenchments in order to draw the defenders from the cover of the defenses. None of these attempts were successful.

Most of the casualties suffered by the Spanish during the fighting occurred in the northwestern section of the entrenchments. Parties of Indians occupied the high ground commanding this sector and were able to fire down on the defenders. Considering the 100- to 150-yard accurate effective range of the Indians' flintlock muskets, the attackers at this point were probably no further than 150 yards from the lines, shooting at the men holding the segment of trench lying between the north and northwest gates.

No attempt seems to have been made to mount a charge or frontal assault on any part of the defense lines. Individual warriors wormed their way up close to the entrenchments, but not in significant numbers. Desertion by the Sac and Fox and the reluctance of the white traders to participate in the attack enraged the Sioux and Winnebago who, it was later reported, would otherwise have tried to storm the lines. The warriors vented their spleen on the bodies of those killed just outside the lines, scalping, mutilating, and dismembering them in full view of the defenders.

Cannon and musket fire kept up for some time with De Leyba personally seeing to the working of the guns. War whoops, the whiz of arrows, and the flat, banging musketry punctuated by the reverberating boom of cannon created a fearsome din. "What was most disconcerting," reported Captain De Leyba, "was the confusion and the lamentable cries of the women and children who could be heard from the . . . [government house] up to the places where the combatants were fighting. . . ."

As the afternoon wore on the Indians became increasingly discouraged, and within about two hours they abandoned the attack. Perhaps they feared a counterattack by George Rogers Clark's 400 American soldiers from the east side of the river. As the Indians withdrew from the fighting several St. Louis citizens asked Captain De Leyba to lead them in a sortie. Prudently fearing an ambush by superior numbers of warriors, De Leyba refused to heed their advice.

Breaking off the attack on the town itself, the Indians scattered through the nearby fields and settled areas, destroying field crops and buildings and killing oxen, cows, horses, pigs, and domestic fowl. A few more *habitants* and slaves were killed and several more were captured by the retreating Indians. By early evening all the attackers had started back to their boat camp north of St. Louis on the east bank of the Mississippi.

Ducharme's attack on Cahokia had also been repulsed, as George Rogers Clark had arrived the previous day with ample American reinforcements. High, gusty winds and their own gunfire had prevented the Americans at Cahokia from hearing the firing at St. Louis.

Captain De Leyba's June 8 report of the attack stated that all the British Indians had gone back up the Mississippi as far north as the mouth of the Illinois River, and thence up the Illinois. Some of them camped at the Indian village of Chicago, where one of the St. Louis captives make his escape. Apprehensions of an ambush by the mistrusted Sac and Fox probably influenced the British-Indian decision to return north by a route different from the one used in approaching St. Louis.

Reports and estimates of casualties sustained by both the Spanish defenders and by the Indians vary considerably. On June 8 De Leyba wrote that 14 whites and seven slaves had been killed, six whites and one slave wounded, and 12 whites and 13 slaves carried off as captives. British reports assert that 33 scalps were taken during the attack on the west side of the Mississippi and that 24 prisoners had been secured. The figure reported for captives tallies with De Leyba's, but the British claimed 12 more killed than are listed by the Spanish captain. The inclusion of hunters killed at some distance north of St. Louis may account for the discrepancy. Only four Indians were reported killed and four others wounded.

Failure of the campaign against St. Louis was a serious blow to British prestige among the vacillating Indians, and at the same time it aroused the Spanish officials and French *habitants* of the "Illinois country" to take action against the English and their Indian allies. George Rogers Clark's second in command, John Montgomery, led a counteroffensive against Britain's erstwhile if reluctant allies, the Sac and Fox. Montgomery assembled a force of 250 American soldiers and Cahokia *habitant* volunteers and 100 Spanish militia under Picote de Belestre and departed from St. Louis about June 13. Pushing north up the Illinois River, the allied expedition reached Peoria and from there marched overland about 100 miles to the village of Saukenuk at the mouth of Rock River. The Sac and Fox hastily fled before the advancing allies, but their abandoned village and crops were burned in retaliation for their participation in the attack on St. Louis.

Following the punitive expedition the Sac and Fox apparently decided to more thoroughly identify themselves with the Spanish and American cause. Late in June, emissaries from the chastened Sac and Fox brought back three whites and three slaves who had been taken captive in the May 26 attack. Much of the Sac and Fox trade had been oriented toward St. Louis before the outbreak of war and, as previously mentioned, their presence among the British Indians on May 26 had only been accomplished by threats and pressure from the British.

A more ambitious St. Louis campaign against the British was launched in January, 1781. During the fall of 1780 reports had reached St. Louis that another British-led Indian campaign was being planned. Supplies for the threatened English strike were being gathered at the post of St. Joseph, Michigan. On January 2 the Spanish expedition, comprised of about 65 men, including 30 St. Louis militia, began a winter march against the unsuspecting British post. Augmented en route by about 60 anti-British Milwaukee Indians, the Spanish task force surprised and captured St. Joseph on February 12. Fearing a strong British counterattack, the Spaniards looted and burned the post and began their return march the next day. The

800-mile strike and return were completed when the successful Spanish expedition reached St. Louis on March 6.

British influence and prestige had met with several reverses as a result of Spanish activities beginning with the defense of St. Louis. It became increasingly difficult for English agents to generate enthusiasm among the Indians for maintaining hostilities against the Americans in the Old Northwest and the Spaniards of Upper Louisiana. The upper Mississippi frontier remained fairly quiet through 1781–1782, and no further British campaigns were sent to the "Illinois country" prior to the end of the Revolutionary War in 1783.

The Spanish Expedition Against Fort St. Joseph in 1781

Lawrence Kinnaird

The Spanish role in the Mississippi valley has been omitted from most accounts of the region, yet it constituted an important force in the area. With the defeat of the Hesse expedition of 1780, the Spanish sought to extend their influence east of the river. A variety of explanations for this effort emerged in the first third of this century. These are summarized and developed in a historiographic analysis by Lawrence Kinnaird, who then comes to his own conclusions relative to the expedition to Fort St. Joseph, Michigan.

Kinnaird (1893———) taught at San Francisco State University and the University of California–Berkeley before his retirement. So thorough is this study that no new interpretation on the rationale for and objectives of the St. Joseph expedition has emerged since the publication of this article over forty years ago.

★ ★

IN THE DAYS of the Revolutionary War a British post named St. Joseph was located upon the river of the same name within the district of Michilimackinac at the present site of Niles, Michigan. This post was captured and plundered, on February 12, 1781, by a band of white men and Indians. Many historians have written of the episode, but there has been marked disagreement among them. Accounts vary in respect both to the participants in the attack and the motives which prompted it, but in general they may be divided into three groups according to the following interpretations. First, the St. Joseph expedition was sent out from St. Louis as a diplomatic move on the part of

From Lawrence Kinnaird, "The Spanish Expedition Against Fort St. Joseph in 1781: A New Interpretation," in the *Mississippi Valley Historical Review*, 19: 173–191, (September, 1932); reprinted without footnotes with permission of the author and the *Journal of American History*.

the Spanish government to establish a claim to territory east of the Mississippi. Second, the affair was merely a frontier foray undertaken against the British by Frenchmen of Cahokia and St. Louis for motives of plunder and revenge. Third, the undertaking was a defensive measure on the part of the Spaniards to prevent a threatened British attack upon St. Louis. The purpose of this article is to examine critically former studies of the St. Joseph episode in an endeavor to arrive at a more complete and more authentic interpretation. [See Map 5.]

St. Joseph was an insignificant post which, in June, 1780, had only fifteen houses and a population of forty-eight French half breeds. The attack upon the place might have been forgotten had it not, at the close of the Revolutionary War, become associated with the claims of Spain to territory east of the Mississippi River. The *Gaceta de Madrid,* on March 12, 1782, published an account of the capture of St. Joseph by a Spanish force sent from St. Louis and supported by a party of Indians. According to the *Gaceta,* Don Eugenio Pouré, the commander of the expedition, "took possession in the name of the King of that place and its dependencies, and of the river of the Illinois, in consequence whereof the standard of his Majesty was displayed there during the whole time." Captain Pouré took the English flag "and delivered it on his arrival at St. Louis to Don Francisco Cruzat, the commandant of that post."

The Spanish diplomats, during the negotiations preceding the peace at the end of the Revolutionary War, made use of the St. Joseph incident to support their claims to territory east of the Mississippi. At that time the American negotiators believed the expedition had been undertaken in accordance with directions from Madrid. They were justified in the belief because the Spanish government had made known to Congress, in 1780, through the French minister, Chevalier de la Luzerne, that it considered the territory lying west of the proclamation line of 1763 as a field for "making a permanent conquest for the Spanish crown." During the peace negotiations of 1782 Spain opposed the efforts of the United States to secure the Mississippi as her western boundary and was supported by France.

The American diplomats finally overcame this opposition by making a separate treaty with Great Britain; but Spain refused to acknowledge officially the western claims of the United States until the signing of Pinckney's treaty in 1795. Under the circumstances both Franklin and Jay naturally regarded the St. Joseph expedition as a deliberate attempt by the Spanish government to establish a title to lands east of the Mississippi in the region north of the Ohio. Franklin did not hesitate to say that he believed the affair was a part of Spain's policy to "shut us up within the Appalachian Mountains." Jay supported this opinion by calling attention to the care with which the Spanish commander of the expedition had taken possession of the territory for Spain.

In fact it was chiefly through Jay that the St. Joseph affair became known to historians in the United States, for he sent both a copy and a translation of the article in the *Gaceta de Madrid* to Secretary of Foreign Affairs Robert R. Livingston. The Spanish narrative in this manner came to be published in the *Secret Journals of Congress,* and in the *Correspondence of the American Revolution,* edited by Jared Sparks. The information contained in these works in turn formed the basis for the accounts of the St. Joseph expedition written by John B. Dillon in the *History of Indiana* (Indianapolis, 1843), James H. Perkins in the *Annals of the West* (Cincinnati, 1846), John Reynolds in the *Pioneer History of Illinois* (Belleville, 1852), Rufus Blanchard in the *Discovery and Conquests of the North-West* (Wheaton, 1879), and others. It was not strange, therefore, that most of the earlier historians who wrote upon various aspects of the Revolutionary War in the West should come to the conclusion that the St. Joseph expedition was prompted by Spain's territorial ambitions.

The diplomatic interpretation of the episode was presented in greatest detail by Edward G. Mason in an article entitled "March of the Spaniards across Illinois." This study, published in 1886 in the *Magazine of American History,* was devoted entirely to the expedition against Fort St. Joseph. Although Mason's chief source of information was the brief account of the affair printed in the *Gaceta de Madrid* of March 12, 1782, his narrative was interesting and colorful. He explained that, as the war in the West progressed, Spain became more and more unfriendly to the United States "until it was apparent that nothing less than the entire valley of the Mississippi would satisfy the ambition of the Spaniards. Their conquests of Baton Rouge and Natchez were made to serve as a basis for title to the whole eastern side of the Lower Mississippi, as far as the Ohio. They needed something more, in order that they might include in their demands what was afterward known as the North-west Territory." Mason was more emphatic than any other historian in his insistence that the St. Joseph expedition could be explained only as a result of diplomatic and political motives. "As an illustration of that crafty diplomacy which sought to control both the Old World and the New, it may repay study," he wrote. "How little did those light-hearted soldiers and their red allies know that they were but the pawns in the great game whereof the players were at Paris and Madrid!"

The diplomatic explanation of the St. Joseph affair was accepted by many historians after Mason. It has been restated with only minor variations by William F. Poole in a chapter of Winsor's *Narrative and Critical History of America* entitled "The West from the Treaty of Peace with France, 1763, to the Treaty of Peace with England, 1783," by Justin Winsor in his *Westward Movement,* by Claude H. Van Tyne in *The American Revolution,* by Reuben G. Thwaites in *France in America,* by Daniel McCoy in an article entitled "Old Fort St. Joseph," by Louis Houck in *History of Missouri,* and by others.

A gradual change in the interpretation of the St. Joseph episode was brought about by the publication of documentary material dealing with the subject. The first volume of the *Calendar of Virginia State Papers* made its appearance in 1875. Douglas Brymner began the publication of the calendar of the Haldimand collection in the 1884 *Report on Canadian Archives.* The Pioneer Society of the State of Michigan in 1886 published the first installment of the Haldimand Papers in volume IX of the *Collections.* Other material found its way into print, chiefly in the *Collections* of the Michigan Pioneer and Historical Society, the State Historical Society of Wisconsin, and the Illinois State Historical Library.

Roosevelt in *The Winning of the West* did not attribute much importance to the capture of Fort St. Joseph. He dismissed the incident with the statement that "in reality it was a mere plundering foray." He explained that after the departure of the enemy "the British at once retook possession of the place, and, indeed, were for some time ignorant whether the raiders had been Americans or Spaniards."

Arthur C. Boggess, writing in 1906, introduced certain new elements into the St. Joseph narrative by a careful study of documentary material already published upon the subject. "According to a Spanish account," he wrote, "the party consisted of sixty-five militia men and sixty Indians, while an American account declares it to have contained thirty Spaniards, twenty men from Cahokia, and two hundred Indians." Boggess indicated that there was a connection between the attack upon St. Joseph in 1781 and the ill-fated expeditions organized among the Illinois French in 1780 by Augustin Mottin de la Balme. Thus a new motive for the undertaking was suggested. "The purpose of the expedition," he stated, "was to retaliate upon the British for the attack on St. Louis and for the defeat of La Balme."

Clarence W. Alvord, late professor of history at the University of Illinois, borrowed the manuscript of Boggess' work, *The Settlement of Illinois, 1778–1830,* before it was published "to use in the preparation of his article on the County of Illinois." Alvord described the St. Joseph expedition briefly in his introduction to the *Cahokia Records* published in 1907, and in December of the same year he read a paper before the State Historical Society of Missouri entitled "The Conquest of St. Joseph, Michigan, by the Spaniards in 1781" in which he elaborated upon the ideas contained in the Boggess study. Although Alvord used in his paper most of the references cited by Boggess upon the subject, he made no mention of the latter's work. His discussion of the St. Joseph expedition, however, was more detailed than that of Boggess and was critical in character. Alvord directed his criticism chiefly against Mason and the historians who had accepted his version. He asserted that Mason had told "the story of this 'March of the Spaniards across Illinois' in eighteen pages with no more information on the subject than is afforded by the brief description in the Madrid Gazette; but his description gives evidence of such detailed knowledge that it has carried conviction with it." Alvord thought that "the demands of diplomacy" were responsible for the article in the *Gaceta de Madrid* and gave it small consideration as a piece of historical evidence.

All accounts of the St. Joseph affair based upon the Spanish narrative emphasized the following points. The expedition was sent out by Cruzat, the Spanish commandant at St. Louis, and was composed of Spanish soldiers and Indians. The post St. Joseph was taken, prisoners were captured, and English goods were seized or destroyed. The commanding officer, a Spanish subject, actually took possession of the territory for the King of Spain. Lastly, the enterprise was all a part of a scheme to strengthen Spain's claim to territory east of the Mississippi. Alvord made the statement that there was "sufficient warrant to suspect the truth of almost every one of these points."

His account of the affair was in substance as follows: In the summer of 1780, there came to the Illinois country a French officer by the name of Augustin de la Balme, who proposed to raise, from among the French population, a force for the purpose of attacking Detroit and invading Canada. He succeeded in collecting a small number of men, and, with one detachment, he reached and occupied Miami about the last of October, 1780. Shortly afterward, the Indians attacked the party, killing De la Balme and thirty of his men. In the meantime his other detachment, composed of men from Cahokia, under the command of Jean Baptiste Hamelin, advanced against St. Joseph. This party succeeded in surprising the post while the Potawatomies, who lived near it, were absent on their hunt. The place was plundered and twenty-two prisoners were taken. The Cahokians then turned toward home, but were overtaken by the British and Indians, who killed four, wounded two, and took seven prisoners.

According to Alvord, the survivors of the expedition returned to Cahokia where they incited the French people to avenge the death of their fellow citizens. The hope of recapturing the lost plunder was an additional incentive for another expedition. Appeals were made to the people of St. Louis, who were also French. Cahokia raised a force of twenty men; St. Louis, thirty; and two hundred friendly Indians joined the expedition. The band set out just twenty-eight days after the first party had met its defeat. The services of Louis Chevalier, who was on very friendly terms with the Potawatomies, were secured, and he succeeded in inducing these Indians to remain neutral. This accomplished, St. Joseph was easily surprised and plundered. The British officers were unable to induce the Potawatomies to pursue the invaders as they had done before.

The foregoing account, Alvord asserted, was the true story of the capture of St. Joseph. This version of the affair was based largely upon a letter written to Colonel Slaughter by Captain McCarty, whom Alvord believed to have been living in Cahokia during the winter of 1780 and 1781. The letter by McCarty, dated January 27, 1781, had been one of the important pieces of evidence previously used by Boggess. Alvord also utilized a story which Governor John Reynolds had heard in Cahokia from one of the survivors of the first expedition against St. Joseph. Alvord stated that the "leader of the expedition was Jean Baptiste Mailhet of Peoria," rather than Eugene Pouré. He believed that the Spaniards had little or nothing to do with the affair and asserted that "there is no evidence that the taking of St. Joseph was in accordance with the instructions from the home government or even from the governor of Louisiana."

Almost simultaneously with the appearance of Alvord's article a Spanish document was published by Reuben G. Thwaites, in his "British Régime in Wisconsin," which contained an expression of satisfaction by the King of Spain himself at the capture of St. Joseph and instructions that the officers in charge be rewarded. The following year Louis Houck, in the *Spanish Régime in Missouri,* published a brief statement of the affair written by Carondelet, governor of Louisiana. At about the same time Robert L. Schuyler, in the *Transition in Illinois from British to American Government,* attempted an interesting combination of certain elements of the accounts of Boggess and Alvord with those of the Spanish version. He explained that, after the defeat of De la Balme, "the Cahokians, eager for revenge, then raised a party of about twenty men. Francisco Cruzat, who had succeeded Leyba as commandant of St. Louis, was at the same time organizing an expedition to attack British posts east of the Mississippi. The two enterprises appear to have been united, and a mixed party of Spaniards, French creoles and Indians, under a Spaniard, Eugenio Pourée, marched to St. Joseph in January, 1781."

Frederick J. Teggart of the University of California wrote for the *Missouri Historical Review* in 1911, an article entitled "The Capture of St. Joseph, Michigan, by the Spaniards in 1781," in which he challenged the accuracy of Alvord's conclusions. Teggart proved by the use of Spanish manuscripts in the

Pinart-Bancroft Collection of Louisiana Papers, Bancroft Library, that the account of the expedition as originally related in the *Gaceta de Madrid* was substantially correct. The most important of the documents used by Teggart were the letters of Malliet to Cruzat, January 9, 1781, and Cruzat to Miró, August 6, 1781, together with the "act of possession" drawn up at St. Joseph by the officers of the expedition on February 12 of the same year. The letter to Miró was especially important because it contained Cruzat's official report of the expedition. Using these Spanish manuscripts, Teggart gave an account of the St. Joseph affair which may be summarized as follows:

A detachment of sixty-five Spanish soldiers and sixty Indians set out from the town of St. Louis on January 2, 1781, to attack the British post of St. Joseph. This force was under the command of Captain Eugene Pouré of the second militia company of St. Louis. Charles Tayon was ensign, and Louis Chevalier was chosen by Cruzat as interpreter. The Indians were led by the chiefs El Heturno and Naquiguen. The expedition set out by boat and ascended the Mississippi and Illinois rivers to a point where the latter was frozen over. A party of twelve Spanish militia men under the command of Jean Baptiste Malliet, who had been stationed on the Illinois River as an outpost against the British, joined Pouré's party en route. Leaving the boats and all unnecessary articles, the band made a twenty day march to St. Joseph, experiencing "all that can be imagined of cold, peril and hunger."

The Potawatomies were persuaded to remain neutral by a promise of half the booty to be taken at the post. At seven o'clock in the morning of February 12, 1781, Pouré led his detachment across the ice of the river, took the post of St. Joseph completely by surprise, and made prisoners all who were found in it. Referring to the manuscripts used by Teggart we learn that Pouré, with his detachment standing at arms, "planted the royal colors in the center of the place" and read a proclamation in which he said: "I annex and incorporate with the domains of his Very Catholic Majesty, the King of Spain, my master, from now on and forever, this post of St. Joseph and its dependencies, with the river of the same name, and that of Islinois, which flows into the Missicipy River." After occupying St. Joseph for one day Pouré led his men back to St. Louis where they arrived on March 6.

This is the version of the capture of Fort St. Joseph given by the Spanish manuscripts and followed by Teggart. There seems to be no good reason to doubt its accuracy. The recent investigations of Abraham P. Nasatir, who is probably the best authority upon the history of Spanish Illinois, have brought to light some new information upon the subject, but, in general, have substantiated Teggart's narrative. Although Nasatir has treated the St. Joseph affair merely as an incident in the study of the *Anglo-Spanish Frontier in the Illinois Country during the American Revolution,* he has written one of the best accounts of it.

The description of the St. Joseph expedition itself now seems to be fairly complete, but the origin of the plan and the motives for it have not been so well determined. Milo M. Quaife in his work, *Chicago and the Old Northwest,* commented upon this fact: "Three detailed studies of this expedition have been made. The conclusions of the first, by Edward G. Mason, were generally accepted by scholars as valid until Professor Clarence W. Alvord's study appeared. His conclusions differ materially from those reached by Mason. More recently Frederick J. Teggart has challenged Alvord's conclusions." Most of the earlier writers who followed the account given in the *Gaceta de Madrid* believed the purpose of the expedition was to establish a Spanish claim to territory east of the Mississippi, although this object was not stated in the Spanish article itself. Developing ideas expressed upon the subject by Roosevelt and Boggess, Alvord succeeded in casting much doubt upon, if not entirely discrediting, the diplomatic interpretation. "It is quite evident," he asserted, "that the expedition was conceived by the Cahokians to revenge the defeat of their friends who had been sent out by De la Balme, and that a second motive was the hope of plundering the property which was known to be unprotected at St. Joseph."

Teggart asserted that Alvord's "explanation of the origin of the expedition must be noticed, not because of its having either merit or probability, but because the author speaks with the prestige of a professor in the University of Illinois." He then proceeded to discredit the evidence used by Alvord in much the same way that Alvord had discredited Mason's article. Teggart believed that Cruzat had devised the scheme to capture St. Joseph in an attempt to prevent an impending expedition of the British against St. Louis. This town had been attacked the year before by the English and Indians. The assault had failed, but it was reported that the British had sent supplies to St. Joseph with which they intended to outfit another expedition in the following year. "The expedition," concluded Teggart, "was the direct result of information Cruzat had received of preparations by the English for a second attack on St. Louis in the spring of 1781." To strengthen his point he called attention to the recapture of Vincennes by the Americans, and stated that "if anything is wanting to complete the evidence it is supplied by the fact that Cruzat had before him the example of George Rogers Clark who, in 1779, had undertaken a similar march for a similar purpose."

A number of questions may be asked which raise doubts as to whether the reason just stated would have been sufficient justification for sending any force upon such a hazardous venture. In the first place, were there sufficient supplies at the little post of St. Joseph to recruit the neighboring Indians and to outfit a second expedition against St. Louis? The stores at the post in all probability had already been damaged considerably, since the Cahokians had captured the place scarcely a month before. If there were sufficient supplies at St. Joseph to equip an expedition against Spanish Illinois, would it be probable that the British would have left them unprotected after having already suffered one raid?

Furthermore, would the destruction of a small post like St. Joseph have given sufficient assurance of the prevention of an attack upon St. Louis to warrant Cruzat in sending a much needed force upon a two months' journey through hostile country in the middle of winter? In regard to this point, Alvord correctly asserted that "the description of the village is sufficient to show that British resources were in no ways impaired, nor could this slight success prevent the British making other military operations in the region." Alvord also made the statement that as late as December 22, only eleven days before the start of the St. Joseph expedition, "Cruzat at St. Louis knew nothing about it." This assertion was given upon the evidently reliable authority of a letter from Barnardo de Gálvez to Cruzat, dated February 15, 1781. If Cruzat planned the expedition as a measure primarily to prevent an attack upon St. Louis the following spring, is it not likely that he would have had it under consideration for more than eleven days, and that he would, at this time, have given Governor Gálvez some definite information about it?

Finally, was there sufficient danger of a British attack upon Spanish Illinois in the spring of 1781 to justify Cruzat's sending any men away upon an apparently reckless venture rather than keeping them at St. Louis and employing them in preparations for defense? Cruzat wrote to Governor Gálvez on November 14, 1780, only seven weeks before Pouré and his men set out from St. Louis: "I have learned that a great number of Indians of different nations, and even of the same nations who came to attack us last spring, are now getting ready to come next spring with the idea of soliciting our clemency and alliance." Apparently other motives than those already stated were involved in the Spanish expedition against St. Joseph. But to determine them obviously would be a difficult task, for, in all probability, Cruzat himself was the only man able to give all the reasons for the undertaking. The only possibility of a solution of the problem seemed to be through the discovery of new evidence.

A careful check of all the documentary material used by previous writers was first made in order to determine whether any fact had been overlooked or misinterpreted. This investigation led to the conclusion that the work had been very well done. The search, however, did result in the finding of one important clue. Cruzat began his letter of August 6 to Miró with the following sentence: "On January 2nd of the present year, as I have written to the governor on the 10th of the same month and year, Don Eugenio Pourre, the captain of the second militia company . . . left this city of San Luis with a detachment of sixty-five militia men and about sixty Indians." The foregoing statement indicated that there had been a letter written by Cruzat to the governor of Louisiana on January 10, 1781.

An examination of other accounts of the St. Joseph affair revealed the fact that the letter of January 10, 1781, had not been used. Written while the expedition was in progress, it would be almost certain to contain valuable information. Was this letter still in existence and if so, where was it likely to be found? The first supposition would be that the manuscript, if still preserved, would be among the Papeles de Cuba in the

Archivo General de Indias, Seville, Spain; but this was only one of many possibilities. The letter might be in one of the other Spanish archives or in another section of the Archivo General de Indias. It might even be in the Archivo Nacional at Havana, Cuba, for certain of the Louisiana manuscripts apparently were overlooked at the time the Spanish government removed 2336 *legajos* of papers from Cuba to the Archivo General de Indias in 1888 and 1889. The search for the document constituted a problem in heuristic that is of no importance here. It is sufficient to say that it was eventually found in the collection of Louisiana Papers now deposited in the Bancroft Library at the University of California. This group of manuscripts was originally a part of the Papeles de Cuba and is of great importance for the study of the history of the Spanish régime in the Mississippi Valley.

The letter justified the search for it. Writing just eight days after Pouré's force had left St. Louis, Cruzat not only explained the origin of the expedition to Governor Gálvez, but carefully stated the reasons why he had been compelled to send it and listed them in the order of their importance. The letter is as follows:

MY DEAR SIR: On the 26th of last month the chief, El Heturnò, arrived, bringing me news of the destruction (by a party of Canadians of the Strait under the leadership of a certain Dequente) of a detachment of seventeen Frenchmen who had set out nearly three months ago from the pueblo of Kaò for the purpose of going to take possession of the Fort of San Joseph, situated in the English dependency fifty-five leagues from the bank of the river. In it there are four persons commissioned by the English, with seventeen men and a considerable quantity of all sorts of merchandise, which they use only to purchase maize and different kinds of provisions from the neighboring Indians, in order to collect in the fort a store of supplies for the expeditions which they are planning against us. In addition to this, they excite and urge the above-mentioned Indian nations to commit in their hostilities their customary cruelties, of which we have had bitter experiences.

The urging of the Indian Heturnò, both on his own account and in behalf of Naquiguen, both chiefs being already known to your Lordship, that I should make an expedition against the English of the Fort of San Joseph, together with the reasons which I shall state to your Lordship, and which I believe to be well founded, compelled me to arrange for the departure from this town, as quickly as possible, on the first of this current month, a detachment of sixty volunteers under the orders of the Captain of Militia Don Eugenio Purè, a person skilled in war and accustomed to waging it in these countries. He, together with the two chiefs mentioned, El Heturnò and Naquiguen, and several others from the bank of the Ylinueses who take their nations with them, form a force sufficient to send to San Joseph endeavoring to destroy everything that the enemy has in it. For if these stores remained in the hands of the English, they would be of assistance in furthering their hostile plans. I believe that the measures I have taken will be effective in realizing our hopes. Indeed, it has been indispensable for me to take this step, as I am going to tell your Lordship.

FIRST. For me not to have consented to the petition of El Heturnò and Naquiguen would have been to demonstrate to them our weakness and to make evident to them our inadequate forces; and perhaps, if they had learned of these facts, it might be sufficient reason for them to change sides, notwithstanding the evident signs of friendship which they have given us. For the Indians are in the habit of following the strongest one, and the English would not have failed to take advantage of this event, nor would we have escaped experiencing the fatal results of the unfriendliness and inconstancy of the two chiefs referred to.

SECOND. To go to San Joseph and seize the fort, the English commissioners, the merchandise, and the provisions would have the effect of terrorizing the surrounding nations. It would take from them the men who are inciting them to evil acts, and would deprive them of powder and merchandise given to them by the English for hunting and making war upon us. By this means would be accomplished both the destruction of the fort and the supply of provisions in it; and, even though the English might not be prevented entirely from carrying out their intentions, it would cut off their resources in part and lessen their hopes of having in that place a store of provisions with which to supply those who may attempt to come by that way to attack us this spring.

By permitting El Heturnò and Naquiguen to go to make war and giving them forces against our enemies we shall succeed in turning our allied nations against those who are opposed to us; and since both sides are bent on sacrificing themselves mutually, it will compel our Indian allies to be loyal during the war because they will have need of our help to defend themselves. The enemy will not then be able to attack us so easily on account of the opposition and resistance which they will meet from the Indians friendly to us.

With the savages it is always necessary, in order to preserve oneself from their destructive inclinations, to keep them occupied by bringing about disagreements among them, and causing them to war among themselves. This has always been experienced in these countries and every day it is proved more and more. These reasons, and many others which your Lordship may think of, compelled me to take the unavoidable step of sending the detachment referred to with the Indians who asked for and were enthusiastic for this expedition. I gave them everything necessary for the success I desire. I am sure that everything that I have done in connection with this affair will meet with your Lordship's approval.

God keep your Lordship many years. San Luis de Ylinueses, January 10, 1781.

I kiss your Lordship's hands. Your most faithful servant,

FRANCO. CRUZAT [rubric].

The foregoing document amplifies the historical work already done upon the St. Joseph affair. It shows the possibility of reconciling, in a measure, two heretofore conflicting opinions concerning the motives of the enterprise. The incentive of the Indian chiefs, who proposed the expedition, and of their followers, was the desire to plunder the stores at St. Joseph. Probably any Cahokians who volunteered went with Pouré for the same reason. On the other hand, one of several motives which induced Cruzat to yield to the urging of the Indians was the hope that a destruction of the supplies at St. Joseph would render more difficult the outfitting of an expedition against St. Louis in the following spring, although this in itself was not sufficient to warrant the undertaking.

The most important points brought out in the letter of January 10, 1781, have not been discussed in former studies. Cruzat's explanation of the St. Joseph episode differs from the three previous interpretations as much as these differ from each other. The expedition was not planned by Spanish diplomats at Madrid, nor by irate Frenchmen at Cahokia; neither was Cruzat himself the originator of the project. The scheme was proposed to the lieutenant-governor by the Milwaukee chiefs, El Heturno and Naquiguen. Cruzat did not decide to send the expedition because he hoped to establish Spanish claims to territory east of the Mississippi, nor because he desired to avenge the defeat of De la Balme; neither did he dispatch it primarily to prevent an expected attack upon St. Louis in the spring of 1782 by the British.

The whole affair was a manifestation of Spain's Indian policy. The very existence of the settlements in Spanish Illinois depended upon maintaining friendly relations with neighboring Indian tribes. Indian alliances for frontier defense had already been used by the Spaniards in Texas and lower Louisiana against both the Apaches and the English. A similar system was later followed in the Old Southwest where Spain attempted to control the Indian nations by means of treaties, subsidies, and agents, and use them as a buffer against the expansion of the United States. Cruzat hoped that the attack upon Fort St. Joseph would bring about hostilities between the Milwaukees and the Indians who adhered to the British, thereby forcing the former in the future to remain loyal to Spain. Above all, the safety of the entire district demanded that the requests of the Indians be complied with lest they learn the weakness of the Spaniards and go over to the British. Cruzat, therefore, yielded to their urging because he dared not refuse.

A Roof for Kentucky

Charles G. Talbert

When most Americans consider the war in the West, they concern themselves with George Rogers Clark and his expedition into the Illinois country and the trek to Vincennes. The war in the West was not ended with the surrender of Henry Hamilton. Rather, this was the opening chapter of the northwestern campaigns. Professor Charles Talbert (1912———) of the University of Kentucky is a native of that state with a long interest in its early history. His concept of the Ohio River forts providing a "roof" to protect Kentucky from Anglo-Indian raids is unique. The "roof" idea, Talbert writes in a note, "refers to the way Kentucky appears on a map. The Licking fort would be the ridge or comb. The Falls and Limestone forts would support the eves. The longer side of the roof, that from the Falls to the Licking, which would measure about eighty miles as compared to forty-five for the side stretching from the Licking to Limestone Creek, would have an additional point of support near its center. This would be the fort at the mouth of the Kentucky River. Some Kentuckians believed this to be the most important of the four." Actually the "roof" stretched farther, involving Fort Jefferson near the juncture of the Ohio and Mississippi and Fort Randolph at the mouth of the Kanawha.

Professor Talbert's description of Clark's troubles after the Vincennes triumph brings into greater focus the problems of frontier defense. Shortages of funds, supplies, and manpower contributed significantly to the failure to exploit the successes of 1778–1779 and resulted in a virtual military stalemate on the northwestern frontier.

* *

COLONEL George Rogers Clark returned to Kentucky from his Shawnee campaign of 1780 [*See* Map 4.] with his desire to capture the British post at Detroit still unrealized. The idea,

---

From Charles G. Talbert, "A Roof for Kentucky," in the *Filson Club History Quarterly*, 29: 145–165 (April, 1955); reprinted without notes with permission of the *Filson Club History Quarterly*.

however, had caught the attention of Virginia's governor, Thomas Jefferson. The governor realized that such a project would reduce the state's support of the continental army. He referred the matter to General George Washington. Jefferson believed that the Virginia regulars under Clark's command, assisted by volunteers or by militiamen from the state's western counties, would be an adequate force for the purpose. He was confident that Virginia could furnish all necessary supplies with the possible exception of powder and asked only that Continental calls upon the state be temporarily reduced.

By January, 1781, Washington had indicated that he was favorable to the plan. Jefferson then suggested to Clark that he come to Richmond to begin his preparations.

Clark, upon his arrival at the capital, received a promotion to the rank of brigadier general. He obtained permission to draft militiamen in several of the western counties. Orders to this effect were forwarded to the county lieutenants. Some of these militiamen were to be at Fort Pitt by March 1. There they would be joined by a battalion of Virginia regulars under the command of Colonel Joseph Crockett. Five hundred men from Lincoln, Jefferson, and Fayette counties were ordered to be at the Falls of the Ohio by March 15. It was believed that Clark would be able to advance upon Detroit at the head of two thousand men.

These plans proved far too optimistic. It was not until the following August that Clark came down the Ohio to the Falls. With him were no more than 250 men. Several factors had combined to produce this disappointing result. Colonel Daniel Brodhead, commandant at Fort Pitt, was not so helpful as Clark had expected him to be. Contemplating a Detroit expedition of his own, Brodhead held back men and supplies. The boundary dispute between Virginia and Pennsylvania had its effect. Men in the Monongahela region refused to volunteer for a Virginia campaign. An attempt to draft them produced a riot. The spring of 1781 brought a British invasion of Virginia. One detachment penetrated so deeply that the government was forced to flee, first to Charlottesville and then across the Blue Ridge to Staunton, for safety. Men and supplies which could have gone to Clark were needed to resist this invasion.

Although Clark did not reach the Falls until August 23, a

report that the Detroit campaign might have to be abandoned preceded him. John Floyd, the county lieutenant of Jefferson, feared that an Indian attack upon his county was imminent. He urged Clark to hasten his return. The strength of the Jefferson County militia frequently was reduced in time of danger by the natural tendency of the people to move to safer parts of the state. As Floyd saw it, only two circumstances prevented his county from being deserted. The Indians had stolen most of the horses, and the Ohio flowed only one way.

Upon his arrival Clark asked the field officers of the militia of the three counties which comprised the region known as Kentucky to meet at the Falls on September 5. He wanted them to help him and his line officers to make plans for defense. The term field officer included all who held the rank of major or higher. Fayette County sent only her county lieutenant, John Todd. Lincoln County sent two representatives, Benjamin Logan, the county lieutenant, and his second-in-command, Colonel Stephen Trigg. Jefferson County, in which the settlement known as the Falls was located, was represented by her county lieutenant, John Floyd, her colonel, Isaac Cox, and her lieutenant colonel, William Pope.

The meeting was held at Fort Nelson in the quarters of one of Clark's line officers, Colonel John Montgomery. Colonel Todd, the senior of the three county lieutenants, presided. Clark presented to this council a prepared statement giving his reasons for having to forego the Detroit expedition and seeking to impress upon the militia officers the seriousness of the situation. Fort Jefferson on the Mississippi already had been abandoned, and it was questionable if the garrison at Vincennes could be maintained much longer. Such withdrawals, thought Clark, would be taken by the Indians as signs of weakness. Thousands more of them would become allies of the British and eventually would descend upon Kentucky.

The general asked the militia leaders to consider the possibility of taking the offensive against the enemy and to suggest possible objectives. He believed that before any expedition could be launched the Indians would have harvested and hidden their corn. In this event the frequently used method of destroying their provisions and thus forcing them to hunt instead of molesting the white settlers would not be applicable.

Success would have to be measured in terms of the number of Indians killed. Since more would be encountered along the Wabash than along the Miami, Clark suggested a campaign in that region. He expressed his willingness to lead them on any expedition that offered hope for success no matter how daring it might seem.

After receiving the general's opinions Todd, Floyd, Logan, and their subordinates began their deliberations. The first question which arose centered around the matter of what measures should be recommended in case an expedition should be deemed inadvisable. It was decided that fuller knowledge of the extent of Clark's authority and of his attitude toward the garrisoning of the Ohio at points above the Falls would help the council to make a wiser decision. Clark having withdrawn, Floyd and Logan were delegated to seek this information. The general made it clear that the State of Virginia had placed him in full command of its western military department, and that he was free to adopt any measures which he considered satisfactory.

When Floyd and Logan returned, the question of attempting a campaign was presented to the council without further delay. There were such differences of opinion that the officers decided to have two distinct reports entered in the minutes. Logan and Todd believed that the wiser policy would be to concentrate upon defense. They suggested that a fort be constructed at the mouth of the Kentucky River. From this point small parties could harass the Indians even in winter. Such a fort also would provide a storage place for provisions for any expedition which might be undertaken in the spring.

The other officers, Floyd, Trigg, Cox, and Pope, saw things differently. They favored an immediate campaign against the Shawnee. If this tribe could be forced to seek peace with the white men others might follow. All of the officers agreed that a Wabash campaign would not be popular. Most Kentuckians considered the Shawnee to be their most dangerous enemy. Furthermore, the Wabash route would be more difficult and probably too long for a successful campaign so late in the season. The officers concluded, however, by offering to furnish for Clark's use any desired number of militiamen up to two-thirds of their total strength.

After he had received the report of the council of militia officers Clark called a meeting of the field officers and captains of the Virginia state troops then stationed at the Falls. This group included Lieutenant Colonel Joseph Crockett, who presided, Lieutenant Colonel John Montgomery, Major George Slaughter, Major George Walls, and eleven captains. The commander offered for their consideration his written instructions from Governor Jefferson, dated January 19, 1781, his address to the field officers of the militia, the written reply to this address, and other information prepared especially for the regular officers.

This board, realizing that the total number of men available for a campaign would not exceed seven hundred, put this question to an immediate vote. Montgomery, Slaughter, and four of the captains wanted to make the attempt, but the other nine officers were opposed. It was agreed unanimously that Kentucky was of sufficient importance to the state to make its defense imperative. The regulars recommended to Clark the continued maintenance of Fort Nelson and the construction of another fort at the mouth of the Kentucky. If a third fort could be supported they would place it just across the Ohio from the mouth of the Miami. It was suggested also that Clark ask the three county lieutenants to provide militiamen to erect the forts and to assist in garrisoning them. The hope was expressed that as the terms of enlistment of the state troops expired some might be re-enlisted for garrison duty. The board closed its session with the further suggestion that the state government be asked to send out enough regulars in the coming spring to capture Detroit and to maintain it as a Virginia outpost.

Before they left the Falls, Todd and Logan joined with Floyd in preparing a letter to Clark. They offered to furnish him with corn and buffalo meat in so far as they were able, but they indicated that they would expect payment. The county lieutenants knew, or believed that they knew, what decision Clark had reached regarding the defense of Kentucky. They concluded: "We wish the General success in his plan which is quite agreeable to our wishes."

Although these meetings ended in a spirit of co-operation, this condition was not to last for long. Within a month Clark called upon Todd and Logan to supply militiamen for the erection of the proposed fort at the mouth of the Kentucky. Todd went over to St. Asaph's, the county seat of Lincoln, to discuss the matter with Logan. On October 13 the two militia officers sent a joint reply to Clark's request. They admitted that they had favored such a fort when they were at the Falls, but charged that the plan then proposed had been so changed that they no longer could support it. By way of explanation they added that they had expected the forts on the Ohio to be built and garrisoned chiefly by regulars. The two county lieutenants described themselves as being ready to assist, but they offered several excuses for declining to do so. They had no tools for digging trenches and constructing earthworks. Their militia forces were small and widely scattered and would not finish harvesting their crops before November.

In offering some of their militiamen to Clark a month earlier Todd and Logan probably were sincere. They may have been thinking of a short campaign as had been suggested by the other militia officers. The arduous task of constructing fortifications and the boresome duty of garrisoning them would not have appealed to their militiamen. In organizations such as theirs, where a private thought himself the equal of his colonel, such objections had to be considered.

As another reason for their change of heart the two officers told of rumors that the Cherokee and Chickamauga were planning an attack upon Lincoln County. They added that it could be taken for granted that the Shawnee would attack Fayette.

A possible explanation for their reluctance can be found toward the end of the letter. They had learned that Jefferson County was not being asked to furnish men for building or garrisoning the fort at the mouth of the Kentucky. "As it is solely intended for our Defense," they wrote, "on calculating the cost we conclude that we are willing to forgoe [*sic*] the many advantages . . . for this season and think it better to defend ourselves near home."

The only concession which the two county lieutenants did make was a promise to send provisions to Clark if this were possible. They made it clear, however, that they expected the provisions to be received "at Lees Town or somewhere on [the] Kentucky."

Eight days later Todd wrote to the new governor, Thomas Nelson, explaining the position which he and Logan had taken. He criticized the state government for keeping regular troops "in the most interior and secure posts," and at the same time seeking to put "the militia on duty at a place distant from 60 to 120 miles from home. . . ." Logan or Daniel Boone, both of whom had sat in the Virginia Assembly in the late spring and early summer, could have told Todd that the interior regions of the state had not remained so "secure" as they were when he journeyed to Richmond as a representative of Kentucky County in the preceding year.

Todd was convinced that if militiamen were sent to garrison a new post Clark would be reluctant to replace them with regulars from Fort Nelson. He was very critical of Clark's contention that the post at the Falls was "the Key of the Country." The mouth of the Kentucky, he thought, was a more logical place for regulars to be stationed. It was nearer to the route which Indians would be likely to follow if they were invading Kentucky. Also the Kentucky River provided a convenient means of transporting supplies to the garrison. It formed the boundary between Fayette and Lincoln from which Todd thought most of the supplies would have to come. The land around the Falls was filled with pools of stagnant water. This he believed to be responsible for the diseases which killed or incapacitated so many of the soldiers: "To say that the Falls is the Key to this Country seems to me unintelligible," he continued. "It is a strong rapid which may, in an age of commerce, be a considerable obstruction to . . . navigation; but as we have no trade, we neither need nor have any keys to trade."

Friction between the leaders of Lincoln and Fayette on the one hand and the state officers at the Falls on the other was not new. Before Clark returned from his visit to Governor Jefferson, Colonel John Montgomery, the senior officer present at Fort Nelson, had complained of it. He had just supervised the evacuation of Fort Jefferson on the Mississippi, and he feared that if money were not provided by the government Fort Nelson too would be lost. There is "not a mouthful for the troops to eat, nor money to purchase it with," he wrote to the governor, "and . . . the credit of the government is worn bare. The counties of Lincoln and Fayette particularly, tho able to supply us, refuse granting any relief without the cash to purchase it on the spot."

The idea of substituting defense for offense was approved by the Virginia Assembly in December, and the governor was urged to take the necessary steps.

The plan as it now stood was to place a roof over Kentucky by strengthening Fort Nelson at the Falls (Louisville) and by building additional forts at the mouths of the Kentucky, the Licking, and Limestone Creek. Although such a roof would have obvious holes any force which entered Kentucky from the North would risk being cut off by the garrisons of one or more of these forts. It was the opinion in the assembly that from six to seven hundred men would be enough to garrison all four posts if each post could be supported by two gunboats. The crews for the gunboats would be obtained from the garrisons.

Two orders pertaining to the situation in Kentucky soon were prepared at the capital. One was a circular letter from Virginia's Commissioner of War, William Davies, to the county lieutenants of Lincoln, Jefferson, and Fayette. It directed these officers to send militiamen to Clark when he requested them. Here was an indication that Virginia's new governor, Benjamin Harrison, who had taken office on November 30, was going to give some attention to the defense of Kentucky, and perhaps to tackle the problem created by a divided command. Although Clark was the supreme military commander in Virginia's western department, his direct authority extended only to the regulars. When dealing with the militia he might make requests, but only during a campaign or upon the direct authority of the Virginia executive could he command.

The other order was a letter from Harrison to Clark. It enclosed the assembly's decision against offensive operations and outlined some plans for defense. Clark was authorized to ask the three county lieutenants for enough militiamen to make, when combined with his regulars, a total of three hundred and four. One hundred of these were to be stationed at the Falls and sixty-eight at each of the other defense points, the mouth of the Kentucky, the mouth of the Licking, and the mouth of Limestone Creek. Additional authority was given to Clark to increase these numbers when he felt that the situation demanded it.

Harrison liked the recommendation of the Assembly regarding gunboats on the Ohio. He urged that three or four such boats be constructed. If Clark could not spare cannon for them the governor thought that a few could be sent down from Fort Pitt in the spring.

Harrison admitted that the work of building forts and gunboats would have to be done on credit. "We have nothing to depend on for the present," he added, "but the virtue of the people."

In his reply to the governor, Clark spoke of having been disappointed by the government's failure to give him adequate support in the past. He denied having either money or credit, but promised to do the best that he could under the circumstances. The practice of raising money by the sale of public supplies which were not urgently needed was generally accepted at the time. Nevertheless, Clark hesitated to employ this method with no knowledge as to when such supplies could be replaced. He approved of the gunboat suggestion, but made it clear that cannon and rigging would have to be sent to him. "The Post of Licking will be Immediately established," he promised, "and the others as soon as circumstances will admit."

Plans for defense continued to be affected by friction between Clark's western military department and the militia of Virginia's three western counties. Joseph Lindsay, who had served as commissary for Kentucky County, was given the same position for the counties of Fayette and Lincoln. In February, 1782, he was appointed by Clark to the post of commissary general. In this capacity he was to procure supplies for the forts which were to be erected along the Ohio.

After receiving this new appointment Lindsay devoted very little attention to militia requirements. The unfortunate effects of this situation were pointed out by Logan and by his militia colonel, Stephen Trigg. Logan believed that Lindsay had in his possession provisions which actually belonged not to the regulars but to the militia. It was his opinion that Fayette County still was being supplied from this source, but that supplies which rightfully belonged to Lincoln County had been forwarded to Clark.

It was unfortunate that such dissension existed at a time when

Kentucky was in danger. The chiefs of some of the Indian tribes had been called to Detroit in the preceding November. They were asked to have their warriors ready to attack the Kentucky settlements in the spring. The British plan, as learned by the Americans, was to capture Fort Nelson and then to lay waste the other settlements. The Indians were urged to bring in prisoners from whom information concerning the state of Kentucky's defenses might be obtained.

When news of the British intentions reached Clark, he made a change in his plans. Instead of building forts along the Ohio, which might require several months, he decided to concentrate upon strengthening Fort Nelson and upon the building of armed boats to patrol the river. Thus the roof for Kentucky, although it would contain large holes, would have movable sections which could be shifted about as conditions might require.

This new plan was referred to in a letter which Clark wrote to Governor Harrison asking that equipment for the gunboats be forwarded as soon as possible. "No vessels they can bring across the portages from the Lakes will be able to face such as we can navigate the Ohio with . . .," he explained.

To implement his new plan Clark asked Logan to have a detachment of the Lincoln militia ready to march to Louisville by March 15. He told his commissary general to be prepared to supply that post with "three hundred Rations of Beef per day . . ." Lindsay was asked to be on the lookout for experienced carpenters and boatbuilders. "We are going to Build Armed Boats to Station at the mouth of [the] Miami," he explained, "to dispute the navigation of the Ohio either up or down."

This time the people of Jefferson County, who stood to benefit most from the proposed strengthening of Fort Nelson, were called upon to furnish their proportionate number of militiamen for the work. Floyd informed Clark that these would be ready on the appointed day. He believed that the people of his county would be very disappointed if no forts were erected above the Falls. They may have felt that this apparent concentration upon Fort Nelson would increase the jealousy of the people of the other two counties, who already believed that Clark was not sufficiently interested in their safety.

The first detachment from Lincoln County went to the Falls in March. It was commanded by Lieutenant Colonel John Logan, a brother of the county lieutenant. Upon arrival John Logan was placed in charge of all militia units which had come to work on the fortifications. The superintending of construction was given to Major John Crittenden, Clark's aide-de-camp.

On March 24 Governor Harrison sent an answer to Clark's request for cannon and other equipment for his gunboats. He promised to supply as much as possible and to deliver it to Fort Pitt. On the following day he wrote to Isaac Zane, who operated an iron foundry, and ordered four cannon. He told Zane that the work would have to be done on credit, but he felt that payment could be made by fall. Within a fortnight William Davies of the Virginia War Office wrote to inform Clark that he expected to send two light three-pounders and a quantity of clothing by wagon to Redstone for shipment down the Ohio.

In April a fresh militia company went to Louisville from Lincoln County. This time Ben Logan went along, probably to see for himself just what was being accomplished. Soon after his arrival he was relieved by his second-in-command, Colonel Trigg, who remained throughout the one-month tour of duty.

Small parties of Indians frequently molested the settlers. John Floyd saw this as part of the British plan to capture Fort Nelson and then to overrun Kentucky. The Indians repeatedly stole the settlers horses. This loss would make flight difficult and pursuit of the invaders impossible.

Floyd blamed the frequent failure of militiamen to report when called for duty upon the talk of a possible separation of Kentucky from Virginia. Some of these delinquents may have believed that a division would be effected very soon, and that it would save them from being brought to justice.

The separation movement was being pushed by Arthur Campbell, John Donelson, and other political leaders and land speculators. These men hoped that separation would be accompanied by the invalidating of Virginia land titles in the Kentucky area. With this in view they sought to influence the Congress to deny Virginia's ownership of Kentucky. In this event speculators might acquire from the United States title to lands which Kentucky settlers now held under Virginia law. Some of the advocates of this scheme sought to hold a meeting at Harrodsburg to draw up a petition to be sent to Congress. On the first attempt the meeting was broken up by a group of Kentuckians led by Major Hugh McGary. Two days later a successful meeting was held with John Donelson presiding. Petitions asking for the separation of Kentucky from Virginia were sent both to Congress and to the Virginia Assembly.

Clark believed that the crest of the wave of agitation for a separate state had passed by the first of May. The Kentuckians had begun to suspect that they were being misled. "I believe," he wrote to the governor, "[that] in a short time it will be dangerous . . . to speak of [a] new government in this quarter . . . The body of the people now seem to be alarmed for fear Virginia will give up their interest."

Meanwhile Clark was continuing the work on his gunboats, or row galleys as he liked to call them. Lindsay, his commissary, was still procuring supplies. The fortifications at Louisville were nearing completion, but Clark was putting his greatest hope in the galleys, the first of which he expected to launch by the end of May. It was seventy-three feet long, was to have forty-six oars and would carry one hundred and ten men. Its gunwales were four feet high, and were surmounted by false gunwales on hinges which could be raised even higher. Both the fixed and the false gunwales were bullet-proof. Thus the boat could "lay within pistol shot of the shore without the least danger." Clark's intention was to mount eight cannon, a two-pounder, six four-pounders, and a six-pounder in each boat.

Governor Harrison in his message to the assembly on May 6 stated that Kentucky was expecting a heavy blow from Detroit, and that artillery and supplies had been sent down the Ohio for her defense. Unfortunately some of the stores failed to reach Clark when he expected them. They were sold by an officer who had them in his charge. This officer had not been granted authority to make such a conversion of public property into cash and had failed to report the incident. He was reprimanded by the governor and ordered to replace all that he had sold.

In spite of Clark's hopes, it was not until July 6 that the first of the row galleys, with a few guns mounted, was ready to move up the Ohio. It was to be used to patrol the river around the mouths of the Licking and the Miami. It was decided that regulars or Jefferson County militiamen would take it to the mouth of the Kentucky. There they would be relieved by a militia company from Fayette. Officers of the Virginia line would remain in command.

On June 27 John Todd started forty of his militiamen, about one-fourth of his total strength, to the meeting place. He promised to relieve them within four weeks. This company was commanded by Captain Robert Patterson. When the boat did not appear at the expected time Patterson and his men camped at Drennon's Lick, a few miles from the mouth of the Kentucky, where they could replenish their supply of meat. Word soon came from Clark that the boat was ready to move. Patterson was ordered to march his company down the Ohio until he met it.

Captain Robert George, who commanded the boat, found it necessary to keep his regulars at the oars. The militiamen met the boat, but they were not very co-operative. They demanded and received double rations of flour. They refused to row, insisting that they were soldiers and not sailors. At the mouth of Big Bone Creek, a few miles below the Miami, they declared that they were going home. This they did, although their period of active duty lacked a week of being completed.

After this unsatisfactory experience the galley was placed under the command of Captain Jacob Pyeatt. It was operated by marines who were enlisted for that express purpose. These men were mostly members of Virginia line companies whose period of enlistment had ended.

Although difficulties had been encountered, the galley had a beneficial effect. The British were expecting another American invasion of Canada. They believed that it would be launched by the summer of 1782, and that their enemies would be assisted by Frenchmen and Indians.

On the day that Patterson and his men took leave of the galley, Indian spies were watching from the hills on the north side of the Ohio. They may have been under the influence of liquor, because they reported to their Loyalist leader, Alexander McKee, that they had seen two large boats both mounting cannon. They said also that these boats were accompanied by the largest army of both Indians and whites which ever had approached their villages. McKee concluded that such a host could not be expected to stop with the destruction of a few Indian villages. Surely this was the expected invasion. He promised his superiors that he and Captain William Caldwell, who was approaching the Ohio with a party of Lake Indians, would try to keep their forces between the enemy and Detroit.

At this time there was little likelihood that British and Indian war parties would attempt to cross the Ohio in the vicinity of the galley. If a few more of these gunboats had been ready for action the Kentuckians might have been safe.

By the first of August Clark must have doubted that an attack was imminent. He was considering an invasion of the Shawnee country in co-operation with General William Irvine who expected to make a thrust from Fort Pitt. These plans were known to the British and caused them to increase their forces protecting Detroit.

Caldwell and McKee must soon have realized that the reports concerning the army which was said to be with the row galley were false. The proposed drive against Detroit had not yet been prepared. Their Indians were hard to retain in a state of inaction. Giving the galley a wide berth, they marched to a point on the Ohio nearly opposite the mouth of Limestone Creek. From that location they crossed into Kentucky. The stated purpose of the two officers was to draw a few of the Kentuckians away from one of the forts. In this way they might take prisoners who could furnish information concerning Clark's intensions. [*See* Map 5.]

By daylight on the morning of August 16 the war party under Caldwell, McKee, and the renegade, Simon Girty, had surrounded Bryan's Station. This settlement was situated in Fayette County, about five miles northeast of Lexington. It was protected by a stockade and blockhouses in a manner common along the frontier. Attempts to lure some of the defenders outside of the fort failed. Realizing that Bryan's could not be taken without artillery, the attackers withdrew on the following morning.

By August 18 a party of 182 mounted men had been raised and had started in pursuit. It was led by John Todd with Stephen Trigg as his second-in-command. On reaching the Licking River at the Blue Licks the Kentuckians saw some of the

Indians on a ridge on the opposite side. The river at this place curves in the form of a horseshoe. Caldwell and McKee had extended their lines from the point where it first changes course to the point where its general course is resumed. The water was deep at all points in the bend except at one spot near the middle of the curve. Here it could be forded without difficulty. Thus a party entering the horseshoe, if beaten, would have but one point of escape.

The Kentuckians crossed the river and advanced in three columns. The one on the right was led by Colonel Trigg. The center was under the command of Major Hugh McGary of Lincoln. The right was commanded by Fayette's lieutenant colonel, Daniel Boone.

When they were within sixty yards of the enemy the men dismounted and tied their horses. Forming their lines parallel to those of the enemy they continued to advance. Heavy firing began on both sides with Boone's men pushing the Indians back nearly one hundred yards. Subsequent events seem to indicate that at least a part of this withdrawal was planned. On the Kentucky right there were some ravines and in these, Indians were hidden. They were overlooked by Trigg's men who soon found that they had the enemy at their backs. In trying to escape from this trap they shifted toward the middle of the ridge. McGary's men then shifted behind Boone's. Within five minutes after the first shot had been fired all was confusion. Escape seemed uppermost in every man's mind. As Major Levi Todd described the scene a few days later: "He that could remount a horse was well off, and he that could not saw no time for delay."

Many were slain while trying to cross the river. The Kentucky losses included Colonels Todd and Trigg, Majors Silas Harlan and Edward Bulger, Joseph Lindsay, the commissary general, four captains, five lieutenants, and about sixty men.

When Benjamin Logan at the head of four hundred and seventy men reached the scene of the battle on August 24 the enemy had departed. Nothing could be accomplished beyond the burial of the dead.

The disaster at Blue Licks occurred at a time when the Revolutionary fighting in the East had ended. The loss of life not only was high, but it included a disproportionate number of

officers, both military and civil. In Lincoln County only three of
the magistrates were left alive.

As might have been expected there was criticism of those who
were responsible for defense. The "roof for Kentucky" had not
been completed. There were those who wanted to know why
this was the case. Friction between the militia officers and the
regulars was in evidence again. As usual it was coupled with a
division between Jefferson County on the one hand and Lincoln and Fayette on the other.

Daniel Boone wrote to Governor Harrison and asked that
five hundred men be sent out for the protection of Kentucky.
He urged that they be stationed wherever the county lieutenants felt that they were most needed. "If you put them under
the Direction of Gen: Clark," he continued, "they will be [of]
Little or no Service to our Settlement, as he lies 100 miles West
of us, and the Indians North East . . ." He complained also that
the men of Fayette frequently were called to the Falls to protect
the people of that area.

Benjamin Logan was even more critical. "I am inclined to
believe," he wrote, "that when your Excellency and Council
become acquainted with the military operations in this
country . . . you will not think them . . . properly conducted . . ." He then told of attending the council of field
officers at the Falls where the decision to build forts instead of
attempting a campaign had been made. From that point on,
Logan was unfair in his selection of facts. He told of being asked
for men to build a fort at the mouth of the Licking. This would
have helped to protect Fayette and Lincoln counties. Logan
charged that these men had been taken to the Falls instead. Not
once did he mention that the first call had been for men to build
a fort at the mouth of the Kentucky. On this occasion he and
Todd had refused to comply.

Logan next criticized the row galley and accused Clark of
"weakening one end [of Kentucky] to strengthen another." He
failed to explain that the galley had not remained at the Falls,
but had been sent to the mouth of the Miami. Neither did he
admit that the refusal of militiamen to serve aboard the galley
had been one of the factors which had hampered its activity.
Logan concluded by reminding Harrison that "a defensive war
cannot be carried on with Indians, and the Inhabitants remain

in any kind of safety." Here again he was forgetting that at the officer's council in September, 1781, he had favored defense rather than offense. "Unless you can go to their Towns and scourge them," he continued, "they will never make a peace; but on the contrary [they will] keep parties constantly in your country to kill, and the plunder they get, answers instead of Trade."

Another criticism of the conduct of military affairs in the West was made by Andrew Steel of Fayette, a survivor of the Battle of Blue Licks. Steel objected to the emphasis placed upon Louisville, located as it was upon the northwestern border of Kentucky. He believed that most of the money and effort which had been expended in defending the Western Country had been applied to Fort Nelson, Fort Jefferson, Kaskaskia, and Vincennes. The amount spent upon the three Kentucky counties, thought Steel, would be in comparison "less than a Mathematical Point."

On September 11 Daniel Boone, Levi Todd, Robert Patterson, and other Fayette officers forwarded to the governor a combined request for aid and criticism of Clark. "Our militia," they wrote, "are called on to do duty in a manner that has a tendency to protect Jefferson County, or rather Louisville—A town without inhabitants, a fort situated in such a manner, that the enemy coming with a design to lay waste our country would scarcely come within one hundred miles of it . . ." They then recommended that, if no campaign could be attempted at the time, the plan of erecting forts at the mouths of the Licking and of Limestone Creek be readopted and carried out."

In October Harrison wrote his replies to the letters which he had received from Logan, Todd, Boone, and the Fayette officers. There were expressions of sympathy for the bereaved, implied criticisms of John Todd and Stephen Trigg as commanders, and suggestions to the effect that revenge might be possible. The governor seemed amazed to learn that the Ohio River forts had not been built. He expressed the belief that they could have prevented the disaster, because the settlers could have been warned in time to collect their total strength.

The governor wrote also to Clark condemning his failure to build the forts. He insisted that it still must be done. Harrison's surprise over the situation in Kentucky would seem to indicate that he had not read Clark's letter of March 7, 1782, very carefully. In it the general had explained the change from the building of additional forts to the strengthening of Fort Nelson and the building of gunboats. He had given the expected attack upon the Falls as his reason.

In his letter to the Fayette militia officers Harrison had said: "Kentucky is as much the object of my care as Richmond, and I shall shew it on all occasions." In his message to the assembly on October 21, 1782, the governor questioned the effectiveness of the defensive measures which were being taken for Kentucky's protection. He suggested that a campaign against the Indians be considered.

Clark, Logan, and Floyd did not wait for a decision to be made at Richmond. Forgetting their differences they ordered their men, to a total of about 1250, to meet at the mouth of the Licking on November 1 in preparation for moving into the Indian country. By November 3 this army had crossed the Ohio, had built and garrisoned a blockhouse, and had started northward. It was divided into two regiments. One, which was composed of men from Jefferson and Fayette, was commanded by Floyd. The other, consisting entirely of Lincoln County men, was led by Logan.

The first objective was the Shawnee town of New Chillicothe or Standing Stone on the Miami River. All hope of taking it by surprise was ended when a few mounted warriors discovered the advancing Kentuckians and hastened to give the alarm. Much of the fighting was with retreating Indians who had left their belongings in their cabins. Parties of men were sent out to destroy the neighboring villages. One of these detachments consisted of 150 mounted men under Logan. This party went to the store of a French Indian trader, Pierre Loramie, at the portage between the waters of the Miami and the waters of the Maumee. Here a large quantity of plunder was taken. The building with the remaining contents was burned.

The Kentuckians remained in the Shawnee Country for four days. Fearing that the weather might change for the worse they then decided to withdraw.

When Governor Harrison learned that Clark was leading an expedition into the Indian country without his permission he was considerably disturbed. Only the realization that these were men whose friends and kinsmen had died at Blue Licks and that they were seeking revenge modified his criticism. Harrison had heard that after that battle the British had ordered their Indian allies to refrain from taking the offensive. He feared now that Clark's action might cause the war to be prolonged. Thus it is not surprising that he mentioned once more the Ohio River forts and insisted that they be built.

When the governor learned that the campaign had been a success his attitude changed. He congratulated Clark and Logan and praised the officers and men who served under them. "It will teach the Indians to dread us," he said, "and [will] convince them that we will not tamely submit to their depredations." He explained that he always had favored offensive operations, but that he had differed in this respect from those to whom he had to answer. This claim at the least was consistent with his message to the assembly in the preceding October.

Most of the military operations west of the mountains had been conducted on credit. The settlers who had furnished provisions or who had gone out on the various campaigns had received only promises of future payment. By 1782 a commission had been authorized to hear evidence and to approve or disapprove claims. Near the end of April, Logan, who may have been urged by people who were anxious to be paid, asked the governor if he would hasten the formation of the commission and speed its departure for Kentucky.

After several Virginians, including William Preston and William Christian, had declined the appointment, a board composed of William Fleming, Samuel McDowell, Caleb Wallace, and Thomas Marshall was named. The first three arrived in Kentucky late in October.

Although little could be accomplished until Clark, Logan, and the other Indian fighters returned from their campaign, the commissioners held short sessions in Harrodsburg and in Lexington.

When Clark arrived he not only submitted his accounts, but asked the opinion of the board of commissioners on the question of forts along the Ohio. The board realized that the Virginia treasury was not then able to support three additional posts, and the same was true of the people of Kentucky. However, the desirability of a fort at the mouth of the Kentucky was recognized. It would lie in the path of those tribes which were most likely to attack Kentucky. Also it would provide protection for Drennon's Lick, a potential source of salt and a favorite place for Indians to kill and cure game while harassing the Kentucky settlements. Fleming, McDowell, and Wallace agreed that posts at the Licking and at Limestone Creek would be difficult to provision. They advised Clark, however, to establish the Kentucky River post as soon as possible.

Thomas Marshall differed from the other members of the board as to the most desirable location for a fort. He favored the mouth of Limestone Creek. This, he believed, was a logical landing place for people who wished to settle in Fayette, which still was the most thinly populated of the three counties.

There were strong indications that, whatever the British attitude might be, the Indians were not yet ready to make peace. In the preceding November twenty chiefs from four of the tribes around Detroit had visited the Chickamauga branch of the Cherokee. They proposed a joint campaign against Fort Pitt, Fort Nelson, and the Kentucky and Illinois posts in the spring. The same idea was then carried to the Choctaw and the Creeks. One of Virginia's Indian agents, Joseph Martin, learned of this plan and reported it to the governor. He wrote also to Logan warning him to be on guard.

Fortunately no such dangerous alliance among the tribes as that which Martin had feared was effected. That the Kentucky settlements could have stood against it is doubtful. Although Clark realized the need for additional forts, he denied being able to spare enough cannon even for one. He asked the commissioners to seek assistance for him in the constructing of one or more forts along the Ohio and in the location of a permanent garrison at Vincennes. If more could be accomplished, he favored a campaign against the Indian tribes along the Wabash.

In believing that this much was possible Clark was more optimistic than some of his officers at Fort Nelson. While he was traveling with the commissioners late in February he received a letter from his subordinate, Major George Walls. A meeting of the officers at Fort Nelson had just been held and the consensus of opinion was that, if men and supplies were not sent, that post would have to be abandoned.

In a letter dated April 9 Governor Harrison informed Clark that peace terms with England had been agreed upon and that hostilities were to cease. If the Indians had received this information they apparently were not impressed. On April 8, John Floyd, his brother, Charles Floyd, and Alexander Breckinridge were traveling from Floyd's Station on Beargrass Creek to a point on Salt River. They were attacked by Indians, and John Floyd was seriously wounded. With his death two days later Kentucky had lost two of her three county lieutenants in less than eight months.

The question of forts on the Ohio still was open. Clark, whose request for an early retirement from the Virginia line had been approved, had, at the request of the governor, gone to Richmond to explain alleged irregularities in the accounts of the western military department. On April 30 he wrote to Logan and the two new county lieutenants, Daniel Boone for Fayette and Isaac Cox for Jefferson. He urged their support of his successor, Major George Walls. Then he gave them some information regarding Virginia's latest plan for Kentucky. All state taxes collected in the three counties of Lincoln, Jefferson, and Fayette were to be used for defense purposes. Posts on the Ohio were to be established as had so often been suggested. The first was to be at the mouth of the Kentucky River. It was to be garrisoned by militia units with the addition of one half of the regulars then at Fort Nelson. This could have led to a renewal of the controversy between the state troops and the militia.

It is not too surprising that the proposed "roof" never was constructed. On September 3, 1783, final peace terms with England were signed and the likelihood of an organized Indian invasion of Kentucky was thereby greatly reduced. By the end of the year Virginia's cession of her lands north of the Ohio to the general government had been accepted by Congress. On March 1, 1784, the deed was presented to the Congress by Thomas Jefferson. It was now the property of the United States to garrison as circumstances might demand and funds might permit. A roof for Kentucky no longer was considered a necessity. From time to time, however, the United States located small garrisons across the Ohio; Fort Harmar at the mouth of the Muskingum, Fort Washington opposite to the mouth of the Licking, Fort Finney at the mouth of the Miami, Fort Massac a few miles below the mouth of the Tennessee, and Fort Knox at Vincennes.

Clark was wise in considering Fort Nelson to be the key to the western country. While the peace negotiations were underway in Paris the Northwest was not strongly held by the Virginians. Clark could not spread his small forces over the entire area. By selecting Louisville as his point of concentration he was in a position to discourage a major attack by Indians who were hesitant about leaving their villages undefended. Also he could reach Vincennes or Kaskaskia more quickly than the British could do so from Detroit. No reference was made to Clark's activities in the diplomatic papers prepared at Paris, but his strong position must have been evident to the British negotiators and to the Prime Minister, the Earl of Shelburne. Governor Harrison, a frequent critic, wrote to Clark on July 2, 1783: "I feel called on . . . to return my thanks and those of my council for the very great and singular services you have rendered your country in wrestling so great and valuable a territory out of the hands of the British enemy, repelling the attacks of their savage allies, and carrying on successful war in the heart of their country."

The Bloody Year in Ohio—1782

Allan W. Eckert

Despite American beliefs to the contrary, the Revolutionary War did not end with the surrender of Cornwallis. Some of the bitterest and bloodiest fighting occurred in the year-and-a-half between Yorktown and the conclusion of peace. From the Carolinas to New England loyalists and patriots exacted vengeance for alledged crimes on one another. Even though regular armies refrained from major combat, dozens of small actions by irregulars left a legacy of tears that remained in the memory of both sides for generations.

Nowhere is this inheritance better illustrated than in Ohio. In the spring of 1782 an American expedition massacred ninety peaceful Moravian Delawares. This opened a season of bloody attack and retaliation that lasted into the fall. Although the British at Detroit realized the implications of Yorktown, they could not restrain the combined Delawares, Iroquois, Shawnee, and Wyandots and their loyalist allies—William Caldwell, Alexander McKee, and Simon Girty. From western Pennsylvania to the bluegrass their raids brought a final agony to the Ohio Valley. Colonel William Crawford of Pennsylvania led a counterattack and buccaneering expedition into Ohio where he hoped to strike at the Indian villages on Sandusky Bay. His defeat, capture, and torture forecast the dozen years of warfare that would be required before American settlement could move into the Lake Erie basin.

Allan W. Eckert (1931———), a former Dayton newspaper correspondent, is now a free lance writer living in Florida. He is the author of numerous television scripts and books dealing with natural history as well as books on the frontier. His outdoor drama Tecumseh! *is performed each summer near Chillicothe, Ohio. Although* The Frontiersmen *uses dialogue which is not historically verifiable, it is accurate and lively reading for those desiring the flavor of the Revolutionary era.*

From Allan W. Eckert, *The Frontiersman: A Narrative* (Boston, 1967), 245–264; reprinted with permission of Little, Brown and Company.

October 19, 1781—Friday

Abraham, chief of the Moravian Indians, listened in disapproving silence to the words of Chief Thayendanega of the Mohawks and the Delaware chiefs, Pimoacan and Pipe. They had failed to convince him he must unite with his Delaware brothers and join the confederation being led by Thayendanega against the white settlements in western Pennsylvania. Now they urged him, for the safety of himself and his three hundred Christian followers, to leave their towns and move to the region of the Upper Sandusky River.

"You know well," Thayendanega said, "that the white chief Brodhead came here and murdered nearly all the residents of Goschachgunk who remained behind while their neighbors fled. Thus was their trust in the white man rewarded. That is what can happen to you. Even Chief White Eyes was murdered by them while in the very act of talking peace!"

Abraham was not impressed. The white men, he said, knowing the Moravian Indians were no longer Delawares and not their enemies, would leave them alone. No, they would not leave. God would protect them as he already had.

Captain Matthew Elliott from Detroit, representing the British, who were demanding that these Indians be moved away, stepped forward with an angry wave of his hand. He had had quite enough of this coaxing; they were not offering a choice but delivering an order. "What do *you* know of God?" he said condescendingly. "Can you really be so ignorant as to believe that because you have been, as they say, 'converted' and changed your name from Chief Netawatwees to Abraham, that this provides you protection of God? I tell you that God will not help you here once we begin to attack these Pennsylvanians in earnest. The whites will try to retaliate and you will be killed. Can't you understand that it is for your own protection that we have requested you to leave? We hoped you would be wise enough to do so without being forced. Instead, we find you a stupid, stubborn old man." He pointed to Thayendanega. "Chief Brant here has three hundred warriors waiting outside the village. Once again I say you *must* take up new residence on the Sandusky River. You have no choice. Go, or we will destroy your homes and your missions."

"But what of our corn, our other crops?"

Elliot shook his head. They would have to leave them behind. But there was no need to worry. He would see to it personally that the Moravian Indians would be given sufficient food to sustain them throughout the winter.

Abraham sighed. He could not believe his friends, the Americans, would hurt them, but this ultimatum worried him. They had worked long and hard, with the missionaries to establish their three towns on the Tuscarawas—Salem, Gnadenhutten and Schoenbrun—and the thought of the homes of his people and their missions being destroyed was distressing to contemplate. There was really no need for him to be unreasonable about it. Perhaps after a winter on the Upper Sandusky River matters would have settled down enough so that they could come back. He nodded resignedly.

"We will go," he said.

November 10, 1781—Saturday

The electrifying news had finally reached Kentucky and the populace was nearly delirious with joy. On October 19 Cornwallis had surrendered his entire army to Washington at Yorktown, Virginia. It had to be the beginning of the end, even though no cessation of British-American hostilities had yet been called and no peace conferences held. For all intents and purposes, America had won her independence as a free nation. The fighting was over. At least that was what they were saying in the east.

They were not so sure in the west.

February 4, 1782—Monday

General Daniel Brodhead returned the salute of the young colonel who had just entered his quarters. He had heard rumors about this young man—that he was cruel and a hothead—and felt that such a temperament might now prove an asset.

"Colonel Williamson," Brodhead said, "the western Pennsylvania settlements, as you know, have been severely harassed all winter long by Mohawks and Delawares. They have stolen, burned and, on occasion, engaged in killing outlying settlers. They have done so with virtual impunity. I intend to change that."

"Yes sir?" David Williamson's dark eyes glittered.

"I'm tied up with details here and can't go myself, but I'm going to give you command of a hundred men. A week from today I want you to move out on a retaliatory expedition against the Delawares. You may have a free hand in this operation. That's all."

Williamson saluted smartly and turned to leave, but then stopped abruptly and swiveled around as Brodhead said, "Colonel!"

"Sir?"

"Do a thorough job. I want those Delawares taught a lesson they won't forget."

"Yes, sir!" Williamson said confidently. "You have my word, we'll give them something to remember."

February 20, 1782—Thursday

Regardless of the British promises to provide food enough to sustain them through the winter, the Moravian Indians suffered severe famine. What supplies did occasionally come out of Detroit were meager in the extreme and nowhere near enough to tide them over, even on far less than adequate rations. The Wyandots and the few Delawares in the vicinity of Upper Sandusky were of little help. Not only had their own crops been skimpy last fall, but they were too engaged in their frequent raids into the Pennsylvania country. Besides, they looked rather scornfully upon any Indian who would willingly renounce his own tribal designation to take up the name Moravian.

Abraham had thrice journeyed to Detroit to plead for food; and now, at last, he returned with good news. No, the British had no food for them, but they had given Abraham permission to lead a hundred and fifty of his followers back to the three Tuscarawas River towns on a temporary visit for the purpose of gathering up what portion of their unharvested corn crop still remained on the stalks.

They would leave at once.

March 8, 1782—Friday

Most of his people had fallen asleep now and Abraham stared unseeingly into the darkness of the big room. During the past two days of talk with the white chief Williamson and many of his men, he was able to reconstruct how such an unbelievable thing had happened. Yet, even as he reviewed it there was something of a nightmare quality about it all, a pervading unreality; in one corner of his mind he still felt that with the dawn he would awaken to find that all that had transpired was nothing but a wild dream.

Exactly two weeks ago he had led his hundred and fifty Moravian Indian followers on the overland journey to the forks of the Muskingum, arriving at the southernmost of their three towns, Salem, late in the afternoon. They had been delighted to find more corn had survived the winter than anticipated, and so Abraham had directed the fifty residents of this town to gather up the corn while he and the remainder continued upriver to Gnadenhutten and Schoenbrun, fifty staying at each of those villages also.

The days had gone by swiftly as the three separate parties worked in their fields, gathering and stripping the corn from the husks during the day and then, around the evening fires, shelling it off the cobs into large buckskin bags.

Meanwhile, Colonel David Williamson and his company of one hundred had arrived within a mile of Gnadenhutten and camped there. In the morning, observing Abraham and some of his followers at work in the cornfield on the opposite side of the river, fifteen volunteers had accompanied Williamson to the location. They crossed the river unseen in a large boatlike sugar-sap trough, two at a time; a vine rope was used by those still on shore to pull the empty boat back to them. When all sixteen were safely across, the remainder of the army marched into Gnadenhutten. There they found only two Indians, a man and his wife, both of whom they killed instantly with tomahawks lest they raise an alarm.

Williamson's squad, on approaching the Indians far out in the cornfield, found them much more numerous than expected. There were forty-eight—men, women and boys— nearly all of whom had weapons with them. His men behind him, Williamson approached in a friendly manner, holding up his hand in greeting. The Indians smiled and waved and followed Abraham as he moved to greet them.

"I come with good news," Williamson said blandly. "We have been sent here to take you back with us to the neighborhood of Fort Pitt where in the future you will be protected from all harm. You may quit your work here now, for there is no need.

Soon you will be given good food in abundance, warm clothing and sturdy shelter.

Abraham broke into a wide smile and shook Williamson's hand warmly and, for those of his followers who had only partially understood, he translated. There were cries of joy and relief from all.

These Indians remembered how last year some of their people had been taken to Fort Pitt in similar manner and had been well treated by the commander of the fort and finally dismissed with fine gifts and tokens of lasting friendship. Under these circumstances it was not at all surprising that Abraham ordered his people, at Williamson's request, to surrender their arms as a token of good faith.

Abraham placed himself and his people under Colonel Williamson's protection and, again at the officer's request, sent a pair of runners to nearby Salem to tell his people at this village to come at once to Gnadenhutten.

Now the entire party recrossed the Tuscarawas, but as they came into the center of the village they found themselves surrounded by men with weapons aimed at them. Puzzled, Abraham asked what was wrong. Williamson refused to answer, but instead ordered the wrists of each Indian bound behind him. The mission and the largest house in the village were side by side and the prisoners were marched into the two buildings, men and boys into the former and the women into the latter. Once inside they were forced to sit on the floor and their ankles were thereupon bound as well.

After two hours the Salem group showed up, walking along happily, talking and laughing. They were greeted outside the town by Williamson and some of his men who shook their hands and smiled and told them their brothers were waiting for them in the mission and that Abraham had said for them to turn over their arms to him. Without suspicion they did so and then followed him into the village, only to have the same scene that had greeted Abraham reenacted.

The chief shook his head sadly as the new prisoners were brought in. How could this have happened? Did it mean that they were to be taken back and held as hostages at Fort Pitt for some purpose? For only one thing was he grateful—that he had not mentioned the third village of Schoenbrun above them, to whom he had planned sending another messenger after crossing the river.

A total of ninety-eight men, women and boys now sat or lay bound in the two buildings. Outside, a strong ring of guards had been stationed and there was no hope of escape. Thus they remained the rest of the day and through the night, being provided with neither food nor water nor toilet facilities. It was a terrible night and few of the captives slept.

In the morning, Colonel Williamson called a meeting of all his men to determine what should be done with the Indians. He spoke to them in a flat, emotionless voice.

"The question before us now," he said, "is whether these Moravian Indians, who are Delawares, should be taken as prisoners to Fort Pitt or be put to death." Some of the men were startled at this, but Williamson went on: "I might remind you of the damage nearly all of you have suffered at the hands of the Indians. And I might further remind you that General Brodhead's strict orders were that the Delawares should be taught an unforgettable lesson. To my way of thinking, imprisonment is hardly such a lesson."

He shot his cold dark glance over the assembled men and then concluded, "I now ask those of you who are in favor of saving their lives to step out and form a second rank." The manner in which he said it, and the thinly masked violence in his eyes, was clear indication that he expected no one to step forward.

A few braved his wrath, but only a few. One at a time they stepped out, but when the movement had ended only eighteen of the hundred had voted for mercy. The majority had ruled; the ninety-eight captives would be executed. It was Williamson himself who told Abraham of the judgment of his "court" and he seemed to revel in the sound of the phrase—"put to death"— as it rolled off his tongue.

Shocked and unbelieving, Abraham finally recovered enough to speak. "I call upon God as witness that my people are perfectly innocent of any crime against you. We are prepared and willing to suffer this death. Yet this much I ask of you: when we were converted from our heathen ways and baptized, we made a solemn promise to the Lord that we would live unto Him and endeavor to please Him alone in this world. But we know, too, that we have been wayward in many respects, and therefore we wish to have the night granted to us to pour out our hearts before Him in prayer and beg His mercy and pardon."

Williamson considered and then shrugged. It made little difference, actually. God had better have mercy on them, because he certainly wouldn't. The request was granted.

As word of the sentence spread through the captives in the mission and then jumped the gap to the women prisoners next door, a great wailing of terror arose which gradually subsided to weeping among the women and some of the smaller boys. Abraham spoke to them at length, reassuring them that God had not forsaken them and that, if it was His will that they should die thus, they should accept it with calmness and a certain joy in the knowledge that they would soon be in the presence of their Heavenly Father. At one point he put his back against the wall and managed to slide himself up along it until he regained his feet.

"My children, hear me," he said. "Our sentence is fixed and we shall soon all depart unto our Savior. This I must say now: I have sinned in many ways and have grieved the Lord with my disobedience, not walking as I ought to have done. But still I will cleave to my Savior, with my last breath, and hold Him fast, though I am so great a sinner. He will forgive me all my sins and not cast me out."

Together then they prayed long into the night, until at last only Abraham remained awake, staring into the darkness and asking himself again how this incredible thing could have happened. But now, as it became lighter in the big mission room, where so many times over the years he and his people had prayed and held services, he could hear them coming and called aloud to his people to awaken and say their final prayers.

Fully twenty men entered the room, led by Captain Charles Builderback who, by the drawing of lots, had been given the honor of starting off the executions. Builderback ordered that the captives be stood on their feet and faced against the walls, shoulder to shoulder around the room. There was just barely space enough for this.

The day before, as the lots were being drawn, the remark had been made that Abraham's long flowing hair would make a fine scalp and so now Builderback, having been handed a large cooper's mallet by one of his men, stepped up behind Abraham and without a word dealt him a blow which caved in the entire back of his skull. The Indian dropped instantly, and even as the chief's legs and arms jerked spasmodically, Builderback cut away the scalp and held it aloft in triumph while his men cheered lustily.

Moving now in a clockwise fashion from Abraham, Builderback felled thirteen more in succession, each blow making a hideous smacking sound. Following this fourteenth execution, however, Builderback blew out a great gust of air and handed the mallet to Private George Bellar.

"My arm's failing me," he said. " You go on in the same way. I think I've done pretty well."

Bellar grinned wickedly and, as Captain Builderback began scalping his last thirteen victims, the private carried on, using both hands and bringing the mallet down with such force that often bits of skull and bloody gray matter splattered his front. But Bellar played out quickly, too, and only managed to murder eleven before he was forced to hand the mallet to the next man. In the distance, sounds of a similar nature could be heard coming from the house next door. But still there were no cries, no pleas for mercy. It was too much for Private Otho Johnston, who abruptly vomited and then fled out the door with the laughter of his companions following him.

But Johnston had left the door ajar and now two of the victims closest to this portal—both of them boys of about fourteen—glanced at one another and nodded. All through the night they had worked on their bonds until they had finally gotten them off. With great care they had replaced them, but so loosely that a single exertion would cast them off both wrists and ankles.

At the instant the club next thudded into the head of a victim, the two boys threw off their ties and leaped out the door. They darted around the building and were practically into the woods before the cry was raised of their escape, but there was no pursuit. The consensus among the soldiers was that once in the woods no one would be able to find them. Besides, they were only boys. Let them go.

And go they did, running as they had never run, until they felt their hearts must burst, and crying as they ran—crying for their lost chief and their lost parents and brothers and sisters and other relatives, crying for their lost companions and neighbors, crying for their lost world.

They ran the full seven miles to Schoenbrun.

Back in Gnadenhutten the massacre continued until all ninety-six of them—thirty-five men, twenty-seven women and thirty-four boys—had been killed and scalped, not including the pair who had been tomahawked on the army's arrival here. Then, Colonel Williamson ordered both the mission and the house containing the women to be set afire. As the roaring flames made ashes of their crime, they set off to the north. While the executions were in progress, a scout had come in to report that he had found another village like this one just a little way upstream.

But when they got there, they found Schoenbrun abandoned.

April 25, 1782—Thursday

Reaction to the Moravian Massacre, as it quickly came to be known, varied in different areas of the country, but mostly it was disapproving at best. The frontiersmen in Kentucky were shocked and dismayed at the barbarism of the act and a distinct undercurrent of fear ran through them that the retaliation, when it came, might spread to involve them. The frontiersmen in Pennsylvania were somewhat awed that such a thing had happened, but there were remarkably few who spoke out against it and many who asserted that the Indians had "got what they deserved." There was even speculation among them of mounting a second invasion of the same type. Leaders in the east were deeply disturbed by the news, but few, if any, had a true realization of what a cold-blooded, premeditated mass murder it had been. Besides which, they had worries of their own; the peace treaty negotiations with Great Britain in Paris were bogging down; political problems were besieging the new states; and the problem of establishing a federal government was rearing its head.

The Moravian missionaries were utterly devastated by the news, scarcely able to comprehend the enormity of what had happened, realizing with guilt that had they stayed at Licktenau with their converts the tragedy might have been averted. The

British in Detroit were appalled by it and yet were quick to assess its propaganda value, using it to light even brighter fires of unrest among the Indians. They even went so far in trying to prove the benevolence of "the great white father across the sea" that a company of Redcoats was dispatched at once to the Upper Sandusky River region to escort the remaining Moravian Indians to a quiet area to build a new village far from danger, a site along the banks of the Thames River in Ontario.

The Indians—all of them in general, and the Delawares in particular—were infuriated as they had never been before. They considered this massacre a wanton outrage of the blackest nature and a clear depiction of the real character of the *Shemanese*. They lived with one thought paramount in their minds now—total annihilation of these enemies. They had more than enough courage and fighting ability for the task. All they lacked were horses, cannons, gunpowder, firearms, food, supplies and manpower.

June 12, 1782—Wednesday

For perhaps the hundredth time since accepting command of this army, Colonel William Crawford berated himself for ever joining the campaign. All his life, it seemed to him, he had been plagued with a sharply critical hindsight of his own actions, coupled with a distinct inability to heed his premonitions, most of which proved correct in the end. This time was no exception.

Ever since David Williamson's massacre of the Moravian Indians, a sort of blood lust had taken over the Pennsylvanians. Instead of seeing it for what it was, these settlers were calling that campaign a "great victory" and clamoring for another of the same to wipe out that other Moravian village along the Upper Sandusky River.

Their wish was granted.

Almost from the start it was dubbed "the Second Moravian Campaign" and, with the exception of Colonels Crawford and Williamson, who were both "loaned" by Fort Pitt for the expedition, the army of four hundred eighty men was made up entirely of western Pennsylvanian volunteers. The object of the campaign was to finish the work of the first one—marching to and destroying the Moravian town on the Upper Sandusky.

After that they would march upstream to the south and wipe out the Delaware and Wyandot towns on the same river, principally the large village of Upper Sandusky.

It was the resolution of all those concerned in the expedition to kill instantly any Indian falling into their hands, Christian or heathen, friend or foe, man, woman or child. No quarter was to be given. Bulletins stressing this were tacked to trees in the campgrounds. The thirst for revenge for the long period of harassment the Indians had given them was all-encompassing.

The rendezvous point for the army was the old Mingo Town on the Ohio. They came mounted on the best horses they could procure, for this was to be a "dash" campaign—in and out before any sizable force could be assembled against them. Each man furnished his own supplies, except for some ammunition provided by the lieutenant colonel of Pennsylvania's Washington County.

Upon assembling on May 25 they held an election for their commander, with Williamson and Crawford the candidates. Crawford won and accepted only with the greatest reluctance. They followed Williamson's Trail, as the route to the Tuscarawas River villages was now being called, and camped at Schoenbrun, where they found much of the unharvested corn still on the stalks. During the evening a pair of Indians was seen by three of the militiamen; the moment the news of the discovery of Indians reached camp, the men rushed out into the woods in a tumultuous mass without any sign of order. It was at tl.is moment that Crawford experienced a definite premonition cf disaster.

The march continued uneventfully to the west until on June 6 they had reached the town of the Moravian Indians on the Sandusky River. Instead of being full of peaceful Christian Indians to murder and plunder to take, however, the village was abandoned. Only the broken remains of a few huts projected from the weeds. [*See* Map 5.]

Now they were confused and no little worried about what to do next. Crawford called a meeting of the officers and a decision was reached to march one day longer in the direction of Upper Sandusky; if the village was not reached by then, they would retreat in all haste.

Thus, on the morning of June 7, they rode through the Plains of Sandusky. About 2 P.M. the advance guard was suddenly attacked by Indians hidden in the high grass. The guard galloped back to the main army and a general engagement broke out. Heavy firing continued incessantly until darkness fell, when it ceased. The casualties were the same on both sides: three men killed. Both armies kindled large fires along the line of battle and then retired some distance from them to prevent surprise attack. Not long after the fires were built, a man bearing a white flag showed himself in the glow between the fires. Crawford sent a man to see him and in a few minutes he returned.

"He talks English, sir," the militiaman reported. "Asked for you by name. Says he wants to talk with you right away but that you're not to come nearer to him than twenty steps."

Crawford went at once, alone, stopping at the required distance and trying to make out the features of the short figure in the flickering light.

"Colonel Crawford," the man called, "do you know me?"

Crawford hesitated. "I seem to have some recollection of your voice," he admitted, "but I can't see your face well enough and those Indian clothes you're wearing don't help. Do I know you?"

"We shared lodgings once," came the reply. "My name is Simon Girty."

Girty! The deserter and renegade. How well Crawford knew him. They had once been very closely acquainted in those months before McDonald's campaign eight years ago.

"A surprise to meet you here, Girty. What do you want?"

Girty's voice lowered. "The Indians think I've come out here to tell you you're surrounded and to demand your surrender. I'll tell them you refused. Crawford, if you don't surrender, the Indians plan to take you tomorrow. They're three times as strong as you are and they'll cut you to pieces. Tonight they really are surrounding you. When the move is completed you'll hear some guns fire all around the ring. But there's a large marshy ground to the east of you. It isn't covered. It'll be hard going, but you have no choice. Listen for the gap in the sound when the firing goes round the ring. Take your men and ride for that gap. It's your only chance."

"Why are you doing this, Girty?" Crawford demanded.

But Girty only threw down the white flag and disappeared back into the darkness. Crawford returned at once to his camp and called a meeting of the officers to discuss this alarming situation.

Williamson and many of the men distrusted Girty and figured the whole business smelled of a trap. They could not believe there were that many Indians about; indeed, Williamson wanted to take a hundred fifty men and move straight into Upper Sandusky, but the commander refused him permission.

"Even if you reached the town, Dave," he said, "all you'd find would be empty dwellings and the army would be weakened by the division. I can't allow it. These Indians don't care anything about saving their town. It's worth nothing. Whatever squaws and children and goods were there have been taken away long ago."

Williamson started to object but Crawford cut him off. "I said no and that's an order, Colonel! These Indians want our lives, our horses and our equipment. If they get us divided they'll soon have them. We've got to stay together and do the best we can."

They continued to talk about the visit from Girty. Crawford and quite a few of the men were inclined to believe the renegade and the scales tilted in their favor when a firing of rifles broke out indicating a circle around them, but with a gap on the east side. A retreat was decided upon along the route suggested by Girty as the only means of saving their army. They would leave as soon as the fires died down. In the meantime, the three dead men were buried and ashes spread over the common grave so the Indians would think it a campfire site and not dig up the bodies for their scalps.

Crawford suddenly gave the order and they moved to the east quickly, expecting ambush at every step. They soon found themselves in the marsh and safely through the Indian lines, whereupon Crawford began swinging the column in a wide circle to the left to get back to their original trail, which they reached in a couple of hours.

During the whole of June 8 the retreat progressed with occasional long-shot harassment of the rear guard. Once again

Williamson and Crawford were arguing. About three hundred of the men sided with their commander in his contention that they must stick together, but Williamson succeeded in convincing the remainder that the best escape possibility lay in breaking into small parties, avoiding the trail by which they had come and making their way back by different directions. The argument turned into near open rebellion until finally Crawford allowed them to go.

Williamson's group split into nine parties of twenty men each, one of which he led, and all nine groups set off in different directions, leaving Colonel Crawford and his weary main army. They calculated the Indians would follow the bigger prize and leave them alone.

They were wrong.

Seven of the small parties were followed and wiped out almost immediately. The remaining two, including the detachment led by Williamson, joined forces and, with severe losses, managed to return to the main army. But now this army was a pitiful thing, weak and straggling and spread out all over the countryside. Many of the men simply fled on their own, alone, and were never seen again.

Toward late afternoon, Crawford suddenly discovered that his son, John Crawford, his son-in-law, Major James Harrison, and his two nephews, James Rose and Bill Crawford, were all missing. He had no way of knowing that all four were already dead, so he halted and called for them as the line of militia passed by—but there was no answer. Then, when he attempted to regain the lead, he found his horse was so weak it couldn't even catch up with the rearguard.

A straggler came along and he saw that it was the army surgeon, Dr. Edward Knight. They stayed together and a little later they were joined by Lieutenant Timothy Downing and another man Crawford didn't know. They traveled all night, directing their course by the light of the north star. On the following morning, June 9, they encountered Captain John Biggs and Lieutenant Bruce Ashley, but the six of them made little headway and camped together early in the evening.

At dawn they were discovered by Indians and Crawford and Knight were captured almost at once; Biggs and Ashley were killed and Downing and the other man escaped. The arms of the captives were bound and rawhide halters placed about their necks and they were led to a Delaware and Wyandot camp less than a mile from their own campsite. Here they found nine other prisoners and seventeen Indians, and here they stayed all day.

On June 11, Crawford and the other ten prisoners were marched to the main Delaware village, called Big Spring, on a bottom land on the east bank of Tymochtee Creek, about eight miles above its mouth at the Sandusky River. And this morning two of the major Delaware chiefs, Pipe and Wingenund, had arrived.

Abruptly Crawford's hopes skyrocketed. Wingenund! Years ago at Fort Pitt, Crawford and Wingenund had become good friends when Wingenund had acted as guide and interpreter for the British under Alex McKee. They had drunk together in Crawford's own quarters and become attached to one another. Now Crawford watched closely and hopefully as the two chiefs talked with the Indians; except for one brief glance in his direction, however, Wingenund paid no attention to him. In a few minutes the chiefs retired to a *wegiwa*.

At once nine of the prisoners—all but Crawford and Dr. Knight—were led to the edge of the village where they were unceremoniously tomahawked and scalped. Knight was left tied where he was but Crawford was now taken by five of the Indians, stripped of all clothing and led to a thick post projecting fifteen feet from the ground. His wrists still tied tightly behind him, a long rawhide cord was run between his arms and then brought around the post and tied firmly in a large loop. In this way he was able to walk around the pole, stand, sit, even lie down, but was unable to move more than four feet in any direction from the pole.

In a little while Pipe came toward him with another man, followed by a large crowd of warriors and squaws. Crawford recognized the other man as Simon Girty and once again his hopes began to rise. But not for long. While the pair stood twenty or thirty feet away, the crowd of Indians rushed up with sticks and switches and beat Crawford unmercifully, withdrawing only when his body was badly welted and bloodstained and he appeared on the verge of unconsciousness.

The group then raced over to where Dr. Knight was tied and

subjected him to the same punishment, while Girty and Chief Pipe watched quietly and in apparent approval. At length Crawford came around enough to call to Girty and both the renegade and the chief approached him.

"Girty,"Crawford said, his voice hesitant with pain, "are they planning to burn me?"

"Yes they are, Colonel."

"My God, Girty, you're a white man, too. Can't you help me?"

Girty shrugged and grimaced, indicating he doubted it but he would try. He turned to Chief Pipe and spoke rapidly in the Delaware tongue. This prisoner, he said, was a good soldier with whom, many years ago, Girty had shared a cabin at Fort Pitt. It was Colonel Williamson, not Crawford, who had murdered the Moravian Indians. Would Chief Pipe sell him this prisoner for three hundred fifty bucks?

Chief Pipe took a step backward, his expression as shocked as if Girty had slapped him. Then a great rage came over him at the effrontery of this white man, at the great insult of his remarks. When he spoke his words hissed between his teeth and were frightening in the malevolence they carried.

"Do you think I am a *squaw*, white man? How dare you make such a proposition to me? If you speak one more word on the subject I will have a stake erected beside his and burn you along with the white chief!"

He stalked away toward his own *wegiwa* at the other edge of town, nearly three quarters of a mile distant. Girty had paled at the threat in the chief's retort and now he blew out a gust of air and came closer to Crawford. He explained what they had said and then shook his head.

"I would like to save you, Crawford, but I will not give up my own life needlessly nor jeopardize my position among the Indians. But there is one thing I can still do. There are two parties of important British traders not beyond reach—one on the Back Fork of Mohican River, the other on the Sandusky below Upper Sandusky. They both have much more influence than I among the Delawares. I'll send runners for them at once. Perhaps they may be able to buy you, but I cannot hold out much hope on that."

Crawford nodded that he understood and Girty started away,

but then turned back. "One thing more," he said. "The death they have in store for you is a very slow and painful one. If all hope becomes lost, I will do what I can to end your suffering more quickly."

Crawford watched him walk away, not cheered by Girty's final remark. He had little hope where the English traders were concerned. There remained, in fact, only one real hope for him.

Wingenund.

June 13, 1782—Thursday

Shortly after sunrise, still shivering from his night of nakedness at the stake, Colonel William Crawford saw Girty threading his way through the crowd already assembling and called him to come over. Girty hesitated and almost walked on, then turned and came toward the captive.

A foot-high circle of kindling had been placed all the way about Crawford's stake at a distance of about five yards. About a hundred dry hickory poles, each an inch or so thick and upwards of twenty feet in length, had been placed so that they lay with one end atop the kindling and the other stretching outward, away from the circle. Girty stepped between them until he could come no closer without stepping upon them and he stopped.

"Any word from your friends, Girty?" Crawford's eyes were pleading.

Girty shook his head and turned to leave but Crawford cried, "Wait!" Girty turned back, and Crawford hurried on. "Listen, do you know Chief Wingenund very well?"

"Well enough."

"He and I used to be friends at Fort Pitt. I don't think he knows who I am. Maybe he could get me out of this."

Girty was shaking his head even as Crawford spoke. "He knows you. That's why he hasn't come to see you. He's afraid you'll ask him to help you. He doesn't think you know who he is."

"Do me one last favor, Girty," Crawford begged. "Go to him right away. Tell him I ask to see him in the name of the friendship we once shared. Tell him he can't deny me this."

"I'll give it a try, Crawford. Don't expect much."

A quarter hour passed before Wingenund finally came up, his embarrassment and agitation obvious. He stepped over the ring of hickory poles and stood in front of Crawford and feigned surprise.

"Are you not Colonel Crawford?"

"I am."

"So! Yes! Indeed!"

Crawford held back his irritation at this play-acting. "Wingenund," he said, "don't you remember the friendship that existed between us? I recollect we were always glad to see each other."

Wingenund smiled. "Yes! I remember all this and that we often drank together and that you have been kind to me."

Crawford relaxed a little. "Then I hope the same friendship still continues."

"It would, of course, were you where you ought to be and not here." Wingenund was frowning now.

"And why not here? I hope you would not desert a friend in the time of need. Now is the time for you to exert yourself in my behalf, as I'd do for you if you were in my place."

"Colonel Crawford! You have placed yourself in a situation which puts it out of my power—and that of others of your friends—to do anything for you."

"How so, Wingenund?"

The chief was becoming angry now. "By joining yourself to that devil,Williamson, and his party. Only the other day, this man murdered a great number of Moravian Indians, knowing them to be friends, knowing that he ran no risk in murdering a people who would not fight and whose only business was praying!"

"Listen, Wingenund, believe me! Had I been with Williamson at the time, this would never have happened. Not I alone, but all your friends and all good men, whoever they are, reprobate acts of this kind."

The Indian nodded. "That may be. Yet these friends, these good men did not prevent him from going out again to kill the remainder of these inoffensive, yet foolish, Moravian Indians. I say foolish because they believed the whites in preference to us. We have often told them they would one day be so treated by those people who called themselves their friends! We told them there was no faith to be placed in what the white man said; that their fair promises were only intended to allure us that they might the more easily kill us, as they had done many Indians before these Moravians."

"I am sorry to hear you speak thus, Wingenund," Crawford said sadly. "As to Williamson's going out again, when I found out he was determined to do it, I went out with him to prevent his committing fresh murders."

Wingenund broke into a harsh, scornful laugh. "This story, my friend, the Indians would not believe were even *I* to tell them so."

"Why would they not believe?"

"Because it would have been out of your power to have prevented his doing as he pleased."

"Out of my power!" Crawford's voice rose indignantly. "Have any Moravian Indians been killed or hurt since we came out?"

"None," Wingenund replied, but now his voice became harsh and bitter, "but do not try to deceive me, Colonel! We know well what you have done. You first went to their town and, finding it deserted, you turned on the path toward us. If you had been in search of warriors only, you would not have gone thither. Our spies watched you closely. They saw you while you were gathering on the other side of the Ohio. They saw you cross the river. Thy saw where you camped for the night there. They visited every one of your camps the moment you were gone from it and they found bits of paper with writing on them that had been stuck to the trees by your men and which said that no Indian—friend, enemy, heathen, Christian, man, woman, boy girl or infant—should be spared. How brave an army! Our spies saw you turn off from the path at the deserted Moravian town. We knew you were going out of your way to attack Upper Sandusky. Your steps were constantly watched and you were permitted quietly to proceed until you reached the spot where we wished to attack you."

Crawford's shoulders slumped and he could not deny the truth of anything Wingenund had said. Those words destroyed his last ray of hope and now his voice was filled with emotion as he asked, "What do they intend to do with me?"

The harshness in Chief Wingenund's features softened. He placed his hand on Crawford's shoulder as he replied. "I tell you with grief. As Williamson, with his whole cowardly host, ran off in the night at the whistling of our warriors' balls—being satisfied that now he had no Moravians to deal with, but men who could fight, and with such he did not wish to have anything to do—I say, as he has escaped and they have taken you, they will take revenge on you in his stead."

"And is there no possibility of preventing this?" Crawford was pleading now and did not see the look of disgust which crossed the Indian's face at such unmanliness. "Can you devise no way of getting me off? You shall, my friend, be well rewarded if you are instrumental in saving my life."

Wingenund shook his head. "Had Williamson been taken with you, I and some friends, by making use of what you have told me, might perhaps have succeeded in saving you; but as the matter now stands, no man would dare to interfere in your behalf. The King of England himself, were he to come on this spot with all his wealth and treasure, could not effect this purpose. The blood of the innocent Moravians, more than half of them women and children, cruelly and wantonly murdered, calls loudly for revenge. The nation to which they belonged will have revenge. The Shawnees, our brothers, have asked for your fellow prisoner and on him, *they* will take revenge. All the nations connected with us cry out, Revenge! Revenge! The Moravians whom you went to destroy, having fled instead of avenging their brethren, the offense is become national and the nation itself is bound to take revenge!"

Numbly, Crawford nodded. "My fate is then fixed and I must prepare to meet death in its worst form?"

Wingenund sighed. "I am sorry for it, but I cannot do anything for you. Had you attended to the Indian principle, that as good and evil cannot dwell together in the same heart, so a good man ought not go into evil company, you would not be in this sorrowful position. You see now, when it is too late, after Williamson has deserted you, what a bad man he must be. Nothing now remains for you but to meet your fate like a brave man. Farewell, Colonel Crawford. They are coming. I will retire to a solitary spot."

Chief Pipe had moved into the center of the milling mass of Indians and stepped up on a log so that he was head and shoulders above them. As he raised his arms the laughter and shrieking and murmur of conversation that had been going on died away. There were about forty warriors in this throng and sixty or seventy squaws and children.

For more than half an hour the chief spoke, his voice filled with controlled anger and emotion. Crawford understood nothing of what was being said and he looked around. In only two faces—and even one of those he was not sure of —did he detect any compassion: Dr. Knight and Girty, the latter sitting close to the tied doctor.

There was a hideous triumphant screaming as Chief Pipe completed his speech and immediately all the warriors and at least half the squaws rushed up until the closest were within a few feet of Crawford. All of them carried flintlock rifles. Into the barrels they poured extra-large quantities of gunpowder but no balls, and now they shot at him in turn.

The grains of powder, saltpeter still burning, peppered his skin, some of it puncturing and continuing to burn just beneath the skin. Crawford screamed until he was hoarse and then only a kind of whimpering grunt issued from him. More than seventy powder charges had struck him everywhere from feet to neck, but the greater majority had been aimed at his groin, and when they were finished the end of his penis was black and shredded and still smoking.

The crowd thinned momentarily as the guns were returned to the *wegiwas*, but as soon as all the Indians had reassembled, Chief Pipe stepped up to Crawford and with two swift movements sliced off his ears. From where he sat watching in horror, fifty feet away, Dr. Knight could see blood flowing down both sides of Crawford's head, bathing his shoulders, back and chest.

Now came squaws with flaming brands and they lighted the kindling all the way around the circle, igniting the material every foot or so until the entire circle was ablaze. The poles quickly caught fire on their tips and the heat became intense, causing the closest spectators to fall back. A peculiar, hair-raising animal sound now erupted from Crawford. He ran around the post in a frenzy, finally falling to the ground and wrapping his body around the stake. After the better part of an hour the fire died down, leaving behind a fanned-out ring of long poles, each with one end a glowing spike.

Crawford's back, buttocks and the skin on the back of his thighs had blistered and burst and then curled up into little charred crisps. The animal sounds from him were fainter now. About this time there was something of a disturbance and the British traders Girty had sent for cantered into the village. They greeted both Pipe and Wingenund in friendly fashion, complimented them on Crawford's capture and moved closer to the fire ring to look. Both men paled at the sight, but they turned back to Chief Pipe and announced their pleasure at being able to witness the execution. In a few moments the chief waved for the continuation of the torture and the traders stepped over to join Girty and watch. As they came up, one of them looked directly at Girty and gave a barely perceptible shake of his head before turning around.

In groups of four the Indians now began taking turns at a new torture. Each of the four would select a pole and jab the glowing end onto Crawford's skin where they thought it would give most pain. Dr. Knight thought Crawford near death by now, but was amazed to see the officer scramble to his feet and begin stumbling about the stake, attempting to avoid the glowing ends which hissed and smoked wherever they touched him. One of the glowing points was thrust at his face and as he jerked to avoid it he ran into another which contacted his open eye, and a fearful shriek erupted from him.

When the poles had all been used and tossed on a pile to one side, some of the squaws came up with broad boards and scooped up piles of glowing embers to throw at him until soon he had nothing to walk upon but coals of fire and hot ashes.

"Girty! Girty! Where are you?" These were the first coherent words Crawford had spoken since before the guns were fired. "Girty, in the name of Christ, kill me! Shoot me. Oh my God, Girty, *kill me!*"

Chief Pipe, hearing Girty's name, shot the renegade a stern glare and Girty neither moved nor replied to Crawford's plea, knowing he was closer to the stake now himself than he had ever thought to be. Most of the Indians did not understand what Crawford was saying, but the beseeching tone of voice pleased them and they clapped their hands and shouted aloud in triumph at having forced the white chief into this outburst.

When there was no answer to his cries, Crawford began a

shuffling walk round and round the stake as if in a trance, scarcely flinching as he stepped on the hot coals. Finally he stopped and slowly raised his head and his voice came out surprisingly loud and clear.

"Almighty God, be with me now. Have mercy upon me God. I pray you end this suffering so that I might be with you where there is no pain and suffering. Oh God, dear God, help me!"

Once more he began the same shuffling walk until at last, two full hours after having been prodded with the glowing poles, he fell on his stomach and lay silent. At once Chief Pipe stepped over the ring of ashes and cut a deep circle on the top of Crawford's head with his knife, wrapped the long dark hair around his hand and yanked hard. The pop as the scalp pulled off was clearly audible to Girty and Dr. Knight.

Chief Pipe now stepped clear of the circle and advanced on the captive doctor. He held the dripping scalp in front of his eyes and shook it. "This is your great captain!' he said. With rapid strokes he whipped the fleshy portion of the scalp back and forth across Knight's face a dozen times or more, stopping only when there came a deep murmur from the crowd behind him.

A squaw had entered the circle of ashes with a board heaped full of brightly glowing coals, and these she scattered on Crawford's back and held them with the board against the officer's bare skull. The murmur that had arisen was occasioned by what seemed wholly unbelievable: Crawford groaned faintly and rolled over and then slowly, ever so slowly, drew up his knees and raised himself to a kneeling position. For perhaps two minutes he stayed like this and then he placed one foot on the ground and stood erect again, beginning anew that queer shuffling walk. A few squaws touched burning sticks to him but he seemed insensitive to them, no longer even attempting to pull away. It was the most appalling sight Dr. Knight had ever witnessed and, unable to control himself any longer, he suddenly vomited and then screamed at his captors, cursing them and calling them murderers and fiends and devils, blaming Girty more than anyone else.

Chief Pipe made a motion and one of the warriors cut the thong binding Knight to the stake at his back and then propelled him toward the Chief's *wegiwa*. When he was gone from sight, Pipe issued some more commands and a bevy of squaws scurried away and returned with armloads of fresh kindling. This was tossed into a pile a dozen yards from the stake and lighted. The hickory poles were thrown atop the new fire.

When the fire reached its peak, two warriors cut the rawhide cord that bound the still shuffling Crawford and, one on each side, let him shuffle toward the fire. When the heat became too intense for them to advance closer, they thrust him from them and he sprawled onto the blaze. His legs jerked a few times and one arm flailed out but then, as skin and flesh blackened, living motion stopped and all that remained was a gradual drawing of arms and legs close to the body in the pugilistic posture characteristic in persons burned to death.

So ended the life of Colonel William Crawford.

The West in the Peace Negotiations

Richard B. Morris

To understand the international aspects of the Revolution and the acquisition of the Old Northwest, one must transfer his attention from North America to the courts and salons of Europe. Here three American negotiators, Benjamin Franklin, John Jay, and John Adams, sought to secure the best possible western boundaries for the new nation. Arrayed against them were some of the shrewdest diplomats of Europe. To understand the story one must have a brief summary of the participants in the dramas, most of whom are unfamiliar to Americans.

Comte de Vergennes, the French foreign minister, masterminded the diplomatic isolation of Britain by bringing the other Bourbon power, Spain, plus Holland actively into the combat and by maneuvering Russia and several Baltic powers into a League of Armed Neutrality to thwart Britain's blockading attempts. Vergennes was one of the principal architects of American independence, but his design did not include the trans-Appalachian region in the domain of the United States.

Joseph-Matthias Gerard de Rayneval, an undersecretary at the foreign ministry, was the principal French authority in relations with the English-speaking world. He designed the plan to curtail American expansion and attempted to negotiate this with the English.

Conde de Aranda, the Spanish ambassador to Paris, sought to keep the Americans as far from the Mississippi valley as possible and thereby protect Louisiana.

Earl of Shelburne, first lord of the treasury and the equivalent of prime minister, was the principal British negotiator. At his Wiltshire estate called Bowood Park he received Rayneval and Benjamin Vaughan representing French and American interests and from these conversations he chartered much of the course leading to the British position in peace negotiations.

Richard Oswald, a Scottish merchant, was Shelburne's envoy to the American delegation in Paris beginning in March, 1782.

Henry Strachey was a British undersecretary of state sent to Paris in October, 1782, to stifle Oswald's excessive generosity in peace terms to the Americans.

269

Baron Grantham was secretary of state for foreign affairs in the British cabinet, his position was mostly perfunctory since Shelburne dominated the negotiations.

Thomas Townshend, secretary of state for home and colonial affairs, was a staunch supporter of Shelburne in the cabinet.

Francois Barbé-Marbois was secretary of the French legation in the United States.

Chevalier de La Luzerne was the French ambassador to the United States.

Alleyne Fitzherbert was the British ambassador to France who negotiated with Vergennes trying to settle the Anglo-French portion of the conflict.

Benjamin Vaughan was a Briton sent by Jay to see Shelburne and explain the American position in the peace negotiations.

Each party to the negotiations played one against the other to secure the best possible treaty. The role of John Jay is particularly important to the understanding of the American diplomacy due to Franklin's illness and Adams's late arrival. The Sage of Passy, as Franklin was known because of his place of residence in Paris, was somewhat distrusted by Jay and Adams as a result of his allegedly excessively Francophile leanings.

Shelburne's decision to be generous to the Americans was crucial to the solution of the western lands. He never seriously considered Rayneval's plan which would have given the Americans little more than Kentucky, West Virginia, and eastern Tennessee. This proposal reasonably corresponded to the actual military situation. Clark's brilliant victories of 1778–1779 were lost because of inadequate financial support from Congress and Virginia, because of the frontiersman's natural desire to remain close to home rather than engage in long campaigns that might endanger his family, and because of an inadequate logistical system that probably could not have supported a Detroit garrison even if the fort had been taken.

Moreover, Clark's efforts had no impact in Paris or London. Rayneval called the Virginian's campaign an "ephemeral raid" having no relevance upon the final boundary question. In this essay, Professor Richard B. Morris (1904———) concludes, "for all the diplomats in Paris seemed to care, the Virginians who had waded the icy waters of the Wabash in their heroic march to Vincennes might just as well have remained by their own firesides."

Fortunately, in Professor Morris's words, Shelburne did not "pant" for the "back-lands." They were a bargaining counter in the stakes over the loyalists and Newfoundland fishing rights. The question was over which basic line to follow: 1) the "Lake Nipissing" line from the New York-Quebec border to this lake north of Lake Huron and thence west to the source of the Mississippi River; 2) the forty-fifth parallel, stretching westward from northern New York to the Mississippi; or 3) the "line-of-the-lakes" which followed the center of the Great Lakes and from Lake Superior west to the Lake of the Woods. The first two would have given the United States the most populated portion of modern Ontario while losing varying amounts of Wisconsin and Minnesota. The line-of-the-lakes provided "logical ground for later negotiations which extended the boundary westward on the 49th parallel" and gave Shelburne some compensation for loyalists in the more temperate areas of Ontario.

Professor Morris, one of America's most distinguished historians, is especially noted for his Government and Labor in Early America *(1946),* John Jay and the Court *(1967), his co-editorship of the scholarly* New American Nation *series, and his editing of the John Jay papers. He always combines a talent for detailed research with felicitous prose.*

★ ★

To LORD SHELBURNE a matchless opportunity now presented itself to exploit the widening rift between the Americans and the French, or, more accurately, between John Jay and Vergennes. To whom would he turn? The answer to that question was in no small measure to shape the Western world emerging out of a great world war. In mid-August [1782], however, the Wiltshire nobleman remained inscrutable to friend and foe alike, his enigmatic posture concealing his own uncertainty about the road to take. Two visitors to Bowood Park would help Shelburne make up his mind.

A condition not a theory confronted John Jay. France could no longer be counted on to support America's revolutionary objectives, aside from independence. As Jay saw it, America's

---

The selection used here is an abridgment of Chapters XIV and XV in *The Peacemakers: An International History of the American Revolution*, Copyright 1965 by Richard B. Morris, and reprinted by permission of Harper & Row, Publishers, Inc.

ambitions were being placed in jeopardy as much by the actions of her ally as by those of her enemy. For Jay the sensible course to adopt—and he was above all else a sensible man—was to pursue a more conciliatory line toward the British adversary while keeping his distance from his ally.

Each of the American commissioners still advanced propositions unpalatable to the British, but the tone of their conversations with Richard Oswald now perceptibly moderated. . . . Franklin, though noncommittal on the notion that America intended to act as guarantor of the peace, [was] still by no means reconciled to dropping his "advisable" articles or to providing for the Tories. The latter business, he pointed out to Oswald, fell within the authority of the states, not Congress. Once more Franklin reminded Oswald of Canada. There could be "no dependence on peace and good neighbourhood," he remarked, so long as Canada continued in British hands, "as it touched their States in so great a stretch of frontier."

Oswald's recent session with Jay had prepared him for the worst, even to being compelled to yield "the whole territory," but Jay appeared in better humor when Oswald next conferred with him, even though he did not budge an inch on the question of treating on the basis of equality. He let Oswald know that he was not content with the latter's instructions of August 3rd, which authorized the acknowledgment of independence in the first article of a treaty irrespective of other articles. The British commissioner may have believed in all sincerity that he had met Jay's conditions, but the New Yorker, as Franklin remarked, thought of "things that did not occur to those who were not lawyers." He did not want to give the adversary that loophole to cut off negotiations which so shrewd an observer of the international scene as Comte Mercy suspected that the British Cabinet was seeking.

Jay and Franklin insisted on clarification of Sir Guy Carleton's role in New York. They had heard that the General had been authorized to make peace proposals directly to Congress. Was this another example of Shelburne's devious tactics? Until they were better informed, they needed to have Oswald's powers clearly delineated. Whether independence could be conceded by King or Parliament constituted a nice legal question. Jay now proposed that, with Parliament prorogued until

November, the King should proceed to grant independence by a "patent" or deed under the Great Seal. He made two drafts of such a "patent," but was persuaded by Franklin and Oswald that this procedural move was unnecessary.

Despite this quibbling over the form by which independence was to be given up, John Jay was "much more open and unreserved" with the British than the doctor. The latter, in George III's biased judgment, "only plays with us and has no intention fairly to treat." Jay was encouraged by the friendly and even optimistic tone of the adversary toward America, and it must have seemed paradoxical to him that Oswald and Vaughan exhibited a sounder understanding of the springs of nationalism and enlightenment in America, of the elements that set the American Revolution apart from all previous wars, than did Vergennes and Rayneval.

Vaughan and Oswald both pressed Jay for a commitment that, once independence was granted, America would not continue the war to support exorbitant claims advanced by France or Spain. To Vaughan, Jay replied cryptically: "Do our business first—as to stirring otherwise, I will not do it." Vaughan was unnerved by this remark. He interpreted it to mean that, while America wanted peace "now and always," she would continue to cultivate France if that nation acted "with ordinary sense" and would proceed "to exterminate the English name in America." Shelburne, as he viewed it, must now see the "good sense" for weighing "the amount of what there is still to grant them." Consider the cost of turning them down, Vaughan argued. Consider how little use we ourselves can make of this territory. Consider the probability that "in an age or two and before it can ripen in our hands," the territory will be "torn away by force or fall by neglect." To be generous will prove the profitable course, he urged, since one would not expect passions to be permanent. The Americans, he instructed Shelburne, are planning "to look deeply into the business of education," and it is unlikely that wrong practices will long be followed "in a country where every human being reads and writes."

When Oswald put to Jay the same question that Vaughan had, the New Yorker answered quite candidly and in a manner that disclosed his whole hand. "You have only to cut the knot of Independence, " he declared, "to get rid of those apprehensions" that America would support the unreasonable demands of the other belligerents. Jay confessed that he had not proceeded very far with the Spanish treaty. Unless Britain "forced" America into this engagement, he volunteered, "he did not see that the people of America had any business to fetter themselves with them." He went so far, in Oswald's account, as to assure the Scot that he would bring the negotiations with Spain to a halt. With studied casualness Oswald remarked that "when America was independent of England," she "would be so also of all other nations." Jay smiled enigmatically. "We will take care of that," he responded, but his manner did not encourage further explorations of the topic at the time.

Shelburne and Grantham were now being showered with a barrage of missives from Paris to conclude quickly with the Americans. A change of the French Ministry was in the offing, erroneous intelligence advised, and this might provide the British Ministry with an opportunity to capitalize on American uneasiness . . . .

John Jay, now convinced that the policy of the Comte de Vergennes was "to keep America in leading strings," set to work feverishly to extricate his country from this entanglement. One day, while riding in his carriage with Vaughan, he remarked, "Why will not your court cut the cord that ties us to France? Why can they suppose we can be quiet, while the very end of the treaty is independence, till independence is granted?" England should not haggle, Jay advised pointedly. She should concede "this one point," for the best deal she could make with France would be "a good agreement with America." Vaughan quickly caught the implication of Jay's remarks. What Jay was really telling him was that France could make better terms with her enemy if America was tied to her apron strings than otherwise. Abruptly Jay switched from this line of conversation. "If your government does not guarantee independence," he warned, there would be "an end to all confidence."

The wettest August of many summers ended on a bright note, and hopes of peace soared again. Prospects of a quick solution to a thorny problem arose from the suddenly enhanced prestige of John Jay in Paris as well as from the increasingly shaky political position of Lord Shelburne at home. In the third week of August Franklin was suddenly stricken with an acute attack of kidney stone, a painful ailment intensified by the doctor's chronic gout. Rumors spread through the diplomatic corps that he had suffered a paralytic stroke. While his mind was not affected, Franklin remained incapacitated for weeks and confined to his home at Passy. Now a strong note of independence from French direction is sounded in the American camp by the solitary bugler on duty.

For Shelburne time seemed to be running out. His political situation at home was perilous. Without commanding support in Parliament he had to make his moves quickly while Parliament was still in recess. At the same time he had to move with circumspection to avoid affronting a stubborn and touchy monarch. . . . He realized the devious course he needed to pursue to win a reluctant King over to accepting a sensible, if humiliating, sacrifice.

To push forward with the peace negotiations at this time involved a military decision. Though barred by Parliament from resuming offensive military action against the Americans, Shelburne was not yet under legal restraints toward the other belligerents. He clearly saw the alternatives. He could make a quick peace with France, thereby avoiding further risky naval and military operations. On the other hand, he could make an immediate settlement with the Americans and continue the war against the European belligerents to strengthen England's diplomatic position. The former course meant cooperating with an ancient foe to keep America a coastal confederacy. The alternative meant treating an errant daughter with generosity, permitting her ample living room, and counting on great commercial advantages from a revivified trade with America. . . .

No one was quite sure which way Shelburne was leaning, but there was a straw in the wind. On August 23rd his Cabinet decided to send a powerful force under Lord Howe to the relief of Gibraltar, a decision which carried the King's hearty approval. At least so far as the Franco-Spanish combination was concerned, Shelburne seemed determined to negotiate from strength.

Still no action was taken in London to comply with John Jay's demand for immediate and unconditional independence. On that point the British government remained inscrutably silent. Impatiently Oswald awaited the return of a courier authorizing him to yield the point, but Shelburne took a fortnight to reply to his latest letters. Meanwhile Jay was taking no chances. He talked freely with Matthew Ridley, an international man of business, then abroad as agent for Maryland, having only just obtained a loan from an Amsterdam banking firm for that state. Already a warm admirer of the New Yorker, and later to become Jay's brother-in-law, Ridley made a note in his diary that Jay advised him to go ahead and ship the supplies to Maryland that he was ordering. "Make preparations for war down to the very hour of signing the treaty," Jay warned, and with his customary realism remarked further that even after the advent of peace it would still be necessary for America to be armed.

Across the Channel Lord Shelburne, having made the decision to reinforce Gibraltar, seemed determined that the King and Cabinet should yield to the Americans on all essentials. Regardless of the political risks to himself, he recognized the commercial advantages to Britain from such a quick settlement and the opportunity it afforded of weakening the grand alliance against his country. . . .

As spelled out in . . . instructions to Oswald, the Cabinet was prepared to concede all of Franklin's necessary articles, literally construed. The Americans would be admitted to the New-foundland and Labrador fisheries, but not given liberty to dry fish on the shores since Franklin had neglected to mention that crucial point. British troops would be evacuated from American territory. Canada would be confined to its historic boundaries prior to the notorious Quebec Act of 1774. By restricting Canada's limits to what they were under the Royal Proclamation of 1763, the British government was prepared to renounce not only the Old Northwest but also the southern half of the future Province of Ontario. Oswald's instructions permitted him to waive stipulating by treaty for payment of prewar debts owing British merchants as well as for compensation to the Loyalists. The government counted on world opinion to bring about an equitable settlement of both issues. On the extent of America's Western claims the instructions were silent, for Franklin in his necessary articles had neglected to stipulate for the Mississippi as the western boundary. . . . [See Map 6.]

A number of new factors conspired to postpone the revelations to the Americans of the crucial portion of the decision reached by the Cabinet at the end of August. First of all, the British were becoming increasingly aware of the views of Vergennes on the American issues. They knew that he was most anxious for England to defer her concession on independence until the treaty itself, fearful that a quick solution of Anglo-American difficulties could seriously compromise the interests of France and Spain. Secondly, they knew too how perturbed Vergennes was about America's fishing claims along the Newfoundland coast. Behind the back of the Americans he was at the very moment asserting French fishing claims, and, as Lord Grantham drily remarked, pressing them "before any American claims may be set forward," and making it almost embarrassingly clear to the British that "there is no doubt of great jealousy between" the French and the Americans "on that score". Moreover, the Comte was becoming increasingly resistant to American expansionist pressures. Convinced that America already had more space than she needed, he pointed out to his envoy in Philadelphia that France could not interfere between Spain and America over the territory east of the Mississippi and around the Ohio. . . .

Aranda . . . denied America's right to the Mississippi as her western boundary, an assertion from which Jay never receded a furlong. America was claiming territory which was never a part of the Thirteen Colonies, Aranda protested. He buttressed his arguments by an appeal to history as well as to the facts of recent conquests by the Spaniards, who had recaptured West Florida and gained certain posts on the Mississippi and the Illinois. Aranda completely ignored the temporary occupation of the Northwest by George Rogers Clark. For all the diplomats in Paris seemed to care, the Virginians who had waded the icy waters of the Wabash in their heroic march to Vincennes might just as well have remained by their own firesides.

On August 23rd Aranda appealed once more to Vergennes. True, Jay's claims seemed extraordinary, the Comte conceded, but, he pointed out, there were actual American settlements located far beyond the red line drawn by the Spaniard. The Conde replied that he was not unbudgeable on that line, and asked Vergennes to work out a compromise. "Talk to Rayneval," the French Foreign Minister advised.

The Conde found the undersecretary even more candid in his criticisms of America's territorial claims than his superior. When Louisiana and Canada had been French, Rayneval pointed out to Aranda, the region lying in between, including the Great Lakes, was also considered as belonging to France. The settlement made at the end of the French and Indian War, Rayneval continued, had embraced as part of Canada the territory lying north of the Ohio, and the land to the south of that river was considered as forming a part of the Floridas which the British had taken over. Encouraged by his appreciative auditor, Rayneval agreed to work out a memorandum on the subject. Just before the conference broke up Vergennes came in. When apprised of the discussion, Aranda records in his Diario, "he seemed to agree."

Vergennes now decided to push for a settlement of the Spanish-American dispute by securing agreement on a compromise line. When he met Aranda two days later, he proposed that the Conde move his red line farther west to the Wabash River and the Western end of Lake Erie. Aranda indicated a willingness to split the difference. For the territory north of the Ohio he was prepared to swing his line forward somewhat to begin not far from the present site of Cincinnati. The Americans would not readily agree to giving up the Wabash, Vergennes pointed out. Accordingly he proposed that river as a boundary line to run south to the Ohio, and below that river suggested the Great Kanawha as a dividing line. This alternative would give the Americans room to exploit their commerce by river courses. For the southern portion of the territory in dispute, Vergennes suggested a line starting from Fort Toulouse on the Alabama. Aranda interrupted to make sure that such a line would include not only the Mobile region of ancient French claims but also the portions of West Florida recently conquered by Spain from Great Britain. . . . [See Map 6.]

Jay made it clear to the Conde at their next conference that a compromise line was unacceptable to the Americans. "We are bound by the Mississippi," he flatly asserted. "I have no authority to cede any territories of it to His Catholic Majesty. . . ."

"That territory belongs to free and independent nations of Indians," Aranda rejoined, "and you have no right to it."

"These are points to be discussed and settled between the Indians and ourselves," Jay retorted. "With respect to the Indians we claim the right of pre-emption; with respect to all other nations, we claim the sovereignty over the territory."

Once more Aranda appealed to Versailles to find some way out of the impasse. Vergennes left the Spanish ambassador with Rayneval. Putting their heads together they drew a new red line running from Fort Toulouse on the Alabama to the Tennessee, and then down that river to the Ohio. Aranda objected that at the mouth of the Tennessee the new line almost touched the Mississippi. Obligingly, Rayneval moved the line eastward, so that it left the Tennessee at the confluence of the Pelisipi [Sequatchie], went up the latter to its source, thence to the source of the Cumberland, and followed that river down to the Ohio. Everything north of the Ohio the Frenchman generously awarded to the British, "because it could not be denied to them that this region had been a dependency of Canada and so recognized by France." Aranda was content, and well he might be, for Rayneval's line would keep the Americans "far away" from the Mississippi. Rayneval then read from a memorandum he was preparing on the territorial question, and gave Aranda a copy. . . .

Rayneval in this memorandum elaborated upon the historical points he had already made in his talks with Aranda. Before the Treaty of Paris of 1763, he argued, the English never asserted pretensions to lands east of the Mississippi, but confined their claims to the lands located around the source of the Ohio, notably along the Allegheny. Once the cessions had been made under that treaty, England no longer regarded the vast territories lying to the eastward of the Mississippi as forming a part of the Thirteen Colonies. The Proclamation of 1763 indicates, so Rayneval contended, that north of the 31st parallel neither Spain nor the American colonists had any rights.

Having demolished the American case to his own satisfaction, Rayneval then proposed his own line for dividing this territory. He would place the Indians dwelling to the west of that line under Spanish protection, while "those to the eastward should be free, and under the protection of the United States; or rather the Americans may make such arrangements with them as is most convenient to themselves." The navigation of the Mississippi must follow with the property, and belongs "to the nation to whom the two banks belong." Thus, if the treaty gives West Florida back to Spain she alone will be the proprietor of the river from the 31st parallel to the sea. "Whatever may be the case with that part which is beyond this point to the north, the United States of America can have no pretensions to it, not being masters of either border of this river." Rayneval's conclusion, if accepted, would have rendered nugatory a major objective of John Jay's diplomatic mission to Spain.

The next day Rayneval placed in Aranda's hands an even longer memorandum, wherein he denied America's claims to the Northwest on the basis of "the ephemeral raid" made by George Rogers Clark in 1779. He did suggest to Aranda the advisability of conceding to the Americans the privilege of navigating the Mississippi, and of granting them a free port near its mouth in return for an American acknowledgment of the proposed boundary. On the other hand, Rayneval seemed prepared to give Spain absolute control over the territory west of the Cumberland-Tennessee-Appalachicola Bay line without obligating Spain to assume a protectorate over independent Indians to the west of that line. These discrepancies between the two memoranda Jay did not know about. Each seemed rather carefully tailored to make the maximum impact on its designated reader.

Rayneval had more pressing business on his hands than the settlement of the Spanish-American dispute. On September 7th he left for England incognito. . . .

Like so many other well-guarded secrets Rayneval's absence was noted almost at once in Paris and caused a buzz of speculation. . . . Word spread quickly, however. By the ninth, two days after Rayneval had set forth on his trip, Jay had learned of it from Matthew Ridley, who got around in the best circles of Paris, as well as from other sources. . . .

To Jay the gossip about Rayneval's secret mission sounded an alarm bell in the night. From his own knowledge he had every reason to fear that a quick deal was in the offing between the other belligerents at the expense of the United States. Distorted accounts of Rayneval's visit which leaked out to the British press seemed to support such an interpretation. Apart from rumor, Jay's suspicions seemed confirmed both by the Rayneval memo-

randum on the West and by a copy of an intercepted cipher
dispatch from Barbé-Marbois to Vergennes, which a member
of the British mission thoughtfully placed in Jay's hands. . . .

Massive evidence in the diplomatic archives reveals that the
views expressed by Barbé-Marbois on the fisheries and Rayneval on the boundaries were not purely personal to the authors
but expressed the deep-seated convictions of their court on
both issues. . . .

On the matter of boundaries Vergennes seemed as restrictive
as had Rayneval. First of all, he was concerned that the Americans should not acquire Canada. "You know our system with
regard to Canada," he wrote La Luzerne. "It is unchanging.
Whatever will halt the conquest of this country accords with our
views. But you will agree, Monsieur, that this way of thinking
ought to be an impenetrable secret from the Americans. It
would be a crime that they would never pardon. It is convenient, then, to make an outward show to convince them that we
share their views, but to checkmate any steps that would put
them into effect in case we are required to cooperate." His
interpretation of Canada was so broad as to exclude the Americans from the Great Lakes, which he considered "a part of
Canada." As regards the claims to the West put forward by Jay,
claims resting on the sea-to-sea provisions of the old charters,
Vergennes dismissed them as "foolishness not meriting serious
refutation." These ideas are for your ears alone, La Luzerne
was again cautioned. Do not reveal this information "because
for the present we do not wish to intervene in the discussion
between Aranda and Jay."

Without being privy to this correspondence John Jay was
convinced that Rayneval's memoir on the boundaries voiced the
official French position. At the proper time, he felt, France was
prepared to assume the role of arbiter between Spain and
America, to contest America's extension to the Mississippi as
well as her claim to the free navigation of that river, and most
"certainly" to support Britain's claims north of the Ohio. In the
event that America would not agree to a division of the West
with Spain along Rayneval's lines, then Jay feared that France
would favor splitting the territory lying north of the 31st
parallel and below the Ohio between Spain and Britain.

With the evidence before him, both direct and circumstantial,

Jay now acted swiftly. On September 9th he learned of Rayneval's secret trip. The next day he was handed the intercepted Barbé-Marbois dispatch. Wasting not a moment, he immediately broke off his discussions with Aranda. Like a woman scorned, the Conde fell into a fury. He accused Jay of bad faith and lacking talent for diplomacy, and put the blame for the breakdown on the New Yorker's exalted opinion of his own public character. . . .

While the Jay-Aranda negotiations were broken off in Paris, the Rayneval-Shelburne talks were proceeding smoothly. Rayneval's visit was prompted, not by the American issue, despite the apprehensions of the French court about America's pretensions, but by the conviction on Vergennes' part that the Allies should now get out of the war if decent terms were offered them. For a certainty the French Minister was as much concerned about Spain's inflexible position on Gibraltar as he was about prolonging the war to satisfy America's demands. . . .

Rayneval was instructed to ask Shelburne point-blank whether the notions about peace he had discussed with Admiral de Grasse conformed to his present intentions. Should Shelburne disavow them, then Rayneval was to demand his passport and leave England. In other words, he was to feel out Shelburne rather than enter into negotiations, and he was to remind the Earl that it was the King of France's intention of treating only in conjunction with his allies. For that assignment a stay of eight or ten days would suffice, Vergennes figured. The Comte gave Rayneval a personal letter assuring Shelburne that the bearer possessed his "full confidence."

Although Rayneval quickly discovered that Shelburne had no intention of making the generous concessions . . . attributed to him, . . . he did not break off his talks and ask for his passport as instructed. The Frenchman was fascinated by his clever host and seemed captive to the conciliatory mood he sought to arouse. Rayneval's stay at Bowood and a subsequent visit some months later converted him into an ardent admirer of Shelburne. He found the Earl "a minister of noble views" and "winning manners," neither "an intriguer" nor an "equivocator," "whatever persons say who imagine that they know him, but imagine wrongly."

Certain later critics have belabored Jay for his assumption

that Rayneval went to England to arrange a deal about the West and the fisheries. . . .

Rayneval's own report of his conversations belies the assertions that he did not advert to America. The subject of America came up almost at once. Shelburne conceded that he had "always been opposed to independence, that it was the hardest pill to digest, but that he recognized the necessity of swallowing it, and that this object would be decided unconditionally." Later on in the talks independence was again referred to, but taken for granted by both parties. . . .

At the closing conference on September 18th the talks again reverted to the Americans, whose pretensions were remarked upon during the course of the opening day's talks. Shelburne confided to Rayneval how much trouble the Americans were stirring up over the boundaries and the fisheries, and expressed the hope that the King of France would not support them. Rayneval answered that he had no doubt of the King's intention to do what could be done to "contain the Americans within the bounds of justice and reason." . . .

Having blasted America's claims to shore rights for drying fish as well as to fishing within coastal waters, Rayneval turned to the boundaries. To sound out Shelburne he expressed his own belief that the Americans would stand on the provisions of their ancient charters. "That would be silly," Shelburne remarked. Rayneval reported that he did not pursue this line of discussion "because I did not wish either to sustain the American pretension or to deny it." He did not switch the subject, however, before pointing out that the British government might find that the negotiations of 1754 relative to the Ohio offered a measuring stick to settle what should be allotted the United States. As Rayneval interpreted it, the rule would have quashed America's claims to the lands north of the Ohio. It is scarcely a coincidence that this same emphasis on the 1754 negotiations appears in the memoir Rayneval had put in Jay's hands before departing for England.

Emboldened by the support of the French court implied in Rayneval's remarks as well as by the heartening news to come from Gibraltar, Shelburne was to renege the Cabinet offer of August 30th, and to put up one more desperate stand along the Ohio. Counting on French support in withholding the "back lands" from America, Shelburne instructed Oswald at later date to learn through Fitzherbert just how Rayneval and his court stood as regards America's territorial claims. . . .

While Rayneval's conversations with Shelburne provided further confirmation for the British of the widening rift between France and America over terms of peace, they also exposed to view the tightrope on which Shelburne himself was teetering. Regardless of his own convictions about the need for American independence, Shelburne had to pursue a political course demanding acrobatic agility of a high order. He had to deal daily with a King unaccustomed to hearing unpalatable truths and to prepare to face some months off a Parliament and a public still ill-prepared to accept terms of submission. Some of these problems Shelburne mentioned to Rayneval in his closing talk. It was terribly difficult to talk to the King, he told the Frenchman. His ministers had never spoken to him save to refer to his grandeur and his power. They had always elevated him above the greatest monarchs, told him that he commanded infinite resources whereas France was exhausted and without credit. He was informed that by continuing the war he would inevitably smash the French Navy. All these ideas, Shelburne explained, had been drummed into the head of George III in the past. To counteract them was indeed a "delicate and difficult" undertaking, but, he reassured his listener, he had the courage to attempt it and up to a point he flattered himself that he had succeeded. With French assistance, he now hoped he could bring about the King's complete conversion.

The letters passing between Lord Shelburne and George III during these fateful weeks disclose how the former constantly sugar-coated the pill and pursued a zigzag course to overcome the King's suspicions. Thus Shelburne found Rayneval "a well-instructed, inoffensive man of business," who stressed Vergennes' eagerness to "expedite everything which can contribute to an instant and final conclusion" of hostilities. When the conferences started, he told the King, he had been "as clearly of opinion against a peace as I ever was against American independence, till in fact the resolutions of the House of Commons decided the point." Now he reminded the monarch of the state of the army and navy, of the troubles in Ireland, and the temper of the Commons. All these factors pointed to the necessity of a quick peace with France. . . .

John Jay had been quick to perceive the peril to American interests at the peacemaking should France and England arrive at a secret understanding. To divine the nature of the Rayneval-Shelburne conversations was beyond the Americans, who lacked the same kind of intelligence service from inside of Bowood Park that Dr. Edward Bancroft had so obligingly provided the British for years from within Franklin's Passy household. Yet the New Yorker was convinced by a perusal of the Rayneval memoir that France was prepared to frustrate America's major aspirations, aside from independence, and his views were shared by Benjamin Vaughan. . . .

Convinced that Vergennes would rather "postpone the acknowledgment of our independence by Britain to the conclusion of a general peace than aid us in procuring it at present," Jay took the most audacious step of his career. He dispatched Benjamin Vaughan to England on a mission so secret that neither Vergennes nor Franklin was apprised of it. Vaughan was sent to counteract Rayneval. He was instructed to tell Shelburne that "the manner as well as the matter of the proposed treaty" was important, and that without unconditional acknowledgement of independence "neither confidence nor peace could reasonably be expected." Such acknowledgment Jay labeled "the touchstone of British sincerity." . . . He . . . gave Vaughan instructions on the boundaries and the navigation of the Mississippi. To contest the American claims to either would be "impolitic," he was told. Shelburne was to be enticed into making these concessions by holding out to him "the profits of an extensive and lucrative commerce." Not "the possession of vast tracts of wilderness," but commerce was the true objective of "a commercial European nation," Jay shrewdly reminded Shelburne, the free trader. Dangling the prospects of an immense amount of trade into the interior of the country, Jay now intimated, and without authority either from Congress or his colleagues on the peace commission, that America was prepared to share that interior trade with England, including the free navigation of the Mississippi. England should abandon any idea of retaining any part of the back country or of insisting on extending the bounds of Canada "so as to comprehend the lands in question." Nothing could prevent the Americans from gradually taking possession of the area, Jay prophesied, and to hold on to it would be to sow the seeds of future war. By implication Jay now waived all claims to ancient Canada itself. In short, Vaughan was instructed to impress Shelburne "with the necessity and policy of taking a decided and manly part respecting America."

That Jay should have picked for so delicate a mission a man who was the unavowed agent of the British First Minister may seem astonishing at this day when there is much less tolerance of divided loyalties than in Jay's time. Yet the New Yorker had complete reliance on Benjamin Vaughan's basic friendliness to the American cause, and his trust was not misplaced. . . .

A week before Jay had decided to send Vaughan over to see Shelburne he had finally hit on a satisfactory formula to end the impasse over independence. On September 2nd he informed Oswald that, if Franklin would consent, he was prepared to accept "a constructive denomination of character to be introduced in the preamble of the treaty" which would merely describe their constituents as "the Thirteen United States of America." While Oswald readily agreed, Jay reminded him that he had no authority to treat with the Americans "under that denomination." Jay now narrowed his insistence down to "an explicit authority" to be stated in Oswald's commission.

"How about using the term 'provinces' instead of 'states,' or the expression 'states or provinces'?" Oswald suggested.

"No, neither will answer," Jay replied.

"Then, let me have in writing a draft of the alteration you propose."

Jay did so at once, and Oswald forwarded the draft of the new commission to the Home Office. Jay's alteration would have empowered the Scot "to treat of Peace or Truce with the Commissioners and Persons vested with equal powers by and on the part of the Thirteen United States of America." Obligingly, Jay also offered to turn over to Oswald a draft of a letter he might send back "to satisfy His Majesty's Ministers of the propriety of their conduct." The draft again stressed America's insistence on being treated on the basis of equality and restated Jay's objections to having such acknowledgment deferred until the first article of a treaty. . . .

In transmitting to the Home Secretary Jay's proposed alteration of the commission along with his draft letter, Oswald warned his government that if they rejected Jay's compromise formula "there will be an end to all further confidence and communication with the Americans." "With great difficulty," Oswald wrote Shelburne, "they have yielded to this mode of compromise. . . . I hope His Majesty will grant it. If it is refused, Mr. Fitzherbert as well as me, may go home, and in my opinion it will not be an easy matter for any other to take up the same clue for extracting the Nation out of its difficulties which I think is within our reach." In that same letter Oswald pointed out that the Spaniards apparently wanted a cession from England before the American treaty was ironed out, and that this was the apparent motive behind Rayneval's visit. . . .

Jay's altered proposal gave an urgency to Vaughan's trip. On September 11th Vaughan wrote Shelburne to inform him of his intention of following "a few hours after the present courier," and apprising him of the rumor that Rayneval's journey had for its object an "underhand bargain" between England and Spain. "This is a crisis of the first consequence," Vaughan declared. He urged Shelburne to hold up his negotiations with the Frenchman, but advised him that he should act with "instantaneous despatch" in dealing with the American commissioners and in modifying the form of Oswald's commission to suit Jay's demands. " 'America must have a character,' to use the words of Mr. Adams," Vaughan remarked. Finally, he cautioned Shelburne in language close to that of Oswald's, "If this moment is rudely managed, or slightly passed over, I conceive peace in consequence takes its flight." In short, in this crisis the alternatives were "good sense" or "ruin." . . .

Vaughan's personal appeal, Oswald's threats, and Jay's sober arguments all added up to compelling reasons for complying with the New Yorker's wishes, and overriding the grumblers within the Ministry. A special meeting of "a considerable number" of the Cabinet who happened to be in town was called for the night of September 18th, less than a week after Vaughan's arrival in England, and on the day of Rayneval's final conference with Shelburne. The Cabinet voted to change the commission and to empower Oswald "to treat, consult, and conclude with any Commissioner or person vested with equal power by and on the part of the Thirteen United States of America," named in geographical order from north to south. Significantly, the Cabinet did not consider the new phraseology to amount to "a final acknowledgment of independence," but merely as providing the American commissioners during the negotiations with "the title they wished to assume." This may have been technically correct, and Shelburne was later to insist on this point in defense of his course before Parliament. Neither Townshend nor Shelburne admitted any such thing to Oswald, however, when on the following day a new commission was sent over to Paris embodying the change that Jay had desired.

How decisive a factor was the Vaughan mission persuading Shelburne to back down on the issue of independence? The motivations of a figure as inscrutable as Shelburne cannot be pinned down with certitude. . . . Shelburne may well have been on the verge, but Vaughan's presence seems to have precipitated the decision to jump. "Mr. Vaughan greatly merits our acknowledgments," Jay reported home.

His business with Shelburne completed, Vaughan returned to Paris on September 27th with word that there was "every disposition in Lord Shelburne for peace." As solid evidence he could point to the new commission for Oswald which the courier had brought and the copy for Mr. Jay. Even Franklin, who had been grumbling about "standing out for the previous acknowledgment of Independency" and been overheard remarking that it was "a pity to keep three or four millions of people in war for the sake of form," was content with the new commission, for which he could scarcely claim credit. Franklin's implied criticism of Jay for stalling the negotiations on a technicality was hardly fair, for as we now know, it was Townshend who kept Oswald from disclosing his full hand, and it was Jay who speedily devised a compromise formula to end the impasse. Despite some reservations on the part of the doctor about legal quibbling, Jay's solo performance did not lessen Franklin's admiration for him one whit, and the pair henceforth worked together in close harmony. . . .

Despite the mental reservations with which the British granted independence, reservations which the rest of Europe did not share, the Gordian knot had at long last been cut. It was inevitable that there should be loose ends, but, as Jay had predicted, the new commission "would set the whole machine in motion." For Great Britain, American independence was now irretrievable in fact, if not in law; for the world, peace was at last in sight.

On the thirteenth of September, 1782, two contrasting scenes of the same drama were being played upon stages almost a thousand miles apart. Bowood Park furnished the setting for the first; Gibraltar, the second. While Gérard de Rayneval seated himself before Lord Shelburne's hearth and took up in conciliatory vein with his host the issues of peace, the Franco-Spanish armada under the Duc de Crillon, conqueror of Minorca, closed in upon a rocky limestone promontory jutting out into the Mediterranean. To soften up the defenses of the great fortress the combined fleet had for several days carried on a tremendous cannonade of the Rock. Then on the morning of the thirteenth a flotilla of ten huge battering ships, designed by the French engineer d'Arçon to be impervious to cannon shot pulled to within less than a thousand yards of Gibraltar's walls. This was to be the *coup de grâce*. Sir George Elliot, commander of the British defenses, replied with a counterfire of red-hot balls, heated in grates and furnaces hastily constructed within the lines. By evening the battering ships were all afire, destined to blow up or burn to the water's edge. The attackers had suffered cruel punishment. Two thousand of their number were killed or captured. By the light from a lurid night sky the invincible fortress still looked down defiantly on the foe. . . .

France's Foreign Minister . . . had the unenviable task of persuading the British to yield the Rock to his Bourbon partner.

Everything happened the way John Adams predicted. "They will make a horrid noise with their artillery against the place; but this noise will not terrify Elliot, and Gibraltar will remain to the English another year, and Lord Howe will return to England, and all Europe will laugh." In this case Adams was blessed with second sight, for Admiral Howe's swifter ships evaded the cumbersome fleets of France and Spain, and succeeded in relieving Gibraltar in October, providing the defenders with all they needed for a prolonged resistance. The Spaniards continued the siege half-heartedly until the following February, but without any constructive effect on the peace negotiation. . . .

The humiliation of the armada before Gibraltar stiffened

Shelburne's stand both toward his European adversaries and toward America. He has now upped his price, the Portuguese ambassador shrewdly observed. Remarking on the halfhearted efforts of the French to capture the Rock, Benjamin Vaughan made the cynical prediction more than a month before the fiasco of the combined fleets "that at a peace it will not be very important to lose what France so much wishes we would keep." In the wake of Gibraltar war weariness gripped France, most noticeably in the impoverished rural areas. Alleyne Fitzherbert relayed the rising sentiment in Paris that France had been the "dupe of her allies, the Americans and the Spaniards."

London learned the good news from Gibraltar on September 30th, just nine days after the new commission was made out for Oswald impliedly acknowledging the United States. In the light of the private reservations that Shelburne held all along, it is not improper to speculate whether he would have yielded the point of independence to Jay had modern means of instantaneous communication been at his command. Prior to learning the news of Gibraltar the Cabinet had made two major concessions, agreeing to Franklin's necessary articles and to Jay's revised commission. Henceforth the British sought to escalate their terms while the Americans fought stubbornly to hold them to their expressed intentions.

Richard Oswald, it must be said, pursued his part in good faith. His counterpart, John Jay, was also ready to iron out the details of the treaty draft. In sending a hasty line to John Adams announcing Oswald's receipt of the commission, Jay added: "I have reasons for wishing that you would say nothing of this till you see me, which I hope and pray may be soon, very soon." With Franklin still in poor physical shape, Jay needed reinforcements for his side badly. Lafayette followed up Jay's letter to Adams with a cautiously optimistic one of his own, in which he predicted that it would be five or six months before the "grand affair of peace" would be concluded. . . .

He would come as soon as he could clear up business in Holland, Adams assured Jay, but "my health is so far from being robust that it will be impossible for me to ride with as much rapidity as I could formerly, although never remarkable for a quick traveler." He added, significantly, "If anything in the meantime should be in agitation concerning peace, in which there should be any difference of opinion between you and your colleague, you have a right to insist upon informing me by express, or waiting till I come."

To the Americans Richard Oswald must have seemed like a pliant instrument sent from heaven rather than Whitehall. Patient and unruffled under trying circumstances, Oswald proved a good listerner. No stickler on etiquette, he treated the commissioners as plenipotentiaries of an acknowledged power. By now he was on the friendliest terms with Jay as well as Franklin, was convinced of the former's essential fairness and deep regard for England, and viewed the not far distant prospect of some "wise association" between England and America generated by common interests. . . .

Surprisingly enough, no differences did develop between Franklin and Jay after the drafting of the provisional terms. Franklin, as Oswald reported, was still "in but an indifferent state of health." Jay carried on the conversations with Oswald alone, and it is apparent that he dropped certain hints to which Franklin may not have been privy. Before making a provisional draft Jay talked terms over with Oswald. They quickly agreed on the four necessary articles, to which Jay was insistent on adding the"privilege in common" of drying fish on Newfoundland shores as well as on the American coast. This is the way Oswald reported it, but Jay used the much stronger word "right." Jay made it clear that the royal domain remaining ungranted within the states would revert to the States and not to the Loyalists, nor could he offer hope of pardon for Tories remaining at posts which the British might still have to evacuate.

In one controversial aspect of his draft Jay allowed his own perturbation over Spanish objections to the navigation of the Mississippi and to America's Western territorial claims to color his judgment. He was anxious to see West Florida in British rather than Spanish hands. . . . With Canada and the Floridas in British hands, it is by no means clear that America would have been better off after 1783 than with West Florida under Spanish control. Considering the diplomatic irritations which later could be laid to what turned out to be a gratuitous, unilateral proposition, this proffer, which won endorsement from Jay's fellow commissioners, was too shortsighted to do them credit. It was prompted by a degree of vindictiveness toward Spain which only compounded France's difficulties in maintaining her precarious bundle of alliances. . . .

That Franklin found no fault with the startling innovations proposed by Jay suggests that the differences between the two Americans lay in tactics not in objectives. Franklin wanted to avoid affronting the French, but advocated propositions as unpalatable to that court as were Jay's. In their continuing dialogue Franklin sought to persuade Jay of the propriety of keeping Vergennes abreast of the discussions. Jay, on guard against leaks to Versailles ever since his conversation with Lafayette less than a fortnight earlier, insisted that no communication be made to Versailles until the draft of the preliminaries was completed and conditionally signed. . . .

Working around the clock, Jay drew up a provisional treaty draft in his own handwriting which he submitted to Oswald on October 5th on behalf of Franklin and himself. Except for a minor reservation included as an alteration to one article, the British commissioner found the draft entirely acceptable. Accompanying Jay's draft was a covering letter which provided for inserting in the treaty an article holding that the treaty was not to be conclusive until the King of France had accepted the terms of peace with England and was ready to conclude such a treaty.

Jay's provisional draft was fated to undergo much surgery, but it constituted the basis of the preliminary treaty. The draft acknowledged American independence and stipulated for the evacuation of troops and the liberation of prisoners. It set the Mississippi as the western boundary, the 31st parallel as the southern. Following the Treaty of 1763, it divided the United States and Canada by the St. Lawrence and the 45th parallel running to Lake Nipissing; on the northeast, the St. John's River from its source to the Bay of Fundy was to separate Maine form Nova Scotia, but an alteration suggested by Franklin deferred the Nova Scotia boundary to a settlement by a commission "as conveniently may be after the war." [*See* Map 6.]

Jay carefully spelled out in his draft "the right to take fish of every kind on the banks of Newfoundland and other places" where the right was exercised before the last war between France and Britain. He was scrupulous to reserve for the

Americans the right to dry and cure fish "at the accustomed places," whether in British or American territory. In accordance with his bid to Oswald for quick action Jay included the free navigation of the Mississippi for both parties, as well as providing free access to "all rivers, harbors, lakes, ports and places" belonging to either nation "in any part of the world," saving only to the British chartered companies—notably the Hudson's Bay and East India Companies—the monopolies they then enjoyed. While Jay did not explicitly stipulate for the free navigation of the St. Lawrence by Americans, such a right was the clear implication of his phraseology. While this clause was destined to suffer drastic mutilation, it may truly be said that the St. Lawrence Seaway stands as a monument to his farsighted statesmanship. . . .

Because Jay set aside for the United States in his draft only a small sector of Ontario lying below the 45th parallel, he has been blamed for having "upset the apple cart in which Franklin had been so patiently and so gently trundling Canada." This argument rests on the unproven assumption that Franklin still seriously entertained hope of securing Canada, and that Jay, in his anxiety to secure the West before Spain laid claim to it, yielded to the British a limitless wilderness without a fight. Jay and Oswald had only recently discussed Canada, along with Franklin's other advisable articles, and the Americans were given to understand that Oswald was not permitted to yield an acre north of the Nipissing line. So much the Cabinet had been prepared to concede at the end of August when in its most generous mood, and not an inch more. By the close of September, when the good news from Gibraltar reached London, the British philanthropic mood quickly evaporated. Had Franklin figured there was a real chance of securing Canada, he would have put up a stout battle. All along he had admitted to Oswald that he did not "insist" on Canada or the other *advisable* articles and that he had no"express directions" from Congress on that head. The Scot accordingly construed this proposal as one personal to Franklin which could be safely ignored. That Oswald had made a shrewd guess was revealed when Franklin went along without protest and backed Jay's 45th parallel boundary.

In their anxiety to stake out a claim to the east bank of the

Mississippi both Americans were prepared to abandon Canada, which was never more than a very misty prospect in any event. To get a quick decision in their favor regarding the West and the back lands the Americans now tossed in their proffer of the free navigation of the American interior waterways. Later, in dispatching the preliminary articles to Congress, the commissioners defended their relinquishment of Canada in these words: "We knew this Court and Spain to be against our claims to the western country, and having no reason to think that lines more favorable could ever have been obtained, we finally agreed to those described in this article; indeed they appear to leave us little to complain of and not much to desire." Few will argue today with this judicious appraisal. . . .

The sage counsel of Oswald and Vaughan failed to cushion the shock to Shelburne and his Cabinet caused by the arrival of Jay's provisional draft, with the British commissioner's endorsement. Oswald had complied in good faith with the Cabinet decision of August 29th. From the reaction of his government it now seemed that the Cabinet's resolve had been nothing more than a bribe to separate America from her French ally. In the light of France's more conciliatory line as revealed by Rayneval and the good news from Gibraltar, the price Britain had been prepared to pay for peace with America on August 29th seemed very high indeed by the second week of October. Within the Cabinet the malcontents girded for battle. There was Oswald over in Paris handing out big chunks of the British Empire in a mood of unchecked generosity. The man simply had to be stopped. Indeed, unless Shelburne "had some secret view," the Duke of Richmond later complained to the King, it was incomprehensible why he had retained as American negotiator a man whom "every other member of the Cabinet had long seen" as pleading "only the cause of America." . . .

With the King's warm approval, a Cabinet meeting was called as soon as Oswald's packet arrived, with its enclosure of the draft treaty. While the discussions of that meeting have not been recorded, it is significant that six days later the Cabinet saw fit to overrule its decision of August 29th. The Cabinet resolve of October 17th reflected what a young delegate to Congress, a fledgling lawyer named Alexander Hamilton, called the "many jarring interests that will not be easily adjusted." These "jarring

interests" comprehended Canadian fur traders, English fish-
ermen, American Tories, and British and Scottish creditors. To
conciliate these very vocal groups the Cabinet directed Townshend to give Oswald a new set of instructions. First of all, he
was told to get a better boundary "to the South West of Nova
Scotia, vizt., Sugadahock and the Province of Maine [*sic*]," or
else refer the northeast boundary to commissioners. In addition, Oswald was instructed to reassert Britain's claims to the
Old Northwest, and "to urge it as a means of providing for the
Refugees." From this stand he could recede only upon condition that the United States made "a just provision for the
Refugees, or in case other means shall occur in the course of our
treaty with France and Spain." He was to deny the right of
drying fish on the coasts of Newfoundland "on account of the
danger of disputes," and while authorized to agree to the
provision for the free navigation of the Mississippi, told that the
remainder of the article providing reciprocal free trading privileges "cannot at present be adopted," but was to be deferred to a
special treaty of commerce. Lastly, he was called upon to urge
the Americans "as strongly as possible" to discharge their
prewar debts.

To stiffen Oswald's backbone the Cabinet dispatched to Paris
a "proper and confidential person," who was not unknown to
the Americans. . . . Henry Strachey had . . . acted as secretary
of Lord Howe's ill-fated peace commission . . . and . . . an Undersecretary of State in the Home Office. . . . [He] was told to
bargain for the boundaries of Canada as fixed by the Quebec
Act, which meant securing the whole of the Old Northwest.
Then, if turned down, he was to try to obtain a cession of Maine
lands to enlarge the territory of Nova Scotia. In neither case,
however, Shelburne told him, should he agree to refer the
boundary issue to a special commission. Thus Shelburne's oral
instruction in this regard ran counter to the new instructions to
Oswald and to the Cabinet resolution, but he refrained from
putting this caveat down in writing. What Shelburne was
seeking was some compensation by way of extra land for the
Tory refugees, and he was anxious to have it appear on the
record that every effort had been exerted in favor of both the
Loyalists and the creditors. Rather than not conclude at all,
however, Strachey was instructed to "bring the treaty back in its

present form," except in the two inadmissible points of drying fish and reciprocal trade.

Henceforth the Tories, the debts, and the fisheries were the chief points at issue. The boundary concessions served as a club to hold over the heads of the American commissioners if they proved obdurate. Shelburne did not really pant for the "back lands." He merely looked upon them as assets to be thrown into a pool to compensate the Tory refugees "either by direct cession of territory in their favor, or by engaging the half, or some proportion of what the Back Lands may produce" when sold or mortgaged. Maine and West Florida were likewise put on the bargaining counter for the same reason. In fact, Shelburne felt less deeply about conserving the Empire's real estate holdings than he did about the debts. . . .

To add a cutting edge to their reproofs Shelburne and Townshend each informed Oswald that they were sending Strachey, ostensibly "to explain the boundaries and the authentic documents," and while not empowered to sign, he was to share the responsibility with Oswald, "which is great." Oswald was to call on Fitzherbert, too, if needed. . . .

While Shelburne and Townshend had been free in their expressions of lack of confidence in their agent in Paris, the negotiations were at too delicate a stage and time was too pressing to risk the dismissal of Oswald who accepted his rebukes with a magnanimity rare in the annals of diplomacy. "I am most pleased that Mr. Strachey is coming over," he told the Earl, and promptly arranged quarters for the undersecretary in his own hotel. He did not apologize for his conduct, and he considered that the issue was too big to allow room for personal feelings. Despite the Cabinet's reversal of instructions he could take consolation from the knowledge that what he had done to date had not been rejected out of hand. . . .

Shelburne's tortuous course was in no small part plotted by his recognition of the gravity of his position at home, and of the need to settle the issue of peace before Parliament reconvened. . . .

Oswald broke the news to Jay on October 24th. He did not enter into particulars, but enough was said to make clear that the cession of the "back lands" was once again being contested by the British, and that despite Oswald's earlier assurances,

Jay's draft was not acceptable. Oswald sought to put the blame on Versailles. "I believe this Court have found means to put a spoke in our wheel," he confessed to Jay. The latter felt that it would be unwise to try to keep Strachey's coming a secret. Declare the truth about it, he told Oswald, "that he was coming with books and papers relative to our boundaries."

The French found out soon enough. That same evening Jay dined at Passy. After dinner Rayneval questioned Jay and Franklin about "how matters stood between us and Oswald." The Americans admitted that they could not agree "about all our boundaries," singling out the line marking off Maine from Nova Scotia.

"What do you demand to the north?" Rayneval asked.

"We insist that Canada be reduced to its ancient bound."

Then Rayneval, according to Jay's Diary, "contested our right to those back lands," as well as "the propriety" of the American contention on the fisheries. The latter the Frenchman attributed to "the ambition and restless views of Mr. Adams." America might do well to content itself with the coastal fishery, he counseled.

On his September visit to Bowood Park, Rayneval had made no secret of his discontent with America's boundary claims. Shelburne remembered these remarks, and now took the occasion to remind Thomas Townshend that it was the intention of France to exercise a moderating influence upon the Americans once independence was conceded. . . .

Strachey, on reaching Paris, proposed to the Americans that "a longitudinal line east of the Mississippi" be drawn to limit America's western extension. Here was the Aranda-Rayneval proposition starkly restated, but now emanating from the British commission. Jay snapped, "If that line is insisted upon, it is needless to talk of peace. We will never yield that point."

The rejection of Jay's provisional draft disabused the Americans on the score of Shelburne's sincerity. . . .

If the British sent reinforcements for their side, the American line was also bolstered. On October 26th John Adams reached Paris, preceding Strachey by two days. Having successfully negotiated a commercial treaty with the Dutch, the New Englander came in response to Jay's urgent call. . . .

On Sunday, the day after his arrival, Adams bathed in the

Seine not far from the Pont Royal. Rested and refreshed, he
looked up Matthew Ridley, and was put abreast of the negotiations. From Ridley's lips he heard praise of Jay's "firmness and
independence" and the New Yorker's refusal to "set his hand to
a bad peace." "I wish he was supported," Ridley remarked
meaningfully. Adams was chagrined to learn that Franklin's
grandson had been appointed secretary of the peace commission with Jay's apparently reluctant consent. . . .

Though not free of the taint of nepotism himself, Adams
resented old Franklin's presumption in this matter, and assumed from Ridley's remarks that there was a good deal more
friction between Jay and the doctor than the facts warranted.
He fancied himself as mediating differences between his colleagues, arising principally out of the binding character of
Congress' instructions, a copy of which, he insisted, had never
come into his hands. "Between two as subtle spirits as any in this
world," he admitted to his Diary, "the one malicious, the other I
think honest, I shall have a delicate, a nice, critical part to act. F's
cunning will be to divide us. To this end, he will provoke, he will
insinuate, he will intrigue, he will maneuvre. My curiosity will at
least be imployed in observing his invention and his artifice."

On Monday the 28th Adams dropped in at the Hôtel
d'Orléans on the rue des Petits Augustins, where the Jays were
residing. Jay apprised his visitor of the state of the negotiations
and offered his own "conjectures as to the views of France and
Spain" and of the ties between Franklin and Vergennes. Adams
enthusiastically concurred in all the New Yorker had done to
date and in the prospective tactics he outlined. "I am pleased,
too, that what is, was done before I came or I might have been
held to be the cause." So delighted was he with the way that Jay
had stood up to the English that he had the presumption to
write Abigail, "Jay and I peremptorily refused to speak or hear
before we were put on an equal foot." He neglected to tell his
devoted spouse that the concession on the point of independence had been made by the British weeks before he arrived in
Paris. Writing years later, Adams observed: "It is impossible for
any man but Mr. Jay and myself to conceive our mutual feelings
upon this sudden discovery, that we had both formed the same
opinions of the policy of the Comte de Vergennes and of Dr.
Franklin; that we were perfectly agreed in our principles, and

our whole system of conduct in the negotiation." In turn, Adams filled Jay's ear with some pretty grim opinions of his own about Franklin. Following dinner the pair continued their animated discussion until well on into the night.

Adams had been in Paris almost four days and still he had not paid his respects to the Sage of Passy. On Tuesday Ridley returned Adams' visit and urged him the necessity of paying a courtesy call upon the renowned peace commissioner, senior by years if not by priority of appointment. "After the usage I have received from him, I cannot bear go near him," Adams said. Ridley very sensibly rejoined that this was no time to be touchy. It would be imprudent for Adams to advertise to the world his differences with Franklin. Such gossip could conceivably jeopardize the negotiations. Adams continued to grumble that the doctor should come to see him. "You are always making mischief," the testy Patriot snapped. But Ridley managed to get Adams to put his overcoat on, then struggled with him as he tried to take it off after having some second thoughts, and got him to ride out that evening to Passy. Franklin, sufficiently recovered from "the cruel gout," was prepared to find that his old colleague had not removed the chip from his shoulder. Adams did not disappoint him. . . . Franklin listened politely but said nothing. Adams' monologue was scarcely soothing medicine for a convalescing septuagenarian. The inscrutable Sage had managed to relieve the tension of these weeks by writing a learned letter on the elements that originally composed the earth, and an essay providing information for prospective emigrants to America. He had long appreciated the importance of keeping one's equilibrium come what may. Nevertheless, Adams' frank outburst, coupled with the independent course that Jay had recently been pursuing, were not without effect on Franklin. Realizing the need to present a solid front to the British negotiators, he surprised his two colleagues by declaring, prior to the start of the first conference with the British negotiating team, "I will go with you, and proceed in the conferences without communicating anything to this Court; and the rather, because they communicated nothing to us."

Talks began on October 29th, when Oswald took Strachey over to meet Jay and Adams, and then to Passy for a chat with the doctor. At eleven o'clock the next morning the first formal conference got under way at Jay's lodgings and continued through dinner. . . .

In the course of the preliminary visit that Oswald, with Strachey in tow, paid upon Jay and Adams, it was made clear that the parties were at odds on the Loyalists, the debts, and the fisheries, and that the West was again in suspense. The new longitudinal line à la Rayneval bisecting the West, which Strachey had thrown out, was rudely dismissed. . . .

The negotiations, which continued round the clock from October 30th through November 4th, brought a few concessions to the British. The new American negotiator, John Adams, contrary to predictions, proved no more inflexible than his colleagues, and perhaps surprised both sides by a readiness to make concessions. . . . Adams persuaded his colleagues to accept a formula whereby Congress would recommend that the states open their courts of justice for the recovery of all just debts. Save for ironing out the phraseology, the British commissioners fell quickly into line. . . . The article agreed upon covered debts contracted by British subjects prior to 1775, but declared those of later date irrecoverable in law on the ground of illegality. It also included a recommendation to the states to correct confiscatory acts respecting lands "belonging to real British subjects." It did not cover debts owing to American Loyalists. This was the very best that could be obtained, Oswald advised his government.

Considering the immensity of the stakes, the struggle over the northern boundary and the "back lands" was over rather quickly. Strachey put up a fight to secure an adequate area in the Old Northwest for the resettlement of Loyalists. . . . No one took very seriously the proposal that Strachey had advanced for a longitudinal line bisecting the West. The Americans attribute this demand to French inspiration, Vaughan hastened to inform Shelburne. He pointed out that the proposal suggested a secret understanding between the courts of France and London, and warned that, if insisted upon, "the treaty will certainly be broke off." This stern warning was hardly necessary since Strachey saw he never had a chance, and quickly settled for much less.

The Americans came to the conference table prepared to offer an alternative northern boundary to Jay's 45th parallel or

"Nipissing Line." They now proposed a line through the St. Lawrence and the middle of the Great Lakes. On its face, this also seemed like a concession, as it yielded southern Ontario to the British and made the Great Lakes accessible to Canadians as well as Americans. Again the maps, notably Mitchell's map of 1755, proved deceptive. Under this alternative proposal the line was described as running from the most northwestern point of the Lake of the Woods due west to the Mississippi. No such line would strike that great river, for, as later exploration revealed, the source of the Mississippi lay 151 miles to the south of the Lake of the Woods. . . . Without realizing what they had accomplished, the American commissioners by this alternative proposal had enlarged the Old Northwest to include what became the state of Minnesota and reserved for posterity the then unknown Mesabi Iron Range. It should be added that the choice of the Lake of the Woods was to provide a logical ground for later negotiations which extended the boundary westward on the 49th parallel. . . . The new alternative had another advantage, in Vaughan's eyes. "It waves down into a better climate." . . . [*See* Map 6.]

Over the Mississippi as the western and the 31st parallel as the southern boundaries there was no dispute. In accordance with the new instructions to Oswald, the Mississippi article was reduced simply to a proposition for free navigation from its source to its mouth. The commercial reciprocity clause in Jay's provisional draft was dropped because it ran afoul of the British Navigation Laws and was simply too radical a proposal to put before Parliament at the moment. Since there was no way of trading down the Mississippi from Canada, and the Ohio was now closed to the British, they sacrificed real for illusory gains by denying reciprocity to America. In fact, it was largely the expectation of securing free access to American markets in the West that had induced Shelburne to yield the Old Northwest to the Americans without putting up a real battle. The parties quickly agreed on awarding Great Britain a more favorable northern boundary for West Florida than either was prepared to allot to Spain. . . .

All in all, the Americans had made substantial concessions in territory, without materially weakening their strategic position. "We have gone the utmost length to favor peace," wrote John

Adams. "We have at last agreed to boundaries with the greatest moderation." What they conceded was minor and sensible. What they held on to, the West as spelled out in Jay's provisional draft, converted a string of coastal provinces into a great nation. After the final peace was made Jay passed through England on route to America. Shelburne asked him what the American commissioners would have done had he refused to yield the West. "Would you have continued the war?" he asked. "I believe so, and certainly should have advised it," Jay replied unhesitatingly. . . .

The Cabinet met on the eleventh of November. After animated discussion it accepted the alternative "line-of-the-Lakes" boundary proposed by the Americans instead of the 45th parallel. . . .

The King accepted the Cabinet's preliminary articles with all the grace of a spoiled child forced to swallow some bitter medicine. Once Parliament to his "astonishment" had granted independence, George contended, he was disabled "from longer defending the just right of this Kingdom." Disclaiming responsibility, he subscribed to the articles out of "necessity not conviction." . . .

Shelburne had the choice of holding up the peace until France obtained further concessions for England from the Americans or presenting Parliament with a *fait accompi*. He realized that to expose the secrets of pending negotiations to the thunderous charges of his foes in Lords and Commons would not only jeopardize the peace, but most certainly bring down his own Ministry. With time now the crucial factor, Shelburne persuaded his Cabinet to have Parliament prorogued from November 26th, when it was scheduled to convene, until December 5th. . . .

The last formal round of talks began on November 25th, when the Americans met at Richard Oswald's lodgings to consider the provisional articles formulated by the British Ministry. . . .

The arguments over the Tories and King Cod continued. . . .

Friday, November 29th, the fourth and next to last day of the renewed discussion, proved memorable for two reasons. The preliminary draft was agreed upon, but not before Henry

Laurens made a last-minute appearance. Thomas Jefferson, fifth commissioner, never did sail for Europe, and neither participated nor signed. . . .

A swarthy, well-knit figure, below middling size, the gout-tortured Laurens now took his seat across the conference table from Richard Oswald, a long-time business associate and perhaps his most intimate friend. Compounding the coincidences, Laurens was indirectly related to Benjamin Vaughan through William Manning, London merchant and Vaughan's father-in-law. Aside from these curious ties to the British on the part of Laurens, the French were understandably cool to the prospect of another descendant of Huguenot refugees joining the American peace delegation. Mr. Jay's prejudices, to their mind, did not need bolstering. In point of fact the anxieties of the French were unwarranted. Laurens, of all the commissioners, seemed the least anxious to sign the preliminary articles without consulting the French. He irritated Adams considerably when he ventured to doubt the authenticity of Barbe-Marbois' letter on the fisheries, and warned against a separate peace. On the score of the Tories he was as deeply uncompromising as Franklin.

The three British and the four American negotiators foregathered at Jay's hotel and spent all of Friday settling the fishing and Tory articles. . . .

Signing was set for the next day, Saturday, November 30th. . . . The parties foregathered at Oswald's lodgings at the Grand Hotel Muscovite, on the same street, rue des Petits Augustins, where the Jays were staying. The principals compared treaty drafts. The Americans pointed out that Strachey had left out the twelve-month limitation of time permitted the refugees to reside in America in order to try to recover their estates. Franklin and Jay looked surprised, and insisted that the limitation be put back, which was done. Laurens managed to get a clause inserted forbidding the carrying off of Negroes or other property of American inhabitants by the evacuating forces. Oswald agreed. . . .

The parties affixed their signatures to duplicate originals of both the preliminary treaty and the separate article. According to protocol, Richard Oswald, representing the more venerable state, signed first on behalf of the erstwhile monarch of a now free and independent people, and then the Americans in strict alphabetical order. . . . Seals were affixed, and a signed original turned over to each side for transmission to their principals. . . .

The signing over, the participants rode out to Passy together to celebrate the event. There they were joined by some French guests, one of whom took occasion to rub salt into the wounds. Turning to the British, he harped on the theme of "the growing greatness of America," and predicted that "the Thirteen United States would form the greatest empire in the world."

"Yes, sir," Caleb Whitefoord replied, "and they will all speak English; every one of 'em."

The great moment had passed, and France was not permitted to share therein. The Americans, in accordance with their settled purpose, had concluded the preliminaries without the advice of the French court. However, the evening before the signing Franklin dashed off a note to Vergennes apprising him of the event about to take place, and promising to forward a copy of the articles of peace. . . .

Privately Vergennes was shocked at the liberal concessions England had made to her rebellious subjects, thereby stripping him of a heavy club he might have wielded against the adversary to secure Gibraltar, concessions in India, and other demands of the Bourbon partners. After looking over the articles he remarked to Rayneval, "The English buy peace rather than make it," adding, "Their concessions exceed all that I could have thought possible." His undersecretary in reply characterized the treaty with the Americans as a "dream." . . .

Without detracting from Shelburne's astute manipulations which resulted in his driving a wedge between the French and American Allies, albeit at a heavy price, one should not minimize the dexterous performance of the Americans who secured peace while maintaining the semblance of the alliance at the same time. As long as the Americans were in a position to make calls upon their French ally, the British could not hope in the final round of talks to water down the vast concessions they had made America by way of preliminaries.

PART III

SOLUTIONS OF THE POSTWAR WESTERN PROBLEM

CONFRONTED with the same problems as the British relative to Indian policy, land title, patterns of settlement, and transmontane government, the Americans sought solutions. In many early instances the American efforts duplicated those of the British. As time changed circumstances, the American policy became innovative and brought about different consequences from those envisioned in London before the Declaration.

Surely one of the more dramatic events of the war years was the cession to the United States of western land claims by the "landed states" of which Virginia, New York, and Connecticut were most conspicuous. This policy was the consequence of a stubborn resistance to large western claims by such "landless states" as Maryland, the result of wheeling and dealing between speculative interests and the Virginia and Maryland legislatures, the need for unity after the military defeats in 1780–1781, and the product of genuine statesmanship by many interested parties.

In the end, the cessions of Virginia and Connecticut were not without conditions. Prior land claims were voided, much to the speculators' dismay, and land title, though not governmental control, was retained for two large "reserves" in what is modern Ohio. The Western Reserve of Connecticut, in the vicinity of modern Cleveland, remained unsettled until the 1790's, because of Indian occupation. The Virginia Military Reserve served as one of the focal points of early Ohio settlement and the locus of an early territorial capital in Chillicothe. Since land there was patented under the Southern system by warrants, the recipient chose the tract by the most desirable shape possible, thereby making this the largest area in the Old Northwest not laid out in rectangular plots.

Once the Virginia cession had been received and the boundaries determined by the Peace of Paris, Congress sought to determine a policy for settling the vast domain under its jurisdiction. The policy followed the recommendations of New Englanders for an orderly survey and purchase in large six mile square townships. The desire was to encourage transmontane settlement by compact communities of settlers rather than by individual farmers and speculators who would be scattered about. The New England model was a noble one, but hardly fit for Southern customs or interests which used warrants to choose the most desirable ground, leaving the remainder unpatented. As a sop for those not concerned with group settlement, Congress allowed purchase of half the first townships in one mile square "sections" of 640 acres. The land was to be auctioned in each eastern state at a minimum price of $1.00 per acre.

The New Englanders failed to re-create the seventeenth-century Puritan villages their statesmen sought. While some migration westward was by like-minded pioneers, the rectangular agricultural plots and American individualism jointly frustrated the dream of a communal agrarian society gathered around a meeting house. Instead the isolated farmstead replaced the medieval rural village after which the New England town had been copied. Only in a few areas such as the Amana communities of Iowa did the older conception of social structure apply in the transmontane region. The effect of the shape of the survey upon our society is unknown, but in the nearly two centuries of our existence, the survey design dictated the right angles at which roads, streets, and highways ran throughout the West. The basic similarity of midwestern towns came from the physical limitations of rectangular land subdivisions. Thus, the land ordinance of 1785 assisted in the development of fragmented communities, economic individualism, and fundamental uniformity that characterized nineteenth-century America.

The governance of Congress's western empire was inextricably linked to the relationship which the region would have to the original states. Fearing the West would dominate the East, or at least dilute its relative influence, many easterners sought to limit the role and number of new states in Congress. Pulling in an opposite direction were the frontiersmen who demanded immediate self-government and equality with the older states or threatened the establishment of a new state or nation in the interior.

Compromising these conflicting interests were the Northwest Ordinances of 1784 and 1787. Collectively they stand as a monument to the creative enterprise of the much maligned Continental Congress. In 1778 Congressmen agreed that all state cessions would receive republican governments and be admitted to the Union on an equal basis with the original members. This was reaffirmed in 1780. Out of the Indian Affairs Committee in 1784 came a preliminary plan for western government. It proposed fourteen states for the trans-Appalachian west where nine now exist. Recent research indicates that the 1784 law was never intended to be more than a temporary measure; it was a policy statement around which the more specific enactment of three years later would be made. It is also apparent that the law more than reflected the "democratic" opinions of Thomas Jefferson, whose authorship of the document has long been advanced. Rather it was a gathering together of ideas on western policy by a number of Americans. One thing was certain, a formal pledge was made to the number of interlopers crossing the upper Ohio into the Indian country and at the same time Congress asserted its authority over the region.

Probably the greatest weakness in the 1784 Ordinance was its division of the Northwest into at least seven potential states requiring a separate governmental apparatus for each several years before they could be expected to assume their own governmental expenses. Such a grandiose scheme could not be afforded. Moreover, the proposed western states north and south of the Ohio River would eventually outnumber the eastern ones, an idea not acceptable to most Congressmen, especially those from New England who anticipated southern dominance in the West.

The 1784 plan contained a four-step process to statehood. The first, unspecified, allowed a state of nature to exist with no governmental organization. Essentially this existed in the region in 1784. A second stage called for all free adult males to form a temporary government based upon that of one of the original states. How all such residents would gather and make such a choice is unclear. When the free residents totaled 20,000 they could call a constitutional convention and draft their own rules of government. Finally, upon attaining a population equal to that of the least populace state, they could petition for admission on an equal basis with the others. Congressmen assumed the smallest state had a population of about 30,000 rather than the 59,000 it actually had in 1784. Admission required the approval of two-thirds of the state congressional delegations. This plan allowed for considerable autonomy for the settlers and denied the national government a major role in territorial governance. Moreover, the progress to statehood might be extremely long. The 1784 enactment never went into effect, although it served as a basis for the 1787 ordinance.

Two persons contributed significantly to the revised territorial government plan—James Monroe of Virginia and Nathan Dane of Massachusetts. Most significant was the creation of one temporary government for the vast region northwest of the Ohio River. Rather than maintain a flexible population requirement of being equal to the least populous state or one-thirteenth of the original states, Congress specified that 60,000 inhabitants be the minimum for statehood. While many thought this requirement too low, it delayed admission of the first state from the region for sixteen years, and the fifth state—Wisconsin—waited sixty-one years.

More important was the direct intrusion of Congress into territorial governance. In effect, the first stage of the 1784 plan was eliminated. The whole region immediately fell under the jurisdiction of a governor and judges appointed by Congress. With a population of 5,000 free males the territory elected an assembly and at 60,000 free inhabitants (or about 15,000 free males) it could frame a state constitution and petition for admission. Approval required only a congressional majority rather than two-thirds as under the 1784 act. Throughout the territorial period Congress appointed the governor and during the second stage it selected a council which advised the governor and served as the upper house of the legislature. All of this, except for admission, was copied from the British colonial experience.

Another section of the 1787 law guaranteed civil liberties and a republican government. Article six prohibited slavery in the Northwest. Instead of Jefferson's idea of universal manhood suffrage, the law required voters to own fifty acres and legislators to have two hundred acres during the territorial period.

There can be little doubt this was the most important legislative enactment of the Continental Congress. It provided for orderly government of the wilderness, for eventual admission of its western colonies into the rising American empire, and for the extension of civil rights and republican government to the West. Only the Declaration of Independence, the Constitution of 1787, and the Bill of Rights have had more important influence upon American development. Congress insured the eventuality of a vibrant republic stretching from the Atlantic to the Mississippi by adopting this most creative colonial policy.

But a major obstacle from the white point of view—the original inhabitants of the region—remained to impede the Americans' progress. The Indians presented a problem which Congress and its agents were unable to solve during the Confederation era. Despite the territorial provisions of the Peace of Paris of 1783, the British maintained several garrisons inside the boundaries of the United States. Niagara, Detroit, and Mackinac affected the Northwest. Governor-General Sir Frederick Haldimand of Canada refused to surrender the posts hoping, he said, to avert a slaughter of Americans and to control the fur trade. Another reason was the failure of the Americans to indemnify the Loyalists for their losses, as the treaty required. There emerged another rationale: the British hoped to create an Indian barrier to their settlements in Upper Canada. During the mid-1780's Haldimand's agents—John Johnson, Joseph Butler, and Joseph Brant—shaped a confederation of Iroquois, Wyandot, Shawnee, Delaware, Miami, Ottawa, Chippewa, and Potawatomi. This group pledged not to cede more territory, to repudiate previous treaties that did so, and to maintain the boundary at the Ohio. Haldimand's scheme floundered on the twin rocks of Indian individualism and American aggressiveness.

In late 1784 American commissioners at Fort Stanwix negotiated a treaty with the Iroquois ceding the Northwest in exchange for lands in New York. This was part of a normal Iroquois diplomatic move to steer settlement away from their homeland. A little later at Fort McIntosh representatives of the Chippewa, Ottawa, Delaware, and Wyandot ceded all their Ohio lands except those between the Cuyahoga and Maumee rivers. Since the Miami and Shawnee did not participate in either of these treaties, the documents were worthless except to provide ammunition for subsequent wars and the basis for subsequent negotiations. For the Americans, their Indian diplomacy went along a line of "what I have is mine, what you have is negotiable." A year later at Fort Finney the Shawnee conceded their claim to all of Ohio except for the Cuyahoga-Maumee reserve in the Fort McIntosh treaty. Claiming they signed under duress, the Shawnee chiefs repudiated the agreement upon returning to their villages. After a three-year interlude, open warfare began in the spring of 1786.

The Indian commissioners sought to forestall all this by sending Colonel Josiah Harmar of the sadly depleted Continental Army—reduced to battalion strength—to clear southeastern Ohio of hundreds of squatters who were swarming into the region in 1785. Even though he established a few blockhouses along the Ohio valley, his patrols were unable to stop the encroachment. Passage of the Indian Ordinance of 1786 established two superintendencies for western Indians and licensed traders to the tribes. Such an act could not stop the inexorable drift towards warfare.

In the summer of 1786 Brigadier General George Rogers Clark and Colonel Benjamin Logan led expeditions of Kentuckians into the Wabash and Great Miami valleys, Logan's troops destroyed ten Shawnee villages and 15,000 bushels of corn before returning home. Clark's militiamen mutinied before meeting a single foe, but they did relieve the beleaguered Americans at Vincennes. This brought the tribes into a common league against the "long knives" who crossed the Ohio.

In the midst of the Indian menace, regular settlement began north of the Ohio between Pittsburgh and Cincinnati. When sales of the seven ranges being surveyed under the Land Ordinance of 1785 were insufficient to provide the income Congress needed, it turned to large sales to speculators for such revenue. Two such purchases—the Ohio Company's and the Miami Purchase of John Cleves Symmes of New Jersey—were reasonably legitimate, but the Scioto Company was pure fraud. In order to ram his Ohio Company scheme through Congress, the Rev. Manasseh Cutler of Massachusetts had to agree to enlarge the size of his purchase and then sell the enlargement to a group of Congressmen headed by William Duer of New York. The Ohio Company received 1,781,760 acres and the Scioto Company 5,000,000 acres.

Because all of this happened at the same time as the Constitution and the Northwest Ordinance of 1787 were being considered, there has long been speculation that a conspiracy existed. For most this involved the speculative interests in Congress against the squatter interests in Ohio. Others saw the Ordinance as a deliberate protection for vested property rights by depriving the "democratic" frontiersmen of self-government. At least one historian sees a complicated arrangement between southern slaveholding interests and New England speculators who exchanged slavery protection clauses in the Constitution for the prohibition of slavery and land deals in the Northwest Territory. Some recent scholars have denied any such agreements, formal or informal, existed. They contend the Ordinance was the natural result of territorial policies evolving in Congress for several years. They see no special role either by the founding fathers in Philadelphia or by Cutler in determining the congressional decision on territorial government.

Whatever the truth, by 1787 Congress had completed much of the process of solving the problem of the transmontane West. They devised a rectilinear survey scheme that would mold western settlement for centuries; they created a governmental system that insured the orderly development and expansion of the American empire; but they left unsolved the role of large speculation schemes and the place of the Native Americans in the United States.

Frontier Diplomacy, 1783–1790

Charles R. Ritcheson

Both their own diplomacy and military activities during the war cost the American Indians dearly. By alienating the victors, they left themselves little maneuvering room when the Peace of Paris left their lands under the control of the United States.

Professor Charles Ritcheson (1925———) discusses the Anglo-American-Indian triangle in a perceptive chapter from a book on British-American foreign policy in the dozen years following the peace treaty. While he places responsibility for frontier hostilities largely upon the Americans, he acknowledges that the absence of any central Indian political authority and the intrigues of Britain and Spain constituted contributory factors. The British faced a series of dilemmas. They occupied military installations inside the new republic, they had allied themselves, deserted, and re-allied themselves with the Indians, and they desired to maintain cordial relations with the United States because of its potential as a market and as a military threat to Canada and the North Atlantic shipping lanes. This explains much of the contradictatory policies of the British government in the 1780's.

Professor Ritcheson now occupies the Lovell Chair of English History at the University of Southern California. His previous teaching positions were at Kenyon College and Southern Methodist University. Besides the book from which the following is taken, he has written British Politics and the American Revolution *(1954),* Lord Grenville's Treaty with Mr. Jay *(1969), and articles on the Loyalists, Edmund Burke, and Anglo-American diplomacy.*

★ ★

T HE PRESENCE of the red man along the western frontier is one of the constants in the American experience from the first coming of the colonists in the seventeenth century to the

From Charles R. Ritcheson, *Aftermath of the Revolution: British Policy Toward the United States, 1783–1795* (Dallas, 1969), 164–170; reprinted without notes with permission of Southern Methodist University Press.

miserable "final solution" of the nineteenth. Almost from the first, hostility between restless, westward-moving, land-hungry Americans and Indians jealous for their forest hunting lands was deep and unrelenting. In the long and savage strife, barbarism was monopolized by neither the one side nor the other.

With the expulsion of the French from Canada in 1763, Britain was faced with the delicate problem of pacifying Indian allies of the defeated enemy. It was the necessary first step toward exploiting the magnificent territorial acquisition in the North American hinterland, and it was made even more urgent in the very year of the Peace by Pontiac's outburst. For a time, success seemed within the grasp of the London government. The Grenville ministry saw the magnitude of the imperial problem and formulated a comprehensive solution which called for troops in the backcountry to guard against Indian attack or French reconquest; a temporary halt to westward expansion from the Atlantic seaboard; an imperial office of Indian affairs with agents in the field to negotiate peaceable acquisition of territory claimed by the natives; and then, systematic settlement, the establishment of government and social institutions in new inland colonies. It is not the least tragic element in Anglo-American history that this sensible, humane, practical plan became hopelessly entangled in the rising constitutional crisis over the question of imperial taxation of the colonies.

While the American government formulated a magnificent plan, in the Northwest Ordinance of 1787, for the exploitation of the backcountry, it never developed an Indian policy beyond the law of the knife. This lamentable failure was due chiefly to the needs, rarely comprehended within the limits of morality, of an expanding population and to the Confederation's weakness—the simple inability to establish effective authority in the West. By the time the United States acquired a reasonably competent federal government, too much blood had flowed, too many wounds had been sustained, too many fundamental challenges had been given and received to permit any solution but the appeal to arms.

There were other contributory factors, however: for example, the absence of any central Indian authority able to negotiate for, and to bind, all—or even a major portion—of the tribes. It may be argued, too, that by 1783 hostility between Indian and American had become so deep and implacable, particularly in view of the Indian participation in the war just concluded, that it was no longer possible to envisage a peaceable settlement. Further, the interests of Spain worked against peace as she intrigued persistently and effectively among the southern Indians, seeking in them a buffer to keep the ever advancing frontiersmen from the Mississippi. The presence of British troops on the soil of the United States also undoubtedly gave encouragement to Indian truculence and hostility in the Old Northwest, as did more active agitations, shadowy and difficult of substantiation, ignited on a considerable scale by private agents, merchants and traders from Canada. It must finally be stated, however, that primary responsibility for the Hobbesian state of nature along the American frontier rested with the government and people of the United States. Putting aside moral considerations, it is obvious that American citizens aggressively seized Indian lands. Their government should have been equally forward in making a decent, humane, and comprehensive settlement. Unfortunately, the Confederation was weak; and by the time a remedy had been found, patterns of conduct, attitudes, immigration, and policy had hardened beyond change.

The Peace of 1783 brought no tranquillity to the frontier. The authority of Congress was legally extended to the Northwest Territory, but establishing it in reality was a very different affair. Several agreements, scarcely important enough to be called treaties, were concluded with the Iroquois and certain other tribes in the southern portion of the trans-Ohio country. The Treaty of Fort Stanwix was made in 1784, and the following year the Treaty of Fort McIntosh, named for a small post, some miles down the Ohio from Pittsburgh, commanded by Lieutenant Colonel Josiah Harmar. Both involved limited cessions of Indian lands, promises to respect Indian rights, and the establishment of a few small posts along the Ohio.

In 1787 efforts were actually made to clear out frontiersmen who had settled along the right bank of the river in defiance of the government's promises to the Indians, but it was a sweeping back of the sea. Newly breveted Brigadier General Harmar went on to occupy Vincennes on the Wabash and points in the

Illinois country; attempts to subordinate the Indians in the area overturned the beehive. Race war spread along the frontier, into Kentucky and even Virginia. Could the savages fight so viciously and destructively without encouragement and assistance from outside? Americans, at the time and subsequently, seeking to explain their country's difficulty in establishing its authority in the western regions, answered the question with an indignant negative and pointed the finger at the British in the Old Northwest. Harmar himself complained in 1787 that the road westward would be blocked until the posts were delivered up: "Villainous emissaries have been continually sallying from thence," he wrote, "poisoning the minds of the Savages & depreciating the character of the Americans." A single treaty at Detroit "would give Dignity & Consequence to the United States and answer every purpose. . . . Elsewhere it would be of little or no effect." The "villains" Harmar had in mind were traders and trappers down from Canada; but those suffering from Indian depredations were not likely to make fine distinctions between private subjects and public authority. In American minds, the Indian troubles were inevitably attributed to British intrigue among the savages.

In reality, British policy and interests called for peace and stability along the frontier with America. This had been true for Shelburne's ministry and for the coalition which succeeded it, and it was true for the Pitt government, too. Shelburne's plan for an Anglo-American economic union—blurring national boundaries, with Canadians and Americans traversing the great forests and trapping and trading with equal freedom—envisaged a "commercial empire of the St. Lawrence." But his successors and the Americans themselves sharply underlined the political reality of the Canadian-American boundary: and the attempt to tie up British, American, and Indian interests in one package failed.

The question inevitably arose of Britain's responsibility to her wartime Indian allies inhabiting the territory of the United States, and with it a dilemma of a powerful and dangerous kind. A withdrawal behind the Canadian frontier, as defined by the Peace of 1783, would clear the arena for a desperate American-Indian struggle, lay the British themselves open to charges of ingratitude to those who had rendered them assistance at a moment of peril, perhaps cause a savage assault upon the Canadian hinterland, and sacrifice the fur-traders and the profits they derived from the area. The early suggestions from Haldimand, noted above—that, for American and British benefit alike, Britain might retain the northwestern posts "for some time" while Indian affairs were placed on a stable basis—coincided with the lobbying of the fur-traders in London and Quebec. A third and more pressing concern—securing justice for British loyalists and creditors—also supported the wisdom of retaining the American posts temporarily. But the constants, the British and Indians, faced a variable: the American advance westward, bringing pressures which were bound to mount steadily and rapidly. Far from courting hostilities, the London government accepted as fundamental the premise that some kind of settlement, peaceably reconciling the interests of all parties, must be achieved lest the balance be overturned. It was a position of the greatest delicacy. If the Americans were allowed to carry their point and to gain possession of the posts unconditionally, Indians and prewar creditors would consider themselves abandoned by the home government: the former would look to British scalps for revenge, the latter to the British treasury for proper indemnities. If the posts were retained too long, however, the consequences would be equally disagreeable: the hostility, open or covert, of the Americans; and, as their people migrated into the disputed territory, an inevitable clash with the Indians, and probably with the British themselves. Timing was vital if the edge of the knife were to be walked to safety. It is not surprising, therefore, that to some British policy should have appeared hesitant and indecisive. But bold decisions and brilliant strokes are not always appropriate; there are times to stand vigilantly on the defensive, to observe the momentum of events, to deflect danger by the timely parry. This was the informing spirit of British policy in the Old Northwest.

In June, 1783, Joseph Brant and John the Mohawk, paramount chiefs of the Six Nations, met General Haldimand in Quebec. Suspicious that Britain had indeed given their hunting lands away to the Americans, they sought from him reassurances he could not give. Embarrassed and apprehensive, the Commander in Chief feared imminent war between the Indians and their new sovereigns. Intending to preserve peace if at all possible, he knew by the end of 1783 that the Indians would insist upon the boundary fixed not by the Anglo-American treaty of peace, but by the Treaty of 1768. As the Americans could not be expected to accept the Ohio River line without a fight, Haldimand's peaceable intentions appeared doomed to failure. His famous recommendation that the forts be retained for a limited time followed. Though based on reasons more complicated than Haldimand knew, the British government's decision to hold the forts calmed the Indians and probably prevented the outbreak of a full-scale frontier war with the Americans.

In spite of this, the Indians remained suspicious of British intentions; and their volatile discontent made the course of events unpredictable and a source of constant worry to the London authorities. In the winter of 1785, Chief Joseph Brant journeyed to England to ask support for the Six Nations if war should come between his people and their enemies to the south. He received assurances of gratitude for past support, compensation for losses suffered during the American war, and advice to remain at peace. Simultaneously, instructions went out to Lieutenant-Governor Hope in Canada: open and avowed assistance to the Indians, in case they went to war with the Americans, "must at all events in the present state of this country be avoided." The balance was, however, to be maintained; it would comport neither with justice nor with good policy "entirely to abandon" the savages, who would inevitably turn against Britain. Within these general limits, the Lieutenant-Governor, on the scene and possessing firsthand knowledge of events, would have to exercise his own judgment and discretion in "a business so delicate and interesting." In short, Hope should assure the Indians of Britain's abiding benevolence, which would involve the continuation of traditional gifts, among them rifles and ammunition for hunting and self-defense; but he should not provide them with the means of making offensive war against the Americans. Indeed, he was ordered to avoid offending the southern neighbor in his dealings with the red men. Here was the very essence of the British dilemma. As long as the two combatants stood beyond arm's length of each other, Britain had room for maneuver; but the distance between them was

steadily diminishing, as Americans moved ever farther westward. Little wonder that British leaders began to dream of an
Indian buffer zone between Canada and the United States,
closed to white settlement, though open equally to traders from
both countries.

The dilemma sharpened after Dorchester arrived in Quebec
in 1786. The new governor of Canada intended to cling to the
middle course, as his predecessors had done; and he promptly
instructed the imperial Indian agent, Sir John Johnson, to make
it clear to the Indians that he had not come to start a war with the
United States, and that he lacked power to do so. Instead, every
effort was to be made to persuade them to make peace with
their new sovereigns. Clearly hinting at a possible cession,
Dorchester also told Johnson to inquire into the attitude of the
Six Nations toward continued occupation of the posts by Britain. The same logic which bade Britain hold the Indians in
check, however, forbade her passive acceptance of an American
assault upon the posts. If, Johnson was told, the former rebels
attempted to overturn the delicate balance, "war must be re-
pelled by war."

The British posture was defensive; but if attack from the
south were not to be invited, Dorchester reasoned, Britain
would have to put her ability to defend herself beyond question.
Cession of the posts, he believed, would deliver the Indians into
the hands of the Americans; and the savages would seek revenge along the Canadian frontier. Abandonment and destruction of the posts would only retard the evil. It was obvious to the
military mind that Britain had to stand firm where she was.
More men and money, Dorchester warned London, were necessary to put the posts in a proper state of preparation. What, he
pointedly asked, should be his course of action in case the
Americans attacked and captured the posts?

It is easy to understand Dorchester's growing preoccupation
with the preparedness of his forces. At the same time, there was
the danger that each side, American and British, might misun-
derstand the intentions of the other and construe defense
measures as preparations for an attack. Mutual suspicion and
apprehension might well escalate into an Anglo-American clash
in the backcountry before the government in London even
knew what was afoot. The delicate balance would go by the
board; and the interests of Indians, Americans, and Britons

would be cast into the crucible of war. The London government, with a view broader than Dorchester's, accordingly told the General that he might disburse funds to put the posts in a "temporary state of defence." The Indians were to be supplied, according to past practice, with the means of defending themselves; but this was to be accomplished in the manner least likely to alarm the Americans or to incite the Indians to an attack. (Dorchester was, thus, being asked to judge the point at which British assistance transcended the capacity for self-defense and became the ability to wage offensive war against the Americans.) As for Dorchester's question, if the Americans should seize the posts and if the Governor believed himself strong enough to recover them, then his duty was clear. If hostilities were confined to the Americans and the Indians, however, it would be imprudent for him to be drawn into rendering active assistance to the savages.

Under the Confederation, the Indian issue was a relatively minor concern in Anglo-American diplomacy. When Minister John Adams saw Foreign Secretary Carmarthen on October 20, 1785, for example, he mentioned that an Indian war was in prospect; but he carefully avoided any charge of official British encouragement of Indian outrages along the frontier. They constituted, he said, only one of the evils occasioned by Britain's retention of the posts. There were more important things on his mind than Indian affairs, and the threatened frontier war was merely a subordinate point in his pursuit of the posts. Even Gouverneur Morris, as late as 1790, used the issue as a subordinate supporting argument in favor of a cession of the posts. Like Adams, he made no charge of complicity against the British government, although he pointed, as Adams had done, at the connection in the minds of the American public between Britain's retention of the posts and Indian hostilities. Every murder committed by the Indians was "attributed to British intrigue; and although some men of liberal minds might judge differently, their arguments would have little weight with the many, who felt themselves aggrieved. . . ." The force of the westward movement and the vigor of the federal government brought the matter to a head. The great western legacy was not to be enjoyed until Indian affairs were settled, and by 1790 the only means to this end appeared to be war.

The Cession of the Old Northwest

Merrill Jensen

The cession of the Northwest to the Continental Congress marked a turning point in the development of the region. Control shifted from several "landed states" to a national agency. Moreover, it constituted the beginning of congressional authority over territory. From the acts of cession came the origins of subsequent important developments in the region—the land Ordinance of 1785 and the revenue system based on land sales which somewhat stabilized the Confederation government.

For years discussion of the problem of land cession revolved around Herbert Baxter Adams's Maryland's Influence upon the Land Cessions to the United States *(1885) which acclaimed the selfless role of Maryland statesmen in refusing to ratify the Articles of Confederation until the grasping landed states gave up their extravagant western claims. This thesis stood unchallenged for half of a century, until young Merrill Jensen (1905———), an instructor at the University of Washington, wrote on the subject.*

Jensen argued that the representatives of the "landless states" had vested interests in speculative companies in these areas and that their motives involved preservation of their claims as much as statesmanship. In the end Congress accepted the Virginia cession with the proviso that the claims of the various land companies be voided. Thus, in exchange for property in the area, Congress disposed of the claims of the Indiana Company and the Illinois-Wabash Company. On all sides statesmanship and partisanship combined for beneficial ends.

*This article of 1936 marks the beginning of Jensen's reinterpretation of the years 1776–1789 which appeared in two seminal books—*The Articles of Confederation *(1940) and* The New Nation *(1950). They constitute a masterful reappraisal of the era which denies the traditionally accepted idea of congressional impotence and which sees the Constitution as a document designed to protect the privilege against the democratic tendencies of the Articles. So pervasive has Jensen's influence been that his thesis is now conventional wisdom among historians.*

Jensen began teaching history at the University of Wisconsin–Madison in 1941 and occupied the endowed Vilas Research Professorship in

History from 1964 until his retirement in 1975. In 1969–1970 he served as president of the Organization of American Historians, successor to the Mississippi Valley Historical Association in whose Review *this and the subsequent Jensen article appeared.*

★★★★★★★★★★★★★★★★★★★★★★★★★★★★★

MORE THAN fifty years ago Herbert Baxter Adams discussed the cession of the Old Northwest in a monograph that has had a pervasive and enduring influence. Maryland's refusal to agree to the Articles of Confederation until Congress should be given some portion of the West was interpreted as a result of the "farsighted policy of Maryland in opposing the grasping land claims of Virginia and three of the Northern States." Rhode Island, New Jersey, and Delaware also opposed the claims of Virginia, but Adams denied that they shared Maryland's vision of a national commonwealth based on western expansion. These lesser states were interested only in sharing the revenues to be derived from the West or in defraying the expenses of the war. He insisted: "The credit of suggesting and successfully urging in Congress that policy which has made this country a great national commonwealth . . . belongs to Maryland, and to her alone."

The determination of Maryland and the other Middle States played a part in the creation of the national domain. But the causes of their determination lay less in patriotic abstraction and national vision than in the jealousy these states felt for Virginia, and in the often thwarted but ever-reviving hopes of the members of speculative land companies within these states. The measure of the influence wielded by such companies is indicated by their membership. Among the members were Governor Thomas Johnson, Charles Carroll, and Samuel Chase of Maryland, and Benjamin Franklin, James Wilson, and Robert Morris of Pennsylvania. Such men ably combined official duties with the furtherance of their hopes of private fortune

From Merrill Jensen, "The Cession of the Old Northwest," in the *Mississippi Valley Historical Review*, XXIII: 27–48 (June, 1936); reprinted without footnotes with the permission of the author and the *Journal of American History*.

in the West, and used their influence to make the official policies of their states conform to their private interests.

Two simple but fundamental and related facts must be kept in mind for an understanding of the course of events that led to the cession of the Old Northwest. The first fact is that land speculation was the major get-rich-quick activity of eighteenth century planters, merchants, and politicians. The second fact is that certain of the colonies— particularly the middle group, Pennsylvania, Maryland, Delaware, and New Jersey—had definite western boundaries within which the opportunities for speculation were relatively limited. The citizens of these landless colonies were at a disadvantage as compared to the citizens of the charter colonies with claims extending to the South Seas. The citizens of the latter were able to secure huge slices of land at no particular personal sacrifice. Thus members of the Virginia aristocracy received vast grants of land in the West, quite certain that it all lay within the bounds of Virginia, and even more certain that Pennsylvania and Maryland speculators would never receive like favors from the Virginia government.

Very early in this game of grab, the speculators of the landless colonies evolved two ideas to neutralize the superior advantage of their more fortunately placed rivals. The first idea was that of the limitation of the area of those colonies which were deemed to have "indefinite bounds" and "inconvenient dimensions." This proposal found expression in the Albany plan of union which owed much to Benjamin Franklin who was both Pennsylvanian and speculator. The second idea, related to the first, involved the formation of new states to the west of Pennsylvania and within the charter bounds of Virginia. Private land companies were to be organized for this purpose and they were to secure grants from the British government, for only through the intervention of a superior power could alien speculators enter into the promised land which seemed to be Virginia's.

There were many abortive schemes for independent colonies and many an abortive land company. Two of the companies, however, were sufficiently long-lived to be able to carry on a campaign of devious character and dubious ethics, one of the most obvious results of which was the delay of the ratification of the Articles of Confederation for three years. These were the Indiana and the Illinois-Wabash companies, both of which were composed mainly of politicians and speculators from Pennsylvania, Maryland, and New Jersey. [*See* Maps 1 and 7.]

The Indiana Company grew out of claims arising from the loss of the goods and the lives of Indian traders through the misfortunes of Indian war. Particularly significant was the fact that much of the goods had been supplied on credit by two Philadelphia firms specializing in furnishing supplies for the western trade. The leaders of these two firms, Samuel Wharton and William Trent, united with some of the surviving traders in an effort to secure compensation for their losses. The Virginia and the British governments ignored their pleas, so the "Suffering Traders" turned to the Indians. Finally at the Treaty of Fort Stanwix in 1768, these "Suffering Traders" secured a grant of land from the Six Nations, not because the Six Nations had been responsible for the losses, but because they had lands to grant. The tract granted became known as Indiana. It lay within the present state of West Virginia and covered approximately the same area which had been granted to the Ohio Company of Virginia in 1749.

Wharton and Trent then went to England to secure official confirmation of the deed from the Six Nations. When they failed in this, they entered into a vast speculative scheme for the erection of the colony of Vandalia within which the Indiana grant was to be included. While engaged in the political intrigues necessary to bring about the creation of Vandalia, Wharton also secured an opinion from Lord Chancellor Camden and from Charles Yorke to the effect that Indian nations were sovereign and that land grants by them did not need the approbation of any other political power. While this gave the Indiana Company a doubtful legal leg upon which to stand, its importance lay in the fillip it gave to speculative enterprise in the colonies. A group of Maryland and Pennsylvania speculators organized the Illinois Company and secured a grant of land north of the Ohio River in 1773. This same group with a few additional members including Lord Dunmore, organized the Oubache or Wabash Company and secured another grant north of Ohio in 1775. Thus at the outbreak of the Revolution two groups of speculators centering in the landless Middle States had staked out large areas lying within the charter bounds of Virginia. [*See* Map 7.]

Just as these speculators had turned to the British government for help before the Revolution, they now turned to what their interest caused them to conceive of as the logical successor to the power of the British government—the Continental Congress. The Congress may have been a weak reed, but was a far more stable support than the Virginia government which soon made it plain that it intended to oppose all deeds and purchases from Indians. In June and July, 1776, the Virginia Convention advised actual settlers in the West to hold their lands until the claims of the land companies could be investigated, appointed a commission to investigate such claims, and declared that all purchases within Virginia's charter limits could be made only with the consent of the Virginia legislature. When the Virginia constitution was written, it declared that the bounds of the state were those set forth in the Charter of 1609 and the Treaty of 1763, "unless, by act of the legislature, one or more territories shall hereafter be laid off, and governments established westward of the Allegheny mountains." These measures forecast the attitude to be taken by the government of the state toward such schemes as the Transylvania purchase of Richard Henderson, the Illinois and Wabash purchases, and the deed of the Indiana Company.

It is difficult to determine just how intimate the connections between the land companies and the members of Congress became at the outbreak of the Revolution. Sufficient evidence exists, however, to indicate tendencies and to demonstrate the stellar rôle played by land speculation. Shares were provided in a proposed land purchase north of the Ohio and some of them were given to Thomas Wharton to distribute among the members of Congress in the hope of inducing Congress to make a declaration in favor of Indian purchases and their validity. Patrick Henry, who had early fallen in with the schemes of the Pennsylvania speculators, later testified that he had been offered and had rejected shares in all the various purchases from Indians. Franklin entered Congress upon his return from England in 1775 and participated both in the work of Congress and in the re-organization of the Indiana Company which assumed its original status upon the collapse of the Vandalia project. In July, 1775, he presented a plan of confederation in which the Congress was given the power of "Planting . . . new Colonies when proper," and thus implying congressional control over the West. In March, 1776, John Adams wrote that union was being delayed by "that avarice of Land, which has made upon this Continent so many votaries to Mammon, that I sometimes dread the Consequences." The first draft of the Articles of Confederation was in the hand writing of John Dickinson of Pennsylvania and Delaware. It gave to Congress the power of limiting and defining state boundaries, of setting up new governments in the regions set aside, and of settling disputes between states over rival land claims. The issue was thus placed squarely before Congress for the first time. And for years it was to remain there as an impediment and even as a threat to union and common action.

The Virginia delegates led in the attack upon these provisions. They denied the right of Congress to interfere within the bounds of the states as defined by their charters. Members from the landless states argued that no state had a "right" to extend to the South Seas. Samuel Chase of Maryland frankly admitted that it was the intention of some of the delegates to limit the size of certain states since their smaller neighbors would not be safe unless such a step were taken. The states with claims were more numerous than those without, and votes rather than arguments settled the question for a time. The obnoxious provisions were stricken from the second draft of the Articles of Confederation.

The Confederation was dropped from consideration after August, 1776, but the land question continued a subject of dispute. In September Congress offered a land bounty in addition to a money bounty for recruits. This met with protest from Maryland who denied that the United States owned any lands, but affirmed that crown lands should become common property. Unless this came to pass, Maryland would be impoverished and at the mercy of her powerful neighbors. After much bickering, Congress again evaded the issue by a fence-straddling resolution to the effect that nothing done was intended either to affirm or deny the claims of any of the states or of the United States to any lands in America.

A few months later Thomas Burke of North Carolina reported that Maryland, Pennsylvania, New Jersey, and others were jealous of the landed states, and expressed the opinion that these landless states would attempt to make the power of

Congress very extensive and then limit the states to the west-ward. By August, 1777, the landless states were beginning to attack the legal validity of Virginia's charter claims, and in October they made a final attempt to write their desires into the Articles of Confederation. They offered a series of motions designed to give Congress power to fix the western limits of the landed states. Each of the motions failed, but they had the effect of arousing the landed states to positive action. An amendment by Richard Henry Lee was added to a long article setting forth the procedure for settling disputes between states. This amend-ment was to the effect that "no State shall be deprived of territory for the benefit of the United States."

Thus the final draft of the Articles of Confederation was sent to the states embodying the desires of the landed states. The reaction of the landless states was immediate. The New Jersey "Representation" queried the intent of the clause providing that no state was to be deprived of territory for the benefit of the United States. Disbelief was expressed that this could mean the "crown lands," for such lands being the property of the common enemy, should become the common property of all the states. Maryland stated her position in a series of amend-ments which she offered to the Articles of Confederation. Congress should be given the power to fix the limits of the states claiming to reach to the South Sea. Maryland demanded a right in common to all the country lying "westward of the frontiers of the United States," but with the significant exception of the property "which was not vested in Individuals at the commence-ment of the present war." But the Maryland delegates had faint hope of success for as one of them wrote: "The bare mentioning of this subject rouses Virginia, and conscious of her own impor-tance, she views her vast Dominion with the surest expectations of holding it unimpaired." Maryland, however, could and did refuse to confederate. By February, 1779, she was the only state which had not yet agreed to the Articles of Confederation.

In fact, the issue around which revolved the refusal of Mary-land to ratify, and the refusal of Congress to accept the Virginia cession of 1781, was the exception of the lands granted to individuals at the beginning of the war. The landless states wanted the West given up for the "good of the whole," except the lands to which their prominent citizens laid dubious claims.

Virginia, when she was ready to cede her claims, insisted upon making sure that the Pennsylvania and Maryland speculators would not preëmpt some of the most valuable territory to be given to Congress.

The events leading to Maryland's agreement to the Confederation center around the measures taken by Virginia, the answer of Maryland to them, and the activity of the various land companies which appealed openly to Congress after their claims had been declared invalid by Virginia. The Virginia Assembly continued the policy toward the West which had been begun by the Convention in 1776. Since then counties had been set up west of the Alleghenies, a commission had been sent out to gather evidence against the purchasers of lands from the Indians, and George Rogers Clark had been sent to the Ohio to bring that region under control. In the fall of 1778, the Assembly declared void all purchases from Indians within Virginia's charter limits and thus in general terms voided the Henderson and Indiana claims south of the Ohio, and the Illinois and Wabash claims north of the Ohio. The news of Clark's success resulted in the establishment of the county of Illinois north of the Ohio River. Finally, lands were set aside for Virginia soldiers in Washington's army, many of whom were more interested in the prospective opening of a land office in Virginia than in the progress of the war. Colonel William Russell was ready to resign from the army rather than to have his hopes of a fortune in western lands thwarted by the opening of a land office during his absence.

The Assembly then turned to the objections of the unconfederated states of Maryland, Delaware, and New Jersey. These states demanded that the ungranted lands in the West should become the common property of the United States. They argued that unless provisions were made for "securing lands for the troops who serve during the war, they [the landless states] shall have to pay large sums to the States who claim the vacant lands to supply their quota of the troops." This was, explained James Duane, "a capital if not the material objection." It was to remove this "capital if not the material objection" that the Virginia Assembly offered to give bounty lands free of cost to the states having no unappropriated lands. Maryland's bluff was further called by instructing the Virginia delegation in

Congress to offer to confederate with less than thirteen states.

Maryland made the next move. On January 6, 1779 her delegation presented to Congress a formal "Declaration" of the attitude of the state. This paper declared that Maryland was entitled to a right in common to all lands lying westward of the frontiers of the United States, excepting those granted to individuals at the beginning of the war; that the state would not accede to the Confederation until Congress was given the power to fix the boundaries of states with western claims. The Virginia delegation replied by laying Virginia's offer of bounty lands before Congress. The fact that the offer was completely ignored is evidence of how little the question of bounty land was the real cause of the attitude of the landless states.

Then in May, 1779 the Virginia delegation made the offer to confederate without Maryland. The Marylanders immediately countered by presenting the instructions which had accompanied their "Declaration" of January 6. Unmarked by even a glimmering of "national vision," these instructions professed to fear that Maryland would become an economic wilderness if the states with western claims were allowed to keep them. If they did so, they would sell the lands on modest terms, draw vast sums of money into their treasuries, and thus lessen taxes. The wealthiest Marylanders would then move to Virginia and Maryland would become depopulated and impoverished and sink in the scale of the union. The argument of some Virginians that the West was too large for a single government and would eventually be carved into independent states, was treated with scorn. Such professions on the part of Virginians were designed only to "lull suspicion asleep, and to cover the designs of a secret ambition," or else the lands were "now claimed to reap an immediate profit from the sale." Congress must be given control of the West. Until then Maryland would not confederate.

A settlement of the issue on the basis demanded by Maryland was impossible. Virginia had control of the West through the moral force of her charter and the practical force of Clark's conquest. If Congress were to be given control over the West, it had to come through the voluntary action of Virginia and only upon Virginia's terms. During May and June of 1779, the Virginia Assembly took certain drastic steps which had the effect of clarifying the dispute and particularly of bringing the land companies out into the open. These companies had made various appeals for redress from Virginia for most of them were realistic and knew that they could succeed most readily if Virginia could be induced to act favorably. Virginia ignored them officially until December, 1778, when she agreed to consider the claims of the Indiana Company. In May, 1779, agents of the Indiana Company, of the now united Illinois-Wabash group, of George Croghan, and of the Ohio Company of Virginia appeared before the Virginia Assembly.

The Indiana Company claim was taken up and supported vigorously both within and without the assembly. In spite of this support, a series of resolutions was passed nullifying the claims of the land companies. It was declared that Virginia had the exclusive right to purchase lands from the Indians within her charter bounds, and that all the purchases made by the King of England within those bounds ought to belong to Virginia. Therefore, the deed from the Indians to the Indiana Company was null and void as were all other such deeds and purchases. Virginia's intentions toward the West were illuminated by the passage of an act validating all the claims of the Virginia speculators—claims that extended back to the Dinwiddie Proclamation of 1754, and the utterly fallacious claims based on the Proclamation of 1763. After doing this, the assembly then agreed that a land office should be opened in October for the sale of all ungranted lands.

Virginia's action is easily understandable. The conflict was one between two speculative groups and Virginia naturally took care of her own speculators. She was well aware that behind the froth of argument and high-sounding declaration from the landless states, there lay the reality of a rival speculative interest. George Mason of Virginia was the leading advocate of the Ohio Company of that state. He wrote that the Maryland "Declaration" merely confirmed suspicions he had long held, and had convinced him that the real cause of the opposition to Virginia's claims was the great land purchase between the Illinois and Wabash rivers "in which Governor Johnston and several of the leading men in Maryland" were concerned, and asked: "Do you observe the care Governor Johnston . . . has taken to save this Indian purchase?" Mason realized the significance of the exception of lands granted at the beginning of the war, from the areas the landless states wanted given to Congress, and he told Richard Henry Lee that if Congress would declare such grants void, it would be more effective in settling the western issue "than all the argument in the world."

George Mason knew the situation very well indeed. The Illinois and Wabash companies had joined forces in the spring of 1779. Some of the original members of both companies were still active, the most notable being Governor Thomas Johnson of Maryland. Since the original purchases, Charles Carroll of Carrollton, and Samuel Chase had been added to the list of influential members. It was Chase who had led in the attacks on Virginia's claims to the West and who had waxed eloquent in picturing the "public good" to be derived from its common ownership. The list of members from Pennsylvania was even more imposing. Leading it was Robert Morris. Next came James Wilson who became president of the united companies, and who was at the same time a leading conservative politician. Other conservative politicians in the company were George Ross and the Reverend Doctor Smith of Philadelphia. Another member was Silas Deane of Connecticut. Conrad Gerard, the French envoy to the United States, and John Holker, the French consul in Philadelphia, were also members. It is well to remember that at the same time this group from the Middle States was demanding that the West be given up to the United States as a whole, it was attempting to deliver the region to Spain as the price of her entry into the Revolution on the side of France and the United States.

The Indiana Company was more exclusively a Pennsylvania affair. George Morgan, Samuel Wharton, and Benjamin Franklin were its most influential members during this period. The influence of this company, like that of the Illinois-Wabash Company was far more widespread than the list of members indicates, for as it stated in a petition to Congress, there were many independent grants "from several proprietors [of the company] to several Persons residing in different States."

The prospective opening of the Virginia land office in October made drastic measures necessary if these land companies were ever to profit from their claims. They well knew that the choicest lots within their claims would go to Virginians. Therefore they appealed to Congress to stay Virginia from selling land. September 14, 1779, George Morgan presented a memorial from the Indiana Company, and William Trent presented a memorial from the Vandalia-Walpole Company. Morgan's memorial stated that since Indiana was a part of Vandalia, and since Vandalia had been separated from Virginia, the region in dispute was not under the jurisdiction of any particular state but under that of the United States as a whole. Congress should consider the plea of the land companies and issue an order to Virginia to stop her land sales until the right to Vandalia "shall be ascertained in such a manner as may tend to support the sovereignty of the United States and the just rights of individuals therein." [*See* Map 1.]

Trent's memorial gave the lie to Morgan's argument for it admitted that the grant to Vandalia had never been completed. But he developed a new argument when he went on to expound the doctrine of the devolution of sovereignty. He proposed that "all the Rights and all the obligations of the Crown of Great Britain respecting the lands and governments . . . devolve upon the United States and are to be claimed, exercised, and discharged by the United States in Congress Assembled." When considered in the light of its thoroughly material origin, this theory has a significance not usually accorded to it by constitutional historians.

These memorials were referred to a committee by the votes of the landless states. Virginia denied that Congress had any jurisdiction in the matter but she was unable to prevent the appointment of a committee consisting of one member each from Maryland, New Jersey, Pennsylvania, New Hampshire, and Connecticut. Virginia did succeed, however, in securing instructions to the committee to first decide upon Congress' rights in the question. The committee ignored the instructions—this was not strange since Jenifer of Maryland was a member—and reported a few days later that it had considered the "facts" and could not find "any such distinction between the question of the jurisdiction of Congress, and the merits of the cause, as to recommend any decision upon the first separately from the last." It then recommended that Virginia and other states with western claims should be requested to "suspend the sale, grant, or settlement" until the end of the war of "land unappropriated at the time of the declaration of independence." Virginia's opposition to this measure was bitter but fruitless. The recommendation was passed by Congress and sent to the states.

The land companies thus achieved their objective, but it was only temporary and completely inadequate. They needed recognition of their claims by some political authority and they were willing to use fair means or foul to get it. Cyrus Griffin of Virginia reported that the Indiana Company had offered Congress ten thousand pounds to confirm its claims. Yet the company was anxious to secure recognition from Virginia and was ready to defend that state against all opposition in return for such recognition. Virginia's claim was the one that really mattered, and the Indiana Company was composed of practical men. In the winter of 1779, George Morgan went to Williamsburg in an attempt to induce the Virginia Assembly to revoke its action of the past summer. The company had much support in the Virginia Assembly, for Virginia politicians, like other men, were susceptible to material lures.

Morgan's hope was quite unfounded. George Mason was in the Virginia Assembly and he was the chief backer of the Ohio Company of Virginia which claimed the same area that the Indiana Company claimed. Mason drew up a remonstrance against the consideration of the land company memorials by Congress which was adopted by the assembly and sent to Congress. This "Remonstrance" pointed out that the Indiana and Vandalia companies included several men of great influence in neighboring states, and that under the guise of creating a common fund these companies had made proposals to Congress which were calculated to guarantee their claims. If these claims were to be confirmed, the greater part of the unappropriated lands would be converted to private use. Only the individual states owned lands, and therefore, if the lands northwest of the Ohio did not belong to Virginia, they belonged to Canada. The document concluded with a suggestion that Virginia might be induced to make concessions. Virginia was ready to listen to "any just and reasonable propositions for removing the *ostensible* causes of delay and to complete ratification of the Confederation." But Virginia remonstrated and protested against any jurisdiction or right of decision on the part of Congress in the case of the Indiana and Vandalia petitions, or in

anything else "subversive of the internal policy, civil government, or sovereignty of this or any other of the United American States, or unwarranted by the articles of the Confederation." Thus so far as Virginia was concerned, the land
companies were her own domestic affair. However, she was
ready to listen to any proposals for a land cession that Congress
might care to make.

The idea of the division of the West into separate and
independent states had been prevalent among one group of
Virginians since 1776. Thomas Jefferson's proposed constitution for Virginia provided that the bounds of the state should
remain as set forth in the Charter of 1609 until the West should
be set off by the legislature into two or more territories which
would become "free and independent of this colony and all the
world." In November, 1778, before Maryland finally refused to
ratify the Confederation, Richard Henry Lee proposed that it
would be wise for Virginia to limit her size. He urged that the
Ohio River should be made the western boundary of the state.
His reasons were as follows: that the Confederation was necessary, that it was diffficult to govern by republican laws a region
so far distant, that it would be economical to create a buffer state
against the Indians, and that it would unmask those who
founded their opposition to the Confederacy upon the extensiveness of Virginia's claims. And as has already been pointed
out, one of the most influential Virginia politicians, George
Mason, had indicated that Virginia would make a cession if
Congress would make suitable proposals.

In the meantime, a train of events was leading to the cession
of New York's uncertain claims. Philip Schuyler arrived in
Congress in November, 1779, and induced it to take up the
problem of making peace with the Six Nations. It was proposed
as a condition of peace that the Six Nations should make the
tender of a land cession to Congress. Congress would reject this
tender as a mark of its magnanimity. The delegates from the
landless states, totally unconscious of the humor involved,
proposed that such cessions be for the benefit of the United
States as a whole—what had been won by the expenditure of
"common blood and treasure" should become common property. Schuyler, who was new to the ways of Congress, was soon
given what he considered convincing proof that New York and

some other states were to be shorn of their lands. He was taken aside and shown a proposed motion to the effect that all lands grantable by the crown before the war, and which had not been granted to individuals, should be considered the property of the United States. He was then shown a map which restricted the southern states to the Alleghenies, or at farthest the Ohio and the Mississippi, while north of the Ohio, New York was to have a western boundary drawn from the northwest corner of Pennsylvania to Lake Ontario and thence down the St. Lawrence.

The effect of this information on Schuyler was such that he got a leave of absence from Congress and hastened to New York where the legislature was in session. He met with it and on February 19, 1780, it ceded to Congress the state's claims to lands west of its present boundaries.

At the same time several forces were working for a cession from Virginia. The South was falling under British control and it was felt in some undefined way that completion of the Confederation would help make the war measures of Congress more effective. The New York cession was an example of conciliation. Many Virginians favored the idea. But Virginia had placed the matter before Congress and the initiative had to be taken by it. In May, James Duane wrote that he was much engaged in an attempt to complete the Confederation and that the Virginia delegates were "warmly disposed to give it all the Aid in their Power." In June, Joseph Jones wrote to Governor Jefferson that the present was the time to complete the Confederation and cited the New York example as worthy of imitation. Virginia was too large for vigorous government. She should cede all her claims northwest of the Ohio River.

Jones also wrote to George Mason asking his opinion of a possible land cession by Virginia. Mason replied that Virginia was still awaiting an answer to the suggestion contained in the Virginia Remonstrance." He believed that if Congress would guarantee the Mason and Dixon line to the Ohio River, and thence down the Ohio to the North Carolina line, Virginia would be willing to cede both the right of soil and sovereignty of the region northwest of the Ohio. Virginia, however, would require compliance with certain conditions before the cession would become final. The condition upon which Mason placed the most emphasis was one requiring that all lands to be ceded should be considered a common fund for the Confederation, and hence, that all purchases and deeds from the Indians of any lands in the region, should be declared as absolutely void as if the region were to remain a part of Virginia. Mason wrote that if this condition were not insisted upon, most of the valuable territory in the region would go to various men in neighboring states. Mason regarded this as an obvious conclusion from the nature of the Maryland Declaration which he felt was designed to save those purchases.

In September, 1780, Richard Henry Lee wrote to Samuel Adams that Virginia might then make a cession if Congress asked her to do so, but predicted that delay would result in failure since many friends of the idea would be retiring from the assembly at the end of the year. Congress had already appointed a committee on June 26 to which had been referred the "Instructions" of the Maryland Assembly, the Virginia "Remonstrance," and the New York cession. On this committee were James Duane, John Henry, Joseph Jones, Roger Sherman, and Willie Jones, a majority of whom favored compromise and confederation. This committee had delivered a report four days later though it was not agreed to until October. The report refused to consider the contention of the landless states that the West belonged to the United States as a whole. Discussion of the questions involved in the Maryland "Instructions" and the Virginia "Remonstrance" had been declined at the time the Articles of Confederation were under debate and therefore it was not necessary to inquire into their merits now. The important thing was to complete the Confederation. The New York cession was a start, and the other states with claims should now pass laws to remove the obstacle to ratification.

As soon as this report was adopted by Congress, the Virginia delegates moved that Congress give certain guarantees for any cession that might be made. They proposed the various conditions which had been supplied by George Mason to Joseph Jones early in the summer. Congress readily agreed to the conditions with the exception of the one relating to Indian purchases and deeds. Faced with reality, the politicians took refuge in generalities. Some members argued that such a guarantee was unnecessary, others that it was improper, implying as

it did that without a previous guarantee Congress would have
the right to surrender the lands to be ceded to private claimants.
Such motives prevailed, wrote Madison, "with more than a real
view of gratifying private interest at the public expense." Jones,
who was now in Virginia, should do as he saw fit.

The danger that Congress might put it out of its power to
help them now aroused the land companies. The Illinois-
Wabash Company and the Indiana Company presented memorials on September 26 and 27. William Trent, who presented
the memorial for the Indiana company, stated that the memorialists had seen a copy of the report on the conditions moved by
Virginia, and in it they had seen the words nullifying all deeds
and purchases within the territory to be ceded. They were
"struck with Apprehension" lest Congress might hastily decide
the question, and asked to be heard before Congress as soon as
possible. Two weeks later Trent presented another memorial in
which he was even more specific. The company had been
informed that Virginia protested against the jurisdiction of
Congress in the case of Indiana and Vandalia. Trent baldly
admitted that since Congress was now the only hope of the
speculators, upheld its sovereignty over that of the states. "Your
Memorialists humbly conceive that this Question, of the Jurisdiction of Congress, is of the very essence of their claims; that it
is of infinite Consequence to the American Union as well as to
your Memorialists."

With more effrontery than wisdom, George Morgan again
approached the Virginia delegates. This time he proposed that
the dispute between Virginia and the Indiana Company should
be submitted to arbitration in the manner laid down in the
Confederation for the settlement of disputes between state and
state. The Virginia delegation scornfully rejected the proposal
on the ground that it was beneath the dignity of a sovereign
state to submit to a "foreign tribunal" a case which involved only
the pretensions of individuals. In forwarding an account to
Governor Jefferson, Theodorick Bland commented that there
was every reason to suspect that "the land Jobbs, of this Comp'y,
the Vandalia, and the Illinois Companies," had "too great an
influence in procrastinating that desireable and necessary event
of Compleating the Confederation." Madison was more
alarmed and urged Jones to call the Assembly's attention to the

necessity of attaching conditions to a cession. Although he did not believe that Congress seriously intended gratifying the "landmongers," he felt that "the best security for their virtue, in this respect," would be "to keep it out of their power."

The land companies now began an attack on Virginia's claims in a series of pamphlets. Samuel Wharton who had written "View to the Title of Indiana" in 1776, now elaborated it in another tract called "Plain Facts." With Benjamin Franklin he wrote what is called the "Passy Memorial." In it was outlined the history of the Vandalia project. Thomas Paine was hired by the Indiana Company to write a pamphlet attacking Virginia's charter claims. This pamphlet, "Public Good," appeared on December 30, 1780, only a few days before the cession of the Old Northwest by Virginia. George Morgan was so jubilant over the recommendations for land cessions that he prophesied: "All the Country, West of Allegany Mountain will probably be put under the Direction of the United States, & Virginia limited to the Waters which fall into the Atlantic from the West & North West." This wishful thought saw no fulfillment.

On January 2, 1781, Virginia ceded all her claims to the region northwest of the Ohio River. Attached to the cession were all the conditions suggested by George Mason to Joseph Jones in July, 1780, including the provision "that all purchases and deeds from any Indian or Indians, or from any Indian nation or nations, for any lands within any part of the said territory" which have been made to private persons, shall be "deemed and declared absolutely void and of no effect" as if the ceded territory were to remain a part of Virginia.

Maryland could no longer delay in spite of the obnoxious conditions. At the end of January her delegates were authorized to sign the Confederation. March 1, 1781 was set for the day of completion and on that day New York delivered its act of cession and the Maryland delegates signed the Articles of Confederation.

The cession of the Old Northwest by Virginia did not result in congressional control of the region. Three years more of increasingly futile controversy occurred for the act of cession had left the Indiana company within the bounds of Virginia, and had excluded the Illinois-Wabash Company from the region ceded. These companies, therefore, used their influence to prevent the acceptance of the Virginia cession. They tried to establish the "sovereignty"of Congress over all the territory west of the Alleghenies by forcing the acceptance of the New York cession as covering all that Virginia claimed, and thus making a cession from Virginia unneccessary. This move had no practical result, nor did the continued assertions that Congress owned the land through a process of "devolution" of powers from the British government.

The cause of the land companies was ably argued by their representatives in Congress. James Wilson, president of the Illinois-Wabash Company, was sent to Congress as a delegate from Pennsylvania. Samuel Wharton of the Indiana Company was sent as a delegate from Delaware. George Morgan of the same company became so influential in the politics of New Jersey that he persuaded the legislature of that state to present the claim of the Indiana Company as a claim of the state of New Jersey and thus, to force Congress to arbitrate the dispute in the manner laid down in the Confederation for the settlement of disputes between states.

Ultimately the acceptance of the Virginia cession was brought about by the appearance of new forces on the horizon of public affairs. With the end of the war, the officers and soldiers were released from duty and they began to demand their bounty lands. Washington appeared before Congress as their spokesman, a role with which his pre-Revolutionary speculative enterprises had made him familiar. He pointed out that while Congress was engaging in bootless argument, the West was being settled by people whom he called "banditti," who were not only depriving the officers of their just reward, but who were also bringing about the danger of Indian war. Such considerations, coupled with the desire for revenue, induced Congress to call upon Virginia for an unconditional cession. Virginia now ceded her claims anew, minus the specific conditions but accompanied by more general though no less binding qualifications. On March 1, 1784 Congress accepted the Virginia cession, three years after the completion of the Confederation. The New Jersey delegation remained faithful to George Morgan and the Indiana Company and voted against the acceptance. The state of Maryland which had played so large a part, was unrepresented in the halls of Congress.

The Creation of the National Domain

Merrill Jensen

In the previous article Professor Merrill Jensen described the initial cession of the Old Northwest by Virginia in 1781. In this one he follows congressional acceptance of that cession in the years 1781–1784.

During this period he found two congressional committee reports to be of particular significance. The first report of November, 1781, reflected the interests of the landless states who sought to validate the territorial claims of various prewar speculators from their states. Since the Virginia cession prohibited such claims, this report relied on New York's cession which was based upon a shadowy title from the Iroquois Indians. This report also validated claims to territory south of the Ohio which Virginia never ceded.

Neither side could muster enough votes to accept or reject the 1781 report. As time went on, the balance of power shifted in Congress toward the southern states. As this occurred, a more favorable attitude toward the Virginians' position developed and in June of 1783 a new committee reported out recommendations favoring most of Virginia's claims. The acceptance of this report by the Virginia assembly in the fall of 1783 finally established the national domain.

* *

THE CREATION of the national domain at the end of the American Revolution entailed the performance of two outwardly simple acts: (1) the cession of western lands by the states laying claim to them; and (2) the acceptance of those cessions by the government of the United States. The apparent simplicity of these actions at once disappears as one turns to the history of the years between the surrender of various state claims to the Old Northwest, and the creation of the national domain by the

---

From Merrill Jensen, "The Creation of the National Domain, 1781–1784," in the *Mississippi Valley Historical Review*, XXVI: 323–342 (December, 1939); reprinted without footnotes with permission of the author and the *Journal of American History*.

Confederation Congress through its acceptance of the claims surrendered. By March, 1781, Congress was in possession of the New York, Connecticut, and Virginia cessions, but Congress did not accept the Virginia cession of the Old Northwest and thereby lay the foundations of the national domain until March, 1784. An account of the causes of this three year delay illuminates a phase of the history of the West and of national politics at the close of the American Revolution.

The cessions of state claims to the Old Northwest came only after a long and confused struggle during the course of which the landless state of Maryland refused to ratify the Articles of Confederation and thus prevented the union of the thirteen states. Maryland refused to ratify the Articles until Congress should be given some control over western lands. In her various demands Maryland consistently exempted from the proposed congressional control and disposition, those areas of land in the West which had been purchased from the Indians before the outbreak of the Revolution. This exemption was designed to protect the Illinois, Wabash, and Indiana companies, which had made such purchases and whose membership was made up largely of important business men and politicians of Maryland, Pennsylvania, and New Jersey.

All the land company purchases and claims lay within the charter bounds of Virginia, and after 1776 that state promptly investigated and declared them null and void. The land speculators therefore turned to the Continental Congress as the only political organization which might be manipulated in their interest. They soon conceived of Congress as a sovereign body which had inherited the powers and prerogatives of the British government, including of course, the power to control lands west of the Appalachians. Such ideas were of little moment at the time. The most effective measure was Maryland's desperate refusal to ratify the Articles of Confederation until the states with western lands could be forced or persuaded to surrender their claims to Congress.

In the course of time and for various reasons, Virginia ceded her claims to the territory northwest of the Ohio River. Prior to her act of cession, however, her delegates in Congress sought from Congress certain guarantees as to the future disposal of the region to be ceded. Congress agreed to these demands with one all-important exception: Congress flatly refused to declare null and void all purchases from Indians in the region to be ceded.

Nevertheless Virginia ceded her claims to the Old Northwest and carefully attached to her act of cession all the conditions previously demanded, including the requirement that Congress nullify the land company purchases. Virginia politicians had no intention of allowing Maryland and Pennsylvania speculators to preempt anything that Virginians might surrender. The Virginia cession was followed by Maryland's ratification of the Articles of Confederation, although Maryland's ratification did not mean that her citizens had surrendered their hopes. The Maryland legislature made it perfectly plain that it still objected to the claims of the landed states and that it still hoped to share in the profits to be derived from the West. Thus the Virginia cession of the Old Northwest did not mark the end of the controversy. The history of the next three years is the history of re-doubled efforts on the part of the land companies and their adherents: efforts directed toward the sole end of evading the obnoxious conditions attached to the Virginia cession and which Congress must accept before the cession could become final, and the national domain a reality.

The requirement that Congress should void all purchases in the territory ceded was aimed directly at the Illinois-Wabash group, which included such leading men of Pennsylvania and Maryland as Robert Morris, James Wilson, Samuel Chase, Thomas Johnson, and Charles Carroll of Carrollton. The required guarantee of Virginia's remaining territory to her was designed to thwart the Indiana Company, which included important men as Benjamin Franklin, Samuel and Thomas Wharton, and George Morgan. Naturally these companies and their representatives in Congress fought to evade the unwelcome conditions attached to the Virginia cession. They attempted to do this in two ways. On the one hand they sought to establish the sovereignty of Congress over the regions at stake. On the other they sought to secure an unrestricted cession from Virginia, thereby leaving the land companies to the none-too-virtuous discretion of Congress. Neither idea was followed consistently and sometimes both were urged at once as expediency seemed to dictate.

When the Virginia delegates delivered the act of cession to Congress in March, 1781, they naively assumed that Congress would soon accept it. One of them wrote Richard Henry Lee, "The Covert manoeuvers of the land Jobbing Companies are so well known, and so fully discovered, that few of their abettors will be hardy enough to oppose it in its fullest latitude." But Richard Henry Lee, who had had more experience with Congress and with land companies, made a far more accurate prediction of what the future was to disclose. Shortly after the Virginia assembly passed the act of cession, Lee explained to Samuel Adams that it would complete the confederation, but that he feared its acceptance would be delayed or defeated in Congress. He wrote:

> It will bar the hopes, of some powerful confederated Land jobbers, who have long had in contemplation immense possessions in this ceded country, under pretence of Indian purchases, and other plausible, but not solid titles. . . . The modes and methods, which these artists pursue, are well understood. . . . They pretend great friendship and concern for the Indepen[den]cy, the Union, and Confederation of America, but by circuitous means, attack and destroy those things, that are indispensible to those ends. Hitherto the avarice and ambition of Virginia, has prevented Confederation—Now when Virginia, has yielded half her Charter Claim, the argument will be applied to the terms as improper, and for certain purposes perhaps it may be said, that the quantity ceded is not enough—in short anything that can operate the delay and defeat of a measure, calculated to sever us completely from Great Britain, and to preclude the avaritious views of certain Land mongers, will be industriously pressed.

Richard Henry Lee's predictions were fulfilled promptly and accurately. Within two weeks of the presentation of the Virginia cession to Congress, Congress received memorials from George Morgan on behalf of the Indiana Company; from James Wilson on behalf of the Illinois-Wabash Company, of which he was now president; from Benjamin Franklin and Samuel Wharton on behalf of the Vandalia Company; and from William Trent, Samuel Wharton, and Bernard Gratz on behalf of George Croghan; these were later followed by yet another memorial from Trent on behalf of the Indiana Company. [*See* Maps 1 and 7.]

The Indiana Company stated that it had presented its case to Congress in the past, and emphasized the present willingness and even anxiety of the company to have the matter decided by Congress, "by whom alone, it is presumed, a proper and competent Decision can be made." The memorial requested the appointment of a day for hearing all the parties concerned. Franklin's and Wharton's petition on behalf of the Vandalia Company was a long recital of the events in the history of that scheme since the treaty at Fort Stanwix in 1768. They maintained that the company had acquired title to the land in question, although they admitted that the instrument of conveyance had never been delivered. But they appealed to Congress for justice as a body having jurisdiction: "Your Honors have now succeeded to the Sovereignty of the Territory in question."

These land company memorials were referred to the same committee to which had been referred the cessions from the various states. The report of this committee made it evident that the land companies had persuasive ways. The original resolutions of Congress asking for land cessions were completely ignored by the committee. Those original resolutions had refused to consider the question of "right" to the West, holding it subordinate to expediency and to the necessity of securing the cessions of all the states, no matter how vague their "rights" might be. Now, the committee on cessions upheld the contentions of the land speculators of the landless states and of the representatives of those states in Congress. Its report declared it inexpedient to accept the cessions with conditions attached. Instead, the committee defied the landed states by proposing a resolution to the effect that there were already lands belonging to the United States and that a committee should be appointed to dispose of such lands for the payment of the debts of the United States.

By dint of much maneuvering, the Virginians brought this report before Congress in October, 1781, and forced it into the hands of a new committee. The issue was clear-cut: should the decision be made upon the basis of the resolutions asking for the cessions, or should the whole question of the territorial rights of the ceding states be reopened for discussion.

The personnel of the new committee made it obvious that the latter was to be the case. It was composed of one delegate each from the landless states of Maryland, Pennsylvania, New Jersey, Rhode Island, and New Hampshire. After some experience with this committee, James Madison declared that apprehensions for Virginia's western interests were not unfounded for "an agrarian law is as much coveted by the little members of the Union, as ever it was by the indigent citizens of Rome." This committee called before it the various claimants including New York, Connecticut, and the land companies. The Virginia delegates flatly refused to present any evidence of their claims and asserted that such jurisdiction on the part of Congress was contrary to the Articles of Confederation. This was perfectly true but it had no effect. The committee continued its work unhindered by constitutional restraints or by Congress, although the Virginia delegates insisted that Congress should interfere.

When the committee delivered its report to Congress on November 3, 1781, it was at once evident that minds capable of evolving such concepts as the devolution of sovereignty, had found with ease a new and far more plausible expedient for evading the unwelcome fact of Virginia's practical control over the West. The old arguments of "common right" to the West arising out of the expenditure of "common blood and treasure" had proven singularly ineffective. The theory of the devolution of sovereign powers from the British government to the Continental Congress was even less convincing. Now, the cession of New York's "shadowy title held from the Six Nations of Indians" was seized upon as covering not only the region ceded by Virginia, but also the region south of the Ohio which Virginia asked to be guaranteed to her. The report recommended acceptance of the New York cession because it was based upon the claims of the Six Nations, and these, the committee declared, were paramount to all other claims. For the same reason the Virginia cession was to be rejected as was the guarantee of her remaining lands to her. Her lands south of the Ohio, said the committee, had been separated from her by the King in Council before the Revolution and then sold to individuals. Thus in theory Virginia was to be confined to the region east of the Alleghenies. The committee, however, recommended that Virginia should reconsider her act of cession and by a "proper act," cede "all claims and pretensions of claims to the lands and country beyond a reasonable western boundary," such cession to be free from all conditions and restrictions.

The report then turned to a consideration of the land company claims. The Indiana claim to land south of the Ohio River was declared valid and Congress was urged to confirm it. Likewise the claims of George Croghan were declared legal. The American members of the Vandalia group were to be reimbursed by new land grants to the extent of their expenses in the Vandalia project. But the Illinois-Wabash petition was rejected on the grounds that the purchases had been made without public authority and because the region in question really belonged to the Six Nations. The denial of the Illinois-Wabash claims in this report is a peculiar maneuver. Its adherents were powerful in Congress at the time, Robert Morris being in the ascendancy as superintendent of finance. Possibly the land company group was ready to surrender the region northwest of the Ohio in the peace negotiations in the hope of getting the lands they desired from Great Britain once the war was over. Such was the belief of James Madison and Luzerne, the French envoy. Furthermore, the votes on the new instructions of June, 1781, which placed the matter of boundaries at the discretion of the peace commissioners, point very strongly in the same direction. Three members of the committee on cession, Livermore, Varnum, and Jenifer, had consistently voted to give discretion to the commissioners, even to the extent of allowing them to give up lands southeast of the Ohio River. While the evidence is circumstantial it is at least worthy of note. Certainly the Illlinois-Wabash Company was not crushed by its apparent failure to receive congressional recognition in the report.

The report thus presented to Congress in November, 1781, was not acted upon for over a year. It was impossible to secure a vote of seven states either for or against it. The Virginia delegates were at last seriously alarmed and asked George Mason and Thomas Jefferson to prepare a statement of Virginia's legal rights in the case. Madison pointed out that the opinion of the committee was not necessarily the opinion of Congress, since the committee was composed of members who he declared were "systematically and notoriously" in opposition to all western claims. He admitted, however, that Virginia had ample cause for the revocation or suspension of her cession, and warned that in making plans for the future, the state should assume that the existing union would not long survive the end of the war.

By the spring of 1782 the question of cessions was badly entangled with the controversy over Vermont and the possibility of its admission to the Confederation. The New England States were said to desire Vermont within the union in order to strengthen the relative position of their section. Hence, they supported the landless states in order to secure support for the admission of Vermont. The landless states on the other hand, supported the admission of Vermont in order to secure New England votes for their western policy. Each group knew full well that the alliance would terminate abruptly once the end of either was achieved, so each was interested in delaying a decision while maneuvering for an advantage. The situation was further complicated because New York had apparently been bidding for support in the Vermont affair by making a cession of her dubious claims. The agents of Vermont and those of "the land-mongers" wrote Madison, "are playing with great adroitness into each others' hands."

The land companies were by this time exceptionally well represented in Congress. James Wilson, president of the Illinois-Wabash Company and one of the great speculators of the day, was a member of Congress from Pennsylvania. Samuel Wharton, a leader in the Vandalia and Indiana companies, was in Congress as a member from Delaware, and, although memorials in his behalf before Congress pleaded the sadness of his bankrupt estate, he yet found funds to treat the members "with magnificent Dinners." Arthur Lee declared, "These Agents are using every art to seduce us and to sow dissention among the States, I think they are more dangerous than the Enemy's Arms. Every Motion relative to Vermont and the Cessions of the other States is directed by the interests of these Companies."

In April the Virginia delegates sought from Congress some decision on the Virginia cession so that they could report to the Virginia assembly during its spring session. Madison insisted that the land companies were "the radical impediment,' and that whenever Virginia proposed a decision, "every artifice that could perplex the case was immediately exerted." Madison failed to tell the whole story, however, for at this time the Virginia delegates were engaging in tactics most offensive to the land companies and their representatives in Congress. When the report on cessions came up for discussion, Arthur Lee moved that its consideration should be postponed until each member of Congress had declared, upon roll-call, whether or not he was interested in any of the land companies affected by the proposed cessions. Lee declared that his "purifying declaration," as he called it, "was evaded by three days chicane." It was met by flurries of counter motions aiming to avoid any such official declaration of holdings in the companies concerned.

From this time on, whenever the report on cessions came up for consideration, the Virginia delegates asked the members of Congress to explain their connections with land companies. Each time the demand was met by a series of counter motions which usually ended with a motion to adjourn when nothing else proved adequate to escape the unpleasant persistence of the Virginians. Finally, on May 6, 1782, consideration of the report was postponed *sine die* as the only way out of the dilemma of the land company members and supporters. The Virginia delegates therefore decided to place the issue before the Virginia assembly and stated that, with regard to the West, the assembly would be fully justified in taking whatever steps Virginia's interests should dictate.

Congress, however, found it impossible to ignore the potential federal revenue to be derived from the creation of a national domain. It needed money and the sale of western lands was its most obvious resource of securing money. In July, 1782, therefore, the committee on finance urged some decision concerning the cessions of the back lands. The only result of this suggestion, however, was to throw Congress once more into a futile debate on the subject of "right" to the West, a basis for discussion which had not in the past and could not in the future be made to square with the facts of practical politics.

In the fall of 1782 the Virginia delegates once more took the offensive when Theodorick Bland moved that Congress accept all the state cessions, regardless of the conditions attached to them. But once more the only result was a series of futile motions and evasions which but thinly disguised the real issue. Some members of Congress realized that such tactics would never result in any profit. It was obvious to the more disinterested that even if Congress did have some legal right to western lands, enough of the states thought the contrary to prevent a vote favorable to its claims. There was even less chance, said Madison, that they would support "coercive measures to render the title of any fiscal importance." It was equally obvious that the states with western land claims might open land offices, as Virginia had done once, issue patents to land, and protect the execution of their claims without any hindrance except "the clamors of individuals within and without the doors of Congress."

It was apparently the realization of this fact that induced John Witherspoon of New Jersey to bring in a series of compromise resolutions. These were to the effect that the states which had not yet made cessions should do so; that the states which had not made cessions in accordance with the wishes of Congress should reconsider their actions; and finally, that the decisions of the ceding states with regard to private property within the ceded areas should not be altered without the consent of the states concerned. This last resolution was the core of the controversy. The members from the landless states attacked and defeated this guarantee that Congress would not interfere with the Virginia decisions nullifying the land company claims.

This was the first open and positive victory that the landless states had won on the floor of Congress and they were confident they could now carry out the rest of their program. As soon as seven states favorable to their plans appeared, they voted acceptance of the New York cession in accordance with the report which had been made almost exactly a year before. By thus accepting the New York cession, Congress in theory escaped the necessity of a cession from Virginia. Practically, however, nothing was done except to add pages to the *Journals* and irritation to the hearts of the Virginians. Virginia was in control of the West. She had no intention of handing it over to the speculators of the landless states, whatever her intentions might be with regard to her own speculators. Virginia did want to surrender the region northwest of Ohio to Congress and her politicians on the whole continued to urge that this end be accomplished in spite of the apparent determination of a majority in Congress to favor the desires of the land speculators.

The land companies engaged in a renewed campaign for congressional help during the spring of 1783. James Wilson, as delegate from Pennsylvania, once more argued the case of his Illinois-Wabash Company. He insisted that there were lands lying beyond the bounds of the particular states. He even argued that the land south of the Ohio had never belonged to Virginia and he urged openly that the Allegheny Mountains should be made the western boundary of that state. His activity was countered by the Virginia delegates, who now offered to compromise by urging Congress to accept the Virginia cession with all its conditions, except the provision which required a guarantee to her of the region south of the Ohio River. The Virginia delegates declared that they took this step in order to sound out the disposition of Congress and because, they said, "We considered it as our duty to produce if possible some decisive determination on a matter so important to the welfare of our state, and of such consequence to the U States in General."

The very next day a memorial of the Indiana Company was read to Congress. The memorial spoke of the "illustrious example of Justice" on the part of the Six Nations and the British King and implied an invidious contrast with the "indecision of Congress." The document sought to pluck hardened congressional heart-strings by pleading that among the memorialists were "numbers of aged and distressed Widows and helpless orphans." Justice so long delayed, it declared, was as injurious as justice denied. The "true Policy, which is always found in National Justice" should move Congress to dictate an order for the immediate settlement of the case in accordance with the committee report in favor of the Indiana Company claim.

This request was ignored and the Virginia proposal was given to a committee which soon decided that Congress should first make a decision on the report of November 3, 1781, so far as that report related to the Virginia cession. Congress immediately turned over the Virginia section of the report to a new committee upon which the extremists of the Middle States were but poorly represented. This committee delivered its report to Congress on June 6, 1783. The report represented the views of those really interested in the creation of a national domain and it wisely referred back to the resolutions of October, 1780, requesting land cessions from the states. One by one it took up the various conditions attached to the Virginia cession of January, 1781, and disposed of them in a manner satisfactory to the Virginians. The committee held that the original resolutions asking for cessions provided for the first condition demanding that the territory ceded should be divided into states not more than one hundred and fifty and not less than one hundred miles square, and that these states should be admitted to the union with the same "rights of sovereignty, freedom and independence as the other states." The committee recommended that commissioners should be appointed to determine the "reasonable" military expenses incurred by Virginia in the Old Northwest and to liquidate the account. The French inhabitants of the region, who had become citizens of Virginia, should be guaranteed their rights and possessions and United States troops should be stationed there as Virginia demanded. The report declared reasonable the fourth and fifth conditions which related to land bounties for George Rogers Clark and his troops, as well as for regular Virginia troops in the region ceded.

The sixth condition required that the lands ceded should be considered a common fund for all the United States, present and future, to be shared according to the "general charge and expenditure." The seventh condition was the famous one demanding the nullification of all land company purchases in the region ceded. The eighth condition asked Congress to guarantee Virginia's remaining territory to her. In discussing these demands the committee arrived at a general formula which gave to Virginia what she demanded without at the same time making any specific guarantees. The sixth condition was declared reasonable and acceptable. This condition was held to be sufficient on the point of land company purchases and therefore a statement on the seventh condition was unnecessary. Finally the committee declared that Congress could not guarantee Virginia's territory to her without entering into a discussion of Virginia's right to the land in question. The committee declared such a guarantee both unnecessary and unreasonable. If the land really belonged to Virginia the Articles of Confederation were a sufficient guarantee. If the land did not belong to Virginia there was no reason for such a guarantee. The important thing, declared the committee, was for Virginia to make a cession in conformity with the report and for Congress to accept such a cession once it was made.

Madison predicted correctly that this report would meet with much opposition as it "tacitly" excluded "the pretensions of the companies." Promptly the delegates from the Middle States demanded postponement. The Delaware delegates declared that they were expecting instructions. A New Jersey delegate said he must first transmit the plan to his constituents. The Maryland delegates were not present and their presence was felt necessary before a decision could be made. Other members of Congress wanted an immediate decision. Alexander Hamilton joined these, but he asserted the "right" of the United States to western lands and moved an amendment to the report in favor of the land company claims. The upshot of the argument was that Congress gave its President permission to send informal notification of the time set for consideration to the land companies, to the Maryland delegates, and to others concerned.

When the report was taken up for further debate on June 20, the New Jersey delegates presented a "representation and remonstrance" from their legislature. This document damned the Virginia cession as "partial, unjust and illiberal," and recapitulated the various proceedings of the New Jersey legislature in which it had stated the "just and incontrovertible claims of this State to its full proportion of all vacant territory." The New Jersey legislature expressed itself as incapable of sitting silent while one state sought to aggrandize itself by keeping property which had been procured "by the common blood and treasure of the whole." "On every principle of reason and justice," it continued, "[the land] is vested in Congress for the use and general benefit of the Union they represent." Therefore, the New Jersey legislature demanded that Congress reject the Virginia cession and call upon Virginia "to make a more liberal surrender of that territory of which they claim so boundless a proportion." Further discussion was shut off, Madison said, "there being seven States only present and the spirit of compromise decreasing."

Consideration was thus finally delayed until September, when the Maryland delegates once more sought to establish the principle that there were lands lying without the bounds of any particular state and that Congress had succeeded to the sovereignty over them. Maryland had not relinquished her rights

and interests in the West when she acceded to the Confederation, declared her delegates. Congress should appoint committees to determine the lands that lay beyond the boundaries
of the several states. Maryland had learned nothing in the
school of practical politics of the past seven years. Only New
Jersey supported her demands. Congress was at last passing
from the control of the landless states whose motives were a
compound of jealousy and private interest. Other problems and
other interests were coming to the fore as the Revolution drew
to a close. For more than a year the financial difficulties of
Congress had caused more and more men to look toward the
sale of western lands as a likely source of revenue with which to
handle the public debt. In fact it was a discussion of the financial
difficulties of Congress which put in motion the train of events
leading to the ultimate creation of the national domain.

Another reality which Congress faced was the necessity of
fulfilling or denying the promises made to the soldiers of the
army back in 1776. At that time Congress had promised land
bounties to those who would enlist for the duration of the war.
It was a promise born of desperation for Congress had then had
no land to give. But now the war was over, and in the Newburgh
Petition the officers of the army demanded fulfillment of the
old promise. Washington backed their demands with the weight
of his vast influence, and when released from the command of
the army, he spent time with Congress furthering the cause of
the army officers who hoped for land grants north of the Ohio
River. He pointed out that which was becoming increasingly
plain: that while Congress and Virginia were debating, the West
was being settled by those whom Washington called "Banditti,"
who were not only depriving the officers of their just rewards,
but who were also sowing the seeds of Indian war. The danger
of Indian war was growing ever greater as uncontrolled emigra-
tion pushed farther and farther into Indian country and came
into violent contact with its inhabitants.

As a result of these various influences and difficulties, Congress accepted the report of June, 1783, which, as Madison said,
"tacitly" excluded the land companies from congressional consideration, and upon the basis of which Virginia was to be asked
for a new cession of the Old Northwest. Massachusetts, Rhode
Island, Connecticut, New York, Pennsylvania, Virginia, and

North and South Carolina voted for the report. Only Maryland and New Jersey persisted in wanting to continue the fruitless struggle. The New York delegates explained their own agreement on the grounds that the matter could be settled only by compromise and that it would leave to Congress an immense tract of country which was "daily overrun by lawless men (who endanger by their Rashness a new Indian War): and which might be improved to great public Advantage." Finally, as they pointed out, the compromise would tend to settle a question which had proven a great obstacle to the conduct of public business,and which might have been a source of internal contention and convulsion.

The issue was at last placed squarely before the Virginia assembly where it had been in dispute for some time. Many Virginians, and particularly George Mason, were bitter against the intrigues of the land companies and were dubious of the intentions of a Congress which was openly charged to be under their influence. A second obstacle proved to be the land-hunger of Virginia officers who looked upon the lands set aside for them south of the Ohio River as barren and inadequate, and who demanded that the assembly grant them lands across the Ohio. A committee of the assembly proposed to grant the officers their desires, and even more, to give them an additional quantity and to pay for the expenses of location as well. This idea met with the hearty support of Patrick Henry, once more on the road back to political favor. Furthermore, he expressed himself in favor of bounding the state reasonably, but instead of ceding the parts beyond the limits established, he was for laying them off into small republics. Joseph Jones, who earnestly desired a cession to Congress, opposed such schemes and was able to stop them temporarily.

Nevertheless, the demand of the Virginia officers for lands northwest of the Ohio caused many members of the assembly to urge the withdrawal of the act of cession. Point was lent to their arguments by the fact that Congress had neither accepted the cession nor assigned any reasons for delay. The best that the friends of the cession could do was to set a date in the future, after which the cession would be withdrawn unless accepted by Congress.

It was at this juncture that the news of the compromise report of June, 1783, reached Virginia. The assembly showed no inclination to take up the matter since it was not an act of Congress. Furthermore, the report did not "fully remove the fears of our people respecting the Indian purchases and grants to companies. Their jealousy of Congress on that head is very strong." Matters stood thus until late in the fall of 1783, when Virginia was faced with the official action of Congress accepting the report which agreed to, in one form or another, the conditions attached to the Virginia cession of 1781. Joseph Jones presented a bill accepting the compromise offered by Congress, and on December 20, 1783, Virginia made a second cession of her claims to the Old Northwest. No specific conditions were attached. The generalities of the act of cession like those of the compromise report of Congress, however, were clearly designed to preserve the West for the United States as a whole.

On March 1, 1784, Congress accepted the second Virginia cession of the Old Northwest and thereby became the owner of a national domain. New Jersey was the only state to vote against acceptance. Maryland was unrepresented in Congress.

The national domain was at last a reality. Congress speedily put in motion measures that led to the adoption of ordinances for the survey and disposal and for the government of the national domain. Military control of the more lawless inhabitants was provided for. A policy of making treaties with the Indian inhabitants was adopted. In all these matters the Confederation Congress showed both vigor and originality and laid a substantial portion of the foundation upon which was based a great deal of the subsequent policy of the government of the United States toward the national domain.

Military Bounty Lands and the Origins of the Public Domain

Rudolf Freund

One of the recurring problems in history involves compensation to veterans for military service. Often the failure to do so adequately has resulted in military dictatorship. This nearly happened in the United States and was only quelled by General Washington's appeal to his officers at the Newburgh cantonment. One of the congressional promises to the veterans was for distribution of public lands as compensation for wartime service. Beginning in 1776 Congress pledged land as an inducement for long-term enlistment in the Continental Army. In this essay the development of the Virginia and United States military reserves as locales in which bounty warrants might be located is traced, and the Ordinances of 1784 and 1787 are shown to have had significant origins in the bounty question.

Before his death in 1955, Rudolf Freund taught in the School of Rural Social Economics, University of Virginia, and at what was then the North Carolina State College of Agriculture at Raleigh. A student of the nature of landed property during the eighteenth century, his publications include "Turner's Theory of Social Evolutions," in Agricultural History *(1945), and "John Adams and Thomas Jefferson on the Nature of Landholding in America," in* Land Economics *(1948).*

* *

THE bounty-land policy of the Revolutionary War has often been criticized on two accounts. Historians seem to agree that the measures adopted did not serve their primary purpose of establishing deserving and needy veterans on farms of their own. Almost 20 years of peace went by before the first titles to bounty lands could be conveyed, and during this long delay

From Rudolf Freund, "Military Bounty Lands and the Origins of the Public Domain," in *Agricultural History,* XX: 8–18 (January, 1946); reprinted without footnotes with permission of the Agricultural History Society.

most of the land warrants had found their way into the hands of speculators and land scouts. Only those veterans who could afford to wait or had pooled their claims were able to reap at least some of the intended benefits. Regarding its second objective, namely an orderly advance of settlement into the new western lands, the military bounty land policy of the United States is held to have failed just as signally. The insistent demands of old veterans and their heirs and assignees forced practically every administration between 1812 and 1862 to relax the stipulations and extend the date lines for the establishment of military claims. The central land office continued to honor these claims up to the end of the nineteenth century in considerable numbers. By that time, between 70 and 100 million acres had been assigned for army warrants of the Revolutionary war and that of 1812 alone, largely on the basis of laws passed as late as 1847 and 1855. If the total of "All Land in Farms" within the four "central" State groups as given in the Census of 1900 is fairly indicative of the farm acreage occupied during the previous hundred years of westward expansion, the military bounty lands alone comprise one-seventh to one-sixth of this acreage. All these lands were acquired, of course, by the bounty claimants without cost.

The incipient stages in the development of this system are said to have had the effect of accustoming the people to "the idea of the government giving away public land." This statement bespeaks the widely held opinion that the westward movement was caused by economic and social forces of overwhelming strength. Consequently, laws and administrative acts are accorded only secondary importance; they must either suit the interests of the pioneer, or be abandoned, or rendered ineffective in some other way. Bounty-land legislation may be viewed as an instance where the original purpose of rewarding the veteran for his services was transformed gradually and unwittingly into a means for helping the people of the frontier to achieve their goal of "free land."

It may be doubted, however, whether this interpretation does not oversimplify the matter. Although the bounty-land policy failed to achieve its intended purposes, nevertheless it contributed to a really remarkable degree toward setting the patterns and erecting the signposts for at least the earlier stages of the westward movement. The cession of western lands, the rules governing the administration of the Northwest Territory and its lands, the preferment of the survey principle over indiscriminate location, and last but not least the first settlements on the Ohio River are cases in point. Furthermore, the question may be raised whether the final stages of the westward movement permit a proper perspective concerning legislation which was forged in the crucible of a fateful war and its hardly less fateful aftermath. Are we to believe that the framers of these laws failed to appraise properly the character and the strength of the forces destined to push open the gate to the promised lands of the west? Did they try to impede these forces by virtue of a narrow and "eastern" conception of the future? And can the colorful and fascinating interplay of personalities, ideas, and events which marked the incipient steps of the land policy of the United States be accorded its proper weight when viewed as but an awkward prelude to the grandiose spectacle of the westward movement?

The recent war and victory have made all Americans conscious of the grave problem of the returning veteran. It is easier for us, therefore, than for peacetime generations to understand the anxiety felt by the Founding Fathers and their helpers on this account. But a still more vexing problem which has no present-day counterpart confronted them and called for immediate solution. Independence had thrown into the lap of a none-too-perfect union the vast and unsettled area between the Great Lakes and the Mississippi and Ohio rivers. It was but natural that the deserving and needy soldiers should expect to receive land in this region. But this prospect was by no means the only stake which the veteran hoped to have in the opening of the west. In the newly won territory, a novel type of colonial government and administration was to be established, in which the veterans, and especially the officers, claimed their due share. Some of them, chiefly from New England, held decided opinions as to the principles which they wished to see incorporated in the new western set-up for their own benefit and that of a strong federal union. Their views were certain to be challenged by Southerners, though adherence to either camp was not necessarily determined by regional interests and outlooks alone. However, some of the basic issues involved in the future administration and land policies of the new west had been tackled, and in part decided, long before the war ended. An early promise of the Continental Congress to the rank and file of its army brought them to a head.

Curiously enough, land was first promised by Congress, in August 1776, to Hessians and other foreigners if they would desert from the English army, but nothing much came of it. The story of the military bounty lands really began somewhat later when Congress decided to offer land to its own nationals as an inducement for enlisting in the new army and for permanent service. The illfated summer campaigns of 1776 made it depressingly clear to everybody concerned that the war could not be waged successfully unless the militia was replaced, at least for the purpose of sustained warfare, by an army of regulars who were willing to serve without interruption until victory was won. This was a radical departure from previous practices, and it was clear that substantial rewards had to be offered to achieve the change from temporary to permanent enlistment. Therefore, when Congress decided in September 1776 to establish 88 regiments on State lines to serve during the war, the former money bounty of $20 was augmented by promises of land, ranging from 100 acres for a private to 500 acres for a colonel. The land was to be provided by the United States, and the expenses connected therewith were to be borne by the States in the same proportion as the other expenses of the war.

These resolutions had been contested hotly in Congress before they were passed, but their execution caused still greater concern. The New England States believed that the land bonus was not sufficient to overcome the aversion to enlistment; civilians and soldiers complained, it was said, of the long engagement as a contract of servitude. These States wanted, therefore, to raise the money bounty, especially for privates, and passed acts to this effect in their assemblies. Maryland protested that it had no land of its own and thought that it would have to buy land for bounties from other States. Its council of safety proposed to raise the money bounty to the Maryland line by $10 instead of offering land. This caused consternation in the Continental Congress where it was feared that this precedent might break the back of all North America. Maryland was officially assured that it would not have to make good the bounty grants in its individual capacity because it was the intention of Congress to provide the bounty lands at the expense of the United States. But Maryland would not recant; and in order to mollify it as well as the New England States, Congress finally permitted enlistment for 3 years under the money bounty system and reserved the land bounty to those soldiers and officers who signed up for the full duration of the war or until they were honorably discharged.

Maryland's decided stand against the land bounty was by no means motivated by petty considerations; this State made it abundantly clear that much larger issues were involved. To an earlier suggestion that land might be bought for $3 per hundred, Maryland's delegates had replied "that an Expectation was formed by the People of our State that what was conquered from an Enemy at the joint Expence of Blood and Treasure of the whole should become their joint property but as Claims had been set up opposite to our Ideas of natural Justice it became a wise people rather to prepare for the worst by giving ten Dollars now than trust to the mercy of a few Venders from whom they would be obliged to purchase . . . at any price, the Case of all Monopolies . . . ." And shortly after the compromise of a 3-year alternative enlistment had been reached, Maryland urged Congress not to close the door on its request "that the back lands acquired from the Crown of *Great Britain* in the present war, should be a common stock for the benefit of the *United States* . . . ."

Though this motion was not carried, the long struggle over the cession of western lands had commenced. While it lasted, Maryland's and even more so Virginia's moves were largely motivated and conditioned by the bounty-land question. In order to "remove the *ostensible* cause" of Maryland's anxiety to share in the common property of the western lands and its subsequent refusal to join the Confederation, the Virginia Assembly offered in December 1779 "to furnish lands out of their territory on the north west side of the Ohio river, without purchase money, to the troops on continental establishment of such of the confederated states as had not unappropriated lands for that purpose. . . ." This offer hardly substantiates Maryland's suspicion of the grasping ambition of its big neighbor. Regardless of whether Virginia's generosity or Maryland's insistence can rightly be called the keystone of the Confederation, there is little doubt that the bounty resolutions of Congress in 1776 must be credited with having inaugurated the train of events which eventually led to perpetual union.

Virginia's "Remonstrance" was only the first step toward actual cession. In the long haggling over the terms under which Virginia was to renounce its claims to the territory across the Ohio River, the bounty lands proved one of the main stumbling blocks. Holding immense tracts of unappropriated land, Virginia had very soon adopted the idea suggested by Congress of granting land bounties to its officers and soldiers, both on the State and continental establishment. And being more able to do so, Virginia was more liberal than Congress with grants. By October 1779, all its officers had been granted ten times, noncoms four times, and privates two times as much land as Congress had stipulated; a year later all bounties were increased by one-third, and new ones were added for generals (following congressional precedent); and in 1782 further increases and bounties for 3-year enlistments were granted. George Rogers Clark and his men had been promised lands in the trans-Ohio region that they were to wrest from the English. Finally, a land office created at Richmond in 1779 was charged with the administration and execution of military bounty warrants and of all other claims pertaining to the unappropriated lands of the State. This step had been greatly resented by Maryland and the other landless states because any definite arrangements made by Virginia might render it still more difficult to obtain its consent to the cession of the northwestern territory under reasonable terms.

Most important of all, as early as December 1778, Virginia had set aside an extensive tract in western Kentucky from which to supply its line officers and soldiers with land. This military reserve became the source of many vexations. When the boundary between Virginia and North Carolina was extended, part of this district fell south of the line. In its final cession offer on January 2, 1781, Virginia stipulated, therefore, that in case the quantity of good lands which it had reserved southeast of the Ohio River proved insufficient, the deficiency should be made up in good lands to be laid off between the Scioto and Little Miami rivers northwest of the Ohio. [*See* Map 7.] Even after this clause and the cession had been accepted March 1, 1784, Congress delayed final action in the matter, until Virginia could prove that its supply of "good land" southeast of the Ohio had really been exhausted. The Senate and the House finally settled the matter by an act of August 10, 1790; the first titles to land in the Military Reserve of Virginia northwest of the Ohio were conveyed in 1791, almost 8 years after peace had been declared and more than 6 years after Virginia had ceded its northwestern territories.

In the protracted struggle over Virginia's claims to bounty lands across the Ohio River, two major issues were involved. The first related to the methods of locating warrants. According to the Land Ordinance of 1785, the lands of the Northwest Territory had to be surveyed and subdivided into rectangular townships and sections before warrants could be located and titles conveyed. An exception was the Virginia Military Reserve, because it was to be settled under Virginia laws which allowed the warrant holder to locate his land himself and to have it surveyed afterward in any shape he and the surveyor thought suitable. Under this practice, good lands, especially the river bottoms, were taken up rapidly. Newcomers pushed farther and farther into the wilderness in search of good lands without bothering about the nearer but second-rate stretches. Thus, new regions quickly became dotted with widely scattered and often unconnected settlements. Determined to give its soldiers the full advantages of "indiscriminate location," Virginia needed large areas in order to satisfy them. This explains why Virginia insisted on making "good land" the measure of its claims to large tracts on both sides of the Ohio and why it grew impatient over the long delay in admitting claimants to its reserve northwest of the river.

In these clashes the ever-present conflict between the North and the South played an important part, though mostly behind the scenes. The Land Ordinance of 1785, just as the famed Ordinance of 1787 for the northwestern territory, was widely hailed as a victory for the decided preference of New Englanders for compact settlement and rectangular surveys. Certain groups of New England officers took the lead in the settlement and administration of the new territory, largely through the Ohio Company. These men feared that the Virginians and their ways would prove a disturbing element once they took up lands in the reserve under the laws of their Mother State. The settlers who eventually entered the Virginia Reserve from the south quickly succeeded in taking up the best lands and soon began to play their full and vigorous part in the political life of the territory and the ascendancy of Ohio to statehood. However, the veterans of the Revolutionary War had a comparatively small share in all this because many of them had tired of the long delay and sold their claims to enterprising Easterners who in time did a thriving business in locating and selling Ohio lands.

Only a few days after the terms of the preliminary peace had been ratified, a shrewd observer in Congress wrote to an eminent officer: "Our circumstances afford an odd Contrast to those we have heretofore experienced. The Difficulty which heretofore oppres'd us was how to raise an Army. The one which now embarrasses is how to dissolve it." Two months later, mutinous soldiers forced Congress to flee from Philadelphia to Princeton. In this open revolt, the officers had not taken part, but they too were discontented and irritable. They hesitated to resort to desperate means, at least as long as there was hope that Congress would act in their favor. In December 1782 they had presented the last of a long list of memorials to that body. This petition demanded the prompt settlement of arrearages and the commutation of half pay for life, promised in 1780, into a lump sum of money to be paid on discharge. Congress had sent a committee to investigate, but having no resources of its own it could only recommend speedy action to the States; but they were slow in adopting appropriate measures. Deeply disturbed by rumors of the approaching peace, even the officers' restraint threatened to give way to open rebellion.

Matters came to a head in early March 1783 at Newburgh. An anonymous officer addressed his comrades in these incendiary terms: " . . . while the swords you wear are necessary for the defence of America, what have you to expect from peace, when your voice shall sink, and your strength dissipate by division? . . . . Can you then consent to be the only sufferers by this revolution, and retiring from the field, grow old in poverty, wretchedness and contempt? . . . . If you can—GO—and carry with you the jest of Tories, and the scorn of Whigs—the ridicule, and what is worse, the pity of the world. Go, starve, and be forgotten!" And then followed a dire threat: ". . . the slightest mark of indignity from Congress now, must operate like the grave, and part you [and Congress] forever: that in any political event, the army has its alternative. If peace, that nothing shall separate you from your arms but death: if war, that. . . you will retire to some unsettled country, smile in your turn, and 'mock when their fear cometh on.' "

Here indeed were the seeds of a serious revolt. The officers were exhorted not to lay down their arms until Congress granted their demands; and if Congress refused an exodus into the western lands was to be the ultimate answer. No doubt, the addresses made a deep impression upon the officers of the cantonment. But at a meeting of their delegates Washington himself unexpectedly appeared. In a speech which moved some of his hearers to tears he reiterated his belief that Congress, though moving slowly, would eventually do full justice to the wishes of the army. He then solemnly pledged his own support in every way which was consistent with his duty to his country. This appeal dissuaded the officers from their dangerous course and set them once more upon the road to orderly appeal, strongly seconded by their commander in chief.

Congress acted quickly and agreed to commute the promise of half pay for life into a sum in gross amounting to 5 years' full pay in money or securities such as those given to the other creditors of the United States. By virtue of this last clause which shows Alexander Hamilton's hand in drawing up the resolutions, the money and pension claims of the army would be treated in exactly the same way as the claims of any other creditor upon the exchequer of the United States. One month later, the proceeds from special imposts on foreign liquors, sugar, etc., a general duty of 5 percent on imports, and contributions from the States were assigned to the service of the total public debt; it is significant that a proposal to appropriate the 5-percent duty to the army claims alone was not adopted at the time. Neither were any provisions made to satisfy the land bounties, the obvious reason being that the cessions of western lands had not been completed. Their consummation was urged in order to hasten the extinguishment of the debts.

Indeed, the officers themselves had not asked Congress to

attend to the land-bounty matter; they had concentrated on obtaining the commutation of their pensions into hard cash. The seeds of the Newburgh addresses were to ripen in this respect also. The appeal to migrate to the west and begin a new semimilitary life there had not fallen on deaf ears, for this idea had been talked about previously, and its combination with the bounty-land question produced a move which was destined to have far reaching, if slowly maturing, consequences. Soon after the Newburgh incident two of the main actors on the scene, Quartermaster Timothy Pickering and Brigadier General Rufus Putnam, together with Brigadier General Jedediah Huntington, were hard at work trying to turn the insidious counsel of the "fellow soldier" into a positive scheme which would utilize the promised bounty lands and other land grants for the establishment of a new state for veterans on the Ohio. By April 1783, elaborate propositions for the settling of such a commonwealth were drawn up for the benefit of those officers and men who were willing to join an association to be founded for the purpose. These propositions called for concerted action along the following lines: purchase by the United States of a tract corresponding roughly to the present State of Ohio; prompt assignment of the bounty lands promised by Congress during the war; grants of additional and larger tracts but with the same scaling as the bounty lands to actual settlers in the purchased district; payment of the initial expenses of settlement and subsistence for 3 years from arrearages due to the members of the association; the preparation of a constitution previous to going west which would exclude slavery; and prompt admittance of this state to the Confederation.

This ambitious plan drew from the supposed author of the Newburgh addresses the caustic remark: " . . . this quixotic idea. It originates with men who wish only to amuse and divert the army from the consideration of more important concerns. They ask, what can not be granted. 'Tis absurd." Whatever sentiments John Armstrong harbored, he was right. Pickering and Putnam had simply proposed that the United States should purchase the tract for the new state from the natives, thereby ignoring, probably intentionally, the thorny problem of the cession of Virginia's northwestern claims. For this and perhaps other reasons, the final petition, signed in June 1783 by almost three hundred officers from New England, merely asked Congress to "assign and mark it out as a Tract or Territory suitable to form a distinct Government (or Colony of the United States) in time to be admitted" to the Confederation and to make provisions for the location and survey of the bounty lands promised.

The petition was sent properly to the commander in chief first, accompanied by a lengthy letter from Putnam. The rugged soldier and pioneer stressed the paramount importance of the Ohio River region as a bastion against England and Spain and the necessity of securing the frontier by a string of forts in order to keep the Indians in check. He then proceeded to voice the expectations of the officers which had been deemed improper to mention in the petition. His comrades, Putnam explained, did not expect to be under any obligation to settle on the bounty lands; if, however, Congress made further and larger grants of land, many were determined to become actual settlers on the Ohio. Putnam went on to emphasize that at least some of the officers held rather decided views as to the manner in which these new lands should be distributed and administered. They were, he declared, much opposed to monopoly and wished to guard against large patents granted to individuals; they hoped, therefore, that no grants would be made except by townships 6 miles square (or multiples), to be subdivided by the proprietor associates themselves and administered after the pattern of a New England town. This township principle was also to apply to private purchasers of land in the region.

Washington forwarded the petition and Putnam's letter to Congress on June 17, 1783, and he himself urged the speedy adoption of the army plan, because its execution would connect the government with the frontier, extend settlements progressively, and plant in the new lands a brave, hardy, and respectable race of people always willing to combat the savages. Despite this endorsement, no action was taken on the proposal by Congress either then or later. During the turbulent days of the insurrection of the Pennsylvania troops, Congress referred the petition to a standing committee, had it read in Congress a week later, and referred back to another special committee which was discharged on October 15, 1783. Upon a pressing inquiry from Putnam, more than a year later, Washington blamed the "want of cession of the land to act upon" as the chief reason for the delay. He was vaguely hopeful that something might be done yet, because the Virginia cession had been accepted, but the plan was never revived in its original form.

Manifestly, it was futile to expect action from Congress in the matter of the bounty lands as long as the squabble over the cessions and their execution lasted. Moreover, Putnam and his comrades had encumbered their plans with political aspirations of pronounced character the open discussion of which would certainly upset the delicate balance of a none-too-perfect union. However, they did plant the proverbial mustard seed when they urged their fellow officers and land claimants to form a voluntary association with the characteristics of a corporate body. True, the idea of a pioneering land corporation was neither new nor without precedent. But only the critical times of the 1780s had engendered strong enough group sentiments to keep this basic feature of the army plan alive, when all other proposals had to be given up. Eight years of war and camp life had rendered many officers unfit for the old ways of life; they were impoverished and despaired of ever again succeeding in living up to the civilian Joneses. On the other hand, the long comradeship in arms had imbued many officers with an esprit de corps which persisted and proved of great psychological value in the troubled times of war and peace alike.

Finally, many believed that the western lands were the destined proving ground for the political principles of independence, self-government, and personal liberty for which the war had been fought. Thus, the lands on the Ohio beckoned with the lure of still another Utopia. In these empty expanses would rise a new community from the seeds of a corporation of New England veterans who had forged their swords into plowshares.

These feelings and expectations, though seldom voiced by the tight-lipped backers of the original army plan, prevented the idea of a pioneering land corporation from vanishing. After 3 years of casting their weights about in various western enterprises, Rufus Putnam and Benjamin Tupper finally launched the Ohio Company of New England which included officers and men who were destined to play a vital part in the opening of Ohio. In the financial and corporate set-up of the company, military bounty claims again loomed conspicuously, and in the early life of Marietta, the first settlement on the Ohio River, some of the dreams of the army plan of 1783 came true. [*See* Map 7.]

The very same routine procedure which buried the army plan in congressional committees obliterated yet another scheme designed to satisfy the soldiers' demands for their bounty lands. Introduced by Theodoric Bland and seconded by Alexander Hamilton, this scheme is of interest here chiefly because it seems to have been a counterproposal to the army plan, though it foreshadows in some respects the system of land sales in Hamilton's famous public credit report of 1790. The plan as presented to Congress in 1783 proposed to merge the army's land claims with the commuted half pay and arrearages, every dollar of which was to be considered equal to a claim for 30 acres of land. The combined land grants were to be assigned within the vacant territory ceded by Great Britain, where districts 2 degrees wide and 3 degrees long, subdivided into townships, were to be laid out. Finally, the United States was to reserve 10,000 acres out of every 100,000 granted as common and unalienable property, their revenues to be used for military and educational purposes. This plan represented one of the several attempts of the "financiers" to fund at least the army debt in toto. It also reflected the fear of the advocates of a strong central government that a new state might upset the delicate balance of the Thirteen Original States, and it combined both political and financial motives in the proposal that the Union keep a permanent interest in the western lands and their future development.

The Bland proposals hinged directly upon the acceptance of the Virginia cession. Indeed, no move in the matter of the promised bounty lands was possible until the United States had acquired clear title to the western lands. As soon as this was accomplished, a gust of fresh air seemed to give new life to this and other questions concerning the future land policy of the United States. The Virginians took the lead, and among them Thomas Jefferson emerged as the leading spirit. True, he did not concern himself much with the bounty-land issue proper; nevertheless, his broad and general approach to the problems of the new west provided a principal solution for this question, albeit one which obliterated most of its political implications. Under his leadership, the legislative framework for the northwestern territory and its administration progressed so far that the lines for future action appeared securely drawn, even though many important changes might occur in carrying out his more detailed plans.

In this respect, one accomplishment stands out clearly before others. Congress agreed (and never deviated from this course) to deal with the problems of the northwest under two headings: the one relating to the form and powers of government, and the other relating to the disposal of land within the territory. This trend of affairs is clearly shown by the sequence of events after Virginia's deed of cession had been accepted on March 1, 1784. On the very same day, Jefferson laid before Congress his proposals for the "Temporary Government of the Northwestern Territory" which had been under consideration by a committee for some time. They provided for the creation and administration of several western territories of rectangular shape and about equal size, established the procedure for their advancing to full statehood and membership in the Union, stipulated the republican form of government, forbade the admittance of citizens with hereditary titles, and abolished slavery after 1800. With the two last mentioned provisions stricken out, these proposals became law on April 23, 1784, but they were never put into effect. The unsettled conditions in the West prevented their early application, and in July 1787, the famous government ordinance for the Northwest Territory was passed which cast Jefferson's ideas, though with important alterations, in a new and permanent form. On April 30, 1784, Jefferson laid before Congress "An Ordinance for ascertaining the mode of locating and disposing of lands in the western territory," the logical sequel and counterpart to the government ordinance just passed. In a measure, the land ordinance shared the fate of its twin; it was assigned to a committee, read in Congress again in the spring of 1785, referred to still another committee from which it emerged in the new and final dress of the renowned Land Ordinance of May 20, 1785. As a matter of course and propriety, the military bounty lands are dealt with in both Jefferson's draft and the Land Ordinance of 1785. However, there seems reason to believe that the broader and political implications of the land-bounty issue were not entirely absent from Jefferson's mind when he drew up the Ordinance of 1784.

The disturbed conditions in the Northwest made it necessary that Congress decide on matters of government first and separately. The Indian claims had to be acquired by Congress, but it seemed impossible that this body should also supervise and enforce the execution of the respective treaties with the Indian tribes. Consequently, the delineation of the territory and its subdivisions as well as the establishment of proper authorities there became more pressing. Likewise, the eager settlers could not be allowed to move into a political vacuum, as the troublesome squatters across the Ohio had done. They had to be made responsible for law and order from the very beginning, and this entailed the framing of govermental rules in advance of their coming. In spite of the expediency of framing a government ordinance first and leaving the land law until later, there still remains the possibility, and even the probability, that Jefferson's move was designed to serve his political ideas also. There seems little doubt that the fight against the Society of the Cincinnati raging at the time prompted him to insist on equal male suffrage in the formation of truly democratic governments within the territory and to insert in his ordinance a clause barring citizens with hereditary titles from settling there. In all probability, he was also aware of the fact that the prime movers behind the army plan were all prominent Cincinnati. Was the thunderer against the aristocracy of wealth and privilege unaware of the possible danger that a landed gentry might rise in the West whose wealth would be based upon bounty lands and additional land grants from Congress and whose privileges would be but a perpetuation of their military merits and insignia? The great civilian among the Founding Fathers was afraid that there would "continue a distinction between the civil & military which it would be for the good of the whole to obliterate as soon as possible. . . ." To attain this goal, he was resolved that the people should be the sole source of democratic government in the East and in the New West. The political realist would know that matters pertaining to land holding might becloud the purity of this principle when included in the same ordinance. Jefferson may have thought it advisable, therefore, to deal with the modes for acquiring land in a separate body of general rules and routine procedures.

That Jefferson was aware of the political implications of the bounty question is shown by a peculiar clause in his land ordinance draft which prescribed that army warrants should pass as lands, by descent and device, but not by assignment or by survivorship. The prohibition of assignment had its precedent in a resolution passed by Congress on September 20, 1776. Both this resolution and Jefferson's clause were intended to prevent speculation in land warrants. In cases of land holding survivorship applied to joint tenancy under a grant and was regarded in Jefferson's time as a survival of feudalism and incompatible with democratic ideas. Of course, this term must have slipped easily from the pen of the author of the laws against entail and primogeniture. The question here is, why just in the case of the bounty lands? True, these alone were grants whereas all other lands had to be acquired by purchase. But again, why should he be so careful if no possible danger threatened from this direction? However, none of Jefferson's provisions in these matters found a place in the Land Ordinance of 1785. On the contrary this law expressly recognized the right to assign bounty warrants. Nevertheless, his proviso that lands in the new territory should pass in dowry and descent according to gavelkind did become the basis of the first section of the Ordinance of 1787, as he had anticipated.

Pertinent features of Jefferson's two ordinances thus appear to reflect his running fight with military and Federalist circles of New England. By no means, however, did he leave this particular battlefield fully victorious. True, the Ordinance of 1787 upheld most of his cherished principles of democratic government. But his draft for the land ordinance underwent such drastic changes that it finally resembled the original draft in little more than name. Again, we are concerned with the land-bounty issue, this time wrapped up with the controversy about the proper way of promoting actual settlement in the West.

Jefferson's land ordinance plan combined the regular survey with a modified form of indiscriminate location. He wanted the new territory laid off in hundreds 10 geographical miles square, which in turn, were to be subdivided in lots 1 mile square; the hundreds were to be offered either entire or in lots. However, the actual surveying was not to begin at a definite location but with the hundreds most in demand. This provision, of course, was closely tied up with the modes of acquiring title to land in the territory. Upon paying to the treasurer or loan officer an unspecified purchase price in specie, loan office, or debt certificates or handing over evidences of military rights to lands, the prospective settler would receive a warrant, go out himself to locate it, and describe to the surveyor the particular lot or hundred chosen. The surveyor would then proceed to lay off the land according to these requests and issue certificates of description which finally became the basis of deeds. Jefferson thus favored a rather liberal method of land allotment, albeit within the frame of regular surveys, and accorded no preferential treatment to soldier warrants; it was the idea of first come, first served applied generally.

In all these respects, the final land ordinance differed widely from Jefferson's scheme. First of all, it authorized the business of surveying and disposing of western lands in a definite and not too extensive area on the upper Ohio River where 7 parallel ranges of townships running due north and south were to be laid off completely before being opened to the location of warrants. The townships were to be 6 miles square and subdivided into lots of 640 acres each. The methods adopted for offering the townships either entire or in lots to prospective settlers and the procedures prescribed for securing warrant and title were rather complicated. Some of the features, especially those relating to the participation of the States in the scheme, were repealed in July 1788 without having had much effect. Here it is sufficient to point out the special treatment accorded to the holders of army warrants. As soon as the Seven Ranges were surveyed, the Secretary of War was to withdraw by lot one-seventh of the townships for the use of the late Continental Army; henceforth, military bounty land claims had to be presented to the Secretary of War and be satisfied by him. The remainder of the townships were to be sold by auction at not less than $1 per acre to be paid in specie or in debt certificates.

In most of these stipulations, the New England viewpoint on the necessity of survey before sale and on more compact settlement and progressive advance into the West had prevailed. In the Seven Ranges it was thought that the United States would acquire a yardstick which would measure and delineate the westward movement in which the veterans would play their due part. In other respects, however, the ordinance clearly represented a compromise between the New England and Southern groups in Congress who had waged a hard battle in committees and on the floor before the measure was finally passed.

To the holders of bounty claims and to prospective settlers in general, the results of the Ordinance of 1785 were disconcerting. Despite all caution, the Indians remained hostile, the chief geographer fell ill, and after 3 years not more than 4 ranges of townships had been laid off. It is not surprising, therefore, that the Secretary of War received incessant inquiries respecting the lands due the late army. In the spring of 1787, he addressed an urgent appeal to Congress. "Too many," he wrote, "have been compelled, by their necessities, to sell the evidences of their public debt, for a small proportion of the nominal sum. These unfortunate men now consider the lands promised them, as their only resource against poverty, in old age, and therefore are extremely solicitous to receive, immediately, their dues in this respect. . . . Assuming the surveys of the last year, as a data, or even supposing double the quantity will be surveyed annually in future, yet a very long period must elapse before the whole quantity due will be delivered. A period, at which very few of those entitled to the land will be living."

Half a year later, when Congress was prodded into high gear by the proposed sale of land to the Ohio Company, an act was passed setting aside 1,000,000 acres north of the Ohio Company lands and west of the Seven Ranges and another tract at the mouth of the Ohio River for the exclusive purpose of satisfying the military bounties of the late army. But only after 7 more years and after the Indian war had been terminated by the Treaty of Granville was Congress able to stipulate the terms and modes under which these lands would be made available for the army, and then 3 more years elapsed before the first deeds were conveyed.

By an act of June 1, 1796, some of the cumbersome procedures of the Land Ordinance of 1785 were relaxed for the military districts. Townships 5 (instead of 6) miles square were divided into quarters of 4,000 acres each; these were assigned entire and by lot to either a single claimant or to groups of veterans who had pooled their warrants for the purpose, the actual locations of their lands to be left to their own care if they so desired. The effect of these stipulations was that many of the quarter townships were carved up in rather irregular fashion and in about the same way as had been feared from the execution of Jefferson's original plan. On the other hand, the "unmilitary U. S. military district," as it has been called, filled up more quickly than the rectangular sections in the Seven Ranges, thus testifying to the merits of Jefferson's plan as well.

Even this rapid survey shows how slowly and cautiously Congress was compelled to move in the matter of satisfying the land bounties of the Revolution. The first 4 ranges could not be opened to claimants before 1787, the Virginia Reserve remained closed till 1791, and the United States military districts did not welcome the first veteran settlers before 1800. Secretary of War Knox's dire prophecy that "few of those entitled to the land will be living" to see their expectations fulfilled did not come true literally, but the long delay had induced many of the veterans—soldiers and officers alike—to sell not only their certificates for half pay and arrearages but also their bounty warrants. The assignment of warrants, forbidden during the war, became legal in 1788, and this helped to hasten the sale of warrants by their original, and often destitute, holders. It is not necessary to reiterate here the well-known facts concerning the speculative mania which seized the moneyed parts of the Nation after the war and enabled a few persons and firms to reap profits from accumulated certificates and the sales of warrants for western lands. There is, however, need to point to the often forgotten circumstance that the existence of a market in debt certificates and land warrants could and did give to vigorous and enterprising men an opportunity and the means for concerted action of considerable public value and portent, even if they thereby advanced their own fortunes.

The Survey of the Seven Ranges

William D. Pattison

One of the most creative ideas to come from the fertile brain of Thomas Jefferson was the rectangular land survey system embodied in the famous Ordinance of 1785. For that majority of modern Americans living in the areas subject to this type of survey it has meant easily determined land titles and rectilinear communities regardless of the topography.

Jefferson's original survey plan called for ten-square-mile townships rather than the six square mile ones that Congress enacted. His plan required that the initial survey begin with the choicest lands and did not demand the rigidity that eventually emerged. The congressional decision requiring a regular survey over a limited area of southeastern Ohio was a wise one. Whether Congress erred in deviating from the decimal system devised by Jefferson is now a moot point. Jefferson's plan was to use geographical miles of 100 chains to the mile, 10 chains to the acre. The congressional solution used the traditional English measurement system. It took the French Revolution to make the type of measurement changes envisioned by the Sage of Monticello.

The first survey in Ohio marked the beginning of a new experiment in property determination. In this article William D. Pattison, (1921 ——), traces the course of the original survey. Under the direction of Thomas Hutchins, geographer of the United States, the survey party consisted of representatives from twelve of the original states (Delaware did not send a surveyor) who reported back to their home state on the nature of the region in order to enhance auction sales there. Many of the state representatives were involved in western land speculation schemes like the Ohio Company or Symmes's Miami Purchase.

Dr. Pattison is associate professor of geography and education at the University of Chicago, where he has taught since 1966. Earlier he taught at the University of California at Los Angeles and San Fernando Valley State College. He is the author of numerous articles on geography and the teaching of geography in the schools.

From William D. Pattison, "The Survey of the Seven Ranges," in *The Ohio History Quarterly*, LXVIII: 115–140 (April, 1959); reprinted without footnotes with permission of *Ohio History*.

THE AMERICAN rectangular land survey system established in the land ordinance of 1785 was first put into effect in the Seven Ranges of eastern Ohio. Despite the publication of important contributions to the history of Ohio which have dealt with various aspects of the Seven Ranges, interesting and significant parts of the survey story have remained untold.

The land ordinance passed by the old Continental Congress in May 1785 was a measure aimed at the raising of revenue through the sale of large quantities of land. Members of congress were persuaded to adopt, in the hope of increased income, a system of property location which required surveyors to divide the land, before either sale or settlement, into squares bounded by "lines running due north and south and others crossing these at right angles." This was the heart of the system. This novel plan, accepted from a committee report of the preceding year, apparently owed its adoption to the successful urging of two beliefs: one, that it would be relatively inexpensive to put into effect, and two, that it would afford security of title to purchasers of the land because of the simple regularity of the property boundaries deriving from it. To save money congress decided to require only the lines bounding townships, six miles square, to be surveyed in the field; on drawings called plats, lines bounding square-mile sections within the townships were to be added at the office of the board of treasury. The township boundaries were to be run according to true north and marked on trees, and their location relative to watercourses "and other remarkable and permanent things" was to be noted, along with the quality of the lands over which they passed.

Often overlooked is the fact that, just as the newly surveyed land was to be made available at auction in each of the thirteen states, so thirteen surveyors were to go west, one from each state, that they might be able "to communicate information to the states for which they were appointed of the quality of the lands, and such other circumstances as may direct the citizens in making their purchases." Over the surveyors congress set the holder of an office which survived from the Revolutionary War, that of geographer of the United States. The incumbent, Thomas Hutchins, was summoned by congress as the time for passage of the land ordinance approached.

The geographer and the surveyors were to proceed to the

country west of Pennsylvania and Virginia of which George Washington had said, "This is the tract which, from local position and peculiar advantages, ought to be first settled in preference to any other whatever." He had in mind, perhaps first of all, its accessibility by way of the Ohio River to Pittsburgh, which in turn was connected with Philadelphia by the Pennsylvania Road. Downstream from Pittsburgh, within a few miles of the point where surveying was scheduled to begin, was a stockaded outpost built during the Revolutionary War called Fort McIntosh. Farther downstream, on the Virginia side of the river, were several very small settlements, where aid and comfort, already being dispensed to emigrants bound for Kentucky, awaited the federal surveyors. The final favorable circumstances were that the Indians had largely evacuated this area by 1785, and that the tribes which might have insisted on their claims to the territory—the Delawares and the Wyandots—had officially yielded those claims in a treaty signed at Fort McIntosh in January 1785. [*See* Map 7.]

Not everything was promising about the country contemplated for survey. The land itself, representing an extension beyond the Ohio River of the Allegheny Plateau, was unusually rugged. The military strength concentrated at Fort McIntosh was slight. Troops stationed there fell below one hundred in number during the summer following passage of the land ordinance, as expected reinforcements of militia failed to arrive and as many of the men, "for want of confidence in the public treasury respecting pay," declined to re-enlist. Settlers downstream from the fort, furthermore, had not all obediently stayed on the Virginia side of the Ohio; those who had made their homes on the federal side were under congressional ban and subject to forcible ejectment. They, of course, had no reason for friendly feeling toward the surveyors. Further afield, the friendship of the Delawares and Wyandots, upon which reliance was placed after the treaty of Fort McIntosh, should have been very little depended upon. As Hutchins and his men were soon to discover, these two tribes could withstand neither the pressure of the hostile Miamis and Shawnees, nor the influence of the British at Detroit.

Congress, with an appreciation of some of the difficulties in store, none the less anticipated a rapid advancement of survey work at the time the land ordinance was passed. A specific beginning point was designated in the ordinance, and, though Hutchins and his men were going to be obliged to wait for others to establish it on the ground, no delay was anticipated as a result. But it was in this connection that the first of many delays developed. The federal surveyors were to start off westward from the north, or right, bank of the Ohio River at the point where Pennsylvania's western boundary intersected it—just as soon as that boundary had been run. The southwestern corner of Pennsylvania had been established in 1784, and the boundary commissioners of Virginia and Pennsylvania had agreed to meet there in the middle of May 1785 to run a line due north to the Ohio River; but they were unable to convene until early in June, and it was not until August 20 that they reached the Ohio River. On that same day field hands were sent across to "set a stake on the flat, the North Side of the River." Many miles of the Pennsylvania boundary remained to be run northward, but public land survey by the United States could now begin.

The summer of 1785 was nearly gone when the geographer, Thomas Hutchins, arrived in Pittsburgh from New York. Receiving an assurance from Colonel Josiah Harmar, commandant at Fort McIntosh, that surveying could be safely undertaken, Hutchins joined several surveyors who had been in the village for a week or more in "engaging Chain Carriers, purchasing provisions, and Buying Horses etc." This was on September 4. Within two weeks a general movement down the Ohio River to an encampment at the mouth of Little Beaver Creek was under way.

Thomas Hutchins was distinguished from the surveyors who accompanied him down the Ohio by more than the fact that he was head of an executive agency of the national government known as the "Geographer's Department." Earlier in his life, as a British officer, he had served at Fort Pitt, and had undertaken exploratory expeditions from that point northward to Lake Erie, overland to Lake Michigan and the upper Wabash Valley, and down the Ohio River to the Mississippi. A general map of the West which he compiled largely on the basis of these expeditions had established Hutchins as an authority on the area. It served in the present instance as the surveyors' guide to the country they were about to enter.

Thirteen surveyors accepted appointments to serve under the geographer in response to invitations sent out by congress during the summer. But of these representatives of the several states, one fell ill, one stayed at home—due probably to a doubt that his services would be needed that year—and three failed to appear for reasons unknown. The eight surveyors who reported for duty in the West were Edward Dowse for New Hampshire, Benjamin Tupper for Massachusetts, Isaac Sherman for Connecticut, Absalom Martin for New Jersey, William W. Morris for New York, Alexander Parker for Virginia, James Simpson for Maryland, and Robert Johnston for Georgia.

Of the first four of these surveyors, in the order named, Dowse alone was a man of minor importance. Tupper was a general recently retired from the Continental Army and a close friend of Rufus Putnam, Isaac Sherman was the son of the influential Roger Sherman, to whom credit is often given for the success of Connecticut's claim to the Western Reserve, and Absalom Martin represented the interests of prominent men in New Jersey and enjoyed the recommendation of the governor of the state. All three of these men were, in fact, harbingers of great colonization movements. Tupper was the first of a series of advance scouts who acted on behalf of the Ohio Company of Associates. The young Sherman, though he may not have gone west primarily to gather intelligence concerning Western Reserve lands, addressed a letter on that subject to the governor of Connecticut before completing his tour of duty as a federal surveyor. In the appointment of Martin we can recognize an early expression of interest in western lands on the part of New Jersey speculators which culminated a few years later in the acquisition by Judge John Cleves Symmes and associates of that large tract in the southwest corner of present-day Ohio known as the Miami Purchase.

The remaining four from among the surveyors who went west in 1785 deserve attention more for their individual attributes and activities than for their significance as representatives of states or special groups. Morris of New York, a young man apparently seeking employment appropriate to his technical training, was the single surveyor who could participate as an equal with Hutchins in what the latter called "the Astronomical business of the Geographer's Department." And he gained the geographer's special commendation for assistance in the field work of 1785. Parker of Virginia appears to have belonged to that class of woodswise men to whose independent surveying activities Virginia already owed the subdivision of much of its own territory. Simpson, though a representative of Maryland, was a surveyor from York County, Pennsylvania. It was through him that the party of federal surveyors made their only known contact with the men occupied in laying out Pennsylvania's boundary north of the Ohio River. He visited the camp of the Pennsylvania commissioners early in October 1785. Johnston, a doctor and resident of Baltimore, who managed to join in the surveying as a representative of Georgia, was apparently a man of means looking for land in which to invest personally. Nearly eighteen square miles of land in the Seven Ranges were later purchased in his name.

By September 30, Hutchins, his eight surveyors, and a retinue of about thirty helpers were all assembled at the mouth of Little Beaver Creek, within easy walking distance of the scheduled initial point of survey. A visitor in camp expected them to progress rapidly with their work, yet he found cause for misgiving. Hutchins was openly apprehensive of Indian hostility, expressing himself as disposed to "instantly quit the business" if danger threatened.

Hutchins made a beginning on September 30 at the post on the north bank of the Ohio River set up by the state boundary commissioners somewhat more than a month earlier. Acting on his instructions in the land ordinance to attend personally to the running of the first east and west line, he proceeded westward until October 8, when, having surveyed less than four miles, he suspended operations due to the receipt of "disagreeable intelligence" concerning the Indians. Though the fact was not yet apparent, the season's surveying had come to an end.

The intelligence which reached Hutchins told of an Indian depredation at "Tuscarawas," a Delaware village located about fifty miles west of the beginning point. At a trading post near the village, according to the report, two traders had been set upon by a band of Indians, who left behind them all the signs of war. Hearing this, Hutchins supervised the shifting of the surveyors' camp to a safer site on the south side of the Ohio; yet hope remained that chiefs of the Delawares and Wyandots would consent to come and attend the surveyors at their work, thereby guaranteeing their safety. Hutchins had dispatched a messenger to these two tribes in the second week of September, but it was not until October 15 that a letter of response, "spoken by Captain Pipe," was received. More apologetic than threatening in tone, it simply declined the invitation. Hutchins, who had placed the greatest reliance upon the chiefs, prepared almost at once to decamp, and within a few days the entire survey company had returned to Pittsburgh, where field hands, recruited earlier in that village, were paid off and discharged.

It might seem strange that the troops at Fort McIntosh, who had been expected by congress to protect the surveyors, were of no help on this occasion. This lack of support was due in part to the reduced strength of the garrison. Unfortunately, the few remaining troops were needed at the site of a prospective treaty conference with the Shawnees farther down the Ohio River. On the day before surveying began, all of the infantry based at Fort McIntosh had floated past the surveyors' camp on their way downstream to the treaty grounds.

Having returned to Pittsburgh about one month after setting forth for the field of survey, the frustrated surveyors started home, traveling once more the Pennsylvania Road, with nothing but debts to show for their time and trouble. Last to depart was Thomas Hutchins, who, upon arriving in New York, submitted a map to congress showing the country along the few miles of line surveyed. Perhaps in an attempt to give congress a sense of value received for money expended, he tendered with the map an unusually copious verbal description.

Despite the inconsequential nature of this first attempt at surveying under the land ordinance, congress had not yet lost faith in the enterprise. Hutchins was given, in effect, a vote of confidence when in May 1786 congress passed a resolution authorizing the geographer to try again.

By the time of the geographer's return to Pittsburgh in June 1786, a new military outpost, Fort Harmar, had been constructed at the mouth of the Muskingum River, the treaty conference with the Shawnees had been brought to a seemingly successful conclusion, and the Wyandots and Delawares, who had attended the conference, appeared to be resigned to the survey of their ceded lands. Prospects for surveying were further brightened by Hutchins' success in dispatching an invitation to chiefs of the Delawares and Wyandots nearly three months in advance of the schedule of the preceding year.

Thirteen ranges of townships, Hutchins now expected, would be surveyed by the end of the season. He seemed justified in this hope for at least three reasons. First, the potential extent of each range had been greatly curtailed by congress. The resolution which had authorized the resumption of field work ordered that surveying be confined to the area south of the east-west line which Hutchins had begun to lay out in 1785. Second, the prospective work involved in surveying had been greatly simplified by the repeal of the requirement that township boundaries be run "by the true meridian," that is, according to true north. Third, Hutchins had been led to expect that thirteen surveyors, one for each range of townships, would come west in this year of renewed effort.

As the surveyors arrived in Pittsburgh, they once more undertook purchasing provisions and hiring field parties. When preparations were complete, each of the states but Delaware was represented by a surveyor equipped and ready to take the field. Four states—Rhode Island, Pennsylvania, North Carolina, and South Carolina—were represented for the first time. Two states—New Hampshire and Virginia—were now served by new men. Of the six men thus added to the roster of pioneer federal surveyors, four deserve special note, beginning with Winthrop Sargent, surveyor for New Hampshire and replacement for Edward Dowse. Major Sargent, whose application for a surveyorship was sponsored by the secretary of war, was a Massachusetts man soon to be elected secretary of the newly organized Ohio Company of Associates. A second noteworthy newcomer was Colonel Ebenezer Sproat, surveyor for Rhode Island, who later became an important stockholder and surveyor of the Ohio Company. He was among the men who landed at the mouth of the Muskingum River to found Marietta in 1788. Thirdly, there was Colonel Adam Hoops, representing Pennsylvania, a professional surveyor and land speculator from Philadelphia and a friend of Hutchins, who probably owed his appointment to Hutchins' influence. Lastly, there was Israel Ludlow, appointed to fill the vacant surveyorship for South

Carolina. A young man from New Jersey who came west in 1786 to make his fortune on the frontier, Ludlow later became actively interested in the Miami Purchase. By the time of his death in the early 1800's he had surveyed more land in the Ohio country than any other federal surveyor.

After a considerable delay, due to the failure of the Indians to send an answer to Hutchins' invitation, and due as well to Colonel Harmar's reluctance to provide an armed escort, surveying began again on August 9, 1786. From that date to September 18, Hutchins pushed steadily westward, marking a course which approximated a parallel of latitude. He reached a point six miles from the Pennsylvania boundary on the second day, and here Absalom Martin of New Jersey directed a line southward, setting out independently to complete the first range of townships. He was followed by other surveyors, in launching off southward from Hutchins' base line, at intervals of six miles in an order determined by lot. An entire range of townships, according to plan, was to be the responsibility of each of these surveyors. [See Map 8.]

By the end of August, Hoops, Sherman, and Sproat had followed Martin's example. Then Sargent and Simpson took their turns, and Morris was about to set off on his assigned strip of country—the Seventh Range—when the first sign of trouble appeared. On September 13 a message reached Hutchins in which the chiefs of the Delawares and Wyandots declined, for the second and last time, to come forward and guarantee the safety of the surveyors. Hutchins pressed westward none the less, dispatching Morris to work on his appointed range and advancing into the Eighth Range himself. Transfer of his headquarters camp ahead to a convenient creek not only brought Hutchins' party into the immediate neighborhood of "Tuscarawas" but separated them by about forty-five miles from their principal military support. Despite the fact that three companies of infantry had been assigned to Hutchins, all but thirty soldiers, under the command of a lieutenant, were confined to a camp on the Ohio River for want of supplies.

The geographer and his followers were now in a dangerously exposed position. On the morning of September 18 they awoke to find that a pole marking the conclusion of the previous day's surveying had been broken during the night, apparently as a warning from hostile natives. Then that afternoon intelligence reached the camp that warriors were gathering at the Shawnee towns, about one hundred and fifty miles to the southwest, intending "to cut off Hutchins and all his men." Thoroughly alarmed, Hutchins abandoned the field and sent messengers to the surveyors on their several ranges asking them to lose no time in following his example. The retreat which followed was almost comic in its confusion. Sargent, on the Fifth Range, hearing that "the Geographer had run away and all the surveyors after him," viewed the proceedings with scorn, and was persuaded only with difficulty to leave his work. At length, however, the surveyors were collected together at the house of one of the pioneers on the Virginia shore, William McMahon, and all of the troops were concentrated at a fortified position on the federal side of the Ohio downstream from the point of beginning.

By the beginning of October, when Hutchins was ready to recross the Ohio, the objective for the season had become a modest four ranges of townships. The troops at Hutchins' disposal were now, for the first time, sufficiently provisioned to take the field, and he assigned about seventy of them to the protection of the surveyors who were to accomplish this objective. The First Range had been completed by Martin before the retreat. Into the next three ranges Hutchins sent six surveyors and as a concession to the headstrong Sargent he allowed that surveyor to venture into the Fifth Range once more. A handful of soldiers went with Sargent, and the remainder were held in reserve in a central position behind hastily erected earthworks. Meantime, in the distant Shawnee country, an expedition of Kentucky militia under the command of Colonel Benjamin Logan was spreading terror and destruction thus preventing the threatened Shawnee attack upon Hutchins and his men. The Kentuckians, in executing an act of local vengeance, apparently made possible the first effective season of national surveying.

By the middle of November four ranges of townships had been successfully surveyed, without Indian incident, though on the Fifth Range Sargent's work was cut short by a small band of Indian marauders who stole nearly all of his party's horses. Hutchins now seriously considered rounding out all of the

seven ranges upon which work had been begun, but the surveyors were generally averse to the idea, nighttime tempera-
tures having dropped to the freezing point. The troops, many
of them "barefoot and miserably off for clothing," were in no
condition to continue in the field. In consequence, the soldiers
were allowed to embark for winter quarters at Fort Harmar,
and the surveyors retired to the comfort and security of
McMahon's house on the Virginia shore.

At McMahon's, Hutchins soon set about marshaling the
documentary evidence of the surveys. Under his direction the
notes which the surveyors had taken for the first four ranges
were transcribed and rearranged in a form suitable for submission to the board of treasury. Martin, Sherman, and Sproat, to
whom had fallen the official responsibility for the first four
ranges, stayed at McMahon's house until their signatures could
be affixed to the completed transcriptions. By the first week in
December most of the surveyors had departed for their homes
in the East, and the final stage of operations had begun—the
preparation of plats, or drawings of boundaries, of each township, as required by the land ordinance. Isaac Sherman, who
withdrew to the house of Charles Wells, about ten miles down
the Ohio from McMahon's, is believed to have prepared the
plats for the Third Range. The remaining plats were very
possibly drawn by Hutchins himself.

Late in January 1787, seven months after his arrival in the
West for a second attempt at surveying, Hutchins departed
from his quarters on the Ohio River. Traveling by way of
Pittsburgh and the Pennsylvania Road, he reached New York
on February 21 with "the Plats and descriptions of four Ranges
completely surveyed into Townships." Hutchins later declared,
in a locution characteristic of the period, that he "flattered
himself that he had performed his duties to the entire satisfaction of Congress."

Hutchins may have vindicated himself to the satisfaction of
congress, but that body had understandably lost faith in the
rectangular land survey system by the spring of 1787. With only
four ranges of townships ready to be advertised for sale after a
lapse of nearly two years, congress was prepared to consider the
sale of large tracts without survey as a means of realizing an
immediate income from the national domain. Finding that

congressional delegates had no intention of supporting surveying beyond the Seven Ranges, Hutchins applied for leave to
fulfill an engagement elsewhere. His request was granted, and
the task of completing the Seven Ranges was left to such of the
surveyors of the preceding year as might be willing to assume
the risks involved in the venture.

First in the field in 1787 were two men who had wintered on
the Ohio River—Absalom Martin and Israel Ludlow. They
went into the woods early in April, and were followed within
two weeks by James Simpson, who had returned to the West
from his home in York County, Pennsylvania. Two other surveyors later appeared on the scene, but these three men had
preempted the surveying which remained to be done.
Throwing caution to the winds, they at first led their survey
parties into the interior without an armed escort, but by the
middle of May they had pulled back and were applying for the
protection of the army.

The surveyors expected aid from a new army post which
seemed ideal to their purposes. This was Fort Steuben, which
had been built on the Ohio River within the First Range and
garrisoned by ninety men during the previous winter. Colonel
Harmar, however, was holding this detachment in readiness for
removal to Vincennes. As a sign of the times, Harmar was more
interested in extending American influence farther down the
Ohio than in accommodating federal land surveyors, but he
responded to their request by sending up sixty men from Fort
Harmar. After making rendezvous at a point opposite
Wheeling, these troops set off with the surveyors to cover them
in the completion of their work.

Within two weeks after resuming operations Israel Ludlow
finished the Seventh Range, striking the Ohio River about seven
miles above the mouth of the Muskingum. Simpson and Martin
brought the Sixth and Fifth ranges, respectively, to completion
soon after, and the escorting troops were able to rejoin their
companies at Fort Harmar before July 10. Although incidents
of scalping and horse-thieving occurred in their vicinity both
during and after this period, the surveyors were untroubled in
their final efforts by Indian marauders.

Records of survey, once again, were prepared at William
McMahon's house on the Virginia shore. Ludlow, Martin, and

Simpson stayed there until the end of August, by which time Ludlow may have been able to complete all of his paper work—both plats and notes—for the Seventh Range. Martin and Simpson were prevented from finishing even their notes for the Fifth and Sixth ranges by the lack of records on hand for surveying done in 1786. After their sojourn at McMahon's the three surveyors made their way to New York, where Hutchins apparently assisted in incorporating the needed earlier data into the records for 1787.

Yet many months still were to pass before final returns would be filed. Martin delayed his work, piqued by the board of treasury's refusal to permit him an extra allowance for "protracting the townships." Hutchins seems to have been diverted by the preparation of a report on the personal surveying assignment which had occupied him during the summer of 1787. After all of the records for the final three ranges were in his hands, Hutchins took additional time to draw up a general plan covering all of the Seven Ranges. At last, on July 26, 1788, Hutchins submitted the general plan and the concluding notes and plats to the board of treasury, and the first phase of United States public land surveying came to an end.

The foundation, so to speak, upon which the Seven Ranges were constructed was the line which Hutchins initiated in 1785, and ran westward in 1786 until caused to flee the field. Called simply the East and West Line at the time of survey, it has come to be known as the Geographer's Line, in honor of Hutchins. In laying it out Hutchins was required by law to determine the latitude of the point of beginning and then to make the line conform to a parallel of latitude.

In meeting the first problem Hutchins took "a great number" of observations on the sun and the North Star, and as a result determined his latitude to be 40° 38' 02" North. He mislocated his position by about 25" of arc, or as measured on the ground, by somewhat less than one-half mile, a magnitude of error which suggests that he employed a sextant, an instrument in common use at that time. The second problem, that of laying down a parallel of latitude, was familiar to Hutchins we can be sure, if only because it is known that he had engaged in extending westward the Mason and Dixon line—a parallel of latitude—in 1784. Whether he attempted to repeat the relatively accurate technique employed in that earlier work or not—and there is strong evidence that to save time he did not—his results were much less satisfactory. The Geographer's Line failed to conform to the proper curve of a parallel of latitude, and it ended fully fifteen hundred feet south of its beginning point.

In laying out township boundaries south of the Geographer's Line the surveyors directed their lines of sight with an instrument called a circumferentor. It was a simple compass, measuring about six inches in diameter, graduated to give readings in degrees, fitted with sight vanes, and mounted by means of a ball and socket upon either a staff ("Jacob's staff") or a tripod. By the time surveying began in earnest, it will be recalled, congress had relieved the surveyors of the necessity of adjusting their lines to "the true meridian." Given this license, the surveyors used the circumferentor's magnetic needle to establish initial direction, and in extending a line they appear to have simply taken a new compass reading at each advance of the instrument. In setting off a right angle at each township corner they almost certainly read directly from the needle instead of turning the angle on the instrument. This was free-style surveying.

In the measurement of distances, approximation again was the rule. The means employed, normal for the period, was a surveyor's chain made of iron wire formed into one hundred straight segments, each segment joined to its neighbor by two rings. The chains were checked for length by Hutchins at the outset of surveying, but their results were far from consistent. While it is well known that such chains were subject to alteration in length through use, a more important source of error was the roughness of the terrain, or, more exactly, the lack of care taken by the surveyors in safeguarding against errors arising therefrom. What with an almost casual determination of distance as well as direction, the surveyed lines generally failed to join satisfactorily at the corners of the townships, as would be expected. The surveyors failed to meet this problem of poor closure, in turn, in any agreed-upon way; they did not regularly complete their townships in one specified corner; and they did not retrace their lines in search of error when a faulty closure occurred.

Inaccuracies in the survey of the Seven Ranges should not be thought of as wholly or even mainly the consequence of an inadequate technology. When the federal rectangular survey system was revived and extended, only about a decade later, distinctly improved results were obtained; and among the sharpest critics of the original surveyors were men who followed after them, with no better instruments, to further subdivide the townships of the Seven Ranges. The work of the original surveyors suffered principally from a lack of regular operating procedures and clearly stated standards of accuracy.

As is well known, the direct contribution of the survey of the Seven Ranges to the settlement of the Northwest Territory was very slight indeed. The first and only sale of land in the Seven Ranges under the land ordinance of 1785 was held in New York City, September 21–October 9, 1787, after an impatient congress had voted to wait for the completion of no more than four ranges of townships, and to offer the parts of those townships not reserved from sale at a central place of auction rather than in the several states, as originally planned. At the sale, land immediately bordering the Ohio River found a fair market, and two townships near the Ohio were sold as whole units, but buyers could not be tempted very far inland nor induced to take up all of the land along the river so long as a minimum price of one dollar per acre, established by law, prevailed. With less than one-third of the land spoken for, the auction was closed. About half of this purchased land was soon forfeited for lack of completed payment, and on the remainder settlement was almost negligible. The single noteworthy extension of the American frontier immediately resulting from this sale occurred on the Ohio a few miles upstream from a point opposite Wheeling late in 1787, when Absalom Martin, official federal surveyor from New Jersey, founded there the settlement known today as Martins Ferry.

To appreciate the indirect and highly important influence of the survey of the Seven Ranges upon the advance of settlement in the Northwest Territory, we must turn our attention to the Ohio Company of Associates, that celebrated organization whose representatives contracted to buy a large tract adjacent to the Seven Ranges a few days after the public auction in New

York was closed. Benefits conferred on this group began in 1785, when General Benjamin Tupper, by adopting the role of surveyor for Massachusetts, found an opportunity for learning at first hand about the route to Pittsburgh and the country downstream from that settlement for a distance of about forty miles. The Ohio Company had not yet been formed, but its prospective organizers, among them Tupper, were known to be comtemplating the founding of a colony. In the summer of 1786, by which time provisional articles of the Ohio Company had been drawn up at a meeting in Massachusetts, federal surveying began to look as though it were specifically meant to serve the exploratory interests of this association. No less than five Ohio Company men, including Tupper, appeared among the surveyors in 1786, and one of them, Winthrop Sargent, detached himself from the rest to reconnoiter the district on the lower Muskingum River which the company was soon to apply for in congress. The fact that this tract of land lay immediately west of the Seven Ranges should not lead one to suppose that Sargent thought of it as an area beyond the scope of federal surveying. Rather, he viewed it at this time as land included within the breadth of the thirteen ranges of townships scheduled for survey in 1786. By 1787, however, the outlook had changed. With only seven ranges of townships begun by the national surveyors, the Ohio Company, apparently impelled by a new determination to obtain land in a single block, threw its influence behind a move in congress to halt any further extension of surveying to the west. Deciding to apply to congress for a direct grant of land, directors of the company declared, "We . . . wish, if possible, to have our eastern bounds on the seventh range of townships." The company succeeded in obtaining a grant with this boundary and went on to conduct township surveying privately, but otherwise in general conformity to the requirements of the land ordinance of 1785. [*See* Map 7.]

In a rather elaborate advertisement of its new purchase, the Ohio Company drew freely upon the opinions and observations of its representatives who had engaged in the survey of the Seven Ranges, a procedure justified by the fact that the Ohio Company lands comprised a continuation of the Allegheny Plateau country wherein the Seven Ranges lay. By way of further reliance upon the federal surveys, this same advertisement exploited the reputation of Thomas Hutchins by including his testimonial that descriptions appearing therein were "judicious, just and true," and consistent with "observations made by me."

Nor did the services rendered to the Ohio Company by the federal surveys end here. In the course of the survey of the Seven Ranges, the army's influence had been brought down the Ohio to the mouth of the Muskingum River, where the Ohio Company's first settlement would soon be made; the Indians had been introduced to the kind of surveying which the Ohio Company would be continuing; and the squatter population of the Ohio country had been confronted by the determination of congress to deny the right of preëmpting land by "tomahawk claim," a legal position which the Ohio Company was resolved to perpetuate.

If the founding of Marietta at the mouth of the Muskingum River by the Ohio Company, in April 1788, is to be accepted as the beginning of organized American settlement in the Northwest Territory, then the Seven Ranges should be recognized with appropriate honor as the bridgehead which made the success of this pioneer venture possible.

The Ordinance of 1784

Robert F. Berkhofer, Jr.

The Ordinance of 1784 marks the beginning of the American territorial system. As such, it has been a subject of considerable interest to historians. Prompting even more interest has been the fact that its authorship has been credited to Thomas Jefferson. Moreover, it has generally been acclaimed a "liberal" document allowing frontier "democracy" in contrast to the "reactionary" Northwest Ordinance of 1784.

These theses permeated historical thought about the Confederation era for over half a century until challenged by Robert Berkhofer (1931 ——) in the past few years. According to Berkhofer, Thomas Jefferson was only one of several Congressmen responsible for the Ordinance, the provisions had been part of congressional thinking for some time before the Sage of Monticello took his seat, and the 1784 Ordinance was not thought of as a final solution but rather as "an incomplete set of resolutions about fundamental principles, . . . while the Northwest Ordinance was a specific system designed to effecuate those principles." His conclusions are largely based upon an investigation of the manuscript journals of the Congress rather than the printed journals in which the sequence of events was confused by the editor.

Berkhofer now teaches at the University of Michigan after a career at Ohio State University, and the Universities of Minnesota and Wisconsin. A man of catholic interests, his writings include Salvation and the Savage: An Analysis of Protestant Missions and American Indian Response *(1965) and* A Behavioral Approach to Historical Analysis *(1969), plus a number of articles dealing with both Native American and frontier history, on the one hand, and historical methodology, on the other.*

From Robert F. Berkhofer, Jr., "Jefferson, the Ordinance of 1784, and the Origins of the American Territorial System," in the *William and Mary Quarterly*, third series, XXIX: 231–262; (April, 1972); reprinted with permission of the author and the *William and Mary Quarterly*.

CURRENT INTERPRETATIONS of the origins of the United States territorial system generally rest upon two fundamental readings of events of the time accepted as fact. Because Jefferson as committee chairman wrote the report that became, as amended by the Continental Congress, the Ordinance of 1784, historians presume he was primarily responsible for the basic governmental policies proclaimed in the document. Therefore they interpret its provisions for new states mainly in light of how they understand his political philosophy. Because the Northwest Ordinance repealed the one of 1784, historians generally portray the latter as a repudiation of the former document specifically and of Jefferson's liberal philosophy in general. Close attention, however, to the chronology of precedents, the evolution of the Ordinance of 1784, and Jefferson's voting record on it challenges the larger role usually attributed to him in the composition of the document. Reexamination of Jefferson's correspondence, the evolution of the Northwest Ordinance, and the opinions of the time raises questions about the relationship between the two ordinances as traditionally ascribed by their leading interpreter. These doubts suggest the need for a newer and more sophisticated history of the origin of the American territorial system.

On March 1, 1784, "the Committee appointed to prepare a plan for the temporary government of the Western territory" presented its report, in the handwriting of Jefferson, to the Continental Congress sitting in Annapolis. It coincided with and was the result of Virginia's cession by deed to Congress of her claim to the territory north and west of the Ohio River. The deed created for the first time a national domain for the "United States in Congress Assembled" to govern and, equally important from the viewpoint of the Confederation treasury, to sell. The deed and the creation of the domain represented the culmination of a long dispute over the Old Dominion's claims to the trans-Appalachian West. Throughout the controversy, but incidental to the main issues, references to the formation of new states in the West served as precedents for Jefferson's report and shaped its main provisions.

Although states other than Virginia also claimed lands in the trans-Appalachian West upon the basis of the vague boundaries stated in their founding charters, no other state's claims embraced so vast a territory as those of the Old Dominion, which included not only the area between the Appalachian Mountains and the Ohio River but also the huge acreage beyond that became known as the Old Northwest. Its very extensiveness made the claim the focus of opposition. Moreover, with seven states "landed" according to charter claims and six "landless," the even balance produced a long drawn out fight that even Virginia's cession in 1784 only partially resolved.

The rhetoric of the controversy focused upon whether Virginia (and by implication other landed states) should retain all rights to the entirety of its claims for its exclusive private advantage or whether, regardless of original charter limits, these lands should benefit all the states fighting the war. Behind the rhetoric lay a diverse set of men and motives on both sides, although both agreed from the beginning upon one principle: whoever controlled the trans-Appalachian West, the area should enjoy new independent governments. As the cession controversy moved through its phases so too did the ideas about the nature of these new governments.

Since the conflict originated in the vagueness of boundaries specified in the colonial charters, the cession dispute was hardly new in 1776. Rather it was in many ways a continuation of the earlier fights among the colonies and their land speculators over rival land claims and political jurisdiction in the trans-Appalachian West. Independence changed the final authority from Parliament to Congress and the official actors from colonies to states. The change shifted concern from how to go about erecting new royal colonies, if any, in the West to whether there would and ought to be new governments in the West as well as what ought to be their nature. The transition in thinking was rapid and may be traced in the documents of 1776.

Although the idea of giving Congress power to limit state boundaries had been discussed earlier in the halls of Congress, the initial draft of the Articles of Confederation first presented the issue officially on July 12, 1776. Composed by John Dickinson from "landless" Pennsylvania, Article XVIII gave Congress the right to limit the boundaries of those states with extended western charter claims. Significantly, he stipulated that Congress would create "new colonies" in these areas "to be established on the Principles of Liberty." Virginians not only opposed in Congress this proposed interpretation of the Confederation's powers but also reasserted their claims in the new state constitution. Jefferson, angered by the attempts to deny his state's sovereignty over the West, was largely responsible for the strong wording of the clause on this subject in the Virginia constitution. In a draft of a proposed constitution for his state, he avowed among other things:

> The western and Northern extent of this country shall in all respects stand as fixed by the charter of [ ] until by act of the Legislature one or more territories shall be laid off Westward of the Alleghaney mountains for new colonies, which colonies shall be established on the same fundamental laws contained in this instrument [i.e., as in Virginia's Constitution], and shall be free and independent of this colony and of all the world.

For Jefferson's strong statement on "new colonies," the Virginia Convention substituted a vaguer wording: the possibility that "one or more Territories shall hereafter be laid off, and Governments established Westward of the *Allegheny* Mountains." Upon learning of this specific provision in their neighboring state's constitution, the Maryland Convention passed unanimously a resolution opposing Virginia's claim to the West and declared that "such lands ought to be considered as a common stock, to be parcelled out at proper times into convenient, free and independent governments." As much as the Maryland and Virginia Conventions differed upon the proper bounds of the Old Dominion, both, however, saw new "governments" arising in the trans-Appalachian West.

After this initial debate, all subsequent references to western governments were in terms of new states rather than colonies—the transition from colonial to independent thinking on the question was completed. Delegates talked about new states when the Articles came up for debate during the next year, and Maryland and other landless states' representatives tried to restore the power of Congress to limit western boundaries. All their efforts failed, and so the final version of the Articles submitted to the states for discussion and ratification in November 1777 followed the wishes of the landed states in regard to boundaries. Without some such provision, however, the

Articles remained unacceptable to Maryland, and by early 1779 she alone remained outside the Confederation.

Resolution of this crisis was to come by means of Virginia's cession of her boundary claims to Congress, because she could cede upon her conditions while Congress gained control of the lands, which was what many of the opposition wanted. In fact, as early as September 1778 a congressional Finance Committee dominated by delegates from landless states suggested such a solution. In its report the committee recommended that Congress call on the several states having "large uncultivated territory" to cede upon certain terms. Among these terms were: "That it be covenanted with the States that the Lands set off shall be erected into separate independent States, to be admitted into the Union, to have a Representation in Congress, and to have free Governments in which no Officers shall be appointed by Congress, other than such as are appointed through the other States." Not until the fall of 1780 did congressmen find a formula acceptable to both sides. On September 6 Congress agreed to a report recommending cession but forbearing to decide on the relative merits of Maryland's and Virginia's claims and counterclaims over the boundary issue. On October 10 Congress further resolved at the behest of the Virginia delegates that all such ceded lands "shall be disposed of for the common benefit of the United States, and be settled and formed into distinct republican states, which shall become members of the federal union, and have the same rights of sovereignty, freedom and independence, as the other states . . . ." The resolution also specified, at Virginia's insistence, "that each state which shall be so formed shall contain a suitable extent of territory, not less than one hundred nor more than one hundred and fifty miles square, or as near thereto as circumstances will admit." This resolution became the basic foundation for subsequent cession and the creation of new states.

Factors other than reports and resolutions, however, caused the Virginia General Assembly to vote on January 2, 1781, to cede all claims northwest of the Ohio River with many conditions attached detrimental to the private land speculators of the landless states. Included in the conditions was the recommendation of October 1780 about the nature and size of the new states. For reasons other than the cession Maryland at long last signed the Articles of Confederation on March 1, 1781. Neither act settled the controversy, for those who opposed Virginia's conditions or hoped to gain territory south of the Ohio River now sought to block congressional acceptance. So successful were they in their tactics that three years were to pass before Congress accepted the cession and thereby created a national domain to sell and to rule. Each side had enough votes to thwart the other's wishes but too few to gain its own ends, and only forces generated by the ending of the war finally brought both cession by Virginia and acceptance by Congress. Both army officers and congressional delegates, with prospects of peace and cession near, discussed the nature of new state goverments in more detail, thereby ushering in the final phase of discussion on the topic before the official report of Jefferson's committee.

A combination of the army officers' specific request for a new state or "colony" in the West and the Virginia condition on the size of new states reached the floor of Congress in mid-1783 by way of Theodorick Bland. As a member of the congressional Finance Committee, which dealt with the so-called Newburgh Conspiracy in the spring, Bland had been concerned about the bounties and back pay owed the army. As a Virginia delegate, he had long fought for congressional acceptance of his state's cession upon her conditions. On June 5, 1783, he combined both ends by moving that Congress accept Virginia's cession in order to finance its promises to the army. As part of his proposal, he requested fellow lawmakers create from the cession a territory of unspecified boundaries and ordain:

> That the said territory shall be laid off in districts not exceeding two degrees of Latitude and three degrees of Longitude each, and each district in townships not exceeding [ ]miles square. . . . That each of the said districts shall, when it contains 20,000 male inhabitants, become and ever after be and constitute a separate, Independent free and Sovereign state, and be admitted into the union as such with the privileges and immunities of those states which now compose the union.

Thus he translated the size of the new states from the Virginia amendment of October 1780 into geographical terms, and he added the number of inhabitants necessary for admission to statehood. All this suggests that Congress may have been considering western government in more specific terms by mid-1783.

Certainly congressmen were discussing new statemaking by the fall of that year. Unfortunately this discussion must be reconstructed solely from the amendments offered during the formulation of postwar Indian policy. George Washington called the interconnection of illegal white settlement, peace with the Indians, and the formation of a new state to the attention of the chairman of the Indian Affairs Committee in a lengthy letter dated September 7, 1783. To maintain peace with the Indians as well as to preserve an orderly, well-regulated white society in the West, Washington recommended the confinement of the unruly frontiersmen to only a portion of the trans-Ohio West. For this purpose, a new state should be established for the white settlers and strict line of separation between red and white men enforced. He also suggested two possible limits for the new state, either a large state embracing Detroit within its bounds or a smaller state. If Congress chose the latter, he thought the remainder of the land that his larger state would have embraced should eventually form a second state.

In accord with Washington's views, the report of the Indian Affairs Committee asked whether Congress should appoint a committee to lay off a new state in the West and devise a plan for its "temporary government." This recommendation led eventually to the appointment of the committee and to Jefferson's report, but congressional debate over this aspect of the Indian report and its implications for the Ordinance of 1784 has been obscured and confused by the particularly bad editing of the report and its amendments in the modern edition of the *Journals of the Continental Congress*. The resultant confusion and scarcity of evidence demand extensive quotation of the relevant portions of the report and the subsequent amendments for clarification.

The Committee on Indian Affairs delivered its report in two parts on two different dates. The original report of September 19 mentioned only the need for a strict separation of Indians and whites, but the idea was not developed to include the possibility of a new state until the further report of September

22. In a long paragraph deserving full quotation, the report followed Washington's reasoning on the unattractive character of frontiersmen and the consequent need for good government and then went on to suggest the appointment of another committee to achieve that purpose:

> And lastly your committee beg leave to observe that they do not offer the measures which they suggested as a sufficient security against the increase of feeble, disorderly and dispersed settlements in those remote and wide extended Territories; against the depravity of manners which they have a tendency to produce, the endless perplexities in which they must involve the administration of the affairs of the United States, or against the calamities of frequent and destructive wars with the Indians which reciprocal animosities, unrestrained by the interposition of legal authority must naturally excite.—Nothing in the opinion of the committee can avert those complicated and impending mischiefs, or secure to the United States the just and important advantages which they ought to derive from those Territories, but the speedy establishment of government and the regular administration of justice in such District thereof as shall be judged most convenient for immediate settlement and cultivation.—Your committee therefore submit it to the consideration, whether it is not wise and necessary that a Committee be appointed to report to Congress on the expediency of laying out a suitable district within the said territory, and of erecting it into a distinct government for the accommodation of such as may incline to become purchasers and inhabitants, as well as for doing justice to the army of the United States who are entitled to lands as bounty or in reward for their services, with instructions to such committee to devise a plan for the temporary government of the inhabitants and the due administration of justice, until their number and circumstances shall entitle them to a place among the States in the Union; when they shall be at liberty, to form a free constitution for themselves not incompatible with the republican principles which are the basis of the constitutions of the respective States in the union. But if Congress conceive it doubtful whether the powers vested by the Instrument of Confederation and perpetual union are competent to the establishment of such government, that then the committee be instructed to prepare and report to Congress a proper address to the respective States for remedying the defects of the said instrument in this respect.

The report ended with Washington's two suggestions for state boundaries. In the minds of committee members, such new states would have to pass through some period of temporary government before achieving permanent government, an idea that received further development during the debate on the second half of the long paragraph.

In the debates on the report what was not amended is as revelatory of congressional thinking on western statemaking as what was amended. The first part of the long paragraph pointing out the desirability of establishing government in the West in light of the nature of the settlement pattern and the character of frontiersmen was never controverted, if lack of amendment reflects lack of discussion. On the other hand, the second part of the paragraph after the second dash was debated extensively on October 14. From the evidence of the journal and the amendment slips in the Papers of the Continental Congress, Elbridge Gerry of Massachusetts offered an amendment apparently to specify more precisely that Congress was solely responsible for the creation of any temporary government in the new state:

> Your committee therefore submit it to consideration, whether it will not be wise and necessary, when the State of Virginia shall close with conditions of Congress in the session of the Western Territory as soon as circumstances shall permit, to erect a part thereof District of the Western Territory into a distinct Government, as well for doing Justice to the Army of the United States, who are entitled to Lands as a Bounty or in reward of their Services, as for the accommodation of such as may incline to become purchasers and Inhabitants, and in the interim to appoint a committee to report a plan, which to be poll [?] consistent with the principles of the Confederation, for connecting with the Union by a temporary Government the said purchasers and Inhabitants of the said District, untill their Number and circumstances shall entitle them to form for themselves a permanent government, [illeg.] permanent constitution for themselves and as citizens of a free sovereign and independent state shall be admitted to a representation in the Union.

Samuel Huntington of Connecticut added a clause to bring Gerry's amendment in line with the stipulations of Congress and the previous conditions of cession: "Provided such Constitution shall not be incompatible with the republican principles which are the basis of the Constitutions of the respective states in the Union." According to the official journal, David Howell of Rhode Island then moved to postpone consideration of the Gerry amendment in favor of his own paragraph allowing the inhabitants of the new state a greater say in their own government:

Y [ou]r Com [mitt]ee recommend it as necessary and expedient as
soon as circumstances will admit to lay off a suitable district within
the said territory and to erect it into a distinct government as well as
for doing justice to the army of the United States, who are entitled to
lands as a bounty or in reward of their services as for the accom-
modation of such as may incline to become purchasers and inhabitants, and for this purpose a com [mitt]ee be appointed ~~with instructions to said committee~~ to devise and report a plan for the
government of the inhabitants and the due administration of justice, which if agreeable to the settlers shall be their ~~form of~~ temporary government until their number and circumstances shall entitle
them to a place among the States in the union; when they shall be at
liberty to form a ~~free~~ constitution for themselves not inconsistent
with the republican principles which are the basis of the constitutions of the republican States in the Union.

Howell's amendment was voted down in favor of Gerry's
amendment by six states to three with three more states insufficiently represented to vote. So the final report as adopted by
Congress and entered upon the journal contains the first half of
the original paragraph before the second dash unchanged and
Gerry's amendment becomes a full second paragraph. The task
of drawing up a plan of temporary government was immediately given to a committee of three. To this committee also
referred the now omitted last part of the original report containing Washington's suggested boundaries.

The process indicates how far congressional thinking had
proceeded in planning the nature and extent of government
for the western territory. All congressmen seemed agreed upon
the necessity, given the nature of frontiersmen, for some form
of good government there. Furthermore, most believed that
Congress should provide such government without consulting
the wishes of the inhabitants. Only five congressmen plus his
fellow Rhode Islander supported Howell's position, while sixteen favored Gerry's position on temporary government. Less
clear from Howell's wording is whether he and his supporters
wished to make any distinction between temporary and permanent government in the new state, but it is certain that those who
followed Gerry did want to provide just such a distinction. In
fact, that reason seems as much behind the Gerry amendment
as his desire to remove the say of the new state's inhabitants in
the planning of their government. Lastly, whether Congress
discussed the number of states is unclear, since Washington's

plan for a single state of whatever size in the beginning was not specifically amended but merely passed along to the new committee.

Only after all this discussion of new statemaking had occurred did Jefferson take his seat in Congress during November 1783. He immediately became chairman of a succession of committees that finally eventuated in the committee to prepare "a plan for the temporary government of the western territory." Also appointed on February 3, 1784, to serve with him were Howell and Jeremiah T. Chase of Maryland. On February 21 committee member Howell, in a long letter to his friend and former congressional colleague, Jonathan Arnold, revealed that the committee had agreed on a report but had not yet presented it to Congress. He then proceeded to give in detail the outline of the report as finally delivered on March 1, the same day on which Congress also formally received the second deed of cession from Virginia. That the report took no more than two and a half weeks for completion during a busy time for all committee members tends to confirm that Congress had discussed western statemaking at length in connection with Indian affairs before Jefferson arrived in Congress. Such certainly was Howell's impression, for he wrote that "the mode of government, during the infancy of these states, has taken up much time, and was largely debated at Princeton last summer." Jefferson reached Princeton just as Congress was preparing to move to Annapolis, so his effective term began at the new location.

Certainly the protracted debate first over cession and then over Indian affairs had dictated the main outlines of the report long before Jefferson arrived on the scene. As a result of the cession controversy, the committee had to operate within a framework that specified the size (and possibly the shape) of the new states, provided for eventual statehood only after some form of temporary government, and required both the temporary and permanent governments to be republican in form. Likewise, the debate over Gerry's and Howell's amendments to the Indian affairs report indicates that congressmen had discussed at some length the possible role of the new settlers' voice in the creation of temporary government. Boundaries had been proposed in the plans of the army officers and in Washington's letter to the Indians Affairs Committee. The subject of prohibiting slavery had come up outside Congress, and the idea of a covenant between Congress and the new states within its chambers. Even the length of time before statehood had been mentioned in a pamphlet by Tom Paine. Thus Jefferson's contribution to the report appears to be less than scholars previously assumed. At the same time, Howell's role may have been greater than merely remembering the congressional debates prior to Jefferson's arrival. Detailed consideration of the report's content and the votes on amendments points further in this direction and enables us to speak more clearly about Jefferson's and Howell's roles. [For Jefferson's proposed states north of the Ohio River, *see* Map 6.]

Regardless of their roles or the previous discussion, the report of March 1, 1784, was the first detailed plan for western government the Congress considered and recorded. The very first resolution fulfilled both the promise made by Congress in event of cession and one of Virginia's conditions for cession: "Resolved, that the territory ceded or to be ceded by Individual states to the United states shall be formed into distinct states. . . ." The remainder of the paragraph specified the boundaries of the proposed states. Each state would extend two degrees of latitude from north to south counting from thirty-one degrees northward. Parallels drawn through the Falls of the Ohio and the mouth of the Great Kanawha River would determine east to west dimensions.

Probably this paragraph contained Jefferson's main contribution to the report. His ideas had evolved from previous proposals for creating only one or two states to forming six to fourteen or more, including, as a result, lands still unceded. As Julian Boyd has pointed out, his originality lay in delineating boundaries on both ceded and yet to be ceded lands. He also showed boldness in recommending immediate division into the full number of states required by the Virginia amendment of October 10, 1780. Thus he rejected the possibility of preliminary government in one or more territories before drawing state boundaries, as Washington and others had suggested.

Jefferson's boundaries included lands south of the Ohio River still claimed by Georgia and North and South Carolina as well as by Virginia. He now advocated that his state should cede more than it already had and incorporated that belief in the report. Even before the report was presented to Congress or the deed executed, he urged James Madison: "For god's sake push this at the next session of assembly."In explanation he argued, "It is for the interest of Virginia to cede so far immediately; because the people beyond that will separate themselves, because they will be joined by all our settlements beyond the Alleghaney if they are the first movers." In a letter to George Washington during debate on the report, he expressed his thoughts even more succinctly: "I hope our country [Virginia] will of herself determine to cede still further to the meridian of the mouth of the Great Kanhaway. Further she cannot govern; so far is necessary for her own well being."

These sentences hint at the reasoning behind Jefferson's proposed geography for the West. The fear of western separation derived from larger considerations of political ideology common to the leaders of the period. For governments to remain republican, he and others believed the size of the state must be small enough to preserve the homogeneity of the interests, opinions, and habits of the citizens; otherwise a stronger, more centralized government than desirable for republicanism would be needed to extend its influence to the far corners of the state. The larger the territory of a government, the more likely that it would embrace diverse interests as a result of different climates and economic concerns. Accordingly, trans-Appalachian settlers would probably break away from eastern control in general and Virginia governance in particular, because they would have different interests from those of the inhabitants on the eastern seaboard. Furthermore, the limited force that a republican government would presumably exert could not possibly reach settlers so far removed from the center of that government. For its own good government as well as that of the trans-Appalachian West, therefore, Virginia ought to cede all territory beyond that which she could govern according to republican ideals of maintaining a homogeneity of interests among the state's population. Such reasoning prompted the original Virginia restriction that states should be no larger than one hundred fifty miles square. Later, in protesting James Monroe's alteration of his proposed state sizes, Jefferson advanced the same reasons for retaining small states.

Small states, in sum, guaranteed the economic and political basis essential to republicanism, for the old states no less than the new ones.

When Jefferson set forth specific boundaries for the new states, however, he violated the sizes stipulated in Virginia's conditions of cession and in the instructions to his committee. According to the maps of the time, particularly one by Thomas Hutchins that Jefferson probably thought most trustworthy, only the states between the meridians of the Great Kanawha and the Falls of the Ohio reasonably approximated the stipulated size. Even they approached the maximum, for they were approximately two degrees latitude by three degrees longitude or roughly 140 by 150 miles. The states between the Falls of the Ohio and the Mississippi generally exceeded the maximum, measuring approximately two by five or six degrees or roughly 140 by 250 or more miles. One may guess that Jefferson deliberately violated the stipulated areas for geopolitical considerations. As Howell explicated the geography of the report, "There are to be three tiers of states:—One on the Atlantic [original thirteen], one on the Mississippi, and a middle tier. The middle tier is to be the smallest, and to form a balance betwixt the two more powerful ones." Jefferson selected his meridian lines for the abstract idea of balance and from fear of conflict between large and small states. He further selected the Great Kanawha as one of the lines, because it provided for the separation of Kentucky that its residents had already threatened and yet gave Virginia access to the western trade by potential canal route from the Ohio River along the Great Kanawha and James Rivers. All in all, the proposed boundaries constituted nothing less than a grand plan for the entire trans-Appalachian West according to Jefferson's ideological geography and his perception of Virginia's interests.

For governing the new settlers, the report established a series of stages, as Howell termed them, from temporary to permanent government to statehood and admission to Congress. The "first stage" allowed the settlers of any new state upon their own petition or by the authority of Congress to meet together to form a "temporary government" by adopting the constitution and laws of one of the original states. When the population of a new state reached twenty thousand free inhabitants, the settlers entered the second stage by receiving authority from Congress to call a convention "to establish a permanent constitution and government for themselves." Admission of delegates from a new state to Congress was possible when the number of its free inhabitants equaled that of the least populated original state, provided two-thirds of the states in Congress consented. Until that time any new state could, after establishment of temporary government, send a delegate to Congress with the right to debate but not to vote.

Though the report distinguished between temporary and permanent government according to the Gerry amendment to the committee's instructions, participation of the settlers in their own governance was definitely more in the spirit of Howell's attempted amendment, as the wording of the provision for the initial stage of government indicated:

> That the settlers within any of the said states shall, either on their own petition, or on the order of Congress, receive authority from them, with appointments of time and place for their free males of full age to meet together for the purpose of establishing a temporary government, to adopt the constitution and laws of any one of these [original] states, so that such laws nevertheless shall be subject to alteration by their ordinary legislature, and to erect, subject to a like alteration, counties or townships for the election of members for their legislature.

Certainly Howell in his long letter to Arnold interpreted these provisions as giving the settlers the initiative in establishing and participating fully in each stage of government.

Scholars have long wondered why the report denied to the settlers the privilege of naming their states if they were granted self-government from the beginning. Again Howell seems to supply the clue, for in his explication of the first stage of government he observed that "settlers will always readily know in which of the states they are, for the states are to be named as well as numbered. . . ." The report named the states, but Jefferson had a map in Paris with the new states numbered. Whether specified as Michigania, Cherronesus, Assinisipia, Pelisipia, and six other classical and patriotic names as in the report or merely located by number, the inference is obvious: such a device seemed necessary precisely to facilitate self-government. Settlers would know exactly, by name or by number, in which little republic they lived, so they could go more quickly about the business of erecting governments. [*See* Map 6.]

The report stipulated five provisos for both temporary and permanent governments. They, like other parts of the report, appeared consistent with much of previous congressional thinking. That the new states "shall for ever remain a part of the United states of America" appears the very reason for the existence of the report, as does the vague wording of the second condition: "That in their persons, property and territory they [the governments] shall be subject to the government of the United states in Congress assembled, and to the Articles of confederation in all those cases in which the original states shall be so subject." The plight of the Confederation treasury and the pressures that generated compromise over cession seem adequate to explain the stipulation that new states pay their share of federal debts, but the long argument over the original states' obligations in financing the Confederation probably reinforced the point. The first part of proviso four, "that their respective governments shall be in republican forms," copied the wording of a number of congressional resolutions and the Virginia cession deed, but the prohibition upon the new states admitting to citizenship a person holding a hereditary title was probably original with Jefferson. He certainly felt strongly upon the subject, especially about the dangers to republicanism of the secret Society of Cincinnati as he indicated when he explained to Washington why Congress later dropped the provision. The prohibition of slavery in any of the new states after 1800, which Timothy Pickering had proposed earlier, was a reform as dear to Howell as to Jefferson.

The last paragraph of the report formed the covenant suggested by the finance committee in 1778:

That the preceding articles shall be formed into a Charter of Compact[,] shall be duly executed by the President of the U. S. in Congress assembled under his hand and seal of the United States, shall be promulgated, and shall stand as fundamental constitutions between the thirteen original states, and those now newly described, unalterable but by the joint consent of the U. S. in Congress assembled and of the particular state within which such alteration is proposed to be made.

No stronger form of language existed at the time to convince the settlers of newer states that Congress intended to carry out its part of the bargain promised in the plan for government in return for their remaining in the Confederation. If the settlers followed the rules outlined, then Congress promised eventual statehood in the union on a par with the original states.

Essentially, then, the report embraced five aspects: a delineation (or bounding) and naming of the proposed states, provisions for the creation of temporary and permanent governments, a set of provisos upon which these governments were to be formed, and a charter of compact. In many ways, the document appears a recapitulation of the original states' political evolution with a colonial agent, taxation without and then with representation, and finally admission to statehood upon attaining a free population equal to that of the least populous original state. The report intended to guarantee the success of republicanism, even to the extent of requiring, during the period of temporary government, the selection of a constitution from one of the original states. It assured the union of the Confederation through the document itself, especially by the promise embodied in the compact. Just how consciously this process imitated the political growth of the colonies into states and confederation must be left to another place.

Debate upon the document proceeded in two phases. The report, according to Secretary Charles Thomson's endorsement, was delivered March 1, read March 3, assigned for consideration March 8, and recommitted March 17. A revised report, again in the handwriting of Jefferson, was delivered and read March 22. From a comparison of the two reports we can tell what was in dispute during the period. The main change was omission of the state names. Subsequent debate suggests that the deletion reflected opposition to the settlers' participation in temporary government, for without self-government at the beginning, the new states need not be designated by name. Another change was the first of many that sought to fix exactly the number of states which had to consent to the admission of a new state as the Confederation enlarged.

It was, however, during consideration of the second report from April 19–23 that Congress revealed in its journal basic disagreements and made major alterations. Soon after debate began Jefferson lost two of his cherished reforms which had been written into the provisos. On the first day the clause prohibiting slavery came under immediate attack. Jefferson and Howell voted for retention of the clause as did all the delegates north of the Mason-Dixon Line, but those from Maryland and South Carolina plus Jefferson's colleagues from Virginia voted for striking the clause. Since North Carolina's representatives divided and New Jersey was insufficiently represented, the antislavery forces lacked but one state of attaining their goal. The next day the delegates struck by a large vote the clause withholding citizenship to persons claiming hereditary titles. As Jefferson explained the defeat to Madison, congressmen did not approve of such honors but they thought the ordinance "an improper place to encounter them."

Obvious concern about the relationship between Congress and the new state governments prompted considerable change in the number and order of the provisos. The ambiguous second proviso gave much trouble in phrasing. In original form, it read: "That in their persons, property and territory they shall be subject to the government of the United states in Congress assembled, and to the Articles of confederation in all those cases in which the original states shall be so subject." Apparently in debate unrecorded in the Journal of Congress, the words "in their persons, property and territory" were deleted. On April 20, the Connecticut representatives moved to simplify the proviso further, leaving it to read simply: "That they shall be subject . . . to the articles of Confederation in all those cases in which the original States shall be so subject." Both Jefferson and Howell voted with Gerry and the majority to adopt this wording; Chase voted against the motion. Subsequently, and again in unrecorded debate, Congress added some words to the end: "and to all the Acts and Ordinances of the United States in Congress assembled conformable thereto." And so what Congress had once voted down, it restored later in another guise.

This teeter-totter of wording probably reflected the course of debate on the degree of congressional authority over the new states as well as on the changing nature of the first stage of government. That it related to the latter question is indicated by the motion to alter even the wording of the heading for all the provisos by striking "temporary and" from the introductory sentence of the section, which read: "Provided that both the temporary and permanent governments be established on these principles as their basis." But only the two sponsors favored such an alteration, and so the words remained. That the argument over the second proviso involved the relationship of congressional authority to the new state governments may be seen in the nature of other provisos added during debate.

Interestingly enough, Jefferson seconded Elbridge Gerry's motion to add another proviso, "That the lands and improvements thereon of non-resident proprietors, shall in no case be taxed higher than those of residents within any new State" before admission into Congress. Howell opposed this attempt to benefit absentee owners and speculators by moving to delete "and improvements thereon." Jefferson with Gerry and Chase and the majority of delegates opposed Howell's motion, but he won because South Carolina's delegates divided. Howell then attempted to amend the wording further by striking that portion of the proviso limiting its effect to the period before statehood but lost overwhelmingly, with Jefferson, Chase, and Gerry all opposing him once again. Finally, on a vote to agree to Gerry's original motion with Howell's first deletion, seven states voted yes, two no, and two divided. In this final tally, Jefferson along with Chase and Gerry voted in favor of prohibiting discriminatory taxation while Howell disapproved the whole proviso.

Thus, by the end of this aspect of the debate, the number, the order, and the content of the provisos upon which the new states' temporary and permanent governments were to be formed had undergone considerable change in the direction of specifying the rights of the Confederation over new state governments. The same tendency also appeared in two additional provisos adopted without record of debate. In the final draft the third proviso prohibited state governments from interfering with prior disposal of the land by Congress or with its conveyance of title to purchasers. The fifth proviso forbade a tax on the lands owned by the federal government.

The climax of the debate came in discussion of the extent of congressional control over settlers before and during the period of temporary government. On April 22 Elbridge Gerry

offered and Jefferson seconded a motion to revise the wording
of the report's paragraph on the subject to read:

> That on the petition of the settlers on any territory so purchased of
> the Indians, or otherwise obtained and sold to individuals, or on the
> order of Congress, authority may be given by Congress with ap-
> pointment of time and place, for all free males of full age, being
> citizens of the United States, and owning lands or residing within
> the limits of their state, to meet together for the purpose of
> establishing a temporary government. . . .

Although Gerry apparently meant to bring the wording in line
with a concurrent Indian affairs report, his motion opened old
wounds from the conflict between landed and landless states
over cession and revived the argument over the original instructions to Jefferson's committee. Five states divided in voting with
only four solidly aye and two nay. The negative votes cast by
Howell and Chase as opposed to Jefferson's aye indicates the
solidarity of the landless states more than who opposed Gerry's
instructions in committee.

With congressmen so divided, Jacob Read of South Carolina
moved to place the settlers under magistrates and laws selected
solely by Congress until the stage of permanent government
was reached. All three members of the committee plus Gerry
voted for this imposition of congressional authority before and
during temporary government. Although three state delegations divided and New Jersey was still insufficiently represented
to vote, the motion failed to pass by only one state, since six
states voted in favor. Thus compromise was indicated, and so
two days later Gerry offered a new paragraph to be inserted
before the final charter of compact: "That such measures as
may from time to time be necessary not inconsistent with the
principles of the confederation are reserved for and shall be
taken by Congress to preserve peace and good order among the
settlers in any of the new States, previous to their assuming a
temporary government as aforesaid." Read again wished to
substitute for this amendment his earlier one to impose congressional officials and laws upon the settlers before and during
the first stage. Only the two landless states of Maryland and
Pennsylvania voted solidly for it this time, but other delegates
favored Read's motion. Howell and Jefferson sided with the
majority against the substitution. According to Boyd, Jefferson

brought forth at this moment the needed substitute compromise amendment, although Gerry received credit for it in the official journal. As finally adopted, it read: "That measures not inconsistent with the principles of the Confederation, and necessary for the preservation of peace and good order among the settlers in any of the said new states, until they shall assume a temporary government as aforesaid, may from time to time, be taken by the United States in Congress assembled." Thus did the argument come around half circle to the original report.

These reversals in position during the debate indicate that congressmen were unsure just how much autonomy they should allow frontiersmen in setting up their own initial governments and how much authority Congress should retain in selecting magistrates and adopting laws, especially before but also during the stage of temporary government. Jefferson's and Howell's vacillation in voting on these two positions proves that they too shared their colleagues' uncertainty. The record shows clearly that both agreed to the strict imposition of congressional authority over the settlers before the organization of permanent government as well as the vaguer, final compromise on authority before temporary government.

More significant than the two men's vacillation, or that of all congressmen, was the remarkable continuity in the controversy from Gerry's and Howell's amendments to the Indian affairs report to the final compromise. Throughout the entire debate the basic alternatives remained the same. Only individuals' specific positions varied at different times. At best, one can only conclude that the final vote and wording was but one point in a continuing debate not yet resolved and that neither Jefferson nor Howell had decided at this particular moment upon the final disposition of the matter any more than had their colleagues in Congress. That this was the case gains added confirmation from the subsequent evolution of the Northwest Ordinance.

Having decided upon the final wording of the paragraph on the extent of congressional authority before the formation of the first stage of government, Congress adopted on April 23, 1784, the amended report as a formal ordinance with all but one state favoring passage. As the New Hampshire delegates explained, because of the conditions of the Virginia cession and the extent of territory involved, establishment of government for the West created "much difficulty" for Congress. In particular, the changed order of the provisos and their contents and the new paragraph on congressional authority inserted before the charter of compact manifested this difficulty. These and other changes tended to establish greater congressional control over the new states before admission to Congress and particularly before the period of temporary government. On the other hand, delegates left major portions of the original report unrevised and presumably did not debate or question them. Although the provisions for the first stage of government received extensive debate, those for the second stage went undiscussed. Neither was there dispute over the population requirement for statehood or the principle of admitting new states into Congress, but congressmen spent much time in wording the exact procedure for admission. The charter of compact and the provisos stipulating that the new states must remain part of the Confederation and maintain republican governments continued into the final ordinance untouched by revision. Similarly, the proviso on sharing the federal debt appeared unchanged in the final ordinance.

Both the altered and unaltered wording and the votes on the various versions provide inferential evidence about the authorship of the original report. Items not discussed imply fundamental agreement upon those aspects of statemaking and perhaps suggest that Congress had considered them before Jefferson's arrival. Absence of debate upon the number of stages in the formation of government and the transition points of each stage likewise hints at previous discussion and perfection of these aspects of the plan before Jefferson took his seat. The continuity in the positions initially represented by Gerry's and Howell's amendments to the Indian affairs report upon the relationship of Congress to the new states and its authority over their inhabitants before statehood shows that Jefferson joined sides already formed upon the issue. Since he voted with Gerry rather than Howell when there was a division of opinion among the two men, one may conclude that he viewed the West and frontiersmen more as did the delegate from Massachusetts than the one from Rhode Island. Moreover, a comparison of his votes with those of Chase and Howell implies he acted as the balance wheel between the two men in preparing the original committee report. Although he shared Howell's outlook more consistently than Chase's, Jefferson did not agree entirely with Howell on congressional authority over the new settlers. Thus we must conclude that the report of March 1, 1784, resulted as much from previous congressional discussion as translated by Jefferson and especially Howell as from the original ideas of the statesman from Virginia.

Not even Jefferson's originality in bounding and naming the new states survived untouched by congressional revision. When Congress moved to assert greater authority over the frontiersmen during initial settlement, the interesting names proposed by Jefferson were no longer necessary to facilitate early participation in self-government and were accordingly struck. Congress retained Jefferson's idea of planning for states to be formed from lands yet to be ceded as well as those already ceded, but it reversed his order of determining latitudinal boundaries in order to avoid appearing to count chicks before they hatched. Instead of fixing boundaries at two degree intervals northward from thirty degrees latitude, the final ordinance specifies that the counting proceed southward from forty-five degrees. Perhaps the change accommodated the feelings of landed states which had yet to cede their claims. Thus the final version of the Ordinance of 1784 retains the basic pattern of Jefferson's geography at the expense of eliminating its two boldest elements. This congressional rebuff to his grand scheme of ideological geography for the West did not prevent Jefferson from drafting an elaborate plan for the disposition of the public domain before he left for France as ambassador. After his departure, Congress adjourned in June 1784, and so the fate of his political ideology as embodied in the restricted size of new states and the land system as well as in the whole ordinance for western government remained in the hands of future congressmen.

The man chiefly responsible for the two major differences between the Ordinances of 1784 and 1787 was Jefferson's young friend James Monroe. He was the first to propose altering the size and number of the states in the West in order that there would be two to five large ones, just as he served as chairman of the committee that produced the first report in a long series that provided a new scheme of temporary and permanent government for those states. Under this plan the inhabitants were to be governed from the beginning of settlement by a governor and secretary, a council of five members, and a court of five judges—all appointed by Congress—under laws of one of the original states. In the new second stage, the people would be governed by their own elected assembly with a governor and council appointed by Congress. During this period the governor could convene, prorogue, or dissolve the assembly at will. Only during this second stage could the territory have a non-voting delegate to Congress. Permanent government based on principles of the inhabitants' choice came only with statehood and admission into Congress. With some changes these proposals regarding the number of states and the nature of the stages survived long debate to become the basis of the Ordinance of 1787.

As was his wont, Monroe reported his activities to his friend in France. After summarizing the new scheme of government proposed by his committee, Monroe concluded that "the most important principles of the act at Annapolis [Ordinance of 1784] are you observe preserv'd in this report." Apparently Jefferson agreed with Monroe's point, for he did not complain in his reply or subsequently about the arbitrary nature of the government provided during the first stage under his fellow Virginian's plan or under the Ordinance of 1787. All the letters usually cited by historians to prove Jefferson's opposition to the extension of congressional authority during the early stages of government, when read in the context of his ideological geography, refer more to the proposed alteration in the size of the new states than to the nature of their government. His reply to Monroe seems ambiguous on this point until read in its entirety:

> With respect to the new states were the question to stand simply in this form, How may the ultramontane territory be disposed of so as to produce the greatest and most immediate benefit to the inhabitants of the maritime states of the union? the plan would be more plausible of laying it off into two or three states only. Even on this view however there would still be something to be said against it which might render it at least doubtful. But it is a question which good faith forbids us to receive into discussion. This requires us to state the question in it's just form, How may the territories of the

Union be disposed of so as to produce the greatest degree of happiness to their inhabitants? With respect to the Maritime states nothing, or little remains to be done. With respect then to the Ultramontane states, will their inhabitants be happiest divided into states of 30,000 square miles, not quite as large as Pennsylvania, or into states of 160,000 square miles each, that is to say three times as large as Virginia within the Alleghaney? They will not only be happier in states of a moderate size, but it is the only way in which they can exist as a regular society. Considering the American character in general, that of those people particularly, and the inergetic nature of our governments, a state of such extent as 160,000 square miles would soon crumble into littles ones. These are the circumstances which reduce the Indians to such small societies. They would produce an effect on our people similar to this. They would not be broken into such small pieces because they are more habituated to subordination, and value more a government of regular law. But you would surely reverse the nature of things in making small states on the ocean and large ones beyond the mountains. If we could in our consciences say that great states beyond the mountains will make the people happiest, we must still ask whether they will be contented to be laid off into large states? They certainly will not; and if they decide to divide themselves we are not able to restrain them. They will end by separating from our confederacy and becoming it's enemies. We had better then look forward and see what will be the probable course of things. This will surely be a division of that country into states of a small, or at most of a moderate size. If we lay them off into such, they will acquiesce, and we shall have the advantage of arranging them so as to produce the best combinations of interest. What Congress has already done in this matter is an argument the more in favour of the revolt of those states against a different arrangement, and of their acquiescience under a continuance of that. Upon this plan we treat them as fellow citizens. They will have a just share in their own government, they will love us, and pride themselves in an union with us. Upon the other we treat them as subjects, we govern them, and not they themselves; they will abhor us as masters, and break off from us in defiance. I confess to you that I can see no other turn that these two plans would take, but I respect your opinion, and your knowlege of the country too much, to be over confident in my own.

In the context of the full paragraph, the conclusion refers to the difference between his plan and Monroe's in terms of the size of states with its long-run implication for republican governments more than the imposition of arbitrary colonial government at the beginning of settlement. Separation would come from the different interests of the settlers beyond the mountains and from their character as frontiersmen, not from the type of government provided by Congress during the initial period of settlement. From Jefferson's point of view, large states increased the probability of diverse interests in a state while the tendency of frontiersmen to disobey any government derived from the wildness of their physical environment. Geography and his view of man's self-interest, not governmental arrangements, lay at the base of his criticism of Monroe's plan.

Jefferson's ideological geography and not the mode of initial government explained his opposition to subsequent developments, too, as when he raised the same issue of state size in discussing the threatened closing of the Mississippi to western commerce:

> I find Congress have reversed their division of the Western states, and proposed to make them fewer and larger. This is reversing the natural order of things. A tractable people may be governed in large bodies; but in proportion as they depart from this character, the extent of their government must be less. We see into what small divisions the Indians are obliged to reduce their societies. This measure, with the disposition to shut up the Missisipi give me serious apprehensions of the severance of the Eastern and Western parts of our confederacy. It might have been made the interests of the Western states to remain united with us, by managing their interests honestly and for their own good. But the moment we sacrifice their interests to our own, they will see it better to govern themselves. The moment they resolve to do this, the point is settled. A forced connection is neither our interest nor within our power.

His fear of separation makes sense only in terms of his assumptions about the geographical determination of men's interests and the necessity for founding republican government upon a population of homogeneous interests and therefore living in a small area.

That Jefferson should disregard the question of arbitrary government was as natural as his spirited defense of his primary contribution to the Ordinance of 1784. The first stage under Monroe's plan provided for a system of government during the period before the formation of temporary government under the Ordinance of 1784 that was consistent with the congressional resolution that Jefferson, Howell, and others supported during the debates upon the original report. Such was Congress's thinking as represented by the new paragraph inserted in the final version of the 1784 ordinance. Thus Monroe's plan apparently seemed to him and to other congressmen an extension and clarification of the basic policy adopted by Congress in the earlier ordinance. The first statement of such a view occurred in May 1785, in the report of an Indian Affairs Committee of which Monroe was chairman. Discussing the reasons for administering an oath of allegiance to the people in the Illinois country, the committee argued:

> The State of Virginia having also relinquished her right of jurisdiction, and no government being as yet established over the said Inhabitants and settlers upon the principles of the resolutions of the 23ᵈ. of April 1784, they are of Course free from any express engagements or allegiance to the Union whatever. The Committee considering it as highly improper, that any body of Men should inhabit any part of the territory within the United States without acknowledging its authority; suggest that the [Indian] Commissioners be instructed to administer to the said Inhabitants an Oath of allegiance or fidelity. . . .

The same notion lay behind Monroe's interpretation of his committee's task of considering the extension of government over the whole of the Old Northwest because of illegal American settlement there. "It will be determin'd," Monroe stated, "what authority Congress will exercise over the people who may settle within the bounds of either of the new Sta[tes] previous to the establishment of a temporary government, whether they will leave them to themselves or appoint majistrates over them." In the mind of Monroe the vexatious problem of congressional authority over the initial settlements in the new states—one that went back to the Gerry and Howell amendments in 1783—had not been resolved in mid-1786. Thus it is apparent why Monroe considered the plan of temporary government proposed by his committee not a violation of "the most important principles" of the Ordinance of 1784, but an extension plugging a loophole in his friend's report that had long posed a perplexing problem to Congress.

Monroe's terminology suggests, moreover, that the Ordinance of 1784 was merely a framework of general rules for the establishment of government in the West and that a specific system had yet to be worked out by further congressional action. Jefferson presented a somewhat similar view of the ordinance in discussing the defects of the Articles of Confederation in the *Encyclopédie Methodique* (1786). He pointed out the need for a general rule for the admission of new states into the Union in the following words: "It becomes necessary to agree what districts may be established into separate states, and at what period of their population they may come into Congress. The act of Congress of April 23, 1784, has pointed out what ought to be agreed on." In this view of the matter, the Ordinance of 1784 represented an incomplete set of resolutions about fundamental principles, or a policy statement, while the Northwest Ordinance was a specific system designed to effectuate those principles. That the latter in accomplishing this implementation moved in the direction of more arbitrary government during the early settlement of the new states meant it followed a trend already well established during the evolution of the Ordinance of 1784 and reflected the political currents of the day toward centralization of government.

Such an interpretation clarifies the legal status of the 1784 Ordinance before the Northwest Ordinance repealed it. The debate has revolved about its application: whether the 1784 Ordinance was or could have been applied to the Old Northwest before the subsequent ordinance superseded it. Thus historians have concerned themselves mainly with how Indian occupation and English influence prevented settlement by many Americans and, more importantly, establishment of congressional jurisdiction over the region. Essentially, then, the issue of legal status is phrased in terms of whether the United States in Congress Assembled exercised de facto control in addition to de jure title in the Old Northwest. According to this view, to the degree that Congress possessed and asserted actual authority, then the 1784 Ordinance was in effect. Although such reasoning may be relevant to the larger history of the ordinance, it is beside the point insofar as its legal status is concerned. It fails to consider the nature of the ordinance as conceived by congressmen of the time. That status was, I argue, a statement of principles that required passage of a more specific system to implement its resolutions on the early phases of settlement in the new states. To the extent that the 1787 Ordinance provided such a system for the principles of 1784, it was an extension of congressional thinking embodied in the original report of Jefferson's committee and the earlier ordinance. Insofar as it duplicated provisions of the 1784 document, it made the previous one unnecessary. To the degree that the Northwest Ordinance created new provisions for the governance of western settlers, it superseded the other ordinance.

For all these reasons, the Northwest Ordinance repealed the set of resolutions passed on April 23, 1784. Thus the 1787 document should be considered more an extension and replacement than a repudiation of the Ordinance of 1784, and the process of transition is best studied in light of the slow evolution of the two documents. No one man was primarily responsible for either document, and consensus upon basic republican goals and principles explains the contents of the two ordinances as much as conflict over the application of those ideas to western inhabitants. That substantial differences exist between the provisions of the two ordinances is undeniable, but these dissimilarities should not obscure the fundamental ideas and attitudes pervading both documents or the consistency of the trend to greater Confederation control over the territories in the period 1783–1784 as well as in the years between then and the adoption of the Northwest Ordinance.

The Compromise of 1787

Staughton Lynd

The coincidental enactment of the Ordinance of 1787 and the drafting of the Constitution involved several issues of momentous import to the young republic. Paramount among these are the questions of territorial development and the protection of slavery. In the first instance particular importance was attached to the population necessary for statehood, the number of potential new states, and the viability of slavery in the West. The latter question affected upon the whole issue of slavery protection which also involved the protection of property in slaves, the continued importation of Africans, and the computation of slaves in the determination of congressional seats in the House of Representatives.

In this article Staughton Lynd (1929——) advances the thesis that the two events of 1787—the Ordinance and the Constitution—involved intercommunications between delegates to both Congress and the Convention which resulted in what he calls the Compromise of 1787. He argues that the South expected to exert influence in the Northwest because southerners would dominate migration there, that the Ordinance implied slavery would be allowed south of the Ohio and prohibited north of it, and that the provisions for speedy admission of western states would bring southern control in the House of Representatives in a few years. Northerners received a prohibition on slavery in the Northwest and the restriction that only three to five states would be created from the region. If kept at three, eastern control of the Senate would continue.

At the convention, southerners received the protection of the fugitive slave clause, they compromised to allow three-fifths of the slaves to be counted for the purpose of representation in the House, and they agreed to a minimum of twenty years before slave importation could be stopped. Both the three-fifths compromise and the twenty-year limit represented a moderate position for eastern interests. Strangely, Lynd does not develop the possibility that the Ohio Company, Scioto Company, and the Symmes purchases might have been part of his compromise.

Lynd is one of the most controversial historians in America. A leader in the "New Left" movement of the 1960's, he and his wife Alice are now doing legal work with workers in the Chicago area. Their most recent publication is an edited collection of interviews, Rank and File:

Personal Histories by Working-Class Organizers *(1974)*.
*Staughton Lynd previously taught American history at Yale University
and Spelman College. In addition to* Class Conflict, Slavery, and the
United States Constitution *(1967), which includes the article here
reprinted, he has written* Intellectual Origins of American Radi-
calism *(1968), and other books.*

* *

On JULY 12, 1787, the Constitutional Convention, meeting
in Philadelphia, adopted the three-fifths compromise regarding apportionment of the House of Representatives. On
July 13 the Continental Congress, meeting in New York City,
adopted the Northwest Ordinance. The three-fifths compromise sanctioned slavery more decidedly than any previous
action at a national level. The Ordinance, on the other hand,
was in Ulrich Phillips' words "the first and last antislavery
achievement by the central government in the period." The
Ordinance has become a symbol of the Revolution's liberalism,
while the compromise, if not a covenant with death and an
agreement with hell, is at least a dramatic instance of its pragmatic conservatism. Why did Congress and Convention act so
differently? The answer to this question, could it be found,
would surely throw much light upon the troubled relation
between the Founding Fathers and the peculiar institution.

Apart from the coincidence of dates, two circumstances make
this problem still more intriguing. One is that the Continental
Congress, at the time it adopted the Ordinance, was controlled
by the South. Its temporary president was a Southerner (William Grayson of Virginia); three of the committee of five which
drafted the Ordinance were Southerners (Richard Henry Lee
and Edward Carrington of Virginia, John Kean of South Carolina); and a Congress with a Southern majority adopted the
Ordinance with a single dissenting vote (by a Northerner,
Abraham Yates of New York). Why these Southern delegates

From Staughton Lynd, "The Compromise of 1787, "in the *Political Science Quarterly*,
LXXXI: 225–250 (June, 1966); reprinted without footnotes with permission from the
Political Science Quarterly.

voted to ban slavery in the Northwest puzzled Nathan Dane of Massachusetts at the time, and has remained a puzzle to historians. Thus B. A. Hinsdale commented that an antislavery clause "had been rejected by Southern men when Mr. Jefferson first brought it forward, and now five of the eight States present are Southern States and eleven of the eighteen men Southern men, and it prevails." Southern support for the Ordinance must puzzle us still more when we set it side-by-side with the determined defense of slavery at the Convention by Deep South delegates such as William Davie of North Carolina and the entire South Carolina group: Pierce Butler, the Pinckneys, and John Rutledge.

A second, less familiar circumstance which thickens the mystery surrounding these events of mid-July is that a number of men were members of both Congress and Convention, and communication between the two bodies was apparently frequent and full. Members of Congress in 1787 who were also named delegates to the Convention were Gorham and King of Massachusetts, Johnson of Connecticut, Blount of North Carolina, Few and Pierce of Georgia, and James Madison of Virginia, who went directly from New York to Philadelphia in early May. A number of men traveled back and forth between the two cities while the Convention was in session. William Pierce returned to New York, where he remained from June 14 to June 18, just after discussion of the rule of representation had begun in Philadelphia, and according to Nathan Dane spoke freely of sectional conflicts at the Convention. Blount and his fellow North Carolinian, Benjamin Hawkins visited Philadelphia from June 19 to July 2, returning to Congress when work on the Northwest Ordinance began. At the same time Pierce again came back from Philadelphia to New York along with his fellow Georgian, Few, like himself a member of both bodies. Others, who, although not members of both groups, very likely carried news from one to the other, included Gouverneur Morris, a Convention delegate who returned to Philadelphia July 2 after a lengthy New York sojourn, and Richard Henry Lee, a member of Congress who took his seat on July 9 after a week in Philadelphia en route. The full text of the Ordinance was, of course, available in Philadelphia soon after it was passed; however, its essential provisions may have been known to some members of the Convention as early as July 11 or 12.

According to his secretary, Edward Coles, Madison years later suggested that there had been a bargain or compromise between the sections involving both the Ordinance and the Constitution. He said, so Coles stated in the eighteen-fifties:

> Many individuals were members of both bodies, and thus were enabled to know what was passing in each—both sitting with closed doors and in secret sessions. The distracting question of slavery was agitating and retarding the labors of both, and led to conferences and inter-communications of the members, which resulted in a compromise by which the northern or anti-slavery portion of the country agreed to incorporate, into the Ordinance and Constitution, the provision to restore fugitive slaves; and this mutual and concurrent action was the cause of the similarity of the provision contained in both, and had its influence, in creating the great unanimity by which the Ordinance passed, and also in making the Constitution the more acceptable to the slave holders.

Coles, speaking shortly after the passage of the Fugitive Slave Act of 1850, may well have exaggerated the importance of that aspect of the compromise of 1787. But it is diffucult to imagine that he misremembered the broad idea that communication and compromise had occurred between Congress and Convention, or that Madison, a member of both bodies, was misinformed.

If other direct testimony exists supporting Madison's account it has not come to my attention. Nevertheless, I believe it is possible to make a tentative reconstruction of Southern motives for accepting the Northwest Ordinance, and of the impact of the Ordinance on the work of the Constitutional Convention.

"The clause respecting slavery was agreed to by the Southern members for the purpose of preventing tobacco and indigo from being made on the N. W. side of the Ohio as well as for sev'l other political reasons." So William Grayson wrote to James Monroe on August 8, 1787. What were the "sev'l other political reasons"? Why did the Southern majority of the Continental Congress unanimously vote for the Northwest Ordinance, despite its antislavery clause?

One answer is as simple as it is surprising: the South expected that the states formed from the Northwest Territory would vote with the South in the sectional conflict then raging in Congress. Late in 1783, when congressional acceptance of Virginia's cession was finally in sight, Thomas Jefferson had written the governor of Virginia: "If a state be first laid off on the [Great] lakes it will add a vote to the Northern scale, if on the Ohio it will add one to the Southern." Jefferson had proposed, and Congress had essentially accepted, a plan to divide the Territory into ten states, some near the lakes and others near the Ohio River. The Ordinance of 1787 provided instead that there be three states running from the river to the lakes, the present Ohio, Indiana, and Illinois. The result was that *both* North and South could hope for their allegiance. Dane of Massachusetts wrote to Rufus King on July 16 that the easternmost state of the three would "no doubt" be settled chiefly from the East, "and there is, I think, full an equal chance of its adopting Eastern politics." A month later he was more confident. Writing again to King on August 12, Dane said:

> Much will depend on the directions given to the first settlements in my opinion, and as the Eastern states for the sake of doing away the temporary governments, etc. established in 1784, and for establishing some order in that Country, gave up as much as could be reasonably expected, I think it will be just and proper in them to establish as far as they can consistently, Eastern politics in it, especially in the state adjoining Pennsylvania.

But the Southern states, too, hoped and expected to dominate the Northwest. On November 3, 1787, the Virginia delegates in Congress wrote to Governor Edmund Randolph:

> Indeed, if it is thought Material to the interest of the Southern States, that their Scale be Strengthened by an accession this quarter, that object will be better secured by the New, than the old plan, because upon the former there may be an early admission of a State [since the states under the new plan would be larger], but upon the latter such an event must be long, or perhaps forever, postponed.

If it was not because they would be slaveholding, it was also not because they were "agrarian" that the South looked forward to the admission of states from the Northwest Territory. Vermont was agrarian, but throughout the seventeen-eighties the South opposed the admission of Vermont because of what Madison called "an habitual jealousy of a predominance of Eastern interest." Clearly the South believed that, unlike Vermont, the Northwest would be settled mainly by Southerners, by an outcropping of the great tide of migrants then flowing over the mountains into Kentucky and Tennessee. Conversely,

Rufus King was relying on a predominance of Easterners in the area to produce the "Eastern politics" for which he hoped. Only the event could prove which section's expectations were correct, and so in July 1787 they could join almost unanimously in promoting the Territory's speedy settlement and organization.

What were the other "political reasons" to which Grayson referred? Richard Hildreth, writing in 1849, supposed that the Southern states were "reconciled" to the Ordinance "by the idea, afterward acted upon, of securing the continuation of slavery in the territory south of the Ohio, under future terms of cession."As we have seen, the South did not need to be reconciled to the Ordinance: it welcomed it in the belief that, even without slaveholding, the Northwest would support the South in national politics. But it is perfectly possible that Hildreth correctly identifies a second motive. For he stresses what many subsequent historians have forgotten, that as late as May 1787 Congress was on the verge of passing an ordinance for the West "the provisions of which extended to the whole western district, both that ceded [the Northwest] and that of which the cession was anticipated [the Southwest]." The ordinance reported on April 26, 1787, was an ordinance "for the government of the western territory." It was read twice but its third and final reading scheduled for May 10 was postponed, and on July 11, "the Committee . . . to whom was referred the report of a committee touching *the temporary government of the western territory* reported an Ordinance for *the government of the territory of the United States North West of the river Ohio,* which was read a first time." [Italics mine.] Thus just at the moment the Convention adopted the three-fifths compromise, Congress for the first time drew an explicit East-West line through the Western territories by legislating for the Northwest alone. What if anything was implied as to the status of slavery south of that line in the region that became the Southwest Territory?

So far as I am aware, at no Southern ratifying convention was any fear expressed that the antislavery portion of the Northwest Ordinance would be applied south of the Ohio River. Southerners presumably knew that North Carolina's cession of the area later called Tennessee read in part: "Provided always, That no regulations made or to be made by Congress shall tend to emancipate slaves, otherwise than shall be directed by the Assembly or legislature of such State or States." Other evidence supports the supposition that in legislating against slavery in the Northwest Congress tacitly legislated for it in the Southwest. South Carolinians at the Constitutional Convention were notoriously apprehensive about their slave property, but on August 9, 1787, the South Carolina legislature, undeterred by the Northwest Ordinance, completed the cession of its Western lands. Richard Henry Lee, who in 1784 voted against Jefferson's proposal to ban slavery throughout the West, was mentioned by both Dane and Cutler as a particularly warm supporter of the 1787 Ordinance which banned it only North of the Ohio.

The Northwest Ordinance legislated against slavery in that part of the West where it did not exist and left it alone in the Southwest where it already was. This was generally recognized. "The Western people are already calling out for slaves for their new lands," George Mason told the Constitutional Convention in August. And forty-seven years later Nathan Dane made a revealing statement in a letter to Daniel Webster:

> . . . in the years 1784, '85, '86, and '87, the Eastern members in the Old Congress really thought they were preparing the North-Western Territory principally for New England settlers, and to them the third and sixth articles of compact more especially had reference; therefore, when North Carolina ceded her western territory, and requested this Ordinance to be extended to it, except the *slave* article, that exception had my full assent, because slavery had taken root in it, and it was then probable it would be settled principally by slaveowners.

Thus, while from the standpoint of the North the Ordinance appeared an antislavery triumph, to the South it may have seemed the end of the national government's attempt to prohibit slavery South of the Ohio.

A third political reason which may have induced Southern congressmen to support the Northwest Ordinance is suggested by a letter of Benjamin Hawkins of North Carolina. Writing to the governor of North Carolina on July 10, Hawkins said that he and William Blount had returned to Congress from the Convention in the

> hope of being able to procure some aid from the Union towards the protection of our Western Citizens, and of securing and preserving

our right to the free and common use of the navigation of the
Miss . . . . the latter which is very interesting to the Western citizens
of the Southern States . . . has at length, from a variety of circumstances unnecessary as well perhaps as improper to relate been put
in a bitter situation than heretofore.

The question of the navigation of the Mississippi was the most
serious sectional issue to come before the Continental Congress.
It had troubled Congress during the war, when Robert Morris
told the French envoy that (in Thomas P. Abernethy's para-
phrase) "the strength of the Confederacy lay in the North and
that the North should be kept in the ascendancy by curtailing
the territory on the Southwest."It took on new intensity in 1786
when John Jay, secretary for foreign affairs, secured congressional approval to sacrifice the right to the navigation in negotiations with Spain. For the South the issue was political as well as
economic. Jay obtained his authorization from Congress by
seven states to five in a strictly sectional vote; and the South
feared, as William Grayson told the Virginia ratifying convention, that "if the Mississippi was yielded to Spain, the migration
to the western country would be stopped, and the northern
states would, not only retain their inhabitants, but preserve
their superiority and influence over that of the southern." The
effort of Northern Congressmen to close the Mississippi had
the same sectional character as the attempt by Northern
members of Congress and Convention to limit the political
representation of new states.

The bitter Mississippi controversy of 1786 became "much
entangled" with the problem of evolving a government for the
West. On May 10, 1786, a five-man congressional committee
with a Southern majority recommended that the number of
states to be formed from the Virginia cession be reduced to not
less than two nor more than five, but that, as in the plan of 1784,
each state should enter the Union when its population was equal
to that of the smallest of the original thirteen. This, as the
Virginia delegates observed in 1787, was a change which would
accelerate the admission of new states. On July 7 Congress
unanimously recommended to the states that they revise their
acts of cession so that three to five states be formed from the
Northwest. But now Northern congressmen began to press to
raise the population requirement for admission to one thir-

teenth of the total population of the original thirteen states at
the last census prior to the request for admission. *This* change
would have slowed down the admission of the new states.
Indeed, had it been applied it would have delayed the admission of Ohio, Indiana, Illinois, Michigan, and Wisconsin an
average of thirty-eight years, with Wisconsin excluded from
statehood until after 1900. On July 19 a personnel change gave
the committee a Northern majority, and on September 19 the
committee reported a revised ordinance including both the
"Northern" population formula for admission to statehood and
a new condition, equally offensive to the South, which provided
for admission if "the consent of so many States in Congress is
first obtained as may at that time be competent to such admission."

Meantime the North was using its congressional majority to
change Jay's instructions regarding his negotiations with Spain
about Mississippi navigation, which led at least three congressmen seriously to contemplate disunion. And on September 1, 1786, a procedural rule was approved which blocked
reconsideration of Jay's instructions unless the same number of
states were present (twelve) that had voted them in August.

During the winter Congressman Madison noted that the idea
of separate confederacies had for the first time reached the
newspapers; and in April, learning that Jay had drawn up a
draft treaty with Gardoqui in which the Mississippi navigation
was given up, Madison launched a frontal attack. On April 18
he moved that negotiations be transferred to Jefferson in
Madrid, a step, he confided to his journal, "which if it should
answer no other purpose would at least gain time." In inconclu-
sive debate on the motion on April 23, Gorham (soon to leave
for the Convention) stated that he thought the Mississippi *should*
be closed to American commerce. On April 25, grasping the
nettle, Madison moved to repeal the rule of September 1786.
Rufus King (another member of both Congress and Convention) led the opposition which forced a postponement. Nevertheless Madison thought it a victory, writing in his journal:

> It was considered on the whole that the project of shutting the
> Mississippi was at an end; a point deemed of great importance in
> reference to the approaching Convention for introducing a change

in the federal Government, and to the objection to an increase of its powers foreseen form the jealously [*sic*] which had been excited by that project.

On May 2 he left for Philadelphia.

The issue of Western government and Mississippi navigation arose once more before Congress lost its quorum in mid-May. On May 9, Congress gave the ordinance for the "western territory" its second reading, but also recorded the receipt of a memorial from Samuel Parsons and his associates which led to the postponement of the third reading ordered for May 10. On May 9 Congress received another letter from Jay requesting "express Instructions on the Points in Difference between the United States and the Crown in Spain." On the tenth Pierce and Few of Georgia (both Convention delegates) carried the motion of April 25 repealing the order of September 1786, and on May 11 a committee on new instructions was appointed with a Southern majority.

Therefore, when Congress regained its quorum July 4 the trend of congressional action was favorable to the South with respect to the Mississippi issue, unfavorable in regard to the admission of Western states. Since both strands of policy directly affected Southern prospects for becoming a majority in Congress, the overall position of the South in the Union was very much in doubt.

The first business of the reactivated Congress was to hear a report from the committee on instructions to Jay which affirmed, predictably, that it was an "indispensable obligation to preserve the right of the United States to their territorial bounds and the free Navigation of the Mississippi from its source to the Ocean . . . ." One Northerner at least was not ready to concede defeat. The next day Nathan Dane wrote to Rufus King, now at the Convention in Philadelphia: "What is best for us to do about procuring an attendance of the Eastern States and to renew the subject of the S[panish] Treaty?" But the stand-off achieved by Madison in April was in fact left undisturbed. "The Mississippi is where you left it; i.e. nothing has been done," Grayson wrote to Monroe on August 8. "I . . . think we are safe for the present." The Mississippi question "has been dormant a considerable time," Madison wrote to

Washington in October, "and seems likely to remain so." In September 1788 Congress referred the matter to the new government with a declaration of opinion that free navigation was a clear and essential right and should be supported, thus belatedly confirming the committee report of July 4, 1787.

Dane himself joined in a more substantial concession to Southern views on Western government. The first full draft of the Northwest Ordinance, in Dane's handwriting, included a provision to admit new states when their population reached sixty thousand and completely dropped the stipulation as to the consent of a competent number of states in Congress. Francis Philbrick comments: "There is no evidence on the subject, but the matter was so bitterly contested as to justify suspicion that some understanding preceded Dane's proposal of the new formula."

To sum up this portion of the discussion: The foregoing pages sketch three lines of reasoning which may have led Southerners to support the Northwest Ordinance, despite its antislavery proviso. The Northwest, even without slavery, was expected to support Southern policies in Congress; the Ordinance may have been construed as a tacit endorsement of slavery in the Southwest; and the negotiations that led to the Ordinance appear to have involved an agreement to speed the admission of new states from the Northwest by lowering the population required for admission. Taken together with the continued stalemate on the issue of Mississippi navigation, the Ordinance could well have seemed a Southern victory to the Southern congressional majority.

Two qualifications need emphasis. First, in speaking of "Southerners" or "Southern attitudes" I mean to suggest only that sectional conflict was already so intense that Southern politicians as a group were conscious of defending commonly-recognized sectional interests. There is no intention of obscuring the difference between Grayson and Lee on the issue of slavery, or between Lee and Blount in regard to Southwestern expansion. Second, thus far I have deliberately ignored Madison's suggestion of cooperation between Congress and Convention, and approached the Northwest Ordinance as the product of sectional compromise within Congress. Whether or not the Ordinance was consciously intended to resolve problems in the Convention, it may have had that effect. We now turn to examine just what those problems were.

The coalition which secured the three-fifths compromise at the Convention was not a combination of "large states." It comprised the states of the South aided now by one Northern state, now by another. The key votes were on July 11, when the three-fifths rule was defeated six-four; on July 12, when it was adopted; on July 13, when it was extended to prospective Western states; and on July 14, when by a five-four vote a motion to limit representatives from the West to a number no greater than that from the original thirteen states, was beaten. The sectional pattern is obscured because South Carolina voted against the three-fifths rule in an effort to have Negroes counted equally with whites. If South Carolina is placed in the "aye" column, one finds Virginia and the states South of it forming a solid South throughout these crucial votes.

The struggle, as Gouverneur Morris observed, was one "between the two ends of the Union." Madison was still more explicit. On June 29 he stated:

If there was real danger, I would give the smaller states the defensive weapons.—But there is none from that quarter. The great danger to our general government *is the great southern and northern interests of the continent, being opposed to each other. Look to the votes in congress, and most of them stand divided by the geography of the country, not according to the size of the states.*

The next day Madison reiterated "that the States were divided into different interests not by their difference of size, but by other circumstances; the most material of which resulted partly from climate, but principally from the effects of their having or not having slaves." By July 14 Madison could say that it was "pretty well understood" that the "institution of slavery & its consequences formed the line of discrimination" between the contending groups of states at the Convention.

Early in July delegates' attention turned from the size of their individual states to the size, actual and anticipated, of the sections to which their states belonged. At first Madison's mention of the sectional issue was rather to soften the conflict between large and small states than to bring forward the problems between North and South. But these problems became inescapable when the committee reports of July 5 and 9 brought the Convention to grips with allotment of representation to the West and to the slave. King said in the ensuing discussion that he "was fully convinced that the question concerning a difference of interests did not lie where it had hitherto been discussed, between the great & small States; but between the Southern & Eastern."

The three-fifths rule had been accepted by a nine-two vote on June 11, but it now became once more problematical, because it was connected with Western expansion. For the South, inclusion of slaves in the basis of apportionment for the House and the admission of Western states represented equally with the old were alternative means of strengthening its power in Congress. This was because, as Bancroft and Alden have noted, it was generally assumed that the South when strengthened by the West would become the most populous part of the country. Delegate after delegate at the Convention asserted that "the Southern & Western population" would "predominate . . . in a few years," that "N.C. [,] S.C. and Georgia only will in a little time have a majority of people in America," or at least that "the people & strength of America are evidently bearing Southwardly & S. westwdly." Later, at the Virginia ratifying convention, no one questioned that (as Grayson put it) "God and nature have intended . . . that the weight of population should be on this side of the continent." Antifederalists reasoned from this assumption that Virginia should wait until a Southern majority in Congress made it safe to transfer power from the states to the national government. Federalist Wilson Nicholas reasoned from the identical premise to a contrary conclusion. "The influence of New England, and the other northern states is dreaded," Nicholas said,

> there are apprehensions of their combining against us. Not to advert to the improbability and illiberality of this idea it must be supposed, that our population, will in a short period, exceed theirs, as their country is well settled, and we have very extensive, uncultivated tracts. We shall soon out-number them in as great a degree as they do us at this time: therefore this government, which I trust will last to the remotest ages, will be very shortly in our favor.

Nicholas' argument did not convince George Mason. Nicholas showed, stated Mason, "that though the northern states had a most decided majority against us, yet the increase of population among us would in the course of years change it in our favor. A very sound argument indeed, that we should cheerfully burn ourselves to death in hopes of a joyful and happy resurrection!"

The generally accepted premise that the weight of numbers was shifting from North to South gave both sections an interest in discarding the existing arrangement which have each state one vote in Congress. Writing to Jefferson, Randolph, and Washington before the Convention met, Madison correctly predicted that proportional representation would be "recommended to the Eastern States by the actual superiority of their populousness, and to the Southern by their expected superiority." This was the basis of compromise at the Convention.

It was a compromise excruciatingly difficult to formulate in detail. What was needed, as Mason said on July 11, was a system which accorded the North its present right to predominate but was so framed that when the Southern states grew larger, power would pass to them. But Deep South delegates feared that the North might use even a temporary majority to force emancipation. Thus Butler of South Carolina stated: "The security the Southn. States want is that their negroes may not be taken from them which some gentlemen within or without doors, have a very good mind to do." Northerners, in their turn, feared that the South and West would employ their eventual majority to oppress commerce and thrust America into needless wars. "He must be short sighted indeed," King said,

> who does not foresee that whenever the Southern States shall be more numerous than the Northern, they can & will hold a language that will awe them [the Northern states] into justice. If they threaten to separate now in case injury shall be done them, will their threats be less urgent or effectual, when force shall back their demands?

Ironically, the South expected to dominate the House of Representatives while the North looked for its security to the Senate. Gouverneur Morris asserted on July 13 that he saw "the Southn. Gentlemen will not be satisfied unless they see the way open to their gaining a majority in the public Councils." This would oblige him "to vote for ye. vicious principle of equality in the 2d. branch in order to provide some defense for the N.

States agst. it." Madison, speaking for the South, was equally alarmed at the idea of equal representation in the Senate because of "the perpetuity it would give to the preponderance of the Northn. agst. the Southn." states. "Should a proprtl. representation take place it was true, the N. side would still out-number the other: but not in the same degree, at this time; and every day would tend towards an equilibrium."

This tangle of anxieties was complicated further by the ordinance for government of the West passed by the Continental Congress in 1784. King reminded the Convention on July 6 that Congress had "impoliticly laid it [the west] out into ten States," and covenanted with the settlers to permit any Western state to enter the Union as soon as the number of its inhabitants equalled the population of the smallest of the original thirteen. Since little Delaware had only thirty-five thousand inhabitants, King concluded, a large number of Western states representing very few people might soon be admitted. The Senate could hardly provide a fortress for Northern interests if in the near future it were overwhelmed with twenty new senators from the West.

Thus by early July the conflict of large and small states had been partially transformed into a conflict of North and South. Georgia, the third smallest state in the Union, and South Carolina, smaller than New York or Connecticut, voted as "large" states because they expected to grow and because they expected the section of which they were a part to grow. Massachusetts and Pennsylvania, the large Northern states, voted on large states when discussion centered on the balance of power in the existing confederacy; but when Western representation came on the floor, what Bancroft called New England's "ineradicable dread of the coming power of the South-west" tended to draw them toward the "small" state position. Section as well as size was involved in the great Convention crisis which led Franklin to suggest prayer and Washington (as Freeman says) to express despair in a tone he had hardly used since the worst days of the war.

What resolved the crisis? Farrand, attempting to account for the change in the tone of the Convention after July 10, was driven to invoke the fact that the weather became cooler. Bancroft, characterizing the passage of the Northwest Ordinance by a Congress racked with sectional strife, concluded that "every man that had a share in it seemed to be led by an invisible hand to do just what was wanted of him." Madison's comment to Coles invites us to search for more adequate explanations by viewing as parts of one whole the events of mid-July in both New York and Philadelphia. Coles' recollection of Madison's memory of events a generation before their conversation can hardly be relied on in detail. What it provides is a fresh point of departure.

The most obvious relationship between the Ordinance and the Constitution is that their fugitive slave clauses are almost identical and their clauses on the sanctity of contracts very similar. There can be little question that the Convention, which worded these clauses of the Constitution in August, had the Ordinance of July in mind.

There were other ways in which the documents, without duplicating each other, were clearly supplementary. Thus the Ordinance said nothing about retaining the right to the Mississippi navigation, although a clause providing that waterways leading into the Mississippi and St. Lawrence "shall be common highways, and forever free," may have been seen as a precedent. But a requirement that treaties be approved by two-thirds of the Senate was inserted in the Constitution "for the express purpose of preventing a majority of the Senate . . . from giving up the Mississippi." Again, the Constitution was vague about the admission of new states. The Randolph Plan said that admission should be "with the consent of a number of voices in the National legislature less than the whole"; the Committee of Detail reported that the admission of new states should require the consent of two-thirds of the members present in each branch of the legislature; and at the insistence of Gouverneur Morris, Article IV, Section 3 merely stated that "New States may be admitted by Congress into this Union." On the other hand, Article I, Section 2 made it clear that the three-fifths rule for the House would apply to "the several States which may be included within this Union," the agreement voted by the Convention on July 13. Southerners reading this clause in conjunction with the provision of the Ordinance that "whenever any of the said States shall have sixty

thousand free Inhabitants therein, such State shall be admitted . . . on an equal footing with the original States, in all
respects whatever," might well feel that they had gained their
points about *both* slave representation and the equal representation of new Western states.

All this is consistent with Madison's idea of a connection in the
drafting of Ordinance and Constitution. One is, therefore, led
to inquire whether consultation between Congress and Convention preceded the drafting of the Northwest Ordinance on July
9–11; whether the nature of the Ordinance was such as to ease
the sectional tension then troubling the Convention; and
whether the essential features of the Ordinance were reported
to members of the Convention in time to influence its voting on
July 12–14. Since the answer to all three questions is probably,
Yes, I think one can justifiably present the hypothesis that there
occurred in July 1787 a sectional compromise involving Congress and Convention, Ordinance and Constitution, essentially
similar to those of 1820 and 1850. The business of a hypothesis,
I take it, is to present a structure of logic which accounts for the
available facts, and is susceptible to proof or disproof. Evidence
proving or disproving the hypothesis of a Compromise of 1787
may come to light, or have (unknown to me) already come to
light, in any of some dozens of manuscript collections. The
hypothesis is brought forward in the hope that such evidence
will be forthcoming.

Were there "conferences and inter-communications" (to use
the words Coles attributed to Madison) between Congress and
Convention in early July? When the Convention adjourned for
three days on July 2 to allow a committee of all the states to seek
a compromise, four congressmen, three of them members of
the Convention, left for New York City. It was this journey of
Blount and Hawkins of North Carolina, Pierce and Few of
Georgia, that enabled Congress to achieve a quorum for the
first time in almost two months. (The accession of the two
Southern states also gave the South a majority in Congress.)
Richard Henry Lee, who arrived on July 7 and took his seat on
July 9, was therefore the fifth prominent Southerner to travel
from Philadelphia to New York in less than a week. Hamilton,
who left the Convention June 29, was in New York City by July
3. On July 5 Manasseh Cutler arrived from Massachusetts.

When one recalls that Pierce, on his earlier return from the convention (June 14–18), had spoken freely of "the plans of the Southern, Eastern, or Middle States," it seems a reasonable conclusion that "conference and inter-communication" occurred.

Was the nature of the Ordinance relevant to the crisis at Philadelphia? If we can assume (as contended earlier) that the prohibition of slavery in the Northwest was not threatening to the South, then the antislavery-fugitive slave clause of the Ordinance may have reassured men like Davie and Butler, just then expressing the first apprehensions about slave property on the floor of the Convention. This was the element in the putative compromise stressed in Coles' recollection. But we have Dane's testimony that the antislavery proviso was added to the Ordinance at the last moment. And Deep South statements of alarm at the Convention continued unabated until the compromise on the slave trade at the end of August.

More significant, surely, were the provisions of the Ordinance concerning the admission of new states. After the Ordinance passed, Dane wrote to King (as already quoted) that "the Eastern states for the sake of doing away the temporary governments, etc. established in 1784, and for establishing some order in that Country, gave up as much as could be reasonably expected." What did the North give up? It gave up its plan to require a large population for admission to statehood, and to make admission depend on the consent of a competent number of states in Congress. The Northwest Ordinance even added that "so far as it can be consistent with the general interest of the Confederacy, such admission shall be allowed at an earlier period, and when there may be a less number of free Inhabitants in the State than sixty thousand." Philbrick, the most detailed commentator on the Ordinance, judged this to be so drastic a change in the ordinance almost passed in May that it raised a "suspicion that some understanding" was involved. If the North rather than the South made the major concession in the drafting of the Ordinance, one could make better sense of Grayson's statement to the Virginia ratifying convention that the Ordinance "passed in a lucky moment," leaving Massachusetts "extremely uneasy about it."

But the admission provisions of the Ordinance spoke to the

needs of North as well as South. On the one hand, given the Southern assumption that the states of the Northwest (even if non-slaveholding) would strengthen the South in Congress, the provisions for easy and early admission to statehood held out hope to the South of swiftly increasing its forces in the House of Representatives. On the other hand, however, the Ordinance wrote into law what had only been approved in principle the year before: that the Northwest would consist of three to five states rather than of ten. Thus it forestalled the prospect, threatening to the North, of losing control of the Senate. This would explain Dane's statement to King that he thought the population requirement for admission too small, "but, having divided the whole Territory into three States, this number appears to me to be less important."

If (as George Mason put it) what the Convention needed was a plan that recognized the present dominance of the North while providing for eventual transition to a Southern majority, a plan, too, which safeguarded the present minority needs of the South and the future minority needs of the North, the Ordinance supplied a *deus ex machina* uncannily appropriate. The beauty of its admission requirements was that they appeared at the time to promote the South's interests in the House while protecting the North's interests in the Senate. Some necessary ambiguity remained. North as well as South hoped for the political allegiance of at least some of the Northwest states. The clause on slavery could be presented to Southern ratifying conventions as a guarantee of property and to Northern ratifying conventions as a bar to the creation of new slave states. In place of a West vaguely attractive or dangerous, the Ordinance made available a West just sufficiently specific that each section could read in it the fulfillment of its political dreams.

Still, could the essential features of the Ordinance have become known in Philadelphia in time to affect the voting of July 12–14? The answer is, Yes. Whatever the catalyst was at the Convention, it was not yet apparent on July 10, when Washington wrote to Hamilton that matters were if anything worse than at the end of June. That same afternoon, after returning to the appropriate congressional committee a draft of the Ordinance with several amendments, Manasseh Cutler left New

York for Philadelphia. Arriving on the twelfth, he spent the evening at the Indian Queen tavern with delegates from the South and Massachusetts—Strong, Gerry, Gorham, Madison, Mason, Martin, Williamson, Rutledge, one of the Pinckneys— together with "Mr. Hamilton of New York," and other, un- named persons. The morning of the fourteenth he spent with Strong, Martin, Mason, Williamson, Madison, Rutledge, and "Mr. Hamilton, all members of the Convention," before re- turning to New York City. What better messenger could have been wished than the promoter of the Northwest Ordinance?

Cutler's references make clear that Hamilton was also in Philadelphia. He was not yet there on July 10, Cutler saw him on the twelfth and fourteenth, he did not represent New York at the Convention, and he was back in New York by the twentieth. The purpose of this brief and unofficial visit is unknown. Conceivably, Hamilton left New York late enough to learn the outlines of the Ordinance and arrived in Philadelphia early enough to influence the voting of the twelfth. Hamilton's good friend Gouverneur Morris closed the Convention session of July 11 on a note of intransigence and opened the next morning's session with a proposal to "bridge" the sectional conflict. But at this point one moves from the realm of legiti- mate speculation to that of uncontrolled fantasy.

If the Northwest Ordinance did in fact influence the com- promises of the Constitution, how bitter a pill for its An- tifederalist sponsors, Grayson, Lee, and Melancton Smith! And that would not be the only irony. It would mean that the South, backing the Ordinance on the doubly-mistaken assumption that its security lay in the House of Representatives and that the states of the Northwest would give it strength there, had pro- duced a charter of freedom for the Negro; but also, that this charter made possible the Constitution, which gave slavery new sanctions.

Finally, why did Congress and Convention act so differently? The evidence suggests that the motives which moved men in making Ordinance and Constitution were essentially the same. The drafters at Philadelphia were troubled about slavery as were the legislators in New York. But in Congress, Southerners who sought to guarantee slave property and to make possible a stronger Southern voice in Congress saw Northwest settlement, even without slavery, as a means to these ends. At the Convention, sanctions for slavery (the three-fifths clause and the slave trade clause) seemed necessary to bring about the same results: protection against emancipation and a Southern majority in the House. In each case the North made the compromises the South demanded, but in Congress, because of the South's mistaken assumptions about the future of the Northwest, an antislavery clause could be included. The fugitive slave clause adopted unanimously by both bodies shows, if not that there was a sectional compromise between Congress and Convention, at least that the makers of both Ordinance and Constitution were ready to compromise the concept that all men are equal. This was the fundamental compromise of 1787.

Origins of the
American Colonial System

Jack E. Eblen

The American colonial system effectively began with the Northwest Ordinance of 1787. Since that time all colonial policies of the United States, including the recent efforts at commonwealth status for Micronesia, have been modifications of the original ideas.

In this essay Jack E. Eblen (1936——) traces the evolution of this famous document through the Continental Congress. Like Professor Berkhofer, Eblen sees the Ordinance as the product of several minds and the consequence of a series of developments in Congress. He finds Nathan Dane of Massachusetts and James Monroe of Virginia modifying the Ordinance of 1784 into a workable colonial policy. He calls the final product the "Jefferson-Monroe-Dane Plan."

Moreover, Eblen discards as unfounded the interpretation that, as he says in a footnote, "conspiratorial land speculators were behind the writing of the Ordinance of 1787 and that the Ohio Company representatives forced Congress to draft the governmental articles the way it did to serve as a mere adjunct to their land grab." He does see the possibility that the Ohio and Scioto grants may have induced some New England Congressmen to support the Ordinance because these schemes offered a chance for eastern influence in an area supposedly inclined toward the South.

For Eblen the 1787 document is not a step backward from the democratic principles of the 1784 ordinance, but rather a constructive solution to the ambiguous and inadequate earlier plan. Of particular importance was Dane's insistence on the inclusion of a list of civil liberties and Monroe's proposals for a limited number of potential states and a precise number of inhabitants required for admission. The coincidence of these developments, combined with congressional insistence on the slavery prohibition, suggests to Eblen the possibility of "logrolling." Nowhere does Eblen see any indication of a conspiracy between Congress in New York and the delegation at the Convention in Philadelphia that Lynd describes in the previous essay.

Professor Eblen's career has involved history teaching assignments at

Northern Illinois University, Fresno State College, the University of Connecticut, and the University of Oklahoma. After the publication of the The First and Second United States Empires, 1784–1912 *(1968), he turned his scholarly endeavors to historical demography. Since 1974 he has been a member of the Sociology Department and the Population Research Center, University of Chicago.*

★★★★★★★★★★★★★★★★★★★★★★★★★★★★★

THE MONTH of July, 1787, was one of the most momentous in American history. In that month the Philadelphia Convention and the Confederation Congress simultaneously resolved fundamental problems of government leading to the formal organization of the first United States empire. The Philadelphia Convention hammered out the basic provisions for a new constitution to establish a stronger central government. In hatching its plan to replace the Articles of Confederation, the Convention also worked out the ideas and mechanics of federalism between the states, and formulated the concept of a federal empire. Controversy over the exact form of the empire was to result in the unanimous adoption, in August, of Gouverneur Morris' vague proposal, which simply granted the new Congress imperial powers without deliniating or delimiting them, rather than James Madison's more detailed plan.

In the meantime, the Confederation Congress, sitting in New York City, had been moving along a parallel line. On July 13, 1787, after more than a year of sporadic debate, it enacted a relatively precise plan of colonial government for the public domain north of the Ohio River. One of the most significant laws in American history, the Northwest Ordinance prescribed the philosophical and structural framework for a United States colonial system based on that of the old British Empire. The Ordinance defined republicanism and specified it to be the only acceptable form of government for the colonies and future states. Its basic ideas were to be applied more or less successfully

From Jack E. Eblen, "Origins of the United States Colonial System: The Ordinance of 1787," in the *Wisconsin Magazine of History*, LI: 294–314 (Summer, 1968); reprinted without footnotes with permission of the *Wisconsin Magazine of History*.

in the United States possessions for over 175 years and its provisions were to lay the foundation for the governments of the thirty-one public lands states and Hawaii. In short, the Ordinance led to the imposition of a uniform system of politics throughout the American empire. Together, then, the Philadelphia Convention and the Confederation Congress in July, 1787, adopted co-ordinate parts of a system for a federal republican empire that was to shape the course of United States history.

Contrary to standard interpretations, the Ordinance of 1787 was not an adjunct of the Ohio Company's land scheme, designed to promote settlement in the Northwest. Nor did the Confederation Congress enact it precipitously under pressure from the Reverend Manasseh Cutler, the Company's lobbyist. Cutler had little if any influence over the final form or content of the Ordinance. Instead, the Northwest Ordinance had distinct pre-Revolutionary colonial origins and evolved in stages. This evolution was the work of the three men—Thomas Jefferson, James Monroe, and Nathan Dane—who successively dominated the congressional committees charged with devising a frame of government for the public domain between early 1784 and July of 1787.

Jefferson was probably the first man to formulate the basic principles for a United States colonial policy. In 1776 Virginia made extravagant claims of ownership to most of the land west of the Appalachian Mountains. By generously interpreting the "west and northwest" sea-to-sea boundary provisions of the 1609 colonial charter, Virginia claimed title not only to Kentucky but also to all of the land west of Pennsylvania north of the Ohio River—that is, the entire Northwest Territory. But Jefferson believed in the classical idea that republican states are inevitably small and did not think democratic republican institutions could flourish in so large a state. Since he was unable or unwilling at this time to reconcile classical republicanism with imperialism, he feared that unless its size was drastically reduced an undemocratic imperial government would develop as the populated area of Virginia increased.

Early in 1776, when drafting a constitution for Virginia, Jefferson acted to insure the permanence of republicanism in his state. He tried to raise to the sanctity of constitutional law his ideas for preventing the emergence of an imperial state by incorporating a compact article between the state and the people who would settle its western land claims. He provided for the settlement of the trans-Appalachian west through the distribution of fifty-acre headrights and the independence of any given colonial area when it became politically mature. In this way Jefferson would have had Virginia voluntarily limit its size to preserve republicanism. Jefferson did not specify the level of political sophistication required for independence, but he did guarantee complete sovereignty once a colony became a state. In contemporary usage "sovereignty" could take any of three forms—independent nation states or a confederation of states in the West, or incorporation into the eastern confederation. Only two of these forms, however, were open to Virginia— if it could make good on its claims—because it obviously lacked authority to incorporate future western states into the existing eastern confederacy. Jefferson did not indicate whether Virginia would create a number of separate nation states or a confederation of states in the West, perhaps implying that the westerners were to choose their own course. Similarly, he was silent on the size and number of states to rise out of the West. As he moved from the second to the third draft of the constitution, Jefferson simply decided there should be several colonies, each of an "appropriate" size.

Western land disposal became a major national issue before Virginia took steps to implement Jefferson's constitutional provisions, and a consensus emerged that rejected the only alternatives Virginia had for the ultimate status of its proposed western colonies. By 1780 the consensus favored the organization of a national inland empire and the full incorporation of western colonies into the existing union. Maryland's persistent refusal to ratify the Articles of Confederation had centered on the western land problem, and on September 6, 1780, the Virginia delegates finally introduced a "recommendation" in Congress intended to meet Maryland's objections. Jefferson, who was then governor of Virginia, undoubtedly had a hand in drafting the recommendation. It surely reflects his new attitude toward the West and marks his emergence as an imperialist. Assuming that a peace treaty ending the war would assure United States sovereignty over all lands north of Florida and east of the

Mississippi River, it urged states claiming western lands to cede them to Congress on the grounds that "the back lands, . . . secured by the blood and treasure of all, ought, in reason, justice, and policy, to be considered a common stock, to be parcelled out by Congress." As passed on October 10, the congressional resolution further stipulated that, under Congress, "the unappropriated lands shall be . . . formed into distinct republican states, which shall become members of the federal union, and have the same rights of sovereignty, freedom and independence, as the other states: . . . each state shall . . . contain a suitable extent of territory, not less than one hundred nor more than one hundred and fifty miles square." This resolution represents the first general statement of a national colonial policy, the first stone laid in the construction of a federal empire.

States claiming western land promptly acted on the congressional resolution. Before the end of 1781 Congress received cessions of the principal claims to land north of the Ohio River, but the Virginia General Assembly attached unacceptable conditions to its act of cession and did not alter them to the satisfaction of Congress for another two years. So Congress did not obtain sole title to the Northwest Territory until it accepted the Virginia deed of cession on March 1, 1784—more than a year after the Treaty of Paris ended the Revolution and Britain recognized United States claims to a Great Lakes-Mississippi River boundary. A national plan for empire was now necessary, and Jefferson introduced one immediately after Congress accepted the Virginia deed of cession.

In February, 1784, Congress had appointed Jefferson chairman of a committee to draft a plan for the temporary government of the West. The committee was to prepare a bill to fulfill the terms of the state land cessions—particularly Virginia's, which Jefferson undoubtedly influenced heavily. Congress had to recognize state land reserves in the Northwest and to divide the West into republican states which would be admitted to the Union as equal and perpetual members. Moreover, both the Congressional resolution of 1780 and the Virginia act of cession required future states to be between 10,000 and 22,500 square miles in area—roughly between the present areas of Maryland (10,577) and West Virginia (24,181).

The report Jefferson presented on March 1 became the Ordinance of 1784. Though he had solicited suggestions, the plan Jefferson offered was his own brainchild. It followed the general principles for a colonial policy laid down in Congress, but in drafting it Jefferson decided to exceed his instructions, to write a compact suitable for imperialistic expansion. His rapid ideological transformation is evident in the various drafts of his report. Starting with George Washington's idea of establishing a single district in the eastern part of the Northwest Territory, he soon chose to carve six states, which he called A, B, C, D, E, and F, out of the territory now occupied by Ohio, Indiana, Illinois, and Kentucky. Kentucky was not within the ceded territory. Not long after drawing geographically unachievable boundaries for these states, he abandoned that plan in favor of one for dividing all the land between the Appalachians and the Mississippi north of Florida into squares, along lines of longitude and latitude, to form small states of 14,000 to 17,000 square miles. In this manner Jefferson moved from the consideration of a governmental policy for the land Congress possessed to the formulation of a broad colonial policy to embrace all the western lands he hoped Congress would someday control. If not yet thinking of expanding the national domain, he was clearly anticipating additional land cessions by the southern states to enlarge the public domain. In particular, he thought Virginia was still too large and ought to cede the area that roughly coincides with the state of West Virginia. [*See* Map 6.]

Although the terms of the state land cessions would seem to have dictated the need to make some provision for the admission of states, Jefferson's instructions were simply to furnish a plan for "temporary government." Instead, he devised a four-stage process through which each of the proposed colonies would progress individually to statehood. He made no provision for government during the early years—or decades—of settlement, suggesting he believed that either rudimentary local government would then be unnecessary or *ad hoc* arrangements would suffice. At an indeterminate point the settlers were to establish a "temporary" government using the constitution and laws of one of the original states. During this second stage they could begin dividing the territory into counties and townships. The second stage would continue until the population within the prospective state reached 20,000. Then, upon receiving proof of the size of the population and of the desire of the people, Congress was to appoint the times and places for the election and meeting of a convention to draw up a permanent state constitution. The third stage began with the inauguration of the permanent state government, but the quasi-state could not apply for admission to the Union, the fourth stage, until its population reached that of the least populous of the thirteen original states. In the meantime, during the second and third stages, the colony could send a representative to Congress who would have the right to debate but not to vote.

Jefferson's plan was paradoxical. On the one hand it gave the appearance of congressional noninterference, yet it set up a half-hearted empire. The settlers were to take the initiative and do all the work. Congress was to assume no financial, administrative, or protective responsibility for the territories. On the other hand, the plan limited western self-determination. It prescribed routes of development and rigidly restricted western actions. Settlers were expected to obtain congressional consent before organizing governments and to enter the successive stages only at the times and in the ways authorized. Congress alone could set the time and place, and presumably the mode, of electing delegates to a constitutional convention. In all stages the colonial governments were to govern the whole area of land within their future state boundaries and to respect the limits imposed on their freedom of action by the Ordinance. One of the most important restrictions was that Congress reserved to itself all matters relating to the disposal of the public lands.

During the debates on Jefferson's report it became clear that the delegates favored more congressional control over the West than he had provided. They added three sections to the compact. These made membership in the confederacy perpetual, required western governments to be republican, and prohibited the higher taxation of lands of nonresidents than of territorial residents. The shift in thinking toward comprehensive congressional participation in the development of the colonies, however, was most evident in the adoption of a general article which compromised the whole idea of western self-determination. On April 21, Jacob Read of South Carolina proposed an amendment to permit Congress to appoint magistrates and other officers for the territories until the settlers formed their own temporary governments. Jefferson voted *for* the amendment, but it lost. Two days later, Elbridge Gerry of Massachusetts offered another amendment, which Jefferson apparently wrote, to give Congress even greater powers. It provided "That measures not inconsistent with the principles of the Confedn. & necessary for the preservation of peace & good order among the settlers in any of the said new states until they shall assume a temporary Government as aforesaid, may from time to time be taken by the United States in Congress assembled." Read immediately moved that Gerry's amendment be laid aside and that Congress reconsider his recently defeated amendment. The delegates denied Read's motion and after altering it slightly adopted the Jefferson-Gerry amendment. On the same day, April 23, by the unanimous vote of ten states, Congress enacted the Ordinance of 1784.

Jefferson may have wanted the Gerry amendment in the Ordinance to provide leeway for future legislative needs and to enable Congress to intervene in territorial affairs if absolutely necessary. But the wording of the amendment suggests a broad construction. In this sense, the Ordinance as he helped amend it both illustrates Jefferson's reconciliation of republicanism with imperialism and demonstrates that he was well on the way to becoming an advocate of a fully centralized empire. Construed broadly, the amended Ordinance did not simply transform the Confederation into an empire. It gave Congress unlimited control over its colonies. Subsequent events were to show that an increasing majority in Congress expected a broad interpretation to be necessary if not desirable.

Although the Ordinance provided for the organization of an empire, it was fraught with defects which made it impossible to implement. As in 1776, when he included the article on the disposal of the West in his constitution for Virginia, so in 1784 Jefferson intended the articles of the Ordinance to "stand as fundamental constitutions between the original thirteen states and each of the several states now newly described," not subject to basic change at the whim of Congress. This raised some serious constitutional problems. In the first place Congress could not make a law part of the constitution, yet the Ordinance may have had to be incorporated in the Articles of Confederation before it could be operative since the Articles did not specifically empower Congress either to create or to admit new states. A more practical problem was that a change in the number of states in the Union would require a change in the constitutional majorities needed for the enactment of laws in Congress, and this could be accomplished only by amending the Articles.

Only by its lack of clarity in some places did the Ordinance evade *ultra vires* difficulties. Jefferson wrote the Ordinance to include "the territory ceded or to be ceded by individual states" and to authorize the organization of states in lands not yet ceded, thereby depriving existing states of territory for the benefit of the United States, despite congressional declarations to the contrary, unless they voluntarily ceded additional lands. Before passing the Ordinance, Congress had deleted two of Jefferson's provisions which lacked constitutional bases: the abolition of slavery and hereditary titles in the West. Apparently none of the above constitutional problems arose when Congress debated the Ordinance. In 1787 and 1788, however, James Madison would use some of them as reasons for adopting the new federal constitution. Unlike the Articles, he then argued, it would give Congress the authority to create and admit new states and take any other actions it considered to be in the national interest. Gouverneur Morris put it more bluntly: the new constitution would provide a sound foundation for the erection of any kind of empire Congress might choose to create.

If Jefferson believed he was writing higher law and sidestepping constitutional issues, others were more pragmatic. Some members of Congress who supported the Ordinance possibly wanted to see if it would work. Probably more considered it to be inadequate but backed it principally because it met the requirements of state land cessions and thereby completed the land transfers. Some of the Congressmen may have opposed a stronger law. With the seemingly inoffensive Ordinance, Congress could avert criticism while giving the states time to adjust to the idea of the stronger general government manifested in congressional administration of the public domain. In time, the states might yield to Congress the additional land as Jefferson and others desired. Such considerations help to explain both the apparently innocuous nature of the Ordinance and Congress' failure to attempt to implement it.

Whatever the thinking in Congress, there were reasons for more positive congressional action than the Ordinance envisioned, and others soon emerged. Some Easterners viewing the Illinois and Kentucky settlements doubted the feasibility of allowing the alien and "half-savage" westerners to have unbridled representative government. On the other hand, if the frontiersmen of the isolated Kaskaskia and Wabash settlements in the Illinois Country had any idea of the provisions of the Ordinance, they might have discovered that their settlements fell in three or four proposed states instead of being united in one. Of more immediate concern, the settlements of the Northwest were too scattered, too poor, and too small to support representative governments even if Congress had authorized them. Western settlers, then, were unable to form temporary governments, even if they were not unwilling or too preoccupied. Yet, they cried for government, protection, and confirmation of their land claims. The Ordinance of 1785, which provided for the survey and sale of land in eastern Ohio, anticipated new settlements in the territory that would add to existing needs for control. Such a migration could only aggravate the Indian problems which were already calling for federal action. Additional settlements in state land reserves in the Northwest would simply compound this anarchy and discord. And congressional declarations alone would neither create order among the frontiersmen nor keep whites and Indians apart.

Congress was unwilling to act under the broad, discretionary Jefferson-Gerry amendment in the Ordinance of 1784 for several reasons. The Ordinance envisioned the creation of at least seven states in the Northwest, and consequently necessitated the organization of at least seven colonial governments. The boundaries of the proposed states, however, were not based on geographic features and contemporary maps were so inaccurate that they could not be used to indicate even their approximate locations. Therefore, the boundaries had to be established by survey. As Congress was soon to find its hands full just surveying the seven ranges provided for in the Land Ordinance of 1785, the idea of undertaking this larger task could not have been appealing. But, since Congress reserved to itself the disposal of the public lands, it would have to provide machinery for the survey and sale of land in each of the proposed states. Moreover, Indian relations and associated military affairs were international in character, so Congress would have to control and co-ordinate their conduct in each state. All this suggests that even if the Jefferson-Gerry amendment had not been in the Ordinance, Congress would have found it absolutely necessary to assume some kind of direct administration over its western colonies, at least during the initial stages of settlement.

No rational person, however, would advocate that the impoverished Congress actually establish and maintain the apparatus necessary to give unity to Jefferson's system. The very idea of continental mercantilism on which the empire rested precluded lavish congressional expenditures for the support of an unwieldy administrative system in a proliferation of territories. Like Parliament, Congress expected its colonies to be self-supporting, not a burden on the national treasury. Congress' primary objectives were to settle the West at the least possible cost to itself and, through the sale of public lands, to raise money to avert financial embarrassment—or bankruptcy. Thus, because of the prohibitive costs implicit in the Ordinance of 1784, Congress would not have acted under it even if it were able to locate the proposed states and even if the settlers assumed the responsibilities of organizing and supporting their own governments.

Since Congress intended to administer some western policies directly, the supposedly autonomous western governments could avoid clashes and congressional interference only if they co-operated closely with the central government. In any case, as creatures of Congress the colonies were its inferiors regardless of what the Ordinance said, and if they did not accept that status voluntarily, Congress could be expected to abridge their autonomy whenever it saw fit to assure the smooth execution of national policies. It is not surprising, therefore, that congressional thinking moved steadily away from the idea of theoretically complete western autonomy to the position that Congress should assume direct control over all sectors of colonial affairs, including local government.

By the end of 1785, a number of American leaders must have

felt a curious sense of identification with Britain's colonial problems. The United States had just won its independence after fighting a war born of the nature of the British colonial system and of Parliament's attempts to enforce centralized administration. Now Congress was on the verge of imposing the same kind of administrative system on its own inland empire. In moving from the denunciation of one empire to the implementation of its own, however, Congress seemed to have solved the British dilemma of what to do with mature colonies. Seemed, because, as a law, especially one of dubious legality Congress could change or repeal the Ordinance at will—and Congress would replace it with another ordinance in 1787. Only time would tell the worth of the Ordinance's guarantees of eventual partnership in the empire, but they undoubtedly made more palatable to former "radicals" the relegation of the territories to an inferior, if temporary, status in the centralized imperial system they were embracing.

In 1785 James Monroe took a tour of the West and returned home convinced that Jefferson's Ordinance should be changed. As it was, the size of the proposed states was too small and the population requirement for statehood was too large. The provisions would impede the growth of the West and might frustrate all efforts to organize state governments. Monroe was especially impressed by the poverty of the Great Lakes area and by its meager prospects for attracting settlers. He concluded that under the Ordinance of 1784 none of the colonies there might ever acquire enough people to gain admission to the Union. If such areas were to be brought into the Union, they would have to be annexed to other areas having a brighter outlook. Therefore, as soon as he returned, Monroe advised Congress to consider reducing the number of states to be created in the Northwest. A division of the territory into three to five states would in his eyes be more judicious. It would equalize resources by giving each of the more promising of Jefferson's states a larger hinterland and a responsibility for developing the poorer areas.

Congress took Monroe's proposal to reduce the number of states under consideration early in 1786. At the same time it set up a new committee to review the whole problem of government for the Northwest. The decision to organize the new committee probably grew out of Monroe's firsthand reports which confirmed doubts about the general suitability of Jefferson's Ordinance. Monroe was sure settlement everywhere in the West was going to be slow at best and thought federal direction would be essential in the early years—at least until frontiersmen could form their own governments—and probably would be desirable until statehood.

Congress made Monroe chairman of the new committee. This was to be expected as he was the heir apparent in Congress to his mentor and fellow Virginian, Thomas Jefferson, who was currently abroad on a mission to France. He was also Jefferson's logical successor by virtue of his recent experiences which had gained him a reputation as an authority on western problems. Finally, Monroe was generally regarded as the Congressman best qualified to draft a practical plan of temporary government acceptable both to northerners and southerners. By early May the committee was hard at work, and Monroe soon gave evidence of his abilities.

On May 9, 1786, Monroe presented his committee's first report. In its refined form the report constituted the governmental articles and part of the compact of the Ordinance of 1787. Monroe unequivocally patterned the system of Colonial government after the British model. At the same time he gave form to Read's proposed amendment to the Ordinance of 1784 and developed the broad imperial construction implicit in the Jefferson-Gerry amendment. Unlike Jefferson, Monroe had kept the object of his work in sight, and his report furnished a relatively precise plan by which the West would pass through two stages of political evolution before admission to statehood. The plan explicitly applied only to the ceded western lands—the Northwest Territory—but Monroe, as had Jefferson, clearly intended that his proposed ordinance would serve as a constitution until statehood. In the first stage, for which Jefferson had provided no government, Monroe, by implication, made the entire Northwest into a single administrative district, thereby centralizing all elements of colonial government. Congress was to appoint a single territorial governor who would hold office for an unspecified number of years. He would be assisted by a five-man council and a secretary, each appointed by Congress for an unspecified term of years. In addition,

Congress was to appoint five judges to a territorial supreme court. They would hold office during good behavior.

During the first, or district, stage the governor was to administer the laws of one of the original states, divide the territory into counties and townships, and appoint all necessary civil officials and militia officers below the rank of major. It would seem that Monroe intended to give the district-stage governor both absolute executive powers and, through the right to issue proclamations, complete legislative powers. In other words, Monroe's first stage was one of pure autocracy.

When the free adult male population reached an unstated number, the territory could enter the second, or representative, stage of colonial government. The transition to the second stage would begin with the first meeting of the General Assembly following the election of a house of representatives. Monroe provided for Congress to assign the time and places of the elections, but the governor would presumably make the initial apportionment of the territory, according to an as yet undetermined, fixed ratio of representatives to free adult males. Prospective representatives would have to meet a property and residence qualification for office, and only those adult males who had a fifty-acre freehold and were citizens or, if aliens, had been residents for one year, were to be eligible to vote. Significantly, neither Monroe nor anyone else seems to have questioned the prudence of transferring these conservative eastern residence and property requirements to western colonies, and this suggests that Monroe and the rest of Congress wanted to guarantee the development of conservative western governments dominated by substantial landholders.

Monroe's second stage was almost identical in concept to the royal colonial governments of the old British Empire. With the appointed governor and council, the house of representatives would form a general assembly. It was to be competent to legislate on all internal affairs insofar as its acts were not inconsistent with the provisions of the Articles of Confederation, acts of Congress, the state land cessions, and other covenants. In essence these restrictions were similar to those of Jefferson's Ordinance. Monroe gave Congress absolute control over representative government through the governor, who had an unqualified veto and the authority to convene, prorogue, and dissolve the assembly at will. Apparently no one questioned the propriety of giving the executive such broad powers, in spite of the complaints they had aroused before the Revolution when they had rested in the hands of the royal governors. In July, 1787, Edward Carrington, then chairman of the committee reconsidering Monroe's plan, perhaps reflected the general attitude in Congress in a letter to Jefferson. Referring to the territorial governor's veto, he observed that during the British colonial period, "The negative which the King of England had upon our Laws was never found to be materially inconvenient." Unlike the British system, however, there was no formal hierarchy of appeals beyond the governor in either stage of Monroe's plan. Under it the governor would lose little if any power in the second stage. He would lose initiative in legislation, for example, only insofar as the requirement that all bills originate in the lower house proved to be significant.

Monroe's May report was vague in several important respects. He did not specify whether the laws of the original state used during the first stage were to continue in force in the second stage until altered or repealed by the general assembly. Nor did he indicate how or when a state constitution was to be formed. His provision for statehood simply stated that a territory could be admitted to the Union by the seating of its delegates in Congress when its population equaled that of the smallest original state. In the meantime, the territory could have a nonvoting delegate in Congress during the second stage as under Jefferson's plan.

Writing to Jefferson on May 11, Monroe noted that "The most important principles of the Act at Annapolis [Ordinance of 1784?] are you observe preserv'd in this report." He added, "It is generally approv'd of but has not yet been taken up." It was not taken up again until July 13, 1786, exactly one year before Congress enacted the Ordinance. In the revised report all the blanks were filled. Monroe gave the governor and secretary three- and two-year terms respectively, and increased the governor's appointive power to include all militia officers below general rank. The second stage could now begin when there were 500 free adult males in the territory. The house of representatives was to be elected annually on the basis of one representative for every fifty free adult males until its membership reached twenty. Thereafter the legislature was to adjust the apportionment to maintain that number. Monroe also reduced the lower house's control over legislation by requiring only money bills to originate in it.

There were two deletions of some consequence in the July report. Either Monroe or Congress, in earlier debates, struck out the requirement that the governor enforce the laws of one of the original states during the first stage. This probably grew out of a belief that the laws of none of the eastern states were likely to meet frontier needs fully. And, though not so stated in the draft ordinance, it may have been understood that the governor would proclaim effective in the territory, or adapt, laws and parts of laws from various existing state codes to fill the statutory void until the second stage. Apparently, the selection of laws was to be left entirely up to the governor. Under the provisions of the May report, he might have chosen laws with the help of the council, but Monroe deleted the first-stage council from the plan in July. In a cost-conscious Congress this was to be expected. During the first stage the council was a superfluous organ. The governor might ask it for advice about important matters, but he was not obliged to consult it. Consequently, Monroe now provided for the council and house of representatives to come into existence simultaneously. At the beginning of the second stage Congress was to appoint five men to serve on the council "during pleasure." Monroe did not prescribe residence or property qualifications for councillors, but since he required as a minimum a 200-acre freehold and three years residence in the territory to qualify for election to the lower house, it may be assumed that the council would represent the territory's largest landowners and speculators.

In the two months after Monroe submitted his revised report, Congress debated the plan several times and the committee restudied it. All this led to further changes but work stopped short of completion early in September. By then Monroe and several other members of the committee had left Congress and nothing more could be done until September 18, when Congress reconstituted the committee. William S. Johnson of Connecticut became chairman of the reorganized committee and Nathan Dane of Massachusetts was among its new members. On the 19th the committee presented a new version of Monroe's plan containing some important changes. Dane's hand was evident in the legal verbiage regarding property rights, and possibly in the inclusion of the first positive guarantees of civil rights, *habeas corpus* and jury trial. In this report the federal judges were empowered to adopt criminal laws for use during the first stage from the existing state codes. In light of Monroe's original provision and its deletion in the July report, this new one suggests that there was some uncertainty in Congress as to who should exercise the legislative authority in the district stage. Now, it seems, the governor was to choose the territory's civil laws, while the court picked its criminal laws.

Other unsettled issues were also manifested in September. The article on representative government regressed almost to its original form. The size of the house, the representation ratio, and the population requirement for initiation of the second stage were again omitted. Finally, there was a new population requirement for statehood reflecting the so-called northern bias of the committee. All reports since 1784 had provided for statehood when a territory's population reached that of the smallest of the original states. Now the committee raised the admission requirement to one-thirteenth of the population of the thirteen original states at the most recent census.

During the debate, Congress reduced the number of federal judges from five to three and filled the blanks in the section on representative government. These provisions would appear unchanged in the Ordinance when it was finally enacted. Congress decided that the territory could not enter the second stage until it had 5,000 free adult male inhabitants. This was a tenfold increase from Monroe's report of July. Similarly, it authorized the election of one representative for every 500 free adult males, whereas in July the ratio had been 1:50. If more conservative, the new formula was more realistic than the earlier one, given the size of the territory and the current wide dispersal of the predominantly French male population which certainly exceeded 500, especially if it were now agreed that the entire Northwest would be a single administrative district, not only in the first stage but also during at least part of the second.

After the September debate, Congress took no further action on the plan for seven months. During this time it witnessed the suppression of Shay's Rebellion and the triumph of the movement for revision of the Articles of Confederation, but it is impossible to say that these events had any political influence on the drafting of the Ordinance of 1787, since its governmental articles were already nearly settled. In April, 1787, less than a month before the Constitutional Convention opened, the committee on western government presented another revision of Monroe's plan. Now the entire Northwest was explicitly made a single administrative district until Congress chose to divide it. The revised report also raised the terms of the secretary and assemblymen to four and two years respectively, and, more importantly, solved the problem of the divided first-stage legislative authority. The governor and judges would exercise it jointly. Meeting together, a majority of them was to adopt those civil and criminal laws from the original states' codes which they thought best suited frontier conditions. These laws were to remain in force until changed by the general assembly in the second stage.

On May 9, 1787, the plan passed its second reading. Its final reading was scheduled for the following day but, for a variety of reasons, Congress did not enact the Ordinance until July 13. Just before its enactment, Congress added property qualifications for all federally appointed offices, changed the tenure of councillors to five-year terms, and lowered the population requirement for statehood. In all other respects the governmental provisions of the Ordinance adopted in July were identical to those in the plan read for the second time on May 9. As has been demonstrated, this plan was hardly more than a refinement of Monroe's original report of May 9, 1786.

On May 9, 1787, the Reverend Manasseh Cutler, lobbyist for the Ohio Company, arrived in New York City, where Congress was meeting. The following morning he appeared before that body to begin promoting his land scheme—a request that Congress grant the Company a vast and choice tract at the junction of the Ohio and Muskingum rivers. [See Map 7.] No other evidence should be needed to show that he did not influence the drafting of the governmental articles of the Ordinance; that, in fact, there was little left in the whole Ordinance for him to affect by the time he arrived. On May 10 Congress also postponed the third and final reading of the Ordinance. This and Cutler's appearance seem to be purely coincidental.

The postponement emanated directly from the long-standing desires of a number of Congressmen to debate adjournment for a vacation and removal of the proceedings to Philadelphia, where the Constitutional Convention was about to meet. Some members of Congress may have wanted Congress to be in Philadelphia to supervise the Convention and keep it in check, but others wanted to be there because they were also delegates to the Convention. In addition, a final southern drive to strike out the one-thirteenth population requirement for statehood may have succeeded on the 10th, thereby raising the need for further examination and amendment of the Ordinance. In any case, Congress took no action on the 11th, and between then and July 6, it lacked a quorum. Obviously, a number of Congressmen were bent on leaving and would not be deterred either by the western need for government or Reverend Cutler's lust for land.

When Congress again had a quorum, it moved quickly to complete the long-overdue business of supplying colonial government for the Northwest. On Monday, July 9, it reorganized the committee on western government to make final revisions in Monroe's plan. The reconstituted committee had three new members, one of whom, Edward Carrington of Virginia, became its chairman, but Nathan Dane remained its most effective member. The reasons for recommitting the Ordinance are reasonably clear. Southerners had not willingly accepted the one-thirteenth population requirement for statehood—written into the plan after Monroe left Congress—and during the debates either of May 10 or of July 9, they secured its deletion. This left the Ordinance without any provision for statehood. Simultaneously, a number of Congressmen from both the North and the South were pressing for amplification of the statehood provision. Like Monroe, they strongly believed the population required for admission should be explicitly tied to the number of states to be created in the Northwest. They were about to have their way. So were those northerners who, since 1785, had wanted to reintroduce Jefferson's proposed prohibition of slavery into the frame of government for the West. The coincidence of these achievements suggests logrolling.

In revising the Ordinance, the committee incorporated Monroe's 1786 proposal for the eventual division of the territory into three to five states. For at least a year and a half this idea for the division of the Northwest had been drifting aimlessly about in Congress attracting only occasional attention. Monroe had proposed it separately and had deliberately omitted it from his plans of government. He did not feel that its inclusion, though desirable, was essential to the adoption of a system of temporary government. On the contrary, he feared that its inclusion would only delay the enactment of a law providing colonial government, since the size of potential western states could not be so increased without the consent of the states which had ceded land to Congress. By 1787, these states were receptive to the idea of creating larger states.

Although Monroe wanted to divide the Northwest into fewer states than Jefferson's Ordinance permitted in order to improve their chances of attaining statehood, he received support from several quarters for very different reasons. Both Cavaliers and Yankees assumed that all western states would have a southern bias. For this reason many northerners were bent on admitting the fewest states possible. So were other easterners who saw in the West a general threat to their power. Together they had labored to amend Jefferson's Ordinance to raise the population requirement for admission and reduce the number of states to be created in the Northwest. It was partially to gain the initiative and forestall attempts to reduce the number to two that Monroe had introduced his proposal in 1786 for a three-to-five-way division of the territory.

After Monroe left Congress, opponents of western statehood obtained the higher admission requirement they desired, but, this having now been struck out of the Ordinance, they returned in mid-1787 with renewed interest to the idea of reducing the number of states. Southerners would certainly have been willing to strike a bargain. Being less interested in the potential number of new states than in increasing their power in Congress with all deliberate speed, they could cheerfully agree to a reduction in the number of states in return for northern acceptance of a smaller population requirement for statehood.

As the statehood article was finally written, everyone could take pride in having accomplished his primary objective. Southerners might anticipate as many as five states emerging from the

Northwest to add considerable strength to their voice in Congress. Northerners, or easterners more generally, could look forward to the eventual division of the territory into only three states. This prospect seems to have made many people jubilant. By so enlarging the size of future states and setting the admission requirement at 60,000 inhabitants, not more than one of the three might ever qualify for statehood, and it might adopt "Eastern politics."

The article, however, also contained the important provision that permitted Congress to admit states with a smaller population if it seemed desirable. Moreover, those people who thought the population requirement was high and possibly prohibitive erred badly. In reality the southerners got a better deal in 1787 than they had in 1784, because the entrance requirement of 60,000 people worked out to fewer than a population equal to that of the smallest original state. This should have been reasonably clear in 1787, but everyone apparently underestimated Delaware's population. In 1790 Delaware, the smallest state in the Union, had 59,096 inhabitants; in 1800 it was still the smallest with 64,273, and the first state was yet to enter the Union from the Northwest. Finally, the Ordinance of 1787 made statehood easier than the Ordinance of 1784 had in that the new plan required only a simple legislative majority in Congress for admission, whereas the old one required the consent of two-thirds of the states in the Union at the time a new state petitioned for admission.

In its final meeting, the committee expanded and added to the compact articles of the Ordinance. One of the new articles restored all the restrictions Jefferson had imposed on western states in 1784. Most of these had been in Monroe's first draft but had been gradually lost in revision. The other articles augmented the list of civil liberties incorporated the preceding September. On July 11, 1787, after two days of work, the committee presented its newly revised and enlarged Ordinance. At this point it might be called the Jefferson-Monroe-Dane Plan. Congress made some minor emendments and, on Friday the 13th of July, after adding an amendment prohibiting slavery in the Northwest, adopted the Ordinance unanimously.

The Ordinance of 1787 provided for three levels of government in place of the four in Jefferson's Ordinance of 1784. The new law both simplified and elaborated elements of the earlier one. It simplified Jefferson's plan by eliminating his third stage. Now a colony was to become a state at the same time that it adopted a permanent state constitution. Part of Jefferson's second and all of his third stage were to be covered by the elongated second stage of the Ordinance of 1787. The new second stage also developed ideas implicit in the Ordinance of 1784 by detailing the structure and operation of the temporary representative government. In this way the new plan furnished a precise definition of republicanism upon which regular state governments were to be built. But the most important change in the new law lay in the complete revision and elaboration of Jefferson's first stage. It is here that the Ordinance of 1787 has been subjected to the most severe criticism, but it was also here that Jefferson's plan was most deficient, and a strong authority was deemed crucial to assure the maintenance of order and the execution of national policies in the territory. The Ordinance of 1787 provided for external direction in the person of the governor, who was intended to act as a stabilizer throughout the colonial period but principally during the first stage. Jefferson's plan did not explicitly provide for continuous congressional direction during any stage of development.

The Ordinance of 1787 was also more in tune with the British colonial experience than was Jefferson's. One can assume Monroe was familiar with the general history of the pre-Revolutionary period and argue that in reviewing it in his mind he extracted what he considered to be the essential elements in the evolution of British colonial government, systematized them, and institutionalized them in his draft Ordinance. The American colonies passed through three stages of political development before the Revolution which roughly but distinctly parallel the three stages of the Ordinance. During the seventeenth century the colonies passed through a stage of strong executive control which can be equated with the first stage of the Ordinance. The first two-thirds of the eighteenth century was a period of executive eclipse and of the real emergence of representative government authorized in the Ordinance's second stage. After 1763 the colonies moved into a period of rebellion leading to independence. The Ordinance sought to avoid rebellion by providing for quasi-independence through statehood as the third stage. In this light, the Ordinance cannot be viewed as innovative in any basic sense, even in the provision for statehood. On the contrary, it was more authoritarian. In the first stage it did not afford even the most meager elements of popular government to be found in colonies during the seventeenth century. And, in the second stage the Ordinance did not simply revert to the second British stage of representative governments with ineffective executives. It incorporated all the changes made in the British system after 1763 to strengthen the governor's office. The British found it to be disastrous to try to do this after representative government was firmly established. Realizing this, Monroe may have considered a strong governor from the beginning of representative government necessary both to get the people in harness and to prevent rebellions before statehood.

To summarize, Monroe designed a relatively precise, operative system of colonial government to implement Jefferson's general principles by returning to the experience of the Old Empire. In adding a positive bill of rights, Dane supplied a valuable but perhaps unnecessary counterweight to the apparently rigid governmental forms and potentially stifling congressional controls. He also gave the Ordinance greater clarity as he rewrote and rearranged parts of Monroe's plan but as he completed his work he unleashed his political conservatism, prescribing property qualifications for all office holders cited in the Ordinance. This was remarkable only in its enthusiasm, for the idea of requiring property qualifications had been in Monroe's first report. Since Monroe had required voters and representatives to own land in the territory, logic must have led Dane to complete the job.

In March, 1830, following the Webster-Hayne debates, Nathan Dane wrote Daniel Webster to explain the origins of the Ordinance of 1787. The law, he contended, was clearly the work of a Massachusetts lawyer, meaning himself. He said *he* had written the *important* parts of the plan and that it owed nothing to the ideas of Jefferson or anyone else. Significantly, he dismissed the governmental articles of the Ordinance as irrelevant. He argued, as other Congressmen may have in the 1780's, that in the history of a nation brief periods of colonialism were inconsequential. Only things that were permanent mattered and, in Dane's eyes, in the Ordinance these were the conveyance article he wrote and those parts of the compact articles he claimed to have written. He thought almost any form of government would suffice temporarily, if at the same time appropriate machinery were provided to guarantee basic property rights and civil liberties. For this reason, in the 1780's as in the 1830's, Dane and others may not have considered it necessary to develop a more satisfactory or democratic system of colonial government for the West, even though it was silly to suppose that colonial institutions of government would not shape those of the states.

Monroe seems to have been well aware of the fundamental relationship between colonial and state institutions and Jefferson must at least have sensed it. Whatever the case, if native Americans from the east were going to settle the Northwest, as Jefferson sometimes anticipated, the Ordinance of 1784 should have been adequate. After the intellectual and physical upheavals and the constitution writing of the preceding decade, Anglo-Americans did not need the more elaborate Ordinance of 1787 to instruct them in their basic rights or in how to set up a republican government. Westerners might demand written guarantees and Congress might respond almost automatically by writing them into law, but, written or not, few Anglo-Americans going to the frontier were likely to believe that their rights and institutions did not accompany them. If, on the other hand, Congress expected the continued settlement of the Northwest by French-Canadians and other aliens unfamiliar with American political and legal institutions, Jefferson's Ordinance would clearly have seemed inadequate—if not a license to anarchy. A more rigid and centralized system of colonial government as in the Ordinance of 1787 would have been deemed desirable. Through it Congress would have sure control over the West during the period of "apprenticeship" in which frontiersmen thoroughly assimilated republican institutions—until they reached the level of conformity requisite for full partnership in the empire.

These considerations apparently loomed large in the decision to rewrite Jefferson's Ordinance and pervaded every stage of the drafting of the Ordinance of 1787. Petitions from the

French settlers of the Illinois Country in the 1780's gave force to arguments that Jefferson's Ordinance needed to be redone in greater detail. But, more important, Monroe said in effect that he wrote his governmental articles specifically for the government of such "foreigners" and to initiate them into the mysteries of republicanism. In the latter sense, the Ordinance of 1787 was intended to teach non-English westerners what constituted a republican government, how it was to be organized, and how it should operate. For Monroe, Dane, and others who seemed to take it for granted that non-English settlers would predominate in the West, then the Northwest Ordinance satisfied the need unmet in the Ordinance of 1784 for concrete congressional supervision and a carefully worked out, clearly defined system of colonial administration.

Similarly, through the article on the descent and conveyance of property, which, as a law, did not belong in a fundamental document such as the Ordinance pretended to be, Dane explained in detail how real and personal properties were transferred and inherited in the United States legal system. Though Dane modestly boasted that this article was the first truly republican inheritance law in history, its inclusion in the Ordinance could be justified only on the assumption that western settlers would import ideas or institutions incompatible with Anglo-American practices and unacceptable to easterners, which should be prevented from taking root. Indeed, Dane was pessimistic about the future of the West. The Northwest, he asserted, would be divided into three districts and only the eastern one was likely to qualify for statehood within the foreseeable future. He was not confident that American institutions would successfully penetrate the western two districts. However, he thought there was some hope for enough easterners to settle in the easternmost district to form a majority, or a controlling minority. Then, by the time it entered the Union there would be an "equal" chance of its adopting a system of government similar to that of the original states and "Eastern politics."

Dane and Monroe, two of the principal architects of the Ordinance of 1787, were supposedly well versed in western problems. They represented different northern and southern perspectives, but they firmly agreed that it would be difficult to transplant republican institutions in the hinterland of the empire and that the success of any attempt was uncertain at best. Add to this their expectation, and Jefferson's, that settlement was going to be slow and statehood for even the easternmost part of the Northwest would be long in coming, and it is small wonder all three decided the Ordinance of 1784 should be redrawn. In fairness, then, politically controversial or deceitful motives cannot be attributed to these men. Their contributions to the Ordinance of 1787 did not emanate foremost from a desire either to further or frustrate whatever democratic tendencies there were on the frontier, but simply out of the felt need to devise a viable system of colonial government for the empire in the West. In more general terms, the governmental articles may be called conservative or reactionary *only* if one is willing to use the same label to describe all American leaders during the mid-1780's. The Ordinance can hardly be considered the work of a band of conspirators since everyone seems to have agreed on its basic content. This is not meant to suggest that there were no compromises between rather fluid factions in Congress or that some of them were unimportant, but it is meant to emphasize the essentially apolitical nature of the governmental provisions. The continuity and consensus of thought are obvious, yet they have been missed in the past because the history of the Ordinance has been overdramatized and its political significance has been obscured by irrelevancies. In light of the aura of intrigue that has surrounded the Ordinance, it is thus surprising to see how its history is apparently nothing more or less than that of a rather ordinary piece of noncontroversial legislation.

Bibliography

Abbey, Kathryn, "Peter Chester's Defence of the Mississippi After the Willing Raid," *Mississippi Valley Historical Review*, XXII (June, 1935), 17–32.

Abbott, Phyllis Ruth, "The Development and Operation of the American Land System to 1800." Ph.D., University of Wisconsin, 1959.

Abel, Annie Heloise, "Proposals for an Indian State, 1778–1878," *Annual Report of the American Historical Association for the Year 1907* (Washington, 1908), I, 87–104.

Abernethy, Thomas P., *Western Lands and the American Revolution* (New York, 1937).

Adair, E. R., "Anglo-French Rivalry in the Fur Trade During the Eighteenth Century," *Culture*, VIII (1947), 434–455.

Adams, Herbert B., *Maryland's Influence Upon Land Cessions to the United States* (Baltimore, 1885).

Adams, John A., "The Indian Trader of the Upper Ohio Valley," *Western Pennsylvania Historical Magazine*, XVII (September, 1934), 163–174.

Adams, Paul K., "Colonel Henry Bouquet's Ohio Expedition in 1764," *Pennsylvania History*, XL (April, 1973), 139–147.

Aiton, Arthur S., "The Diplomacy of the Louisiana Cession," *American Historical Review*, XXXVI (July, 1931), 701–720.

Alden, George H., "The Evolution of the American System of Forming and Admitting New States into the Union," *Annals of the American Academy of Political and Social Science*, XVIII (November, 1901), 469–479.

Alden, George H., "New Governments West of the Alleghenies Before 1780," University of Wisconsin *Bulletin, Economics, Political Science, and History Series*, II (1899).

Alden, John R., *General Gage in America* (Baton Rouge, 1948).

Alden, John R. "The Albany Congress and the Creation of the Indian Superintendencies," *Mississippi Valley Historical Society*, XXVII (September, 1940), 193–210.

Alden, John R., *Pioneer America* (New York, 1966).

Altsheler, Brent, "The Long Hunters and James Knox, Their Leader," *Filson Club History Quarterly*, V (October, 1931), 169–180.

Alvord, Clarence W., "The British Ministry and the Treaty of Fort Stanwix," Wisconsin State Historical Society, *Proceedings*, LVI (1908), 165–183.

Alvord, Clarence W., "The Conquest of St. Joseph, Michigan, by the Spaniards in 1781," *Missouri Historical Review*, II (1908), 195–210.

Alvord, Clarence W., "The County of Illinois," Illinois State Historical Library, *Publications* (1907).

Alvord, Clarence W., "The Daniel Boone Myth," *Journal of the Illinois State Historical Society*, XIX (April, 1926), 16–30.

Alvord, Clarence W. "Genesis of the Proclamation of 1763," *Michigan Pioneer and Historical Collections*, XXXVI (1909), 20–52.

Alvord, Clarence W., *The Illinois Country, 1673–1818* (Springfield, 1920).

Alvord, Clarence W., ed., *The Illinois-Wabash Land Company* (Chicago, 1915).

Alvord, Clarence W., *The Mississippi Valley in British Politics: A Study of Trade, Land Speculation, and Experiments in Imperialism Culminating in the American Revolution*, two volumes (Cleveland, 1917).

Alvord, Clarence W., "Virginia and the West: An Interpretation," *Mississippi Valley Historical Review*, III (June, 1916), 19–38.

Ambler, Charles H., *George Washington and the West* (Chapel Hill, 1936).

Ambler, Charles H., and Summers, Festus P., *West Virginia: The Mountain State*, second edition (New York, 1958).

Anson, Bert, *The Miami Indians* (Norman, Oklahoma, 1970).

Appel, John C., "Colonel Daniel Broadhead and the Lure of Detroit," *Pennsylvania History*, XXXVIII (July, 1971), 265–282.

Baerreis, David A., Voegelin, Erminie W., and Wycoco-Moore, Remedios, *Anthropological Report on the Chippewa, Ottawa, and Potawatomi Indians in Northeastern Illinois and the Identity of the Mascoutens* (New York, 1974).

Bailey, Kenneth P., *The Ohio Company of Virginia and the Westward Movement, 1748–1792: A Chapter in the History of the Colonial Frontier* (Glendale, California, 1939).

Bailey, Kenneth P., *Thomas Cresap, Maryland Frontiersman* (Boston, 1944).

Bakeless, John E., *Background to Glory: The Life of George Rogers Clark* (Philadelphia, 1957).

Bakeless, John, *Daniel Boone* (New York, 1939).

Balls, H. R., "Quebec, 1763–1774: The Financial Administration," *Canadian Historical Review*, XLI (September, 1960), 203–214.

Bannon, John Francis, "The Spaniards and the Illinois Country, 1762–1800," *Journal of the Illinois State Historical Society*, LXIX (May, 1976), 110–118.

Barber, William D., "The West in National Politics, 1784–1804." Ph.D., University of Wisconsin–Madison, 1961.

Barnhart, John D., "A New Evaluation of Henry Hamilton and George Rogers Clark," *Mississippi Valley Historical Review*, XXXVII (March, 1951), 643–652.

Barnhart, John D., *Henry Hamilton and George Rogers Clark in the American Revolution* (Crawfordsville, Indiana, 1951).

Barnhart, John D., "The Southern Element in the Leadership of the Old Northwest," *Journal of Southern History*, I (May, 1935), 186–197.

Barnhart, John D., "The Southern Influence in the Formation of Ohio," *Journal of Southern History*, III (February, 1937), 18–42.

Barnhart, John D., "Sources of Southern Migration into the Old Northwest," *Mississippi Valley Historical Review*, XXII (June, 1935), 49–62.

Barnhart, John D., *Valley of Democracy: The Frontier Versus the Plantation in the Ohio Valley, 1775–1818* (Bloomington, Indiana, 1953).

Barrows, Harlan H., *Lectures on the Geography of the United States as Given in 1937*, Department of Geography Paper Number 77 (Chicago, 1962).

Barrett, Jay A., *Evolution of the Ordinance of 1787* (New York, 1891).

Bartlett, Richard A., *The New Country: A Social History of the American Frontier, 1776–1890* (New York, 1974).

Bayard, Charles J., "The Development of the Public Land Policy, 1783–1820, with Special Reference to Indiana." Ph.D., Indiana University, 1956.

Beals, Ellis, "Arthur St. Clair, Western Pennsylvania's Leading Citizen, 1764–1818," *Western Pennsylvania Historical Magazine*, XII (April–July, 1929), 75–96, 175–196.

Bell, Whitfield J., Jr. "Washington County, Pennsylvania, in the Eighteenth Century Antislavery Movement," *Western Pennsylvania Historical Magazine*, XXV (September–December, 1942), 135–142.

Belote, Theodore, *The Scioto Speculation and the French Settlement at Gallipolis* (Cincinnati, 1907).

Belting, Natalia M., *Kaskaskia Under the French Regime*, University of Illinois, *Studies in the Social Sciences*, XXIX (Urbana, 1948).

Bemis, Samuel F., "Canada and the Peace Settlement of 1783," *Canadian Historial Review*, XIV (September, 1933), 265–284.

Bemis, Samuel F., *The Diplomacy of the American Revolution* (New York, 1935).

Bemis, Samuel F., "The Reyneval Memorandum of 1782 on the

Western Boundaries and Some Comments on the French Historian Donoil," American Antiquarian Society, *Proceedings*, new series, XLVI (1937), 15–92.

Bennet, John, *Blue Jacket: War Chief of the Shawnees* (Chillicothe, Ohio, 1943).

Berthrong, Donald J., *An Historical Report on Indian Use and Occupancy of Northern Indiana and Southwestern Michigan* (New York, 1974).

Berkhofer, Robert F., Jr., "Barrier to Settlement: British Indian Policy in the Old Northwest, 1783–1794," in David M. Ellis, ed., *The Frontier in American Development: Essays in Honor of Paul Wallace Gates* (Ithaca, 1969), 249–276.

Berkhofer, Robert F., Jr., "Jefferson, the Ordinance of 1784, and the Origins of the American Territorial System," *William and Mary Quarterly*, third series, XXIX (April, 1972), 231–262.

Berkhofer, Robert F., Jr., "The Northwest Ordinance and the Principal of Territorial Evolution," in John Porter Bloom, ed., *The American Territorial System* (Athens, Ohio, 1973), 45–55.

Berkhofer, Robert F., Jr., "The Republican Origins of the American Territorial System," in Allan G. Bogue, *et al.*, eds., *The West of the American People* (Itasca, Illinois, 1970), 152–160.

Berthoff, Rowland, *An Unsettled People: Social Order and Disorder in American History* (New York, 1971).

Bestor, Arthur, "Constitutionalism and the Settlement of the West: The Attainment of Consensus, 1754–1784," in John Porter Bloom, ed., *The American Territorial System* (Athens, Ohio, 1973), 13–44.

Billington, Ray Allen, *American Expansion: A History of the American Frontier*, fourth edition (New York, 1974).

Billington, Ray Allen, *America's Frontier Heritage* (New York, 1966).

Billington, Ray Allen, "The Historians of the Northwest Ordinance," *Journal of the Illinois State Historical Society*, XL (December, 1947), 347–413.

Billington, Ray Allen, "The Fort Stanwix Treaty of 1768," *New York History*, XXV (April, 1944), 182–194.

Blair, Emma Helen, ed., *The Indian Tribes of the Upper Mississippi Valley and the Region of the Great Lakes*, two volumes (Cleveland, 1911–1912).

Bodley, Temple, *George Rogers Clark* (Boston, 1926).

Bodley, Temple, "Our First Great West: In the Revolutionary War, Diplomacy and Politics," Filson Club, *Publications*, Number 36, (Louisville, 1938).

Boehm, Robert B., "Fort Gower," in Thomas H. Smith, ed., *Ohio in the American Revolution*, Ohio American Revolution Bicentennial Conference Series, Number 1 (Columbus, 1976), 26–30.

Boggess, Arthur C., *The Settlement of Illinois, 1778–1830* (Chicago, 1908).

Bomberger, Christian M., *A Short History of Westmoreland County, The First County West of the Appalachians* (Jeanette, Pennsylvania, 1941).

Bond, Beverly W., Jr., "An American Experiment in Colonial Government," *Mississippi Valley Historical Review*, XV (September, 1928), 221–235.

Bond, Beverly W., Jr., *The Foundations of the Civilization of the Old Northwest* (New York, 1934).

Bond, Beverly W., Jr., *The Correspondence of John Cleaves Symmes, Founder of the Miami Purchase* (New York, 1926).

Bond, Beverly W., Jr., *The Foundations of Ohio* (Columbus, 1941).

Bond, Beverly W., Jr., "Some Political Ideals of the Colonial Period as They Were Realized in the Old Northwest," in *Essays in Colonial History Presented to Charles McLean Andrews by His Students* (New Haven, 1931), 299–325.

Boyd, C. E., "The County of Illinois," *American Historical Review,* IV (July, 1899), 623–635.

Boyd, Thomas, *Simon Girty, The White Savage* (New York, 1928).

Branch, E. Douglas, "Henry Bouquet: Professional Soldier," *Pennsylvania Magazine of History and Biography*, LXXII (January, 1938), 41–51.

Brebner, John B., *The Explorers of North America, 1492–1806* (New York, 1933).

Brown, Margaret Kimball, "Cultural Transformation Among the Illinois: The Application of a Systems Model to Archaeological and Ethnohistorical Data." Ph.D., Michigan State University, 1973.

Brunet, Michel, *Les Canadiens apres la Conquete 1759–1775* (Montreal, 1969).

Brunet, Michel, *La Presence Anglaise et les Canadiens* (Montreal, 1958).

Bryce, Peter H., "Sir John Johnson, Baronet: Superintendent-General of Indian Affairs, 1743–1830," New York State Historical Association, *Journal*, IX (July, 1928), 233–271.

Buck, Elizabeth H., and Buck, Solon J., *The Planting of Civilization in Western Pennsylvania* (Pittsburgh, 1939).

Buck, Solon J., "The Story of Grand Portage," *Minnesota History Bulletin*, V (February, 1923), 14–27.

Buffington, Arthur H., "The Policy of Albany and the English Westward Expansion," *Mississippi Valley Historical Review*, VIII (March, 1922), 327–366.

Burgess, Charles E., "John Rice Jones: Citizen of Many Territories," *Journal of the Illinois State Historical Society*, LXI (Spring, 1968), 58–82.

Burghardt, Andrew F., "The Origin and Development of the Road Network in the Niagara Peninsula, Ontatio, 1770–1851," *Annals of the Association of American Geographers*, LIX (September, 1969), 417–440.

Burpee, Lawrence J., *The Search for the Western Sea: The Story of the Exploration of North-Western America*, revised edition, two volumes (Toronto, 1935).

Burson, Caroline M., *The Stewardship of Don Esteban Miro, 1782–1792* (New Orleans, 1940).

Burt, Alfred L., *Guy Carleton, Lord Dorchester*, revised edition (Ottawa, 1957).

Burt, Alfred L., "A New Approach to the Problem of the Western Posts," Canadian Historical Association, *Report for 1931* (Ottawa, 1932), 61–75.

Burt, Alfred L., *The Old Province of Quebec* (Toronto, 1933).

Burt, Alfred L., *The United States, Great Britain, and British North America from the Revolution to the Establishment of Peace after the War of 1812* (New Haven, 1940).

Burton, Clarence M., *John Connolly, A Tory of the Revolution* (Worcester, Massachusetts, 1909).

Bushnell, David I., "The Virginia Frontier in History—1778," *Virginia Magazine of History and Biography*, XXIII (April–December, 1915), 113–123, 256–268, 337–351, XXIV (January–April, 1916), 44–55, 168–179.

Butterfield, Consul W., *History of George Rogers Clark's Conquest of the Illinois and Wabash Towns* (Columbus, Ohio, 1904).

Butterfield, Consul W., *An Historical Account of the Expedition Against Sandusky Under Col. William Crawford in 1782* (Cincinnati, 1873).

Butterfield, Consul W., *History of the Girtys* (Cincinnati, 1890).

Caldwell, Norman W., "Fort Massac: The American Frontier Post, 1778–1805," *Journal of the Illinois State Historical Society*, XLIV (Spring, 1951), 47–60.

Caley, Percy B., "Dunmore, Colonial Governor, New York and Virginia, 1770–1782." Ph.D., University of Pittsburgh, 1940.

Caley, Percy B., "The Life-Adventures of Lieutenant-Colonel John Connolly: The Story of a Tory," *Western Pennsylvania Historical Magazine*, XI (January–October, 1928), 10–49, 76–111, 144–179, 225–259.

Caley, Percy B., "Lord Dunmore and the Pennsylvania-Virginia Boundary Dispute," *Western Pennsylvania Historical Magazine*, XXII (June, 1939), 87–100.

Callahan, James Morton, *History of West Virginia: Old and New*, three volumes (Chicago, 1923).

Campbell, Marjorie W., *The Northwest Company* (New York, 1957).

Carey, Lewis J., "Franklin is Informed of Clark's Activities in the Old Northwest," *Mississippi Valley Historical Review*, XXI (December, 1934), 375–378.

Carpenter, Helen M., "The Origins and Location of the Fire Lands of the Western Reserve," *Ohio Archaeological and Historical Quarterly*, XLIV (April, 1935), 163–203.

Carstensen, Vernon, ed., *The Public Lands* (Madison, 1963).

Carter, Clarence E., *Great Britain and the Illinois Country, 1763–1774* (Washington, 1910).

Cartlidge, Anna M., "Colonel John Floyd: Reluctant Adventurer," *Register of the Kentucky Historical Society*, LXVI (October, 1968), 317–366.

Caruso, John A., *The Applachian Frontier: America's First Surge Westward* (Indianapolis, 1959).

Caruso, John A., *The Great Lakes Frontier: An Epic of the Old Northwest* (Indianapolis, 1961).

Caughey, John W., *Bernardo de Galvez in Louisiana, 1776–1783* (Berkeley, 1934).

Caughey, John W., "Willing's Expedition Down the Mississippi," *Louisiana Historical Quarterly*, XV (January, 1932), 5–36.

Chalmers, Harvey, and Monture, Ethel B., *Joseph Brant: Mohawk* (East Lansing, 1955).

Christelow, Allan, "Proposals for a French Company for Spanish Louisiana, 1763–1764," *Mississippi Valley Historical Review*, XXVII (March, 1941), 603–611.

Clark, Thomas D., "Boonesborough—Outpost of the American West," *Register of the Kentucky Historical Society*, LXXII (October, 1974), 391–397.

Clark, Thomas D., *Frontier America* (New York, 1959).

Clark, Thomas D., *A History of Kentucky* (Lexington, 1954).

Coffin, Victor, *The Province of Quebec in the Early American Revolution: A Study in English-American Colonial History* (Madison, 1896).

Coleman, J. Winston, Jr., *The British Invasion of Kentucky* (Lexington, 1951).

Cone, Mary, *Life of Rufus Putnam* (Cleveland, 1886).

Cook, Ray Bird, *Washington's Western Lands* (Strasberg, Virginia, 1930).

Copland, R., *The Quebec Act: A Study in Statesmanship* (Oxford, 1925).

Corbitt, D. C., "James Colbert and the Spanish Claims to the East Bank of the Mississippi," *Mississippi Valley Historical Review*, XXIV (March, 1938), 457–472.

Cotterill, Robert S., *History of Pioneer Kentucky* (Cincinnati, 1917).

Cox, Isaac J., "The Indian as a Diplomatic Factor in the History of the Old Northwest," *Ohio Archaeological and Historical Quarterly*, XVIII (October, 1909), 542–565.

Cribbs, George A., *The Frontier Policy of Pennsylvania* (Pittsburgh, 1919).

Creighton, D. G., *The Commercial Empire of the St. Lawrence, 1760–1850* (Toronto, 1937).

Cruikshank, Ernest A., "Early Traders and Trade-Routes in Canada and the West, 1760–1783," Royal Canadian Institute, *Transactions* (1886–1892), 253–274.

Cruikshank, Ernest A., *The Story of Butler's Rangers and the Settlement of Niagara* (Welland, 1894).

Crumrine, Boyd, "The Boundary Controversy Between Pennsylvania and Virginia," *Annals of the Carnegie Museum*, I, 505–524.

Crumrine, Boyd, *History of Washington County, Pennsylvania* (Philadelphia, 1882).

Curry, Richard O., "Lord Dunmore and the West: A Re-evaluation," *West Virginia History*, XIX (July, 1958), 231–243.

Curry, Richard O., "Lord Dunmore—Tool of Land Jobbers or Realistic Champion of Colonial 'Rights'?: An Inquiry," *West Virginia History*, XXIV (April, 1963), 289–295.

Cutler, J. P., and W. P., *The Life, Journals, and Correspondence of Rev. Manasseh Cutler*, two volumes (Cincinnati, 1888).

Danglade, James K., "John Graves Simcoe and the United States, 1775–1796: A Study in Anglo-American Frontier Diplomacy." Ph.D., Ball State University, 1972.

David, Joseph S., *Essays in the Earlier History of American Corporations* (Cambridge, 1917).

Davidson, George R., *The North West Company* (Berkeley, 1918).

Davis, Andrew M., "The Employment of Indian Auxiliaries in the American War," *English Historical Review*, II (October, 1887), 709–728.

Del Papa, Eugene M., "The Royal Proclamation of 1763: Its Effect upon Virginia Land Companies," *Virginia Magazine of History and Biography*, LXXXIII (October, 1975), 406–411.

Dendy, J. O., "Frederick Haldimand and the Defence of Canada." Ph.D., Duke University, 1974.

Derleth, August, *Vincennes: Portal to West* (Englewood Cliffs, New Jersey, 1968).

Dick, Everett, *The Lure of the Land: A Social History of the Public Lands from the Articles of Confederation to the New Deal* (Lincoln, 1970).

Donnelly, Joseph P., "Pierre Gibault, and the Critical Period of the Illinois Country, 1768–78," in John Francis McDermott, ed., *The French in the Mississippi Valley* (Urbana, Illinois, 1968), 81–92.

Donnelly, Joseph P., *Pierre Gibault, Missionary, 1737–1802* (Chicago, 1971).

Douds, Howard C., "Merchants and Merchandising in Pittsburgh, 1759–1800," *Western Pennsylvania Historical Magazine*, XX (June, 1937), 123–132.

Downes, Randolph C., "Dunmore's War: An Interpretation," *Mississippi Valley Historical Review*, XXI (December, 1934), 311–330.

Downes, Randolph C., *Council Fires on the Upper Ohio: A Narrative of Indian Affairs in the Upper Ohio Valley Until 1795* (Pittsburgh, 1940).

Downes, Randolph C., "George Morgan, Indian Agent Extraordinary, 1776–1779," *Pennsylvania History*, I (October, 1934), 202–216.

Downes, Randolph C., "Indian War on the Upper Ohio, 1779–1782," *Western Pennsylvania Historical Magazine*, XVII (June, 1934), 93–115.

Downes, Randolph C., "Ohio's Squatter Governor: William Hogland of Hoglandstown," *Ohio Archeological and Historical Quarterly*, XLIII (July, 1934), 273–282.

Downes, Randolph C., "The Treatment of the Indians in the Coshocton Campaign of 1781," *Western Pennsylvania Historical Magazine*, XVII (September, 1934), 287–290.

Downey, Fairfax, *Indian Wars of the United States Army, 1778–1865* (New York, 1963).

Driver, Harold E., *Indians of North America*, second edition (Chicago, 1969).

Dunbar, Willis, *Michigan: A History of the Wolverine State* (Grand Rapids, 1965).

Dunn, Walter S., Jr., "The Frontier on the Eve of the Revolution," *Niagara Frontier*, XX (Winter, 1973), 96–111.

Dunn, Walter S., Jr., "Western Commerce, 1760–1774." Ph.D., University of Wisconsin, 1971.

Dunnignan, Brian L., *King's Men at Mackinac: The British Garrisons, 1780–1796*, Reports in Mackinac History and Archaeology, Number 3 (Mackinac, Michigan, 1973).

Durrie, Daniel S., *The Early Outposts of Wisconsin* (Madison, 1872).

Dyer, A. M., "First Ownership of Ohio Lands," *New England Historical and Geneaological Register*, LXIV (1910), 167–180, 265–282, 356–369, LXV (1911), 51–62, 139–150, 220–231.

Eblen, Jack E., *The First and Second United States Empires: Governors and Territorial Government, 1784–1912* (Pittsburgh, 1968).

Eblen, Jack E., "The Origins of the United States Colonial System: The Ordinance of 1787," *Wisconsin Magazine of History*, LI (Summer, 1968), 294–314.

Eckert, Allan W., *Blue Jacket: War Chief of the Shawnee* (Boston, 1969).

Eckert, Allan W., *The Frontiersmen: A Narrative* (Boston 1967).

Edmunds, R. David, "Pickawillany: French Military Power Versus British Economics," *Western Pennsylvania Historical Magazine*, LVIII (April, 1975), 169–184.

Edson, Obed, "Brodhead's Expedition Against the Indians of the Upper Allegheny, 1779," *Magazine of American History*, III (November, 1875), 649–675.

Ernst, Joseph, "With Compass and Chain: Federal Land Surveys in the Old Northwest, 1785–1816," Ph.D., Columbia University, 1958.

Evans, Emory G., "The Colonial View of the West," *Journal of the Illinois State Historical Society*, LXIX (May, 1976), 84–90.

Farrell, David, "Settlement along the Detroit Frontier, 1760–1796," *Michigan History*, LII (Summer, 1968), 89–107.

Ferguson, Russell, *Early Western Pennsylvania Politics* (Pittsburgh, 1938).

Fitting, James E., and Cleland, Charles E., "Late Prehistoric Settlement Patterns in the Upper Great Lakes," *Ethnohistory*, XVI (Fall, 1969), 289–302.

Flexner, James T., *George Washington*, four volumes (New York, 1965–1972).

Flexner, James T., *Mohawk Baronet: Sir William Johnson of New York* (New York, 1959).

Flick, Alexander C., *The Sullivan-Clinton Campaign in 1779* (Albany, 1929).

Ford, Amelia Clewley, *Colonial Precedents of Our National Land System as It Existed in 1800*, Bulletin of the University of Wisconsin, Number 352 (Madison, 1910).

Fouse, Russell L., *The Western Reserve and Early Ohio* (Akron, 1920).

Franklin, W. Neil, "Pennsylvania-Virginia Rivalry for the Indian Trade of the Ohio Valley," *Mississippi Valley Historical Review*, XX (March, 1934), 463–480.

Frass, Elizabeth, "An Unusual Map of the Early West," *Register of the Kentucky Historical Society*, LXXIII (January, 1975), 61–69.

Freeman, Douglas Southall, *et al.*, *George Washington: A Biography*, seven volumes (New York, 1948–1957).

Freund, Rudolph, "Military Bounty Lands and the Origins of the Public Domain," *Agricultural History*, XX (January, 1946), 8–18.

Friis, Herman R., *A Series of Population Maps of the Colonies and the United States, 1625–1790* (New York, 1940).

Gates, Charles M., *Five Fur Traders of the Northwest* (St. Paul, 1965).

Gates, Paul W., "The Role of the Land Speculator in Western Development," *Pennsylvania Magazine of History and Biography*, LXVI (July, 1942), 314–333.

Gates, Paul W., "Tenants of the Log Cabin," *Mississippi Valley Historical Review*, XLIX (July, 1962), 3–31.

Geiser, Karl F., "New England and the Western Reserve," Mississippi Valley Historical Association, *Proceedings*, VI (1912–1913), 62–78.

Gerlach, Don R., *Philip Schuyler and the American Revolution in New York* (Lincoln, 1964).

Gerlach, Don R., "Philip Schuyler and the New York Frontier in 1781," *New York Historical Society Quarterly*, LIII (April, 1969), 148–181.

Gerlach, Larry R., "Firmness and Prudence: Connecticut, the Continental Congress, and the National Domain," Connecticut Historical Society, *Bulletin*, XXXI (July, 1966), 65–75.

Gilman, Rhoda R., "The Fur Trade in the Upper Mississippi Valley, 1630–1850," *Wisconsin Magazine of History*, LVIII (Autumn, 1974), 3–18.

Gipson, Laurence H., *The British Empire Before the American Revolution*, fifteen volumes (New York, 1936–1970).

Goodrich, Carter, *The First Michigan Frontier* (Ann Arbor, 1940).

Graham, Gerald S., *British Policy and Canada, 1774–1791: A Study in Eighteenth Century Trade Policy* (New York, 1930).

Graham, Louis E., "Fort McIntosh," *Western Pennsylvania Historical Magazine*, XV (May, 1932), 93–119.

Grant, Charles S., "Pontiac's Rebellion and the British Troop Moves of 1763," *Mississippi Valley Historical Review*, XL (June, 1953), 75–88.

Grant, William L., "Canada *Versus* Guadeloupe, An Episode of the Seven Years War," *American Historical Review*, XVII (July, 1912), 735–743.

Gray, Elma F., and Gray, Leslie R., *Wilderness Christians: The Moravian Missions to the Delaware Indians* (Ithaca, 1956).

Graymont, Barbara, *The Iroquois in the American Revolution* (Syracuse, New York, 1972).

Green, Ernest, "The Niagara Portage Road," Ontario Historical Society, *Publications*, XXIII (1926), 260–311.

Greenman, Emerson F., *The Indians of Michigan* (Lansing, 1961).

Griffin, J. David, "Historians and the Sixth Article of the Ordinance of 1787," *Ohio History*, LXXVIII (Autumn, 1969), 252–260.

Guthrie, Dwight R., *John McMillan: The Apostle of Presbyterianism in the West, 1752–1833* (Pittsburgh, 1952).

Guzzardo, John C., "The Superintendent and the Ministers: The Battle for Oneida Allegiances, 1761–75," *New York History*, LVII (July, 1976), 255–284.

Hackett, Charles W., Hammond, G. P., and Mecham, J. L., eds., *New Spain and the Anglo-American West: Historical Contributions Presented to Herbert Eugene Bolton*, volume one (Los Angeles, 1932).

Hagan, William T., *The Sac and Fox Indians* (Norman, Oklahoma, 1958).

Hall, Charles S., *Life and Letters of General Samuel Holden Parsons* (Binghamton, 1905).

Hammon, Neal O., "Captain Harrod's Company, 1774: A Reappraisal," *Register of the Kentucky Historical Society*, LXXII (July, 1974), 224–242.

Hammon, Neal O., "The Fincastle Surveyors at the Falls of the Ohio, 1774," *Filson Club Quarterly*, XLVII (January, 1973), 14–28.

Hammon, Neal O., "The Fincastle Surveyors in the Bluegrass, 1774," *Register of the Kentucky Historical Society*, LXX (October, 1972), 277–294.

Hanna, Charles A., *The Wilderness Trail*, two volumes (New York, 1941).

Harlow, Charles T., *The Founding of the Second British Empire, 1763–1793*, two volumes (London, 1952–1964).

Harris, Marshall, *Origin of the Land Tenure System of the United States* (Ames, 1953).

Harrison, Lowell H., *George Rogers Clark and the War in the West* (Lexington, 1976).

Hassler, Edgar W., *Old Westmoreland: A History of Western Pennsylvania During the Revolution* (Pittsburgh, 1900).

Hatcher, Harlan, *The Western Reserve: The Story of New Connecticut in Ohio* (Cleveland, 1966).

Hauser, Raymond E., "The Illinois Indian Tribe: From Autonomy and Self-Sufficiency to Dependency and Depopulation," *Journal of the Illinois State Historical Society*, LXIX (May, 1976), 127–138.

Havighurst, Walter, *Wilderness for Sale: The Story of the First Western Land Rush* (New York, 1956).

Hayden, Edwin Horace, "Oliver Pollock, His Connections with the Conquest of Illinois," *Magazine of History*, XXII (1893), 414–420.

Haynes, Robert V., "James Willing and the Planters of Natchez: The American Revolution Comes to the Southwest," *Journal of Mississippi History*, XXXVII (February, 1975), 1–42.

Helderman, Leonard C., "The Northwest Expedition of George Rogers Clark, 1786–1787," *Mississippi Valley Historical Review*, XXV (December, 1938), 317–334.

Henderson, Archibald, *The Conquest of the Old Southwest* (New York, 1920).

Henderson, Archibald, "The Creative Forces in American Expansion: Henderson and Boone," *American Historical Review*, XX (October, 1914), 86–107.

Henderson, Archibald, "Dr. Thomas Walker and the Loyal Land Company of Virginia," American Antiquarian Society, *Proceedings*, new series, XLI (1931), 77–178.

Henderson, Archibald, "The Transylvania Company: A Study in Personnel," *Filson Club Historical Quarterly*, XXI (January–October, 1947), 3–21, 228–242, 327–349.

Hibbard, Benjamin H., *A History of Public Land Policies*, second edition (Madison, 1965).

Hildreth, Samuel P., *Pioneer History: Being an Account of the First Examinations of the Ohio Valley, and the Early Settlement of the Northwest Territory* (Cincinnati, 1848).

Hoberg, Walter R., Early History of Colonel Alexander McKee," *Pennsylvania Magazine of History and Biography*, LVIII (January, 1934), 26–36.

Hodge, Frederick W., ed., *Handbook of North American Indians*, two volumes (Washington, 1907–1910).

Horsman, Reginald, "American Indian Policy in the Old Northwest, 1783–1815," *William and Mary Quarterly*, XVIII, third series (January, 1961), 35–53.

Horsman, Reginald, *The Frontier in the Formative Years, 1783–1815* (New York, 1970).

Horsman, Reginald, "Great Britain and the Illinois Country in the Era of the American Revolution," *Journal of the Illinois State Historical Society*, LXIX (May, 1976), 100–109.

Horsman, Reginald, *Matthew Elliott: British Indian Agent* (Detroit, 1964).

Horsman, Reginald, "United States Indian Policy and the Expansion of Ohio," in Randall L. Buchman, ed., *The Historic Indians in Ohio*, Ohio American Revolution Bicentennial Conference Series, Number 3 (Columbus, 1976), 6–13.

Houk, Louis, *A History of Missouri*, three volumes (Chicago, 1908).

Houck, Louis, *Spanish Regime in Missouri* (Chicago, 1909).

Howland, Henry, "Navy Island and the First Successors to the *Griffin*," Buffalo Historical Society, *Publications*, VI (1903), 17–33.

Hoyt, William D., Jr., "Colonel William Fleming in Dunmore's War," *West Virginia History*, III (January, 1942), 99–119.

Hoyt, William D., Jr., "Colonel William Fleming on the Virginia Frontier." Ph.D., Johns Hopkins University, 1940.

Huber, John P., "General Josiah Harmar's Command: Military Policy in the Old Northwest, 1784–1791." Ph.D., University of Michigan, 1968.

Hulbert, Archer B., "Andrew Craigie and the Scioto Associates," American Antiquarian Society, *Proceedings*, new series, XXIII (1913), part 2, 222–236.

Hulbert, Archer B., "The Methods and Operations of the Scioto Group of Speculators," *Mississippi Valley Historical Review*, I (March, 1915), 502–515, II (June, 1915), 56–73.

Hulbert, Archer B., *Ohio in the Time of the Confederation* (Marietta, Ohio, 1918).

Hulbert, Archer B., *Red Men's Roads: The Indian Thoroughfares of the Central West* (Columbus, Ohio, 1900).

Humphreys, Robert A., "Lord Shelburne and British Colonial Policy, 1766–1768," *English Historical Review*, L (April, 1935), 257–277.

Humphreys, Robert A., "Lord Shelburne and the Proclamation of 1763," *English Historical Review*, XLIX (April, 1934), 241–264.

Humphreys, Robert A., and Scott, S. Morley, "Lord Northington and the Laws of Canada," *Canadian Historical Review*, XIV (March, 1933), 43–54.

Hunt, George T., *The Wars of the Iroquois: A Study in Intertribal Trade Relations* (Madison, [1940]).

Hurt, N. Franklin, "Growth of Local Action During the British Rule at Detroit, 1760–1774," *Michigan History*, XL (December, 1956), 451–464.

Huston, John W., "The British Evacuation of Fort Pitt, 1772," *Western Pennsylvania Historical Magazine*, XLVIII (October, 1965), 317–329.

Hutchinson, William T., "Military Bounty Lands of the Revolution in Ohio." Ph.D., University of Chicago, 1927.

Hutson, James H., "Benjamin Franklin and the West," *Western Historical Quarterly*, IV (October, 1973), 425–434.

Innis, Harold A., *The Fur Trade in Canada: An Introduction to Canadian Economic History* (New Haven, 1930).

Innis, Harold A., "Peter Pond and the Influence of Capt. James Cook on Exploration in the Interior of North America," *Proceedings and*

Transactions of the Royal Society of Canada, 3rd series, XXII (May, 1938), 135–137.

Jackson, Harvey H., "General Lachlan McIntosh, 1727–1806: A Biography." Ph.D., University of Georgia, 1973.

Jacobs, James Ripley, *The Beginning of the U.S. Army, 1783–1812* (Princeton, 1947).

Jacobs, Wilbur R., "The Indian Frontier of 1763," *Western Pennsylvania Historical Magazine*, XXIV (September, 1951), 185–198.

Jacobs, Wilbur R., *Diplomacy and Indian Gifts: Anglo-French Rivalry Along the Ohio and Northwest Frontiers, 1748–1763* (Stanford, 1950).

Jacobs, Wilbur R., "Was the Pontiac Uprising a Conspiracy?," *Ohio State Archaeological and Historical Quarterly*, LIX (January, 1950), 26–37.

Jacobs, Wilbur R., *Wilderness Politics and Indian Gifts: The Northern Colonial Frontiers, 1748–1763* (Lincoln, 1966).

Jaebker, Orville John, "Henry Hamilton: British Soldier and Colonial Governor." Ph.D., Indiana University, 1954.

Jahns, Patricia, *The Violent Years: Simon Kenton and the Ohio-Kentucky Frontier* (New York, 1962).

Jakle, John A., "The American Bison and the Human Occupance of the Ohio Valley," *Proceedings of the American Philosophical Society*, CXII (1968), 299–305.

James, Alfred P., "The First English-Speaking Trans-Appalachian Frontier," *Mississippi Valley Historical Review*, XVII (June, 1930), 55–71.

James, Alfred P., "George Mercer of the Ohio Company: A Study in Frustration," *Western Pennsylvania Historical Magazine*, XLVI (January–April, 1963), 1–43, 141–183.

James, Alfred P., *The Ohio Company: Its Inner History* (Pittsburgh, 1959).

James, James A., "An Appraisal of the Contributions of George Rogers Clark to the History of the West," *Mississippi Valley Historical Review*, XVII (June, 1930), 98–115.

James, James A., "Detroit: The Key to the West During the American Revolution," Illinois State Historical Society, *Transactions* (1909), 154–164.

James, James A., "Indian Diplomacy and the Opening of the Revolution in the West," Wisconsin State Historical Society, *Proceedings*, LVII (1909), 125–142.

James, James A., *The Life of George Rogers Clark* (Chicago, 1928).

James, James A., "The Northwest: Gift or Conquest?," *Indiana Magazine of History*, XXX (March, 1934), 1–15.

James, James A., "Oliver Pollock and the Free Navigation of the Mississippi River," *Mississippi Valley Historical Review*, XIX (December, 1932), 331–361.

James, James A., "Oliver Pollock, Financier of the Revolution in the West," *Mississippi Valley Historical Review*, XVI (June, 1929), 67–80.

James, James A., *Oliver Pollock: The Life and Times of an Unknown Patriot* (New York, 1937).

James, James A., "The Significance of the Attack on St. Louis, 1780," Mississippi Valley Historical Association, *Proceedings*, II (1908–1909), 199–217.

James, James A., "Some Problems of the Northwest in 1779," in *Essays in American History Dedicated to Frederick Jackson Turner* (New York, 1910), 57–83.

James, James A., "Spanish Influence in the West During the American Revolution," *Mississippi Valley Historical Review*, IV (September, 1917), 193–208.

James, James A., "To What Extent Was George Rogers Clark in Military Control of the Northwest at the Close of the American Revolution?," American Historical Association, *Annual Report for 1917* (Washington, 1920), 313–329.

Jensen, Merrill, *The American Revolution Within America* (New York, 1975).

Jensen, Merrill, *Articles of Confederation* (Madison, 1940).

Jensen, Merrill, "The Cession of the Old Northwest," *Mississippi Valley Historical Review*, XXIII (June, 1936), 27–48.

Jensen, Merrill, "The Creation of the National Domain, 1781–1784," *Mississippi Valley Historical Review*, XXVI (December, 1939), 323–342.

Jensen, Merrill, *The New Nation* (New York, 1950).

Johnson, Hildegard Binder, *Order Upon the Land: The United States Rectangular Land Survey and the Upper Mississippi Country* (New York, 1976).

Johnson, Ida, *The Michigan Fur Trade*, Michigan Historical Publications, University Series, V, part 1 (Lansing, 1919).

Johnson, Roy H., "Frontier Religion in Western Pennsylvania," *Western Pennsylvania Historical Magazine*, XVI (February, 1933), 23–37.

Jones, Eldon L., "Sir Guy Carleton and the Close of the American War of Independence: 1782–1783." Ph.D., Duke University, 1968.

Kellogg, Louise P., *The British Regime in Wisconsin and the Northwest* (Madison, 1935).

Kellogg, Louise P., "A Footnote to the Quebec Act," *Canadian Historical Review*, XIII (June, 1932), 147–156.

Kellogg, Louise P., "France and the Ohio Valley," *Mississippi Valley Historical Review*, XVIII (September, 1931), 3–22.

Kellogg, Louise P., "Indian Diplomacy During the Revolution in the West," Indiana State Historical Society, *Transactions*, XXXVI (1929), 47–57.

Kelsay, Isabel T., "Joseph Brant: The Legend and the Man," *New York History*, XL (October, 1959), 368–379.

Kenton, Edna, *Simon Kenton* (Garden City, New York, 1930).

Kerby, Robert L., "The Other War in 1774: Dunmore's War," *West Virginia History*, XXXVI (October, 1974), 1–16.

Kincaid, Robert L., *The Wilderness Road* (Indianapolis, 1947).

King, James C., "Indian Credit as a Source of Friction in the Colonial Fur Trade," *Western Pennsylvania Historical Magazine*, XLIX (January, 1966), 57–66.

Kinnaird, Lawrence, "American Penetration into Spanish Territory, 1776–1803." Ph.D., University of California, Berkeley, 1928.

Kinnaird, Lawrence, *New Spain and the Anglo-American West*, two volumes (Los Angeles, 1932).

Kinnaird, Lawrence, "Introduction," *Spain in the Mississippi Valley, 1764–1794, Part I, Annual Report of the American Historical Association for the Year 1945* (Washington, 1946), II, xv–xxxi.

Kinnaird, Lawrence, "The Spanish Expedition Against Fort St. Joseph in 1781: A New Interpretation," *Mississippi Valley Historical Review*, XIX (September, 1932), 173–191.

Kinnaird, Lawrence, "The Western Fringe of Revolution," *Western Historical Quarterly*, VII (July, 1976), 253–270.

Kerr, Charles, ed., *History of Kentucky*, five volumes (Chicago, 1922).

Kinietz, W. Vernon, *The Indian Tribes of the Western Great Lakes*, University of Michigan Museum of Anthropology, Occasional Contributions, Number 10 (Ann Arbor, 1940).

Kinietz, W. Vernon, *The Indians of the Western Great Lakes: 1615–1760* (Ann Arbor, 1966).

Klett, Guy S., "Charles Beatty, Wilderness Churchman," Presbyterian Historical Society, *Journal*, XXXII (September, 1954), 143–159.

Klett, Guy S., "The Presbyterian Church and the Scotch-Irish on the Pennsylvania Colonial Frontier," *Pennsylvania History*, XVIII (April, 1951), 97–190.

Knopf, Richard C., " 'Cool Cat George' and the Indian Wars in Ohio," in Randall L. Buchman, ed., *The Historic Indians in Ohio*, Ohio American Revolution Bicentennial Conference Series, Number 3 (Columbus, 1976), 20–28.

Knopf, Richard C., "Fort Miamis: The International Background," *Ohio Archaeological and Historical Quarterly*, LXI (April, 1951), 146–166.

Kohonva, Marie J., "The Moravians and Their Missionaries: A Problem in Americanization," *Mississippi Valley Historical Review*, XIX (December, 1932), 348–361.

Lambaert, Joseph I., "Clark's Conquest of the Northwest," *Indiana Magazine of History*, XXXVI (December, 1940), 337–350.

Lanctot, Gustave, *Canada and the American Revolution, 1774–1783* (London, 1967).

Lass, William E., "How the Forty-Ninth Parallel Became the International Boundary," *Minnesota History*, 44 (Summer, 1975), 209–219.

Laub, C. Herbert, "British Regulation of Crown Lands in the West: The Last Phase, 1773–1775," *William and Mary Quarterly,* second series, X (January, 1930), 52–55.

Laub, C. Herbert, "The Problem of Armed Invasion of the Northwest During the American Revolution," *Virginia Magazine of History and Biography*, XLII (January–April, 1934), 18–27, 132–144.

Leavitt, Orpha E., "British Policy on the Canadian Frontier, 1782–1792: Mediation and an Indian Barrier State," Wisconsin State Historical Society, *Proceedings,* LXIII (1915), 151–185.

LeRoy, Perry E., "Sir Guy Carleton as a Military Leader During the American Revolution: Invasion and Repulse, 1775–1776." Ph.D., Ohio State University, 1960.

Lester, William S., *The Transylvania Colony* (Spencer, Indiana, 1935).

Lewin, Howard, "A Frontier Diplomat: Andrew Montour," *Pennsylvania History*, XXXIII (April, 1966), 153–186.

Lewis, Anthony M., "Jefferson and Virginia's Pioneers, 1774–1781," *Mississippi Valley Historical Review,* XXXIV (March, 1948), 551–588.

Lewis, George E., *The Indiana Company, 1763–1798: A Study of Eighteenth Century Frontier Land Speculation and Business Venture*, Old Northwest Historical Series, IV (Glendale, California, 1941).

Lewis, Virgil A., *History of the Battle of Point Pleasant* (Charleston, West Virginia, 1909).

Leyland, Herbert T., *The Ohio Company: A Colonial Corporation*, Historical and Philosophical Society of Ohio, *Publications*, XVI (Cincinnati, 1921).

Livermore, Shaw, *Early American Land Companies: Their Influence on Corporate Development* (New York, 1939).

Lutz, Paul V., "Land Grants for Service in the Revolution," *New York Historical Society Quarterly*, XLVIII (July, 1964), 221–236.

Lydekker, John W., *The Faithful Mohawks* (Cambridge, England, 1938).

Lynd, Staughton, "The Compromise of 1787," *Political Science Quarterly*, LXXXI (June, 1966), 215–250.

MacDonald, Kenneth R., Jr., "The Battle of Point Pleasant: First Battle of the American Revolution," *West Virginia History*, XXXVI (October, 1974), 40–49.

Mahon, John K., "Anglo-American Methods of Indian Warfare, 1676–1794," *Mississippi Valley Historical Review*, XLV (September, 1958), 254–275.

Malone, Miles S., "The Distribution of Population on the Virginia Frontier in 1775." Ph.D., Princeton University, 1935.

Manley, Henry S., *The Treaty of Fort Stanwix, 1784* (Rome, New York, 1932).

Marshall, Peter, "Colonial Protest and Imperial Retrenchment: Indian Policy, 1764–1768," *Journal of American Studies*, V (April, 1971), 1–17.

Marshall, Peter, "Imperial Policy and the Government of Detroit: Projects and Problems, 1760–1774," *Journal of Imperial and Commonwealth History*, II (January, 1974), 153–189.

Marshall, Peter, "Imperial Regulation of American Indian Affairs." Ph.D., Yale University, 1959.

Marshall, Peter, "The Incorporation of Quebec in the British Empire, 1763–1774," in Virginia B. Platt and David C. Skaggs, eds., *Of Mother Country and Plantations: Proceedings of the Twenty-Seventh Conference in Early American History* (Bowling Green, Ohio, 1972), 43–62.

Marshall, Peter, "Lord Hillsborough, Samuel Wharton and the Ohio Grant, 1767–1775," *English Historical Review*, LXXX (October, 1965), 717–739.

Marshall, Peter, "Sir William Johnson and the Treaty of Fort Stanwix, 1768," *Journal of American Studies*, I (July, 1967), 149–179.

Martzolff, Clement L., "Zane's Trace," *Ohio Archaeological and Historical Quarterly*, XIII (April, 1904), 297–331.

Mason, Kathryn H., *James Harrod of Kentucky* (Baton Rouge, 1951).

Mason, Kathryn H., "Harrod's Men—1774," *Filson Club Historical Quarterly*, XXIV (July, 1950), 230–233.

Massay, G. F., "Fort Henry in the American Revolution," *West Virginia History*, XXIV (April, 1963), 248–257.

Mason, Philip, *Detroit, Fort Lernault, and the American Revolution* (Detroit, 1964).

McAdams, Donald R., "The Sullivan Expedition: Success or Failure," *New York Historical Society Quarterly*, LIV (January, 1970), 53–81.

McArthur, Duncan, "The British Board of Trade in Canada, 1760–1774, I: The Proclamation of 1763," Canadian Historical Association, *Report* (1932).

McDermott, John Francis, "The Myth of the 'Imbecile Governor'— Captain Fernando de Leyba and the Defense of St. Louis in 1780," in John Francis McDermott, ed., *The Spanish in the Mississippi Valley, 1762–1804* (Urbana, Illinois, 1974), 314–405.

McManus, John, "An Economic Analysis of Indian Behavior in the North American Fur Trade," *Journal of Economic History*, XXXII (March, 1972), 36–53.

McIlwraith, Jean N., *Sir Frederick Haldimand*, second edition (London, 1926).

Miller, J. Jefferson, II, and Stone, Lyle M., *Eighteenth-Century Ceramics from Fort Michilimackinac*, Smithsonian Studies in History and Technology, Number 4 (Washington, 1970).

Merriam, John M., *The Legislative History of the Ordinance of 1787* (Worcester, Massachusetts, 1888).

Metzger, Charles H., "An Appraisal of Shelburne's Western Policy," *Mid-America*, XIX (July, 1937), 169–181.

Metzger, Charles H., *The Quebec Act: A Primary Cause of the American Revolution* (New York, 1936).

Meyer, Larry L., *Shadow of a Continent: The Prize that Lay to the West—1776* (Palo Alto, 1975).

Mohr, Walter H., *Federal Indian Relations, 1773–1788* (Philadelphia, 1933).

Mood, Fulmer, "Studies in the History of American Settled Areas and Frontier Lines, 1625–1790," *Agriculture History*, XXVI (January, 1952), 16–34.

Moore, Arthur K., *The Frontier Mind: A Cultural Analysis of the Kentucky Frontiersman* (Lexington, 1959).

Morgan, Lewis H., *League of the Ho-De-No-Sau-Nee- or Iroquois*, two volumes (New York, 1901).

Morris, Richard B., *The Peacemakers: The Great Powers and American Independence* (New York, 1965).

Murphy, Orville T., "Charles Gravier de Vergennes: Profile of an Old Regime Diplomat," *Political Science Quarterly*, LXXXIII (September, 1968), 400–418.

Musick, James B., *St. Louis as a Fortified Town* (St. Louis, 1941).

Nasatir, Abraham P., "The Anglo-Spanish Frontier during the American Revolution, 1778–1783," *Journal of the Illinois State Historical Society*, XXI (October, 1928), 291–358.

Nasatir, Abraham P., "The Anglo-Spanish Frontier on the Upper Mississippi, 1786–1796," *Iowa Journal of History and Politics*, XXIX (April, 1931), 155–232.

Nasatir, Abraham P., "Anglo-Spanish Rivalry on the Upper Mississippi," *Mississippi Valley Historical Review*, XVI (December, 1929–March, 1930), 359–382, 507–528.

Nasatir, Abraham P., *Borderland in Retreat: From Spanish Louisiana to the Far Southwest* (Albuquerque, 1976).

Neatby, Hilda, *Quebec: The Revolutionary Age, 1760–1791* (Toronto, 1966).

Nettles, Curtis P., *The Emergence of a National Economy, 1775–1815* (New York, 1962).

Nollenberg, Bernhard, *George Washington: The Virginia Period, 1732–1775* (Durham, 1964).

Norris, John, *Shelburne and Reform* (New York, 1963).

Norton, Thomas Elliot, *The Fur Trade in Colonial New York, 1686–1776* (Madison, 1974).

Notestein, Wallace, "The Western Indians in the Revolution," *Ohio Archaelogical and Historical Quarterly*, XVI (July, 1907), 269–291.

Nyland, Keith R., "Doctor Thomas Walker (1715–1794): Explorer, Physician, Statesman, Surveyor and Planter of Virginia and Kentucky." Ph.D., Ohio State University, 1971.

O'Donnell, James, "The Plight of the Ohio Indians During the American Revolution," in Randall L. Buchman, ed., *The Historic Indians in Ohio*, Ohio American Revolution Bicentennial Conference Series, Number 3 (Columbus, 1976), 14–20.

O'Donnell, James, "Who Is There To Mourn for Logan? No One! The Native American Crisis in the Ohio Country, 1774–1783," in Thomas H. Smith, ed., *Ohio in the American Revolution*, Ohio American Revolution Bicentennial Conference Series, Number 1 (Columbus, 1976), 17–21.

Ogg, Frederick A., *The Old Northwest* (New Haven, 1921).

Onuf, Peter S., "Sovereignty and Territory: Claims Conflict in the Old Northwest and the Origins of the American Federal Republic." Ph.D., Johns Hopkins University, 1973.

Ouellet, Fernand, *Historie Sociale et Economique de Quebec, 1760–1850* (Montreal, 1966).

Palmer, Frederick, *Clark of the Ohio: A Life of George Rogers Clark* (New York, 1919).

Pare, George, "The St. Joseph Mission," *Mississippi Valley Historical Review*, XVII (June, 1930), 24–54.

Parish, John Carl, "The Emergence of the Idea of Manifest Destiny," in *The Persistence of the Westward Movement and Other Essays* (Berkeley and Los Angeles, 1943), 54–59.

Parker, John, *The Great Lakes and the Great Rivers: Jonathan Carver's Dream of Empire* (Lansing, 1965).

Parkins, Almon Ernest, *The Historical Geography of Detroit*, Michigan Historical Publications, University Series, III (Lansing, 1918).

Parkman, Francis, *The Conspiracy of Pontiac and the Indian War After the Conquest of Canada*, two volumes (Boston, 1882).

Patterson, John G., "Ebenezer Zane, Frontiersman," *West Virginia History*, XII (October, 1950), 4–45.

Pattison, William D., *The Beginnings of the American Rectangular Land Survey System, 1784–1800*, University of Chicago, Department of Geography, Research Paper Number 50 (Chicago, 1957).

Pattison, William D., "The Survey of the Seven Ranges," *Ohio Historical Quarterly*, LXVIII (April, 1959), 115–140.

Pease, Theodore C., "The Mississippi Boundary of 1763: A Reappraisal of Responsibilities," *American Historical Review*, XL (January, 1935), 278–286.

Pease, Theodore C., "1780—The Revolution at Crisis in the West," *Journal of the Illinois State Historical Society*, XXIII (January, 1931), 664–681.

Pease, Theodore C., "The Ordinance of 1787," *Mississippi Valley Historical Review*, XXV (September, 1938), 167–180.

Pease, Theodore C., and Pease, Marguerite J., *George Rogers Clark and the Revolution in Illinois, 1763–1787* (Springfield, 1929).

Peckham, Howard H., "Books and Reading on the Ohio Valley Frontier," *Mississippi Valley Historical Review*, XLIV (March, 1958), 649–663.

Peckham, Howard H., "Josiah Harmar and His Indian Expedition," *Ohio Archaeological and Historical Quarterly*, LV (July–September, 1946), 227–241.

Peckham, Howard H., *Pontiac and the Indian Uprising* (Princeton, 1947).

Philbrick, Francis S., "Introduction," *The Laws of Illinois Territory, 1809–1818*, Collections of the Illinois State Historical Library, XXV (Springfield, 1950), ix–cccclxxvii.

Philbrick, Francis S., "Introduction," *The Laws of the Indiana Territory, 1801–1809*, Collections of the Illinois State Historical Library, XXI (Springfield, 1930), ix–cclxxxii.

Philbrick, Francis S., *The Rise of the West, 1754–1830* (New York, 1965).

Phillips, Paul C., "American Opinion Regarding the West, 1778–1783," Mississippi Valley Historical Association, *Proceedings*, VII (1913–1914), 286–305.

Phillips, Paul C., "The Fur Trade in the Maumee-Wabash Country," in *Studies in America History Inscribed to James Albert Woodburn* (Bloomington, 1926), 91–118.

Phillips, Paul C., *The West in the Diplomacy of the American Revolution* (Urbana, 1913).

Phillips, Paul C., *The Fur Trade*, two volumes (Norman, Oklahoma, 1961).

Pieper, Thomas, and Gidney, James B., *Fort Laurens, 1778–1779* (Kent, Ohio, 1976).

Plath, Raymond, "British Mercantilism and British Colonial Land Policy in the Eighteenth Century." Ph.D., University of Wisconsin, 1939.

Platt, Myles M., "Detroit Under Siege, 1763," *Michigan History*, XL (December, 1956), 465–497.

Prucha, Francis P., *American Indian Policy in the Formative Years: The Indian Trade and Intercourse Acts, 1790–1835* (Cambridge, 1962).

Prucha, Francis P., *The Sword of the Republic: The United States Army on the Frontier, 1784–1846* (New York, 1969).

Quaife, Milo M., *The Capture of Old Vincennes* (Indianapolis, 1927).

Quaife, Milo M., *Chicago and the Old Northwest, 1673–1835* (Chicago, 1913).

Quaife, Milo M., "The Ohio Campaigns of 1782," *Mississippi Valley Historical Review*, XVII (March, 1931), 515–529.

Quaife, Milo M., "The Royal Navy of the Upper Great Lakes," *Burton Historical Collection Leaflet*, II (May, 1924), 49–64.

Quaife, Milo M., "The Significance of the Ordinance of 1787," *Journal of the Illinois State Historical Society*, XXX (January, 1938), 415–428.

Quaife, Milo M., "When Detroit Invaded Kentucky," *Filson Club Historical Quarterly*, I (1927), 53–57.

Quimby, George I., *Indian Culture and European Trade Goods* (Madison, 1966).

Quimby, Geroge I., *Indian Life in the Upper Great Lakes, 11,000 B.C. to A.D. 1800* (Chicago, 1960).

Radike, Floyd, *Detroit: A French Village on the Frontier* (Detroit, 1951).

Ranck, George W., *Boonesborough* (Louisville, 1901).

Randall, Emilius O., *History of Ohio*, six volumes (New York, 1912–1915).

Randall, James G., "George Rogers Clark's Service of Supply," *Mississippi Valley Historical Review*, VIII (December, 1921), 250–263.

Reeve, J. C., "Henry Bouquet: His Indian Campaigns," *Ohio Archaeological and Historical Quarterly*, XXVI (1917), 489–506.

Reibel, Daniel B., "The British Navy on the Upper Great Lakes, 1760–1789," *Niagara Frontier*, XX (Autumn, 1973), 66–75.

Reibel, Daniel B., "A Kind of Citadel: 1764–1805," *Michigan History*, XLVII (March, 1963), 47–71.

Reid, Marjorie G., "The Quebec Fur Traders and Western Policy, 1763–1774," *Canadian Historical Review*, VI (March, 1925), 15–32.

Rice, Otis K., *The Allegheny Frontier: West Virginia Beginnings, 1730–1830* (Lexington, 1970).

Rice, Otis K., *Frontier Kentucky* (Lexington, 1975).

Rice, Otis K., "The Ohio Valley in the American Revolution: A General View," in Thomas H. Smith, ed., *Ohio in the American Revolution* , Ohio American Revolution Bicentennial Conference Series, Number 1 (Columbus, 1976), 5–13.

Rich, Edwin E., *Montreal and the Fur Trade* (Montreal, 1966).

Richardson, James B., III, and Kirke C. Wilson, "Hannas Town and Charles Foreman: The Historical and Archeological Record," *Western Pennsylvania Historical Magazine*, LVIII (April, 1976), 153–184.

Rickey, Don, Jr., "The British-Indian Attack on St. Louis, May 26, 1780," *Missouri Historical Review*, LV (October, 1960), 35–45.

Riddell, W. R., *Michigan Under British Rule, Law and Law Courts, 1760–1796* (Lansing, 1926).

Riegel, Robert E., and Athearn, Robert G., *America Moves West*, fifth edition (New York, 1971).

Ritzenthaler, Robert E., and Ritzenthaler, Pat, *The Woodland Indians of the Western Great Lakes* (Garden City, New York, 1970).

Robbins, John E., "The Fort Gower Resolves, November 5, 1774," in Thomas H. Smith, ed., *Ohio in the American Revolution*, Ohio American Revolution Bicentennial Conference Series, Number 1 (Columbus, 1976), 21–26.

Robbins, Leroy K., *St. Louis in the War for American Independence* (St. Louis, 1940).

Robbins, Roy M., *Our Landed Heritage* (Princeton, 1942).

Roberts, Edward G., "The Roads of Virginia, 1607–1840." Ph.D., University of Virginia, 1950.

Robertson, John E. L., "Fort Jefferson," *Register of the Kentucky Historical Society*, LXXI (April, 1973), 127–138.

Robinson, Percy J., *Toronto During the French Regime: A History of the Toronto Region from Brule to Simcoe, 1615–1793* (Toronto, 1965).

Rohrbough, Malcolm J., *The Land Office Business: The Settlement and Administration of American Public Lands, 1789–1837* (New York, 1968).

Rossie, Jonathan G., "The Northern Indian Department and the American Revolution," *Niagara Frontier*, XX (Autumn, 1973), 52–65.

Russell, Nelson V., *The British Regime in Michigan and the Old Northwest*, (Northfield, Minnesota, 1939).

Russell, Nelson V., "The French and British at Play in the Old Northwest," *Journal of the Illinois State Historical Society*, XXXI (March, 1938), 22–53.

Russell, Nelson V., "The Governmental Organization of Michigan, 1760–1787," *Michigan History Magazine*, XXIII (Winter, 1939), 93–104.

Russell, Nelson V., "The Indian Policy of Henry Hamilton, A Re-valuation," *Canadian Historical Review*, XI (March, 1930), 20–37.

Russell, Nelson V., "Transportation and Naval Defense in the Old Northwest During the British Regime, 1760–96," *University of Michigan Historical Essays*, XI (1937), 113–139.

Saum, Lewis O., *The Fur Trader and the Indian* (Seattle, 1965).

Savelle, Max, *George Morgan: Colony Builder* (New York, 1932).

Scanlan, Peter L., *Prairie du Chien: French, British, American* (Menasha, Wisconsin, 1937).

Schafer, Joseph, "Beginnings of Civilization in the Old Northwest," *Wisconsin Magazine of History*, XXI (December, 1937), 213–226.

Schoolcraft, Henry R., *Information Respecting the History, Condition, and Prospects of the Indian Tribes of the United States*, six volumes (Philadelphia, 1852–1855).

Schuyler, Robert L., *The Transition in Illinois from British to American Government* (New York, 1909).

Scholarman, Joseph H., *From Quebec to New Orleans: The Story of the French in America* (Belleville, Illinois, 1929).

Schweinitz, Edmund de, *Life and Times of David Zeisberger* (Philadelphia, 1870).

Severance, Frank H., *An Old Frontier of France: The Niagara Region and Adjacent Lakes Under French Control*, Buffalo Historical Society, *Publications*, XX–XXI (1917).

Severance, Frank H., "The Peace Mission to Niagara of Ephrain Douglas in 1783," Buffalo Historical Society, *Publications*, XXIII (1919), 117–134.

Sheeler, J. Reuben, "The Negro on the Virginia Frontier," *Journal of Negro History*, XLIII (October, 1958), 279–297.

Shepard, Claude L., "The Connecticut Land Company: A Study of the Beginnings of Colonizations of the Western Reserve," Western Reserve Historical Society, *Tracts*, Number 96 (1916), 65–221.

Sherman, C. E., "Original Land Subdivisions," *Ohio Cooperative Topographical Survey*, III (Columbus, 1925).

Shimmell, Lewis S., *Border Warfare in Pennsylvania During the Revolution* (Harrisburg, 1901).

492

ION

Shy, John, "Dunmore, the Upper Ohio Valley, and the American Revolution," in Thomas H. Smith, ed., *Ohio in the American Revolution*, Ohio American Revolution Bicentennial Conference Series, Number 1 (Columbus, 1976), 13–16.

Shy, John, *Towards Lexington: The Role of the British Army in the Coming of the American Revolution* (Princeton, 1965).

Siebert, Wilbur H., "The Loyalists and the Six Nation Indians in the Niagara Peninsula," Royal Society of Canada, *Transactions*, third series, IX (1915), 79–128.

Siebert, Wilbur H., "The Loyalists of Pennsylvania," Ohio State University, *Bulletin*, XXIV (1920), *Contributions in History and Political Science*, Number 5.

Silveus, Marian, "Churches and Social Control on the Western Pennsylvania Frontier," *Western Pennsylvania Historical Magazine*, XXIX (June, 1936), 123–134.

Sioussat, St. George L., "The Chavalier de la Luzerne and the Ratification of the Articles in Maryland, 1780–1781," *Pennsylvania Magazine of History and Biography*, LX (October, 1936), 391–407.

Skaggs, David C., "Between the Lakes and the Bluegrass: An Overview of the Revolution in the Old Northwest," *Northwest Ohio Quarterly*, XLVIII (Summer, 1976), 89–101.

Slick, Sewell E., *William Trent and the West* (1947).

Slocum, Charles Elihu, *Ohio Country Between 1783 and 1815* (New York, 1910).

Smith, Alice E., *The History of Wisconsin, Volume I: From Exploration to Statehood* (Madison, 1973).

Smith, Dwight L., "Provocation and Occurence of Indian-White Warfare in the Early American Period in the Old Northwest," *Northwest Ohio Quarterly*, XXXIII (Summer, 1961), 132–147.

Smith, Marc Jack, "Joseph Brant, A Mohawk Statesman." Ph.D., University of Wisconsin, 1946.

Smith, W. Roy, "Sectionalism in Pennsylvania During the Revolution," *Political Science Quarterly*, XXIV (June, 1909), 208–235.

Smoot, Joseph G., "Freedom's Early Ring: The Northwest Ordinance and the American Union." Ph.D., University of Kentucky, 1964.

Snow, Alpheus H., *The Administration of Dependencies: A Study of the Evolution of the Federal Empire, With Special Reference to American Colonial Problems* (New York, 1902).

Snyderman, George S., *Behind the Tree of Peace: A Sociological Analysis of Iroquois Warfare* (Phildelphia, 1948).

Sonne, Neils H., *Liberal Kentucky, 1780–1828* (New York, 1938).

Sosin, Jack M., *Agents and Merchants: British Colonial Policy and the Origins of the American Revolution* (Lincoln, 1965).

Sosin, Jack M., "The British Indian Department and Dunmore's War," *Virginia Magazine of History and Biography*, LXXIV (January, 1966), 34–50.

Sosin, Jack M., "The French Settlements in British Policy for the North American Interior, 1760–1774," *Canadian Historical Review*, XXXIX (September, 1958), 185–208.

Sosin, Jack M., *The Revolutionary Frontier, 1763–1783* (New York, 1967).

Sosin, Jack M., "The Use of Indians in the War of the American Revolution," *Canadian Historical Review*, XLVI (June, 1965), 101–121.

Sosin, Jack M., *Whitehall and the Wilderness: The Middle West in British Colonial Policy, 1760–1775* (Lincoln, 1961).

Sosin, Jack M., "The Yorke-Camden Opinion and American Land Speculators," *Pennsylvania Magazine of History and Biography*, LXXXV (January, 1961), 38–49.

Stanley, George F., "The Six Nations in the American Revolution," *Ontario History*, LVI (December, 1964), 217–232.

Stealey, John E., III, "George Clendinen and the Great Kanawha Frontier: A Case Study of the Frontier Development of Virginia," *West Virginia History*, XXVII (July, 1966), 278–296.

Steckmesser, Kent L., *The Westward Movement: A Short History* (New York, 1969).

Stevens, Wayne E., *The Northwest Fur Trade, 1783–1800* (Urbana, 1928).

Stevens, Wayne E., "The Organization of the British Fur Trade, 1760–1800," *Mississippi Valley Historical Review*, III (September, 1916), 172–202.

Stone, Frederick D., "The Ordinance of 1787," *Pennsylvania Magazine of History and Biography*, XXV (September, 1938), 167–180.

Stone, Lyle M., *Fort Michilimackinac, 1715–1781: An Archaeological Perspective on the Revolutionary Frontier*, Publications of the Museum, Anthropological Series, Michigan State University (East Lansing, 1974).

Stone, William L., *Border Wars of the American Revolution*, two volumes (New York, 1874).

Stoz, Charles M., "Defense in the Wilderness," *Western Pennsylvania Historical Magazine*, XLI (Autumn, 1958).

Sutton, Robert M., "George Morgan, Early Illinois Businessman: A Case of Premature Enterprise," *Journal of the Illinois State Historical Society*, LXIX (August, 1976), 173–184.

Swanton, John R., *The Indian Tribes of North America*, Smithsonian Institution Bureau of American Ethnology, Bulletin Number 145 (Washington, 1952).

Swiggett, Howard, *War Out of Niagara: Walter Butler and the Tory Rangers* (New York, 1933).

Talbert, Charles G., *Benjamin Logan: Kentucky Frontiersman* (Lexington, 1962).

Talbert, Charles G., "Kentucky Invades Ohio—1780," *Register of the Kentucky Historical Society*, LII (October, 1954), 291–300.

Talbert, Charles G., "Kentucky Invades Ohio—1782," *Register of the Kentucky Historical Society*, LIII (October, 1955), 288–297.

Talbert, Charles G., "A Roof for Kentucky," *Filson Club History Quarterly*, XXIX (April, 1955), 145–165.

Tatter, Henry, "State and Federal Land Policy During the Confederation," *Agriculture History*, IX (October, 1935), 176–186.

Teggart, Frederick J., "The Capture of St. Joseph, Michigan, by the Spaniards in 1781," *Missouri Historical Review*, V (1911), 214–228.

Thomas, Charles M., "Successful and Unsuccessful Merchants in the Illinois Country," *Journal of the Illinois State Historical Society*, XXV (January, 1928), 429–437.

Thrower, Norman J. W., *Original Survey and Land Subdivision*, Association of American Geographers, Monograph Number 4 (Chicago, 1966).

Thwaites, Reuben G., *Daniel Boone* (New York, 1902).

Treat, Payson J., *The National Land System, 1785–1820* (New York, 1910).

Trudel, Pierre, "L'attitude du Gouverneur Louis-Frederick Haldiman a L'egard des Canadiens francais (1778–1781)," *Revue de l'Universite d'Ottawa*, XXXVI (1966), 5–14.

Tucker, Sara Julia, and Temple, Wayne C., *Indian Villages of the Illinois Country*, Illinois State Museum, *Scientific Papers*, II, two volumes (Springfield, 1942–1958).

Turner, Frederick J., "The Character and Influence of the Fur Trade in Wisconsin," *Proceedings of the State Historical Society of Wisconsin*, XXXVI (1889), 52–98.

Turner, Frederick J., "Western State-Making in the Revolutionary Era," *American Historical Review*, I (October, 1895–January, 1896), 70–87, 251–269.

Upton, Harriet T., *History of the Western Reserve* (New York, 1910).

Van Alstyne, Richard, *Empire and Independence: The International History of the American Revolution* (New York, 1965).

Van Alstyne, Richard, "The Significance of the Mississippi Valley in American Diplomatic History, 1686–1890," *Mississippi Valley Historical Review*, XXXVI (September, 1949), 215–238.

Van Every, Dale, *Ark of Empire: The American Frontier, 1783–1803* (New York, 1963).

Van Every, Dale, *A Company of Heroes: The American Frontier, 1775–1783* (New York, 1962).

Van Every, Dale, *Disinherited: The Lost Birthright of the American Indian* (New York, 1966).

Van Every, Dale, *Forth to the Wilderness: The First American Frontier, 1754–1774* (New York, 1961).

Van Every, Dale, *Men of the Western Waters: A Second Look at the First Americans* (Boston, 1956).

Virtue, George O., *British Land Policy and the American Revolution: A Belated Lecture in Economic History*, University of Nebraska, *Studies*, new series, XI (Lincoln, 1955).

Vivian, James F., and Vivian, Jean H., "Congressional Indian Policy During the War for Independence: The Northern Department," *Maryland Historical Magazine*, LXIII (September, 1968), 241–274.

Vivian, Jean H., "Military Land Bounties during the Revolutionary and Confederation Periods," *Maryland Historical Magazine*, LXI (September, 1966), 231–256.

Voegelin, Erminie Wheeler, *Indians of Northern Ohio and Southeastern Michigan: An Ethnohistorical Report* (New York, 1974).

Volwiler, Albert T., *George Croghan and the Westward Movement, 1741–1782* (Cleveland, 1926).

Wainwright, Nicholas B., *George Croghan: Wilderness Diplomat* (Chapel Hill, 1959).

Wainwright, Nicholas B., "An Indian Trade Failure: The Story of Hockley, Trent, and Croghan Company," *Pennsylvania Magazine of History and Biography*, LXXII (October, 1948), 343–375.

Waite, Mariella D., "Political Institutions in the Trans-Appalachian West, 1770–1800." Ph.D., University of Florida, 1961.

Walker, Mabel G., "Sir John Johnson, Loyalist," *Mississippi Valley Historical Review*, III (December, 1916), 318–346.

Wallace, Paul A. W., *Indian Paths of Colonial Pennsylvania* (Philadelphia, 1965).

Wallace, W. Stewart, "The Beginnings of British Rule in Canada," *Canadian Historical Review*, VI (September, 1925), 208–221.

Wallace, W. Stewart, "Pedlars from Quebec," *Canadian Historical Review*, XIII (December, 1932), 387–402.

Waller, Geroge M., *The American Revolution in the West* (Chicago, 1976).

Waller, George M., "George Rogers Clark and the American Revolution in the West," *Indiana Magazine of History,* LXXII (March, 1976), 1–20.

Washburn, Wilcomb E., *The Indian in America* (New York, 1975).

Watlington, Patricia, "Discontent in Frontier Kentucky," *Register of the Kentucky Historical Society,* LXV (April, 1967), 77–93.

Walton, John, *John Filson of Kentucky* (Lexington, 1956).

Webster, Eleanor M., "Insurrection at Fort Loundon in 1765: Rebellion or Preservation of Peace?," *Western Pennsylvania Historical Magazine,* XLVII (April, 1964), 125–139.

Weslager, C. A., *The Delaware Indians: A History* (New Brunswick, New Jersey, 1972).

Wesley, Edgar Bruce, "The Military Policy of the Critical Period," *Coast Artillery Journal,* LXVIII (April, 1928), 281–290.

West, Elizabeth H., "The Indian Policy of Bernardo de Galvez," Mississippi Valley Historical Association, *Proceedings,* VIII (1915).

Whitaker, Arthur P., *The Spanish-American Frontier, 1783–1795* (New York, 1927).

Whitney, Ellen M., "Indian History of the Indians of Illinois," *Journal of the Illinois State Historical Society,* LXIX (May, 1976), 139–146.

Whittemore, Charles P., *A General of the Revolution: John Sullivan of New Hampshire* (New York, 1961).

Wiener, Frederick B., *Civilians Under Military Justice: The British Practice Since 1689, Especially in North America* (Chicago, 1967).

Wilcox, Frank, *Ohio Indian Trails,* William A. McGill, ed. (Kent, 1970).

Wilkinson, Norman B., "Land Policy and Speculation in Pennsylvania, 1774–1800." Ph.D., University of Pennsylvania, 1958.

Williams, Edward G., "Fort Pitt and the Revolution on the Western Frontier," *Western Pennsylvania Historical Magazine,* LIX (January, 1976), 1–37.

Winger, Otho, "The Indians Who Opposed Harmar," *Ohio Archaeological and Historical Quarterly,* L (January–March, 1941), 55–59.

Wood, George A., "Celoron de Blainville in French Expansion in the Ohio Valley," *Mississippi Valley Historical Review,* IX (March, 1923), 302–319.

Woodress, James, *A Yankee's Odyssey: The Life of Joel Barlow* (Philadelphia, 1958).